T0371858

The Economics of Developing and Emerging Markets

This textbook presents an innovative new perspective on the economics of development, including insights from a broad range of disciplines. It starts with the current state of affairs, a discussion of data availability, reliability, and analysis, and an historic overview of the deep influence of fundamental factors on human prosperity. Next, it focuses on the role of human interaction in terms of trade, capital, and knowledge flows, as well as the associated implications for institutions, contracts, and finance. The book also highlights differences in the development paths of emerging countries in order to provide a better understanding of the concepts of development and the Millennium Development Goals. Insights from other disciplines are used to help understand human development with regard to other issues such as inequalities, health, demography, education, and poverty. The book concludes by emphasizing the importance of connections, location, and human interaction in determining future prosperity.

Charles van Marrewijk is Professor of Economics and Department Head of Utrecht University School of Economics. He has studied, worked, and/or taught in the Netherlands, the United States, China, Australia, Russia, and the Philippines. Charles is (co-) editor for three journals and has published widely in top journals on economic development, growth, migration, trade, comparative advantage, inequality, location, foreign direct investment, urbanization, resilience, transfers, and so on. He has also published more than 10 books for Cambridge University Press and Oxford University Press and is probably best known for his work in geographical economics and a spiky world (with Steven Brakman and Harry Garretsen).

Steven Brakman is Professor of International Economics at the faculty of Economics and Business at the University of Groningen. His main research areas are International Economics and Regional Economics. He is a research fellow of the CESifo institute in Munich, and Managing-editor of the *Journal of Regional Science*. He is academic partner of the Netherlands Bureau for Economic Policy analysis.

The Economics of Developing and Emerging Markets

Charles van Marrewijk

Utrecht University, The Netherlands

Steven Brakman

University of Groningen, The Netherlands

CAMBRIDGE
UNIVERSITY PRESS

Shaftesbury Road, Cambridge CB2 8EA, United Kingdom

One Liberty Plaza, 20th Floor, New York, NY 10006, USA

477 Williamstown Road, Port Melbourne, VIC 3207, Australia

314–321, 3rd Floor, Plot 3, Splendor Forum, Jasola District Centre, New Delhi – 110025, India

103 Penang Road, #05–06/07, Visioncrest Commercial, Singapore 238467

Cambridge University Press is part of Cambridge University Press & Assessment, a department of the University of Cambridge.

We share the University's mission to contribute to society through the pursuit of education, learning and research at the highest international levels of excellence.

www.cambridge.org
Information on this title: www.cambridge.org/highereducation/isbn/9781107043336

DOI: 10.1017/9781107338036

First published 2023

Printed in the United Kingdom by TJ Books Limited, Padstow Cornwall

A catalogue record for this publication is available from the British Library

Library of Congress Cataloging-in-Publication Data
Names: Marrewijk, Charles van, author. | Brakman, Steven, author. | Swart, Julia, author.
Title: The economics of developing and emerging markets / Charles van Marrewijk, Rijksuniversiteit te Utrecht, The Netherlands, Steven Brakman, Rijksuniversiteit Groningen, The Netherlands, Julia Swart, Rijksuniversiteit te Utrecht, The Netherlands.
Description: New York, NY : Cambridge University Press, 2023. | Includes bibliographical references and index.
Identifiers: LCCN 2022031227 (print) | LCCN 2022031228 (ebook) | ISBN 9781107043336 (hardback) | ISBN 9781107618589 (paperback) | ISBN 9781107338036 (epub)
Subjects: LCSH: Economic development. | International finance. | Social interaction.
Classification: LCC HD82 .M3677 2023 (print) | LCC HD82 (ebook) | DDC 338.9–dc23/eng/20220815
LC record available at https://lccn.loc.gov/2022031227
LC ebook record available at https://lccn.loc.gov/2022031228

ISBN 978-1-107-04333-6 Hardback
ISBN 978-1-107-61858-9 Paperback

Additional resources for this publication at www.cambridge.org/vanmarrewijk.

Contents

Figures

Tables

Boxes

Preface

> Most people in the world are poor. If we knew the economy of being poor, we would know much of the economics that really matter.
>
> Theodore Schultz (1981, p. 3)

Title of the Book and Terminology

One of the most central questions in economics concerns why some nations become rich and others stay poor. This is the focus of one of the most famous books in economics: *An Inquiry into the Nature and Causes of the Wealth of Nations*, by Adam Smith. The current textbook tackles the same question and demonstrates what has been learned since the publication of Smith's famous work in 1776. However, it focuses largely on the developing world because, in these countries, the problem of staying poor is not simply a matter of lagging behind: it is a matter of extreme poverty, and this makes the answer to the question incredibly urgent.

This book is entitled *The Economics of Developing and Emerging Markets*. This understandably raises the question: What are developing and emerging markets? The answer is not simple. The quote from Schultz, above, suggests that it is about poverty, and it is. But it is about much more than that. Today, the average person in Macao earns about 160 times more per year than the average person in Burundi. That is already an enormous difference, but it gets worse. Male life expectancy in Burundi today is around 59 years, compared to roughly 81 years in Macao. So in terms of lifetime earnings, the difference is around 220 times as high. In addition, income inequality is high in Burundi. According to the World Income Inequality database (https://wid.world/data/), the poorest half of the population earn about 15 percent of all income, which is the same as the figure shared by the richest 1 percent of the population. For the bottom half in Burundi, the lifetime earnings ratio relative to the average person in Macao has now risen above 700. And it seems to be getting worse over time: in 2002, the average income level in Macao was only 65 times higher than in Burundi, compared to today's 160 times.

As shown throughout this book, many issues play a role in poverty and development, including health, education, the environment, trade flows, uncertainty, capital accumulation, agricultural transition, institution building, firms, demography, urbanization, and the environment. The existence of reliable datasets on these phenomena is one of the big changes compared to the days of Adam Smith, and this hugely increases the knowledge of economic development. As this textbook shows, all these issues are highly correlated with levels of income per capita. Since reliable income data is available for most countries, it is used as a benchmark in most of the analyses. The terms "North" and "South" have been used in the past to describe advanced and poor countries respectively, but this is geographically incorrect: various countries in the south have high income levels and some countries in the north have low income levels. It was also customary at some stage to use numbers: First World (Western Europe and North America), Second World (Communist Bloc of the Soviet Union and China), and Third World (all other countries). This system became obsolete over time.

It is now customary to use the term "developing countries" to refer to poorer nations, suggesting that it is a matter of time before these countries can deal with their development problems. It is not viewed as a derogatory term, as all countries are developing in one way or another.

Many authors use the term "developed countries" to differentiate from developing countries, but this has three disadvantages. First, it is a static term, suggesting that developed countries have reached some end point and stop developing. Second, it is a derogatory term relative to developing countries, many of which in certain aspects of human development and cultural finesse reach higher levels of development than some "developed" countries. Third, the terms "developing" and "developed" are too similar, which can easily cause confusion.

For these reasons, the terms "developing" and "advanced" are used throughout this textbook when referring to countries. The difference in sound and looks leads to clarity, and being advanced also implies there is still room for improvement. The focus here is on being economically advanced – not necessarily advanced in other areas. (To distinguish between developing and economically advanced countries would be too cumbersome, however, so developing and advanced are used for brevity.) The authors apologize in advance to anyone who may be offended in some way.

Development is a dynamic and relative term, depending on time and with whom the comparison is made. The focus in this textbook is the world as a whole, so countries are usually compared to all other countries for which data are available. The figure below is an illustration. Since countries can be large or small in terms of land area, population, and income. These differences are also taken into consideration, for example, by comparing to the world average or relative to the size of the population.

Figures – and for that matter, tables – are often used to demonstrate a point. Much can be learned from a good figure or table. What can be learned from this figure, for example? And, importantly, when should caution be exercised when drawing conclusions from figures like the Preface Figure? Take a moment to inspect it. Note that the situation is compared regarding incomes per capita of 1995 (horizontal axis) and 2019 (vertical axis).

- First, the figure could show that a country is emerging if it moves from the low to the middle category. This method would imply that four countries (China, Armenia, Sri Lanka, and the Philippines) have been emerging from 1995 to 2019.

Figure 0.1 Income per capita; percentile ranking, 1995 and 2019
Source: Created using World Development Indicators online.
Notes: Income per capita is GNI PPP in constant 2017 $; 109 countries included; dashed line is diagonal; dotted lines at one-third and two-thirds; squares have long-run growth above 4 percent; triangles have percentile rise above 0.15.

- Second, it could show that a country has to have a high growth rate for a significant time period to be classified as emerging. The average longer-term compounded growth rate from about 1990 to 2019 for 154 countries is 2.0 percent. So the figure could show that a country is emerging if its growth rate is above 4.0 percent over a period of 20 years or more. There are nine countries that meet this criterion, identified by a square symbol. The Philippines would no longer qualify, but the other countries above are joined by Vietnam, India, Cambodia, Bangladesh, Latvia, and South Korea.
- Third, the figure could show that a country is emerging over some time period if its percentile ranking rises sufficiently fast. Suppose an increase of 0.15 or more is required. Five countries meet this criterion, namely Armenia, China, and Latvia, as well as Belarus and Ireland (identified by triangles).
- Fourth, the figure could show that a country is emerging if it meets all three requirements above, in which case only Armenia and China would qualify.

Each method above has its disadvantages. The first method fails to identify rapidly developing countries like India and Vietnam. The second method avoids this problem, but also identifies more advanced countries, like South Korea, which should no longer be thought of as emerging. The third method avoids arbitrary cut-off lines, but includes advanced countries like Ireland and countries that do not perform spectacularly, but rise in the rankings because countries in their distribution range do poorly, like Belarus. The fourth method is too restrictive. Perhaps the second criterion in combination with the requirement that it is a low- or middle-income country initially would be most appropriate. It would identify eight countries: Cambodia, Bangladesh, India, Vietnam, China, Armenia, Sri Lanka, and Latvia.

The main goal of the textbook is that you, based on evidence that is provided in the literature and based on available data, and after studying the material in this book, can form your own informed opinion of what is important in the development process of countries.

Overview of the Book

Many issues play a role in determining a country's competitiveness, and hence its level of economic development. This textbook delves deep into most of them. It does so in four main parts divided into 19 chapters, outlined briefly below.

Part I: Introduction and Deep Roots

Part I consists of four chapters to provide an introduction to economic development and an analysis of deep roots. Chapter 1 focuses on the current state of economic development in the world, with a discussion of global regions, land area, population, income level, trade flows, and competitiveness. Chapter 2 evaluates data and methods, with a discussion of the reliability of data sources, an overview of statistics, the importance of creating graphs, and a review of regressions and main problems, and methods to deal with these problems. Chapter 3 starts the *deep roots* discussion on the (initial) main (biogeographic) causes of differences between countries and regions in the level of economic development. It takes us to the origins of life on Earth and human development, with an emphasis on the import- ance of the *Agricultural Revolution* for creating the conditions for building institutions and more rapid economic growth. Chapter 4 concludes the deep roots discussion by emphasiz- ing the role of geographic-human interaction for properly understanding the evolution and shifts in economic development. It focuses on the role of incorporated institution building in migration flows in relation to geo-human interaction to properly understand these effects.

Part II: Human Interaction

Part II consists of five chapters and shifts focus from geo-human interaction to human interaction, which becomes relatively more important as time progresses. Chapter 5 pro- vides an overview of globalization and economic development from a longer-run perspec- tive (2,000 years). The chapter covers different types of globalization, price wedges, and trade-, migration-, and capital flows. Chapter 6 focuses on a better understanding of the causes and consequences of trade flows between nations. It covers comparative advantages based on differences in technology and factor abundance, as well as competitive advan- tages related to intra-industry trade flows, imperfect competition, and firm heterogeneity.

Chapter 7 continues with an overview of the main causes of economic growth and development based on (human) capital accumulation, total factor productivity, knowledge flows, and endogenous growth, as well as the dynamic costs of trade restrictions. Chapter 8 analyzes institutions and contracts, with a discussion of the nature of the firm, social costs, property rights, and the relationship between institutions and economic development (do institutions cause growth?). Chapter 9 concludes, outlining money and finance issues, with a particular focus on exchange rates, forward markets, interest parity, the policy trilemma, and the links between finance, investment, and development.

Part III: Human Development

Part III consists of five chapters with a focus on important aspects of human development. Chapter 10 opens, with a discussion on measuring poverty and the speed of its decline, as well as gender equality, and measuring income inequality with an overview of recent changes, both globally and within and between countries. Chapter 11 introduces *poor economics*, which attempts to better characterize and understand the economic lives of the poor and the decisions they make. This approach uses randomized control trials as its main methodology, briefly discussed in terms of advantages and disadvantages and applied in other chapters. Chapter 12 analyzes population and migration issues by discussing developments in world population, birth rates, death rates, and population pyramids. The impact of demographic transition is then linked to present and future demographic dividends. Problems of migration in terms of refugees and internally displaced persons can be big, but are usually small relative to the demographic forces analyzed previously. Chapter 13 focuses on the importance of education for economic development by discussing the biology of learning and the links with development. The chapter addresses the gender gap in education and the quality of university and basic skills education before discussing a teaching model on tracking students, peer effects, and teacher payoffs (which is then taken to the data). Chapter 14 concludes with a discussion of health issues, including life expectancy, its links with development, differences in health care, and a characterization of the main causes of death. The chapter includes an evaluation of infant-, child-, and maternal mortality, before discussing two health experiments on deworming and providing school meals.

Part IV: Connections and Interactions

Part IV also consists of five chapters and focuses on connections and interactions between different parts of the development process. Chapter 15 opens with a discussion of agriculture in connection with (rural) development by reviewing agricultural production and employment in an historical perspective in relation to the Lewis model of development. After an evaluation, the chapter continues with a discussion of development in the agricultural sector, before concluding with agricultural policies. Chapter 16 evaluates the rising importance of location for economic development by analyzing the role of urbanization and agglomeration in the development process, both from an historical perspective and more recently. Chapter 17 continues in this spatial direction by discussing regularities

(Zipf's Law and the Gravity Equation) in a geographical economics framework with multiple equilibria and path dependence. A discussion in a broad historical perspective emphasizes the rising importance of human interaction over time, while building on geo-human interaction, as noted above. Chapter 18 discusses firm heterogeneity and focuses on the rising importance of multinational firms for economic development. It provides an overview of empirical regularities before explaining the Melitz model, which helps to understand horizontal and vertical foreign direct investment (fragmentation). The chapter reviews the links with (wage) inequality and concludes with a discussion of measuring supply chains. The book concludes in Chapter 19 with a discussion of sustainability in connection with development and the environment by analyzing scale, competition, and technology effects, and multilateral agreements and the natural resource curse, as well as the main differences between renewable and nonrenewable natural resources.

Authorship

Charles van Marrewijk has authored or co-authored all chapters in this book.
Steven Brakman has co-authored Chapters 9, 15, 16, 17, and 18 of this book.
Julia Swart has co-authored Chapter 19 of this book.

PART I
Introduction and Deep Roots

Part I consists of four chapters to provide an introduction to economic development and an analysis of deep roots. Chapter 1 focuses on the current state of economic development in the world, with a discussion of global regions, land area, population, income level, trade flows, and competitiveness. Chapter 2 evaluates data and methods, with a discussion of the reliability of data sources, an overview of statistics, the importance of creating graphs, and a review of regressions and main problems, and methods to deal with these problems. Chapter 3 starts the *deep roots* discussion on the (initial) main (biogeographic) causes of differences between countries and regions in the level of economic development. It takes us to the origins of life on Earth and human development, with an emphasis on the importance of the *Agricultural Revolution* for creating the conditions for building institutions and more rapid economic growth. Chapter 4 concludes the deep roots discussion by emphasizing the role of geographic-human interaction for properly understanding the evolution and shifts in economic development. It focuses on the role of incorporated institution building in migration flows in relation to geo-human interaction to properly understand these effects.

1 Economic Development Today

1.1 Introduction

This chapter paints a broad picture of the current state of economic development. Section 1.2 provides a brief overview of the World Bank classification in global regions. Section 1.3 discusses the importance of countries in terms of (agricultural) land area and population. Section 1.4 does the same for income levels and evaluates the differences between domestic product and national income. This section also points out the importance of correcting for price differences when comparing income levels between countries. On that basis, section 1.5 analyzes the differences in income per capita in more detail for a large range of countries. Section 1.6 briefly reviews trade flows of goods and services and evaluates the size of imports relative to exports. Section 1.7 provides an overview of the range of issues which are important for determining the global competitiveness of a country. Section 1.8 concludes.

1.2 World Bank Regions

The World Bank provides detailed free information at the country level in the World Development Indicators online (www.worldbank.org). This information will be used as a basis for discussion throughout this textbook. For presentation and discussion purposes, it is sometimes useful to group countries together in bigger regions. Based on historical, cultural, and geographic information, the World Bank identifies seven main global regions: see Table 1.1.

The East Asia and Pacific (EAP) region consists of 32 countries and includes diverse countries like China, Indonesia, and Australia. Occasionally, this group will be subdivided into smaller parts (East Asia, Southeast Asia, and Oceania). The Europe & Central Asia (ECA) region consists of 49 countries, including the core European countries, such as France, Germany, and the UK, and Central Asian countries, such as Kazakhstan and Russia. This group is also occasionally split into smaller parts (Europe and Central Asia).

The Latin America & Caribbean (LAC) region consists of 35 countries. It includes virtually all American countries south of the US border, such as Mexico, Brazil, and Argentina. From a geographical point of view, a cut at Panama would have been

Table 1.1. Overview of the World Bank regions

Code	Region	Example countries	#
EAP	East Asia and Pacific	China, Japan, Indonesia, Australia	32
ECA	Europe & Central Asia	UK, Germany, France, Russia	49
LAC	Latin America & Caribbean	Brazil, Mexico, Argentina	35
MNA	Middle East & North Africa	Egypt, S. Arabia, Algeria	21
NAM	North America	USA, Canada, Bermuda	3
SAS	South Asia	India, Pakistan, Bangladesh	8
SSA	Sub-Sahara Africa	Nigeria, S. Africa, Ethiopia	48

Source: World Development Indicators online.
Note: # = number of countries.

understandable. The World Bank decided to include Mexico and the Central American countries in the LAC region in view of the historical and cultural links. As a consequence, the North American (NAM) region consists of only three countries: the USA, Canada, and Bermuda.

As a connection between Europe and Africa, the Middle East & North Africa (MNA) region consists of 21 countries, including Egypt, Saudi Arabia, and Algeria, and stretches partly over the African and Asian continents. The remainder of Africa (48 countries) is grouped together in the Sub-Sahara Africa (SSA) region. It includes Nigeria, South Africa, and Ethiopia. The final region is South Asia (SAS), which consists of eight countries, including India, Pakistan, and Bangladesh. A general word of caution for putting together different countries in one group is provided at the end of this chapter in Box 1.2.

1.3   Land Area and Population

There are many countries in the world. In the World Development Indicators (WDI), the World Bank distinguishes between 217 different countries. Some of them are so small in terms of land area, population, and economic clout that you may never have heard of them. The small Polynesian island state of Tuvalu, for example, has a land area of 26 km^2 and a population of about 12,000 people. Even the tiny land area of Washington DC is more than six times as large, while its population is about 60 times as large. As usual, when information is gathered, some data are missing. Taiwan, for example, is considered by China to be one of its provinces. As a result, Taiwan was expelled from the United Nations in 1971 when China took its place. There are, therefore, no official data available for Taiwan at the World Bank. Similarly, for some countries some data is lacking or somewhat older. For the purposes of this chapter, the most recently available information from the WDI is used in the period 2017–2019. For all countries with missing information and a population of at least 300,000 people, information was gathered from the CIA World

Factbook (www.cia.gov/library/publications/resources/the-world-factbook/). In this way, a complete dataset for 196 countries was created.

This chapter focuses attention on the most important countries. Important in what sense? Clearly, if you are one of the few inhabitants of Tuvalu, this is an important country to you and your family. However, for the world as a whole, this chapter assumes that "large" countries are important. Again, the question is raised: large in what sense? There are, of course, several options available, their suitability depending on the object of study. In general terms, land area or population can be looked at. Since this is a book on economic development, various income measures can be examined. Since this book analyzes in an international context, exports or international capital flows can be used. In the rest of this chapter, all these aspects are briefly examined, together with some of their interactions.

1.3.1 Land Area and Agricultural Land Area

As the central piece left over after the break-up of the Soviet Union, the Russian Federation, henceforth Russia for short, is still by far the largest country in the world in terms of land area. With 16.4 million km^2, as indicated in Table 1.2, or 12.6 percent of the world total, Russia is about 75 percent larger than China, the world's second-largest country. Other nonsurprising large countries are Canada, the USA, and Brazil. Perhaps more remarkable in the top 10 list is the ninth place for Kazakhstan (formerly a part of the Soviet Union) and Algeria (tenth) in Africa. Other African countries follow: Sudan (eleventh) and DR Congo (Zaire, twelfth). (There are two "Congo" countries in Africa, the largest of which in terms of both population and size, a former Belgian colony, might also be known under the old name Zaire.) As a result of the most frequently used methods for projecting the world globe

Table 1.2. Top 10 countries in land area and agricultural land area, 2019

Rank	Country	Land area	%	Country	Agricultural	%
1	Russia	16.38	12.6	China	5.28	10.9
2	China	9.39	7.2	USA	4.06	8.3
3	USA	9.15	7.0	Australia	3.71	7.6
4	Canada	9.09	7.0	Brazil	2.84	5.8
5	Brazil	8.36	6.4	Russia	2.18	4.5
6	Australia	7.69	5.9	Kazakhstan	2.17	4.5
7	India	2.97	2.3	India	1.80	3.7
8	Argentina	2.74	2.1	S. Arabia	1.74	3.6
9	Kazakhstan	2.70	2.1	Argentina	1.49	3.1
10	Algeria	2.38	1.8	Mongolia	1.11	2.3
	World	129.94	100	World	48.62	100

Sources: Based on the most recently available information in the World Development Indicators online for the period 2017–2019 and CIA World Factbook for missing data.
Notes: Land area and agricultural land area in million km^2; % is relative to world total.

on a flat piece of paper, most people tend to underestimate the size of the African land area. To avoid this problem and get a better indication of the land area at different locations, panel a of Figure 1.1 provides a simple equilateral projection of bubbles proportional to a country's total land area, where the center of the bubble is located at the country's geographic center. Similar diagrams for other variables for the same reason are provided in the remainder of this chapter. For discussion purposes, the figure displays individual country data and at the same time groups the countries together in the seven regions of the World Bank (see Table 1.1).

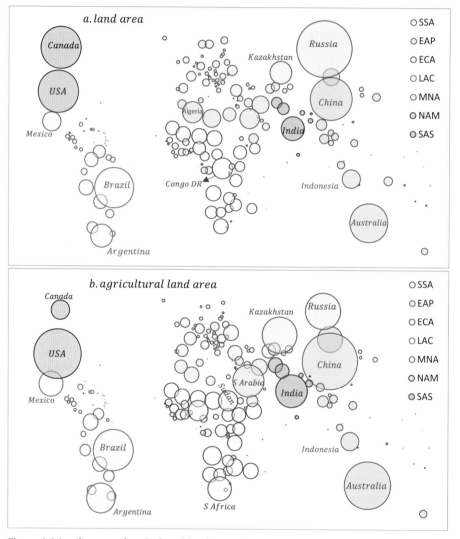

Figure 1.1 Land area and agricultural land area, 2019
Source: See Table 1.2.
Notes: Bubbles are proportional to a country's land area (panel a) and agricultural land area (panel b), located at the geographic center (except for the USA, which is at the geographic center of the 48 contiguous states) (CIA World Factbook), equilateral projection. For the world as a whole, agricultural land area is about 38 percent of total land area; 196 countries; see Table 1.1 for the World Bank region abbreviations.

The top six countries in Table 1.2 clearly stand out in panel a of Figure 1.1. Together, these six countries already account for 46 percent of the world's total land area. This graph also clearly illustrates the size of the African continent. Only one African country makes it to the top 10, but there are many African countries and they tend to be large in size. Taken together, the African countries account for more than 23 percent of the world's total area. If we realize that Russia (for its land area at least) and Kazakhstan are located in Asia, we also note that Europe is rather small in total land area (the sum of the other bubbles is not so large).

Since there are large land areas which consist of deserts, are almost permanently frozen, or receive hardly any rain at all, one may wonder how useful the land area is for humans. A first indication is to look at agricultural land area rather than total land area. This is done in panel b of Figure 1.1, where the bubbles are proportional to agricultural land area rather than total land area. For the world as a whole, agricultural land area is about 38 percent of total land area. Note, therefore, that comparing the bubbles in panel b with the bubbles in panel a only gives an indication of a country's relative importance (as a share of the world's total) in one case compared to the other. It can be observed that Russia and Canada are not nearly as important in terms of agricultural land area. The reverse holds for China, Kazakhstan, Australia, Argentina, and South Africa, which all are significantly more important in terms of agricultural land area. As a group, the East Asia & Pacific region and the Sub-Sahara Africa region gain in importance. It is important to realize, of course, that this provides no information regarding the intensity of agricultural production, which is low in Kazakhstan, Australia, and Mongolia.

1.3.2 Population

As an indicator of economic importance, a country's land area is of limited use. Many of the countries listed in Table 1.1 incorporate vast stretches of desert, rocks, swamps, or areas frozen solid all year round. Such uninhabitable land cannot be used to sustain and feed a population engaged in commerce, production, and trade. In this respect, the total population of a country is a better indicator of its fertility and potential economic viability. Table 1.3 lists the top 15 countries in terms of total population.

Two Asian countries, China and India, clearly stand out in terms of total population. Together, they have 2.76 billion inhabitants, which is about 36 percent of the world's total population. The USA, ranked third with 328 million inhabitants, has only about 24 percent of the Indian population, which is ranked second. Asian countries dominate the population list. Apart from China and India, this includes Indonesia (fourth), Pakistan (fifth), Bangladesh (eighth), Japan (eleventh), the Philippines (thirteenth), and Vietnam (fifteenth). Note that Russia (ninth) is not included in this list of Asian countries, despite the fact that its largest land mass is in the Asian continent, because the largest share of its population is on the European continent. This makes it the only European country on the list (Germany is eighteenth). The Americas (the USA, Brazil, and Mexico) and Africa (Nigeria, Ethiopia, and Egypt) both have three countries on the list.

Table 1.3. Top 15 countries in population, 2019

Rank	Country	Population (millions)	%
1	China	1,398	19.1
2	India	1,366	17.6
3	USA	328	4.4
4	Indonesia	271	3.5
5	Pakistan	217	2.8
6	Brazil	211	2.6
7	Nigeria	201	2.4
8	Bangladesh	163	2.2
9	Russia	144	2.0
10	Mexico	128	1.8
11	Japan	126	1.7
12	Ethiopia	112	1.4
13	Philippines	108	1.3
14	Egypt	100	1.3
15	Vietnam	96	1.2
	World	7,700	100

Source: See Table 1.2.

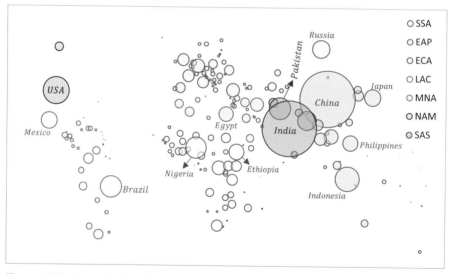

Figure 1.2 Total population, 2019
Sources: See Table 1.2 and Figure 1.1.
Notes: Bubbles are proportional to a country's total population located at the geographic center; 196 countries; see Table 1.1 for the World Bank region abbreviations.

Figure 1.2 provides an indication of the distribution of the world population across the globe. When compared with Figure 1.1 on the distribution of land area, the Americas shrink substantially (from 30.2 percent of land area to 13.2 percent in terms of population). Asia, in contrast, becomes much more important. This holds in particular for South Asia (from

3.8 percent in terms of land area to 23.9 percent in terms of population) and the countries in East Asia and Southeast Asia. Together, the EAP and SAS countries account for 54.5 percent of the world population.

1.4 Income

The best indicator of the economic power of a nation is, of course, obtained by estimating the total value of the goods and services produced in a certain time period. Actually doing this and comparing the results across nations is a formidable task, which conceptually requires taking three steps. First, a well-functioning statistics office in each nation must gather accurate information on the value of millions of goods and services produced and provided by the firms in the economy. This will be done, of course, in the country's local currency, that is dollars in the USA, rupee in India, yuan in China, and so on. Second, we have to decide what to compare between nations: gross domestic product or gross national income? Third, we have to decide *how* to compare the outcome for the different nations. The second and third steps are outlined in further detail below.

1.4.1 Domestic Product or National Income?

As mentioned above, we can compare either gross domestic product (GDP) or gross national income (GNI) between nations. GDP is defined as the market value of the goods and services produced by labor and property *located* in a country. GNI is defined as the market value of the goods and services produced by labor and property of *nationals* of a country. If, for example, a Mexican worker is providing labor services in the USA, these services are part of American GDP and Mexican GNI. The term "located in" sometimes has to be interpreted broadly, for example if a Filipino sailor is providing labor services for a Norwegian shipping company, this is part of Norwegian GDP despite the fact that the ship is not actually located in Norway most of the time. The difference between GNI and GDP holds for all factors of production, including capital, such that:

$$\text{GDP} + \text{net receipts of factor income} = \text{GNI} \qquad 1.1$$

Does it really matter whether we compare countries on the basis of GDP or GNI? Essentially: no. This is illustrated in Figure 1.3 using a logarithmic scale,[1] with the size of the bubbles proportional to the size of GNI. Almost all observations are close to a straight 45° line through the origin, at least for the large countries. This implies that the

---

[1] A logarithmic scale uses order of magnitudes, such that each step is the previous step multiplied by a value. It allows us to depict a wide range of values in one graph. In Figure 1.3, the multiplicative value is 10, so we go from 1 to 10, then from 10 to 100, then from 100 to 1,000, and so on. Obviously, some other multiplicative value can also be used.

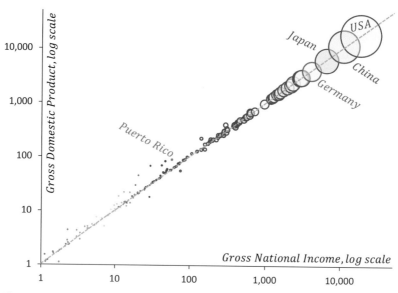

Figure 1.3 Gross national income and gross domestic product, 2019
Source: World Development Indicators.
Notes: GNI and GDP in billion constant 2010 USD (most recent up to 2019); the dashed line is a 45° line; logarithmic scales; bubbles are proportional to the size of GNI; 195 countries.

values of GDP and GNI are usually close to each other. When restricting attention to the 30 largest countries, which together account for 87 percent of total GNI and GDP, the (unweighted) average absolute deviation between GNI and GDP is only 2.6 percent. The maximum deviation for this group of countries is in Switzerland, where GDP is 10.2 percent higher than GNI. The figure also illustrates that for some smaller countries the deviation between GDP and GNI can be more substantial. This is shown in the graph for Puerto Rico, where GDP is 50 percent larger than GNI because of the investments by American multinationals.

1.4.2   Comparison

The left part of Table 1.4 reports the top 10 countries in terms of GNI level when the outcome for each nation in local currency is simply converted to the same international standard currency on the basis of the average exchange rate in the period of observation (referred to as GNI xrate). The total value of all goods and services produced in the world in 2019 was about $86 trillion. Taken together, the top 10 countries account for about 68 percent of world GNI in exchange rate terms.

Based on exchange rates, the USA is by far the largest economy in the world, producing about 25 percent of all goods and services. This is about 50 percent more than China, which is ranked second (at 16.6 percent), followed by Japan (6.1 percent). There are four European countries in the top 10, namely Germany (fourth), the UK (sixth), France (seventh), and Italy (eighth). None of these European countries makes it to the land area top 10 of Table 1.2 or the population top 15 of Table 1.3.

Table 1.4. Top 10 countries GNI and GNI PPP, 2019

Rank	Country	GNI xrate	%	Country	GNI PPP	%
1	USA	21,625	25.1	China	23,403	17.7
2	China	14,308	16.6	USA	21,625	16.3
3	Japan	5,264	6.1	India	9,507	7.2
4	Germany	3,958	4.6	Japan	5,654	4.3
5	India	2,844	3.3	Germany	4,796	3.6
6	UK	2,788	3.2	Russia	4,147	3.1
7	France	2,768	3.2	France	3,379	2.6
8	Italy	2,018	2.3	Indonesia	3,230	2.4
9	Brazil	1,791	2.1	UK	3,211	2.4
10	Canada	1,719	2.0	Brazil	3,135	2.4
	World	86,278	100	World	132,306	100

Source: See Table 1.2.
Notes: GNI and GNI PPP in billion current USD; xrate = exchange rate; 194 countries.

1.4.3 Purchasing Power Parity

The ranking of production value in the left part of Table 1.4 is deceptive because it tends to overestimate production in the high-income countries relative to developing countries. To understand this, it is necessary to distinguish between *tradable* and *nontradable* goods and services. As the name suggests, tradable goods and services can be transported or provided in another country, perhaps with some difficulty and at some costs. In principle, therefore, the providers of tradable goods in different countries compete with one another fairly directly, implying that the prices of such goods are related and can be compared effectively on the basis of observed (average) exchange rates. In contrast, nontradable goods and services have to be provided locally and do not compete with international providers. Think, for example, of housing services, getting a haircut, or going to the cinema.

Since (i) different sectors in the same country compete for the same laborers, such that (ii) the wage rate in an economy reflects the average productivity of a nation (see also Chapter 6), and (iii) productivity differences between nations in the nontradable sectors tend to be smaller than in the tradable sectors, converting the value of output in the nontradable sectors on the basis of observed exchange rates tends to underestimate the value of production in these sectors for developing countries. For example, on the basis of observed exchange rates, getting a haircut in the Netherlands may cost you $18 rather than the $4 you pay in China or the $2 you pay in the Philippines, while going to the cinema in Sweden may cost you $12 rather than the $2 you pay in Jakarta, Indonesia. In these examples, the value of production in the high-income countries relative to the low-income countries is overestimated by a substantial amount.

To correct for these price differences, the UN Internationaal Comparison Project (ICP) collects data on the prices of goods and services for virtually all countries in the world and calculates "purchasing power parity" (PPP) exchange rates, which better reflect the true value of goods and services that can be purchased in a country for a given amount of dollars. Reporting PPP income levels therefore gives a better estimate of the actual value of total production in a country.

Suppose, for example, that people in America and China spend about 70 percent of their income on nontraded goods and 30 percent on traded goods. Also assume that if exchange rates are used to compare income levels, the average Chinese person earns $7,000 and the average American $49,000, or *seven* times as much. When calculating PPP income levels, the average American still earns $49,000, since it is the benchmark country. The average Chinese person spends $4,900 on nontraded goods (70 percent of 7,000) before correcting for PPP and $2,100 on traded goods (30 percent of 7,000). After correcting for PPP, spending on traded goods is still $2,100, but spending on nontraded goods will rise because the price for nontraded goods is lower in China than in the USA. Suppose that nontraded goods are on average about twice as expensive in the USA, such that spending on nontraded goods by the average Chinese person is $9,800 (= 4,900 × 2) after PPP correction. Average income in China after PPP correction is then $11,900 (= 9,800 + 2,100). As a consequence, income in the USA is no longer seven times higher, but only 4.12 times higher (49,000/11,900). The PPP correction raises income in China by 11,900/7,000 = 1.70, since prices are the same for traded goods and twice as high in the USA for nontraded goods (0.3 × 1 + 0.7 × 2 = 1.70).

The right part of Table 1.4 lists the top 10 countries in terms of income corrected for PPP. By construction, the value for the USA remains the same. Since the world income level is about 53 percent higher for GNI PPP than for GNI exchange rates, the share of the US economy in the world's total declines from 25.1 to 16.3 percent. Note that the ordering in the right part of Table 1.4 has changed compared to the left part. Russia and Indonesia are the only new countries in the table at the expense of Italy and Canada. In PPP terms, total income in China is *higher* than in the USA, such that China is actually the world's largest economy (since 2015). India moved up from five to three, while Russia moved up from twelve to six.

Figure 1.4 illustrates the distribution of world income across the globe using similar bubbles located at a country's geographic center as used in Figures 1.1 and 1.2. Panel a is based on GNI exchange rates and panel b on GNI PPP. When comparing the income bubbles in panel a with the land area bubbles of Figure 1.1 or the population bubbles of Figure 1.2, it can be noted immediately that Africa virtually disappears: it is important in terms of land area, somewhat less important in terms of population, and almost unimportant in terms of income level. A similar observation holds for South Asia (particularly relative to population) and for Latin America (particularly relative to land area). The opposite holds for North America and Europe: these regions are more important in terms of income levels than in terms of population and land area (the latter particularly for Europe).

When comparing panel b of Figure 1.4 with panel a, note that the above observations are mitigated. Sub-Sahara Africa is somewhat more important when correcting for PPP and South Asia is substantially more important. In contrast, Europe and North America become

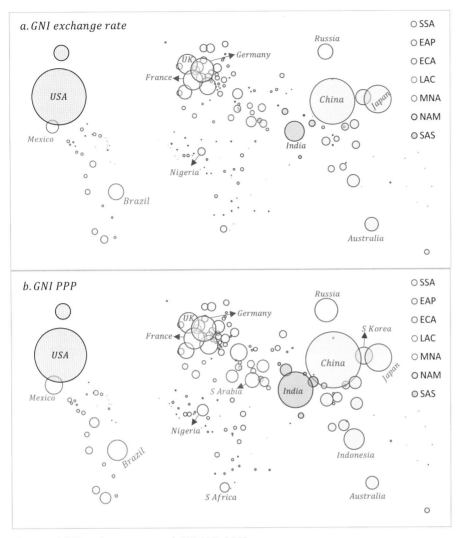

Figure 1.4 GNI exchange rate and GNI PPP, 2019
Source: See Table 1.2.
Notes: Bubbles are proportional to a country's GDP exchange rate (panel a) and GDP PPP (panel b); 196 countries; see Table 1.1 for the World Bank region abbreviations.

somewhat less important. This is, of course, an indication of the generally high price levels in these regions. All these observations are related to differences in income per capita for the various countries. This issue is addressed in the next section.

1.5 Income Per Capita

For an individual inhabitant of a country, the total production value of the country is hardly relevant. More important is the production value per person (per capita). It should be noted that income per capita gives an idea of the well-being for the "average" person in the country, but gives no information on the distribution of the income level within the country (see Chapter 10). If Juan and Pedro together earn $100, the average income level is $50, which holds if they both earn $50 *and* if Juan earns $1 while Pedro earns $99. The average income level is thus a poor indicator of the situation in a country if the distribution of income is more uneven. In general, income is more evenly distributed in Europe and Japan than in the USA, where it is more evenly distributed than in many developing nations.

Table 1.5 gives an overview of income per capita for a selection of (more populous) countries, corrected for purchasing power. The table also provides the rank of the country, the size of the population, and income per capita relative to the world average and relative to Burundi, the poorest country in the data. The associated Figure 1.5 provides an overview of the cumulative order of income per capita for 191 countries, taking population size into consideration. The average income level in the world in 2019 was $16,672 per person (in constant 2017 international $). The highest income level ($120,376, more than seven times the world average) was generated in the tiny casino-rich state of Macao (Asia). The lowest income level ($754, about 5 percent of the global average) was measured in Burundi (Sub-Sahara Africa). To put this into perspective: the average income level in Macao is about 160 times higher than in Burundi and the world average is about 22 times higher.

The visualization in Figure 1.5 shows how high the differences in income per capita really are, even without taking within-country income inequality into consideration (as the

Table 1.5. Income per capita, selected countries; GNI PPP, 2019

Rank	Country	Code	Income / capita	Population	Rel world	Rel BDI
1	Macao	MAC	120,376	0.6	7.22	159.7
11	United States	USA	62,513	328	3.75	82.9
16	Germany	DEU	55,155	83	3.31	73.2
29	Japan	JPN	42,564	126	2.55	56.5
56	Russia	RUS	26,157	144	1.57	34.7
69	Mexico	MEX	19,160	128	1.15	25.4
	World average / total		16,672	7507	1.00	22.1
80	China	CHN	15,187	1398	0.91	20.1
88	Brazil	BRA	14,263	211	0.86	18.9
108	Indonesia	IDN	11,459	271	0.69	15.2
130	India	IND	6,681	1366	0.40	8.9
142	Pakistan	PAK	5,005	217	0.30	6.6
143	Bangladesh	BGD	4,976	163	0.30	6.6
145	Nigeria	NGA	4,929	201	0.30	6.5
191	Burundi	BDI	754	12	0.05	1.0

Source: World Development Indicators online.
Notes: Income per capita is GNI PPP in constant 2017 $ (2019 or most recent); 191 countries included; world average is population-weighted; rel world = income per capita relative to world average; rel BDI = income per capita relative to BDI.

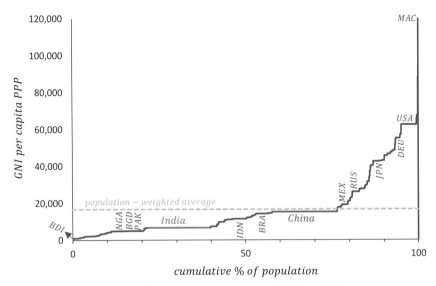

Figure 1.5 Cumulative ranking of income per capita; GNI PPP, 2019
Source: Created using World Development Online data.
Notes: Income per capita is GNI PPP in constant 2017 $ (2019 or most recent); 191 countries included; ordered from low to high; cumulative percent of population (2019) based on included countries only; see Table 1.5 for country codes; figure based on country averages.

figure is based on country averages). To properly see the differences, the vertical axis does *not* use a log scale, in contrast to most of the remainder of this book. Because of the size of their populations, India and China are easily identifiable. Other countries are identified by their codes.

The 10 poorest countries are all located in Sub-Sahara Africa, namely (in order, starting with the poorest): Burundi, Central African Republic, Malawi, DR Congo, Niger, Mozambique, Liberia, Chad, Sierra Leone, and Madagascar. The 25 poorest countries are almost all located in Sub-Sahara Africa, with three exceptions: Haiti, Solomon Islands, and Afghanistan. At the other extreme, the 10 richest countries are all small countries in Asia and Europe, namely (in order, starting with the richest): Macao, Qatar, Singapore, Luxembourg, Switzerland, United Arab Emirates, Norway, Ireland, Brunei, and Hong Kong. Of the populous countries identified in Figure 1.5, Nigeria, Bangladesh, and Pakistan earn about 30 percent of the world average, India about 40 percent, Indonesia about 70 percent, Brazil and China close to 90 percent, Mexico about 15 percent more than the world average, Russia about 57 percent more, Japan about 2.5 times the world average, and Germany and the USA more than three times the world average.

1.6 International Trade

An important component of economic development consists of international interaction through trade flows. An important reason for developing countries to impose restrictions on such flows is to generate revenue for the government, see Box 1.1. Before continuing, it should be noted that the comparison problems between countries discussed in sections 1.4 and 1.5 arising from the distinction between tradable and nontradable goods do not occur when investigating and discussing trade flows, which can readily be compared using the exchange rates.

1.6.1   Large Trading Nations

So what are the large trading nations? Table 1.6 provides the largest exporting nations in terms of goods (on the left) and in terms of services (on the right). The total value of goods exports is $18,757 billion. The total value of services exports is $6,156 billion. This implies that about 75 percent of all exports is in terms of goods and the remainder is in terms of services.

China was the world's largest goods exporter (12.8 percent of total exports), followed by the USA (8.8 percent) and Germany (7.8 percent). Taking into consideration the USA's share of world production (see section 1.4), the American share of world exports is rather modest. Most countries in Table 1.6 have a larger share in world exports than in world production. To some extent, this can be explained by the artificiality of drawing borders between nations on the globe. For example, if a Russian firm in St. Petersburg sells goods 6,500 km away in Vladivostok, this is not counted as exports because both cities are located in Russia. Compare this to a firm in Singapore selling goods to a consumer in Kuala Lumpur just 300 km away, which, of course, is part of Singapore exports.

Table 1.6. Top 15 exporting countries; goods and services, 2019

Rank	Country	Export goods	%	Country	Export services	%
1	China	2,399	12.8	USA	876	14.2
2	USA	1,652	8.8	UK	418	6.8
3	Germany	1,464	7.8	Germany	347	5.6
4	Japan	698	3.7	France	294	4.8
5	France	597	3.2	Ireland	248	4.0
6	South Korea	562	3.0	China	244	4.0
7	Netherlands	553	2.9	India	215	3.5
8	Hong Kong	548	2.9	Japan	207	3.4
9	Italy	511	2.7	Singapore	205	3.3
10	UK	476	2.5	Netherlands	203	3.3
11	Mexico	461	2.5	Spain	157	2.6
12	Canada	449	2.4	Belgium	122	2.0
13	Singapore	441	2.4	Italy	122	2.0
14	Russia	420	2.2	Switzerland	122	2.0
15	Switzerland	337	1.8	Luxembourg	111	1.8
	World	18,757	100	World	6,156	100

Source: See Table 1.2.
Notes: Values in billion current USD; based on BoP items for goods and services.

Consequently, some countries in Table 1.6 are relatively small, high-income open economies, such as the Netherlands, Hong Kong, Singapore, and Switzerland.

The right part of Table 1.6 lists the top 15 services exporters. Relative to the left-hand part there are five new countries on the list, namely Ireland, India, Spain, Belgium, and Luxembourg, which replace South Korea, Hong Kong, Mexico, Canada, and Russia. Although large goods exporters are generally also large services exporters, the order on the list differs quite remarkably. The USA, for example, moves up to first place (from second) and the UK moves up to second place (from tenth). China, on the other hand, drops from first to sixth place, while Japan drops from fourth to eighth. Evidently, the USA and the UK specialize to some extent in exporting services, while China and Japan specialize in exporting goods.

1.6.2   Exports Relative to Imports

Figure 1.6 illustrates the international exports and imports of goods in 2019 for 181 countries using a logarithmic scale. It also depicts a 45-degree line where exports are equal to imports and the goods trade balance is zero. The bubbles are proportional to a country's share in total trade flows (exports and imports of goods). The four largest goods trading nations (together accounting for 34 percent of total trade) are listed in the figure: China (11.8 percent), USA (11.2 percent), Germany (7.2 percent), and Japan (3.7 percent). Although a country's export value is generally roughly in line with its import value, the deviations between the two are clearly more substantial than the deviations between GDP and GNI illustrated in Figure 1.3. For China and Germany, exports are substantially larger than imports. The reverse holds for the USA.

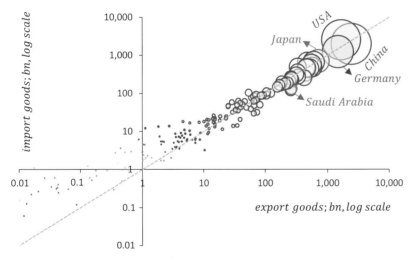

Figure 1.6 Exports and imports of goods, 2019
Source: See Table 1.2.
Notes: Values in billion current USD; based on BoP items; 181 countries included; bubbles are proportional to the country's percentage of total goods trade (exports and imports); dashed line is the diagonal.

BOX 1.1 TARIFFS AS A SOURCE OF GOVERNMENT REVENUE

Chapter 6 analyzes the economic forces underlying international trade flows, the welfare impact for different agents in the economy, and the consequences of restricting trade flows. In general, it is shown not only that international trade flows lead to efficiency gains and welfare improvements for a country as a whole, but also that policy measures restricting trade flows deteriorate welfare and reduce efficiency, sometimes in unexpected and covert ways. In view of these observations, the question arises *why* countries impose (welfare-deteriorating) trade restrictions. In this respect, it is necessary to point to the problems facing the governments of many developing nations which do not have an efficient tax-collecting system available. After all, tax collection requires detailed information on the inhabitants of the country, their income level, specific circumstances that may be relevant for an individual, and many public servants to gather and process the information. The governments of all nations, however, require funds to perform basic duties, such as protecting the country, providing law, order, and education, and so on.

In the absence of an efficient tax-collecting apparatus, it is thus tempting to collect government revenue by imposing tariffs on the (relatively easily controlled) international trade flows (imports duties, export duties, exchange profits, and the like). This is illustrated in Figure 1.7, which ranks countries in terms of taxes on international trade as a percentage of government revenue. It shows not only that the countries imposing high tariffs are generally developing nations, but also that some countries are highly dependent on taxing international trade flows for their tax revenue. This holds in

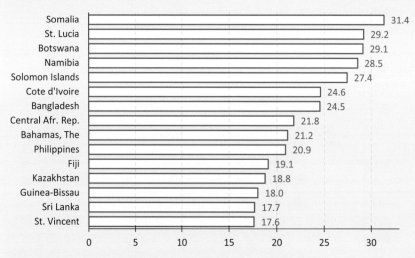

Figure 1.7 Taxes on international trade (% of revenue), 2019
Source: World Development Indicators online.
Notes: 2019 or most recent since 2016; top 15 countries; St. Vincent = St. Vincent and the Grenadines; Central Afr. Rep. = Central African Republic.

BOX 1.1 (cont.)

particular for Somalia, St. Lucia, Botswana, and Namibia, where it is about 30 percent of revenue. For all countries in the figure, it is above 17 percent. Even for a large country such as the Philippines, dependence of taxes on international trade for government revenue can be as high as 21 percent.

Figure 1.6 also indicates that the oil-exporting nation Saudi Arabia has much larger exports than imports ($262 versus $132 billion, respectively). Similar observations hold for other oil-exporting nations. Note that for many small trading nations in the lower part of the diagram, the import value exceeds the export value (the observations are above the 45° line). Most of these observations are developing nations which can finance their high imports through foreign aid flows and remittances from workers abroad.

1.7   Global Competitiveness

Many aspects that are important for economic growth and development are not yet discussed in this chapter. Chapter 7 provides an overview of the forces of economic growth. The role of institutions is analyzed to lay a solid foundation for the economic growth process in Chapters 4 and 8. In order to invest and innovate, firms and individuals need access to sources of finance, an issue analyzed in Chapter 9. Workers need to be healthy, well-trained, and educated in order to function properly in our increasingly complex society. Education is discussed in Chapter 13 and health in Chapter 14. An idea of what is needed to create a competitive economy is provided annually by the World Economic Forum in the Global Competitiveness Report. The 2019 framework distinguishes between 12 so-called pillars of competitiveness (see Table 1.7), subdivided under four main headings.

Under the heading *Enabling environment*, there are four pillars, namely institutions, infrastructure, ICT adoption, and macroeconomic stability. Under the heading *Human capital*, the pillars are health and skills. Under the heading *Markets*, the pillars are product market, labor market, financial system, and market size. Finally, under the heading *Innovation ecosystem*, the pillars are business dynamism and innovation capability.

This approach acknowledges that many different aspects are important for determining a country's competitiveness and economic growth. The relative importance of individual components for total competitiveness is, of course, up for discussion. The report, however, uses detailed information to estimate how well a country is scoring on each of the individual components. The institutions pillar, for example, is estimated using 26 different indicators, including property rights, freedom of the press, terrorism incidence, judicial independence, organized crime, e-participation, and so on. To take another example, the business dynamism pillar is estimated using eight different indicators, including cost of

Table 1.7. Pillars of Global Competitiveness Report, 2019

Pillar	Abbreviation	Full
Enabling environment		
1	Inst	Institutions
2	Infr	Infrastructure
3	ICT	ICT adoption
4	Stab	Macroeconomic stability
Human capital		
5	Heal	Health
6	Skill	Skills
Markets		
7	Prod	Product market
8	Lab	Labor market
9	Fin	Financial system
10	Size	Market size
Innovation ecosystem		
11	Bus	Business dynamism
12	Inno	Innovation capability

Source: World Economic Forum 2019.

starting a business, insolvency recovery rate, willingness to delegate authority, growth of innovative companies, and so on – similarly for the other 10 pillars.

The competitiveness report scores all 12 pillars on a scale from 0 to 100 and calculates an overall competitiveness score based on that for 141 countries (together accounting for 99 percent of world income). The highest score in 2019 was received by Singapore (84.8), followed by the USA (83.7), Hong Kong (83.1), and the Netherlands (82.4). The lowest scores were received in Chad (35.1), followed by Yemen (35.5), DR Congo (36.1), and Haiti (36.3). Rather than focusing on these scores for individual countries, it is more appropriate for this book to analyze the scores for the global regions discussed in section 1.2 (see Box 1.2 for a warning on grouping countries together). To do so, the high-income countries of Europe and North America are combined in one group (and excluded from the Europe & Central Asia region, which is labeled Eurasia in the report, but the term ECA continues to be used here). The report then calculates averages for each of the 12 pillars for seven global regions. The scores then range from a minimum of 29.4 for innovation capability in Sub-Sahara Africa to a maximum of 92.6 for macroeconomic stability in Europe & North America. The maximum scores vary substantially per pillar (from 58.1 to 92.6). For illustration purposes, scores are therefore calculated *relative* to the maximum for that pillar.

Figure 1.8 shows the relative score for the six global developing regions in a radar diagram which ranges from 40 in the center to 100 at the end. The further away the score is from the

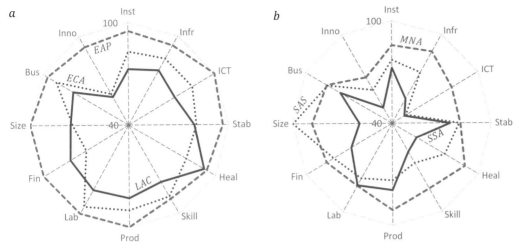

Figure 1.8 Global competitiveness for global regions; relative score, 2019
Source: Based on information from World Economic Forum 2019, table 1.
Notes: See Table 1.1 for global region abbreviations (ECA excludes high-income countries); see Table 1.7 for pillar abbreviations; Europe and North America (EUNAM) not included; scores for all pillars are defined relative to maximum score for that pillar, which is EUNAM for all pillars except Prod, Lab, Fin, and Size; axis ranges from 40 in the center to 100.

center, the higher the score for that pillar. The graphs thus show relative performance for each region for all pillars. The scores for Europe & North America are not included in the figure; they receive the highest score of 100 for all pillars, except for the four market pillars, where East Asia & Pacific receives the highest score (see panel a). Since the average score for the four market pillars in Europe & North America is 95.0, Figure 1.8 more or less indicates how the global developing regions are doing relative to Europe & North America.

From panel a, it is clear that East Asia & Pacific (including Japan, China, and Australia) scores highest on the four market pillars and close to the relative maximum on all other pillars. Its relative weakest points are for the human capital pillars health and skills. The Europe & Central Asia global region (including Russia and Ukraine) scores reasonably well on most pillars (the simple average is 82), but particularly poorly on the pillars innovation capability, financial system, and market size. It seems wise to focus efforts for improvements on these areas. The Latin America & Caribbean region scores somewhat weaker than Europe & Central Asia on most pillars and on average (about 78 points), although it does somewhat better on market size and much better on health and financial system.

From panel b, it is clear that the scores for the Middle East & North Africa are more balanced than in the other two regions, and therefore on average higher (about 85 points). Its relative weakness is on innovation capability. South Asia scores high on market size, but mediocre or poorly on the other pillars. It scores particularly low on ICT adoption and innovation capability, and relative to the other regions it scores lowest on product market and labor market. Even Sub-Sahara Africa scores higher in the latter two pillars, which immediately identifies its relative strongest points. The overall score is lowest for Sub-Sahara Africa (about 65 on average), with ICT adoption and innovation capability as its weakest points, just like South Asia.

BOX 1.2 THE BRIC(S) EMERGING MARKET ECONOMIES

The term BRIC countries, which later changed to BRICS countries, is based on the first letter of four (later five) countries and was introduced in 2001 by consultancy firm Goldman Sachs to refer to major emerging market economies. The included countries are Brazil, Russia, India, China, and South Africa. The term BRICS countries quickly became popular in the media as a catch-all term for major emerging market economies which are then grouped together in subsequent discussions. Figure 1.9 provides information on the income developments in these countries using GNI PPP in constant 2017 international dollars with a log scale, both per capita (panel a) and in total (panel b). Based on this information, it is remarkable how these countries have been grouped together and how popular the term BRICS is.

First, as panel a of Figure 1.9 shows, there have been enormous differences between the countries in terms of the development of income per capita. The compounded growth rate of income per capita over the period 1990–2019 ranges from a meagre 0.7 percent per year for Russia and South Africa to a remarkable 8.1 percent for China (based on the period 1995–2018). The growth rate for Brazil is mediocre (1.1 percent) and for India substantial (4.5 percent), but not as spectacular as for China. Also note the high variability of growth rate for Russia and, to a lesser extent, for Brazil. On the basis of this information alone, it seems unwise to group China and India together with the other three countries; see also the figure in the Preface to this textbook.

Second, as panel b of Figure 1.9 shows, there is an enormous difference between the countries in terms of total economic power and the speed at which this power is rising. In 2018, for example, total income in South Africa is only 3.3 percent of total income in China, which makes it difficult to understand the inclusion of South Africa. The total economic power of Brazil and Russia is also modest compared to that of China (about 14 and 18 percent of China's in 2018, respectively). In this respect, only India comes close

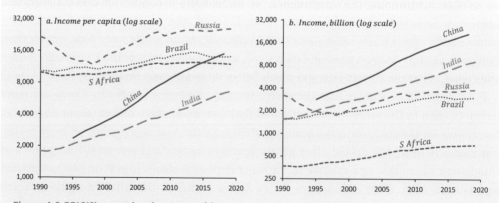

Figure 1.9 BRIC(S) countries; income and income per capita, 1990–2019
Source: Based on data from World Development Indicators.
Note: GNI PPP in constant 2017 international $.

BOX 1.2 (cont.)

(about 41 percent of China's total income in 2018, or more than twice as important as Brazil and Russia). The difference relative to panel a is based on differences in the size of population and its growth rate (which is fast in India and South Africa, negative in Russia, and in between in China and Brazil). Future demographic differences are also substantial.

In short, when listing "major emerging market economies," it seems wise to only include the I and C countries India and China of the BRICS acronym. The term IC is, of course, not "catchy" enough to become popular.

1.8   Conclusions

This chapter provides a snapshot of the state of economic development today. There are many countries (more than 200) which vary enormously in land area, population, international trade flows, and income level. Based on the World Bank classification, countries are frequently grouped together in (seven) "global regions" to better characterize the economic circumstances in different parts of the world. Throughout, this textbook emphasizes that economic development is positively, but imperfectly, correlated with the level of income per capita. Even after correcting for differences in local prices, which are higher for nontraded goods in high-income countries than in low-income countries, the variation in per capita income levels remains enormous. Taking income inequality within countries into consideration, the variation in income per capita is even higher. Your country of birth matters a great deal for determining your economic future.

Many issues play a role in determining the global competitiveness of a country, which is instrumental for explaining its level of economic development. This includes the building of reliable institutions, the construction of infrastructure connections, macroeconomic stability, access to health care, education, and training, the functioning of product, labor, and financial markets, and the innovative capabilities of a country. These aspects are analyzed in detail in the remainder of this book. But before this, the next chapter clarifies the steps to be taken to collect and statistically analyze economic data in combination with theoretical and methodological developments.

Further Reading

A solid source for weekly up-to-date economic information and analysis is provided by *The Economist*. There is a student discount for subscription, while most university libraries will either have physical copies or an online subscription available. See: www.economist.com.

The International Monetary Fund publishes two reports each year on global economic and financial developments, including emerging markets. Under the heading *World Economic Outlook*, these publications describe the global economy and highlight special topics that affect the world economy at the time of writing the reports. See: www.imf.org/en/Publications/WEO.

The World Bank publishes research on the current state of affairs, with a focus on developing countries. See: www.worldbank.org/en/research.

The Groningen Growth and Development Centre provides long-run-time series on economic growth, as well as trade data. See: www.rug.nl/ggdc/historicaldevelopment/. You can, for example, also find the complete Penn World Tables, with information for 183 countries since 1950 on relative levels of income, output, input, and productivity.

Specialist Branko Milanovic provides a technical account of how to correctly measure income inequality. See: Milanovic, B. 2005. *Worlds Apart: Measuring International and Global Inequality* (Princeton University Press).

2 Data and Methods

I often say that when you can measure what you are speaking about, and express it in numbers, you know something about it; but when you cannot measure it, when you cannot express it in numbers, your knowledge is of a meagre and unsatisfactory kind; it may be the beginning of knowledge, but you have scarcely, in your thoughts, advanced to the stage of science, whatever the matter may be.

Lord Kelvin (William Thompson, 1883)

There is nothing more practical than a good theory.

Kurt Lewin (1952, p. 169)

In the fields of observation, chance only favours the prepared mind.

Louis Pasteur (1854)

2.1 Introduction

It is almost excessive to start a chapter with three quotes, but their combination adequately reflects the essence of scientific understanding and continuous improvement. All three quotes are well known, although Lord Kelvin's is too long to be remembered verbatim. The process of scientific improvement is shown as a virtuous circle in Figure 2.1, explained briefly below.

The first quote by Lord Kelvin relates to statistics and argues that your knowledge and depth of scientific reasoning rises substantially when you are able to measure what you are analyzing and express it in numbers. There are, obviously, many things you cannot measure accurately or express in numbers, but economic science has over the last century made great progress in providing much better and more detailed statistical information on many relevant issues, including prices (and correcting for purchasing power), production (including more detailed disaggregation), consumption (and allowing for new goods and services), trade flows (including value-added trade), investment flows (including cross-border flows), and so on.

The ability to measure something and express it in numbers allows you to characterize it, summarize it, and better appreciate differences in characteristics for different sources or entities. The essence of such characterization is usually summarized in statistical properties, like mean, median, variance, and so on. This is discussed briefly in section 2.3 on simple statistics. The ability to compare is crucial at this stage. After all, you only know that a mean of 14 for some variable is high or low if you can compare it with a range of mean

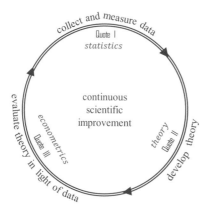

Figure 2.1 Virtuous cycle of continuous scientific improvement

observations for other entities. Before you can engage in this step of analysis, you have to collect data from appropriate sources, as explained briefly in section 2.2.

The second quote above by Kurt Lewin ("There is nothing more practical than a good theory") relates to theory. Variations of the quote attributed to other people are also available. The essence here is on the value of theoretical development when analyzing data as a good theory provides a coherent framework – a miniature world, so to say – which helps you to understand the relationships between variables. In short, with a good theory in mind, you know what to look for when analyzing data, which is tremendously valuable. It is difficult to fully appreciate the value of a good theory if you are new to a specific field, like the economics of developing and emerging markets. Only after working in a field for some time and analyzing relevant data do you start to realize how important a good theoretical framework is for doing your job. (Note that this chapter does not provide a theory of economic development, since this is done in all remaining chapters.)

The third quote above by Louis Pasteur ("In the fields of observation, chance only favours the prepared mind") relates to critical observation, the need to be prepared, and the ability to draw the right conclusion. In my view "Observation" could refer to collecting and measuring data (statistics) and a "prepared mind" could refer to analyzing these data from the perspective of a relevant theory. This brings us into the realm of econometrics, where theories are evaluated in light of the data. Chance favors the prepared mind by drawing the correct conclusion on what is needed to adjust our theories to better understand the data. At this step, therefore, the theories sometimes need to be revised, which requires more data collection to evaluate these new theories using appropriate econometric tools in a virtuous cycle of endless improvement, as illustrated in Figure 2.1.

After the discussion of data sources in section 2.2 and of simple statistics in section 2.3, the remainder of this chapter briefly reviews some econometrics models and issues. One chapter is, of course, too short to study econometrics, so the interested reader is referred to relevant books by Stock and Watson (2019), Wooldridge (2015), or Verbeek (2017) for further reading. Section 2.5 reviews the steps to go from theory to econometrics, section 2.6 explains regressions, and section 2.7 reviews hypothesis testing. Section 2.8 addresses some regression problems and section 2.9 some more advanced issues. Section 2.10 concludes.

2.2 Data Sources

If you want to analyze an economic phenomenon in the spirit of Lord Kelvin, you need to be able to measure the subject somehow and gather *reliable* data. Reliability is the key issue here, in particular if you are interested in relationships between variables. If, for example, you measure variable X with bias and inaccurately (see section 2.8) as well as variable Y, then an attempt to investigate the relationship between variables X and Y with any accuracy is doomed from the start. This principle is also known as: *garbage in, garbage out*.

There are many problems associated with the primary data collection process. The second edition of the Emergency Food Security Assessment Handbook of the World Food Programme (WFP), for example, mentions these common problems (WFP 2009, box 3.5; see Box 2.1 for recent changes):

- interviewers lack knowledge or skills;
- information is incomplete or inaccurate;
- questionnaires or checklists neglect key issues;
- interviewers and informants are biased;
- interviewers and informants become bored;
- interviewers experience assessment fatigue.

The handbook addresses these and related issues, including sampling problems and methods, conceptual issues, planning, interpreting, and analyzing the data in about 300 pages. Clearly, professional agencies where people are trained and organized to deal with data collection problems have a great advantage over individuals and nonprofessional organizations as a source of data. The simple advice when searching for reliable data is therefore: always go to official international organizations and statistical agencies of individual countries. Only if the type of data you are looking for is not available should you start to look for other sources of data. Any analysis you perform on data downloaded from dubious internet sources is questionable. Remember: garbage in, garbage out.

Since this book focuses on international development, Table 2.1 provides an overview of some relevant data sources in this perspective for certain types of data as listed by *The Guardian* in 2016 (in no particular order). As noted above, most of the listed sources are international organizations, like the World Bank, the OECD (Organisation for Economic Co-operation and Development), the IMF (International Monetary Fund), the UN (United Nations, including sub-organizations), and the IEA (International Energy Agency). Two

BOX 2.1 THE TABLET AND MOBILE PHONE TECH REVOLUTION IN DATA COLLECTION

When measuring poverty indicators, the World Bank is facing similar problems in the primary data collection process as listed by the World Food Programme in section 2.2. Technological innovation, however, is alleviating some of these problems. As the World Bank (2017) notes:

> It wasn't long ago that to conduct household surveys, data collectors from national statistical offices would set off on a journey across the country to interview respondents on a set of questions, equipped with nothing but a paper questionnaire on which to jot down the information. Most were incredibly diligent. Others, less so. Either way, these data collectors would return to the statistical office, their hand-written notes would be transferred to a computer system, and after a bunch of data calculations, voila: a country's poverty rate.

The World Bank continues by describing how this process is transformed and improved by using tablets and mobile phones for data collection. Data collectors still travel to towns, but survey answers are entered on tablets and automatically synced to a centralized system. GPS trackers ensure that collectors go to the right place and interview the right people. Alternatively, when certain areas cannot be reached, for example, for safety reasons, mobile phone surveys can be used instead without the need for the data collector to travel as a complement to household surveys. One way to facilitate this is by handing out mobile phones and solar chargers to respondents. As Alvin Etang Ndip, a World Bank economist, says: "The tech revolution is really changing the way we work. For the better."

other listed sources are based at reputable academic institutions, namely Harvard University and Uppsala University, which also tend to be trained to deal with data collection problems, and thus are also reasonably reliable sources of information. The most questionable entry in the list is the Transnational Land Database, which attempts to give an overview of international land transactions. This is a difficult task as it is based on sensitive and private data. The entry also serves as an indication that for certain types of data it is hard to find information from official statistical agencies. Rather than not analyzing the problem at all, it is then worthwhile to look for the best, most reliable, and objective data available. As the table indicates, an excellent primary source of information on all economic-development-related issues is the World Bank's World Development Indicators (WDI), which has a wide range of user-friendly, reliable, and publicly available information. If the type of data you are searching for is not available in the WDI, you will have to look elsewhere. This may be the case, for example, if you are interested in the performance of different regional parts (provinces or cities) within a country, as the WDI is country-based.

Table 2.1. *The Guardian's* top 10 sources of data on international development, 2016

Source	What
Economic Atlas and Globe of Complexity	See http://atlas.cid.harvard.edu/ and http://globe.cid.harvard.edu/ at Harvard University, USA, for a visualization of world trade and industrialization data; note that visualization can be complex to understand.
International Energy Agency Atlas	See http://energyatlas.iea.org/#!/tellmap/-1118783123 for an overview of energy use and production data.
Transnational Land Database	See https://landmatrix.org/ for an overview of international transactions in land ("land grab" according to some sources); guesstimates only, because this is based on sensitive and private data.
IMF Data	See www.imf.org/en/Data for all sorts of financial information, including debt levels and capital flows.
Uppsala Conflict Data Program	See www.pcr.uu.se/research/UCDP/ at the University of Uppsala, Sweden, for information on organized violence and conflicts affecting the lives of millions of people.
World Bank Doing Business Database	See www.doingbusiness.org/en/rankings for a range of business environment indicators and the actual costs of trade.
World Development Indicators Database	See https://datacatalog.worldbank.org/dataset/world-development-indicators for World Bank information on almost anything at the country level; a user-friendly database that is an excellent first source of information.
UNDP Human Development Index	See http://hdr.undp.org/en/data for information on a broader range of human development indicators, including education and health.
UN Comtrade Database	See https://comtrade.un.org/ for detailed raw data on trade flows; for easier access (if your institution has it), see: https://wits.worldbank.org/default.aspx.
OECD Aid Database	See www.oecd.org/dac for information on aid and international development finance data.

Source: Based on *The Guardian* 2016.

2.3   Statistics

The first step in the analysis after gathering information on an economic phenomenon is always to characterize the data using some simple statistics. Table 2.2 gives an overview of the most commonly used statistics, subdivided into simple statistics (part a) and more advanced statistics (part b). These statistics are briefly discussed below, with the outcome of a fair dice as an example, as indicated in the table.

The main simple statistics are minimum, maximum, mean, and median. For a fair dice, the *minimum* (lowest) value is 1 and the *maximum* (highest) value is 6 and the *range* encompasses the integers from 1 to 6. If we roll the fair dice there is 1/6 probability (chance) for each of the six outcomes from 1 to 6. The *expected value* of rolling the dice (the mathematical expectation of the outcome before rolling the dice) is equal to

Table 2.2. Some statistics; fair dice example

Statistic	Description	Fair dice
(a) Simple		
Minimum	Lowest value	1.00
Maximum	Highest value	6.00
Mean	"Average" value; first raw moment, see Table 2.4	3.50
Median	Value separating lower half from upper half of observations	3.50
(b) More advanced		
Variance	Measure of dispersion; second central moment, see Table 2.4	2.92
Standard deviation	Measure of dispersion; $\sqrt{variance} \equiv \sigma$, see Table 2.4	4.18
Skewness	Measure of asymmetry; third standardized moment, see Table 2.4	0.00
Kurtosis	Measure of "tail fatness"; fourth standardized moment, see Table 2.4	1.73

Table 2.3. Calculating some statistics for a fair dice

Outcome X	$X - \mu$	$(X - \mu)^2$	$(X - \mu)^3$	$(X - \mu)^4$
1	−2.5	6.25	−15.63	39.06
2	−1.5	2.25	−3.38	5.06
3	−0.5	0.25	−0.13	0.06
4	0.5	0.25	0.13	0.06
5	1.5	2.25	3.38	5.06
6	2.5	6.25	15.63	39.06
$\dfrac{sum}{6} = 3.5 \equiv \mu$	$\dfrac{sum}{6} = 0$	$\dfrac{sum}{6} = 2.92 \equiv \sigma^2$	$\dfrac{sum}{6} = 0$	$\dfrac{sum}{6} = 14.73$
Mean μ		St. Dev. $\sqrt{2.92} = 1.71$	Skewness $\dfrac{0}{\sigma^3} = 0$	Kurtosis $\dfrac{14.73}{\sigma^4} = 1.73$

$\frac{1}{6} \times 1 + \frac{1}{6} \times 2 + \frac{1}{6} \times 3 + \frac{1}{6} \times 4 + \frac{1}{6} \times 5 + \frac{1}{6} \times 6 = 3.5$. This number is known as the *mean* or *average* value and is commonly denoted by μ. Note that in this case the actual outcome (an integer) cannot be equal to the mean (which is 3.5). The *median* value divides the number of observations in two equal parts, with 50 percent of the observations lower than the median and 50 percent higher than the median. With six outcomes (an even number), the median is somewhere in between the third and fourth outcome (in this case, between 3 and 4); it is common to just take the simple average (3.5). In this case, the mean and median values are the same. This is always the case for a *symmetric* distribution (with the same shape to the left and the right of the mean).

Calculating the more advanced statistics of Table 2.2 is a little more cumbersome. The principles are provided in Table 2.4 and discussed below. The calculations for the fair dice example are provided in Table 2.3. The first column indicates that there are six possible outcomes, namely 1 through to 6. If we sum these values and multiply by 1/6 (which is the equal probability of each outcome), we get the mean value $\mu = 3.5$ (see also the calculation above). This provides us with an indication of *where* the distribution is located (namely around 3.5). The more advanced statistics provide us with information on the distribution *relative* to the mean value μ. The second column of Table 2.3 therefore calculates the deviation $X - \mu$ between the outcome and the mean. If the outcome is 1, the deviation is -2.5, while if the outcome is 4, the deviation is 0.5, and so on. If we sum these values and multiply by 1/6, we get the expected deviation between the outcome and the mean, which is, of course, zero.

The more advanced statistics use the information from column 2 of Table 2.3 to provide information on the shape of the distribution around the mean. Column 3 calculates the *variance* σ^2 and the *standard deviation* σ (which is simply the square root of the variance). Both are measures of the *dispersion* around the mean of the distribution; the higher these numbers, the further away from the mean the observations tend to be. The variance is calculated as the expected value of the squares of the deviation from the mean. If the outcome is 2, for example, the deviation is -1.5 and the deviation squared is 2.25. This outcome occurs with probability 1/6, so if we sum column three and multiply by 1/6, we get the variance $\sigma^2 = 2.92$. If we take its square root, we get the standard deviation $\sigma = 1.71$.

Following a similar procedure, columns four and five of Table 2.3 provide information on the skewness and kurtosis of the distribution. Note that both measures are normalized by dividing by σ^3 and σ^4, respectively (see Table 2.4 and the discussion below). *Skewness* provides a measure of *asymmetry* of the distribution around the mean. If the distribution is symmetric, skewness is zero. If the distribution is skewed to the right (as is the case for many economic variables), skewness is positive. If the distribution is skewed to the left, skewness is negative. In the fair dice example, skewness is zero because the distribution is symmetric. *Kurtosis* provides a measure of the *fatness* of the *tails* (the extreme

Table 2.4. Overview of raw, central, and standardized moments

Moment k	*Raw* moment Expected value about 0	*Central* moment Expected value about μ	*Standardized* moment Central moment normalized σ^k
1	$E(X) \equiv \mu$; *mean*	$E(X - \mu) = 0$	$\dfrac{E(X - \mu)}{\sigma} = 0$
2	$E(X^2)$	$E\big((X - \mu)^2\big) \equiv \sigma^2$; *variance*	$\dfrac{E\big((X - \mu)^2\big)}{\sigma^2} = 1$
3	$E(X^3)$	$E\big((X - \mu)^3\big)$	$\dfrac{E\big((X - \mu)^3\big)}{\sigma^3}$; *skewness*
4	$E(X^4)$	$E\big((X - \mu)^4\big)$	$\dfrac{E\big((X - \mu)^4\big)}{\sigma^4}$; *kurtosis*

Moments of random variable X, where E is the expectations operator.

observations) of the distribution. By definition, kurtosis is positive. To get an idea of whether or not the tails are "fat," it is customary to compare to the normal distribution, which has a kurtosis of 3. If, therefore, kurtosis is higher than 3, the tails are "fat," whereas the opposite holds if kurtosis is lower than 3 (as is the case for the fair dice example). For confusion's sake, some statistical programs report *excess kurtosis* (which is defined as *kurtosis* − 3) under the heading *kurtosis*, so one should be careful in correctly interpreting the outcome.

In the case of rolling a fair dice there are only six possible (discrete) outcomes, each with a probability of 1/6. In the case of flipping a fair coin there are only two possible outcomes (heads or tails), each with a 50 percent probability. If the dice or coin is not fair we need to adjust the probability of a certain outcome, while making sure the total adds up to one. In many other, economically relevant cases there are many possible outcomes and it is easier to treat the variable as a continuous outcome. This is the case, for example, for income levels, which may take on a wide range of possible outcomes. If the random variable X is continuous we do not work with discrete possibilities of certain outcomes, but rather with a *probability density function* $f(x)$ (pdf for short), that gives the likelihood of a certain outcome x. This is briefly discussed in Box 2.2, together with its counterpart the *cumulative distribution function* (cdf, for short).

Note that if $f(x)$ is a pdf over some domain A we must have: $\int_A f(x)dx = 1$, which means the total of all probabilities must add up to one.[1] Moreover, if $g(X)$ is a well-defined function, its *expected value* or *mathematical expectation* is defined as: $E(g(x)) \equiv \int_X f(x)g(x)dx$, where E is the expectations operator. Many statistics are expected values of simple functions, frequently based on *moments* as indicated in Table 2.4. The first (raw) moment is the expected value of the function $g(X) = X$ and is thus simply the mean μ. The second (raw) moment is the expected value of the function $g(X) = X^2$, the third moment is the expected value of X^3, and so on. Instead of *raw* moments (which is the expected value about zero), we can also calculate *central* moments, which is the expected value about μ. The first central moment is therefore the expected value of $X - \mu$, which is simply zero. The second central moment is the expected value of $(X - \mu)^2$, which is the variance σ^2, and so on. Finally, we can calculate *standardized* moments, which are the central moments normalized by the standard deviation σ to the relevant moment power (leading to a dimensionless number). The third standardized moment is therefore the expected value of $(X - \mu)^3/\sigma^3$, which is equal to the skewness of the distribution. Similarly, the fourth standardized moment is kurtosis. All of this is summarized in Table 2.4.

Figure 2.3 illustrates the above discussion for three example density functions in the range from 0 to 1.

---

[1] In our applications the set A will always be an interval on the real line. If you are not comfortable with integrals you may replace them with summations over a set of discrete outcomes indexed by i with outcome probability p_i associated with x_i, in which case $\sum_i p_i = 1$ and $E(g(X)) = \sum_i g(x_i)p_i$.

BOX 2.2 UNCERTAINTY, DENSITY, AND DISTRIBUTION

When you flip a coin the outcome is uncertain. If the coin is fair the chance that *tails* will appear is 50 percent, indicating that if you flip the coin infinitely many times half of the outcomes will be tails. The other outcomes will be *heads* as these are the only two possibilities. This can be represented mathematically by defining the (discrete) random variable $x = 1$ if heads occurs and $x = 0$ if tails occurs. For the fair coin we then write $P(X = 1) = 0.5$ as well as $P(X = 0) = 0.5$ to indicate the probability P of an outcome. If the coin is not fair, say $P(X = 1) = 0.6$, then we conclude that $P(X = 0) = 0.4$ as the total probability must sum to unity (*some* outcome must occur).

The variable x of outcomes may also take on a continuum of possibilities, say any value in the interval $[0, 1]$. Rather than focusing on a particular outcome, we now focus on the probability that the outcome falls in a certain range as dictated by the *probability density function* (pdf), say $f(x)$. The probability that the outcome is then below a certain value x, referred to as the *cumulative distribution function* (cdf), say $F(x)$, is given by $F(x) \equiv P(X \leq x) = \int_0^x f(x)dx$. This is illustrated in Figure 2.2, where the area under the curve of $f(x)$ between 0 and x gives the probability that the outcome is below the value x, which is equal to the value of the cdf. Relevant properties are: (i) $F'(x) = f(x)$, (ii) the probability that the outcome is in between the values x_0 and x_1 is given by the area under the pdf between those points: $\int_{x_0}^{x_1} f(x)dx = F(x_1) - F(x_0)$, and (iii) the probability that the outcome is equal to a specific value is zero.

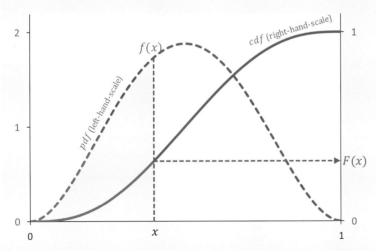

Figure 2.2 Cumulative distribution (cdf) and probability density (pdf)

- The solid line with a peak in the middle is a *normal* distribution with mean 0.5 and standard deviation 0.14 denoted by $N(0.5, 0.14)$. It is a symmetric distribution where the mean is equal to the median, such that the skewness is equal to 0. Like all normal distributions, kurtosis is 3.

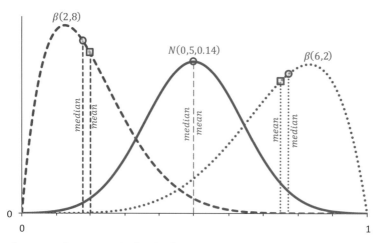

Figure 2.3 Three example density functions

- The dashed line with a peak on the left is a *beta* distribution with parameters 2 and 8 denoted by $\beta(2, 8)$. It is an asymmetric distribution where the mean (0.200) is *higher* than the median (0.179), such that the distribution is skewed to the right as indicated by the *positive* skewness (0.83). Kurtosis is 3.49, such that the tails are somewhat *fatter* than for the normal distribution.
- The dotted line with a peak on the right is a *beta* distribution with parameters 6 and 2 denoted by $\beta(6, 2)$. It is an asymmetric distribution where the mean (0.750) is *lower* than the median (0.773), such that the distribution is skewed to the left as indicated by the *negative* skewness (–0.69). Kurtosis is 3.11, such that the tails are slightly *fatter* than for the normal distribution.

The next section illustrates the use of statistics with an income per capita example.

2.4   Income Per Capita

Chapter 1 discussed the wide variations in income per capita at the country level, even after correcting for price differences (PPP – purchasing power parity, here in constant 2011 $). The summary statistics described in the previous section for this case are reported in Table 2.5 (ignore the information in natural logs for the moment). The range is from a minimum of $663 per capita in the Central African Republic to a maximum of $116,799 in Qatar (more than 176 times as much). The mean value of $18,081 is close to the income level of Argentina, while the median value of $11,348 is equal to that of Sri Lanka. (Note that the population-weighted mean value of $15,265 is significantly less than the simple mean of $18,081 reported here. Taking the size of the population into consideration provides a more accurate picture of the average income level per capita but requires, of course, more information (namely the population size of all countries). The population-weighted average is about equal to the income level in China.) Since there are 193 countries

Table 2.5. Summary statistics for income per capita, 2017

	income per capita	ln (*income per capita*)
Minimum	663	6.497
Maximum	116,799	11.67
Mean	18,081	9.22
Median	11,348	9.34
Standard deviation	19,289	1.17
Skewness	1.97	–0.26
Kurtosis	7.99	2.30

Source: Based on World Development Indicators online data.
Notes: Income is GNI PPP per capita in constant 2011 $, most recent observation in 2011–17 period; 193 countries included.

included in the data, this means that 96 countries have a lower income level than $11,348 (Sri Lanka) and 96 countries have a higher income level. The fact that the median is substantially lower than the mean indicates that the distribution is skewed to the right, as discussed below. Indeed, alternative measures of skewness are based on the deviation between mean and median.

The standard deviation of income per capita is $19,289. This is a measure of dispersion of the observations around the mean. Based on the normal distribution, a rule of thumb is that about 68 percent of the observations are within one standard deviation from the mean. In this case, however, 85 percent of the observations are within one standard deviation, which indicates that this distribution cannot be characterized by a normal distribution (see below). The skewness is positive and large (1.97), indicating again that the distribution is skewed to the right. Finally, kurtosis is large (7.99), indicating that the tails are *fat* compared to the normal distribution.

The summary statistics provided in Table 2.5 provide some indication of the shape of the distribution, but a better picture is provided if the distribution itself is examined more closely. We proceed in two steps: first, by looking at discrete so-called *bins*; and, second, by using a continuous framework. This also illustrates the advantages of the admittedly more complicated continuous approach.

For the discrete picture we divide the range into 15 *bins* of equal size. The first bin ranges from 0 to 8,000; the second from 8,000 to 16,000; and so on. The result is illustrated in a histogram of income per capita in panel a of Figure 2.4. Starting with the Central African Republic and ending with Jamaica, no fewer than 77 countries (40 percent of the total) are classified in the first bin from $0 to $8,000. Another 42 countries are in the second bin, 21 countries are in the third bin, and 17 countries are in the fourth bin. Taken together these four bins in the range from $0 to $32,000 account for 81 percent of all countries (and 86 percent of total population). The rest is spread out over the remaining 11 bins. Some of these have no observations at all (bins 13 and 14), while others have only one observation (bins 11, 12, and 15, with Singapore, Macao, and Qatar, respectively).

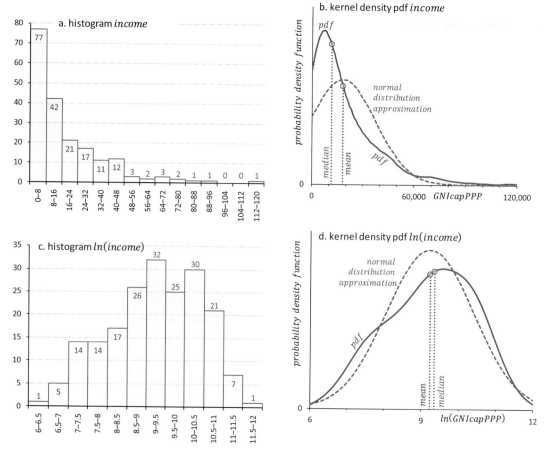

Figure 2.4 Histogram and probability density of income per capita, 2017
Source: Created using World Development Indicators online.
Notes: Income is GNI PPP per capita in constant 2011 $, most recent observation in 2011–17 period; 193 countries included; panel a labels ×1,000; normal distribution approximations based on sample mean and standard deviation.

The histogram helps us to understand how skewed the distribution of income per capita is, with many countries to the left and a few countries to the right. More precisely, 125 countries have an income level below the mean (which is 65 percent of all countries, representing 78 percent of total population), while only 68 have an income level above the mean. However, the histogram does not provide any information on the shape of the distribution for low values of income per capita, simply because so many countries are lumped together in the low-number bins. To improve our understanding in this respect, it is preferable to use a continuous approach based on kernel densities, as explained in detail in Box 2.3.

Panel b of Figure 2.4 shows the kernel density pdf of income per capita in combination with the mean and median values and an approximation based on the normal distribution (with sample mean and standard deviation). The kernel density first rises, reaches a peak at about $7,000, and then mostly declines (with a brief increase beyond $100,000 based on the Qatar outlier). The skewness of the distribution, with a mean substantially above the

BOX 2.3 KERNEL DENSITIES

A disadvantage of histograms is their discrete nature. For all values of *x* within a certain interval all observations receive an equal weight, while all values outside of the interval receive a weight of zero. *Kernel density* smoothing procedures give a varying weight to all observations based on the distance between *x* and the observations, see Dinardo and Tobias (2001) for a discussion. The kernel function is a non-negative function that integrates to one. Various options are available, but the normal distribution is used in this book. The smoothing procedure implies the choice of a bandwidth parameter $h > 0$ that one would like to choose as small as the data will allow. Its choice involves a trade-off between the bias of the estimator and its variance. This book uses the rule of thumb that if there are *N* data points a suitable choice is: $h = (4/3N)^{1/5}\hat{\sigma}$, where $\hat{\sigma}$ is the standard deviation of the sample.

So how exactly is the kernel density pdf in Figure 2.4 constructed? Recall that we have data points x_i on the level of income per capita for each of 193 countries ($i = 1, \ldots, 193$). To calculate the kernel density at a particular point, we first have to choose these points. Let's denote them by z_j. In panel b of the figure starting from 0 we increase in steps of 100 up to 1,000; followed by steps of 200 up to 20,000; concluding with steps of 1,000 up to 120,000 (for a total of 206 points). Let φ be the standard normal density function, $N = 193$, and define *h* as above, then the kernel density *g* at point z_j equals:

$$g(z_j) = \frac{1}{Nh} \sum_{i=1}^{N} \varphi \left(\frac{z_j - x_i}{h} \right)$$

Panel b of Figure 2.4 simply connects all these data points. Panel d does the same for the natural log of income per capita in equal-sized steps. Obviously, standard statistics and econometric packages have software incorporated to calculate kernel densities, but the advantage of doing it yourself is that you know what you are doing.

median, is clearly illustrated by the kernel density. When comparing the actual pdf with the normal distribution approximation, it is clear that this does no justice to the distribution on either side of the mean. The difficulty with the wide scale of income per capita (from 663 to 116,799) and the lack of detail at the low-income level can also be tackled by using a natural logarithmic scale, in particular since this is used in many theoretical explanations of differences in income levels. Our next step is therefore to analyze the *log* of income regarding statistics, histogram, and kernel density.

2.4.1 The Log of Income Per Capita

When analyzing the statistics of the natural logarithm of income per capita in Table 2.5, we see that the range is from about 6.5 to almost 12, the mean is 9.22, and the median is 9.34. Since the median is slightly higher than the mean, the distribution in slightly skewed to the left (–0.26). The kurtosis is somewhat lower than for the normal distribution (2.30) and the standard deviation is 1.17. According to the rule of thumb for the normal distribution, about 68 percent of the observations should be within one standard deviation, which is approximately true for the sample distribution (64 percent).

Looking at the histogram in panel c of Figure 2.4, which is divided into 12 bins of equal size starting with the bin from 6 to 6.5 (with one country) and concluding with the bin from 11.5 to 12 (also with one country), we see that the distribution is more symmetric, slightly skewed to the left, and with a suggestion of two peaks (for bins 7 and 9). Looking at the kernel density pdf in panel d of Figure 2.4, the suggestion of two peaks disappears. Instead, there is a single peak at around 9.7 (which translates to a per capita income of around $17,000). The kernel density is not symmetric, but at least much better approximated by a normal distribution than the density of income per capita in panel b. Comparing the kernel density with the approximation for the log of income per capita in panel d, note that the kernel density is higher than the approximation below 8 (around $3,000) and in the range from 10 to 11.5 (around $22,000 to close to $100,000). In any case, this illustrates that it may be useful to analyze monotone transformations (like the natural logarithm) to investigate the impact on the distribution properties of the sample. The next section continues with a brief discussion on the required steps to confront our theories with the data.

2.5   From Theory to Econometrics

When we are developing different theories to try to better understand various economic phenomena, we often assume that the relationships between the economic variables we are analyzing are exact. In principle, our theories should lead to results, that is propositions or predictions that should hold empirically if the theory is true. If we gather economic data to test if the theoretical implications do indeed hold in reality, we need a method to determine whether or not a theory is refuted. This is the work of econometricians. In practice, things are, as usual, not quite that simple, for four main reasons.

First, we must recast the theory in a manner suitable for empirical evaluation and testing. This means we have to acknowledge the fact that the relationships between the economic variables of our theories are not exact due to simplifications and disturbances. There may be, therefore, deviations from the exact relationships which we can contribute to other phenomena, such as measurement errors or the weather, which do not immediately refute the theory. The point is, of course, that these deviations should not be *too large*.

Second, it can be complicated, even after overcoming the first problem, to actually test the implications of a theory for technical or econometric reasons. Numerous examples can be given of the many hurdles econometricians sometimes have to jump and traps they have to avoid before they can devise an adequate test of what may initially look like a simple implication of a theory (see sections 2.6 to 2.9).

Third, it can be virtually impossible, even after overcoming the first and second problems, to pinpoint the nature of an observed friction between theory and empirics.

Remember that our theories are usually based on a range of assumptions. In many cases, economic theorists may be convinced by the arguments of econometricians that an implication of a theory does not hold in practice, but disagree strongly on the particular assumption on which the theory was based which caused this friction. It can take several decades of scientific research, involving the development of new theories, new tests, and so on, before some, if any, consensus on the nature of the problem is reached.

Fourth, even if an empirical test confirms our theory, this does not necessarily prove it. Perhaps some other theory can also explain the observations; we are never really sure.

2.6 Regressions

This section focuses on the simplest version of the first problem mentioned in section 2.5. Suppose there is an economic theory which predicts a linear relationship between the economic variables y and x, such that $y = \alpha + \beta x$, where α and β are unknown parameters (representing the underlying *truth*). Since all theories are simplifications of reality (which is what makes it theory), there is always a range of other phenomena which might influence the actual relationship between the variables y and x. There can be other, more complicated economic forces not modeled in the theory which could affect the relationship, there can be forces outside of economics (such as the weather, volcanic eruptions, or political changes) which could affect the relationship, there can be errors in measurement, and so on. This leads us to posit that the observed relationship is as follows:

$$y_i = \alpha + \beta x_i + \varepsilon_i \qquad\qquad 2.1$$

The subindex i denotes different observations (for example, different time periods or different countries) and the variable ε_i denotes the deviation between the structural linear part of an observation and the actual value of the observation. This deviation should not be too large, so when it is averaged over many observations, its value should be zero (it is, for example, normally distributed with mean 0 and variance σ^2).

An econometrician is, of course, not given the *true* parameters α and β of the structural linear equation (although there may be implied theoretical values). Instead, she is given a number of observations, that is joint pairs (x_i, y_i) of the economic variables x and y. These are depicted as the dots (or balls) in Figure 2.5. Her task is then to find the best line to fit these empirical observations, that is estimate an intercept (say a) and a slope (say b) to minimize the (quadratic) distance from the observations to the line, the so-called Ordinary Least Squares (OLS) estimation.

$$b_{OLS} = \frac{\sum_{i=1}^{N}(x_i - \bar{x})(y_i - \bar{y})}{\sum_{i=1}^{N}(x_i - \bar{x})(x_i - \bar{x})} = \frac{cov(x, y)}{var(x)} \qquad\qquad 2.2$$

$$a_{OLS} = \bar{y} - b_{OLS}\bar{x} \qquad\qquad 2.3$$

Technical Note 2.1 shows how this problem is solved in general. If there are N observations on the pairs (x_i, y_i) and we denote the sample averages with $\bar{x}$ and $\bar{y}$, then for the simple

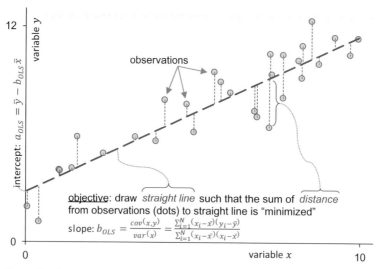

Figure 2.5 Basic econometrics; observations and regression line

two-dimensional case discussed above and illustrated in Figure 2.5 the solution is quite intuitive. The estimated slope (b_{OLS}) of the regression line (see equation 2.2) is the ratio $cov(x, y)/var(x)$, where $cov(x, y)$ denotes the covariance between the variables x and y. (The covariance is: $cov(x, y) = E((x - \bar{x})(y - \bar{y}))$.) The estimated intercept (a_{OLS}) corrects the average of the endogenous variable ($\bar{y}$) using the estimated slope times the average of the exogenous variable: $a_{OLS} = \bar{y} - b_{OLS}\bar{x}$, see equation 2.3. Box 2.4 briefly discusses under which conditions this OLS procedure leads to *good* results.

2.7 Hypothesis Testing

This section outlines briefly how hypotheses can be tested using OLS regressions. Figure 2.5 was artificially constructed using a *true* model with intercept 2 and slope 1 ($\alpha = 2, \beta = 1$) by adding (normally distributed) disturbances ε_i using a random number generator. Since the econometrician is only given the observations and not the true parameters, she tries to estimate their values (a_{OLS} and b_{OLS}) based on the observations. The terminology is to "run a *regression*," where y is the *endogenous* variable (the variable to be explained) and x is the *exogenous* variable (the explanatory variable). She finds the results depicted in equation 2.4. The numbers in parentheses are estimated standard errors of the estimated coefficients: see below. Instead of the true parameter 2 the econometrician therefore estimates the intercept to be 2.776 and instead of the true parameter 1 she estimates the slope to be 0.872. Well, we don't expect her to find the exact parameters, but how far off is she? Is this within acceptable limits? And how good is the *fit* of the estimated line?

BOX 2.4 ON THE BLUE-NESS OF OLS: GAUSS-MARKOV ASSUMPTIONS

One may wonder, of course, under which conditions the OLS procedure of section 2.6 gives *good* results? The term *good* focuses on two main aspects, namely (i) *unbiased* – which means that the expected value of the parameter is equal to the truth – and (ii) *best* – which means that the estimator has minimum variance. To keep the search controllable, it is customary to look for these aspects for a certain class of estimators, in this case the class of *linear estimators*. The question thus becomes: what is the Best Linear Unbiased Estimator (BLUE)? This can be summarized as: when is OLS BLUE?

The answer to this question is given by the four so-called *Gauss-Markov conditions*, named after the German mathematician Carl Friedrich Gauss (1777–1855) and the Russian mathematician Andrey Markov (1856–1922). These conditions, listed as assumptions A1–A4, are:

- A1 – *mean zero*; the error terms have mean zero, or $E(\varepsilon) = 0$.
- A2 – *independence*; the error terms are independent of the exogenous variables.
- A3 – *homoskedasticity*; the error terms have the same variance, or $var(\varepsilon_i) = \sigma^2$.
- A4 – *no autocorrelation*; the error terms are mutually uncorrelated, or $cov(\varepsilon_i, \varepsilon_j) = 0$ for $i \neq j$.

Note that conditions A3 and A4 can be written as: $var(\varepsilon) = \sigma^2 I_N$, where I_N is the $N \times N$ identity matrix. In combination with assumption A1, assumption A2 then implies $E(\varepsilon|X) = E(\varepsilon) = 0$, where X is the matrix collecting all exogenous variables; see Technical Note 2.1. Section 2.8 briefly discusses how to deal with problems that arise if these assumptions are violated.

$$y = \underbrace{2.776}_{(0.4730)} + \underbrace{0.872}_{(0.0744)} x \qquad\qquad 2.4$$

It is clear that the fit of the line is better the closer the observations are to the line. A popular measure for this fit is the share of the variance of the variable y explained by the estimated line, the so-called R^2. In this case, 83.1 percent of the variance is explained by the regression ($R^2 = 0.831$). In general, the higher the R^2, the better the fit. It should be noted, however, that the share of the variance that can be explained differs widely per application, with some areas of economics where researchers are happy if they can explain 20 percent of the variance and others where less than 90 percent is considered bad.

In this respect, the standard errors reported in equation 2.4 are more useful as they indicate the reliability of the estimated coefficients. They can be used for hypothesis testing. Based on the so-called t-distribution, we can calculate the probability that the true parameter has a particular value, given the observations on the pairs (x_i, y_i) available to us and the associated regression line. As a rule-of-thumb: hypotheses within two standard deviations of the estimated coefficient are accepted; in this case, this means a slope in between 0.7232 and 1.0208 and an intercept in between 1.830 and 3.722. Note that the true values α and β (equal to 1 and 2) are within these limits. Alternatively, the rule of thumb implies that an absolute t-value (which equals the estimated coefficient divided by the estimated standard error) larger than two denotes a *significant* parameter as the estimated coefficient differs from the hypothesis *equal to zero* by more than two standard deviations.

2.7.1   Capital Per Worker and Income Per Capita

Section 2.4 briefly analyzed the enormous differences in income per capita at the country level. One simple reason for these differences that comes to mind is that workers in high-income countries have more advanced and better functioning capital at their disposal, which raises their productivity. Construction workers in developing countries, for example, have only simple tools to work with, while construction workers in advanced countries have equipment available, such as cranes and drills, to help them lift heavy loads or destruct hard obstacles. This is analyzed in more detail in Chapter 7. For now, this section illustrates how regression analysis may be helpful in analyzing this relationship and how some simple hypotheses could be tested.

Figure 2.6 illustrates the relationship between capital per worker and income per capita using a log scale for both variables. The overall impression is that the linear relationship in the figure does a fairly good job at explaining most of the variance in the log of income per capita. Indeed, the share of explained variance is more than 87 percent, indicating that capital per worker is certainly an important component in explaining income differences.

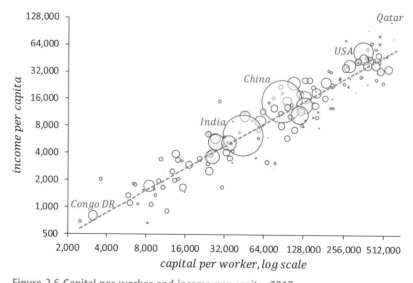

Figure 2.6 Capital per worker and income per capita, 2017
Sources: Created using World Development Indicators for income per capita and Penn World Table 9.0 for capital per worker.
Notes: Income in GNI PPP per capita (constant 2011 $), most recent observation in 2011–17 period; capital per worker in 2014 (constant 2011 $); slope regression is 0.8288; standard error of estimated slope is 0.02486; $R^2 = 0.8714$; bubbles proportional to population in 2017.

The estimated slope of the regression line is 0.8288 with an estimated standard error of 0.02486. Since both variables are measured in logs, the slope of the line indicates the relative change in the endogenous variable (in this case income per capita) as a consequence of a relative change in the exogenous variable (in this case capital per worker). The estimate 0.8288 therefore indicates that if capital per worker rises by 1 percent, then income per capita rises by about 0.83 percent.

Regarding hypotheses testing for the estimated slope of the regression line, the first focus here is on statistical significance itself. In this case, we hypothesize that there is *no* effect of capital per worker on income per capita. This is the so-called null hypothesis H_0 that assumes $\beta = 0$. Since the estimated standard error is quite small, the t-value is large (namely $0.8288/0.02486 = 33.34$) and the null hypothesis is soundly rejected. We therefore conclude that $\beta \neq 0$ (the estimated coefficient is significant).

Suppose a theoretical model has been developed in which the relationship (in logs) between capital per worker and income per capita is one-for-one, such that a 4 percent rise in capital per worker leads to a 4 percent rise in income per worker. In this case, our null hypothesis H_0 assumes $\beta = 1$. As before, we can use the regression information to test if this hypothesis is valid. To determine the associated t-value for this hypothesis, we take the (absolute) difference between the estimated coefficient and the hypothesized value and divide by the estimated standard error (note that the above procedure on significance is a special case of this more general procedure). Filling in the relevant information from above, we get: $(1 - 0.8288)/0.02486 = 6.89$. This value is much higher than our rule-of-thumb value of 2 (associated with 5 percent probability), which makes it highly unlikely that the true value of β is equal to one given our test results. We therefore reject the hypothesis $\beta = 1$ and in principle also the theory we developed that gave rise to this hypothesis.

2.8   Regression Problems

Many things can, of course, go wrong when performing regression analysis. In the spirit of *Murphy's Law* (what can go wrong will go wrong), it is therefore good to know some of the caveats. This section discusses some relatively simple problems directly related to the Gauss-Markov conditions A1–A4 listed in Box 2.4, while the next section addresses more advanced issues. The key solution for any violation of the Gauss-Markov conditions to keep in mind is to re-specify the model such that the conditions *do* hold and OLS is BLUE again (see Box 2.4).

2.8.1   Heteroskedasticity – A3
Heteroskedasticity arises if the variance of the error terms is not the same. We can expect this violation of condition A3 to occur in cross-section models where the variance depends on one or more explanatory variables, like firm size, income level, or gender. Alternatively, it may arise with time-varying volatility in financial markets. The OLS estimate is still

unbiased, but the estimated standard errors are incorrect. Popular solutions are to use robust standard errors (standard in econometrics software), to reconsider the model (for example, by using logs or by changing variables), or to use Generalized Least Squares (namely, transform the model such that Gauss-Markov applies and use OLS; this requires an estimate of the degree of heteroskedasticity). In general, heteroskedasticity is a fairly simple problem to deal with.

2.8.2   Autocorrelation – A4

Autocorrelation arises if the errors of different observations are correlated. We can expect this violation of condition A4 to arise with time series data if the error in this period is correlated with the error in the previous period, for example because of a seasonal pattern, overlapping samples, or a misspecification. It also occurs in so-called *panel data* (where observations differ both across section and over time) with repeated observations of the same economic agents (such as workers or firms), where the observations for the same agent can be correlated. As with heteroskedasticity, OLS is still unbiased, but the estimated standard errors are incorrect. *First-order* autocorrelation arises if (using sub-index t to denote time) $\varepsilon_t = \rho\varepsilon_{t-1} + v_t$ for some parameter ρ, where v_t is an error term with mean zero and constant variance. Higher-order autocorrelation can always be transformed into first-order autocorrelation. The procedure is to estimate ρ, transform the model such that the Gauss-Markov conditions hold, and use OLS to estimate it (similar to Generalized Least Squares; only the first observation is lost). One can also try to reformulate the model such that autocorrelation does not occur. In general, autocorrelation is a little more involved in terms of handling than heteroskedasticity, but it is still fairly easy to deal with.

2.8.3   Endogeneity – A2

Endogeneity arises when an explanatory (x) variable is correlated with the error term, such that $E(x_i\varepsilon_i) \neq 0$. We can expect this violation of condition A2 to occur under various circumstances. It arises, for example, if there is measurement error in an explanatory variable, if you have a dynamic model with a lagged dependent variable and autocorrelation, if an important explanatory variable is ignored in the regression (omitted variable bias), or if *simultaneity* occurs, which means that x not only affects y, but y also affects x (*reverse causality*). The simultaneity problem arises frequently in economics: just think of price and quantity being jointly determined by the intersection of demand and supply curves. The consequences of endogeneity are much more severe than of heteroskedasticity and autocorrelation since (with endogeneity) the OLS estimates become biased and inconsistent (which means that even if you have arbitrarily many observations available, you still do not find the *true* coefficients).

Dealing with endogeneity problems is (by now) theoretically straightforward, but empirically challenging. Suppose we try to estimate equation 2.1, but there is an endogeneity problem such that $E(x_i\varepsilon_i) \neq 0$. In theory, we need to find a suitable *instrumental variable z* satisfying two conditions:

1. *Exogeneity*; $E(z_i \varepsilon_i) = 0$, which means that the instrument is uncorrelated with the errors.
2. *Relevance*; $cov(z, x) \neq 0$, which means that the instrument is correlated with the endogenous regressor x.

Recall from equation 2.2 that the OLS estimate for β is equal to: $b_{OLS} = cov(x, y)/var(x)$. This estimate is biased and inconsistent. All we have to do now is to replace the variable x with the instrument z in the numerator and once in the denominator to get the Instrumental Variable (IV) estimate for β as provided in equation 2.5, which is a consistent estimate of β. The principle works the same in a more general setting in which we have K explanatory variables of which $R < K$ have endogeneity problems. We now need to find R suitable instruments for the endogenous explanatory variables satisfying the above two conditions (exogeneity and relevance). The $R - K$ exogenous explanatory variables can serve as their own instruments in this more general setting.

$$b_{IV} = \frac{cov(z, y)}{cov(z, x)} = \frac{\sum_{i=1}^{N}(z_i - \bar{z})(y_i - \bar{y})}{\sum_{i=1}^{N}(z_i - \bar{z})(x_i - \bar{x})} \qquad 2.5$$

In the matrix notation of Technical Note 2.1, the OLS estimate is $b_{OLS} = (X'X)^{-1}X'y$. If Z is the $N \times K$ matrix of instruments, the IV estimate is simply $b_{IV} = (Z'X)^{-1}Z'y$. An alternative, not discussed here, is Generalized Instrumental Variables or Two-Stage Least Squares.

The empirical challenge of endogeneity problems is to find suitable instruments. This is a difficult problem because statistical theory is of little use (see section 2.9.2). Finding instruments is based on economic arguments to explain why an instrument is exogenous. (Only if there is *over-identification* [more instruments than endogenous explanatory variables] can we test the exogeneity of instruments.) In contrast, it is fairly easy to test if an instrument is relevant. If an instrument is *weak* (only weakly correlated with the endogenous regressors), the properties of the instrumental variable estimator can be poor and severely biased.

2.9 More Advanced Methodology Issues

The discussion of some more advanced methodology issues in this section is based on chapter 3 of Brakman, Garretsen, and van Marrewijk (2019), who analyze the spatial agglomeration of economic activity at different spatial scales. These issues are revisited in Chapters 16 and 17. For now, this section simply notes that there is abundant empirical evidence of a *positive* relationship between the size of a location (city or urban agglomeration) and its level of income per capita.

$$ln(w_{it}) = \gamma ln(pop_{it}) + \eta c_{it} + \varepsilon_{it} \qquad 2.6$$

Equation 2.6 summarizes this positive relationship, where i denotes a location and the dependent variable is $ln(w_{it})$, the log of wage or income per capita at location i at time t.

The explanatory variables are $ln(pop_{it})$, which is the log of population size as a measure of urban scale, and a series of control variables $c_{i,t}$. The error term is $\varepsilon_{i,t}$ and a time index t is added since one may be interested in this relationship over time and not only in a cross-section analysis. This is an example of a *panel data* specification, with observations varying both cross-section and over time. The key coefficient of interest is γ as it summarizes the relationship between population size and income per capita. The next subsections discuss some methods for correctly trying to estimate this parameter.

2.9.1   Omitted Variables and Fixed Effects

The correct specification of the relationship often follows from the model of interest. If a multiplicative link between, for example, wages and location relevant variables can be derived, a log-linear specification should work. The exact specification of the relationship thus depends on the theory at hand. Also note that theory drives the choice of variables. The *omitted variable* problem deserves special attention as it is almost always present in empirical research. The specification of interest in equation 2.6 is between income and population. It would, however, be naïve to assume that population is the only variable that affects income levels. Countries with a harbor, for example, have easy access to the rest of the world, enabling international trade flows and a more efficient international division of labor, which stimulates income. Including an indicator variable that captures the presence of an international harbor can be important. There are many other variables of interest like this and omitting them from the empirical specification leads to biased estimates of γ (see section 2.8.3). The error term becomes a catch-all for all the omitted effects. The ideal in research is to correct for all these biases in order to get a clean estimate of the parameter γ. In practice this is possible only to a certain extent. Some effects are clearly important, but the information could be missing in statistical sources, not available on the correct spatial scale, or not available for the relevant period.

$$ln(w_{it}) = \gamma ln(pop_{it}) + \eta c_{it} + L_i + T_t + \varepsilon_{it} \qquad 2.7$$

A standard solution for the omitted variables problem is to include so-called *fixed effects* in the regression specification. This solution requires a panel dataset. A fixed effect is a dummy variable that takes on the value zero or one. Adding fixed effects to equation 2.6 leads to equation 2.7, where L_i is a location fixed effect and T_t is a time fixed effect. The dummy variable L_4, for example, is equal to 1 if, and only if, the location i is equal to 4. It is equal to zero in all other cases. This location-specific fixed effect is thus only operative for the observations of location 4. Similarly, the time fixed effect T_{2018} is only operative for observations in the year 2018.

Suppose countries are our unit of observation, so the location fixed effect L_i is a country fixed effect. Countries differ in many ways. They have different institutions, different political systems, different ideas on taxes, and many other differences that could affect wages and urban population. A fixed effect controls for all these differences that are specific for a country in a general way; the location dummy captures all idiosyncrasies of that particular country relative to the other countries. The assumption is that these differences between countries are constant over time. The benefit of this solution is that all variables that could affect wages – and are constant over time – are controlled for and no longer lead to a bias in the estimate of parameter γ. The downside of this approach is also evident; the fixed effect is a catch-all variable. This is the reason that in many empirical studies only the use of fixed effects is indicated in the empirical tables and not the coefficients themselves. This is because it is difficult to interpret these coefficients, as there is no information on the contribution of the underlying variables separately.

The use of location fixed effects L_i assumes that the location differences are constant over time. However, some factors that could affect wages are not constant over time. The Great Recession that started in 2008, for example, may have affected wages across all countries. To correct or neutralize influences that change over time, a time fixed effect T_t can be included, just like for the location fixed effect L_i. The assumption underlying this time fixed effect is that it is the same for all countries.

2.9.2 Cause and Effect

As noted above, equation 2.6 suggests a causal relationship from population size to income per capita, but the reverse is also possible. Both relations are plausible and could be valid at the same time. Technically, this is the issue of endogeneity discussed in section 2.8.3, which can be solved with instrumental variables. The main problem with selecting an instrument is finding a good and convincing story that motivates the selection of instruments. Furthermore, from a technical point of view, the instrument should be (highly) correlated to the right-hand-side variable, but not to the error term. So, the presumed exogeneity of the instrument needs careful motivation and discussion. This is illustrated by the example in Table 2.6, which also serves to illustrate the use of instruments.

Table 2.6. Wages in France as a function of density with different instruments

Estimated equation: $ln(w_{it}) = \gamma ln(dens_{it}) + \varepsilon_{it}$

	None	Instruments		
Variable		Historical	Soil	Both
$ln(dens)$	0.033[*a]	0.027[*a]	0.050[*b]	0.020[*c]
Historical instruments				
$pop(1831)$		Yes	No	Yes
$pop(1881)$		Yes	No	No
Soil instruments				
Ruggedness		No	Yes	Yes
Depth to rock		No	Yes	No

Source: Combes *et al.* 2010, [a] table 1.6, [b] table 1.7, [c] table 1.9.

Notes: [*] indicates significance at 1 percent level; the authors use various ways to define wages. (The table above shows results for W^3 only; these are wages after controlling for sector effects, observable time-varying individual characteristics, and all fixed individual characteristics.)

Combes *et al.* (2010) are interested in the relationship between wages and density in France. They note (as Adam Smith and Alfred Marshall already observed) that wages are higher in denser places because of all sorts of technical or knowledge spillovers. However, it is also possible that more productive places attract more workers and as a result become denser, or that more productive people choose to live in denser places because they can afford it, or that the benefits of dense places accrue especially to high-skilled people. Whatever the reason, this is a classic example of reverse causation.

The authors suggest two types of instruments: historical population density variables and geological variables, such as the nature of soils. Historical variables are obviously not correlated with current error terms, while geological variables can be expected to be key drivers of population settlements. Soil quality is important for agricultural productivity and thus is likely to have determined settlement patterns in agricultural France thousands of years ago. The pairwise correlation between historical population density variables and current employment density ranges between 0.46 and 0.88. For the soil quality these correlations range between 0.01 and 0.13 (given the amount of work involved in constructing the soil quality data this must have been a disappointment for the authors).

Table 2.6 shows a few results to illustrate the point about the importance of using instruments. First, note that the use of instruments has an effect on the estimated impact of density on wages as they affect the parameter γ. Second, note that the impact of density is smaller if only historical instruments are used, larger if only soil instruments are used, and smaller again if both instruments are used. After an extensive discussion, the authors prefer estimates in which both types of instruments are used, and conclude that the best estimate is about 0.020.

2.9.3   Natural Experiments

Reverse causation and missing variables are major topics in empirical urban economics and geographical economics research. Another solution is provided by the use of *natural* experiments. This is not an experiment in a laboratory setting where the circumstances of the experiment can be carefully organized and controlled in order to assure that only the factor of interest is influencing the outcome. A natural experiment is a sudden change in circumstances that changes the environment of a group of firms, workers, and locations such that they have to adapt to the new circumstances. This is the so-called *treatment* group. There is also another group of firms, workers, and locations that is *not* affected by the change. This is the so-called *control* group. Comparing the outcome for the two groups provides us with information on the effects of the shock. A natural experiment is ideally an exogenous *shock*. If the shock is truly unexpected, the reverse causality problem should not bias the outcome. Examples are floods, hurricanes, or the fall of the Berlin Wall.

To evaluate the impact of the shock, two periods are needed to compare the situation before and after the shock for both groups, which helps us to control for all sorts of systematic differences between the treatment group and the control group. There are thus four groups in total: the treatment group before and after the change, as well as the control group before and after the change.

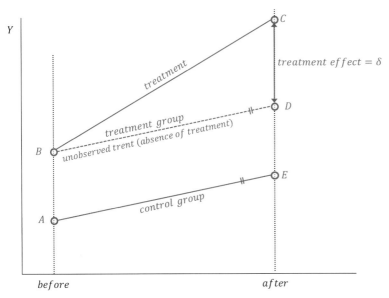

Figure 2.7 Diff-in-diff estimation

Figure 2.7 illustrates the basic set-up of this estimation procedure. The variable Y could be some regional development variable – for example, regional growth stimulated by central government subsidies aimed at regional infrastructure projects. The central government is interested in whether the subsidies indeed stimulate regional growth. There is a treatment group (that is, the regions that receive infrastructure subsidies) and a control group (that is, regions that do not receive these subsidies). Both groups are observed before and after the treatment.

We are interested in the treatment effect $C − D$; the effect of the infrastructure subsidies on the treatment group. From Figure 2.7 it is obvious that we cannot estimate $C − D$ because we cannot observe what would have happened to the treatment group if they would *not* have received the treatment; that is, situation D simply does not exist. We can, however, identify the treatment effect if we make a strong assumption; introduce a control group that does not receive the treatment, but has a common trend with the treatment group. This is reflected by lines AE and BD having the same slope; even without the infrastructure subsidies both groups would have grown anyway.

The treatment effect δ can now easily be calculated; $\delta = (C − E) − (D − E) = (C − E) − (B − A)$. The last equality follows from our assumption that the development of the control group also reflects the development of the treatment group if they would not have been treated, that is $(D − E) = (B − A)$. Therefore, it is crucial for this method to work to find a control group that is identical to the treatment group in all respects, except for the treatment itself. This estimator is called a *diff-in-diff estimator*; it is the result of two differences: the difference between treated groups versus nontreated groups, and the difference between these groups in both periods (before and after the shock). Note that *other factors* that might affect regional growth no longer have an influence; they are differenced away. This implies that the missing variable problem no longer needs to be solved and there is no need to gather information on other variables that affect (in this case) regional growth.

2.9.4   Regression Discontinuity Design (RDD)

The use of natural experiments to infer causality makes sense when the shock or event that is supposed to set apart the treatment and control group is truly exogenous and is also the only aspect in which the two groups differs. As noted above, spatial events or shocks like natural disasters, but also changes to economic integration and the associated borders, have been used as examples of (quasi-) natural experiments. With a natural disaster like a flooding or hurricane, the experiment literally falls out of the sky. Researchers in the social and medical sciences, however, typically do not wait for Mother Nature to enable them to conduct such an experiment. Instead, they create these conditions themselves via so-called Randomized Control Trials (RCTs). In medicine, the most well-known and straightforward application of RCTs is to test the effectiveness of a medicine by using two groups of trial participants that are identical in all but one respect: the treatment group gets the real medicine and the control group gets a placebo.

The use of RCTs has also become popular in the field of economics. RCTs are increasingly used as a research design and as the main strategy to make identification of cause and effect feasible. This is also true for the social sciences at large where, in both lab and field experiments, RCTs are by now the leading research design. A related strategy to infer causality is the so-called *Regression Discontinuity Design* (RDD). The main difference with the RCTs is that there is no exogenous shock or event that makes for a split between the units of interest. With the RDD, one looks for conditions that create a clear discontinuity in terms of some outcome variable across the sample. The classic example, as discussed by Lee and Lemieux (2010, 2014) in their survey of the use of RDDs in economics and the social sciences, is a class of students where every student with an average grade above a certain cut-off gets a scholarship or sizeable reward. The discontinuity is to see if for some outcome variable for the total class of students (like future income or career development) the intervention or assignment of the scholarship creates a discontinuity (jump) when the average grades of all students are plotted against the outcome variable of interest. The RDD aims to show whether a discontinuity can be observed exactly at the point where the intervention kicks in (see Figure 2.8 with the assignment variable on the x-axis and the outcome variable on the y-axis). Ideally, when the intervention is as clear cut as in Figure 2.8, the RDD is basically equivalent to the RCT (and natural experiment) approach in the sense that it yields the possibility to infer causality.

A good example of an RDD is the study by Dachis, Duranton, and Turner (2012), which analyzes the impact of a land transfer tax in Toronto on the local real estate market. The authors concentrate their analysis on houses and localities that fall just inside the administrative border of the city of Toronto (where the land transfer tax applies), as well as on houses and localities that are just outside the city of Toronto (where the tax does

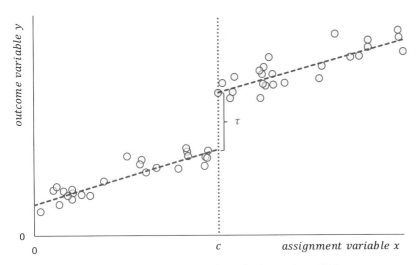

Figure 2.8 The basic idea of Regression Discontinuity Design – RDD
Sources: Based on Lee and Lemieux 2010, 2014.

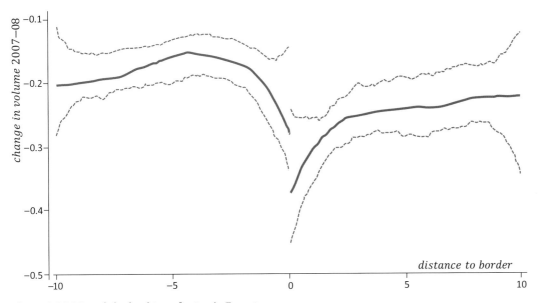

Figure 2.9 RDD and the land transfer tax in Toronto
Source: Based on Dachis *et al.* 2012.
Note: Thin-dashed lines indicate confidence interval.

not apply). The two sets of localities are deemed equal in nearly all respects (distance to downtown Toronto, jobs, and amenities, as well as in other social-economic respects). The right line in Figure 2.9 depicts the volume of housing sales transactions in the city of Toronto (y-axis) when one moves away from the border (point 0 on the x-axis) toward Toronto (x-axis). The left line shows the volume of similar transactions (from right to left on the x-axis) for areas just next to but marginally *outside* the city of Toronto. The message is clear: there is a marked discontinuity precisely at the city of Toronto border, with housing sales transactions falling more sharply for areas in Toronto that are just within the city limits.

2.10   Conclusions

This chapter has briefly analyzed a range of data and method issues. Using three quotes, it first described the virtuous cycle of continuous scientific improvement based on collecting and measuring data (statistics), developing a framework to look at these data (theory), and evaluating this framework in light of the data (econometrics). The chapter highlighted the importance of gathering reliable data for economic analysis, which (if possible) is best left to (official) professional organizations. It also emphasized the importance of developing theories to analyze data, but did not develop any such theories (although all subsequent chapters will return to this question). Instead, the remainder of this chapter reviewed some basic statistical and econometric issues.

From a statistical perspective, the importance was emphasized of looking at and characterizing data using simple statistical measures (minimum, maximum, mean, and median) and somewhat more advanced distribution measures (variance/standard deviation, skewness, and kurtosis). The chapter provided an overview of raw, central, and standardized moments and discussed discrete and continuous distributions. It illustrated the use of statistics with a discussion of income per capita differences at the country level, where it emphasized the importance of graphical analysis using histograms and kernel densities, as well as the possibility of transforming variables (analyzing the log of income per capita rather than the level of income per capita).

From an econometric perspective, the chapter discussed the steps to be taken to confront theories with data and provided a brief analysis of regressions – in particular, Ordinary Least Squares (OLS). It reviewed the Gauss-Markov conditions under which OLS regressions are *good* (Best Linear Unbiased Estimator – BLUE) and analyzed how to test hypotheses using regressions. It illustrated the use of regressions with a discussion of the impact of capital per worker on income per capita. Finally, it analyzed some regression problems based on the Gauss-Markov assumptions (heteroskedasticity, autocorrelation, and endogeneity) and more advanced issues for panel data (omitted variables and fixed effects, cause and effect [instrumental variables], natural experiments [diff-in-diff estimation], and Regression Discontinuity Design – RDD).

The remainder of Part I of the book analyzes the *deep roots* of economic development in Chapter 3 ("Uneven Playing Field") and Chapter 4 ("Geo-Human Interaction"). This takes us far back in history. Readers less interested in such historical developments can skip Chapters 3 and 4 and jump to Chapter 5 in Part II of the book without affecting the main line of argument. (Such readers do risk, of course, the loss of a fundamental appreciation for the long-lasting, deep roots of economic development in a multi-disciplinary framework involving geology, geography, biology, anthropology, climate, and their interactions with economic forces and human beings.) The data and method issues discussed in this chapter should be of use to better understand all future chapters.

Further Reading

The reliability of some data sources is discussed in the chapter, which also provides *The Guardian*'s top 10 sources of data on international development. Reliable textbooks on statistical and econometric methods include: Verbeek, M. 2017. *A Guide to Modern Econometrics*, 5th edn. (Chichester: John Wiley) and Wooldridge, J. M. 2020. *Introductory Econometrics: A Modern Approach*, 7th edn. (Boston, MA: Cengage Learning).

An entertaining and useful book on the basic insights for the proper use of (descriptive) statistics is provided by: Smith, G. and J. Cordes. 2019. *The 9 Pitfalls of Data Science* (Oxford University Press).

TECHNICAL NOTE 2.1   Ordinary Least Squares – OLS

The most-used regression method is Ordinary Least Squares (OLS). Let y_i be the i-th observation of (endogenous) variable Y for $i = 1, \ldots, N$ and let y be the $N \times 1$ column vector of all observations. We assume that the variable Y is explained by K exogenous variables, one of which is a constant. Let x_{ij} be observation i of (exogenous) variable j used to explain Y for $i = 1, \ldots, N$ and $j = 1, \ldots, K$. We can collect all observations in the $N \times K$ matrix X. Similarly, let β_j be the unknown parameter associated with variable j and let β be the $K \times 1$ column vector of these parameters. Finally, let ε_i be the error term associated with observation i and let ε be the associated $N \times 1$ column vector. We can now write the linear regression model as provided in equation A2.1.

$$y = X\beta + \varepsilon \qquad\qquad \text{A2.1}$$

If we hypothesize $\beta = b$, then we define the residuals $e = y - Xb$. These can be viewed as estimates of the errors ε. OLS chooses b such as to minimize the squared sum of the residuals, which can be written as $e'e = (y - Xb)'(y - Xb) = y'y - 2y'Xb + b'X'Xb$. Differentiating with respect to b and collecting terms, we get the first order conditions: $-2(X'y - X'Xb) = 0$. If the matrix $X'X$ has full rank and can be inverted, we get the OLS estimator: $b_{OLS} = (X'X)^{-1}X'y$. In the two-variable case with a constant included, this reduces to the expression provided in the main text.

3 Uneven Playing Field

3.1 Introduction

We now discuss the "deep roots" of economic development by taking a very-long-run perspective. Although this is fascinating, the book is organized such that readers less interested in events that happened hundreds or even thousands of years ago can skip Chapters 3 and 4 without affecting the flow of the argument in the remainder of the book.

This chapter starts with an ultra-long perspective. First, it provides a sense of the dimensions of space and time from an astronomical point of view (section 3.2). Second, it discusses life on Earth from a geological point of view (section 3.3). Third, it reviews human development from an anthropological point of view (section 3.4).

The analysis in the subsequent sections focuses merely on the more recent 12,000 years of human history, which is ultra-recent compared to the previous discussions. This discussion is based on the work of Jared Diamond. It highlights the importance of the Agricultural Revolution for the development of mankind (section 3.5). This involved the domestication of plants and animals, which allowed for the transition from a hunter-gatherer society to a farmer society. This revolution took place at different locations on Earth at different times, starting in the Fertile Crescent around 8500 BC. The section then analyzes why the revolution started there and not at some other location. The answer is given by the title of this chapter: the playing field for the transition to farming was very uneven for different parts of the world, with exceptionally good circumstances at the Fertile Crescent. This held for the availability of domesticable plants (section 3.6), animals (section 3.7), and the spread of knowledge (section 3.8). The biogeographic circumstances thus play an important role in explaining the start of the transition to farming.

This chapter concludes with a discussion of the relevance of the above information for explaining *current* levels of economic development (section 3.9). Perhaps to the surprise of many readers, the biogeographic circumstances of different locations on Earth still play an important role in determining today's development level. This holds in particular for the Old World (which excludes the Americas and Oceania from the analysis), where biogeographic circumstances are able to explain more than 64 percent of the variance in current income per capita levels. Chapter 4 will explain why it is appropriate to exclude the Americas and Oceania.

3.2   A Sense of Time and Space

Apparently, according to today's astronomical insights, the universe was created by a *Big Bang* some 13.8 billion years ago.[1] At the start, all matter was concentrated at a single point. Space then expanded incredibly fast and temperatures dropped, creating light, atoms, and later on more massive particles in the process. Gravity and collision then created the galaxies and large-scale structures (clusters of galaxies with a mass of 10 million billion Suns and more) we observe today. The Milky Way is actually part of a very large super cluster, now called Laniakea (Tully *et al.* 2014).

Our own *Milky Way* galaxy has about 200 billion stars and consists of three components. First, there is the central *bulge* at the core, which consists of older, mostly red stars (about 10 billion years old). Second, there is the *disk* with four spiral arms, which consists of younger, mostly blue stars (between 1 million and 10 billion years old). The Sun is a quite standard star in the disk (about 4.6 billion years old), which takes roughly 240 million years to complete one orbit of the galaxy (a galactic year). Third, there is an encompassing *halo*, a diffuse spherical region surrounding the disk with low-density older stars in clusters and composed mainly of dark matter. Recent explorations have discovered hundreds of planets orbiting the stars in the vicinity of our Sun. If this is indicative for the rest of the universe, there should be even more planets than stars.

In view of all these billions and billions of galaxies, stars, and planets, one would expect the world we live in to be busy and crowded with particles and matter. On the contrary, however, space is largely *empty*. A good way to illustrate this is to know that the speed of light is almost 300,000 kilometers per second (fast enough to circle the Earth more than seven times in one second). The distance from the Earth to the Sun is about 150 million kilometers, so it takes light from the Sun just a little more than eight minutes to travel this distance. A light-year is the distance traveled by light in one Earth year's time (about 9,461 billion kilometers, or some 63,241 times the distance from the Earth to the Sun). Space is, in fact, so empty that the *nearest* other star is more than four light-years away from the Sun.

The *Solar System* consists of the Sun and eight planets (plus: asteroids, clouds, and belts). Earth is the largest of the four inner planets (in distance from the Sun: Mercury, Venus, Earth, and Mars), which are rocky and close to the Sun. The four outer planets are gas giants, much heavier than Earth and much further away (in distance from the Sun: Jupiter, Saturn, Uranus, and Neptune). The largest is Jupiter, which has a mass of 318 times that of Earth. Indeed, if the mass of all planets is added together, then the Earth comprises only 0.2 percent of the total. The whole Solar System is, however, appropriately dominated by the Sun: its diameter is 109 times that of Earth and its mass is 330,000 times as much. Of all the mass in the Solar System, 99.86 percent is contained in the Sun itself. As time passes by, the Sun will start to shine brighter and expand. As a consequence, all of the Earth's water

---

[1] The information in this section is based on: www.damtp.cam.ac.uk/research/gr/, the cosmology website of the University of Cambridge, and NASA: www.nasa.gov, accessed June 17, 2014.

will evaporate and escape into space within a billion years or so, making current life impossible. In about 5.4 billion years, the Sun's main sequence phase will be over. It will become a red giant and engulf the Earth by that time.

3.3 Life on Earth

Earth itself is about 4.6 billion years old. The geological time scale is divided into four main *eons* (see Figure 3.1). In the Hadean eon, which lasted until 4 billion years ago, the conditions on Earth were "hellish," with volcanism, high temperatures, partially melted surfaces, and frequent collisions with other bodies of the Solar System. (The eon is thus named after Hades, the ancient Greek god of the underworld.) The oldest known rocks were formed during the Archean or "beginning" eon. At the end of the Archean, some 2.5 billion years ago, plate tectonic activity was probably similar to that of contemporary times. During the Proterozoic or "early life" eon, which lasted until 541 million years ago, oxygen built up in the atmosphere and the first advanced single-cell and multi-cellular life was created. The most recent Phanerozoic or "visible life" eon started 541 million years ago. During this eon, abundant animal life was developed.

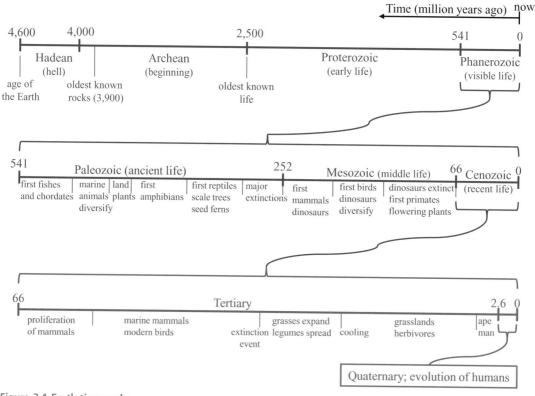

Figure 3.1 Earth time scale
Source: Based on Geological Society of America, Time Scale v. 4.0, 2012.

The second part of Figure 3.1 shows that the visible life eon is subdivided into three main eras. In the Palaeozoic or "ancient life" era there was a widespread diversification of life, starting in the ocean with fishes, but eventually transiting onto land with amphibians and reptiles. Great tracts of forest covered the Earth, forming our current coal beds. This era ended in a mass extinction some 252 million years ago, from which it took life millions of years to recover. The second Mesozoic or "middle life" era is also called "the age of reptiles," as these were the dominant animal species on land. It was the time in which the first (small) mammals arrived and the supercontinent *Pangea* separated into the different continents we know today. This era ended with another mass extinction event (caused by an asteroid impact) killing off the dinosaurs some 66 million years ago. The last era is the Cenozoic or "recent life" era.

The third part of Figure 3.1 shows that the recent life era is subdivided into two main periods. The Tertiary period lasts until 2.6 million years ago and is subdivided into several epochs, during which the appearance of a proliferation of mammals, modern birds, grasses, herbivores, and the predecessors of humans can be observed. The quaternary period focuses on the evolution of humans and starts 2.6 million years ago with the earliest tools used by our ancestors.

3.4 Human Development

The time scale of human development is illustrated in Figure 3.2, this time in thousands of years instead of millions. The oldest finds of our predecessors are for Tschadensis, one of the earliest human species which lived in West Africa 6 to 7 million years ago.[2] He had a chimpanzee-sized brain and walked (partially) upright on two legs. Kaddaba lived in wooded areas and also walked upright, which therefore did not evolve only in an open savannah environment. By about 4 million years ago, Anamensis walked mostly bipedal. The Afarensis species was mostly vegetarian and includes the famous "Lucy" find. The Africanus species was the first early human species to be discovered in 1924.

The first species of the Homo genus, to which we all belong, was Habilis, who lived 2.4 to 1.4 million years ago. The name means "handy man" because it was thought to be the first stone toolmaker. More recent finds now date the earliest tools (stone flakes and cores) to some 2.6 million years ago. Boisei and Robustus lived largely parallel to Habilis. All species and finds discussed so far were exclusively in different parts of Africa, which is therefore without doubt the birthplace of mankind. The longest-surviving Homo species so far (but now extinct) was Erectus, from 1.89 million to 143,000 years ago. They were the first species to make hearths, eat lots of animal meat, and care for the old and dead. They were also the first to live not only in Africa, but also in West and East Asia. Heidelbergensis

---

[2] For brevity, the genus names Sahelanthropus, etc. of the different species are not listed in this section. See the notes below Figure 3.2 for details.

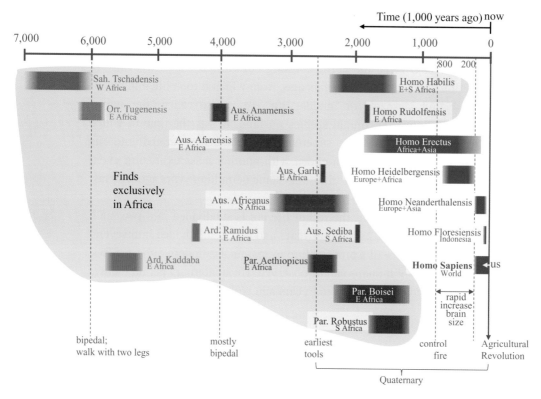

Figure 3.2 Human evolution time scale

Source: Based on information from Smithsonian National Museum of History website, June 16, 2014, http://humanorigins.si.edu.

Notes: Genus abbreviations: Sah. = Sahelanthropus; Orr. = Orrorin; Ard. = Ardipithecus; Aus. = Australopithecus; Par. = Paranthropus.

were the first species to live in Africa as well as in the cold climate of Europe, where they built shelters and hunted big game animals with wooden spears. The European species of Heidelbergensis were the ancestors of Neanderthalensis, who lived from 200,000 to 28,000 years ago and were the first to make clothing, bury the dead, develop language, and use symbols. The African species of Heidelbergensis were the ancestors of Homo sapiens some 200,000 years ago. This is our species, the only Homo species to survive to this day. (The most recent Homo species to become extinct is Floresiensis, a small, "hobbit"-like species who lived in Indonesia from 95,000 to 17,000 years ago.) Evolved in Africa, Homo sapiens spread out across the globe starting some 100,000 years ago, now occupying all parts of the world.

Figure 3.2 also highlights six major milestones in human evolution. The first evidence of bipedal walking dates back some 6 million years ago. After some 2 million years, so about 4 million years ago, the human species walked upright most of the time, but still climbed trees, allowing them to live near open areas *and* in dense woods. The dawn of technology started some 2.6 million years ago with the use of simple stone tools. The control of fire about 800,000 years ago allowed for cooking of food and led to a fundamental change in the early human diet. It also enabled humans to gather around campfires, socialize, find

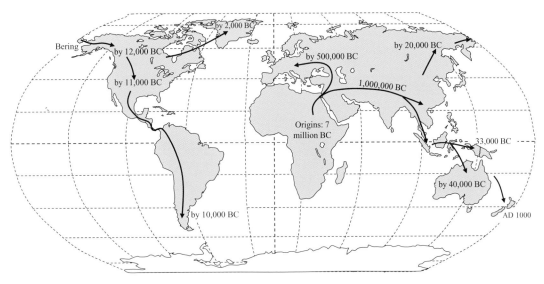

Figure 3.3 The spread of humans across the world
Source: Based on Diamond 1997, figure 1.1.

comfort and warmth, share food and information, and find safety from predators. Associated with these changes there was a rapid increase in human brain size from 800,000 to 200,000 years ago, enabling early humans to interact with one another and their surroundings in new and different ways. The last of the six major milestones was the Agricultural Revolution (also referred to as the "Neolithic Revolution" or "the turning point"), which allowed humans to control the growth and breeding of certain plants and animals and led to farming and herding animals. This milestone dates back only 12,000 years. On the scale of Figure 3.2, that is essentially *on* the "0/now" line. The remainder of this chapter will focus on this 12,000-year history, but it is important to keep the time scale information of sections 3.3 and 3.4 in mind and realize that from a life-on-Earth or human development perspective, the entire discussion is *ultra*-recent.

Figure 3.3 illustrates the spread of humans across the world. For a long time, human evolution only took place in Africa. Around 1 million years ago, humans spread across West, South, and East Asia.[3] About half a million years ago, humans reached (cold) Europe. The tools available at the time did not yet allow humans to fish, build watercraft, and protect from the cold. A major improvement in standardized tool making and tools of bone (suitable for shaping into fish hooks) arose about 50,000 years ago. The seawater level varied substantially over time (with lots of water locked in glaciers during the Ice Ages) such that New Guinea was at times connected to Australia and the Bering Strait was at times a Bering Bridge. About 40,000 years ago, humans were able to cross the sea into Australia using watercraft. (The oldest watercraft elsewhere in the world date back only

---

[3] All time indications in this section are open to some discussion, but only the most robust present claims are reported.

13,000 years (in the Mediterranean).) Some 20,000 years ago, protective clothing allowed humans to enter into Siberia and from there across the Bering Bridge or Strait into Alaska and North Canada some 12,000 years ago. They spread across the USA some 1,000 years later and reached the southern tip of South America in another 1,000 years.

In Europe, Africa, and Asia, big mammals lived and evolved alongside humans for hundreds of thousands or millions of years. The human hunting skills were gradually improving over time and the animals evolved a fear for humans and adapted their evasive and defensive techniques accordingly. By the time humans reached Australia and the Americas, the local big mammals had no such fear and were quite suddenly confronted with advanced human hunting skills. The most likely consequence is that this confrontation resulted in the extinction of large animals, which were easy prey for humans,[4] first in Australia, where the megafauna disappeared quickly after humans arrived and there are currently no larger mammals than 100-pound kangaroos.[5] Similarly, the Americas had been full of big mammals before the humans arrived, with "herds of elephants and horses pursued by lions and cheetahs, and joined by members of such exotic species as camels and giant ground sloths" (Diamond 1997). Again, those animals disappeared shortly after humans arrived. These extinctions might have had important consequences later in history, as discussed below (section 3.7).

3.5 The Agricultural Revolution

By about 11,000 BC, Homo sapiens were spread around the globe, the glaciers had retreated, resulting in a warmer and wetter climate, and technologies for harvesting, transporting, preparing, and storing cereals were in place (see Olsson and Hibbs 2005). These conditions enabled the start of the Agricultural Revolution, where the domestication of plants and animals allowed for the transition from a hunter-gatherer lifestyle to sedentary agriculture. The domestication of a species is defined by Smith (1998) as: "the human creation of a new plant or animal – one that is identifiably different from its wild ancestors and extant wild relatives . . . [which] . . . has been changed so much that it has lost its ability to survive in the wild." This transition started independently in at least five different places in the world with a time difference of at least 6,000 years (see Figure 3.4 for an overview). One of the questions addressed in sections 3.6 and 3.7 is thus why this revolution occurs so much earlier in some places than in others.

The first transition occurs in the Fertile Crescent/Near East, consisting of parts from present-day Israel, Lebanon, Syria, Jordan, and Iraq. For plants (wheat, pea, and olive), this was around 8500 BC, and for animals (sheep and goat), this occurred around 8000 BC. The

---

[4] Alternative theories on these extinctions seem less likely (see Diamond 1997).

[5] The disappearing animals include giant kangaroos, rhino-like marsupials the size of a cow, a marsupial leopard, a 400-pound ostrich-like flightless bird, and some big reptiles, like a one-ton lizard, a giant python, and land-dwelling crocodiles (see Diamond 1997).

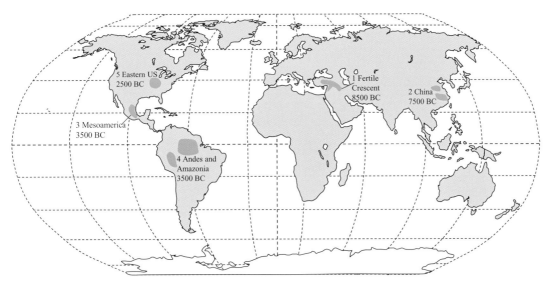

Figure 3.4 Centers of origin of food production
Source: Based on Diamond 1997, figure 5.1.

second transition occurs about 1,000 years later in China (around 7500 BC; plants: rice and millet; animals: pig and silkworm). The third and fourth transition take place 4,000 years later (around 3500 BC) in Mesoamerica (plants: corn, beans, squash; animals: turkey) and the Andes and Amazonia (plants: potato and manioc; animals: llama and guinea pig). The fifth transition occurs another 1,000 years later (around 2500 BC) in the eastern United States (plants: sunflower and goosefoot; animals: none).

There are four disputed places for the independent origin of domestication. Although it is clear that local plants (and in one case animals) were domesticated, this may only have occurred after the adoption of so-called founder crops from elsewhere. These places include Sahel (5000 BC; plants: sorghum and African rice; animals: guinea fowl), Tropical West Africa (3000 BC; African yams and oil palm), Ethiopia (unclear; coffee and teff), and New Guinea (7000 BC; sugar cane and banana). Three other important locations where local domestication surely only followed after the arrival of founder crops are Western Europe (6000–3500 BC; poppy and oat), the Indus Valley (7000 BC; plants: sesame and eggplant; animals: humped cattle), and Egypt (6000 BC; plants: sycamore fig and chufa; animals: donkey and cat).

As the above description clearly shows, the population of a certain location may benefit from the start of an agricultural transition even without making the first step itself. Through human interaction and trade contacts, knowledge about the domestication of plants and animals and their benefits spread from one location to another location, and so on. Indeed, this spread of knowledge allowed pretty much all of Europe, most of Northern Africa, and all of West-South Asia to go through an agricultural transition thousands of years before the Americas, based on adoption rather than invention. This is illustrated in Figure 3.5 and further discussed in section 3.8.

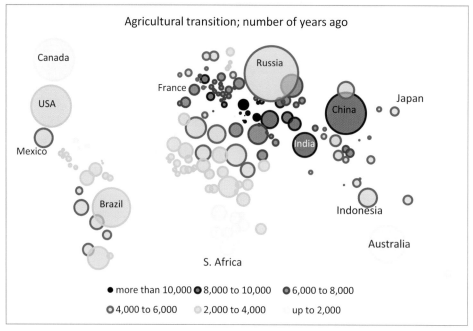

Figure 3.5 Start of agricultural transition, number of years ago
Source: Author construction; agricultural transition from Putterman and Weil 2010.
Note: Bubbles are proportional to a country's land area, located at the geographic center (CIA World Factbook), equilateral projection, except for the USA (which is at the geographic center of the 48 contiguous states) and Russia (which is at the population-weighted geographic center).

3.6   Farmer Power

The term "Agricultural Revolution" is actually quite inappropriate. It suggests a rapid transition from one lifestyle (nomadic hunter-gathering) to another (sedentary farming). The real picture is much more gradual and much more blurred.[6] First, not all hunter-gatherers are nomadic, such as in North America's Pacific Northwest coast, and not all farmers are sedentary, such as the nomads of New Guinea's Lakes Planes, who farm bananas and papayas and also live as hunter-gatherers. Second, hunter-gatherers can manage their land intensively – in New Guinea, for example, by clearing away competing trees, keeping channels in swamps clear, and cutting down mature sago trees to promote growth of new shoots. Australia is another example, where burning of the landscape encourages the growth of edible plant seeds and replacing the stems and tops of the tubers of wild yams in the ground allows them to regrow. Both cases are only a small step away from farming. Third, the actual transition involves many small steps and it took thousands of years to switch from complete dependence on wild foods to a diet with very few wild foods.

---

[6] This section is largely based on Diamond 1997, chs. 6–8.

What individuals and families are facing is actually an economic problem surrounding what to do with the available time (a budget restriction) in order to stay alive and not starve to death (the objective function). On the verge of the transition you may, for example, choose between the following alternative competing strategies: (i) hoeing your garden to have low-risk vegetables in a couple of months, (ii) gathering shellfish to have a little low-risk meat today, or (iii) hunting deer to have a lot of very high-risk meat today, but more likely nothing. Over the course of a couple of thousand years, the factors involved in deciding what to do led to a worldwide switch from the nomadic hunter-gathering lifestyle to that of sedentary farming.

There are five important factors that played a role in the switch to farming (see Diamond 1997). First, the decline in the availability of wild foods made hunter-gathering less attractive: think of the disappearance of large mammals in the Americas or the decline of wild gazelles in the Fertile Crescent. Second, climate change expanded the area of habitats of wild cereals, the precursors to the domestication of the earliest crops, for example, in the Fertile Crescent. Third, technologies for collecting, storing, and processing wild foods were developed as a prerequisite for farming. This included sickles for harvesting wild grains, baskets to carry the grains home, mortars and other means to remove the husks, roasting grains to store them without sprouting, and underground storage pits. Fourth, the interconnection between a rise in population density and a rise in food production was self-reinforcing: farming can feed more people per acre such that population density rises, which puts pressure on raising food production even more, and so on. Fifth, and finally, the denser and larger populations of food producers either displaced or killed hunter-gatherers by their sheer numbers. In places suitable for food production, the hunter-gatherers either survived as farmers or were replaced. Only important geographic and ecological barriers allowed hunter-gatherers to co-exist for a long time along with farmers, such as the deserts in the Western USA or a Mediterranean climate zone unsuitable for the crops of Bantu farmers in South Africa.

The first crops to be domesticated in the Fertile Crescent were wheat, barley, and peas because they were easy to grow by sowing or planting, they were already edible in the wild with high yields, and they grew quickly and could be harvested within a few months. Wheat and barley are cereals or grains, members of the grass family. These crops grow fast, are high in carbohydrates, and have high yields per acre. Consequently, five of the world's leading crops today are cereals: wheat, corn, rice, barley, and sorghum. Cereal crops tend to be low in protein, however. In contrast, pulses (such as peas, lentils, and soybeans) are high in protein. A combination of cereals and pulses, such as wheat, barley, and peas in the Fertile Crescent, thus allowed for a balanced diet.

Why, then, did farming first start in the Fertile Crescent? The short answer is that the circumstances were exceptionally good at this location. Its Mediterranean climate with mild, wet winters and long, hot, dry summers is suitable for annual plants which dry up and die in the dry season. Most of the energy of these plants is put into producing big seeds that sprout when the rains come. These seeds are edible by humans and can be harvested and stored. Cultivation thus leads to a fairly quick return on investment. It is part of by far the largest Mediterranean climate area (smaller areas are in California, Chile, South Africa, and

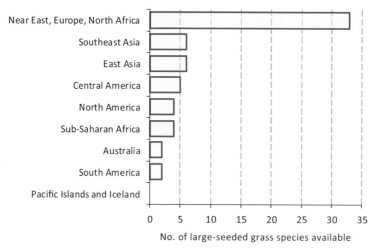

Figure 3.6 Distribution of large-seeded grass species
Source: Based on Olsson and Hibbs 2005, table 2.
Note: 56 heaviest-seeded wild grass species, grain weight from 10 to more than 40 milligrams, about 10 times greater than the median value for all grass species.

Australia), with an enormous variation in altitude such that harvesting along the slopes of hills and mountains can occur at different times of the year rather than all at once.

Most importantly, however, the Fertile Crescent was enormously abundant relative to other locations in terms of plants suitable for domestication. There are about 200,000 wild plant species, but most are not suitable for eating (too woody or no edible fruit, roots, or leaves). Although we eat a few thousand plants and cultivate a few hundred, only 12 species account for 80 percent of the tonnage of all crops today (that is, wheat, corn, rice, barley, sorghum, soybeans, potato, manioc, sweet potato, sugar cane, sugar beet, and banana – see also Chapter 15). The most important among these are cereals, from the grass family of plants. Figure 3.6 vividly illustrates the relative abundance of the Fertile Crescent by providing the distribution of the 56 large-seeded grass species. There are no less than 33 of them in the area of the Fertile Crescent (Near East, Europe, and North Africa), or more than five times as many as in the second two most abundant locations (Southeast Asia and East Asia). There were 23 grasses available in the Jordan Valley alone, and its population selected the two very best for cultivation (barley and emmer wheat). Agriculture started in the Fertile Crescent with the early cultivation of eight founder crops (emmer wheat, einkorn wheat, barley, lentil, pea, chickpea, bitter vetch, and flax). Only two of these crops (flax and barley) were widely available outside of the Fertile Crescent, while another two (chickpea and emmer wheat) were not available outside the Fertile Crescent at all.

3.7 Domesticable Animals

Big domestic mammals are important to humans possessing them for many reasons. They can provide meat, milk products, transportation, fertilizer, leather, and wool. Some can also be used in the military and to pull ploughs. Humans have, of course, also domesticated small mammals and birds for various products and tasks (such as meat, eggs, and feathers, to pull sleds or to kill rodents). Think of the domestication of chickens in China, ducks and geese in Eurasia, turkeys in Mesoamerica, wolves (to become dogs) in Eurasia and North America, rabbits in Europe, the guinea pig in the Andes, and cats in North Africa and Southwest Asia. None of these smaller mammals and birds can pull ploughs, be used in war, or were as important for food as the big domestic mammals. The remainder of this section thus focuses only on big mammals, where "big" is defined as a terrestrial, herbivorous, or omnivorous mammal weighing on average more than 45 kg.[7]

Using the above definition of big mammals, "candidate" species for domestication are easily identifiable as the wild species meeting the criteria. Jared Diamond divides the world in four parts and notes that the distribution of candidate species is skewed, namely 72 in Eurasia, 51 in Sub-Sahara Africa, 24 in the Americas, and 1 in Australia. On the face of it, this looks promising for both Eurasia and Sub-Sahara Africa. The number of actual domesticated big mammals is, of course, much smaller. In fact, out of the 148 candidates listed above, only 14 big mammals were domesticated before the twentieth century. The first big mammals were domesticated around 8000 BC (sheep, goat, and pig). The last big mammals were domesticated around 2500 BC (Bactrian camel and Arabian camel), so more than 4500 years ago. The 14 domesticated mammals are subdivided into the "Major Five" that became widespread and important around the world (cow, sheep, goat, pig, and horse) and the "Minor Nine" that became important only in limited areas of the globe (Arabian camel, Bactrian camel, llama/alpaca, donkey, reindeer, water buffalo, yak, banteng, and gaur). Note that none of the animals from this list originates from Sub-Sahara Africa, so out of its 51 candidates *none* was domesticated. (African elephants were never domesticated even though they were used by Hannibal in his army when crossing the Alps. These were wild animals that were captured and tamed; they were not bred in captivity. The same holds for Asian work elephants.) How can this be explained? Why were zebras, for example, not domesticated?

To answer the above questions, it is important to realize that to be suitable for domestication a big mammal must meet a range of conditions. Failing any one of these conditions already means that the mammal is not suitable for domestication. This section focuses on six conditions. First: *diet*. The conversion of food biomass into consumer biomass is around 10 percent. To grow a 600 kg cow you thus need 6,000 kg of grass or other biomass. To grow a 600 kg carnivore, you would need to feed it 6,000 kg of cow, requiring about 60,000 kg of grass or other biomass. This is too inefficient, hence carnivores are ruled out. Second: *growth rate*. Elephants and gorillas are vegetarians, but they grow too slowly to be of interest to farmers. Third: *problems of captive breeding*. Animals may not be willing to go through their courtship ritual in captivity. This holds, for example, for cheetahs and vicuñas. Fourth: *nasty disposition*. A sufficiently big mammal can injure or kill a human.

---

[7] This section is largely based on Diamond 1997, ch. 9.

Some large mammals are particularly nasty and dangerous and are thus not suitable for domestication. This holds, for example, for the grizzly bear, African buffalo, and hippo. It also holds for zebras, which have the nasty habit of biting and not letting go. Fifth: *tendency to panic.* When they perceive danger, big herbivore mammals either respond by instant flight or by holding their ground in the herd and not running until necessary. The nervous, instant-flight species, such as the gazelle, are difficult to keep in captivity as they are likely to panic and batter themselves to death against the fence. Sixth: *social structure.* The ideal social structure for domesticated large mammals has three characteristics: (i) they live in herds; (ii) there is a well-developed dominance hierarchy; and (iii) the herds occupy overlapping home ranges. Under those conditions, the animals are tolerant of one another (there is no fighting) and humans can take over the dominance hierarchy. Instead, if the animals are solitary territorial they do not tolerate one another and are not instinctively submissive. This rules out, for example, most deer and antelope species.

As discussed above, only 14 animals passed the above six conditions and were already domesticated 4,500 years ago. Figure 3.7 provides an overview of the number of large domesticable mammals for the same nine geographic regions listed in Figure 3.6. The distribution is again much skewed in favor of the Near East, Europe, and North Africa, with 9 of the 14 available species present. East Asia follows with seven, Southeast Asia with two, and South America with one. The other five regions have no large domesticable mammals at all. As discussed at the end of section 3.4, for the Americas and Australia this may have been because of the mass extinction of large mammals due to hunting by the sudden appearance of humans prior to the start of domestication efforts. There are immediate consequences of this for farming as well. Since there were no cows or horses to pull ploughs in the Americas, all tilting had to be done by hand. As a result, only mixed fields were farmed and no monoculture arose.

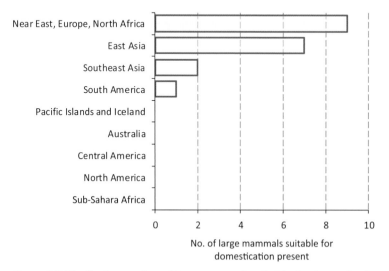

Figure 3.7 Distribution number of large mammals suitable for domestication
Source: Based on Olsson and Hibbs 2005, table 2.
Note: 14 domesticable herbivorous or omnivorous terrestrial mammals weighing on average more than 45 kg.

3.8 North–South or East–West?

As emphasized in various chapters throughout this book, one of the most important benefits of human interaction, through trade, investment, and knowledge flows, is that you can enjoy the fruits of inventions and human ingenuity originating from one location at very low costs at another location. To use a popular phrase, this avoids the need for "reinventing the wheel" at high cost and effort (see below). The domestication of plants and animals has important benefits that spread beyond the inventor's use by adoption elsewhere (more on this in Chapter 7). Jared Diamond notes that there is a great difference between the speeds at which domestication spread in the Americas compared to that in Eurasia.[8] In his calculations, the llama spread from Peru to North Ecuador at a speed of about 0.2 miles per year and corn and beans spread from Mexico to the Southwest of the USA at less than 0.3 miles per year. In contrast, all sorts of domesticated plants and animals spread quite rapidly from the Fertile Crescent to Europe, Egypt, and the Indus Valley of India at an average rate of about 0.7 miles per year (and from the Philippines to Polynesia at about 3.2 miles per year).

One of the most important consequences of the quick spread of crops from the Fertile Crescent is that the domestication is based on just one wild variant of the original species, indicating a single domestication that was adopted at all other locations, from Spain and France to Egypt and India. After all, if farmers have a productive crop available, they will not trouble themselves with finding a wild relative and re-domesticating it. In contrast, there is ample evidence of crops domesticated at least twice at different locations in the Americas, such as lima beans, common beans, and chili peppers in Mesoamerica and South America, as well as squash and goosefoot in both Mesoamerica and the eastern USA. This double domestication at two different locations indicates that the speed of spreading from the earliest location was so slow as not to prevent a second domestication at the other location.

The main reason for the slow speed of spreading domesticated plants and animals in the Americas and Africa compared to Eurasia lies in the *orientation* of the continents either along the North–South or East–West axis, as illustrated in Figure 3.8. In the Americas, the distance from North to South is about 9,000 miles and the widest distance from East to West is 3,000 miles (the narrowest distance is 40 miles in Panama). The major orientation of the Americas is thus North–South. The same holds, although less extreme, for Africa. In contrast, the major orientation of Eurasia is from East to West along 10,000 miles. Locations at the same latitude have the same daylight and seasonal variation and tend to have similar vegetation, temperature, and rainfall. Local circumstances thus tend to be rather similar when you go from East to West. In contrast, locations at different latitudes have different daylight and seasonal variation and tend to have different vegetation, temperature, and rainfall. Local circumstances thus tend to be rather different when you go from North to South. Since plants have adapted to the local circumstances for

---

[8] This section is largely based on Diamond 1997, ch. 10.

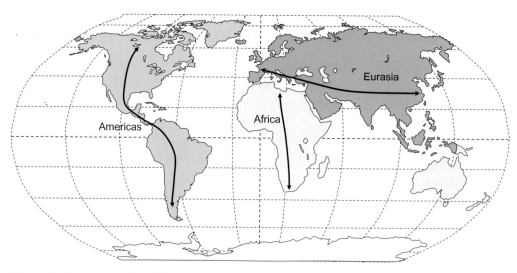

Figure 3.8 Major orientation of the continents
Source: Brakman *et al.* 2009, figure 1.11.

germination, growth, and disease resistance, it is much easier to spread domesticated crops from East to West than it is to spread from North to South.

After food production arose in the Fertile Crescent around 8500 BC, it spread for thousands of miles to Greece, Cyprus, and the Indian subcontinent by 6500 BC, Egypt by 6000 BC, Central Europe by 5400 BC, Spain by 5200 BC, and Britain around 3500 BC (see Figure 3.5). In contrast, many domesticated plants and animals did not spread from Mesoamerica to the Andes, even though the distance between Mexico's highlands and Ecuador's is only 1,200 miles and the local conditions are quite similar. The reason is that the spread would have to go from North to South or vice versa through the hot lowlands of Central America unsuitable for those crops. Thus, no llamas, guinea pigs, or potatoes reached Mexico from the Andes and no turkeys reached the Andes from Mexico. For the same reason, Fertile Crescent crops quickly spread to Egypt and reached the cool highlands of Ethiopia, but never reached South Africa's perfectly suitable Mediterranean climate because of the 2,000 miles of tropical conditions in between these two locations. Agriculture could thrive in South Africa only after European settlers brought with them the whole Fertile Crescent package in the seventeenth century.

Associated with the human interaction through trade, investment, and knowledge flows incorporated in domesticated plants and animals is the spread of technological advancement. Originating from within or near the Fertile Crescent spread the knowledge of writing, metalworking, milking, fruit trees, and beer and wine production. The same holds for the invention of the wheel, which has obvious advantages for transportation purposes, although its invention is not that simple (see Wolchover 2012). Once successful at one location in Eurasia, it spread quickly from there. In the Americas, however, the wheels invented in prehistoric Mexico never spread to the Andes region. In addition to the orientation of the continents, local climatic fluctuations also seem to play a role in the diffusion of agriculture (see Box 3.1).

BOX 3.1 **CLIMATIC FLUCTUATIONS AND THE DIFFUSION OF AGRICULTURE**

In addition to the orientation of the continents as an important determinant for the diffusion of agriculture emphasized in section 3.8, Ashraf and Michaelopoulos (2015) argue that local climatic fluctuations also play a role. The main argument is that under moderately volatile environments, hunter-gatherers are "forced to take advantage of their productive endowments at a faster pace, thereby accumulating tacit knowledge complementary to the adoption of agriculture" (p. 607). In contrast, under static climatic conditions, foragers are not induced to exploit marginal resources in their habitat, while under extreme climatic fluctuations the resource base is drastically altered and foragers use radically different subsistence strategies (which delays the adoption of agriculture). The diffusion of agriculture is thus hump-shaped: low under static climatic conditions, rising under moderately volatile conditions, and declining again under extreme climatic fluctuations. The empirical analysis in the paper indeed finds strong support for this prediction after controlling for the effects discussed in this chapter.

3.9 Biogeography and Income

The above discussion summarizes part of Jared Diamond's argument that the inhabitants of Eurasia enjoyed a series of biogeographic advantages that allowed for an early transition from a hunter-gatherer society to farming and a rapid spread of knowledge. Building on this transition, population rose rapidly and more complicated social structures were possible. This in turn allowed for specialized crafts to develop, leading to technological innovation with long-term consequences for comparative development (more on this in Chapter 16). Among the advantages of Eurasia were the large size of its land mass, the diversity of animals and plants available for domestication, and its East–West instead of North–South orientation.

To what extent is current income per capita explained by the biogeographic conditions discussed above? Many people have pointed out the importance of biogeographic conditions prior to Diamond. In their excellent overview article, Spolaore and Wacziarg (2013) mention Machiavelli, Montesquieu, Marshall, Myrdal, and many others. They also distinguish between a direct channel, where biogeographic conditions have a direct impact on current productivity and development, and an indirect channel, where these conditions built up to sustained advantages over a longer time period (with Jared Diamond as one of the representatives). These issues are discussed in the next chapter.

Olsson and Hibbs (2005) provide the most important direct test of Diamond's work. The discussion here is based on an update of their work by Spolaore and Wacziarg (2013) (see Table 3.1). It starts with the explanatory power of four simple biogeographic factors, namely: (i) absolute latitude; (ii) percent land area in the tropics; (iii) landlocked dummy

Table 3.1. Biogeography and current income

Dependent variable: log per capita income, 2005 (PWT 6.3), OLS estimates

Variable	1 World	2 OH[#]	3 OH[#]	4 OH[#]	5 OH[#]	6 Old world
Absolute latitude	0.044[***]	0.052[***]				
Percent land area in the tropics	−0.049	0.209	−0.410	−0.650[**]	−0.421	−0.448
Landlocked dummy	−0.742[***]	−0.518[***]	−0.499[**]	−0.572[**]	−0.505[**]	−0.226
Island dummy	0.643[**]	0.306	0.920[***]	0.560[**]	0.952[***]	1.306[***]
Geographic conditions[a]			0.706[***]		0.768[***]	0.780[***]
Biological conditions[b]				0.585[***]	−0.074	0.086
Observations	155	102	102	102	102	83
Adjusted R^2	0.440	0.546	0.521	0.449	0.516	0.641

Source: Spolaore and Wacziarg 2013, table 1.

Notes: Constant and t-statistics not reported.

Shaded cells with [***], [**], and [*] are significant at the 1, 5, and 10 percent level, respectively.

[#] OH = Olsson-Hibbs sample; this excludes Australia, Canada, New Zealand, the USA, and countries whose current income is based primarily on extractive wealth (Olsson and Hibbs 2005).

[a] First principal component of absolute latitude, climate suitability to agriculture, rate of East–West orientation, and size of landmass in million km^2.

[b] First principal component of the number of annual or perennial wild grasses and the number of domesticable big mammals.

(equal to one if the country has no direct access to a sea or ocean); and (iv) an island dummy (equal to one if the country is an island). Column 1 of Table 3.1 shows that for the world as a whole these factors explain about 44 percent of the variance in current income levels. The higher the absolute latitude (so the further North or South from the equator), the higher the current income. Current income is higher for island countries (with easier trade contacts across the sea) and lower for landlocked countries. The percent of land area in the tropics is not significant. Column 2 of Table 3.1 repeats the analysis of column 1 for a selection of countries, the Olsson-Hibbs sample (referred to as OH in the table). This sample excludes neo-European countries (Australia, Canada, New Zealand, and the USA) and countries whose current income is primarily based on extractive wealth (mainly oil production based on foreign technology and skilled labor). It is thought to be a better representation of the true biogeographic forces and the explained variance indeed rises to about 55 percent.

The remaining columns of Table 3.1 try to estimate more directly the impact of Diamond's biogeographic conditions. They are grouped together into two components, namely geographic conditions and biological conditions. The geographic conditions are based on the first principal component of absolute latitude, climate suitability to agriculture, rate of East–West orientation, and size of landmass in million km^2. The biological conditions are based on the first principal component of the number of annual or perennial wild grasses and the number of domesticable big mammals. Since absolute latitude is part of the geographic conditions, it is no longer included separately in the analysis in columns 3–6. When entered separately, both geographic conditions and biological conditions are highly significant in determining current income levels: see columns 3 and 4 of Table 3.1 (note that the percent of land area in the tropics becomes negative significant in column 4, basically because it picks up the importance of the excluded variable absolute latitude [which is not incorporated in the geographic conditions for this column]). When entered together (see column 5), the geographic conditions appear to be more important than the biological conditions (which are not significant). The last column (6) restricts attention even further by including only the countries of the Old World (excluding the Americas and Oceania). The explanatory power of the biogeographic conditions in this case further improves to more than 64 percent of the variance.

The above analysis shows that biogeographic conditions still play an important role in explaining current income levels, either through their direct impact on current productivity or through their indirect impact on accumulating knowledge. Empirical estimates seem to indicate that the impact of geographic factors is stronger, or longer-lasting, than the impact of biological factors. This probably reflects the fact that it is harder to change the geographic factors than the biological factors. After all, you cannot relocate a country to alter its absolute latitude or climate, but you can import biological species from other parts of the world that may be useful at this location even though they do not originate from it.

3.10   Conclusions

The discussion in this chapter focused on three main issues. First, it provided a sense of the dimensions of space and time, the development of life on Earth, and the origins and spread of human beings from Africa. Second, it discussed the main developments in human history over the past 12,000 years, focusing on the importance of the Agricultural Revolution, which allowed for a transition from a hunter-gatherer society to a farmer society. The uneven distribution of domesticable plants and animals gave some regions a head start, in particular the Near East, Europe, and North Africa. The chapter explained how the spread of agricultural knowledge is easier East–West than North–South and how this benefited the Eurasian continent relative to Africa and the Americas. These biogeographic circumstances thus play an important role in explaining the start of the transition to farming at any particular location. Third, and finally, the chapter showed that this transition is still relevant today as it helps explain differences in current levels of income per capita, particularly for the Old World. The next chapter explains why it is appropriate to exclude the Americas and Oceania on the basis of geographic–human interaction (geo-human interaction for short).

Further Reading

A must-read on the deep roots of economic development is Jared Diamond's *Guns, Germs, and Steel* (London: Vintage Books, 1997). Differences in the environmental circumstances are amplified by positive feedback loops into gaps in power and technology.

A well-written account of human history and what factors have stimulated growth and inequality, including how and why humanity has only recently escaped the Malthusian poverty trap, is provided by Oded Galor in *The Journey of Humanity: The Origins of Wealth and Inequality* (New York/London: Dutton/Penguin, 2022).

David Graeber and David Wengrow argue that the history of humanity does not progress in a linear fashion. Hunter-gatherer societies, for example, were far more complex than people like Jared Diamond or Stephen Pinker give them credit for. See: Graeber, D. and D. Wengrow. 2021. *The Dawn of Everything: A New History of Humanity* (London: Allen Lane). It is an engaging read, although at times tiresome, because Diamond and Pinker are sometimes described as the "villains" in this book.

4 Geo-Human Interaction

4.1 Introduction

Biogeographic conditions are important for explaining the Agricultural Revolution and current income levels, particularly for the Old World (see Chapter 3). This chapter focuses on some aspects of geographic–human interaction (geo-human interaction) to provide a better understanding for current income levels for the world as a whole. As discussed above, an example of such geo-human interaction is the East–West or North–South orientation of the continents which facilitated the spread of agricultural knowledge. Another example is the extent to which nations have access to navigable waterways (rivers or seas) to facilitate human interaction in terms of trade and knowledge flows.

The chapter starts with a discussion of the relationship between per capita income levels and biogeographic factors, like distance to the equator, climate zone, and having access to the sea (section 4.2). It then provides a more detailed discussion of malaria, an important example of the connections between a tropical climate, health (or death), and income levels (section 4.3). Next, it shows that biogeographic conditions can help explain human development levels for the whole world up to the year 1500 (section 4.4).

Up until this point, biogeographic conditions have been important for explaining income per capita levels. This importance can be questioned on the basis of the Reversal of Fortune discussion (sections 4.5 and 4.6). Some researchers argue that the role of man-made institutions is more important than of biogeographic factors. To support this claim, they point at initially rich countries in 1500 (such as Peru) that have become relatively poor 500 years later because of "bad" institutions imposed by European powers, and vice versa for initially poor countries in 1500 (such as the USA). Hence the name "reversal of fortune." The chapter will briefly outline sample selection effects associated with this discussion and note that the reversal of fortune is not observed if European countries are included in the sample and is reversed (hence initially rich countries tend to be still rich today) for countries that were not former European colonies or for indigenous countries (with more than 50 percent of the current population descending from people who already lived in the country in 1500).

Finally, the chapter notes how geo-human interaction can explain the empirical observations (sections 4.7 and 4.8): first, by discussing the size and consequences of international migration flows in the period 1500–2000 for the structure of the present-day population of a country; and, second, by showing how the agricultural and institutional knowledge that is incorporated in the people and descendants of these migration flows is important for explaining current income per capita levels for the whole world, including Oceania and the Americas. Biogeographic factors are therefore important for determining income levels today, either directly or indirectly through geo-human interaction.

4.2   The Geography of Population and Income

The distance from the equator to a country can be measured by the absolute value in degrees latitude from its geographic center. A simple but effective illustration of the relationship between geography and income is provided in Figure 4.1. Using data for 2019, the figure shows that, on average, income per capita levels increase the further away you move from the equator (see also Chapter 3). Tanzania, for example, is close to the equator (2.15 degrees) and has a low income level ($2,473). Germany, on the other hand, is much further away from the equator (48.16 degrees) and has a high income level ($55,155). The same holds for other high-income countries in the North, such as the USA and Japan. It also holds in the South, with higher income levels for Australia and South Africa. Not all countries close to the equator are poor. A clear example is Singapore at 1.36 degrees and with a high income level ($88,155). This city-state is a thriving harbor benefiting from many international connections (see also Box 4.1 and Chapters 6 and 16). Why do countries close to the equator tend to perform worse economically? The tropical climate zones, which are concentrated around the equator, are thought to be a primary reason for the poor economic performance of countries located there. Let's have a closer look at this aspect of the geography of population and income.

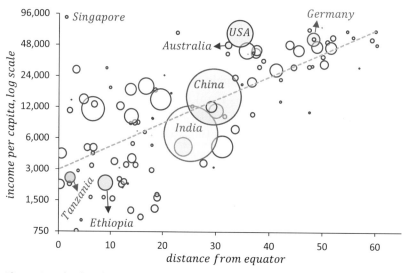

Figure 4.1 Absolute latitude and income per capita, 2019
Sources: Created using Olsson and Hibbs (2005) data for distance from equator (in degrees absolute latitude) and World Development Indicators online.
Notes: Income per capita is GNI PPP in constant 2017 $, log scale (2019 or most recent); bubbles proportional to population (2019); 109 countries included; dashed line is a regression.

Table 4.1. The Köppen climate classification letters

First letter		Second letter		Third letter	
A	Tropical	f	Fully humid	h	Hot arid
B	Dry	m	Monsoon	k	Cold arid
C	Mild temperate	s	Dry summer	a	Hot summer
D	Snow	w	Dry winter	b	Warm summer
E	Polar	W	Desert	c	Cool summer
		S	Steppe	d	Cold summer
		T	Tundra		
		F	Frost		

Source: Based on Chen and Chen 2013.

Your geographic location on the globe has consequences for the climate you live in. It can be hot or cold, wet or arid, windy or calm, and all of this may vary substantially over the year, or not. Climate zones can be identified on the basis of the Köppen classification system, which uses up to three letters to characterize a climate (see the explanation in Table 4.1). The *Af* climate is thus tropical – fully humid; the *As* climate is tropical – dry summers; the *BSk* climate is dry – steppe – cold arid; the *Cwa* climate is mild temperate – dry winter – hot summer, and so on. The various relevant combinations together lead to 31 different climates (see Figure 4.2 for a recent global overview). This was a bit too much for Sachs, Mellinger, and Gallup to handle when they wanted to summarize the geography of population and income, so they grouped them together into five major types, see Sachs *et al.* (2001):

- Tropical – subtropical
- Desert – steppe
- Temperate – snow
- Highland
- Polar

Since there are virtually no people living in the polar climate, this leaves us with four main climate types, which are henceforth referred to as tropical, desert, temperate, and highland, for short.

In this section, the four main climate types interact with another important geographical aspect of prosperity, namely that coastal regions usually do better than inland areas because of their easy access to sea trade. This was already noted by Adam Smith in a by now well-known quote in the first book of *The Wealth of Nations* (Smith 1776):

As by means of water-carriage a more extensive market is opened to every sort of industry than what land-carriage alone can afford it, so it is upon the sea-coast, and along the banks of navigable rivers, that industry of every kind naturally begins to subdivide and improve itself, and it is frequently not till a long time after that those improvements extend themselves to the inland parts of the country.

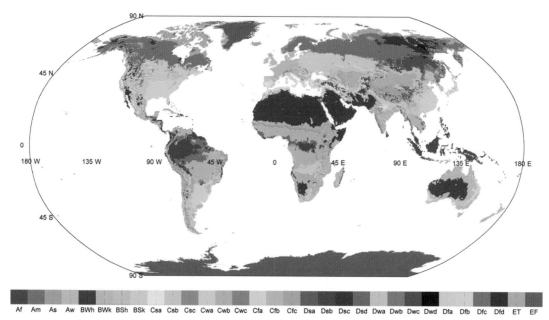

Af Am As Aw BWh BWk BSh BSk Csa Csb Csc Cwa Cwb Cwc Cfa Cfb Cfc Dsa Dsb Dsc Dsd Dwa Dwb Dwc Dwd Dfa Dfb Dfc Dfd ET EF

Figure 4.2 The Köppen climate classification system for 1901–2010
Source: Chen and Chen 2013; see http://hanschen.org/koppen/ and Table 4.1 for further explanation.
Note: The resolution is 0.5 degrees latitude/longitude.

To illustrate the interaction between geography, population, and income, Sachs, Mellinger, and Gallup use information of a country's income level, the distribution of its population across the country, the climate zones, and the extent to which an area is near to the sea. They do this by dividing the world map into five-minute by five-minute sections (equal to about 100 km^2 at the equator). For each section, they determine the size of the population, the level of gross national product (GNP) per capita (based on the relevant country's national average), and the GNP density (income per km^2). They also determine for each section to which of the four climate zones it belongs and whether or not the section is near to the sea. The latter is done by labeling a section *Near* to the sea if it is within 100 km of a seacoast or a sea-navigable waterway (a river, lake, or canal in which ocean-going vessels can operate) and labeling it *Far* if it is not. In combination with the four climate zones, there are therefore eight different geographical types: Tropical-Near, Tropical-Far, Desert-Near, Desert-Far, Temperate-Near, Temperate-Far, Highland-Near, and Highland-Far.

Sachs, Mellinger, and Gallup then report for each of the eight types the land area, population, and GNP as a percent of the world total. In terms of climate zones: the largest area is for the temperate zone (39.2 percent), followed by Desert (29.6), Tropical (19.9), and Highland (7.3); the largest population is in Tropical (40.3), followed by Temperate (34.9), Desert (18.0), and Highland (6.8); the largest GNP is in Temperate (67.2), followed by Tropical (17.4), Desert (10.1), and Highland (5.3). In terms of Near or Far from the coast:

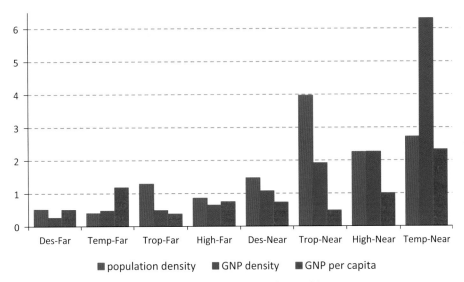

Figure 4.3 Population and income density relative to the world average
Source: Based on Sachs *et al.* 2001.
Notes: Trop = Tropical; Des = Desert; Temp = Temperate; High = Highland.

the smallest land area is Near (17.3 percent), but it has about the same population level as Far (49.4) and much higher GNP (67.5).

Based on this information, calculations were made regarding the population density, GNP density, and GNP per capita level for each of the eight geographical types relative to the world average, as illustrated in Figure 4.3 (ordered by GNP density). Even for such broad geographical types, the figure shows enormous differences in income level per km^2 (GNP density). It is above the world average for all Near types and below the world average for all Far types. It is by far the highest for the Temperate zone Near the coast (6.3 times the world average, or almost 25 times as high as for the Desert zone Far from the coast). The Temperate zone Near the coast also has the highest income per capita level (2.3 times the world average or more than six times higher than for the Tropical zone Far from the coast). The highest population density is for the Tropical zone Near the coast (almost four times the world average, or more than 10 times in the Temperate zone Far from the coast). The above shows that being Near to the coast gives large benefits in terms of income per capita and income density. It also shows that being in the Tropical zone leads to high population density (note that it is also above the world average Far from the coast), but low income per capita. The next section discusses one possible explanation.

4.3   Example: Malaria

Malaria is one of the most important infectious diseases affecting, in particular, people living in tropical climate zones. It is a mosquito-borne disease caused by a parasite of the

BOX 4.1 SINGAPORE, LEE KUAN YEW, AND AIRCONDITIONING

In March 2014, Lee Kuan Yew passed away at the age of 91 years old.[1] Born when Singapore was a British colony, Mr. Lee studied in London and Cambridge. He returned to Singapore after the Second World War, where he co-founded the People Action Party (PAP) and became the first prime minister in 1959 when Singapore won self-government from Britain. He led Singapore to a federation with Malaysia in 1963 and was heartbroken when the country was expelled and became independent in 1965. Mr. Lee was prime minister until 1990 and remained an important influence until shortly before his death.

Under Mr. Lee's guidance, Singapore became an economic success story. (Dutchman Albert Winsemius also played an important role as Chief Economic Advisor from 1961 to 1984.) In 1960, GDP per capita in Singapore was 94 percent of the world average in that year. By 2019, it was 531 percent of the world average, an astounding relative income rise of more than 7 percent points per year for six decades (see Figure 4.4). The rise is all the more remarkable since Singapore is located in the tropics, very close to the equator, has no natural resources (no oil or precious metals; it initially even lacked its own water supply), and nonetheless currently has a higher income per capita than the USA (see Figure 4.1). Its success is built on a record of honest and pragmatic government and its ideal location as a harbor, making trade relations with other nations the source of its prosperity. (At the personal level, Mr. Lee could be relentless; he used defamation suits to tame the press and sometimes to bankrupt his opponents.) At the end of the second millennium, Mr. Lee himself, however, saw things differently (The Economist 2014a, 2014b):

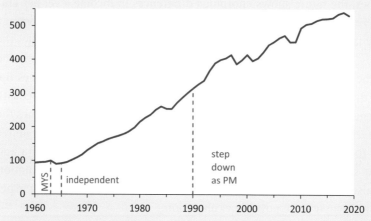

Figure 4.4 Singapore income per capita as a percent of the world average, 1960–2019
Source: Created using World Development Indicators.
Notes: Income is GDP in constant 2010 USD; MYS = Malaysia.

---

[1] Information is taken from *The Economist* (2014a, 2014b).

BOX 4.1 (cont.)

In some ways, Mr Lee was a bit of a crank. Among a number of 20th-century luminaries asked by the *Wall Street Journal* in 1999 to pick the most influential invention of the millennium, he alone shunned the printing press, electricity, the internal combustion engine and the internet and chose the air-conditioner. He explained that, before air-con, people living in the tropics were at a disadvantage because the heat and humidity damaged the quality of their work.

This inspired journalist Cherian George to start a website (www.airconditionednation .com) and write a book entitled *The Air-conditioned Nation: Essays on the Politics of Comfort and Control* as a metaphor for the comfort Mr. Lee brought to his people at the expense of the control he took.

Plasmodium type.[2] The mosquitos (of the *Anopheles* species) are referred to as malaria vectors. Early symptoms include fever, headache, chills, and vomiting. Severe cases can cause acute anaemia, respiratory distress, cerebral malaria, and death. There are four species of Plasmodium that can infect and be spread by humans, the most deadly of which is *P. Falciparum*. An estimated 198 million cases of malaria occurred worldwide in 2013, resulting in about 584,000 malaria deaths (World Health Organization 2014). In view of the uncertainty associated with collecting data under difficult circumstances, the number of cases ranges between an estimated lower bound of 124 million and an upper bound of 283 million. Similarly, the number of deaths ranges between a lower bound of 367,000 and an upper bound of 755,000. These ranges are illustrated in Figure 4.5, which also shows the number of malaria cases and deaths since the year 2000. The point estimates indicate that there was a modest decline in the number of cases in this millennium (by 13 percent, from 227 million in 2000 to 198 in 2013) and a more substantial decline in the number of deaths (by 33 percent from 882,000 to 584,000).

The malaria burden still extends to subtropical regions in five continents. Attempts to eliminate or suppress the disease have been successful already early in the twentieth century, particularly in temperate zones with seasonality and cold winters.[3] The reason is that the period required for the life-cycle change that the parasite must undergo within the mosquito becomes much longer if the temperature declines, while development stops completely below 16°C and mosquitos stop biting at low temperatures. Cold winters thus made it easier to eliminate malaria from much of the temperate zone. In tropical regions, however, exposure to mosquitos is perennial and temperatures are high.

---

[2] Information is taken from the World Health Organization fact sheet no 94, updated December 2014; see www .who.int/mediacentre/factsheets/fs094/en/.
[3] This paragraph is based on Sachs and Malaney 2002.

Table 4.2. Estimated number of malaria cases and malaria deaths, 2013

Region	Estimated number of			Deaths < 5 as % of total
	Cases (×1,000)	Deaths	Deaths < 5	
Africa	163,000	528,000	437,000	83
Americas	700	800	220	28
Eastern Mediterranean	9,000	11,000	3,900	35
Europe	2	0	0	–
Southeast Asia	24,000	41,000	11,000	27
Western Pacific	1,000	3,300	1,600	48
World	198,000	584,000	453,000	78

Data source: World Health Organization 2014, table 8.2; see the report for details on the regions.

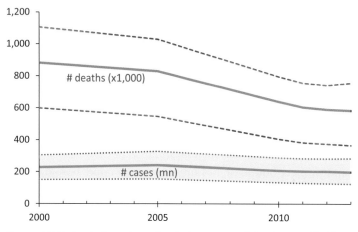

Figure 4.5 Estimated number of malaria cases and deaths, worldwide
Source: Based on World Health Organization 2014, table 8.3.
Note: Ranges show lower and upper bound.

The malaria burden is unevenly distributed in several ways. First, only about half the world population is at risk, mostly in tropical regions. Second, within the tropical climate zone two regions are most affected, namely Sub-Sahara Africa and Southeast Asia. Third, within these regions young children are most affected as they have not yet developed protective immunity. Table 4.2 provides the relevant information. Of the 198 million malaria cases, 163 million (82 percent) occurred in Africa and 24 million (12 percent) in Southeast Asia. Regarding the number of deaths: 528,000 (90 percent) occurred in Africa and 41,000 (7 percent) in Southeast Asia. Most of these deaths were for young children under the age of 5 years old (453,000 or 78 percent of the total deaths). Of the number of deaths under 5 years old 437,000 (96 percent) occurred in Africa and 11,000 (2 percent) in Southeast Asia. To summarize: on average, 377 new cases of malaria arose every minute, resulting in the death of one person: a young child in Africa.

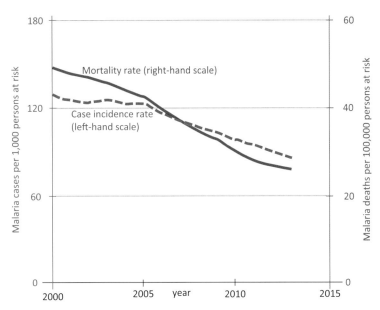

Figure 4.6 Estimated malaria case incidence rate and mortality rate, 2000–13
Source: Based on World Health Organization 2014, figure 8.8.
Note: Point estimates only.

In addition to the direct costs of malaria (the medical costs and foregone income), there are indirect economic costs through (i) changes in household behavior and (ii) macroeconomic costs.[4] Regarding (i), you can think of high fertility rates associated with high infant and child mortality rates (since parents have additional children to replace the ones that they lose) and low investments in education per child (the quality–quantity trade-off), resulting in lower levels of human capital. Regarding (ii), you can think of reduced international connections through lower trade and investment flows between regions with and without malaria, particularly with respect to tourism. When malaria transmission was suppressed in Greece, Portugal, and Spain in the 1950s, a process of rapid economic development started, driven by increased foreign investment from Northern Europe and greatly increased tourism.

In cooperation with many other organizations, the World Health Organization has made significant progress since 2000 in reducing the malaria burden. The most important benefits have arisen from progress in vector control, such as insecticide-treated mosquito nets and long-lasting insecticidal nets. It is clear from Figure 4.5 that the burden reduction holds for the number of deaths (which has declined), but it is not evident for the number of cases. Keep in mind, however, that Figure 4.5 is based on the *absolute* number of deaths and cases. As such, this figure ignores the fact that the population at risk has grown rapidly in this time period, particularly in Africa. For that reason it is better to look at the case *incidence rate* (the number of cases per 1,000 persons at risk) and the *mortality rate* (the number of deaths per 100,000 persons at risk) (see Figure 4.6). From 2000 to 2013, the

---

[4] This paragraph is also based on Sachs and Malaney (2002).

mortality rate has declined by about 47 percent and the case incidence rate by about 30 percent. The decline has been more rapid since 2005.

4.4   Development by 1500

As will be discussed in sections 4.7 and 4.8, the worldwide migration flows into the Americas, Oceania, and parts of Africa over the past 500 years have had important consequences for the level of economic development for the receiving nations. This makes it worthwhile to briefly investigate what the level of economic development was before these migration flows started, say around 1500 AD. Associated with this investigation is another problem: how do we estimate the level of economic development 500 years ago? Economic historians have tackled this question for quite some time. Chapters 5 and 7 provide an overview of the fruits of their labor. More or less reliable estimates are, however, only available for a limited number of countries or regions. More importantly, it appears that until around 1500 the "Malthusian theory" was still empirically valid (see Ashraf and Galor 2011). This theory argues that technological progress and resource expansion primarily lead to a rise in an area's population and not to a rise in income per capita. As a consequence, economists tend to use estimates of population densities in countries or regions as an early indicator of economic development. These estimates are also more widely available (and probably more reliable) than the early income per capita estimates.[5]

Biogeographic factors are, indeed, correlated with population density in 1500 (see column 2 of Table 4.3), but some (such as the number of wild grasses and domesticable big mammals) mainly through their influence on the timing of the adoption of agriculture (Ashraf and Galor 2011). The first step taken in Table 4.3 is therefore to determine the influence of biogeographic factors on the timing of the agricultural transition (column 1; this is a first-stage regression). Most of the effects are highly significant and together they account for 71 percent of the variance in the date of adoption. The next step taken in Table 4.3 is then to determine the influence of the number of years since the agricultural transition on population density in 1500, both using OLS (column 3) and IV (instrumental variables, column 4). The estimated effects are positive (population density rises as the number of years since the agricultural transition rises) and economically significant. (A one standard deviation increase in the years of agriculture results in a 63 percent standard deviation change in log population density in 1500.) Building on their Neolithic advantages countries with early adoption of agriculture thus create a technological lead that gives them an economic advantage by 1500. Note, however, that although these effects are economically significant and explain about 40 percent in the variance of population density (see column 3 of Table 4.3), this still leaves enough room for other factors to be important for explaining the remaining 60 percent.

---

[5] This section is largely based on Spolaore and Wacziarg 2013, table 2.

Table 4.3. Geography and development in 1500

Dependent variable	Years since agricultural transition	Population density in 1500		
Estimator	OLS (1)	OLS (2)	OLS (3)	IV (4)
Absolute latitude	−0.074***	−0.022	0.027**	0.020*
Percent land area in the tropics	−1.052**	0.997**	1.464***	1.636***
Landlocked dummy	−0.585**	0.384	0.532	0.702***
Island dummy	−1.085***	0.072	0.391	0.508
# wild grasses	0.017	0.030		
# domesticable big mammals	0.554***	0.258***		
Years since agricultural transition			0.426***	0.584***
Observations	100	100	98	98
Adjusted R^2	0.707	0.439	0.393	−

Source: Spolaore and Wacziarg 2013, table 2.
Notes: Constant and t-statistics not reported. Shaded cells with ***, **, and * are significant at the 1, 5, and 10 percent level, respectively.

4.5   Institutions and Reversal of Fortune

There are, of course, many crucial human interactions involved in raising the level of economic development for a nation, as discussed in more detail in Chapters 6–9. This section highlights the importance of "institutions" in this process (see also Chapter 8). Countries with better institutions, such as more secure property rights, less distortionary policies, and a more reliable government, create an environment in which people have a bigger incentive to invest in physical capital, in themselves through education (human capital), and in research and innovation (to develop new goods and services) since it is more likely that they can reap the fruit of their own efforts and investments. As a consequence, in the longer run better institutions lead to higher levels of economic development.

The present discussion will be based on the work of Acemoglu, Johnson, and Robinson (2001 and 2002; AJR in the remainder of this section). They focus on the current economic consequences of colonization by European countries for former European colonies through differences in institutions. Their main argument runs roughly as follows.

- First, there were different types of colonization policies. Some colonies were regarded as "extractive states," such as the Congo colonized by Belgium. In those cases, the colonial power did not provide checks and balances for the government or sufficient protection of private property. Other colonies were regarded as "Neo-Europes," possible destinations for migration and settlement. Examples are Australia, New Zealand, Canada, and the USA. In those cases the colonial power imposed more or less the same "good" institutions as at home.

- Second, the colonization strategy was influenced by the feasibility of settlement. If the disease environment was unfavorable, such as in the tropics where malaria and yellow fewer resulted in high settler mortality, the formation of extractive states rather than Neo-Europes is more likely.
- Third, institutions change slowly over time. So the colonial state and institutions persisted even after independence.

As a consequence of these three premises: high settler mortality influenced the likelihood of settlement, which influenced the likelihood of extractive institutions, which influenced the quality of current institutions, which influences current economic performance.

To get an indication of potential settler mortality, AJR gather information on the number of deaths among 1,000 soldiers measured by the number of replacements for European troops in different locations, mostly in the period from 1818 to 1848. The variation is enormous, ranging from less than nine replacements in Australia and New Zealand to more than 1,000 for Gambia, Mali, and Nigeria. To get an indication of the quality of current institutions, AJR gather information on the average protection against expropriation risk in the period 1985–95. This is combined with current income per capita levels (GNI per capita PPP in constant 2017 $, most recent available in the period 2017–19). Panel a of Figure 4.7 shows that there is indeed a strong negative association between the current income level and settler mortality in the nineteenth century. Similarly, panel b of Figure 4.7 shows that there is a negative association between settler mortality and the current level of institutional quality. Note that Figure 4.7 depicts the information for two groups of countries, namely the countries included in the AJR sample to be discussed in Table 4.4 and other countries (see also section 4.6). (Note that three countries are excluded in panel a for lack of current income per capita data, namely Argentina in the AJR sample and Djibouti and Myanmar in the other countries sample; in panel b, 10 of the other countries are missing for lack of protection against expropriation data.)

The main results are summarized in Table 4.4 using two-stage regressions. Panel b shows the first-stage influence of settler mortality on the quality of institutions, where higher settler mortality leads to significantly worse institutions. Panel a shows the second-stage influence of institutions on current income per capita, where better institutions lead to significantly higher income levels. According to the estimates, the difference in institutional quality between Chile and Nigeria, for example, leads to an estimated seven-fold difference in income per capita (see Acemoglu *et al.* 2001).

Column 2 of Table 4.4 adds dummy variables for British and French colonies, with colonies from other nations as the omitted group. It has been pointed out that British colonies tend to have better institutions and perform better (see La Porta *et al.* 1998). As column 2 shows, however, it is important to control for settler mortality: Britain colonized places where settlements were possible, leading to better institutions, which in turn resulted in better performance.

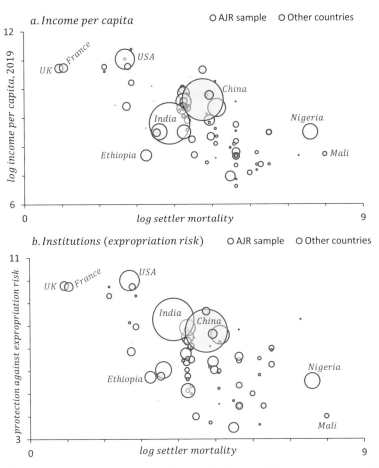

Figure 4.7 European settler mortality, institutions, and income per capita, 2019
Sources: Based on data from Acemoglu *et al.* 2001 and World Development Indicators online.
Notes: Income per capita is GNI PPP in constant 2017 $ (2019 or most recent available); European settler mortality per 1,000; expropriation risk = risk of expropriation of private foreign investment by government (index from 0 to 10, where a higher score means lower risk); 86 observations in panel a and 74 in panel b.

Table 4.5 summarizes two simple versions of a more controversial aspect of AJR's work, known as the "reversal of fortune" phenomenon (see Acemoglu *et al.* 2002). Here the main argument is as follows. European colonies that were relatively rich in 1500, such as the Mughals in India and the Aztecs and Incas in the Americas, were confronted with worse institutions after colonization than previously poor places, such as North America, Australia, and New Zealand. As a consequence of the institutional reversal, a reversal of fortune can be observed in terms of income per capita: previously rich places become relatively poor and vice versa. AJR argue explicitly that their findings are indicative of institutional quality as the crucial variable for determining prosperity and are not supported by a simple geography hypothesis on the prosperity of nations, since geographic variables that do not change over time cannot explain a reversal in relative incomes.

AJR use two indicators of economic prosperity in 1500, namely the degree of urbanization and population density, and analyze their influence on current income levels. Column

Table 4.4. Institutions and development

	AJR sample (1)	AJR sample, colonial dummies (2)
Panel a Second stage; dependent variable: log GDP per capita		
Institutions (expropriation risk)	0.94***	1.10***
British colonial dummy		-0.78**
French colonial dummy		-0.12
Panel b First stage; dependent variable: institutions (protection against expropriation risk)		
Log settler mortality	-0.61***	-0.53***
British colonial dummy		0.63*
French colonial dummy		0.05
R^2	0.27	0.31
Observations	64	64

Source: Acemoglu *et al.* 2001, tables 4 and 5.
Notes: t-statistics not reported; shaded cells with ***, **, and * are significant at the 1, 5, and 10 percent level, respectively.

Table 4.5. Reversal of fortune

Dependent variable: Log per capita income 1995; estimator OLS

	AJR base sample	AJR base sample
Urbanization in 1500	-0.078***	
Log population density in 1500		-0.38***
Observations	41	91
R^2	0.19	0.34

Source: Acemoglu *et al.* 2002, tables III and V.
Notes: t-statistics not reported; shaded cells with ***, ** and * are significant at the 1, 5, and 10 percent level, respectively.

1 of Table 4.5 focuses on urbanization. It shows that countries with a higher urbanization level in 1500 tend to have a lower income level today. There are only 41 observations and the share of current income variance explained is 19 percent. Although AJR prefer urbanization as an indicator of prosperity in 1500, they also use population density estimates since this is correlated with urbanization and available for more countries (91 instead of 41). Column 2 of Table 4.5 shows that countries with a high population density in 1500 tend to have a lower income level today, another indicator of the reversal of fortune that explains 34 percent of the variance in current income.

4.6 Selection Effects

One can raise various objections to the reversal of fortune phenomenon discussed in section 4.5. First, one may wonder how appropriate is it to compare economic development per capita today, which is measured relatively precisely in real dollars, with economic development measured relatively imprecisely by urbanization or population density 500 years ago. Second, the standard neoclassical growth model discussed in Chapter 7 also gives rise to a reversal of fortune without any need for a change in institutional quality. Third, perhaps countries with high economic development have good institutions because of the way institutional quality is measured – namely, ex post, with a tendency to see better institutions in richer places. Fourth, and the topic of the remainder of this section, the selection of countries to be included in the analysis plays a crucial role (Spolaore and Wacziarg 2013).

The main selection effects are summarized in Table 4.6. The beta coefficients in the table indicate how many standard deviations a dependent variable will change per standard deviation increase in the exogenous variable (based on a regression where all exogenous variables are standardized to have a variance of one). Spolaore and Wacziarg use extended information for a broader sample of countries and updated to 2005 in terms of "current"

Table 4.6. Selection effects

Dependent variable: Log per capita income 2005; estimator OLS

Panel a Including European countries

	Whole world (1)	Europe only (2)	Not former European colony (3)	Indigenous countries (4)
Log pop dens 1500	0.027	0.117	0.170[**]	0.193[**]
Beta coefficient (%)	3.3	22.8	22.3	20
Observations	171	35	73	138
Adjusted R^2	0.001	0.052	0.050	0.040

Panel b Excluding European countries

	Whole world (5)	Former European colony (6)	Not former European colony (7)	Indigenous countries (8)
Log pop dens 1500	−0.246[***]	−0.393[***]	−0.030	−0.117
Beta coefficient (%)	−27.8	−47.9	−3.1	−11.7
Observations	136	98	38	103
Adjusted R^2	0.077	0.229	0.001	0.014

Source: Spolaore and Wacziarg 2013, table 3.
Notes: t-statistics not reported; indigenous countries have more than half of the current population descended from people who lived there in 1500 (see section 4.7 for details); shaded cells with [***], [**], and [*] are significant at the 1, 5, and 10 percent level, respectively.

income per capita. Panel b column 6 shows that the reversal of fortune effect holds if attention is restricted to former European colonies (a negative and significant coefficient). This also holds for the world as a whole if European countries are excluded (column 5). The effect does not hold, however, for countries that were not former European colonies (column 7), and for non-European indigenous states (column 8). An "indigenous state" is defined as a country with more than half of the current population descended from people who lived there in 1500 (see section 4.7 for a discussion).

Panel a of Table 4.6 shows that when Europe is included there is no evidence of a reversal of fortune. The effect is not significant for the world as a whole (column 1) and if attention is restricted to European countries only (column 2). The effect is significant and *positive*, thus indicative of persistence rather than a reversal of fortune, if former European colonies are excluded (column 3) or only indigenous countries are looked at (column 4). Spolaore and Wacziarg (2013) note on page 335: "In other words, the reversal of fortune is a feature of samples that exclude Europe and is driven largely by countries inhabited by populations that moved there after the discovery of the New World, and now constitute large portions of these countries' populations – either European colonizers (e.g. in North America and Oceania) or African slaves (e.g. in the Caribbean)."

The estimates thus suggest that the composition of a country's population may play a role in determining the prosperity of nations. After all, when people move to other countries, such as Europeans settling in North America or Africans forcibly transported to Brazil, they bring with them their human capital and all aspects of their country's culture and history (see Glaeser *et al.* 2004). Before discussing the potential contribution of these migration flows to economic development today in section 4.8, it is necessary to discuss the size and impact of these migration flows in section 4.7.

4.7   Migration Flows since 1500

Putterman and Weil (2010) are the first to provide a structural and detailed account of the migration flows in the world in the past five centuries. They use information for 172 countries, together comprising almost the entire world population. The focus is on determining to what extent the current population living in a particular country descend from people who already lived there in 1500 and from ethnicities from other countries. The 1500 benchmark date is taken as the starting point of the era of European colonization of other continents, which resulted in large-scale population movements. Both the direct and indirect consequences of these movements are referred to here as "migration" flows; the term therefore includes voluntary migration, the transport of slaves, and forced relocation. If a person migrated recently from one country to another, the direct consequence for the current population is just one additional person. If a person migrated from one country to another several decades or even centuries ago, the consequences for the current population add up indirectly as well through their offspring (their children, grandchildren, and so on). Putterman and Weil use detailed country-level studies and genetic information to estimate both the direct and indirect consequences of migration flows.

To analyze the consequences of the main migration flows since 1500, (i) the detailed 172 country-level data of Putterman and Weil (2010) are used, which is (ii) combined with the current population size for these countries, and then (iii) grouped together in larger global regions for illustration purposes. The World Bank identifies seven global regions on the basis of geography, history, and development (see Table 4.7). Two of those regions are further subdivided. First, the large East Asia and Pacific region (31.3 percent of the world population) is subdivided into three parts: East Asia (including China, Korea, and Japan), Southeast Asia (including Indonesia and the Philippines), and Pacific (including Australia and New Zealand). Second, the Europe and Central Asia region is subdivided into Europe (including the UK, Germany, France, and Italy) and Central Asia (including Russia) separately. There are therefore 10 different global regions. (As a UN organization, the World Bank does not include Taiwan in its global regions. It has been included here in the East Asia region.)

Figure 4.8 illustrates the consequences of the migration flows since 1500 for the 10 global regions, while further detail is provided in Table 4.8. First, note that the population of only three global regions currently consists largely of nonindigenous population, namely North America (97 percent), Pacific (94 percent), and Latin America (68 percent). Of the 351 million people currently living in North America, for example, only 11 million descend from people who lived there in 1500. For the remaining seven global regions, the nonindigenous population is less than 6 percent (even 0 percent for East Asia). To the extent that migration flows have an impact on current development, this therefore has an impact only for the Americas and Pacific. There are a few exceptions at the country level. In contrast to

Table 4.7. Global regions

World Bank regions – further subdivided

Region	Code	Population				# countries
		Million	%	Million	%	
East Asia and Pacific	EAP	2,225	31.3			36
Pacific	PAC			31	0.4	17
East Asia	EAS			1,570	22.1	7
Southeast Asia	SEA			624	8.8	12
Europe and Central Asia	ECA	899	12.7			57
Europe	EUR			542	7.6	45
Central Asia	CAS			357	5.0	12
Latin America and Caribbean	LAC	615	8.7			41
Middle East & North Africa	MENA	403	5.7			21
North America	NAM	351	4.9			3
South Asia	SAS	1,671	23.5			8
Sub-Sahara Africa	SSA	937	13.2			48
Total		7,101	100			214

Source: Based on World Bank Development Indicators classification, 2015.

Table 4.8. Region-wide global migration flows in the past five centuries

Lives in	Originates from										sum
	CAS	EAS	EUR	LAC	MENA	NAM	PAC	SAS	SEA	SSA	
						(millions of people)					
CAS	352	1	3	0	1	0	0	0	0	0	357
EAS	0	1,593	0	0	0	0	0	0	0	0	1,593
EUR	7	0	524	0	4	0	0	2	1	1	540
LAC	1	2	328	196	3	0	0	1	0	81	613
MENA	4	0	5	0	378	0	0	3	0	7	398
NAM	6	8	264	20	2	11	0	4	5	31	351
PAC	0	1	24	0	1	0	2	1	1	0	28
SAS	4	0	0	0	0	0	0	1,666	0	0	1,670
SEA	0	31	0	0	0	0	0	4	589	0	624
SSA	0	0	12	0	1	0	0	2	0	909	925
Origin	375	1,636	1,160	216	389	11	2	1,684	596	1,030	7,099

In percent of total world population

Origin	5.3	23.0	16.3	3.0	5.5	0.2	0.0	23.7	8.4	14.5	100

Source: Calculations based on migration matrix (Putterman and Weil 2010) and population in 2013.
Notes: 172 countries included; CAS = Central Asia; EAS = East Asia; EUR = Europe; LAC = Latin America and the Caribbean; MENA = Middle East and North Africa; NAM = North America; PAC = Pacific; SAS = South Asia; SEA = Southeast Asia; SSA = Sub-Sahara Africa.

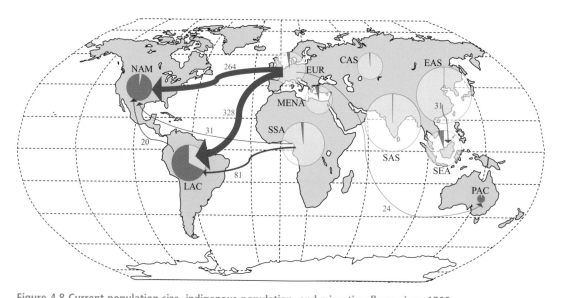

Figure 4.8 Current population size, indigenous population, and migration flows since 1500
Sources: Authors' calculations based on Putterman and Weil 2010 data and World Bank Development indicators.
Notes: GDP per capita in 2013. Region abbreviations: see Table 4.7; bubbles proportional to population size in 2013; light-shaded area is indigenous population (descended from people who lived in the region in 1500); dark-shaded area is nonindigenous population; weight of migration line is proportional to size of population flow (in millions); only flows of 15 million or more people are shown; see Table 4.8 for further details.

the largely nonindigenous population in the Pacific and Latin America, more than half of the population *is* indigenous in Fiji, Bolivia, Ecuador, Guatemala, Honduras, Mexico, and Peru. With the exception of Mexico, which benefits from being in the neighborhood of North America, all these countries with a high indigenous population have a lower income per capita than their region average. Similarly, in contrast to the largely indigenous population in their region, there are only two countries where the nonindigenous population is more than half, namely Mauritius and Singapore. Both these countries have a (substantially) higher income level than their region average.

Second, note that by far the largest global regional migration flows originate from Europe. Of the 1,160 million people currently alive originating from Europe in 1500, only 524 million live inside Europe (see Table 4.8). The remaining 636 million moved to Latin America (328 million), North America (264 million), Pacific (24 million), and other regions. Sub-Sahara Africa is a distant second global region for the origin of migration flows. Of the 1,030 million people currently alive originating from Sub-Sahara Africa in 1500, most live inside Sub-Sahara Africa (909 million), while 81 million migrated to Latin America and 31 million to North America. The only remaining substantial migration flow is from East Asia to Southeast Asia (31 million).

4.8   Ancestry

This section briefly discusses the historical influence of geographic *locations* as well as the historical legacy of the *populations* inhabiting these locations for current economic development. Two measures of early economic development are used, namely *state history* and the number of *years of agriculture* (Putterman and Weil 2010). The state history variable measures the extent to which what is now a country had a supra-tribal government, the geographic scope of that government, and whether this was indigenous or by an outside power in the 15 centuries prior to 1500. It discounts the past by reducing the weight for each half century by 5 percent. Ethiopia, for example, achieves the maximum value of 1; China reaches 0.906; Spain reaches 0.562; while the USA has a value of 0. The number of years since the agricultural transition has already been discussed in Chapter 3. It is measured in thousands, with, for example, a highest value of 10.5 for Israel; a value of 9 for China; a value of 4 for Ecuador; a value of 3.5 for Ivory Coast; and a value of 1 for Haiti.

State history and years of agriculture are both examined in their original form and adjusted to take account of migration flows since 1500. These variables are labeled *ancestry-adjusted* state history and *ancestry-adjusted* years of agriculture. The principle for the adjustment is simple: migrants bring with them the state history and years of agriculture of their old country to their new country. The historical influences of state history and years of agriculture on current development is thus incorporated in the migrants and (partially) passed on to their offspring. The adjustment is a population-weighted average of the historical experiences of the entire population. If, for example, the population of country A consists of 90 percent population from country A with a state history of 0.6 and of 10 percent population from country B with a state history of 0.2,

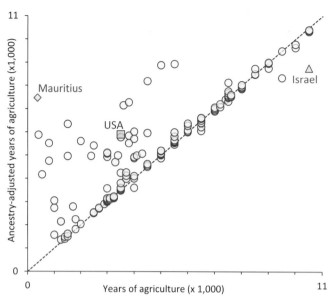

Figure 4.9 Years of agriculture and ancestry-adjusted years of agriculture
Source: Authors' calculations based on Putterman and Weil 2010 data.
Note: The dotted line is a 45° line.

then the ancestry-adjusted state history of country A is: $0.9 \times 0.6 + 0.1 \times 0.2 = 0.56$; similarly for years of agriculture.

Figure 4.9 illustrates the differences between years of agriculture and ancestry-adjusted years of agriculture. For many countries there is hardly any difference between these two variables: the observations are close to the 45° line. Most of these countries are in one of the seven global regions largely consisting of indigenous population (see section 4.7). For a range of other countries, mostly in the Americas and the Pacific, the ancestry-adjusted years of agriculture is much higher than without the adjustment. An example is the USA, where the ancestry-adjusted state history is 5.9 instead of 3.5. Occasionally this also holds for countries outside these regions, such as Mauritius (7.5 instead of 0.4) and Singapore (8.2 instead of 4.5, not shown). Only in two cases are the ancestry-adjusted variables significantly lower than the original variables, namely for Israel (8.8 instead of 10.5) and Kuwait (8.3 instead of 9.5, not shown).

The importance of adjusting for migration flows for the historical influence on current economic development is summarized in Table 4.9. All regressions estimate current income levels and include four geographic components, namely absolute latitude, percent land area in the tropics, landlocked dummy, and an island dummy. The two measures of early economic development, state history and years of agriculture, are then added to the regression in turn, both in their original form and ancestry-adjusted. In their original form, both variables are not significant (columns 1 and 3). When using ancestry-adjusted variables, however, both measures of early development are highly significant and economically important (columns 2 and 4). A one standard deviation increase in years of agriculture raises the log of income by 17 percent, while a one standard deviation increase in state history raises this by 22 percent (see Putterman and Weil 2010). These results

Table 4.9. Ancestry-adjusted geography, state history, and development

Dependent variable: Log per capita income 2005; estimator OLS; beta coefficient in parentheses

Main regressor	Years of agriculture (1)	Ancestry-adjusted years of agriculture (2)	State history (3)	Ancestry-adjusted state history (4)
Years of agriculture	0.019 (3.8)			
Ancestry-adjusted years of agriculture		0.099[**] (17.2)		
State history			0.074 (1.5)	
Ancestry-adjusted state history				1.217[***] (21.6)
Absolute latitude	0.042[***]	0.040[***]	0.047[***]	0.046[***]
Percent land area in the tropics	−0.188	−0.148	0.061	0.269
Landlocked dummy	−0.753[***]	−0.671[***]	−0.697[***]	−0.555[***]
Island dummy	0.681[**]	0.562[***]	0.531[**]	0.503[**]
Observations	150	148	136	135
Adjusted R^2	0.475	0.523	0.558	0.588

Source: Spolaore and Wacziarg 2013, table 5.
Notes: t-statistics and constant not reported; shaded cells with [***], [**], and [*] are significant at the 1, 5, and 10 percent level, respectively.

indicate that economic development today is at least partially based on the characteristics of human populations. The people who migrated voluntarily and forcibly to another country brought with them their characteristics, human capital, and familiarity with certain types of institutions and norms of behavior. All these aspects seem to be important for explaining current levels of economic development.

4.9   Conclusions

The importance of geo-human interaction for explaining current development levels is analyzed in four steps. First, by pointing out the connections between current economic development and biogeographic factors in general, particularly for the Old World (excluding Oceania and the Americas). Second, by showing how these factors can help explain the agricultural transition and human development levels for the whole world up to the year 1500. Third, by discussing the role of man-made institutions and selection effects in the reversal of fortune discussion, which is not observed if European countries are included in the analysis and reversed for indigenous countries and countries that were not former European colonies. Fourth, by analyzing the role of international migration flows from 1500 to 2000 for the structure of the present-day population of a country and by showing how the institutional knowledge incorporated in these flows helps explain current economic development levels for the whole world, including Oceania and the Americas. Eventually, biogeographic factors are thus important for economic development levels, either directly or indirectly through geo-human interaction.

In the man-made institutions versus biogeographical factors analysis associated with the reversal of fortune discussion, it can be seen that biogeographic factors are crucial in at least two ways.

First, there is a direct effect, since European countries only established "good" institutions in countries that were conducive to their own well-being; that is, countries with similar circumstances, a similar climate, and a lower disease burden. Biogeography is thus important for determining where to impose the good institutions.

Second, there is a geo-human interaction effect. Chapter 3 showed that the transmission of knowledge was easier across the Eurasian axis such that people there could benefit from discoveries and knowledge generated elsewhere, which in turn was important for developing good institutions. After 1500, the Europeans colonized large parts of the world and settled in many places. The parts that had good climatic conditions for benefiting from the earlier developments in Eurasia were: North America, Oceania, South Africa, and parts of Latin America. Those are the parts that are prosperous today – either through the institutional structure imposed (which depends to a large extent on the biogeographic conditions) or from the indirect benefit of transferring thousands of years of accumulated historical knowledge to these places through migration flows.

This concludes the discussion in Part I on the importance of biogeographic factors in general and of geo-human interaction in particular for explaining current economic development. The next part focuses on the importance of human interaction for economic development, through globalization (Chapter 5), trade (Chapter 6), economic growth (Chapter 7), institutions (Chapter 8), and finance (Chapter 9).

Further Reading

A well-written account of human history, what factors have stimulated growth and inequality, including how and why humanity has only recently escaped the Malthusian poverty trap, is provided by Oded Galor in *The Journey of Humanity: The Origins of Wealth and Inequality* (New York/London: Dutton/Penguin, 2022). As is forcefully put forward in this book, apart from the quality of institutions, geography is one of the crucial factors. The book also discusses Acemoglu, Johnson, and Robinson (2001 and 2002) in a nontechnical way. Edward Glaeser provides an accessible introduction to the role of cities in economic development in *Cities, Agglomeration, and Spatial Equilibrium* (Oxford University Press, 2008).

Nathan Nunn looks at the influence of different "values, beliefs and traditions" on the (economic) success of countries. Some of these are successful in some periods, but not necessarily in others, with new challenges to solve (for example, climate change). See: Nunn, N. 2022. "On the Dynamics of Human Behavior: The Past, Present, and Future of Culture, Conflict, and Cooperation," *AEA Papers and Proceedings*, 112, 15–37.

PART II
Human Interaction

. . . .

Part II consists of five chapters and shifts focus from geo-human interaction to human interaction, which becomes relatively more important as time progresses. Chapter 5 provides an overview of globalization and economic development from a longer-run perspective (2,000 years). The chapter covers different types of globalization, price wedges, and trade-, migration-, and capital flows. Chapter 6 focuses on a better understanding of the causes and consequences of trade flows between nations. It covers comparative advantages based on differences in technology and factor abundance, as well as competitive advantages related to intra-industry trade flows, imperfect competition, and firm heterogeneity. Chapter 7 continues with an overview of the main causes of economic growth and development based on (human) capital accumulation, total factor productivity, knowledge flows, and endogenous growth, as well as the dynamic costs of trade restrictions. Chapter 8 analyzes institutions and contracts, with a discussion of the nature of the firm, social costs, property rights, and the relationship between institutions and economic development (do institutions cause growth?). Chapter 9 concludes, outlining money and finance issues, with a particular focus on exchange rates, forward markets, interest parity, the policy trilemma, and the links between finance, investment, and development.

Globalization and Development

5.1 Introduction

Chapter 1 provides a brief overview of the current state of international economic affairs. Before starting to analyze how the current economic interactions can be better understood, it is useful to provide a brief, nontechnical overview of the long-run developments of the world economy, which is done under the term "globalization."[1] Section 5.2 shows that there are different types of globalization and that the term is interpreted in different ways by different people. This book will focus on economic globalization. Sections 5.3 and 5.4 then provide an overview of "recent" history by analyzing the development of global trade and income flows since 1960, both in total and per capita. Most of the remainder of this chapter focuses on "long-run" history. First, by providing an overview of the developments of income per capita over a 2,000-year period (section 5.5). Second, by discussing globalization in history and the two waves of globalization for trade flows (section 5.6). Third, by analyzing the role of the price wedge in globalization for trade flows (section 5.7) and for capital and migration flows, both with their own waves of globalization (section 5.8). Section 5.9 concludes. Note that the link between globalization and income inequality is analyzed in Chapter 10.

5.2 What Is Globalization?

The short and uninformative – but correct – answer to the question "what is globalization?" is: everything you want it to be. Many of the heated disputes on the streets and in the media about the advantages and disadvantages of the globalization process arise from the fact that this phrase means different things to different people. At the infamous 1999 meeting of the World Trade Organization (WTO) in Seattle, the environmentalists dressed in sea-turtle outfits cared about different issues than the French farm leaders protesting against the "McDonaldization" driving out the consumption of Roquefort cheese. Similarly for the trade unionists and the human right activists. Five key debates can be identified (see also McDonald and Burton 2002).

---

[1] This chapter is partially based on Beugelsdijk *et al.* 2013; I am grateful to my co-authors Sjoerd Beugelsdijk, Steven Brakman, and Harry Garretsen for permission to use our joint work.

- *Cultural globalization.* This debate asks whether there is a global culture or a set of universal cultural variables and the extent to which these displace embedded national cultures and traditions. To an unprecedented extent, we have similar cultural experiences in virtually all countries of the world: we see similar (American) movies, listen to similar (American and British) music, eat at McDonald's, drink Coca-Cola, drive Toyotas, and so on. The carriers of culture globalization are argued to be large multinationals, hence the term "McDonaldization." Some people are afraid that this will lead to a boring, homogeneous global culture at the expense of local cultures and traditions. Others are not so gloomy, and see enough room for local traditions and new developments against a globally oriented background. After all, there is great regional cultural variety in China even after thousands of years of common experiences, and similarly for Europe. Cultural globalization is not the focus of this book.

- *Economic globalization.* This debate centers on the decline of national markets and the rise of global markets, be it for the production and sale of final and intermediate goods and services or for the procurement of inputs (labor and capital). Driven by fundamental changes in technology which permit new, complicated, and more efficient ways of internationally organizing production processes, the rules of competition are being redefined along the way and firms and governments will have to learn how to adapt. This chapter *does* analyze the consequences of economic globalization: the increased interdependence of national economies, and the trend toward greater integration of goods, labor, and capital markets (Neary 2003).

- *Geographical globalization.* This debate refers to the sensation of compressed time and space as a result of reduced travel times between locations and the rapid (electronic) exchange of information. Knowledge and production previously confined to certain geographical areas may now cross borders and can be made available anywhere because of the rapid transfer of information and transport innovations. Some argue that this leads to the "end of geography" in which the "world is flat" such that location no longer matters and "footloose" global capital can quickly cross borders. But Chapter 17 shows that declining trade and interaction costs make location/geography more important and lead to the agglomeration of economic activity. Think, for example, of the clustering of international finance in three global centers (London, New York, and Tokyo).

- *Institutional globalization.* This debate relates to the spread of "universal" institutional arrangements across the globe. In the aftermath of the neo-liberal policies of Ronald Reagan (USA) and Margaret Thatcher (UK), in combination with the collapse of communist Soviet-type economic systems, an increasing number of countries adopted similar reforms (Albert 1993), with an emphasis on making markets more flexible, privatizing former state-owned organizations (SOEs), reducing the size of welfare arrangements, and so on. In an international context, these policies were promoted by institutions like the International Monetary Fund (IMF) and the World Bank, which some said forced the "Washington Consensus" upon the developing world (Stiglitz 2002). In a similar vein, micro-level business institutions are influenced by global trends. Multinationals adopt similar policies under the pressure of competition and regulation. For instance, benchmarking practices are promoted by global consultancy businesses such as the Boston Consulting Group and McKinsey, and the regulations of the New York Stock Exchange (NYSE) are imposed on many non-American enterprises (Sorge and van Witteloostuijn 2004).

- *Political globalization.* This debate refers to the relationship between the power of markets and (multinational) firms versus the nation-state, which is undergoing continuous change and updating in reaction to economic and political forces – from counter-cyclical national demand policies and international cooperation after the Second World War to the renaissance of the belief in the power of the price mechanism and market forces for efficient allocation of resources in the 1970s. The globalization process is conditioned by the (financial) institutions and the dominant market players, such as multinational corporations and large investment firms. Some argue that the competitive pressure of international markets will "hollow out" the functions of the nation-state and lead to an erosion of sovereignty and a race-to-the-bottom (be it in corporate tax rates or environmental policies).

5.3 World Income and Trade since 1960

The world income level, measured as GDP in constant 2010 dollars for all countries of the world combined, rose from $11,356 billion in 1960 to $88,944 billion in 2019 (see Figure 5.1). This is a substantial 7.5-fold increase over six decades with a compounded growth rate of 3.4 percent per year.

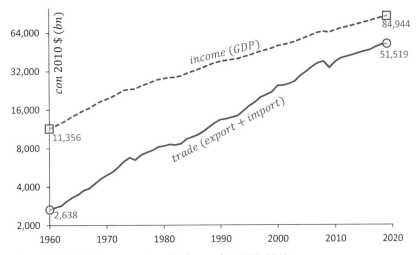

Figure 5.1 World income and trade; log scale, 1960–2019
Source: Calculations based on World Development Indicators online.
Note: Values in constant 2010 billion USD.

One important aspect of globalization is the international trade of goods and services, measured here as the sum of exports and imports. (Even at the world level the balance of trade is not zero, for example, as a result of statistical errors or because goods are en route to their destination during a particular time period. Over the period 1960–2013, the average world external balance is –0.11 percent of GDP, indicating that the value of measured imports is slightly higher than the value of measured exports.) The world trade volume, measured in constant 2010 dollars for all countries of the world combined, rose from $2,638 billion in 1960 to $51,519 billion in 2019 (see also Figure 5.1). This represents an even more substantial 19.5-fold increase over six decades at a compounded growth rate of 5.0 percent per year. Trade flows thus rise more quickly than income flows. In percentage terms the difference between income growth and trade growth seems modest (namely, 3.4 versus 5.0 percent per year). Over a 60-year period, this modest difference nonetheless adds up to substantial differences as a result of compounded growth, as indicated (see Box 5.1 on a rule of thumb and the use of log scales).

As a consequence of the rapid increase in trade flows, trade relative to income rises from 23 percent in 1960 to 61 percent in 2019. Relative to either exports or imports only, this

BOX 5.1 LOGARITHMIC GRAPHS AND A RULE OF THUMB

To graphically analyze the growth rate of income and trade, Figure 5.1 uses a logarithmic scale. The important advantage is that the *slope* of the income line reflects the growth rate of income (and similarly for trade), since:

$$y \equiv ln(Y) \quad \Rightarrow \quad dy = dln(Y) = \frac{dY}{Y} \qquad 5.1$$

If the slope of a logarithmic graph is thus relatively stable over time, then the long-run growth rate is also relatively steady. A careful look at the graphs for trade and income in Figure 5.1 suggests that the slope is declining for income, indicating that income growth slows down, but not for trade. This is further analyzed in the main text.

A disadvantage of logarithmic graphs is the large step-wise increase in values along the vertical axis. The vertical distance from 1,000 to 4,000 in Figure 5.1 is the same as from 4,000 to 16,000. One such step therefore represents a 4-fold increase, two steps represent a $4 \times 4 = 16$-fold increase, three steps represent a $4 \times 4 \times 4 = 64$-fold increase, and so on. The increase in the level values is extremely rapid as you go up a graph, which is not always fully appreciated by a careless reader.

Rule of thumb: a growth rate of x percent per year implies a doubling in 70/x years.

In evaluating the impact of seemingly small differences in growth rates, it is useful to apply the rule of thumb above. According to the rule, which is surprisingly accurate, output doubles in 70 years if the growth rate is 1 percent, whereas output doubles in 35 years if the growth rate is 2 percent, and so on.

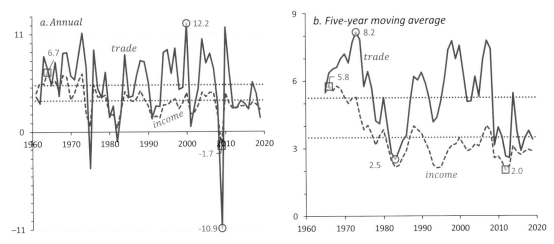

Figure 5.2 World income and trade growth rates; percent, 1960–2019
Source: See Figure 5.1.
Notes: Panel b five-year moving averages located at most recent year; average growth rate for income is 3.5 percent per year, for trade 5.2 percent per year (see dotted lines); st. dev. is 1.6 and 3.9.

thus represents an increase from 11.5 percent in 1960 to 30 percent in 2019. Figure 5.1 also suggests that the development of trade flows is more volatile than the development of income: there are larger fluctuations in the trade graph than in the income graph. This is confirmed and illustrated in Figure 5.2, where panel a depicts annual growth rates and panel b depicts five-year moving average growth rates.

The average growth rate for income is 3.5 percent per year; ranging from a minimum of –1.7 percent in 2009 to a maximum of 6.7 percent in 1964, with a standard deviation of 1.6 percent. In contrast, the average growth rate for trade is 5.2 percent per year; ranging from a minimum of –10.9 percent in 2009 to a maximum of 12.2 percent in 2000, with a standard deviation of 3.9 percent. Trade flows are thus substantially more volatile than income levels, but on average grow much faster.

There is only one year in which the world income level declines, namely in 2009 by 1.7 percent as a result of the Great Recession. There are three years in which the world trade level declines, namely in 1975 by 4.1 percent as a result of the first oil crisis, in 1982 by 1.1 percent as a result of the second oil crisis, and in 2009 by 10.9 percent as a result of the Great Recession.

To get a better view of the longer-term growth rates of world trade and income, panel b of Figure 5.2 depicts five-year moving averages. This illustrates three main points. First, none of the five-year moving average growth rates is negative. Second, in all cases the moving average for trade growth is higher than for income growth. So over five-year periods for the past half century trade has always grown more rapidly than income. Third, the growth rate of income seems to decline over time, certainly before 1980 and perhaps more slowly after that. A similar conclusion cannot be drawn for world trade flows. (The variance of five-year moving averages for world trade is still quite high; looking at longer-year moving averages does not lead to clear changes for world trade growth over time either.) The next section analyzes this aspect in more detail.

5.4   World Trade and Income Per Capita since 1960

Over the period 1960 to 2019, world population increased from 3.03 billion people to 7.67 billion people, a 2.5-fold increase over six decades at an annual compounded growth rate of about 1.6 percent per year. Disasters aside, population growth does not vary much from one year to the next, but it does change significantly over longer time periods. At the world level, population growth peaked at 2.11 percent per year in 1969; it was above 2 percent per year for each year of the ten-year period 1963–1972. In 2019, population growth was about 1.07 percent per year; it was below 1.25 percent per year since 2005. Population growth is thus declining over time, which may be one of the reasons a declining growth of income can be observed over time, as illustrated in panel b of Figure 5.2.

Why does declining population growth lead to declining GDP growth? This is simple arithmetic. Let y be income per capita and let p be the population. Total income is then given by $Y = p \cdot y$. If we let a tilde indicate a relative change, so $\tilde{p} = dp/p$ and so on, then this implies that $\tilde{Y} = \tilde{p} + \tilde{y}$, so the growth rate of GDP is the sum of the population growth rate and per capita GDP growth. (Differentiating gives $dY = ydp + pdy$; divide both sides by Y to get: $\tilde{Y} \equiv \frac{dY}{Y} = \frac{dp}{p} + \frac{dy}{y} \equiv \tilde{p} + \tilde{y}$.) Since the population growth rate is declining over time, total income growth will decline over time even if per capita income growth is steady. To analyze if this is true, we thus have to investigate the development of world trade and income in per capita terms.

A logarithmic graph of the developments over time of income and trade per capita looks, of course, very similar to Figure 5.1 since we are dividing both graphs by total population. Trade per capita thus rises from 23 percent of income per capita in 1960 to 61 percent of income per capita in 2019. The slopes of the graphs are, of course, less steep, since we are dividing by a total population that rises over time. In particular, income per capita rises from $3,746 in 1960 to $11,070 in 2019, a 3.0-fold increase in 60 years at a compounded growth rate of about 1.8 percent per year (= 3.4–1.6; income growth minus population growth). Trade per capita rises from $870 in 1960 to $6,714 in 2019, a 7.7-fold increase at a compounded growth rate of 3.5 percent per year.

When we calculate growth rates of income and trade per capita (see Figure 5.3), the annual data per capita look similar to a shifted-down version of the total data (see Figure 5.2a, so this is not provided separately). Our main interest lies in the five-year moving averages depicted in Figure 5.3. This shows that income per capita growth slowed down considerably before 1980 and fluctuated around a stable rate since then. The high growth rates in the 1960s and 1970s are generally attributed to a recovery catch-up process after the Second World War, in particular for Europe and Japan. In fact, the peak in income per capita growth was 3.7 percent per year over the period 1961–1966. The average

Table 5.1. Trend analysis of world income per capita and trade per capita since 1960

	1960–1980		1980–2019	
	coefficient	p-value	coefficient	p-value
Income per capita	−0.1376**	0.0179	0.0232	0.1733
Trade per capita	−0.0784	0.5479	0.0039	0.9441
Observations	20		40	

Source: See Figure 5.1.

Notes: Dependent variable is annual growth rate in percent for world income per capita and trade per capita; ** significant at the 5 percent level. The "p-value" in the table refers to probability values. It estimates on the basis of standard errors the probability that the coefficient does *not* differ significantly from zero. For income per capita in the period 1960–1980, this value is 0.0179, or 1.79 percent. This is such a low probability that we conclude instead that the coefficient *does* differ significantly from zero. It is customary to have certain cut-off levels of significance; in this case, the coefficient is significant at the 5 percent level as indicated by ** since 1.79 percent is lower than 5 percent. See Chapter 2 on basic econometrics for further details.

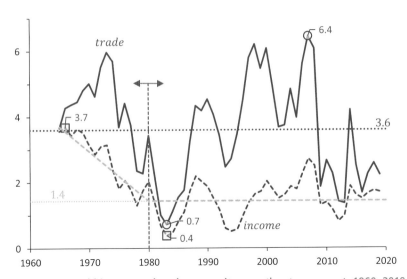

Figure 5.3 World income and trade per capita growth rates; percent, 1960–2019
Source: See Figure 5.1.
Notes: Five-year moving averages located at most recent year; average growth rate for income per capita is 1.8 percent per year, for trade 3.5 percent per year.

income per capita growth rate before 1980 (the period 1960–1980) is 2.6 percent per year, which declines to 1.4 percent per year since 1980 (the period 1980–2019). In contrast, there seems to be no noticeable slowdown in the growth rate of trade per capita, which is much more volatile.

Table 5.1 confirms the impression provided by Figure 5.3 using a trend analysis. The growth rate of world income per capita declined significantly over the period 1960–1980, namely by about 0.1376 percentage points per year. Since 1980, the growth rate of world income per capita stabilized at about 1.4 percent per year (the estimated coefficient is low at 0.0232 percentage points per year and not significant, with a high p-value of 0.1733). If the same exercise is repeated for the growth rate of trade per capita, note that the estimated coefficient is small both before and after 1980 and not significant in either period (high p-values of 0.5479 and 0.9441, respectively), which indicates there is no time trend for trade per capita.

It can be concluded that the worldwide growth rate of income per capita declined over the period 1960–1980 and fluctuates around 1.4 percent per year since 1980. The worldwide growth rate of trade per capita fluctuates around 3.6 percent per year since 1960. This implies that since 1980 trade per capita grows about 2.2 percent per year faster than income per capita.

Chapter 18 analyzes supply chains, another aspect of international trade flows which is based on international fragmentation (see Box 5.2).

BOX 5.2 **FRAGMENTATION**

Another noteworthy globalization phenomenon is "fragmentation." Part I of Figure 5.4 depicts a traditional production process in which firm 1 located in country A uses inputs to produce a final good. International economics can help to clarify under what circumstances the firms of a country have a comparative advantage in the production of a certain type of good, which will then be exported. However, technological and communication advances have enabled many production processes to be subdivided into different phases which are physically separable, a process known as fragmentation. This enables a finer and more complex division of labor, as the different phases of the production process may now be spatially separated and undertaken at locations where costs are lowest.

Part II of Figure 5.4 shows an example of fragmentation in which the production process consists of four phases, performed in three countries by two firms. Service links – such as transportation, telecommunications, insurance, quality control, and management control – facilitate the fragmentation process. International economics can help to clarify in this more complex setting why the firms in a country will have a comparative advantage in a phase of the production process, where the coordination (service links) will take place, why some phases of the production process will be internally organized (phases 1, 2, and 4 in part II of Figure 5.4), and why outsourcing is better for some other phase of the production process (phase 3 in part II of Figure 5.4). It is clear that these more complex production processes lead to increased *interdependence* of national economies and more intricate international connections, as well as to large exports (and re-imports) of parts of products (as holds, for example, for country A in part II of Figure 5.4).

BOX 5.2 (cont.)

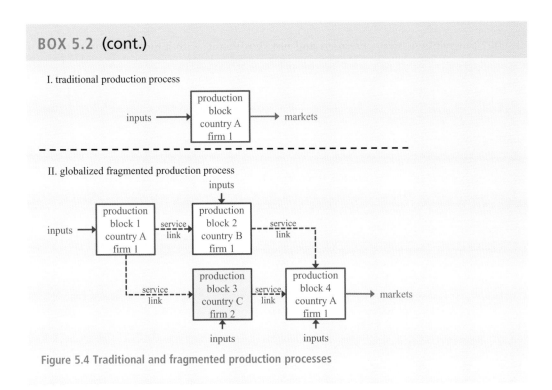

Figure 5.4 Traditional and fragmented production processes

5.5 A Longer-Term Perspective: 2,000 Years

In his impressive work full of historical detail entitled *The World Economy: A Millennial Perspective* (2001), Angus Maddison collects detailed statistics on a wide range of economic variables – such as income, population, international trade, and capital flows – for all the major regions and countries in the world over the past 2,000 years. To describe the evolution of income over time, Maddison uses "1990 international Geary-Khamis dollars" (which correct for PPP) and takes great care to ensure transitivity, base-country invariance, and additivity. He collects data for virtually all countries in the world.

The development of world *per capita* income is illustrated in Figure 5.5 using a logarithmic scale. As explained in Box 5.1, the advantage of using a logarithmic scale is the simultaneous depiction of the *level* of a variable (measured by its vertical height) and the *growth rate* of that variable (measured by the slope of the graph) in one figure. Average world *per capita* income in year 0 was estimated to be $467. The subsistence income level is $400. Where the governing elite could maintain some degree of luxury and sustain a relatively elaborate system of governance, Maddison estimates the income level in year 0 to be higher, as was the case for Italy ($809), North Africa ($550–600), the Fertile Crescent ($500–550), and China and India ($450).

As shown in Figure 5.5, there was no advance in *per capita* income on a global scale in the first millennium. From the year 1000 to 1820, global *per capita* income started to increase in what is now considered a slow crawl – the world average rose by about

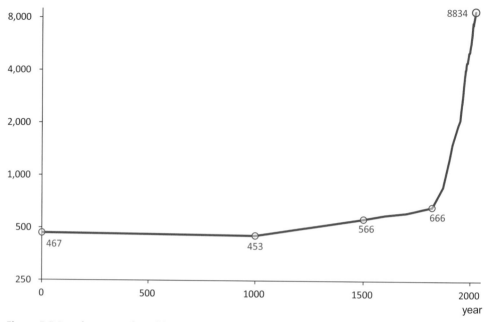

Figure 5.5 Development of world income per capita; 0–2019, log scale
Data sources: Maddison Historical Statistics 1-2008 AD and World Development Indicators.
Note: 1990 international Geary-Khamis dollars.

50 percent in 820 years, to $666. A clear increase in the global economic growth rate started in 1820 with the Industrial Revolution. Since then, *per capita* income rose more than 11-fold in a period of 188 years. The nineteenth and twentieth centuries have been unprecedented in terms of economic growth rates. Moreover, as Maddison argues (2001, p. 17): "*Per capita* income growth is not the only indicator of welfare. Over the long run, there has been a dramatic increase in life expectation. In the year 1000, the average infant could expect to live about 24 years. A third would die in the first year of life, hunger and epidemic disease would ravage the survivors … Now the average infant can expect to survive 66 years." According to the World Bank data, average life expectancy increased from 52.5 years in 1960 to 72.6 years in 2018 (see Chapter 14 for more details).

The focus now turns to the leading and lagging nations and regions in *relative* terms over the last 2,000 years, by calculating a deviation index of income *per capita* above the world average (with the world average as base) and below the world average (with the country as base). The asymmetric construction of the index for leading and lagging nations is for comparability of the degree of deviation; if both indices used the world average as the base, there is no upper bound for leading nations, while there is a lower bound (of 100 percent) for lagging nations. The calculations over this long period are available for 28 individual countries (15 in Europe, 6 in Asia, 3 in the Americas, 2 in Africa, and 2 in Australia) and six country groups, together comprising the global economy. Figure 5.6 summarizes the conclusions for leading and lagging nations.

At the beginning of our calendar (the year 0), the leading country by far was Italy (+73 percent) while there were many countries and regions lagging behind (in Europe, the

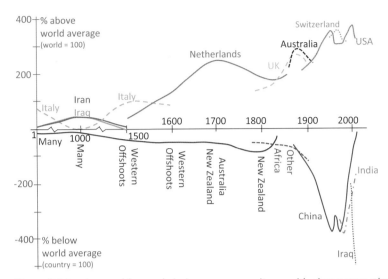

Figure 5.6 Leaders and laggards in income per capita: a widening perspective
Data source: Maddison Historical Statistics 1-2008 AD.
Notes: Deviation relative to world average; world index = 100 for positive deviations; country index = 100 for negative deviations.

Americas, and Australia; namely –17 percent). During the first millennium there was a convergence of income per capita: in the year 1000, Iran and Iraq became the world leaders (+43 percent), while many countries still qualified as laggard (–13 percent). The second millennium witnessed increasing divergence. The leading nations in terms of per capita income were, in turn: Italy (+94 percent), the Netherlands (+246 percent), the UK (+260 percent), Australia (+276 percent), the USA (+353 percent), Switzerland (+353 percent), and the USA again (+371 percent). The lagging nations were, in turn: the "Western Offshoots" (Australia, Canada, New Zealand, and the USA; –49 percent), Australia and New Zealand (–54 percent), New Zealand (–66 percent), Africa (–74 percent), China (–371 percent), India (–381 percent), and Iraq (–626 percent). A clear common feature for both positive and negative deviations is that the gap has been widening considerably over the past 1,000 years (see also Chapter 10 on income inequality).

5.6 Globalization in History

The relative rise of international trade flows is not something new. Trade flows have always been central in economic interactions: for the ancient cultures of Egypt and Greece, as well as for China, India, and Mesopotamia. According to Maddison, trade has been most important for the economic rise of Western Europe in the past millennium. Based on improved techniques of shipbuilding and navigation (the compass), Venice played a key role from 1000 to 1500 in opening up trade routes within Europe and the Mediterranean, and to China (via the caravan routes), bringing in silk and valued spices, as well as technology (glassblowing, also used for making spectacles, the cultivation of rice, and sugar cane cutting). Venice's role in the development of banking, accounting, and foreign exchange and credit markets was equally important, thus establishing a system of public finance which made it the lead economy of the period. The fall of Byzantium and the rise of the Ottoman Empire eventually blocked Venetian contacts with Asia.

Portugal began more ambitious interactions between Europe and the rest of the world in the second half of the fifteenth century by opening up trade and settlement in the Atlantic islands and developing trade routes around Africa, to China, Japan, and India. It took over the role of Venice as the major shipper of spices. Portugal's location on the South Atlantic coast of Europe enabled its fishermen to gather knowledge of Atlantic winds, weather, and tides. Combined with maritime experience, the development of compass bearings, cartography, and adjustments in ship design to meet Atlantic sailing conditions, this allowed the Portuguese (such as Vasco da Gama) to embark on their explorations and play a dominant role in intercontinental trade. As Maddison (2001, p. 19) puts it: "Although Spain had a bigger empire, its only significant base outside the Americas was the Philippines. Its two most famous navigators were Columbus who was a Genoese with Portuguese training, and Magellan who was Portuguese." Portugal was able to absorb Jewish merchants and scholars, who were required to undergo a pro forma conversion and who played an important role in science, as intermediaries in trade with the Muslim world and in attracting foreign capital (Genoese and Catalan) for business ventures. Unfortunately, Portugal also initiated the slave trade to the New World and carried about half of the slaves from Africa to the Americas between 1500 and 1870.

From 1400 to the middle of the seventeenth century, the Netherlands was the most dynamic European economy, using power from windmills and peat, creating large canal networks, and transforming agriculture into horticulture, but most of all developing shipping, shipbuilding, and commercial services. As illustrated in Figure 5.7, by 1570, the carrying capacity of Dutch merchant shipping was about the same as the combined

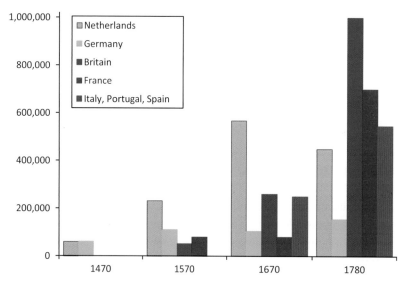

Figure 5.7 Carrying capacity of European merchant fleets; 1470–1780, metric tons
Data source: Maddison 2001, p. 77.
Note: Absence of a bar in a year for a particular country/group indicates that no data are available.

fleets of Britain, France, and Germany. The Dutch were then able to maintain this lead for a century by more than doubling this capacity. Holland created a modern state which provided property rights, education, and religious tolerance, and had only 40 percent of the labor force in agriculture. This attracted a financial and entrepreneurial elite from Flanders and Brabant, which emigrated to Holland on a large scale and made it the center for banking, finance, and international commerce.

Britain became the leading economy in the eighteenth century, initially by improving its financial, banking, fiscal, and agricultural institutions along the lines pioneered by the Dutch, and subsequently by a surge in industrial productivity. The latter was based not only on the acceleration of technical progress and investments in physical capital, education, and skills, but also on commercial trade policy, which in 1846 reduced protective duties on agricultural imports and by 1860 had unilaterally removed all trade and tariff restrictions. The British willingness to specialize in industrial production and import a large part of its food had positive effects on the world economy and diffused the impact of technical progress, but most of all it allowed Britain to achieve unprecedented rates of economic growth and establish itself as a global economic and political power by taking over the lands that the French and Dutch had lost in Asia and Africa. The soundness of its monetary system (the gold standard) and public credit gave Britain an important role in international finance. At the end of the nineteenth and beginning of the twentieth centuries, there was a massive outflow of European capital (French, Dutch, and German, but most of all British – up to half of British savings) for overseas investment, mostly in the Americas and Russia. The British economist John Maynard Keynes (1919, ch. 2) summarized the high degree of global economic progress and development in this epoch as follows:

> What an extraordinary episode in the economic progress of man that age was which came to an end in August 1914! . . . The inhabitant of London could order by telephone, sipping his morning tea in bed, the various products of the whole earth, in such quantity as he might see fit, and reasonably expect their early delivery upon his doorstep . . . But, most important of all, he regarded this state of affairs as normal, certain, and permanent, except in the direction of further improvement, and any deviation from it as aberrant, scandalous, and avoidable.

The old liberal order came to end, as indicated by Keynes's quote, as a result of two world wars (1914–18 and 1939–45) and the Great Depression in the 1930s, with its beggar-thy-neighbor policies, which drastically raised trade impediments and led to a collapse of trade, capital, and migration flows. As a consequence, the world economy grew much more slowly from 1913 to 1950 than it had from 1870 to 1913 – that is, 0.91 percent per annum rather than 1.30 percent. (Although this difference might seem small, world income would have been 15 percent higher in 1950 if the slowdown had not occurred and the economy had maintained its 1.30 percent growth rate.) The institutional arrangements with codes of behavior and cooperation set up after the Second World War, such as the General Agreement on Tariffs and Trade (GATT), the International Monetary Fund (IMF), the Organisation for Economic Co-operation and Development (OECD), and the World Bank, created a new liberal international order which abolished beggar-thy-neighbor policies in favor of liberal trading. In the post-Second World War

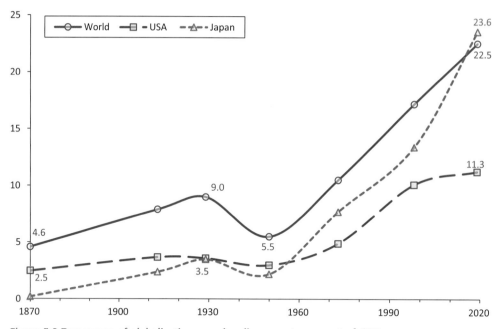

Figure 5.8 Two waves of globalization; merchandise exports, percent of GDP
Data sources: Maddison 2001, table F-5.
Note: In constant 1990 prices, extended to 2019 using World Development Indicators Online.

period, this contributed to remarkable growth rates of income *per capita* (3 percent per year), total world income (5 percent per year), and world trade flows (8 percent per year). At the same time, the world economy became more closely connected than ever before, as illustrated in Figure 5.8.

This type of globalization is not a monotone process, as clearly illustrated in Figure 5.8, which depicts the development of merchandise exports relative to income for the world as a whole, the USA, and Japan from 1870 to 2019. It is now customary to identify two "waves" of globalization: the first wave at the end of the nineteenth and the beginning of the twentieth centuries; and the second wave after the Second World War. Evidently, international trade rose much more rapidly than output for the period as a whole, but there was a long and substantial interruption as a result of two major international conflicts and economic policy changes.

5.7   The Price Wedge and Trade Flows

The most basic economic picture consists of a downward-sloping demand curve (on the assumption that people buy less of a good if its price is higher) and an upward-sloping supply curve (on the assumption that firms produce more of a good if its price rises). International trade flows can also be depicted in this most basic framework, with two twists. Assume there are two countries, America A and Britain B, and attention is focused on Britain's import market. The first twist is that Britain's downward-sloping demand curve for *imports* actually consists of Britain's demand for the good *not* provided by its domestic suppliers (it is therefore

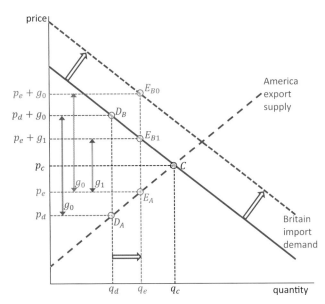

Figure 5.9 International trade and market integration

also called Britain's *net* demand curve). The same applies, necessary changes being made, for America's export supply curve (or net supply curve). The second twist is that there may be a number of reasons for a deviation between the price received by American producers and the price paid by British consumers, which is called a *price wedge* – for example, because American firms have to overcome transport costs, tariffs, trade impediments, cultural differences, and all sorts of other extra costs before exporting to the British market.

Figure 5.9 illustrates international trade equilibrium, which results from the intersection of the downward-sloping British import demand curve and the upward-sloping American export supply curve, taking the price wedge into consideration. Suppose the initial equilibrium is situation D, where trade volume is q_d, the price received by American exporters is p_d, and the price paid by British consumers is $p_d + g_0$. The difference between the price paid in Britain and the price received in America is thus the price gap g_0.

International trade flows can now increase for two main reasons.

- First, a shift to the right in either America's export supply curve or Britain's import demand curve at a constant price wedge g_0 will result in increasing trade flows. As an example, Figure 5.9 shows that a shift in Britain's import demand curve to the right as a result of a demand shock (as indicated by the arrows) for a given price wedge g_0 raises the price received by America's producers to p_e, the price paid by British consumers to $p_e + g_0$, and the volume of trade to q_e. The demand shift might, for example, be caused by changing preferences, population growth, or per capita income growth.
- Second, a decrease in the price wedge between what consumers pay and what producers receive will also lead to rising trade flows. Figure 5.9 shows that the same increase in trade volume from q_d to q_e can be obtained if the price wedge decreases from g_0 to g_1; in that case, the price received by America's producers is again p_e, but the price paid by

British consumers falls to $p_e + g_1 < p_e + g_0$. The decrease in the price wedge may be caused, for example, by lower transportation costs, lower tariffs, a reduction in other types of trade restrictions, lower communication costs, and so on.[2]

Globalization, as measured, for example, by the rising volume of trade or increased capital flows, may thus be caused by volume effects or a decrease in the international price wedge. O'Rourke and Williamson (2002) argue that early growth of international trade was mostly of the first kind: rising trade in noncompeting goods, such as spices, special dyes (indigo), coffee, tea, and sugar, which could not be produced in substantial amounts in the importing countries themselves. Usually, these were expensive luxury items and their buyers could afford to pay for the price wedge. The discovery of the New World and its commodities created a market for these goods, shifting the British import demand curve to the right without necessarily reducing the price wedge. O'Rourke and Williamson then provide evidence that the post-1492 trade boom was most likely caused by the demand for luxury items and population growth and hardly reduced the price wedge on traded goods, as measured by changes in the mark-up. Moreover, there is some evidence that the retreat of China and Japan from world markets from the mid-fifteenth century to the mid-nineteenth century further stimulated European–Asian trade. See Box 5.4 for evidence of the (asymmetric) benefits of trade linkages for economic growth.

The two waves of globalization illustrated in Figure 5.8 provide examples of the second kind of growth in international trade. During the first wave of the nineteenth century there was an increase of trade in basic and homogeneous commodities. During the second wave after the Second World War there was an increase of trade in basic and differentiated manufactured products. Decreases in transports costs, technology improvements, falling trade restrictions, international cooperation, and improved communication possibilities have all been important underlying forces in these two waves of globalization. The spectacular decline in transport costs in the nineteenth century is considered to be the most important cause for increased trade flows. The railway and the steamship revolutionized the means of transportation, while the opening of the Suez Canal and the Panama Canal dramatically cut travel times and meant that traders could avoid the dangerous routes around the Cape of Good Hope and Cape Horn.[3] Technological inventions, such as effective means of refrigeration, which enabled the transportation of perishable goods (meat and fruit) across the Equator, further stimulated trade, as did reductions in protectionist measures. Table 5.2 provides empirical estimates from O'Rourke and Williamson (2002) for both the declining transport costs and the reduction

---

[2] If the price wedge completely disappears, trade flows increase to q_c in Figure 5.9 and the price consumers pay in Britain becomes equal to the price producers receive in America (equal to p_C).

[3] The size and speed of Atlantic liners, for example, increased spectacularly: it took the *Britannic* (using a combination of steam power and sails) 8 days and 20 hours to cross the Atlantic with 5,000 tons of pay load in 1874, whereas it took the *Mauritania* (using steam power only) 4 days and 10 hours to cross the Atlantic with 31,000 tons of pay load in 1907. During the same period railway mileage also increased dramatically: from 1850 to 1910 railway mileage in the UK increased from 6,621 to 23,387 miles, in the USA from 9,021 to 249,902 miles, and in Germany from 3,637 to 36,152 miles (O'Rourke and Williamson 1999).

Table 5.2. Price convergence and declining transport costs, 1870–1913

Transport cost reductions (index)		
American export routes, deflated freight cost	1869/71–1908/10	100 to 55
American east coast routes, deflated freight cost	1869/71–1911/13	100 to 55
British tramp, deflated freight cost	1869/71–1911/13	100 to 78
Commodity price convergence at selected markets (% deviation)		
Liverpool–Chicago, wheat price gap	1870–1912	58 to 16
London–Cincinnati, bacon price gap	1870–1913	93 to 18
Philadelphia–London, pig iron price gap	1870–1913	85 to 19
London–Boston, wool price gap	1870–1913	59 to 28
London–Buenos Aires, hides price gap	1870–1913	28 to 9

Source: O'Rourke and Williamson 2002, table 1.

Table 5.3. Tariffs on manufactures for selected countries; 1820–2010, percent

	1820[a]	1875[a, b]	1913[a, b]	1931[c]	1950[c]	2010[c]
Denmark	30	15–20	14	–	3	1.9 (EU)
France	Prohibition	12–15	20	30	18	1.9 (EU)
Germany	–	4–6	13	21	26	1.9 (EU)
Italy	–	8–10	18	46	25	1.9 (EU)
Russia	Prohibition	15	84	Prohibition	Prohibition	6.0
Spain	Prohibition	15–20	41	63	–	1.9 (EU)
Sweden	Prohibition	3–5	20	21	9	1.9 (EU)
Netherlands	7	3–5	4	–	11	1.9 (EU)
UK	50	0	0	–	23	1.9 (EU)
USA	45	40	44	48	14	3.0

Sources: [a] Baldwin and Martin 1999, table 8; [b] O'Rourke and Williamson 1999, table 6.1; [c] Beugelsdijk *et al.* 2013, table 1.6.
Note: – = data unavailable.

in the price wedge for commodities produced in different markets, indicating closer market integration.

The rise in trade during the first wave of globalization was also caused by reductions in protectionist measures. Under the influence of Adam Smith's doctrine of free trade, many restrictions to trade were removed during the nineteenth century. By 1860, the UK and the Netherlands had unilaterally virtually removed all trade restrictions. Special bilateral arrangements were made between the UK and France (the Cobden–Chevalier Treaty of 1860).[4] Other bilateral arrangements involving other countries soon followed. Table 5.3

---

[4] The treaty was also important because it introduced the most-favored-nation (MFN) principle as the cornerstone of European trade policies (Findlay and O'Rourke, 2001).

shows that tariffs were very high at the beginning of the nineteenth century and declined considerably until 1875. Around the 1880s, the tariff reductions more or less came to a stop. Cheap Russian grain increased competition in agricultural markets. The real earnings of British farmers, for example, declined by more than 50 percent between 1870 and 1913 (Findlay and O'Rourke 2001). Soon, Britain, France, Germany, Sweden, and other countries returned to protectionist practices and tariffs were raised again. Perhaps the integration of product markets, due to better transport systems, was so successful that it undermined its own success. In general, it seems that the transport revolution could flourish in an environment that already tended toward free trade, but that the income consequences led to adverse reactions. The continued efforts of the GATT/WTO after the Second World War to reduce trade barriers has now driven tariff measures to unprecedented low levels.

The reduction in trade cost and the narrowing of the price gap are driving forces of the globalization process, to a large extent based on international fragmentation (see Box 5.2). It should be noted at this point that the country where the final product is manufactured is not necessarily the most important country in terms of created value-added. This is analyzed in Box 5.3, which shows that an iPad assembled in China may have "made in China" written on the product, although China receives only a small fraction of the total retail price.

BOX 5.3 WHO EARNS WHAT WHEN AN IPAD IS SOLD?

In 2011, the retail price of an iPad was about $500 in the USA. But who earns what when you buy an iPad? In a thought-provoking analysis of the entire value chain of the iPad, Linden, Kraemer, and Dedrick (2009, 2011) show that most of the value-added goes to American shareholders and workers (see Figure 5.10).

The costs of material inputs are about 31 percent of the retail price, while Apple's profits of the iPad are about 30 percent of the retail price. Apple's design, software development, and marketing are located in the USA. Moreover, distribution and retail costs are about 15 percent, meaning that for each iPad sold in the USA another 15 percent goes to American workers. The remaining 24 percent of the retail price is divided over a number of other contributors. About 7 percent goes to South Korean firms, like Samsung and LG, which provide key components. The production of an iPad takes place at the Taiwanese Foxconn firm located in China, which explains the Taiwanese profits of about 2 percent. The most striking observation is the fact that although production takes place in China, only 2 percent of the retail price goes to Chinese labor (for assembling). This analysis triggered a response by many economists, business scholars, and policymakers, in particular because of the finding that production may take place in China, but the value-added generated there is pretty small.

BOX 5.3 (cont.)

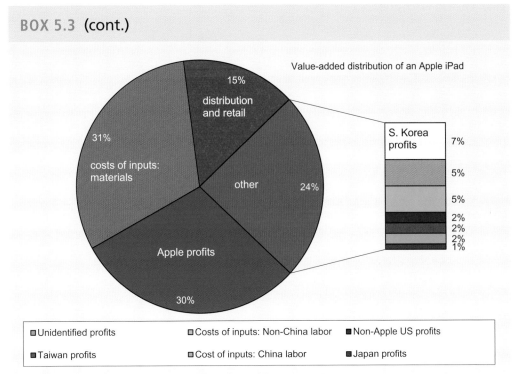

Figure 5.10 Value-added distribution of an Apple iPad, 2011
Sources: Beugelsdijk *et al.* (2013); the figure is based on data provided by Linden *et al.* (2009, 2011).

5.8   More Waves: Capital and Migration Flows

The reduction in the price wedge for international trade flows during the first wave of globalization and the increase in the interwar years analyzed in section 5.7 is also visible on the capital market. This is illustrated in Figure 5.11 by depicting the mean bond spread for 14 core and empire countries surrounded by a measure of dispersion (a band equal to ± 2 standard deviations).[5]

Obstfeld and Taylor (2003) study government bonds traded in London, focusing exclusively on bonds denominated in gold or in sterling so as to isolate the effects of default risk. The interest rate spread for these countries was small, usually within 1 or 2 percentage points of Britain's. Moreover, there was a convergence in bond spreads up to 1914, and a widening in spreads and increased volatility in the interwar years. As with international trade flows, it is customary to identify two "waves" of globalization for capital flows as well. This is illustrated in Figure 5.12, where foreign capital stocks relative to world GDP

---

[5] The core and empire countries are Australia, Belgium, Canada, Denmark, France, Germany, India, the Netherlands, New Zealand, Norway, South Africa, Sweden, Switzerland, and the USA.

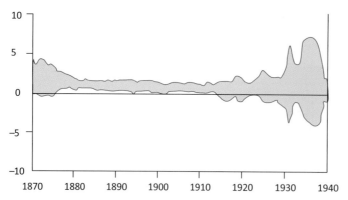

Figure 5.11 London external bond spread; 1870–1940, 14 core and empire bonds
Source: Beugelsdijk *et al.* 2013, based on Obstfeld and Taylor 2003.
Note: Units are percentage points.

Figure 5.12 Foreign capital stocks; assets/world income, 1860–2000
Source: Beugelsdijk *et al.* 2013, based on Obstfeld and Taylor 2003.

are relatively high toward the end of the nineteenth and the beginning of the twentieth centuries, then drop dramatically in the interwar years, only to reach unprecedented heights after the capital market liberalizations beginning in the 1960s.

The idea of the price wedge can also be applied to international migration flows. In principle, real wage differences between countries explain the direction of migration flows to a large extent. Large wage differences between countries exist (see Chapter 1). These are caused, for example, by migration quotas, the perceived probability of actually finding a job in the destination country, or lack of knowledge of foreign countries. Such factors contribute to the size of the wedge and to the absence of labor market integration.

UN evidence indicates that although the absolute migration numbers have increased, world migrants – that is foreign-born – comprise only about 3.1 percent of the world

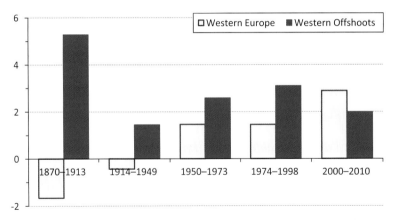

Figure 5.13 Relative migration flows; Western Europe and Western Offshoots, 1870–2010
Source: Maddison 2001, table 3.4.
Notes: Net migration in the period (Maddison 2001, table 3.4) is divided by the (simple) average population and length of the period, normalized per 1,000 inhabitants; updated for the period 2000–2010 with data from UN Population Division, Migration Section; Western Europe consists of Belgium, France, Germany, Italy, the Netherlands, Norway, Sweden, Switzerland, and the UK.

population in 2010.[6] This relatively low number seems inconsistent with popular opinion that the level of migrants is large, primarily as a result of the low number of migrants in developing countries. Indeed, in some individual countries, these numbers are much larger. The share of foreign-born as a percentage of the labor force is relevant, as this number gives an impression of competition on the labor markets. In Australia, for example, 26.5 percent of the labor force in 2008 was foreign-born; in the USA this number was 16.5 percent; in the UK 12.6 percent; in the Netherlands 11.4 percent; and in Denmark 6.8 percent.[7] In addition, the UN High Commissioner for Refugees estimates that there are some 15.4 million refugees in the world in 2010.

Historians have also identified two modern "waves" of migration (see Figure 5.13). The first took place between 1820 and 1913. More than 50 million migrants departed (mostly) from Europe to Australia, Canada, South America, and the USA. Almost 60 percent of the migrants went to the USA. Most were young and relatively low-skilled. After 1850, most migrants came from Ireland.

The second "wave" started after the Second World War and has not yet ended. Between 1913 and 1950, migration was only a fraction of what it had been during the nineteenth century. The USA remained the main destination country. Immigration grew from a low of 252,000 per year in the 1950s to 916,000 in the 1990s, but the source countries changed dramatically. Before the 1950s, most immigrants came from Europe, in the 1990s most came from Asia and (from 1990 onward) also from eastern European countries. During this second wave, immigration restrictions became more binding than before. Many countries use a quota, and allow in migrants for reasons such as a family reunion or specific labor needs. In Europe, most migration flows are in the form of intra-EU migration. From 1990 to

---

[6] Based on UN Population Division, Migrant Section data.　　[7] Based on OECD labor force statistics.

BOX 5.4 OPEN-TO-CLOSED OR CLOSED-TO-OPEN ECONOMIES AND (ASYMMETRIC) GROWTH

As shown throughout this book, many factors play a role in determining the efficiency of firms and their incentives to innovate and invest in R&D, and thus ultimately a country's welfare level and rate of growth. In the end it is an empirical issue to determine the extent to which globalization benefits or harms a country. One way to do this is by analyzing the consequences of countries that decide to enforce a radical globalization policy change, by either opening up to the world economy or closing down. This is done by developing a model that predicts an asymmetric adjustment process, with a more rapid increase in economic growth after a decrease in trade restrictions than the decrease in economic growth after an increase in trade restrictions (see Marrewijk and Berden 2007). To test this implication of the model the authors combine Sachs and Warner's (1995) trade openness indicators with the Maddison income data.

Sachs and Warner classify a country as closed or open based on tariff rates, nontariff barriers, a black market exchange rate, a state monopoly on major exports, and a socialist economic system (see the main text). The emphasis in this work is on trade liberalization, as it is in an update by Wacziarg and Welch (2008), which concludes: "the effects of increased policy openness within countries are positive, economically large, and

Table 5.4. Trade policy adjustment; time trend of ln(income per capita), 1950–2001

	From open to closed[*]	From closed to open[**]
Number of observations	15	32
Average time trend 10 years before policy change plus year of policy change	0.0191	0.0053
Average time trend 10 years after policy change plus year of policy change	0.0162	0.0233
Average change in time trend	−0.0030	0.0179
standard error of change in time trend	0.0076	0.0036

Notes:
[*]Sri Lanka (1957), Venezuela (1960), El Salvador (1961), Nicaragua (1961), Costa Rica (1962), Guatemala (1962), Honduras (1962), Morocco (1965), Syria (1966), Kenya (1968), Peru (1968), Jamaica (1974), Bolivia (1979), Ecuador (1984), Sri Lanka (1984).
[**] Japan (1962), Taiwan (1964), South Korea (1969), Indonesia (1971), Chile (1976), Sri Lanka (1978), Botswana (1979), Morocco (1985), Bolivia (1986), Colombia (1986), Gambia (1986), Ghana (1986), Costa Rica (1987), Guinea (1987), Guinea-Bissau (1987), Mexico (1987), Uganda (1988), Guatemala (1989), Philippines (1989), Tunisia (1989), Benin (1990), El Salvador (1990), Jamaica (1990), Paraguay (1990), Turkey (1990), Venezuela (1990), Argentina (1991), Brazil (1991), Hungary (1991), Mali (1991), Poland (1991), and Uruguay (1991).
Source: van Marrewijk and Berden 2007.

BOX 5.4 (cont.)

statistically significant" (p. 189). Using a similar within-country-through-time analysis, van Marrewijk and Berden also investigate the opposite movement from an open to a closed trading system. They analyze the time trend of the log of income per capita for the year of the policy change and the 10 years before and after the policy change separately for all developing countries going through a regime change as indicated by Sachs and Warner for which these data are available (see Table 5.4).

There are 15 developing countries going from an *open to a closed* trade regime. The average *decrease* in the time trend of the rate of growth was 0.3 percent per year. There are 32 developing countries going from a *closed to an open* trade regime. The average *increase* in the time trend of the rate of growth was 1.79 percent per year. This increase is statistically significant at the 10 percent level, as is the difference between the decrease following a rise in trade restrictions and the increase following a decline in trade restrictions, thus providing support for an asymmetric adjustment process. Also note that closed economies grow more slowly than open economies both before the policy change (0.53 versus 1.91 percent) and after the policy change (1.62 versus 2.33 percent).

2010, the stock of migrants in Europe increased from 49 million to 70 million, compared to an increase from 28 to 50 million in North America. In contrast to globalization with respect to trade and capital, labor markets are thus less globally integrated.

5.9 Conclusions

This chapter explained that there are different types of globalization and that the term is interpreted in different ways by different people. It then showed that at the global level trade flows have risen considerably faster than income flows since 1960. It also noted that there is a slowdown in total income growth which is related to the declining population growth rate. On a per capita basis, income growth slowed down from 1960 to 1980, but has fluctuated around 1.3 percent growth per year since then. Trade flows per capita have fluctuated around 3.8 percent per year since 1960, implying that trade per capita has been growing more rapidly than income per capita by about 2.5 percent per year since 1980. From a long-run perspective, the chapter noted that income per capita growth has been particularly fast for the last two centuries and that the gap between the leading and lagging nations seems to have been rising for the past 1,000 years. It also discussed the role of the price wedge in globalization and the waves of globalization for trade flows, capital flows, and migration flows. The rest of the book returns to the issues raised above. The next chapter starts with a more thorough analysis of international trade flows.

Further Reading

The role of trade in economic development is analyzed by: Atkin, D. and D. Donaldson. 2022. "The Role of Trade in Economic Development," in G. Gopinath, E. Helpman, and K. Rogoff (eds.), *Handbook of International Economics: International Trade* (Amsterdam: Elsevier), vol. 5. The main question addressed in this state-of-the art survey surrounds whether international trade is beneficial for economic development. The question is important given the recent backlash against globalization.

For an account of this recent backlash, see: Colantone, I., G. Ottaviano, and P. Stanig. 2022. "The Backlash of Globalization," in G. Gopinath, E. Helpman, and K. Rogoff (eds.), *Handbook of International Economics: International Trade* (Amsterdam: Elsevier), vol. 5.

6 International Trade

6.1 Introduction

Chapters 1, 3, 4, and 5 already indicated several times that countries that are relatively open to influences from the outside world tend to benefit in the economic development process. This chapter focuses on one particular aspect of open-ness,[1] namely through the flow of international trade in goods and services. Other aspects of open-ness are discussed in other chapters; for migration, see Chapter 3, for investment, see Chapters 7, 9, and 17, and for ideas, see Chapters 7, 8, 16, and 18. This chapter focuses on three main aspects. First, it provides information on the size and direction of international trade flows. Second, it explains the underlying reasons for these flows, based on market size, love-of-variety, heterogeneous firms, and differences in technology and factor abundance. Third, it highlights the benefits from trade flows, the so-called gains-from-trade, associated with the underlying reasons for these trade flows.

Before starting the discussion, Figure 6.1 provides some evidence for the positive association between trade flows and economic development as measured by income per capita (panel a) and for the negative association between obstacles to trade flows, as measured by tariffs, and income per capita (panel b). In both panels the size of the bubble is proportional to the population of the country. Panel a uses double logarithmic scales to show for 181 countries that in general the more open a country is to trade flows (as measured by the export of goods and services as a percent of income) the higher its per capita income level tends to be. The figure highlights this for four (small) open economies that are relatively rich: Macao, Singapore, Hong Kong, and Luxembourg.

The association between trade and income is far from perfect (a formal regression explains about 28 percent of the variance in income per capita). Measured this way, some countries, such as the USA, are rich even though they are relatively closed. The opposite does not occur: there are no relatively open but poor countries (the bottom-right part of the panel is empty). The observation for the USA is related to the size of its economy: it is a relatively large country. A closer look at the panel shows that large countries are relatively clustered in the upper-left part of the panel. This should make us realize that export as a share of income is an imperfect measure for open-ness. If a company from New York sells

---

[1] This chapter is partially based on earlier work: see van Marrewijk 2017 and Beugelsdijk *et al.* 2013.

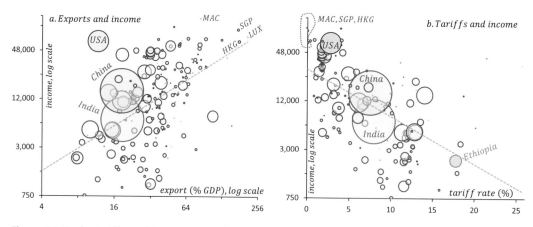

Figure 6.1 Trade, tariffs, and income per capita, 2019
Source: Created using World Development Indicators online data.
Notes: Income is GNI PPP per capita in constant 2017 $ (2019 or most recent); exports of goods and services as % of GDP (2019 or most recent); tariff rate applied, simple mean, manufactured products (%, 2018 or most recent); bubbles proportional to population (2019); 181 countries for panel a, 170 countries for panel b; MAC = Macao; SGP = Singapore; HKG = Hong Kong; LUX = Luxembourg; dashed lines are trendlines.

something 5,000 kilometers away in California, it is not counted as international trade since it is still sold in the same (large) country. In contrast, if a company from Rotterdam (the Netherlands) sells something to a customer in Antwerp (Belgium), it is counted as international trade (since two different countries are involved), even though the distance is only about 100 kilometers.

Panel b of Figure 6.1 highlights for 170 countries that it may not be a good idea to create artificial obstacles to international trade flows. Countries can create obstacles in many different ways, such as tariffs (making the price of imported goods higher), quotas (limiting the supply of imported goods), domestic content requirements (benefiting domestic suppliers), rules and regulations (imports of certain products are, for example, cleared by customs in one small office in a particularly awkward location with limited capacity), and so on. Panel b focuses on a simple artificial obstacle: the average tariff rate (in percent) imposed by a country on its imported goods (simple mean, all products). The association is clearly negative (but again far from perfect; a formal regression explains about 35 percent of the variance in income per capita). Three countries in this panel are particularly noteworthy as their average tariff rate is zero. This holds for Macao, Singapore, and Hong Kong. All three are small countries which, because of their open trade policies (panel b) leading to high trade flows (panel a), benefit from the gains-from-trade described in this chapter and enjoy high levels of income per capita (both panels).

6.2   International Trade Flows

To characterize the size and direction of international trade flows, this section will aggregate countries into global regions based on the World Bank classification discussed

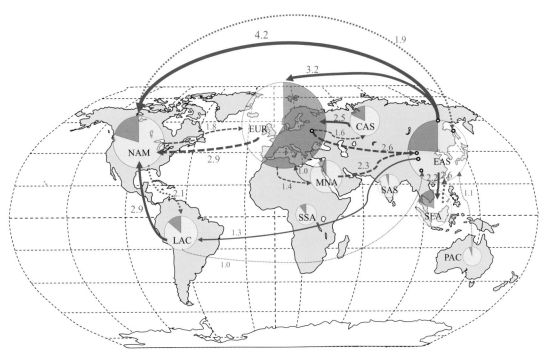

Figure 6.2 Global intra- and inter-regional trade flows, percent of total
Source: van Marrewijk 2017, figure 5.2.
Notes: Bubbles proportional to size of trade flows; light-shaded area is extra-regional trade; dark-shaded area is intra-regional trade; weight of inter-regional trade flow is proportional to size (in percent); only flows of 1 percent or more are shown.

in Chapter 4. Total trade within a global region is the sum of all trade flows for the countries that are part of that global region. These flows can be subdivided into *intra*-regional flows (within the same region; so from a country in the region to another country in the same region) and *inter*-regional flows (between regions; so from a country in the region to a country in some other region). The results of our calculations are visualized in Figure 6.2, while more details on the size of the flows is provided in Table 6.1.

The visualization in Figure 6.2 uses a map for reference, and circles are located more or less at the geographic center of a region on that map and proportional to the size of the region's total trade flows (average of exports and imports). Arrows between circles indicate trade flows from one region to another. In order not to clutter the diagram only inter-regional flows of one percent or more are shown in the figure. To get an indication of the importance of these flows the thickness of the line is proportional to the size of the flow. To get an indication of the size of the intra-regional versus the inter-regional trade flows, each circle is subdivided into a light-shaded part and a dark-shaded part. The intra-regional flows are represented by the dark-shaded part.

A number of important observations can be made by looking at Figure 6.2 and the details provided in Table 6.1 regarding the trade flows as a whole.

Table 6.1. Current intra- and inter-regional trade flows

a. Including intra-regional trade; percent of total trade

		Exporting region										
		CAS	EAS	EUR	LAC	MNA	NAM	PAC	SAS	SEA	SSA	Sum
Importing region	CAS	1.0	0.8	1.6	0.1	0.1	0.2	0.0	0.1	0.1	0.0	3.9
	EAS	0.6	6.3	2.6	1.0	2.3	1.9	1.1	0.3	2.6	0.7	19.3
	EUR	2.5	3.2	25.9	0.8	1.0	1.8	0.1	0.5	0.8	0.6	37.2
	LAC	0.1	1.3	0.8	0.9	0.1	2.1	0.0	0.1	0.2	0.1	5.8
	MNA	0.3	0.8	1.4	0.1	0.5	0.4	0.1	0.4	0.2	0.0	4.3
	NAM	0.3	4.2	2.9	2.9	0.7	3.4	0.1	0.3	0.8	0.5	16.1
	PAC	0.0	0.5	0.3	0.0	0.1	0.2	0.1	0.0	0.3	0.0	1.7
	SAS	0.1	0.7	0.6	0.1	0.9	0.2	0.1	0.1	0.3	0.2	3.3
	SEA	0.1	2.2	0.7	0.1	0.6	0.6	0.2	0.2	1.6	0.1	6.4
	SSA	0.0	0.5	0.6	0.1	0.1	0.1	0.0	0.1	0.1	0.3	2.0
	Sum	5.0	20.6	37.4	6.1	6.3	11.0	1.8	2.2	7.0	2.5	100

b. Excluding intra-regional trade; percent of total trade

		Exporting region										
		CAS	EAS	EUR	LAC	MNA	NAM	PAC	SAS	SEA	SSA	Sum
Importing region	CAS		1.3	2.6	0.2	0.2	0.4	0.0	0.1	0.2	0.1	4.9
	EAS	1.0		4.4	1.7	3.8	3.1	1.8	0.6	4.3	1.1	21.8
	EUR	4.2	5.4		1.3	1.7	3.0	0.2	0.8	1.3	1.0	18.9
	LAC	0.1	2.2	1.4		0.2	3.5	0.1	0.2	0.3	0.2	8.1
	MNA	0.4	1.4	2.3	0.2		0.8	0.1	0.7	0.3	0.1	6.3
	NAM	0.5	7.0	4.8	4.8	1.1		0.2	0.5	1.4	0.8	21.1
	PAC	0.0	0.9	0.6	0.1	0.1	0.4		0.0	0.6	0.1	2.7
	SAS	0.1	1.2	1.0	0.1	1.5	0.3	0.2		0.6	0.3	5.3
	SEA	0.2	3.7	1.3	0.2	1.0	1.0	0.3	0.3		0.1	8.1
	SSA	0.1	0.9	0.9	0.1	0.2	0.2	0.0	0.2	0.2		2.9
	Sum	6.7	23.9	19.2	8.6	9.8	12.7	2.9	3.4	9.1	3.7	100

Sources: van Marrewijk 2017, table 5.2; calculations based on UN Comtrade data for 2011.
Notes: Lightest shade are flows between 1 and 2 percent; next shade between 2 and 4 percent; next shade between 4 and 8 percent; darkest shade and in bold are flows above 8 percent; 166 countries included; for region abbreviations, see Chapter 4.

- Europe is by far the most important region for international trade flows; it represents more than 37 percent of global trade. Other important regions are East Asia (China and Japan) with 20 percent of global trade and North America with 13.5 percent. Together these three regions account for 71 percent of all trade flows.
- There is a limited number of sizeable inter-regional trade flows. Out of the 90 possible flows, only 18 exceed the 1 percent threshold.

- There are large flows between the three main centers; from East Asia to North America (4.2 percent), from East Asia to Europe (3.2 percent), from Europe to North America (2.9 percent), and so on.
- There are large flows from regions in the vicinity of the main centers to the main center; from Latin America to North America (2.9 percent), from Southeast Asia to East Asia (2.6 percent), from Central Asia to Europe (2.5 percent), and so on. Chapter 17 revisits this geographical component.
- Two or three global regions are rather isolated with relatively little interaction with the rest of the world. This certainly holds for Sub-Sahara Africa and South Asia (without any connecting arrow to any other region in Figure 6.2). To a somewhat smaller extent, it also holds for Pacific (with one connecting arrow), which is geographically isolated, but in view of its relatively small population has a reasonable interaction with the world economy, particularly with East Asia (the destination of 59 percent of its export flows).

To provide some more perspective on the relative interaction of some regions: the share of Pacific in world trade flows is 1.7 percent, of Sub-Sahara Africa is 2.2 percent, and of South Asia is 2.7 percent. The share of the Netherlands, a small European country with a population of 16.8 million people, in world trade flows is 3.6 percent. This is 30 percent larger than South Asia (with a population that is 99 times larger), 60 percent larger than Sub-Sahara Africa (with a population that is 54 times larger), and 110 percent larger than Pacific (with a population that is twice as large). An alternative visualization at the country level (without connecting arrows) is provided in Figure 6.3. The reader

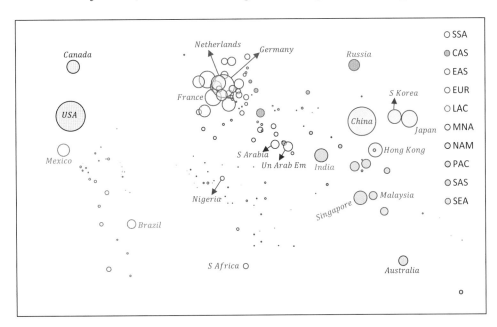

Figure 6.3 International trade flows, 2019

Source: See Table 6.1.

Notes: Bubbles are proportional to a country's trade flows in 2019 located at the geographic center; 164 countries included; for region abbreviations, see Chapter 4.

may want to compare the size of a country's trade flows with the country's area or population in Chapter 1.

When evaluating the performance of our trade theories it is important to keep in mind to what extent they are able to explain the main trade flows discussed above. There is, however, one important aspect which has not yet been discussed – namely, the extent of intra-regional trade relative to inter-regional trade flows. For the world as a whole, the intra-regional trade flows are substantial: if all intra-regional trade flows are excluded from the analysis (as is done in panel b of Table 6.1), total trade falls by 40 percent. What remains is a slightly different picture of the importance of some regions. More conclusions can be drawn as follows:

- Europe has by far the largest intra-regional trade flows: more than 25 percent of world trade flows from one European country to another European country, while 69 percent of Europe's exports flow to another European country. This is by far the highest for all regions; the main trading regions are a distant second and third: 31 percent of North American exports are destined for North America and 30 percent of East Asian exports are destined for East Asia. The simple average for the other regions is only 12 percent.
- If intra-regional trade flows are excluded from the analysis, the importance of Europe in global trade drops substantially, namely from 37.3 to 19.0 percent. All other regions become more important; in relative terms this holds particularly for South Asia, Pacific, Middle East & North Africa, and Sub-Sahara Africa.
- All major observations discussed above still hold if intra-regional trade flows are excluded: (i) there are three main trade regions (Europe, East Asia, and North America); (ii) there are large flows between these main regions; (iii) there are large flows between the main regions and the regions in the vicinity; and (iv) there are three rather isolated regions (Pacific, South Asia, and Sub-Sahara Africa).

6.3   Comparative Advantage: Technology

The theory of comparative advantage is one of those ideas that separates economists from other people: it is a remarkable insight that, once understood, should remain in the toolbox of every economist. In the words of Paul Samuelson (as cited in Krugman 1992), "comparative advantage is one of the few ideas in economics that is true without being obvious." To avoid unnecessary complications, a number of simplifying assumptions are made. There is only one factor of production: labor. This factor of production is perfectly mobile within countries, but cannot migrate across national borders. As a consequence, the factor reward, in this case the wage rate, is the same in different sectors within a country, but may differ between countries. Markets are characterized by perfect competition. This implies that we don't have to deal with strategic interactions between firms or consumers. In imperfectly competitive markets, where firms have market power, the action of one firm might trigger a reaction by other firms, which may result in, for example, price cartels or price wars. In the

Table 6.2. Hypothetical labor productivity; production per hour

	USA	EU
Cloth	6	1
Wine	4	2

perfect competition case, individual firms are too small relative to the whole market to affect the behavior of others. For the simplest international trade model, at least two commodities are needed, one to export and one to import, and two countries; otherwise there could be no *international* trade.

The famous British economist David Ricardo (1772–1823) focused on technology differences as a prime reason for countries to engage in international trade. Table 6.2 summarizes a hypothetical state of technology for two regions: the USA and the EU. Each is able to produce two goods, cloth and wine. It measures labor productivity by indicating how much cloth and wine can be produced in either America (USA) or Europe (EU) with one hour of labor. In the USA, one hour of labor produces either six units of cloth or four bottles of wine. In the EU, one hour of labor produces either one unit of cloth or two bottles of wine. Note that the USA is more efficient than the EU in the production of both cloth and wine – that is, the USA has a higher labor productivity for both sectors. It can be said that the USA has an *absolute* cost advantage for both sectors. Given that the USA is more efficient in the production of both goods, one might wonder why the USA would engage in international trade at all: why import products from another country if you can produce these more efficiently yourself? The answer is surprising: by focusing on the production of those goods in which a country is *relatively* more efficient, both countries can gain from international trade, even if goods are imported from a less productive trade partner.

To see this, first note that in a relative sense the USA is six times more efficient in the production of cloth (6/1) and two times more efficient in the production of wine (4/2) than the EU. It can be said that the USA has a *comparative* advantage in the production of cloth, where it is relatively the most efficient. It can also be said that the EU has a comparative advantage in the production of wine, where it is least disadvantaged compared to the USA. The next step is to show that if countries start trading with each other according to their comparative advantages, this is beneficial for both countries.

Suppose that the USA has four hours of labor available for the production of wine or cloth and the EU 12 hours of labor (you might assume these are billions of hours, but this does not change the underlying principles). In autarky (that is, without international trade), the USA could, for example, use two hours of labor for the production of cloth and two hours of labor for the production of wine. Similarly, the EU could, for example, use eight hours of labor for the production of cloth and four hours of labor for the production of wine. As indicated in Table 6.3, this implies that the USA produces 12 units of cloth and 8 bottles of wine, while the EU produces 8 units of cloth and 8 bottles of wine. Total world production is therefore 20 units of cloth and 16 bottles of wine.

Table 6.3. Production of cloth and wine in the EU and USA

a Autarky

	USA (4 labor hours)	EU (12 labor hours)	World production
Cloth	12	8	20
Wine	8	8	16

b Specialization according to (against) comparative advantage

	USA	EU	World production
Cloth	24 (0)	0 (12)	24 (12)
Wine	0 (16)	24 (0)	24 (16)

Now suppose that both countries specialize according to their comparative advantages: that is, the USA starts producing only cloth and the EU starts producing only wine. As shown in Table 6.3, this implies that the USA produces 24 units of cloth and 0 bottles of wine, while the EU produces 0 units of cloth and 24 bottles of wine. Total world production for *both* goods has therefore increased: from 20 to 24 units of cloth and from 16 to 24 bottles of wine. This extra production of both cloth and wine in the world economy can be used to ensure that both countries gain from international trade. Specialization according to comparative advantage is, therefore, in principle, beneficial for both trading partners, even if one country is less efficient than the other country for the production of all goods. Finally, note that if the countries were to specialize *against* their comparative advantage – that is, the USA started to produce only wine and the EU started to produce only cloth – the world production level for both goods would fall, as indicated by the production figures between brackets in Table 6.3b.

Although it is demonstrated above that the world welfare level increases if countries specialize according to their comparative advantages, the crucial question of why comparative advantage works in practice has not been answered: consumers are not familiar with the theory of comparative advantage when they go shopping, so how can we be sure that specialization takes place according to comparative advantage? The answer is provided by looking directly at something consumers do care about: *prices*. Under perfectly competitive conditions, with constant returns to scale and only one factor of production (labor), it follows that:

$$price\ of\ a\ commodity = \frac{wage\ rate\ (per\ hour)}{labour\ productivity\ (per\ hour)} \qquad 6.1$$

Consumers considering the purchase of a unit of cloth compare the price for a unit of cloth from the USA with the price of a unit of cloth from the EU. Since labor productivity in the USA is six units of cloth per hour worked (see Table 6.2), only 1/6 hours of labor are needed to produce a unit of cloth in the USA, implying a price equal to 1/6 times the wage rate in the USA. Similarly, labor productivity in the EU is one unit of cloth per hour worked, implying a price for a unit of cloth produced in the EU equal to the wage rate in the EU. If we let p denote the price of a good and w the wage rate per hour worked, and use subindices US, EU, cloth, and wine to identify the various possibilities, we see that consumers buy cloth produced in the USA if the price there is lower. That is:

$$p_{US,cloth} < p_{EU,cloth} \quad or \quad \frac{1}{6}w_{US} < \frac{1}{1}w_{EU} \qquad \qquad 6.2$$

Clearly, if this inequality does not hold, the production of cloth is cheaper in the EU and consumers would buy their cloth there. Note in particular that this holds if the wage rate in the EU is sufficiently low. Similarly, consumers purchasing wine will buy wine from the EU only if wine is cheaper in the EU than in the US, or:

$$p_{EU,wine} < p_{US,wine} \quad or \quad \frac{1}{2}w_{EU} < \frac{1}{4}w_{US} \qquad \qquad 6.3$$

Again, if this inequality does not hold, the production of wine is cheaper in the USA and consumers would buy their wine there. Combining the two inequalities for the wage rates in the EU and the USA ensures that production takes place according to comparative advantage as given in equations 6.2 and 6.3, and leads to a range of possibilities for the wage rate in the US relative to the wage rate in the EU:

$$2 = \frac{(1/2)}{(1/4)} < \frac{w_{US}}{w_{EU}} < \frac{(1/1)}{(1/6)} = 6 \qquad \qquad 6.4$$

 Equation 6.4 informs us that the wage rate in the USA can be two to six times higher than the wage rate in the EU for production to take place in accordance with comparative advantage. If the relative wage is within the indicated range, consumers can simply enforce specialization according to comparative advantage by comparing prices and buying from the cheapest source. (Note that the exact wage ratio is not determined unless the international equilibrium prices for cloth and wine are known, which cannot be determined without specifying the demand side of the economy.) The fact that the wage rate in the USA will be higher than in the EU reflects the fact that the USA is more efficient in all lines of production. This shows that wages are to a large extent determined by international productivity differences.

What happens if wages are not in this range – for example, if wages in the USA are eight times higher than in the EU? This implies that the EU will attract all consumers, because both commodities will be cheaper in the EU than in the USA. The massive demand for EU products and the reduction in demand for US products will increase labor demand and thus wages in the EU and will force wages down in the USA, until wages are in the range described by the inequality above. So, in the end, international trade will stimulate specialization according to comparative advantage. As long as this is not the case, profitable alternatives exist for both consumers and firms. The conclusion is that countries can always compete in world markets, even if they are less productive than their trading partners, if they compensate lower productivity by lower wages (see Box 6.1). Furthermore, in principle, all countries gain from international competition and specialization.

BOX 6.1 COMPARATIVE COSTS, ABSOLUTE COSTS, AND INTERNATIONAL WAGES

This section argues that differences in comparative costs are crucial for determining international trade flows and gains from trade. Absolute cost advantages, however, are crucial for determining a country's per capita welfare level, and thus help explain differences in international wages. With this in mind, the information given in Figure 6.4 for 47 different countries can help us to understand the world economy. The bubbles are proportional to population size in order to quickly identify the main observations. Countries with a low labor productivity, such as Brazil ($11.48 per hour) or Mexico ($17.26 per hour), have a low income level per capita ($15,037 and $16,370, respectively). Countries with a high labor productivity, such as the USA ($58.98 per hour) and Norway ($76.76 per hour), have a high income level per capita ($53,042 and $64,406, respectively). The (regression) line in Figure 6.4 (which explains about 77 percent of the variance in income per capita and is highly significant) summarizes this relationship. On average, a 10 percent higher income level leads to a $3.2 higher wage rate per hour.

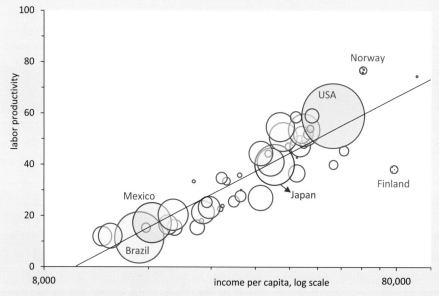

Figure 6.4 Labor productivity and income per capita
Source: Adapted from Beugelsdijk *et al*. 2013, figure 3.1.
Notes: Income per capita GDP PPP, log scale (World Development Indicators); labor productivity per hour worked in USD (2009), based on Conference Board Total Economy Database; bubbles proportional to population; dotted line is a regression line; 47 countries.

6.4 Comparative Advantage and Competitiveness

Sometimes comparative advantage of countries is confused with the *competitiveness* of firms. Conventional wisdom holds that nation-states, just like firms, can benefit from competitive advantages or suffer from competitive disadvantages, as argued by some politicians. In the West, for instance, the argument that the rich countries are harmed by a competitive disadvantage as a result of (too) high wages is widespread. Following this logic, politicians and other opinion-makers then argue that wages must be reduced in order to avoid loss of jobs as a consequence of the relocation of many activities by multinationals to low-wage countries. In addition, it is often claimed that lower productivity levels at home compared to those abroad imply that the race for competitiveness has been lost. This kind of rhetoric has often led, and still does lead, to heated and confusing debates about the relations between countries and firms, which makes it useful to point out the main differences between countries and firms when it comes to competitiveness. Countries and firms are not the same. What holds for firms is therefore not necessarily relevant or important for countries, as pointed out, for example, by Krugman (1995) and Irwin (2002).

First, if a firm is more expensive than another firm which makes a similar product, it cannot sell its product in the market, and will no longer be able to pay its workers, its owners, or its bank. The bottom line is that it will probably go out of business unless it changes its strategy. In our example in section 6.3, this means that if the wage rate in the USA is between two and six times higher than the wage rate in the EU, a cloth-producing firm in the EU will not be able to sell cloth and will go bankrupt, as will the wine producer in the USA. In each country, however, the other sector will flourish: output of wine in the EU will increase, as will output of cloth in the USA.

Second, note that it might be bad news for the competitive position of a firm if its main (foreign) competitor gains market share, but that this does not hold for countries. For a Japanese multinational like Toyota, the growth of a main competitor such as Hyundai from Korea may be a sign that Japanese production costs are too high relative to Korean production costs. This holds, for example, if wages in Japan are too high for producing cars in Japan. In this case, given productivity levels and wages, Toyota will eventually have to close its doors, or will have to move (part of) production to a country with a comparative advantage in the car sector. This type of reasoning does not hold for countries. A high growth rate in Korea is in fact good news for Japanese firms as they will face a larger export market in Korea, which will enable them to increase export sales. If (relative) labor productivity does not change, this will not affect relative wages between the countries.

Third, note that the process of specialization according to comparative advantage may seem unfair to individual firms. In the 1980s, for example, Lee Iacocca, then CEO of the Chrysler car manufacturer, complained that Chrysler was at least as "competitive" as its Japanese rivals, but was still losing market share (see Irwin 2002). He therefore argued that competition had to be "unfair" in some sense. In this period, many popular books were written on the economic struggle between the USA, Japan, and Europe, often with gloomy conclusions regarding the competitive position of "old" economies such as the USA and Europe (for an example, see Thurow 1993). In present-day discussion, the role of Japan is often taken over by China, and it seems that the present discussion with respect to China is similar as it was with Japan in the 1980s. But our example regarding comparative advantage shows that it is perfectly sensible – or at least explainable – that such a firm could lose market share if another sector in the economy, such as cloth or chip production, is relatively *more* productive than the car industry. It is important to understand that the theory of comparative advantage demonstrates that even if a firm is *more* productive than a foreign counterpart, it might still lose market share because other domestic firms might have an even *higher* productivity advantage relative to foreign firms. Failing to understand this line of reasoning may unintentionally stimulate counterproductive discussions about unfair competition and the need for protectionist measures.

Fourth, the Toyota example also highlights an aspect of multinational firm behavior. Many multinational firms in OECD countries move – or plan to move – their often low-skilled assembly activities to low-wage countries. This is often seen as an unwelcome aspect of globalization as it forces wages down in the home countries. This may happen for two reasons. Firms relocate to low-wage countries and the original workers in these companies become unemployed. The simple threat to relocate production to low-wage countries may also force wages down at home in order to prevent such relocation from happening. Below the surface, however, comparative advantage is still at work. What often happens in these cases is that a low-wage (and relatively low-productivity) country is specializing in a sector in which it has a comparative advantage (in this case, assembly), while the high-wage country is losing a sector in which it has a comparative *dis*advantage.

6.5   Comparative Advantage: Factor Abundance

The model of comparative advantage based on technology differences discussed in section 6.3 explains that trade is welfare-enhancing for all participants as a result of benefiting from differences in labor productivity between countries. These differences, however, were given exogenously and not explained by the model. In the 1930s, economists felt uneasy with this assumption. Why should productivity differ between technologically similar countries, such as the UK and the USA? These countries had more or less the same access to equivalent technologies. Economists, therefore, increasingly became unhappy with the notion that trade was explained by productivity differences alone. They started to realize that technology itself might not be too different between countries, but other factors could be responsible for productivity differences – such as differences in *factor endowments*. France exports wine to the Netherlands not because potential wine producers in the Netherlands are less productive than farmers in France, but because abundant sunshine in combination with hills that are ideal for planting grapevines are better suited for wine production than the wet climate in the Low Countries (in this example, climate is a production factor).

The so-called Heckscher–Ohlin model, also known as the Heckscher–Ohlin–Samuelson (HOS) model or the factor abundance model, takes this idea to its extreme by explaining international trade only through differences in factor endowments between countries. The reasoning of the model is quite simple, although its mathematics can be complicated. First, the following six assumptions are made:

- There are two countries, 1 and 2, each producing two homogeneous goods, cloth (C) and steel (S), using two factors of production, capital (K) and labor (L). Country 1 is assumed to be relatively well endowed with labor, compared to country 2.
- Production functions for cloth and steel are identical in the two countries, but they have different factor intensities – that is, for given factor prices the cost-minimizing input combination differs. We simply assume that steel is relatively more capital-intensive to produce than cloth at given factor prices.
- The (relative) supply of capital and labor differs between the two countries, and is perfectly mobile between sectors within a country, but perfectly immobile between countries. This implies that factor prices are the same in the two sectors within a country, with or without international trade.
- Production is perfectly competitive and characterized by constant returns to scale.
- Consumer tastes and preferences are identical in the two countries such that, for the same price of cloth relative to steel, the ratio of cloth consumption to steel consumption is the same in the two countries. (These are called identical and "homothetic" preferences.)
- There are no barriers to trade of any kind – that is, no transport costs and no tariffs or other policies restricting or influencing international trade flows.

The sections below first analyze what these six assumptions imply for an individual country in autarky. They then investigate the consequences for the economy if international trade is possible.

6.5.1   Autarky

Perfect competition in combination with constant returns to scale implies that the market price for a good is equal to the costs of producing that good. If profits are positive, a new firm will enter the market, which increases supply and reduces profitability. This will continue until profits are zero. The costs of production consist of the amount of labor necessary to produce a unit of good i, say a_{Li}, multiplied by the wage rate w, and the amount of capital necessary to produce a unit of good i, say a_{Ki}, multiplied by the rate of return on capital r.

$$p_i = costs = a_{Li}w + a_{Ki}r; \quad or \quad a_{Ki} = \frac{costs}{r} - \frac{w}{r}a_{Li} \qquad 6.5$$

Equation 6.5 simply states that the market price of cloth or steel equals the cost of production. Evidently, the assumption is that capital and labor are perfectly mobile within

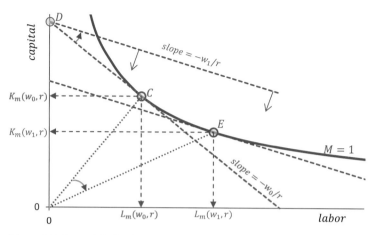

Figure 6.5 Cost minimization

countries as factor prices w and r are the same in both sectors. Taking the wage rate and the rental rate as given, the second part of the equation provides all combinations of labor and capital inputs with the same costs of production. In Figure 6.5, these are represented as straight (isocost) dashed lines. Each isocost line represents different combinations of capital and labor with the same total costs, given the wage rate and rental rate. The latter determine the slope of the isocost line, which is equal to *minus* the wage rate divided by the rental rate: $-w/r$. The total cost of production determines the intercept of the isocost lines. Obviously, the more capital and labor is used, the higher the total costs; lines closer to the origin correspond to a lower cost of production. An isoquant ($M = 1$ in the figure) depicts different combinations of capital and labor yielding the same level of production for a particular good, and is indicated by the solid-line curve.

Once a firm has determined its optimal production level, say the level indicated by the isoquant in Figure 6.5, it will choose the lowest possible cost of production. Graphically, this holds for the isocost line tangent to this isoquant, as indicated by point C in the figure for slope $-w_0/r$. This is the minimum cost combination of capital and labor to produce the good. The figure also illustrates what happens if the relative factor rewards change, say if labor becomes relatively less expensive such that $w_1/r < w_0/r$. This implies that the isocost line rotates counter-clockwise, shifting the point of tangency with the isoquant to point E. As capital has become relatively more expensive, firms do what they can to avoid rising costs by substituting cheap labor for expensive capital in the production process. It is important to realize that this reasoning can also be applied to the two-country case if relative factor rewards differ between countries – say, if one country is relatively abundant in labor, which is therefore relatively cheap, ensuring that this country produces at point E in Figure 6.5 and the other country is relatively abundant in capital, implying that labor is relatively expensive and ensuring that this country produces at point C in Figure 6.5. This is discussed further below.

This section now examines the relationship between goods prices and factor prices. The simplest way to do this is a method introduced by Abba Lerner in the 1930s. Figure 6.6

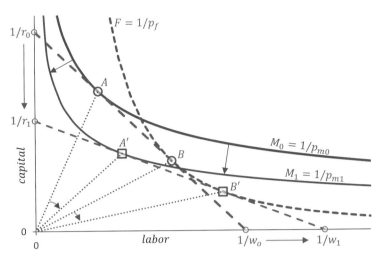

Figure 6.6 The Lerner diagram

depicts special isoquants for both food and manufactures: the so-called *unit value* iso-quants. These isoquants represent the production level of each good that is worth one dollar of revenue when sold in the market. In this way, it's not necessary to know how much the country under consideration actually produces of each good; for given prices the unit value isoquants are the same irrespective of the actual amount that is produced. We have drawn the unit value isoquants for both food and manufactures, assuming that the price of food is p_f and the price of manufactures is initially p_{m0}. Obviously, if the price of food is equal to p_f we have to produce only $1/p_f$ units of food to get one dollar of revenue, as $p_f \times 1/p_f = 1$. The unit value isoquant is therefore *inversely related* to the price of a commodity; the more expensive a good is, the fewer units have to be produced to get one dollar's worth of revenue.

Now suppose that both commodities are produced. What does this imply for factor prices? Since the prices of final goods must be equal to the total costs of production and both goods are produced, the minimum cost combinations of capital and labor for the unit value isoquants must be points of tangency with a unit isocost line. Because both sectors are confronted with the same wage rate and capital returns, this implies that the two optimal production points must lie on the same *unit value isocost* line, representing combinations of capital and labor that cost one dollar. These points are labeled A and B in the figure. As an aside, note that the figure also reflects the fact that, for given factor rewards, the production of manufactures is more capital-intensive than the production of food: the capital/labor ratio (equal to the slope of a line from the origin to the production points) is larger for manufactures than for food.

It is now possible to analyze what happens if relative goods prices change. Suppose, for example, that the price of manufactures rises to $p_{m1} > p_{m0}$. This implies that fewer units of manufactures need to be to produced to create a dollar's worth of revenue, so the unit value isoquant for manufactures shifts toward the origin from $1/p_{m0}$ to $1/p_{m1}$. As explained above, equilibrium in which both goods are produced is only possible if the optimal production points are tangent to the unit isocost line. Obviously, this implies that the unit isocost line must rotate counter-clockwise, leading to the new optimal production points A' and B' in the figure. As can be seen from the intercepts of the isocost line, the rental rate has increased (because $1/r_0 > 1/r_1$) and the wage rate has fallen (because $1/w_0 < 1/w_1$). An increase in the price of manufactures, therefore, leads to a higher rental rate and a lower wage rate. Intuitively, this makes perfect sense. Since manufactures are capital intensive, the return to capital (the rental rate) benefits from the price increase (the so-called Stolper–Samuelson theorem).

Figure 6.6 summarizes the relationships between factor prices and goods prices. It shows the link between the relative goods price p_f/p_m and the wage/rental ratio w/r for two ratios. Clearly, this exercise can be repeated for many different ratios. As noted above, this is a positive relationship: a rise in the price of (capital-intensive) manufactures lowers the wage-rental ratio. Similarly, a rise in the price of (labor-intensive) food raises the wage-rental ratio. This also works in the opposite direction: a rise in the wage-rental ratio raises the price of food relative to manufactures. It is a one-to-one correspondence, provided there is no factor-intensity reversal.

6.5.2   Trade

We are now in a position to analyze what happens in a trading equilibrium. We reinterpret points A and B for country 0, as well as A' and B' for country 1, in Figure 6.5 with the tangent unit cost curves in representing differences in factor endowment between the countries. It is now straightforward to derive the Heckscher–Ohlin theorem as explained in Figure 6.7. Because country 1 is relatively labor-abundant, we have in autarky: $(w/r)_1 < (w/r)_0$. Note, in principle, there are two different versions of factor abundance – the *physical* definition, arguing that country 1 is labor-abundant if the labor/capital ratio is higher than in country 2, and the *price* definition, arguing that country 1 is relatively labor-abundant if its wage/rental ratio is lower than in country 2.[2]

From Figure 6.7, it can be inferred that in this case the relative price of labor-intensive food is lower in country 1 than in country 0: $(p_f/p_m)_1 < (p_f/p_m)_0$. Intuitively, this makes perfect sense. In the labor-abundant country, labor-intensive food is less expensive than in the capital-abundant country because its relatively high supply of labor leads to lower relative wages, which makes food production less expensive.

This relative price difference is the basis for international trade, as summarized in Figure 6.7 by the points AU_0 and AU_1. Once costless international trade of final goods is possible, individual consumers exploiting arbitrage opportunities between the two countries will ensure that the price of food and the price of manufactures is the same in both

---

[2] The two definitions are not necessarily identical, because the price definition reflects not only supply conditions, but also demand conditions. Since it has been assumed that countries are identical in all aspects, except with respect to relative factor endowments, the two definitions give the same result in this case.

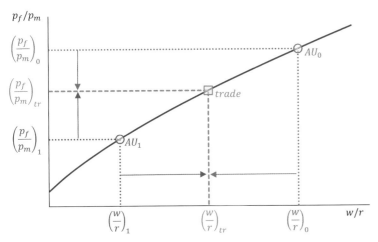

Figure 6.7 The impact of international trade

countries, and so will the relative price of food compared to manufactures. As illustrated in the figure, the trade equilibrium price – say $(p_f/p_m)_{tr}$ – will be somewhere in between the two autarky prices. The relative price of food will therefore be higher in the trade equilibrium for country 1 and lower for country 0. Consumers and producers will react differently to these price changes. In particular, consumers in country 1, where the price of food has risen, will purchase relatively less food, while producers will increase the production of food. Since production was equal to consumption in autarky, the result is that production will exceed consumption in country 1 in the trade equilibrium. Consequently, labor-abundant country 1 will export food. The reverse reasoning holds for capital-abundant country 0, which exports manufactures.

Heckscher–Ohlin / Factor Abundance theorem:

A country will export the good that intensively uses its relatively abundant factor of production. It will import the other good.

Trade ensures that the (relative) good prices become identical in the world market. As noted above, the price of food increases in country 1, while the price of manufactures declines. The reverse holds for country 0. Since the technology in the two countries is the same, Figure 6.6 depicts the determination of factor prices in *both* countries simultaneously and there is no need to draw an additional figure for the second country: they are identical. The two unit value isoquants for manufactures and food can also be uniquely determined. If both goods are produced in equilibrium in both countries, the unit value cost line must be tangent to *both* unit value isoquants, which can be done only in one way (see Figure 6.6). From the points of intersection of the unit value cost line with the axes, we can determine the wage rate and the rental rate, which must thus be the same in both countries. Equalization of the final goods prices through international trade thus leads to equalization of the return to the factors of production in the two countries. This is called *factor price equalization*. In country 1, the relative wage rate rises; in country 0, it falls. On average, both countries gain from trade: the reward for the abundant factor of production increases and the reward of the scarce factor decreases. So, the net effect is positive.

It is important to understand the main difference between the Ricardian model and the Heckscher–Ohlin model. In the Ricardian model, technology differences, resulting in wage differences between countries, cause international trade flows. In the Heckscher–Ohlin model, differences in factor endowments trigger international trade. Although in both models the prices of final goods will be equalized, factor prices will be the same in the trade equilibrium only in the Heckscher–Ohlin model.

6.6   Intra-Industry Trade

European countries are intensively involved in international trade flows, but a large share of these flows is to other European countries (Figure 6.2 and Table 6.1). Intra-industry trade is the export and import of goods in the same sector. The intra-industry trade phenomenon was first noted empirically when a group of European countries formed the European Common Market, which has now grown into the European Union (EU) and consists of 27 countries. It was soon realized that most EU trade was with other EU countries involved in the simultaneous import and export of similar types of goods. Figure 6.8 illustrates that in 2019 about 59 percent of the EU's merchandise exports of €5,193 billon was destined for other EU countries and about 61 percent of the EU's imports of €4,996 billion came from

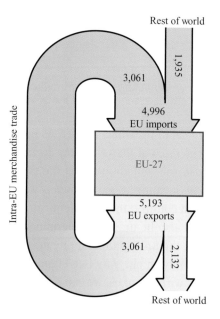

Figure 6.8 European Union (EU-27) merchandise trade flows, 2019
Source: Calculations based on Eurostat data (ec.europa.eu/eurostat).
Note: Values in billion euro.

other EU countries. Intra-industry trade is a general characteristic of trade flows, see Verdoorn (1960), Balassa (1966), and Grubel and Lloyd (1975).

How can intra-industry trade be measured – the extent of trade in similar goods? Although various options are available, the most often used measure is the Grubel–Lloyd index, which is simple and intuitively appealing. Let Ex_i be the exports of industry i and let Im_i be the imports of industry i, then the Grubel-Lloyd index GL_i for industry i is defined as

$$GL_i = 1 - \frac{|Ex_i - Im_i|}{Ex_i + Im_i} \qquad 6.6$$

If a country only imports or only exports goods or services within the same industry, such that there is no intra-industry trade, the second term on the right-hand side of equation 6.6 is equal to one, such that the whole expression reduces to zero. Similarly, if the exports of goods or services are exactly equal to the imports of those goods or services within the same industry ($Ex_i = Im_i$), the second term on the right-hand side of equation 6.6 is equal to zero, such that the whole expression reduces to one. The Grubel–Lloyd index therefore varies between zero, indicating no intra-industry trade, and one, indicating only intra-industry trade.

The distinction between sectors in trade data is based on "digits." At the two-digit level there are only 96 different sectors. At the three-digit level each of these may be subdivided into 10 more subsectors, and so on. Figure 6.9 depicts the global weighted average evolution of the Grubel–Lloyd index over a period of 45 years (1962–2006), and measured at both the three-digit and the five-digit level. It is clear that the measured degree of

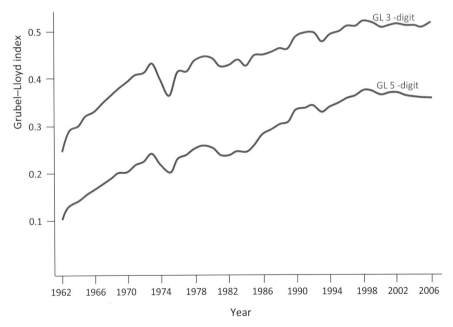

Figure 6.9 Evolution of intra-industry trade; global weighted average, 1962–2006
Source: Figure based on Brülhart (2008) data at SITC (third revision) three-digit and five-digit levels.
Note: Depicted graphs are global weighted averages.

intra-industry trade falls if more sectors are identified (the five-digit line is below the three-digit line). Nonetheless, it is equally clear that the evolution over time is similar using either measure, where in both cases intra-industry trade is becoming more important over time, rising from about 10 percent in 1962 to about 35 percent in 2006 at the five-digit level and from about 25 percent in 1962 to about 52 percent in 2006 at the three-digit level. The "dip" in both lines at around 1973–75 shows that the large rise in oil prices at that time shifted the balance from intra- to inter-industry trade temporarily.

6.7 Imperfect Competition

The explanations for international trade flows based on comparative advantage (driven by differences in technology or factor abundance) greatly enhance our understanding of the benefits of international (partial) specialization, the division of labor, and the implications for international trade flows. These theories, however, are especially useful to explain *inter*-industry trade flows – that is, trade in different types of commodities, such as wine for cloth, or iron ore for tuna fish. However, a large part of international trade flows is of the *intra*-industry type – that is, similar trade within one broader category, such as the exchange of television sets for television sets, cars for cars, or engineering services for engineering services (see section 6.6). This type of trade might seem wasteful at first sight. Why would you import something that not only can you produce yourself, but that you are also exporting? It was not until the late 1970s and the early 1980s that trade theorists were able to meet this challenge by incorporating imperfect competition into their models to explain intra-industry trade. These models are characterized by the simple fact that a single firm has *some* market power, by being able to influence the market-clearing price to some extent.

Various measures have been put forward to give an indication of the degree of competition in a particular market, usually based on the number of firms active in that market. (Examples are concentration ratios, which measure the sum of the market shares of the top four, five, or eight firms in a market, and the Herfindahl index, which measures the sum of the squared market shares of all firms in the market.) Such measures are far from perfect because a market can display monopoly power even if there are many active, but colluding, firms, or a market can be quite competitive even if there are only a few active firms, but the mere threat of entry into the market by outsiders can prevent monopolistic behavior. Unfortunately, there are many ways in which a market can behave in accordance with *im*perfect competition, even though there is only one way in which it can behave in accordance with perfect competition. This implies that the theory of international trade dealing with imperfect markets consists of many different models. Some core models are outlined here.

The underlying main cause for most international trade models of imperfect competition is the presence of internal increasing returns to scale. This implies that if a firm's production volume increases, the average costs of production fall. The presence of fixed costs at the firm level, like overhead costs, is a main reason for average costs to fall when production expands, since the fixed costs can be divided over more units of production. In the constant returns world of the Ricardo and Heckscher–Ohlin models, even the smallest profit in a market is an incentive for a new firm to enter, no matter how small the scale of production. After all, under constant returns to scale conditions, the size of a firm's production has no implications for a firm's unit costs, which are identical whether the firm produces two units or 2 million units. In reality, this is often not the case. In the aircraft industry, for example, large initial investment costs prevent the easy entry of new aircraft manufacturers.

Suppose that there is only one firm active on a specific market. This firm is called a monopolist. Like any other firm, it will be interested in maximizing its profits, probably camouflaged in its brochures as a commitment to efficiency, service to society, and eagerness to deliver high-quality goods and services to its customers. Since it is the only firm active in the market, it will realize that its actions have a large impact on the market. In particular, the firm will realize that there is a negative relationship between the price charged for its products and the quantity sold on the market. The monopolist's profit maximization problem is therefore more sophisticated than the problem facing a perfectly competitive firm which treats the output price as a parameter. A monopolist must gather information not only about its own production processes and cost structure, but also about the market for its product and the responsiveness of this market to changes in the price charged by the firm.

Figure 6.10 illustrates the monopolist's problem. The market demand curve is given by the downward-sloping solid line. It is assumed to be linear, which implies that the marginal revenue (MR) curve is also linear, with the same intercept and a slope twice as steep. The marginal revenue curve is steeper than the demand curve because the firm has to lower its

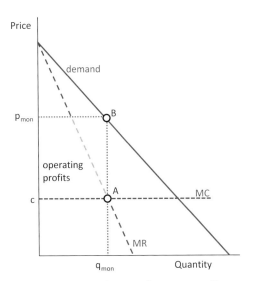

Figure 6.10 Optimal output for a monopolist

price if it wants to sell more goods, which also lowers the revenue on the initially sold output. Assume that the firm's marginal costs (MC) are constant, as indicated by the dashed horizontal line in Figure 6.10.

To maximize its profits, the firm will set its marginal costs equal to its marginal revenue, as indicated by point A. It will therefore produce the monopoly output indicated by q_{mon} in Figure 6.10. To determine the price the firm will charge at this output level, we have to go back to the demand curve; see point B, which gives us price level p_{mon}. The most important thing to note about Figure 6.10 is that the price charged by the monopolist is *higher* than the marginal cost of production. In determining the optimal price for its products, the monopolist thus charges a *mark-up* over the marginal cost of production. This mark-up depends on the price elasticity of demand $\varepsilon(q) \equiv -(dq/dp)(p/q)$:

$$p\left(1 - \frac{1}{\varepsilon(q)}\right) = c(q) \qquad\qquad 6.7$$

where $c(q)$ is the marginal cost of production. The deviation between price and marginal cost of production is in stark contrast to a perfectly competitive market, in which the market clearing price is always equal to the marginal cost of production. The fact that a monopolist's market power enables the firm to charge a higher price than the marginal cost of production also implies that the firm is able to make a profit. Since the marginal cost of production was assumed to be constant, the firm's profits are represented by the shaded rectangle in Figure 6.10 as $(p_{mon}-c)q_{mon}$ (that is, price minus cost times quantity sold).[3]

How does trade enter into this picture? Assume that the Home market is characterized by a monopoly and that there exists an identical foreign firm with the same cost structure and the same demand function in the Foreign market. Note that this is an extreme form of similar products; if it can be shown that trade arises, then there is an explanation for intra-industry trade. Figure 6.11 partially repeats information from Figure 6.10. It shows, in particular, that in autarky (without international trade) the Home firm, as a monopolist, will equate marginal revenue and marginal cost at point H, charge a price determined by point I and achieve total profits equal to $IJKL$. So what happens if international trade is possible and the foreign firm can also sell goods in the Home market? To facilitate the analysis a simplifying *assumption* is made: the Foreign firm assumes that the Home firm will continue to produce the same quantity as before. (This is a standard assumption in many game-theoretic models of competition, known as the Cournot assumption.)

Once the Home market is open to competition from the Foreign country, a Foreign firm may enter the market. This firm knows that the *residual* demand curve it faces is from point I downwards, because the amount JI is supplied by Home. This is the potential demand that is left over after the Home firm supplies the market. The associated marginal revenue curve of residual demand is indicated by *MR Foreign* in Figure 6.11. Consequently, equating marginal revenue and marginal cost at point A in Figure 6.11, the entrant charges a price determined

---

[3] The shaded area represents operating profits. This may be required to recuperate the initial (fixed cost) outlays if there are increasing returns to scale.

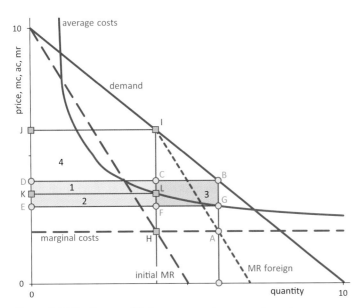

Figure 6.11 Trading equilibrium; monopoly versus duopoly

by point *B*. As the Home and Foreign firm produce a homogeneous good, this becomes the new market-clearing price in the Home market. Total production is equal to *DB*, of which *DC* is produced by the domestic firm and *CB* is imported. It is only necessary to show what happens in the Home market, because by assumption the analysis for the Foreign market is identical. So for both firms total sales are equal, *DB*, of which the amount *CB* is exports.

What can be concluded from this analysis? First, profitability for the Home firm has decreased, because the market price has fallen from *J* to *D*. The reason for this is simple: increased competition – a new entrant to the market – results in a price decrease that affects the profits of the Home firm, which is able to hold on to its domestic sales only at a lower price. The Foreign firm is able to enter the market and make a profit in its export market. In the end, both firms expand production and profits are based on the average cost curve at point *G*. The reason is that total sales of both firms equal *DB*, because both firms export to each other's market and average cost is determined by total sales: Home sales plus exports to the Foreign market.

The *change* in total profits as a result of introducing international trade flows is the net result of four different effects, as indicated in Figure 6.11:

- Area 1 *KDCL* – the part of the initial monopoly profits that is unaffected by the new entrant;
- Area 2 *EKLF* – an increase in initial monopoly profits resulting from a larger sales volume which reduces average costs;
- Area 3 *FCBG* – an increase in profits resulting from sales to the export market;
- Area 4 *DJIC* – a decrease in initial monopoly profits due to increased competition.

Note that Area 3 is the export profits of the Foreign firm that has entered the Home market, but because the two countries are identical, we know that the profits of the Home firm in the export market are also equal to Area 3. The net effect of the increased competition must be a reduction in total profits, as the Home firm was initially a profit-maximizing monopolist. The consumers in both countries gain from this increased competition by being able to purchase more goods at a lower price. The net welfare effect for the two countries under these circumstances is positive as the consumers' gain is larger than the domestic firm's loss.

In the final equilibrium, total sales in the Home market are higher and the price is lower than in the situation of a monopoly. At this point, there is a simple explanation for intra-industry trade. Both firms have an incentive to enter each other's market. Each individual firm thinks that it can consolidate profits in the Home market and gain some extra profits in the Foreign market. However, both firms are identical and use the same kind of reasoning, and both will enter the other market. The result is not only more competition, but also trade in similar (in this case, identical) final goods.

6.8 Monopolistic Competition

Section 6.7 analyzes a situation in which both firms are initially monopolists in their home markets and produce identical products. Trade changes this situation into a duopoly, which reduces the market power of both firms in both markets. The assumption that firms produce identical products is strong and almost never holds in practice. A different framework, that of *monopolistic competition*, does not rely on the assumption of identical goods, and thus takes us a step closer to most actual situations. The central idea is simple. Two countries, A and B, each produce many varieties of a single product, such as different types of cars or different varieties of beer. In essence, consumers love to have a choice between different varieties: once a new variety becomes available, there is always a market for this new product as it caters to the needs of specific customers. This is known as the "love-of-variety" effect.

Each car manufacturer, for example, has monopoly power in its own market in the sense that it offers a unique variety. However, it faces competition from other car manufacturers who sell similar, though slightly different, products. Each variety of a car has a unique number in Figure 6.12. Both countries produce n varieties. The resources of each country are not large enough to produce the whole range of varieties, indicated by letting country A produce all odd varieties and B all even varieties. The gap between each variety indicates that product characteristics are not the same. Some consumers will find their ideal variety in this market, while others have to look for product varieties that are as close as possible to their preferences. Assume that consumers are evenly distributed over a horizontal line which indicates the market area of a specific variety. This could be called the "product-characteristics" line. Consumers in A who prefer variety 3 can buy their ideal variety from the producer of variety 3, but consumers between, say, varieties 1 and 2 have to choose to buy either variety 1 or 3, whichever product has characteristics that serve them best,

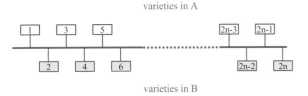

Figure 6.12 The varieties approach of monopolistic competition

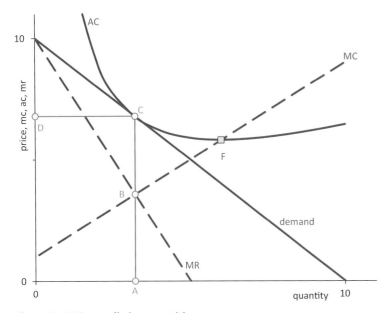

Figure 6.13 Monopolistic competition
Notes: AC = Average Costs; MC = Marginal Costs; MR = Marginal Revenue.

given the prices to be paid for each product. This may not be their ideal variety, but they always look for the closest alternative – that is, close to their ideal product. This set-up implies that if the gap between each pair of neighboring varieties is the same and if they all have the same price, all producers will serve exactly the same amount of consumers. Consumers in country *B* face similar choices regarding the even varieties. How does a firm in such a market behave?

The situation of a typical firm in this market is illustrated in Figure 6.13 for the monopolistic competition equilibrium, which is based on three assumptions:

1. The number of sellers is sufficiently large so that each firm takes the behavior of other firms as given.
2. Products are heterogeneous; buyers have preferences for all types of products.
3. There is free entry and exit of firms into and out of this market.

Figure 6.13 shows the market demand and cost conditions for a representative firm. Each firm assumes that its competitors do not react if it lowers its price. The location of the demand curve facing the producer of a variety depends on the pricing behavior of all other producers. If they decide to reduce their price, the demand curve will shift downwards. New firms entering the market will also shift the demand curve downwards because a number of customers will abandon this firm to purchase from the new firm. Similarly, the demand curve will shift upwards if other firms exit the market, thereby increasing the customer base for the firm. The differences with perfect competition and monopoly are clear. In the case of perfect competition, the demand curve will be a horizontal line and there is no need to consider the actions of other firms. In the case of a monopoly, the firm will be faced with a downward-sloping demand curve, but the firm does not have to take the actions of other firms into account, because there are no other firms.

Figure 6.13 depicts the monopolistic competition outcome of this process. The firm behaves as a monopolist in its market segment by equating marginal cost and marginal revenue at point B, leading to price D and quantity A. However, as indicated by the tangency of the average cost curve to the demand curve at point C for the production quantity A, the price the firm charges is exactly equal to the average costs of production. The firm therefore does not make (excess) profits. This aspect of the monopolistic competition equilibrium is caused by the competitive pressure of other firms in similar market segments in combination with the assumption that firms can freely enter and exit the market. If the representative firm made a profit, other firms would enter the market until these profits disappeared. Similarly, if the representative firm would make a loss, some firms would leave the market, which would increase the market share for the remaining firms, which in turn would allow them to reduce their loss. This process continues until the loss disappears. In equilibrium, therefore, the representative firm makes zero profits, as illustrated in Figure 6.13.

The situation illustrated in Figure 6.13 is Chamberlain's famous tangency solution of monopolistic competition (see Chamberlain 1933). In the situation depicted in the figure there is a difference between equilibrium average costs (at point C) and minimum average costs (at point F).[4] This implies that there are unexploited economies of scale, which raises the question of whether this is a waste of resources.[5] The answer to this question is both yes and no. Yes, in the sense that there is excess capacity. No, in the sense that product differentiation introduces variety, which expands the extent of consumer choices and thereby welfare.

What happens in the monopolistic competition model if it becomes possible for the two countries to engage in international trade? Several changes may occur simultaneously, but the most important thing to remember is that consumers love variety – that is, they always prefer more varieties of a good to fewer. Since consumers in country A after international trade will have access to varieties produced both at home and abroad, the number of varieties to choose from, and thus their welfare level, will increase. In the simplest version of the model, the total number of varieties remains the same $(2n)$. Each producer, both at home and

---

[4] Herein lies a difference with the average cost curve of Figures 6.10 and 6.11, where the average costs continue to fall as production expands. Note that the intersection of the marginal cost curve and the average curve is at the minimum of the average cost curve (why?).

[5] This simplified treatment does not distinguish between short-run and long-run (average) cost curves.

abroad, will lose half of its domestic sales to foreign competitors, since those domestic consumers can now import a variety that serves their needs better than locally produced varieties. (Remember that consumers in A between varieties 1 and 3 have with trade an additional variety: 2. For some consumers this is the ideal variety.) At the same time, each producer will gain half of its previous sales by entering the foreign market and selling to foreign consumers. In this case, therefore, Figures 6.12 and 6.13 still represent the monopolistic competition equilibrium, but total sales now consist of domestic sales and exports in equal amounts. Obviously, this gives rise to two-way trade in similar products (intra-industry trade) and gains from trade through the increase in the number of varieties to choose from.

Under more general circumstances, the increase in the number of available varieties may attract new customers. Customers that initially found the distance between their preferred variety and what the market had to offer too large and did not enter this market may now enter because a wider range of products is available. Simultaneously, the entry of the new (foreign) firms increases competition between suppliers, making the demand curve faced by an individual supplier more elastic as each firm faces closer substitutes to the product it supplies and also because more competition shifts the intersection with the vertical axes downwards. Higher elasticity implies, in this context, that consumers will decrease (increase) demand for firm x's product more in response to a price increase (cut) by this firm x.

What did the model of monopolistic competition add to the conclusions outlined in section 6.7?

- There is another elegant explanation for intra-industry trade flows. Firms no longer have to sell identical products, but can offer close substitutes to consumers. This adds some reality to the model.
- The number of suppliers is large, but limited. This is also a characteristic that can be observed in reality. A disadvantage of the model of monopolistic competition is that it assumes that varieties are different from a consumer's utility point of view, but not from a producer's cost point of view.
- Consumers love variety: once new varieties become available, they will buy them. The implication of the monopolistic competition model is that consumers will now also buy varieties from foreign suppliers, leading to intra-industry trade.
- Producers will experience more competition from foreign suppliers, implying that the demand curve for individual suppliers becomes more elastic and shifts downward. In the trade equilibrium, each firm produces a larger output (now also serving foreign consumers) and charges a lower price due to more competition and better exploitation of scale economies.

6.9 Heterogeneous Firms

Casual observation shows that firms differ in many aspects: what they produce, how they are organized, how productive they are, how much they sell, and for which markets they produce. Productivity differences have been intensively analyzed recently, both empirically and theoretically, and for both advanced and developing countries (see Bernard *et al.* 2003, Melitz 2003, and Bergeijk and van Marrewijk 2013). There is now overwhelming evidence that most sectors or industries are characterized by firms with large productivity differences that co-exist simultaneously. This contrasts with the models outlined so far. The question arises to what extent such "representative firm" models can accurately describe the stylized facts of firm heterogeneity. In the seminal theoretical contribution of Marc Melitz (2003), who developed a monopolistic competition model in which firms differ in terms of productivity, the answer to this question is: no. The model developed by Melitz is beyond the scope of this textbook, but given the analytical tools already available it is possible to sketch the basics of his approach.

Figure 6.14 repeats the demand, marginal revenue, and profit maximization information from Figure 6.10, but at the same time it simplifies by assuming that there are no fixed costs. The investigation relates to three firms faced with a particular demand curve that have different productivity levels, leading to marginal cost curves c_1, c_2, and c_3. Assume that firm 1 is the most efficient and firm 3 is the least efficient: $c_1 < c_2 < c_3$. The left panel of the figure depicts the profit maximization decision. Marginal revenue equals marginal costs for firm 1 at point E_1, such that the firm produces quantity q_1, charges price p_1, and earns operating profits $(p_1 - c_1)q_1$, as indicated by the light-shaded area in Figure 6.14. Similarly, marginal revenue equals marginal costs for firm 2 at point E_2, such that the firm produces quantity q_2, charges price p_2, and earns operating profits $(p_2 - c_2)q_2$, as indicated by the (smaller) hashed area in Figure 6.14. Since firm 2 is less efficient than firm 1 it is confronted with higher costs and thus charges a higher price (with a lower mark-up), sells a smaller quantity, and earns considerably lower profits. Firm 3 is the borderline firm. Its marginal costs are so high that it charges a price equal to its marginal costs and sells a

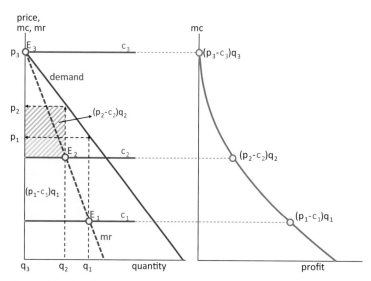

Figure 6.14 Firm heterogeneity, prices, and profits

quantity of zero, leading to zero profits. The right panel of Figure 6.14 depicts the relationship between efficiency (marginal costs) and firm profits. They are equal to zero for firm 3 at marginal cost level c_3 and rise to the higher levels indicated for firms 2 and 3. The (quadratic) solid curve in the right panel connecting these three profit levels provides the relevant information for all possible productivity levels.

What happens to the individual firms depicted in Figure 6.14 if the country opens up to international trade flows? There will be a larger total market, an increase in the number of firms, and increased competition for the individual demand for each firm. As a consequence, the price-responsiveness for the individual demand curves will increase, such that a firm lowering its price will be able to sell more products. The consequences are depicted in Figure 6.15. The demand curve for an individual firm rotates counter-clockwise around point c_5 in the left panel of the figure, as indicated by the dotted line. The profit levels associated with different marginal cost levels therefore also change, as indicated by the dotted curve in the right panel of the figure. The maximum price a firm can charge is lower than before. As a result, the least efficient firms, namely those with marginal costs in between c_4 and c_3, are no longer able to make positive profits and will be forced to exit the market. The remaining firms can be divided into two groups. The firms with rather low productivity, namely with marginal costs in between c_6 and c_4, are able to survive in the market, but at the expense of lower profits. The most efficient firms, however, are able to expand their production levels and earn higher profits. This holds for all firms with marginal costs below level c_6. The inefficient surviving firms have less opportunity to lower prices in response to foreign competition (high marginal costs limits price reductions), while the most efficient firms can lower prices and gain market share as a consequence (more elastic demand curve). Open economies are usually found to be more productive than more autarkic countries. The reason for this finding is not that individual firms become more efficient as a result of more foreign competition, but that less efficient

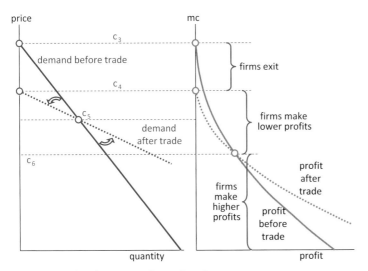

Figure 6.15 Firm heterogeneity and trade

firms are driven out of the market, while more efficient firms are able to expand production.

What the figures don't show, but what is now easy to understand, is the empirical finding that exporting firms are "a happy few" and that multinational firms are even happier than exporting firms. Suppose, as found in many empirical studies, that entering the domestic market is relatively cheap for firms, but that entering a foreign market is more expensive. Setting up a sales network, learning a different language, or getting familiar with a different culture is more expensive than doing business in a local market. Becoming a multinational firm is even more expensive because running a foreign firm requires additional investments. In the model above, this can easily be incorporated by introducing different levels of fixed costs; say, zero for domestic firms, somewhat higher for exporting firms, and the highest for multinational firms. These fixed costs have to be deducted from operating profits. If this is done in the right panel, the intersection of the profit curve with the vertical axis shifts downward. This indicates that some firms can profitably serve the domestic market, but are not efficient enough to export, and that some firms are profitable enough to export (and serve the domestic market), but not efficient enough to become a multinational firm. Box 6.2 outlines evidence for Latin American firms to illustrate these findings. See Chapter 18 for a further discussion.

BOX 6.2 FIRM HETEROGENEITY IN LATIN AMERICA

Chang and van Marrewijk analyze firm heterogeneity in 15 Latin American countries using data from the World Bank Enterprise Survey: Argentina, Bolivia, Chile, Colombia, Ecuador, El Salvador, Guatemala, Honduras, Mexico, Nicaragua, Panama, Paraguay, Peru, Uruguay, and Venezuela (see Chang and van Marrewijk 2013). They investigate the impact of both export intensity and foreign ownership by identifying four types of firms: (i) national domestic firms (nationally owned, producing for the domestic market); (ii) national exporting firms (nationally owned, also exporting); (iii) foreign domestic firms (partly foreign-owned, producing for the domestic market); and (iv) foreign exporting firms (partially foreign-owned, also exporting). The cut-off level to identify partial foreign-ownership and also exporting is 10 percent in both cases.

Figure 6.16 illustrates the main findings of this study for the 15 countries and 13 sectors taken together. Although there is considerable overlap in productivity levels for the different firm types regarding normalized productivity levels (which range from zero to one), the national domestic firms are least productive while the foreign exporting firms are the most productive. In between are the national exporting firms and the foreign domestic firms, in that order of productivity. A more detailed analysis, as provided in Table 6.4, substantiates most of these findings. After controlling for different sectors,

BOX 6.2 (cont.)

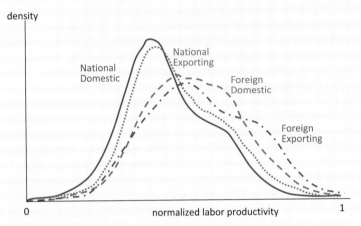

Figure 6.16 Productivity and firm type in Latin America
Source: Chang and van Marrewijk 2013.
Note: Data are for 2006.

Table 6.4. Productivity, exports, and foreign ownership in Latin America, 2006

Normalized productivity	Manufactures			Services		
	1	2	3	4	5	6
National Exporter	0.046 (8.53)**	0.039 (7.43)**	0.043 (8.03)**	0.020 (1.79)	0.013 (1.13)	0.013 (1.17)
Foreign Domestic	0.081 (9.80)**	0.070 (8.79)**	0.070 (8.80)**	0.103 (11.70)**	0.087 (9.96)**	0.087 (9.91)**
Foreign Exporter	0.092 (10.12)**	0.076 (8.53)**	0.075 (8.39)**	0.109 (5.63)**	0.078 (4.15)**	0.082 (4.32)**
Size Medium	0.042 (10.19)**	0.038 (9.60)**	0.036 (8.97)**	0.024 (3.99)**	0.018 (3.03)**	0.019 (3.20)**
Size Large	0.069 (12.83)**	0.065 (12.36)**	0.063 (11.91)**	0.009 (1.23)	0.008 (1.05)	0.009 (1.22)
Ln(GDP/cap)	0.115 (33.15)**	0.126 (21.66)**	0.080 (6.97)**	0.067 (11.69)**	0.049 (4.61)**	0.032 (1.12)
Constant	−0.670 (21.56)**	−0.715 (13.74)**	−0.174 (1.35)	−0.206 (4.00)**	0.103 (1.05)	0.187 (0.71)
Observations	6146	6146	6146	3075	3075	3075
R-squared	0.23	0.29	0.32	0.09	0.17	0.20

BOX 6.2 (cont.)

Table 6.4. (cont.)

Normalized productivity	Manufactures			Services		
	1	2	3	4	5	6

Test if coefficients are significantly different, F-test (Prob > F)

NE v FD	0.000**	0.001**	0.002**	0.000**	0.000**	0.000**
NE v FE	0.000**	0.000**	0.001**	0.000**	0.002**	0.001**
FD v FE	0.330	0.635	0.705	0.761	0.660	0.801

Source: Chang and van Marrewijk 2013.
Notes: Dependent variable: normalized productivity; robust t statistics in parentheses; [*] significant at 5 percent; [**] significant at 1 percent; the specification in columns 2, 3, 5, and 6 include sector and country fixed effects; the third and sixth specification also include sector-country interaction fixed effects; NE = National Exporter; FD = Foreign Domestic; FE = Foreign Exporter.

countries, firm size, development level, and country-sector interaction effects, they find the following statistically significant ranking of productivities (from low to high):

National Domestic < National Exporter < Foreign Domestic < Foreign Exporter

Chang and van Marrewijk therefore conclude that the so-called foreign ownership premium is more important than the exporter premium.

6.10   Conclusions

International trade flows are positively associated with economic development levels. It is thus not surprising that Europe, North America, and East Asia are the most active trade centers, which tends to also benefit countries and regions in the vicinity of these centers, such as Mexico, Southeast Asia, the Middle East, and North Africa. Developing regions are in general less active in trade flows. This holds in particular for Sub-Sahara Africa and South Asia. As such, these regions do not fully benefit from the potential welfare gains associated with trade flows.

This chapter explained the underlying reasons for trade flows and the associated gains from trade. Comparative advantages, associated with differences in technology or factor abundance, lead to efficiency gains from trade. Competitive advantages, associated with market size, firm power, love of variety, intermediate goods, and heterogeneous firms, lead to pro-competitive gains from trade, gains from effective market size, and selection gains in productivity. Countries imposing trade restrictions, which lead to lower trade flows, thus miss out on a large range of potential gains from trade.

The chapter has also provided a snapshot of trade flows at a certain moment in time and discussed various reasons for the size and direction of these trade flows. As such, it provides a picture of the static gains from trade, international interaction, and openness. Chapter 7 focuses on the dynamic aspects of economic development, both within a country and as a result of interaction with other countries.

Further Reading

Elhanan Helpman analyzes in detail how the contributions that are discussed in this chapter contribute to our understanding of global inequality. See Helpman, E. 2018. *Globalization and Inequality* (Cambridge, MA: Harvard University Press). In earlier work, Helpman reviews the models that are also discussed in this chapter in somewhat more detail, without becoming (too) technical. See Helpman, E. 2011. *Understanding Global Trade* (Cambridge, MA: Harvard University Press). An intermediate source is van Marrewijk (2017).

Recent research points out that (internal) geography and trade are closely related. See: Redding, S. 2022. "Trade and Geography," in G. Gopinath, E. Helpman, and K. Rogoff (eds.), *Handbook of International Economics: International Trade* (Amsterdam: Elsevier), vol. 5.

7 Economic Growth

7.1 Introduction

Chapter 1 already demonstrated that there are big differences between countries in terms of income per capita. Figure 7.1 provides an indication of how big those differences really are using a logarithmic scale for 191 countries, together accounting for more than 97 percent of the world population. The population-weighted average income level is $16,672. This ranges from a low of $754 for Burundi to a high of $120,376 for Macao. The average income level in Qatar is thus 160 times higher than in Burundi. Macao has a small population (about 0.6 million people) and is the casino capital of China. There are also large differences, however, for countries with large populations that do not depend on a single economic activity for generating their income. The USA is the richest sizeable country in terms of population (about 328 million people). It has a per capita income level of $62,513; this is 83 times as much as Burundi (12 million people), 28 times as much as Ethiopia (112 million people), 13 times as much as Nigeria (201 million people), nine times as much as India (1,366 million people), and more than four times as much as China (1,397 million people). This chapter explains to some extent the main causes of these big differences.

In trying to confront the performance of theoretical models with the empirical evidence some economists have constructed lists of *stylized facts*. Five "facts" from two of these lists are shown below.

The *Kaldor* (1961) list of stylized facts is:[1]

1. The continued growth in the aggregate volume of production and in the productivity of labor at a steady trend rate.
2. A continued increase in the amount of capital per worker.
3. A steady rate of profit on capital.
4. Steady capital-output ratios over long periods.
5. A steady investment coefficient and a steady share of profits and wages.

Figure 7.2 illustrates Kaldor's stylized fact 1 for the USA, using data for the period 1850–2010. Over a period of 160 years the income per capita increased 16.5 times (from

---

[1] Kaldor also noted that countries have very different long-run growth rates.

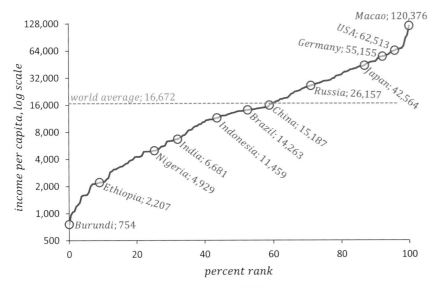

Figure 7.1 Ordering of real income per capita, 2019
Source: Created using World Development Indicators online.
Notes: Income is GNI PPP in constant 2017 $ (2019 or most recent); 191 countries included; world average is population-weighted.

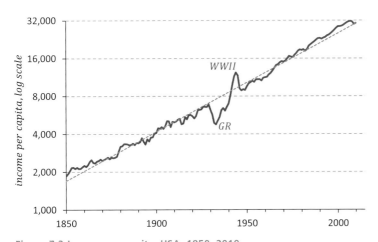

Figure 7.2 Income per capita; USA, 1850–2010
Source: Based on Maddison Project Database (www.ggdc.net).
Notes: Income in 1990 international GK $ (ppp corrected); the thin line is a regression line; GR = Great Recession; WWII = Second World War.

$1,849 to $30,491, measured in so-called 1990 international Geary-Khamis dollars, which corrects for purchasing power parity). That is a formidable increase indeed, within about five generations. Figure 7.2 uses a logarithmic scale and also shows a thin regression line to illustrate how stable the development of income per capita has been, except for a dip during the Great Recession and a peak during the Second World War. According to the regression line, per capita income growth is a little over 1.8 percent per year, which is a doubling of the income level within 40 years. However, this stability does *not* hold for many other countries, and as such is questionable. Kaldor's stylized facts 2–4 hold reasonably well empirically, but stylized fact 5 is also questionable (see Box 7.3).

The foundations of the endogenous growth theory were laid by Paul Romer, who in response to Kaldor's stylized facts produced a list of his own. The *Romer* (1994) list of stylized facts is:

1. There are many firms in a market economy.
2. Discoveries differ from other inputs in that many people can use them at the same time (nonrival goods).
3. It is possible to replicate physical activities.
4. Technological advance comes from things that people do.
5. Many individuals and firms have market power and earn monopoly rents on discoveries.

The empirical validity of Romer's stylized facts is hardly disputed. They turn out to be useful for constructing a proper theoretical model (see section 7.7). First, sections 7.2 and 7.3 discuss the role of physical and human capital in the economic growth process and how economic agents make forward-looking decisions (section 7.4). Section 7.5 explains what total factor productivity is and how it is measured. Sections 7.6 and 7.7 then outline the meaning of the terms accumulability, rivalness, and excludability and how these are useful for explaining the role of knowledge spillovers in the economic growth process. Section 7.8 covers Dupuit triangles and the dynamic costs of trade restrictions. Finally, section 7.9 provides an indication of the size of these costs for China.

7.2   Capital Accumulation

On a typical construction site in a developing country such as the Philippines there are an impressive number of workers laboring in the heat using relatively simple tools. On a typical construction site in Australia, on the other hand, there is a fairly small number of workers operating impressive looking cranes and other machinery, in many cases from an air-conditioned cabin. One important explanation for differences in per capita income is therefore related to differences in the amount and quality of tools available for the average worker (or capital per worker). The neoclassical growth model focuses on capital accumulation over time as the main driving force of economic growth (see Solow 1956). As discussed below, the neoclassical model is based on strong restrictions regarding technology and type of competition.

Output Y is a function $F(K, L)$ of the inputs capital K and labor L. Since the neoclassical production function has constant returns to scale, we can write the variables in *intensive* form, which is per worker units. We use lower case letters to denote these variables, so $y = Y/L$ is output per worker, $k = K/L$ is capital per worker, and so on. The production function is then $y = f(k) \equiv F(k, 1)$. We denote its first derivative by $'$ and its second derivative by $''$. A neoclassical production function has a positive marginal product of

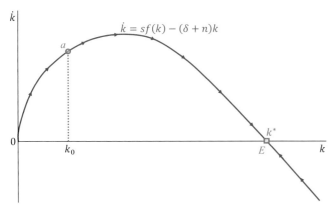

Figure 7.3 Capital accumulation in the neoclassical model

capital which diminishes as the capital stock increases, so: $f' > 0$ and $f'' < 0$. We also impose the Inada conditions: $f(0) = 0$, $\lim_{k \downarrow 0} f'(k) = \infty$, and $\lim_{k \to \infty} f'(k) = 0$.[2]

We are interested in changes of the variables over time. We denote these changes by a dot over the variable; $\dot{k} = dk/dt$ is thus the change of capital per worker over time, and so on. The gross capital stock K increases if we invest I in new capital and decreases as a result of the depreciation rate δ times the capital stock K, such that: $\dot{K} = I - \delta K$. Assume that the working population grows at a constant rate n, such that: $\dot{L}/L = n$. Differentiation of the definition $k = K/L$ over time gives the first part of equation 7.1.[3] It says that capital per worker increases if investment per worker i is higher than $(\delta + n)k$, which is what is needed to keep the amount of capital per worker constant.[4] The second part of equation 7.1 follows by assuming that a constant fraction s of income is saved and invested in the capital stock ($I = sY$ or $i = sy = sf(k)$).

$$\dot{k} = i - (\delta + n)k = sf(k) - (\delta + n)k \qquad 7.1$$

The implied dynamics of the amount of capital per worker given in equation 7.1 is illustrated in Figure 7.3. Since capital is essential for production ($f(0) = 0$), the curve starts at zero. It then becomes positive (since the marginal product of capital is arbitrarily large if the capital stock is arbitrarily small), reaches a peak, and becomes negative (since the marginal product of capital becomes arbitrarily small if the capital stock becomes arbitrarily large). If we start out with a given stock of capital per worker k_0, then this stock first increases rapidly (as indicated by point a in Figure 7.3) and then gradually slower and

---

[2] Named after Ken-Ichi Inada (see Uzawa 1963). In words: capital is indispensable for positive production, the marginal product of capital becomes arbitrarily large if the capital stock becomes arbitrarily small, and the marginal product of capital becomes arbitrarily small if the capital stock becomes arbitrarily large.

[3] Note that $\dot{k} = \frac{\dot{K}}{L} - k\frac{\dot{L}}{L} = \frac{I - \delta K}{L} - nk = i - (\delta + n)k$.

[4] Since you have to replace depreciated capital δk and provide new workers with capital nk just to keep k constant, the term $(\delta + n)k$ is the minimum investment level required to keep k constant.

slower until long-run equilibrium point E is reached. At that point the amount of capital per worker is constant, denoted by k^*.

The steady state capital per worker k^* depends on the parameters in equation 7.1. In particular, it rises if the savings rate s increases, the depreciation rate δ falls, or the population growth rate n falls. Countries with a high savings rate thus converge to a high capital stock per worker and countries with a high population growth rate to a low capital stock per worker. Furthermore, output per worker y^* of course increases if k^* increases since $y^* = f(k^*)$. The same does not hold, however, for consumption per worker c^*, since $c^* = y^* - i^* = f(k^*) - sf(k^*)$. In fact, it is easy to determine the "optimal" savings rate that maximizes consumption per worker in the steady state. This so-called *golden rule of accumulation* must ensure that $f'(k^*) = (\delta + n)$, so the marginal product of capital must be equal in the steady state to the population growth rate plus the depreciation rate.[5]

One problem of the neoclassical model outlined above is that in the steady state the amount of capital per worker and the output per worker do not actually increase, which is in contrast to facts 1 and 2 on the Kaldor list (section 7.1). To remedy this shortcoming, it is possible to impose *exogenous labor-augmenting technical change* (at a constant growth rate g). The term exogenous indicates that this technical change will increase production but is not explained within the model. The term labor-augmenting indicates that this technical change makes the input labor more productive (see below). Let A denote our measure of the level of technology. Assume it grows at a constant rate $g = \dot{A}/A$. Gross output Y is now given by the production function $Y = F(K, AL)$, which has all the neoclassical properties. We can again write the model in intensive form, but this time all variables are in *effective* worker units. We thus have $y = Y/AL$, $k = K/AL$, and so on. All results above still hold, provided we change equation 7.1 to: $\dot{k} = sf(k) - (g + \delta + n)k$. The economy thus moves over time to a constant level of capital per *effective* worker. In *worker* units this means that the capital stock is ultimately growing at the exogenous rate g (and so is output per worker), which allows us to explain all five stylized facts on Kaldor's list. The *golden rule of accumulation* must now be adjusted to ensure that $f'(k^*) = (g + \delta + n)$.

So how important are differences in the amount of capital per worker for explaining differences in output per worker? This question is not so easy to answer because it requires us to aggregate many different types of capital into one aggregate measure. The construction of a consistent data set that can be compared for a large number of countries is therefore complicated and involves a lot of work. The data used here are from the Penn World Table (see Feenstra *et al.* 2015). Table 7.1 provides information on the capital stock per worker for a selection of countries. It also provides information on the income level per capita and the population size of the country. For the countries in the table income per capita ranges from $1,063 for DR Congo to $67,462 for the United Arab Emirates, or 63 times as large. The variation in capital stock per worker is even larger, ranging from $6,000 for DR Congo to $690,000 for the United Arab Emirates, or 123 times as large. In general, countries with low capital per worker, such as Pakistan and Nigeria, have low

---

[5] Note that $c^* = f(k^*) - sf(k^*) = f(k^*) - (\delta + n)k^*$ in the steady state from equation 7.1.

Table 7.1. Income, capital per worker, and population; selected countries, 2019

Country	Income per capita	Capital per worker	Population
DR Congo	1,063	6	87
Pakistan	5,005	28	217
Nigeria	4,929	34	201
India	6,681	56	1,366
China	15,187	120	1,398
Mexico	19,160	143	128
Russia	26,157	196	144
UK	45,686	326	67
USA	62,513	364	328
UAE	67,462	690	10

Sources: Penn World, Table 9.1; and World Development Indicators.
Notes: Income per capita is GNI PPP in constant 2017 $ (2019 or most recent); capital per worker $\times 1,000$ in constant 2011 USD (rnna/emp; 2017); population in million (2019).

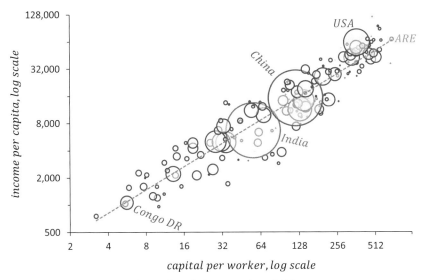

Figure 7.4 Income per capita and capital per worker, 2019
Source: Calculations based on sources mentioned in Table 7.1.
Notes: 167 countries included; bubbles proportional to population; dashed line is a regression line; ARE = United Arab Emirates.

income per capita, while countries with high capital per worker, such as the UK and the USA, have high income per capita. It is not always true, however, that higher capital per worker leads to higher income per capita: Nigeria, for example, has a lower income per capita than Pakistan despite higher capital per worker.

Figure 7.4 illustrates the relationship between capital per worker and income per capita for 167 countries using logarithmic scales. It clearly shows the strong (but imperfect) positive association between these two variables. The estimated regression line shown in

BOX 7.1 DO PEOPLE IN RICH COUNTRIES WORK LONGER HOURS?

Economics is about choosing optimally given the restrictions that you face. One such choice is, given that you want to work, to determine how many hours you want to work. Occasionally, you may enter conversations where somebody argues that the income level in country X is low because the people in country X do not like to work long hours (the terms "lazy" or "lying on the beach" may pass by). Keep in mind, however, that people in different countries face different circumstances, and for that reason alone may make different choices.

The Penn World Table provides reliable information on the average annual number of hours worked per person engaged for 65 countries, which excludes most developing countries. Figure 7.5 ranks these countries from low to high. The simple average is 1,859 hours worked per year. This is close to the Turkish average of 1,832 hours (Turkey is the median). People in Cambodia work the longest: 2,456 hours per year. People in Germany work the shortest: 1,354 hours per year. This is about 45 percent less than people in Cambodia.

Figure 7.6 provides a clearer picture on the relationship between the number of hours worked and income per capita. In general, people in high-income countries work *less*, not more. This suggests that spare time is a luxury good of which you start to consume more if income rises. Germany (which works the shortest hours) is a high-income country, while Myanmar and Cambodia (which work the longest hours) are developing countries. There are exceptions, however, as indicated by Hong Kong and Singapore, where income is high, but people work long hours. As a result, the trendline only explains

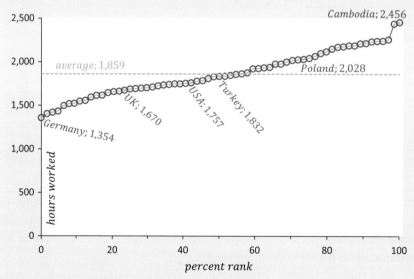

Figure 7.5 Ordering of hours worked per year, 2017
Source: Created using data from PWT 9.1.
Notes: Hours worked is average annual hours worked by persons engaged (2017); 65 countries included; simple average.

BOX 7.1 (cont.)

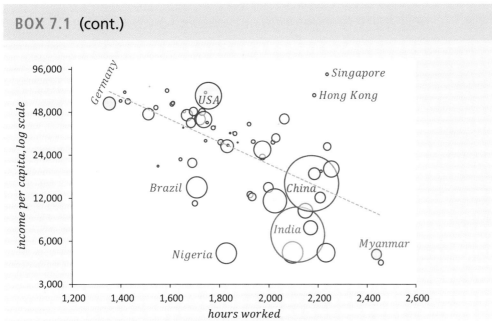

Figure 7.6 Income per capita and number of hours worked per year, 2019
Sources: Created using data from PWT 9.1 and World Development Indicators online.
Notes: Hours worked is average annual hours worked by persons engaged (2017); income per capita is GNI PPP in constant 2017 $ (2019 or most recent); bubbles proportional to population size (2019); 65 countries included; dashed line is a trendline.

about 38 percent of the variance in income per capita. In any case, this information shows clearly that the hypothesis that people in developing countries are poor because they work shorter hours can be ruled out. Instead, the opposite holds in general: people in advanced countries have high income levels despite the fact that they work shorter hours.

the figure explains 86.4 percent of the variance in income per capita and has an estimated slope coefficient of 0.85. This implies that, on average, when the capital stock per worker rises by 10 percent the income per capita level rises by about 8.5 percent. DR Congo and the United Arab Emirates are close to the regression line, as are some big countries like India, China, and the USA. It is safe to conclude that capital per worker is an important determinant of income per capita.

7.3 Human Capital

Section 7.2 showed that the accumulation of capital over time is crucial for understanding differences in per capita income levels. The discussion so far has focused attention implicitly on *physical* capital. This section addresses two main issues. First, it describes

Table 7.2. Income, human capital per worker, and population; selected countries, 2019

Country	Income per capita	Human capital per worker	Population
Niger	1,201	1.21	23
Ethiopia	2,207	1.41	112
India	6,681	2.12	1,366
China	15,187	2.57	1,398
Philippines	9,778	2.69	108
Argentina	21,190	3.04	45
Italy	42,776	3.12	60
Russia	26,157	3.40	144
USA	62,513	3.74	328
Singapore	88,155	3.97	6

Sources: Penn World Table 9.1 and World Development Indicators.
Notes: Income per capita is GNI PPP in constant 2017 $ (2019 or most recent); human capital per worker is an index based on years of schooling and returns to education (2017); population in million (2019).

the large differences between countries in terms of *human capital* levels. Second, it shows how both types of capital can be incorporated in the neoclassical growth model.

Penn World Table 9.1 provides an index of human capital per worker based on years of schooling and returns to education. Table 7.2 provides information on the human capital per worker, income per capita, and population size for a selection of countries. The ranking is based on human capital per worker from low to high. The variation in human capital per worker is substantial, ranging from 1.21 in Niger to 3.97 in Singapore, or more than three times as high. This is significantly less, however, than the variation in income per capita (which differs by a factor of 73). In general, countries with low human capital per worker, such as Niger, Ethiopia, and India, have low income per capita, while countries with high human capital per worker, such as the USA and Singapore, have high income per capita. The relationship is less clear cut, however, than for capital per worker; for examples of countries with lower income per capita despite higher human capital per worker, see China and the Philippines and Italy and Russia.

Figure 7.7 illustrates the relationship between human capital per worker and the log of income per capita for 140 countries. It clearly shows the strong (but imperfect) positive association between these two variables. The estimated regression line shown in the figure explains 67 percent of the variance in income per capita and has an estimated slope coefficient of 1.4165. This implies that, on average, when the human capital per worker rises by 0.1, the income per capita level rises by about 14 percent. Most big countries, such as India, China, and the USA, have observations close to the regression line. Some rich countries, such as Qatar (oil) and Macao (casinos), have higher income per capita levels than expected on the basis of human capital per worker only. Other countries, such as DR Congo, Uganda, and Kyrgyzstan, have lower than expected income per capita, In any case, it is safe to conclude that human capital per worker is an important determinant of income per capita.

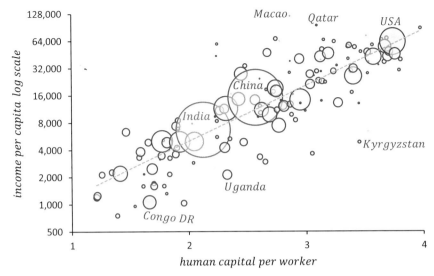

Figure 7.7 Income per capita and human capital per worker, 2019
Sources: Created using data from PWT 9.1 and World Development Indicators online.
Notes: Human capital per worker is an index based on years of schooling and returns to education (2017); income per capita is GNI PPP in constant 2017 $ (2019 or most recent); bubbles proportional to population size (2019); 140 countries included; dashed line is a trendline.

The relationship between capital per worker and income per capita is somewhat stronger than between human capital per worker and income per capita, where the former explains 86 and the latter 67 percent of the variance in log income per capita. There is, obviously, a high correlation between the two explanatory variables: countries with a high stock of capital per worker also tend to have a high index of human capital per worker (the correlation coefficient is 0.75 for the countries in Figure 7.7).

The easiest way to accommodate human capital in the neoclassical growth model is by treating it essentially the same as physical capital (see Barro 1991; see section 7.5 for a critical evaluation of this approach). Suppose, therefore, that there are two types of capital: physical capital K and human capital H. We ignore technical change, so output Y is a function of physical capital, human capital, and (unskilled) labor L, with the standard neoclassical properties (and Inada conditions for both types of capital): $Y = F(H, K, L)$. We can write this in per worker terms as: $y = f(h, k)$. As before, physical capital rises because we save and invest a constant fraction of income s_k and falls as a result of depreciation and the rising work force. Equation 7.1 is thus replaced by equation 7.2. Similarly, human capital rises because we save and invest a constant fraction of income s_h and falls as a result of depreciation and the rising work force. (For simplicity, the depreciation rate of human and physical capital is the same, but this is not essential.) This gives us equation 7.3. Both equations together determine how capital accumulates over time.

$$\dot{k} = s_k f(h, k) - (\delta + n)k \tag{7.2}$$

$$\dot{h} = s_h f(h, k) - (\delta + n)h \tag{7.3}$$

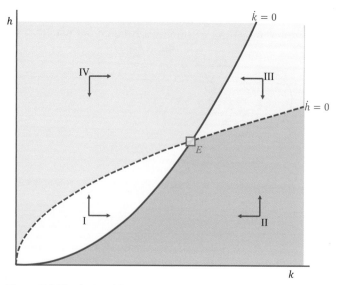

Figure 7.8 Physical and human capital accumulation

Figure 7.8 illustrates the dynamics in physical capital – human capital (k, h)-space.[6] The curve $\dot{k} = 0$ depicts combinations of (k, h) for which the physical capital per worker is not changing. Physical capital rises to the left of this curve and falls to the right of it, as indicated by the horizontal arrows. The curve $\dot{h} = 0$ depicts combinations of (k, h) for which the human capital per worker is not changing. Human capital rises below this curve and falls above it, as indicated by the vertical arrows. Taken together, the two curves divide the (k, h)-space into four different areas, labeled I–IV. Starting from any point on the plane, we will evolve over time to the stationary point E. During this process self-reinforcing dynamics are important: as physical capital accumulates, the marginal product of human capital rises; as human capital accumulates, the marginal product of physical capital rises, and so on. In the end, this approach implies that a larger share of total output is accounted for by accumulable inputs (capital).[7] The distinction between these types of input is not really important.

7.4   Forward-Looking Behavior

Sections 7.2 and 7.3 assume that a constant fraction of income is saved and invested. This is, of course, not true in reality: there are large differences across time for most countries (see Box 7.3). Economic agents (consumers and entrepreneurs) make a *choice* at each point

---

[6] It is based on a simple production function: $y = h^{0.30}k^{0.35}$, with depreciation 10 percent, population growth rate 2 percent, savings for physical capital 30 percent, and savings for human capital 25 percent.

[7] In the example of Figure 7.8, note that 35 percent of output is attributed to physical capital and 30 percent to human capital, so in total 65 percent to accumulable inputs.

in time of how much to save and invest, depending on the expected future returns to savings and investments. Proper economic modeling of this forward-looking behavior by economic agents thus implies dynamic optimization over time (Ramsey 1928) in a framework of uncertainty and expectations formations (Muth 1961). This requires technical analysis beyond the scope of this textbook, but the main issues that are at stake can nonetheless be illustrated in a simple framework.

The framework here is the same as in section 7.2, without exogenous technological change. In a dynamic setting, consumers try to choose their consumption level c optimally at any point in time from now until the indefinite future, to maximize the discounted value of (instantaneous) utility $u(c)$, which depends on their consumption level c at that point in time. Discounting the future at some exogenous rate of time preference $\rho > 0$ reflects the fact that consumers prefer to consume now rather than tomorrow, or it reflects the inherent uncertainty associated with future outcomes. Let $\sigma(c) > 0$ be the intertemporal elasticity of substitution, indicating how difficult it is to substitute consumption now for consumption tomorrow.[8] The crucial equations for the optimization problem are given by:

$$\dot{k} = f(k) - c - (\delta + n)k \qquad\qquad 7.4$$

$$\dot{c}/c = \sigma(c)[f'(k) - (\rho + \delta + n)] \qquad\qquad 7.5$$

Equation 7.4 is essentially the same as equation 7.1; the only difference is that we have replaced i by $f(k) - c$ to highlight the fact that we can choose the consumption level c optimally. Equation 7.5 dictates the dynamic behavior of consumption over time. The most important thing to note is that $\dot{c}/c$ can only be equal to zero if $[f'(k) - (\rho + \delta + n)]$ is equal to zero (since $\sigma(c) > 0$). This holds for a particular level of the capital stock per worker. We denote this by k^{**} as determined by: $f'(k^{**}) = (\rho + \delta + n)$. In other words, the consumption level is constant if, and only if, the marginal product of capital is equal to the sum of the rate of time preference, the depreciation rate, and the population growth rate. This so-called *modified golden rule of accumulation* simply adds the rate of time preference to the earlier condition, such that $k^{**} > k^*$.

The equilibrium dynamics for the economy are illustrated in Figure 7.9. It is constructed by looking at combinations of (k, c) for which $\dot{k} = 0$ and $\dot{c} = 0$. Capital per worker is rising below the $\dot{k} = 0$ curve and falling above it, as indicated by the horizontal arrows. Consumption per worker is rising to the left of the $\dot{c} = 0$ curve and falling to the right of it, as indicated by the vertical arrows. As in Figure 7.8, this divides the plane into four areas, I–IV. This time, however, some arrows point toward the long-run equilibrium at point E where (k, c) is stationary and some arrows point away from it. At first, this may seem to be a problem as it seems unclear how the economy would move over time toward the stationary point. It turns out, however, that forward-looking agents *ensure* that the stationary point is reached over time, as it is part of the necessary conditions for solving the optimization problem.

---

[8] It is defined as: $\sigma(c) = -u'(c)/cu''(c)$.

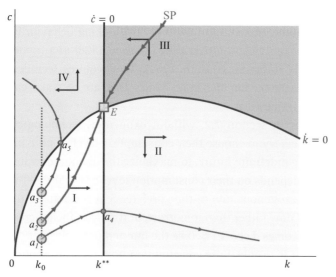

Figure 7.9 Economic growth and forward-looking behavior

Suppose that we are initially *not* at the equilibrium point E, but rather have an initial level of capital per worker k_0 below this equilibrium level: $k_0 < k^*$. We know that the capital stock can only be gradually adjusted over time through investments and depreciation while we can choose optimal consumption at any point in time. This implies that at time 0 the capital stock–consumption level combination must be somewhere along the vertical line given by k_0 in Figure 7.9. We now discuss where on this line the consumption point should be. Figure 7.9 illustrates three possible trajectories out of an infinite number of possibilities to assist us in determining this equilibrium.

- First, suppose that the initial capital stock–consumption level combination is given by point a_1 in the figure. As this point is in area I, we know that the capital stock is increasing, as is the consumption level. The speed at which this occurs is determined by equations 7.4 and 7.5. As we follow the trajectory from point a_1 in Figure 7.9, we note that at some time in the future we reach point a_4 and cross over from area I to area II, such that henceforth the capital stock is increasing and the consumption level is falling. This trajectory moves away from the long-run equilibrium at point E. Instead, we start to consume less as we need to invest more and more resources to increase the capital stock. Asymptotically, we are no longer consuming anything, so this trajectory cannot possibly solve our optimization problem.

- Second, suppose that the initial capital stock–consumption level combination is given by point a_3 in the figure. Again, this point is in area I such that the capital stock and consumption level are both increasing. As we follow the trajectory from point a_3 in Figure 7.9, we note that at some time in the future we reach point a_5 and cross over from area I to area IV, where the consumption level is rising and the capital stock is falling. Again, this trajectory will not lead us to the long-run equilibrium at point E. Instead, it ensures that the capital stock is completely depleted at some time in the future, at which time production becomes zero and consumption must jump to zero too. Such a trajectory also cannot possibly solve our optimum problem.

- Third, suppose that the initial capital stock–consumption level combination is given by point a_2 in the figure, a well-chosen point in between the points a_1 and a_3. It is determined such that all points below a_2 will eventually cross over from area I to area II, while all points above a_2 will eventually cross over from area I to area IV. Point a_2 is therefore very special as the trajectory determined by equations 7.4 and 7.5 does not cross over from area I to area II or from area I to area IV. Instead, the trajectory will lead us on a delicate path to the long-run equilibrium at point E. It is "delicate" because if the initial consumption level is just a little higher or a little lower, the trajectory will lead us in a completely different direction. Such a path is called a saddle path (SP).

The economic agents with forward-looking behavior thus *choose* the right consumption level given by point a_2 in Figure 7.9 to ensure that the long-run equilibrium point is reached. They know that the saddle path leading to this point is the only viable solution. Note that the fact that the saddle path is "delicate" (there is only one solution leading to point E) is actually not a problem, but helps the economic agents to determine the equilibrium. If there were several solutions leading to point E, the agents would have to somehow determine the optimal path or they would have to coordinate their actions in determining which one to pick. This principle of selecting the saddle path which leads to some balanced growth or stationary equilibrium underlies all dynamic optimization models.

7.5 Total Factor Productivity (TFP)

Section 7.2 emphasizes the importance of physical capital accumulation K to explain rising output Y, while section 7.3 emphasizes the importance of human capital accumulation H. The importance of the accumulation of knowledge A to explain rising output per capita has also been emphasized. One simple way to summarize the discussion so far is thus to define output Y as a function of these different inputs: $Y = AF(K, H, L)$. If we have data available on all of these variables, we can also estimate the contribution of the individual components to explain actual economic growth, an exercise known as "growth accounting." If we define the *growth rate* of a variable by a tilde above it (such that $\tilde{Y} = \dot{Y}/Y$, $\tilde{K} = \dot{K}/K$, and so on), we can differentiate the production function above to determine the growth accounting exercise in terms of growth rates:

$$\tilde{Y} = \alpha_K \tilde{K} + \alpha_H \tilde{H} + \alpha_L \tilde{L} + \tilde{A} \qquad 7.6$$

In equation 7.6, the variable α_K is the elasticity of output with respect to capital, defined as the marginal product of physical capital times the amount of capital used, divided by total output (that is, $\alpha_K = (\partial F / \partial K)(K/F)$). Similar definitions hold for α_H and α_L. The term $\alpha_K \tilde{K}$ in equation 7.6 reflects the contribution of the change in physical capital to rising output. In a neoclassical framework of perfect competition the return to capital is equal to its marginal product, in which case α_K is simply the share of output paid for using the input physical capital, and so on. In that case the shares sum to one $(\alpha_K + \alpha_H + \alpha_L = 1)$ and the growth of output is the weighted average of the growth of inputs plus technical change.

In practice, we have reasonably reliable information on the growth of output Y, the contribution of the inputs K, H, and L, and ways to estimate the elasticities. We lack, however, reliable information for measuring the level of knowledge A. The growth accounting exercise now turns equation 7.6 around: rather than using it to explain rising output levels it is used instead to estimate changes in the level of knowledge A, referred to as *Total Factor Productivity* (TFP): $\tilde{A} = \tilde{Y} - \left(\alpha_K \tilde{K} + \alpha_H \tilde{H} + \alpha_L \tilde{L}\right)$.

Table 7.3 provides information on the contribution of different components for explaining economic growth for 120 countries over the period 1990–2014 using data from the Conference Board, a business membership and research association. The data provides estimates of the contribution from the quantity and the quality of labor (similar to our variables L and H) and two types of capital goods (a subdivision into two parts of our variable K), namely ICT capital and nonICT capital.

Table 7.3a shows that the median growth rate of output over the period 1990–2014 is 3.6 percent per year, ranging from a low of 0.7 percent to a high of 10.2 percent. The median growth rate of labor quality is 0.3 percent, of labor quantity is 1.7 percent, of ICT capital is

Table 7.3. Income, inputs, and total factor productivity (percent growth); averages, 1990–2014

	average	median	min	max	count
a. Period-average growth rates					
GDP	3.75	3.63	0.68	10.17	120
Labor quality	0.34	0.30	−0.06	1.37	111
Labor quantity	1.64	1.70	−1.97	7.77	120
ICT capital services	14.35	13.84	1.46	27.90	69
NonICT capital services	3.67	3.41	−1.85	13.10	120
b. Contribution to GDP growth					
Labor quality	0.19	0.16	0.01	0.69	111
Labor quantity	0.71	0.75	−1.45	3.88	120
ICT capital services	0.67	0.58	0.00	2.31	69
NonICT capital services	1.68	1.44	−1.18	7.07	120
c. Total Factor Productivity (TFP) growth; part of GDP growth not explained by input growth					
TFP	0.75	0.49	−2.88	5.43	120

Source: The Conference Board Total Economy Database, May 2015.
Notes: Reported values are country-level averages for the period 1990–2014; min = minimum; max = maximum; count = number of countries; the "average" column for GDP thus reports the average GDP growth rate for 120 countries in the period 1990–2014 (equal to 3.75 percent), and so on for other rows and columns.

13.8 percent, and of nonICT capital is 3.4 percent per year. (Note that the growth rate of output is roughly the same as the growth rate of nonICT capital, which is in line with Kaldor's stylized facts; see section 7.1.) On the basis of this information alone, the contribution from labor quality to economic growth would appear to be lowest and of ICT capital would appear to be highest. This would ignore, however, the importance of the elasticity terms in equation 7.6. ICT capital grows the fastest, but its importance as an input into the production process is still smaller than that of nonICT capital. Table 7.3b gives estimates of the contribution of the four types of input taking the elasticity terms into consideration. From low to high the median values are 0.2 percent for labor quality, 0.6 percent for ICT capital, 0.8 percent for labor quantity, and 1.4 percent for nonICT capital. This implies that nonICT capital explains the largest part of actual economic growth, followed by increases in the quantity of labor.

The part of economic growth that is left unexplained by rising quality or quantity of inputs is used to estimate changes in total factor productivity in panel c of Table 7.3. The median value is about 0.5 percent and the average value about 0.75 percent of economic growth. The lowest TFP estimate is –2.9 percent (for Senegal) and the highest is 5.4 percent (for Armenia). The average and median contribution of the different components to explain economic growth is shown in Figure 7.10 for the 69 countries for which all relevant information is available, including ICT capital information. As explained in Box 7.2, total factor productivity estimates tend to fall if more detailed information on the quantity and quality of inputs becomes available. For the countries in Figure 7.10, the median growth rate is 2.9 percent. The contribution of labor quality to economic growth remains the lowest (0.2 percent) and the contribution of nonICT capital remains the highest (1.2 percent). The contribution of labor quantity and ICT capital is now about equally important (around 0.6 percent). The contribution of TFP to economic growth is about 0.2 percent. The average values are a little higher, but the picture remains the same.

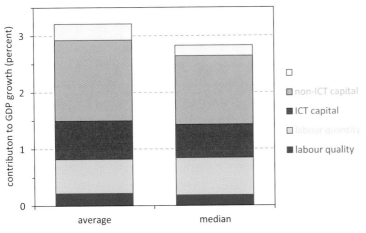

Figure 7.10 Decomposition of economic growth, 1990–2014
Source: See Table 7.3.
Note: Only 69 countries with complete information are included.

BOX 7.2 AVAILABLE INFORMATION AND TFP ESTIMATES

Table 7.3 provides total factor productivity (TFP) summary statistics for 120 countries, while Figure 7.10 provides a decomposition of the contribution to economic growth for the four different types of input and TFP for 69 rather than 120 countries. The reason for doing this for a smaller group of countries only is that care needs to be taken in drawing conclusions regarding TFP if limited information is available. By construction, TFP is measured as a residual: it is the part of output growth that cannot be explained from a rise in input quantity or quality. (Indeed, before the term TFP became popular, this estimate used to be called the "Solow residual.") If limited information is available regarding these inputs, the missing information is thus automatically allocated to TFP changes, thereby tending to overestimate the contribution of TFP.

This tendency to overestimate TFP if limited information is available is illustrated in Table 7.4. The table identifies three groups of countries. The first group consists of 69 countries for which all information on the four inputs is available (labor quality, labor quantity, ICT capital, and nonICT capital). For this group of countries the average share of economic growth that is "explained" by TFP is a modest 8.9 percent and the median is 6.4 percent. The second group consists of 42 countries for which no ICT capital information is available. For this group of countries, the share of economic growth that is attributed to TFP is a substantial one-third of total output growth. The rather small third group consists of nine countries for which no information on ICT capital and no information on labor quality is available. For this group of countries the share of economic growth that is attributed to TFP is about one-quarter or one-fifth. Compared to the group of countries with complete information on all inputs available, the TFP estimates are substantially higher for both the second and the third groups.

Table 7.4. Available information, TFP estimates, and contribution to growth, 1990–2014

Country group	TFP estimate percent per year		TFP contribution to growth, % total	
	average	median	average	median
69 all input information	0.29	0.19	8.9	6.4
42 no ICT capital info	1.44	1.29	34.5	30.7
9 no labor quality or ICT capital info	0.99	1.36	17.4	25.9

Source: See Table 7.3.

7.6   Accumulability, Rivalness, and Excludability

Section 7.5 shows that nonICT *capital accumulation* is the most important component for rising output, since it explains about 42 percent of output growth (see Figure 7.10). As

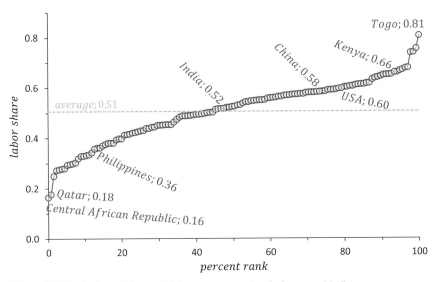

Figure 7.11 Ordering of share of labor compensation in income, 2017
Source: Created using PWT 9.1.
Notes: Data for 2017; simple average; 136 countries.

such, the neoclassical focus on capital accumulation is understandable. However, this can also be viewed from a different perspective: the sum of the *other* components is even more important! Recall that these components are labor quantity, labor quality, ICT capital, and TFP. It is possible to argue that this is the *human* component of the contribution to output growth, which as a whole is thus more important than capital accumulation. (ICT capital is included as it largely consists of software written by humans. There may also be a human component in capital accumulation arising from poorly measured improvements in quality.) Since both components must be compensated for their contribution somehow, a crude indication of their relative importance for a specific country is to analyze the share of labor compensation in total income (see Figure 7.11).

The average share of labor compensation in income is about 51 percent, close to the level of India. There is substantial variation between the countries, ranging from a low of 16 percent in the Central African Republic and 18 percent in Qatar to a high of 81 percent in Togo. The Philippines is below this average, while large countries like India, China, and the USA are above the average. There is, however, considerable variation across per capita income levels, as shown for developing countries by Central African Republic, Kenya, and Togo in Figure 7.11. In fact, a figure with the logarithm of income per capita on the one axis and the share of labor compensation on the other axis shows that there is virtually *no* relationship between these two variables. To understand why this is the case, it is useful to distinguish between the three main types of sectors that together comprise the economy, namely agriculture, services, and industry. It turns out that (see Chapter 15):

- The share of agriculture in total output *falls* if per capita income rises.
- The share of services in total output *rises* if per capita income rises.

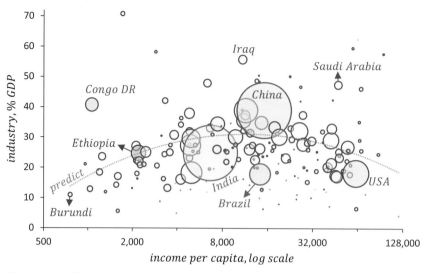

Figure 7.12 Industry and income per capita, 2019
Source: Created using World Development Indicators online data.
Notes: Income per capita is GNI PPP in constant 2017 $ (2019 or most recent); industry (including construction) value-added as percent of GDP (2019 or most recent); bubbles proportional to population (2019); 182 countries included; predict is based on population-weighted quadratic regression using log income.

Industry activity is basically the residual of these two main trends; its share tends to be small both at low levels of income per capita (because most people work in agriculture) and at high levels of income per capita (because most people work in services). This suggests that there is a tendency for industry activity to peak at intermediate income levels. As Figure 7.12 illustrates, this is true to some extent. For example, the share of industry in total output is low for Burundi (11 percent), substantially larger for Ethiopia and India (25 percent), and even larger for China (39 percent), but then declines and is much lower for the USA (18 percent). As Figure 7.12 shows, the effect is not so strong if all countries in the world are considered and the variation is substantial. Since industrial activity tends to be relatively capital intensive, such that the share of labor compensation is low if the share of manufacturing activity is high, this partially explains why there is no overall relationship between income per capita and the share of labor compensation in income.[9]

Before section 7.7 analyzes the importance of the human component in continued economic growth through knowledge creation, the current section discusses three important characteristics of inputs, namely *accumulability*, *rivalness*, and *excludability* (see Romer 1990).

An input is *accumulable* if its value can potentially increase without bound. This holds, for example, for the (economic) value of the capital stock. (The physical amount of the capital stock may be limited. Its economic value in the production process is not.) The labor force, interpreted as the number of people at work, has been increasing for thousands of years. Nonetheless, given the finite space available on Earth (and ignoring extraterrestrial

---

[9] The correlation between the labor share in income and the industry share in GDP is −0.50 in 2019 for the 129 countries with data on both variables.

BOX 7.3 GROSS SAVINGS RATES

In order for an economy to grow fast it has to invest intensively in order to accumulate physical capital (section 7.2), accumulate human capital (section 7.3), or improve technology (sections 7.5–7.7). All these investments require access to savings in order to make them possible. The International Monetary Fund (2015) provides statistical information on the gross savings rate as a percentage of income for all years in the period 1980–2014 for 136 different countries. (There is additional information for 37 other countries for part of this period.) The average savings rate for these countries is about 20 percent of income. There is, however, considerable variation across countries and over time (in contrast to Kaldor's stylized fact in section 7.1; see Figure 7.13).

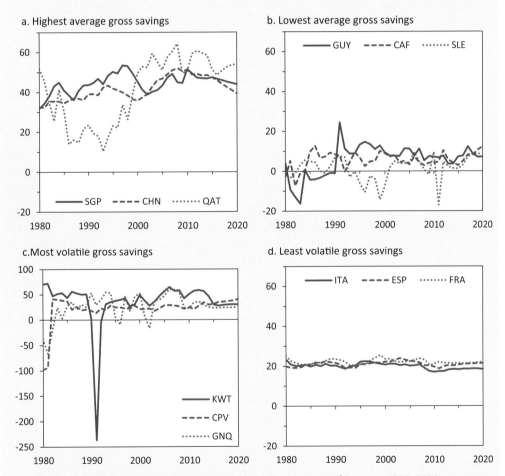

Figure 7.13 Gross savings rates; high, low, and volatility, percent of income, 1980–2020
Source: Data from IMF 2015.
Notes: Data for 2015–2020 are estimates; volatility measured by standard deviation; SGP = Singapore; CHN = China; QAT = Qatar; GUY = Guyana; CAF = Central African Republic; SLE = Sierra Leone; KWT = Kuwait; CPV = Cape Verde; GNQ = Equatorial Guinea; ITA = Italy; ESP = Spain; FRA = France; note that the vertical scale is different for panel c.

BOX 7.3 (cont.)

The three countries with the highest average savings rates (around 40 percent of income) are Singapore, China, and Qatar (see panel a). This has been consistently high for rapidly developing Singapore and China. It is much more volatile for Qatar, which depends on the fluctuating oil price for its main source of revenue. The three countries with the lowest average savings rates (around 5 percent of income or less) are Guyana, Central African Republic, and Sierra Leone (panel b). All three are developing countries. The three countries with the most volatile gross savings rates (measured by the standard deviation) are Kuwait, Cape Verde, and Equatorial Guinea (panel c). Note that the vertical scale of this panel differs from that of the other three panels in order to accommodate the enormous fluctuations, in particular associated with the Gulf War after the Iraq invasion in 1990. The three countries with the most stable gross savings (around 21 percent of income) are the European countries Italy, Spain, and France.

possibilities), the labor force cannot continue to rise forever. It is therefore ultimately nonaccumulable. Analyzing in per capita terms, the labor force is already fixed at one. The production value of a worker may, of course, rise indefinitely if she is working with ever-rising amounts of capital or ever-more available knowledge. Section 7.3 discussed the importance of human capital, focusing on the level of schooling for workers in order to be able to work with new knowledge and more complex capital goods. In that section, human capital was essentially treated the same as physical capital and could accumulate indefinitely. Paul Romer, however, convincingly points out that human capital is incorporated in a person and that this person cannot pass on that human capital to someone else when she dies. Ultimately, therefore, human capital is *not* accumulable.

An input is a *rival* good if only one person can use it at a given point in time. I can work on a computer, and so can you. But we cannot work on the same computer at the same time. A computer is therefore a rival good, as is a desk, a chair, a copy machine, and so on. In principle, labor and capital are rival inputs. Knowledge, however, is special as it is in general a nonrival good. I can apply the principles of addition, subtraction, or double-entry bookkeeping at the same time as you can. And we can do this in different sectors.

An input is *excludable* if the owner can prevent others from using it. Most rival goods are excludable. Most knowledge, such as a newly invented intermediate good, is partially excludable. You may try to keep your design a secret or the patent office grants you exclusive rights to your new invention for a number of years. Eventually, however, others may benefit from the new knowledge you created because the secret is leaked or the patent runs out. The creation of knowledge thus usually leads to knowledge spillovers that are valuable to other people.

On the basis of the rivalness and accumulability characteristics, it is possible to identify three major types of input for the analysis in section 7.7 (see van Marrewijk 1999):[10]

- Rival, not accumulable inputs, such as *labor L* (or human capital).
- Rival, accumulable inputs, such as *capital K*.
- Nonrival, accumulable inputs, such as *knowledge A*.

7.7 Knowledge and Endogenous Growth

To explain rising levels of output and capital per worker, section 7.2 introduced *exogenous* technical change. As a result, the growth rate of output per worker is g because we assumed it to be g. This is, of course, not satisfactory because technical change, the development of new goods and services, and the creation of new knowledge is the outcome of costly and risky investment decisions by firms, governments, and individuals. All these investment decisions taken together must somehow determine the growth rate of knowledge (and the economy). The objective of the endogenous growth literature is to explain this growth rate within the framework of the model itself, rather than imposing it exogenously. There are important contributions regarding the invention of new varieties of goods (Romer 1990), the introduction of quality improvements (Aghion and Howitt 1992), and an integration of both approaches (Grossman and Helpman 1991). For simplicity, this section focuses on the variety approach.

Paul Romer starts by pointing out that on the basis of two of his stylized facts (see section 7.1), namely nonrivalness of knowledge (fact 2) and a replication argument (fact 3), there *must* be increasing returns to scale in the aggregate. This gives rise to imperfect competition (fact 5), although to a limited extent as there are many firms in a market economy (fact 1). Since accumulating knowledge, testing and developing new products, and achieving scientific breakthroughs is costly and takes a lot of effort from talented individuals (fact 4), he argues that a proper model of economic growth should allow these efforts to be determined and remunerated within the model.

Romer identifies three sectors: (i) a perfectly competitive final goods sector; (ii) an intermediate goods sector with monopolistic competition; and (iii) a research and development (R&D) sector for inventing new varieties of intermediate goods. There is free entry in the R&D sector to ensure that the expected return is equal to the expected revenue. The development of a new variety is equivalent to the creation of new knowledge A. Entrepreneurs can recover the costly development of a new variety by using their market power in the intermediate goods market to earn positive operating profits. A slightly simplified version of the model can be summarized in equations 7.7 and 7.8, where the intermediate goods sector is represented by the capital stock K.

---

[10] The fourth possibility (nonrival and not accumulable) can be trivially included.

$$Y = F(L_Y)A^a K_Y^{1-a} = C + \dot{K} \qquad\qquad 7.7$$

$$\dot{A} = R(L_A)A \qquad\qquad 7.8$$

There are three inputs: a rival and nonaccumulable input labor L (which is taken as constant), a rival and accumulable input capital K, and a nonrival and accumulable input knowledge A. There are two production functions: one for output Y and one for new knowledge $\dot{A}$. For the rival inputs L and K there is a subindex Y or A to indicate in which sector this input is used. There is no subindex for the nonrival input A since the same knowledge can be used *simultaneously* in both sectors. If we use certain knowledge in the output sector we can still use the same knowledge in the R&D sector. It is, after all, a nonrival input.

The production function for output uses labor, capital, and knowledge as inputs. Output can be consumed or added to the capital stock. The production function in the R&D sector is special in two ways. First, it does not use capital as an input, only labor and knowledge. We thus have: $K_Y = K$. Second, the nonexcludable part of new knowledge leads to knowledge spillovers in the R&D sector. Entrepreneurs only pay for the use of labor in R&D, and this labor becomes more productive as A rises. As a result of these assumptions, only the allocation of labor across the two sectors is relevant (since capital is only used in the final goods sector and knowledge is nonrival): $L_Y + L_A = L$. This allocation depends, of course, on the return to labor in the two sectors. Note that for a given level of labor the growth rate of knowledge is constant ($\tilde{Y} = R(L_A)$, because of the imposed knowledge spillovers and constant returns to scale for the accumulable factor A). If we impose $\tilde{Y} = \tilde{K}$ (Kaldor's stylized fact 4), it follows easily from equation 7.7 that the growth rate of output is equal to the growth rate of knowledge ($\tilde{Y} = \tilde{A}$ because of constant returns to scale to the accumulable factors A and K). The growth rate is thus determined endogenously within the model based on the investment decisions of entrepreneurs who use their monopoly power in the intermediate goods market to cover the R&D costs. The process is self-sustaining as a result of constant returns to scale knowledge spillovers in the R&D sector. The decentralized economy is not socially optimal since the entrepreneurs do not take these spillovers into consideration when making their investment decisions (the economy grows too slowly and the government should stimulate innovation).

Some of the restrictions on the production functions imposed in the Romer model are not necessary. We can allow for a framework where the rival inputs labor and capital are used in all sectors: to produce output, intermediate goods, and R&D (van Marrewijk 1999). Such a setting allows for a nontrivial role for both (neoclassical) capital accumulation and (endogenous growth) knowledge spillovers. In this framework capital accumulation and innovation are complementary processes, neither of which would take place in the long run without the other. The restrictions needed to make this work are intuitive. There must be constant returns to scale to accumulable factors (A and K) for both output and R&D and there must be labor-augmenting knowledge spillovers in the intermediate goods sector and the R&D sector.

7.8   Dupuit Triangles and the Costs of Trade Restrictions

It appears that the first analysis of the value of a new good to society, that is the first attempt to try to measure the value of something that does not yet exist, was provided by the French engineer Jules Dupuit in 1844. As head of an engineering district, he was responsible for building roads, bridges, and canals. He was therefore interested in developing practical rules for determining if a specific project should be built, for which he described a demand curve and a revenue curve, which allowed him to identify an important problem associated with the introduction of new goods.

The main issue is illustrated in Figure 7.14, depicting a downward-sloping demand curve for a good, say a bridge, that has not yet been introduced. The vertical axis represents the price to be paid each time the bridge is crossed. If the price is too high (above p_{max}), nobody will use the bridge. If the price is zero, the bridge will be used most intensively at q_{max}. According to standard microeconomic theory, the area under the demand curve measures the value of the bridge to the consumers at any given quantity. At a price of 0, for example, the total value of the bridge to consumers is equal to the triangle area $0q_{max}p_{max}$.

Suppose that a private company is interested in building this bridge, and evaluates whether or not it is worthwhile to go ahead with the project. In Figure 7.14, we assume that the firm charges price p, resulting in q crossings of the bridge and total revenue pq, equal to the area $0pAq$. How the firm determines the price p it charges for one crossing of the bridge is immaterial for our argument. What is important is the fact that the total area under the demand curve at q, that is the area $0p_{max}Aq$, is strictly larger than the revenue generated by the firm from the crossings of the bridge, the area $0pAq$. The difference between the value to consumers and the revenue for the firm, that is the triangle $p_{max}Ap$, represents a welfare gain for which the firm building the bridge is not compensated in terms of revenue. If the firm decides that the total revenue generated by the bridge is not enough to compensate it

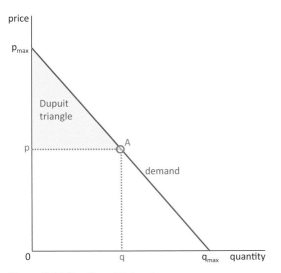

Figure 7.14 The Dupuit triangle

for the costs of building and maintaining the bridge, it will decide not to build the bridge. Romer calls the area $p_{max}Ap$ the Dupuit triangle and argues that it is equal to the welfare loss to society of not building the bridge (see Romer 1994).

In general, the above reasoning shows that there are costs involved, in terms of a welfare loss to society as a whole, of *not* introducing a good on the market. The Dupuit triangle can be interpreted as a measure for this welfare loss. (Actually, the Dupuit triangle probably overestimates this loss. If the bridge is not built, an alternative means of crossing the river, such as a ferry, will be viable. The ferry will have a similar Dupuit triangle which mitigates the welfare loss of not building the bridge.) Moreover, it is evident that market forces can't be relied on to ensure that all new goods that are valuable to society will actually be introduced, because the firm introducing a new good can only appropriate part of the surplus it generates. (Price discrimination cannot solve this problem; see Romer 1994.) Romer continues by pointing out that one of the most important consequences of imposing trade restrictions is the fact that they might lead to new goods and services not being available on the market. He illustrates his argument for a small developing economy, say Developia, which does not invent its own capital goods. Instead, those intermediate capital goods and services are invented abroad. After a successful innovation, the foreign inventors face the decision whether or not to introduce the intermediate good on Developia's market, which gives them an operating profit as the price they charge will be higher than the marginal costs of production and transport. They will only introduce the new intermediate good on Developia's market if the operating profits are higher than the fixed costs of introduction, say for setting up a local consulting office. This criterion determines the number of varieties introduced on the market. Romer discusses the impact of "expected" versus "unexpected" tariffs for Developia's market. This approach has been extended to a dynamic setting by van Marrewijk and Berden (2007).

Suppose the government of Developia imposes an ad valorem tariff T on the purchases of all foreign goods. This section discusses the consequences of the welfare loss (measured as the percentage reduction in output relative to the output level without tariffs) for a specific numerical example (see Figure 7.15). The *static costs* of this policy assumes that all capital goods continue to be introduced on the market; this leads to a welfare loss of 8 percent if the tariff level is 10 percent. The *maximum costs* of this policy assumes that all inventors at any point in time already know that this policy will be imposed (also into the indefinite past) and thus maximizes the number of goods not introduced on the market; this leads to a welfare loss of 50 percent if the tariff level is 10 percent. The *dynamic costs* of this policy assumes that inventors are completely taken by surprise at the time the policy is introduced, hence only a range of newly developed goods will not be introduced on the market; this leads to a welfare loss of 25 percent if the tariff level is 10 percent. The important thing to remember is that the true costs of trade restrictions should include the dynamic costs of trade restrictions (goods not introduced on the market), which are much larger than the static costs of trade restrictions. Moreover, these costs rise rapidly if trade restrictions increase. If the tariff level is 20 percent, the dynamic costs already amount to a welfare loss of 45 percent (rather than the static costs of 17 percent). Section 7.9 incorporates a case study of these costs.

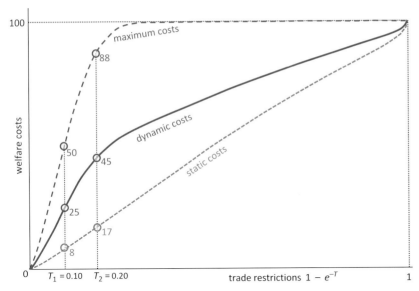

Figure 7.15 Dynamic costs of trade restrictions
Source: van Marrewijk and Berden 2007.

7.9 China: A Case Study

The main difficulty of calculating the dynamic costs of trade restrictions as explained in section 7.8 is the fact that even if you think that these costs are important it is almost impossible to estimate their size. How do you estimate the size of the welfare loss as a result of goods and services that are not introduced using a generally accepted methodology? It is virtually impossible. However, circumstantial evidence that the dynamic costs are important can be provided. An example is the difference in economic development between North Korea and South Korea after the Korean ceasefire in 1953. North Korea isolated itself economically from virtually all outside influences, thus not benefiting from the knowledge increases and inventions of new goods and services in the rest of the world. The result was a stagnant, or slowly deteriorating, North Korean economy for more than five decades, eventually resulting in large famines. The developments in North Korea contrast sharply with those in South Korea, which focused aggressively on expansion on the world market, using knowledge and capital goods from all over the world. Unfortunately, lack of reliable data on the North Korean economy prevents the provision of further detail here.[11] Instead, this section will briefly focus attention on the developments in mainland China.

---

[11] Similar examples of neighbors with different openness of economic systems, and corresponding differences in economic development, are: East versus West Germany, and Thailand versus Myanmar.

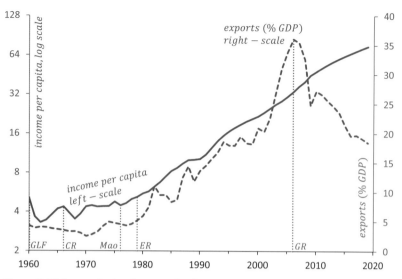

Figure 7.16 Economic development in China, 1960–2019
Source: Created using World Development Indicators online.
Notes: Income per capita is GDP in constant 2010 USD (relative to world average of that year in percent); exports of goods and services as percent of GDP; GLF = Great Leap Forward; CR = Cultural Revolution; Mao = Mao's death; ER = Economic Reform; GR = Great Recession.

China is a large country with an impressive cultural, economic, and military history dating back thousands of years. According to recent estimates, there are about 1.4 billion Chinese inhabitants. Since we want to gauge the importance of international trade and capital flows, and openness to the outside world, even for such a large country as China, economic development in China relative to the outside world will be measured. To this end, Figure 7.16 depicts China's income per capita as a percentage of world average income per capita in any given year.

In 1949, Mao Zedong proclaimed the founding of the People's Republic of China and installed a new political and economic order modeled on the Soviet example. In 1958, Mao broke with the Soviet model and started a new economic program called the *Great Leap Forward*. Its aim was to raise industrial and agricultural production by forming large cooperatives and building "backyard factories." The results of the market disruption and poor planning, leading to the production of unsaleable goods, were disastrous. Within a year, starvation appeared even in fertile agricultural areas, resulting in the *Great Famine* from 1959 to 1961. The relationship with the Soviet Union deteriorated sharply, leading to the restriction of the flow of scientific and technological information to China, and the withdrawal of all Soviet personnel in 1960. When compared to the world average, the impact of the Great Leap Forward is shown in Figure 7.16 as a deterioration of China's living standards from an already low 5.12 percent in 1960 to an even lower 3.30 percent in 1962 (a relative decline of 36 percent!).

In the early 1960s, Liu Shaoqi and his protégé Deng Xiaoping took over direction of the party and adopted pragmatic economic policies at odds with Mao's revolutionary vision.

In 1966, when the Chinese economy had almost recuperated from the consequences of the Great Leap Forward and Chinese per capita GNP had bounced back to 4.37 percent of the world average, Mao started the *Cultural Revolution*, a political attack on the pragmatists who were dragging China back toward capitalism. The Red Guards, radical youth organizations, attacked party and state organizations at all levels. Again, Mao's insightful ideas were disastrous to the Chinese standard of living, which dropped to 3.51 percent of the world average in 1968 (this time a relative decline of "only" 20 percent). The Chinese political situation stabilized after some years along complex factional lines, resulting in living standards of around 4.5 percent of the world average. Deng Xiaoping was reinstated in 1975, but he was then stripped of all official positions one year later by the Gang of Four (Mao's wife and three associates).

Mao's death in September 1976 set off a scramble for succession, leading to the arrest of the Gang of Four and the reinstatement of Deng Xiaoping in August 1977. In a pivotal meeting in December 1978, the new leadership adopted *Economic Reform* policies to expand rural incentives, encourage enterprise autonomy, reduce central planning, open up to international trade flows with the outside world, establish foreign direct investment in China, and pass new legal codes in June 1979. The positive consequences of the economic reforms, which were continued with some interruptions by successive governments, for the Chinese standard of living were enormous, dramatically illustrating the dynamic costs of trade restrictions. In relative terms, income per capita in China increased 15-fold in 41 years, from 5 percent of the world average in 1978 to 74.6 percent in 2019. A monumental achievement indeed, with enormous consequences for more than a billion people.

The policy of openness is illustrated in Figure 7.16 by exports relative to income, which rose from 4.6 percent in 1978 to 36 percent in 2006. Remember that this is a sharply increasing share of a rapidly rising income level. These trade flows have been vital for Chinese development. Relative exports declined once the *Great Recession* started in 2007 (to 18.4 percent in 2019), but this has not slowed down Chinese development. Apparently, China was rather successful in its transition process to the next stages of economic development, such that it can also rely on domestic factors for continued economic growth.

Another indicator of the policy of openness is provided by the foreign direct investment (FDI) flows relative to income in Figure 7.17. There are no data available before 1980, but it is certain that FDI flows were virtually absent before that time. After the economic reforms, FDI into China rose rapidly from 0.03 percent of income in 1980 to a peak of 6.2 percent in 1993. Inflows remained high until 2010 (when they were 4 percent of income). Associated with these investments is an enormous transfer of knowledge by multinational firms. Inflows have fallen substantially since 2010 to reach 1.1 percent in 2019. China is now also increasingly active as an investor in the rest of the world. FDI outflows increased from about 0.24 percent of income in 1996 to a peak of 1.9 percent in 2016. In short, the more decentralized and outward-oriented economic

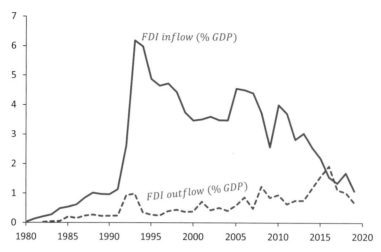

Figure 7.17 China; FDI inflows and outflows (% of GDP), 1980–2019
Source: Created using World Development Indicators online data.
Notes: FDI = foreign direct investment; net inflows and net outflows as percent of GDP.

policies that started around 1980 have been enormously important for China's economic development.

7.10   Conclusions

Many issues play a role in determining a country's level of economic development. The main issues at stake are summarized in Chapter 1 on the basis of the Global Competitiveness Report. Many of these issues are discussed in more detail in other chapters. This chapter has focused on the main theories of economic growth. First, it stressed the importance of investing in (physical and human) capital accumulation for maintaining economic growth and explained how economic agents make forward-looking decisions. A disadvantage of this approach is that *exogenous* technical change has to be imposed in order to keep the economy growing on a per capita basis. Second, the chapter outlined the important role of innovation and firms with market power which invest in R&D, as well as the role of knowledge spillovers for explaining total factor productivity and per capita economic growth *endogenously*, discussing the terms accumulability, rivalness, and excludability, which are important for modeling the structure of the economy and firm behavior. Capital accumulation and innovation are complementary processes, neither of which would take place in the long run without the other. Third, the chapter discussed the role of openness by evaluating the dynamic costs of trade restrictions using Dupuit triangles, illustrated with a case study for China. The Global Competitiveness Report (discussed in Chapter 1) emphasizes the role of basic requirements as a foundation for economic growth in its first four pillars. The first pillar is *Institutions*, which will be discussed in Chapter 8 in more detail.

Further Reading

. . . .

Classic contributions in the field of economic growth are Robert Solow (1956), Frank Ramsey (1928), and Paul Romer (1990). The work of Solow and Romer (with William Nordhaus) is clarified on the Nobel Prize website. See: www.nobelprize.org/prizes/economic-sciences/1987/summary/ and www .nobelprize.org/prizes/economic-sciences/2018/summary/.

For an explanation on the link between innovation (a driver of growth) and globalization, see: Akcigit, U. and M. Melitz. 2022. "International Trade and Innovation," in G. Gopinath, E. Helpman, and K. Rogoff (eds.), *Handbook of International Economics: International Trade* (Amsterdam: Elsevier), vol. 5. This chapter provides a state-of-the-art survey of the recent literature and is a good starting point for further research.

For readers who are not afraid of a solid mathematical treatment, see: Acemoglu, D. 2009. *Modern Economic Growth* (Princeton University Press).

8 Institutions and Contracts

8.1 Introduction

According to Nobel Prize laureate Douglass North (1990, p. 3): "Institutions are the rules of the game in a society or, more formally, are the humanly devised constraints that shape human interaction." The definition emphasizes that the "rules of the game" are devised by humans (so we can control them), that they impose constraints on our behavior, and that they provide incentives for human interaction. It is immediately clear that this definition of institutions is broad, can be applied to many different types of rules, regulations, or customs, and includes contracts, and through their impact on economic incentives must be important for economic development (see sections 8.4–8.8). It should also be clear that the wide applicability of institutions as the rules of the game does not allow us to study it in depth in one brief chapter. Codified law, for example, is certainly only a small part of institutions and it takes law students many years of detailed study to know and better understand this small part. Evidently, this chapter only touches the surface here.

Even if attention is restricted to only the most important "economic" aspects of institutions, the field is huge, enormously fruitful, and has been developing rapidly. The best way to illustrate this is by pointing out that in the most recent three decades (the period 1990–2019) no fewer than 8 of the 30 Nobel Prizes awarded in economics are related to institutions and contracts (see Table 8.1). This illustrates that institutions and contracts play a crucial role in different fields of economics, analyzing issues like institutional structure, property rights, history, quantitative methods, institutional change, economic incentives, asymmetric information, economic governance, the commons, the boundaries of the firm, search frictions, market power, regulation, and contract theory. Clearly, this chapter does not have sufficient room to cover all these issues adequately. So what *can* it cover?

The chapter starts with the two key contributions of Nobel laureate Ronald Coase regarding the nature of the firm (Coase 1937) in section 8.2 and the problem of social cost and property rights (Coase 1960) in section 8.3. Section 8.4 continues with a general discussion of the links between institutions and economic development, based on the *World Development Report* (World Bank 2002). To provide some measures of the quality of specific types of institutions, section 8.5 discusses the (inverse) World Press Freedom Index and section 8.6 discusses the Economic Freedom Index and its components. Section 8.7 analyzes the connections between the Economic Freedom Index type of institutions and the level of income per capita, as well as its growth rate. Section 8.8 provides a deeper

Table 8.1. Recent Economics Nobel laureates for Institutions and Contracts

Year	Recipients	Excerpts from press release statements
1991	Ronald Coase	"for his discovery and clarification of the significance of transaction costs and property rights for the institutional structure and functioning of the economy"
1993	Robert Fogel Douglass North	"for having renewed research in economic history by applying economic theory and quantitative methods in order to explain economic and institutional change"
1996	James Mirrlees William Vickrey	"for their fundamental contributions to the economic theory of incentives under asymmetric information"
2001	George Akerlof Michael Spence Joseph Stiglitz	"for their analyses of markets with asymmetric information"
2009	Elinor Ostrom	"for her analysis of economic governance, especially the commons"
	Oliver Williamson	"for his analysis of economic governance, especially the boundaries of the firm"
2010	Peter Diamond Dale Mortensen Christopher Pissarides	"for their analysis of markets with search frictions"
2014	Jean Tirole	"for his analysis of market power and regulation"
2016	Oliver Hart Bengt Holmström	"for their contributions to contract theory"

Source: www.nobelprize.org/.
Note: Period 1990–2019.

discussion of these connections based on the work of Glaeser *et al.* (2004). This analysis returns to the Reversal of Fortune discussion of Chapter 4 (see section 8.8) and attempts to answer the question: do institutions cause growth? The answer is in line with the empirical findings in section 8.7 and the analysis in Chapter 4, as summarized in section 8.9.

8.2   The Nature of the Firm

Coase (1937) analyzes the nature of the firm. He observes that production is directed outside the firm by price movements through exchange transactions on markets. Within the firm, however, production is directed by the entrepreneur-coordinator as market transactions are eliminated. Coase wonders why coordination is the work of prices in one case and of entrepreneurs in the other case. In essence, this raises the question of why firms exist at all. A related question is what determines the size of a firm.

Coase's main argument is straightforward (1937, pp. 390–1). Firms exist because there are *transaction costs* associated with using the price mechanism, which includes the cost of organizing production by discovering what the relevant prices are. In some cases, these costs may be lowered by specialized agents, but they cannot be eliminated. Moreover, it is necessary to take into account the costs of negotiating and writing a separate contract for each market transaction. Again, standardization is possible in some cases to lower these costs, but they cannot be eliminated.

The owners of factors of production cooperating within a firm do not have to make a series of contracts, but use only one contract. The nature of this "open" agreement is that for a certain reward the owner of a factor of production follows the instructions of the entrepreneur within certain limits. Within these limits the entrepreneur can direct the factors of production. In general, these contracts are for the longer term, where the exact details are determined at a later stage within the limits provided. This is what Coase calls a *firm*, which is "a system of relationships which comes into existence when the direction of resources is dependent on an entrepreneur" (1937, p. 393). A firm thus essentially lowers transaction costs and is more likely to arise if short-term contracts are not satisfactory, as is the case for labor services. Note that firms will not arise without transaction costs.

As firms get larger there may be decreasing returns to entrepreneurship, which implies rising costs of organizing transactions within the firm. The size of firm is then simply determined by the point where "the costs of organising an extra transaction within the firm are equal to the costs involved in carrying out the transaction in the open market, or, to the costs of organising by another entrepreneur" (Coase 1937, p. 394). This work created an incentive to analyze the type of contract structure which characterizes firms, the associated distribution of rights and obligations (property rights, see section 8.3), and research on principal–agent relationships.

8.3   Social Cost and Property Rights

Building on the analysis of the nature of the firm discussed in section 8.2, Coase (1960) analyzes the next step in discussing the institutional structure of the economic system. His main method is to discuss details of specific examples of externalities and then draw general conclusions based on this knowledge. One example is of a farmer whose cattle stray onto the cropland of his neighbor, thus causing damage to the crops. Coase argues that the traditional view is that since the farmer inflicts harm on the neighbor, we have to decide how to restrict the farmer. He points out that this is wrong because of the reciprocal nature of the problem. Instead, we should ask ourselves: is the farmer allowed to harm the neighbor or is the neighbor allowed to harm the farmer? It appears at first sight that in the first case we have more meat and less crops, while in the second case we have more crops and less meat. This turns out to be wrong under certain conditions. In any case, from an efficiency point of view, the answer should depend on the value of meat versus crops and other circumstances. Suppose, for example, that the construction of a fence is cheaper than the loss in the value of crops from straying cattle. The efficient outcome is then to construct a fence.

Coase continues to argue for his examples, that if the property rights are well-defined and there are no transaction costs at all, the economically efficient outcome will be reached through bargaining, independent of the distribution of property rights. For the cattle stray example: the neighbor will pay for the fence if the farmer is allowed to harm the neighbor, while the farmer will pay for the fence if the opposite holds. In both cases, the efficient outcome is reached, although the distribution of property rights does, of course, affect the distribution of income and wealth. This is summarized below.[1]

Coase Theorem

If property rights are well-defined and there are no transaction costs at all, voluntary negotiations between economic agents will lead to an efficient outcome. The outcome is independent of the distribution of property rights, but will affect the distribution of income and wealth.

Nobel laureate George Stigler apparently coined the phrase Coase Theorem, but Ronald Coase himself seems to have become frustrated by its use for two main reasons (see also below). First, he emphasized the importance of transaction costs, not their absence. As a consequence, the economic outcome is usually not efficient and the allocation of property rights is important. Second, since transaction costs lead to inefficient outcomes, the role of the government by creating a proper institutional framework is important, but its knowledge and power should not be overestimated.

Regarding the first reason above, Coase points out that market transactions are, in fact, costly (as he did in the "nature of the firm" discussion in section 8.2). Once these costs are taken into account, a rearrangement of property rights will only be undertaken if the increase in value is greater than the costs involved. As a consequence (Coase 1960, p. 16, emphasis added):

> In these conditions the initial delimitation of legal rights *does* have an effect on the efficiency with which the economic system operates. One arrangement of rights may bring about a greater value of production than any other. But unless this is the arrangement of rights established by the legal system, the costs of reaching the same result by altering and combining rights through the market may be so great that this optimal arrangement of rights, and the greater value of production which it would bring, may *never* be achieved.

Regarding the second reason above, although Coase has now argued that there is room for beneficial government intervention, he points out both the advantages and disadvantages of the government and repeatedly mentions its fallibility and costs (Coase 1960, pp. 17–18):

> The government is, in a sense, a super-firm ... able, if it wishes, to avoid the market altogether, which a firm can never do ... It is clear that the government has powers which might enable it to get some things done at a lower cost than could a private organisation ... But the governmental administrative regime is not itself costless ... there is no reason to suppose that the ... regulations, made by a fallible administration subject to political pressures and operating without any competitive check, will necessarily always ... increase the efficiency with which the economic system operates.

---

[1] The main text uses the common terminology in the literature, although the use of the word "theorem" is problematic under these circumstances. Perhaps the term *Coase Claim* would be more appropriate.

After discussing how the distribution of property rights in certain examples might affect the economic outcome and how the government, depending on the conditions, might improve the economic outcome through certain institutions, contracts, and laws, the (policy) recommendation is to start the analysis with an examination of reality as it exists today, then examine the effect of proposed policy changes, and finally determine if the implied outcome is better, or worse than the original one.

8.4   Institutions and Development

The World Bank's annual *World Development Report* is always an important and rich source of information on development-relevant topics. The discussion in this section is based on the *World Development Report* (World Bank 2002). As the title indicates, the focus of the report is on enhancing opportunities for poor people in markets by empowering them, making market activity more rewarding to boost economic growth and reduce poverty. Institutions play an important role in this process in three ways.

1. Institutions channel *information* about market conditions, goods, and participants. This information is crucial, for example, for identifying business partners, determining high-return opportunities, and verifying creditworthiness.
2. Institutions define and enforce *property rights* and *contracts*. Knowing and protecting your rights to assets and income is critical for market development and the efficient allocation of factors of production as it determines who gets what under which circumstances. Economic agents are only willing to invest in new opportunities if their property rights are well-protected.
3. Institutions will affect market *competition*. For efficiency and equity purposes, *good* institutions should increase competition to invest in projects based on merit, promote equal opportunity, and stimulate innovation and economic growth. *Bad* institutions, in contrast, reduce competition and create privileged interest groups – for example, when overregulation prevents new firms from entering a market or when activities are organized around a small group of participants.

Before this chapter moves on to the general principles of building institutions, there are two important observations.

First, institutions are *not* a one-size-fits-all phenomenon. The conditions of different countries with different cultures in different geographical regions during different time periods differ markedly, and so do the institutions that work in these different countries, cultures, regions, and time periods. Small vendors interacting with consumers on rural vegetable markets, where the quality of the product can be easily verified, have different institutional and incentive compatibility requirements than large multinational firms interacting for components of complicated differentiated products with other firms in remote countries separated in time, which makes credit and quality verification challenging. Evidently, the set of institutions which make the market of an economy work efficiently must be adjusted to the varying circumstances and requirements.

Second, the building of institutions is a *cumulative* process which takes time and effort to evolve according to the needs of developing nations and regions. It is in general a time-consuming, slow process of trial and error with ups and downs caused by political conflicts and economic or social conditions. An example is provided in Box 8.1, which emphasizes the timely development of the protection of property rights to create a balance of power during England's Glorious Revolution.

Chapter 3 discussed the time dimension of institution building, analyzing the importance of the transition around the world from hunter-gatherer societies to human settlements as a result of the Agricultural Revolution, in part based on the local availability of large-seeded grasses and large domesticable mammals. This allowed humans to organize themselves in villages, which evolved into small cities, rising in size to large cities, and

BOX 8.1 THE GLORIOUS REVOLUTION IN SEVENTEENTH-CENTURY ENGLAND

North and Weingast (1989) analyze the evolution of institutions, property rights, and the consequences for government finance in seventeenth-century England. Prior to the so-called *Glorious Revolution* of 1688, the Stuart monarchy used "forced loans" to finance its expenditures, where the lender had no recourse if loans were not repaid. This was one of various signs that the regime was not committed to protecting property rights, other indicators being the confiscation of land, forced public procurement, the sale of monopoly rights, and the removal of judges ruling against the Crown.

The winners of the Glorious Revolution (the Whigs) made a series of fundamental changes in political institutions to make credible the government's ability to honor its commitments. The Crown now had to obtain Parliamentary assent to change its agreements. Since Parliament represented wealth holders, this reduced the king's ability to renege. Moreover, the Bank of England exercised independent control over public finances, resulting in a more equitable division of powers between the branches of government.

The importance of the restraints on the arbitrary exercise of power and the protection of property rights is illustrated by the substantially improved ability of the government to finance public expenditure by issuing debt. Before 1688, the Crown was only able to place public debt equal to 2 or 3 percent of total income (GDP) at very short maturity and high interest rates. As North and Weingast show, within nine years of the institutional changes the Crown was able to finance debt equal to 40 percent of income at longer maturity and lower interest rates. It undoubtedly helped the private capital markets to prepare for the adequate financing of the upcoming Industrial Revolution.

ultimately resulted in today's enormous metropolitan areas (see Chapter 16). Along with this evolution, institutional development evolved according to the needs of the era to the ever-more refined and complicated institutional structures to enhance information flows, protect property rights, respect contracts, and foster competition, as outlined above. The importance of cumulative institutional development measured by the number of years of agriculture and state history in Chapter 4 is therefore emphasized (see the discussion in section 8.8).

Supported by numerous examples discussed in detail throughout the report, the World Bank emphasizes four main aspects in building *effective institutions* for development.

1. *Complement what exists.* The involvement of the state in institution building must be consistent with its capacity. In line with the discussion above, what works for advanced countries may not work for developing countries because of the available complementary institutions, existing levels of corruption, costs relative to income per capita, administrative capacity, and technology. As a consequence, to be successful regulatory systems in developing countries need to be simpler, less information intensive, and less burdensome on the court.

2. *Innovate to identify institutions that work.* Innovation through experimentation can help identify institutions that work effectively under existing conditions. In Bangladesh, for example, Mohammed Yunus observed that very small loans could make a disproportionate difference to a poor person. Because of the size of the loans and the lack of collateral, such loans were not interesting for regular banks, so in 1976 he started Grameen Bank and used his government connections to pioneer the concepts of microcredit and microfinance. He earned the Nobel Peace Prize in 2006 for his "efforts through microcredit to create economic and social development from below" (see www.nobelprize.org/).

3. *Connect communities through information flows and trade.* Open trade flows not only foster allocative efficiency, but also (i) expose participants to a diverse group of trading partners, (ii) help firms learn about organization and management, (iii) expose markets to competition, changes in returns, and different risks, and (iv) bring in market participants from other countries. All these changes ask for related changes in institutions to provide information, enforce contracts, manage the new risks, and support the market transactions.

4. *Promote competition – among jurisdictions, firms, and individuals.* Existing institutions may inhibit competition as it benefits closed groups who have superior access to information (see also section 8.5). Promoting competition can make institutions more effective by changing the incentives of individuals and firms – for example, if increased land disputes create a demand for more formal procedures for recording land transactions. Competition also affects the distribution of gains within the economic system and to some extent may be a substitute for regulation. Jurisdictional competition, for example in international capital markets, has raised demand for better institutions, such as accounting standards and prudential regulation.

The main aspects of the importance of institutional quality and development in general terms have been summarized above. It is now time to look in more detail at certain aspects of institutional quality. Section 8.5 starts with a discussion of the institutional quality of freedom of information as measured by the World Press Freedom Index. Section 8.6 continues with a range of institutional aspects related to economic freedom.

8.5 The (Inverse) World Press Freedom Index

An important aspect of institutional quality related to the competitive provision of information is the extent to which reporters are free to express themselves and report the facts. Founded in 1985 in Montpelier, France, and now based in Paris, Reporters without Borders is the world's leading organization defending freedom of information. The organization reports daily about the media freedom situation worldwide, mobilizes public and government support to promote press freedom, organizes activities to free journalists taken hostage, and compiles the World Press Freedom Index annually for 180 countries to evaluate the level of freedom available to the media.

As illustrated in Figure 8.1, the World Press Freedom Index is a country score ranging from 0 to 100. For confusion's sake, it is actually a *reverse* World Press Freedom Index because the higher the score the worse the press freedom situation, something to keep in mind in the discussion below. As indicated in the figure, Reporters without Borders uses five broader categories to summarize the Press Freedom Index, ranging from good (14 countries) to very bad (23 countries). The best score is for Norway, which is joined in the "good" range by mostly European countries, as well as Jamaica and Costa Rica (see Figure 8.2). The worst score is for North Korea, which is joined in the "very bad" range by

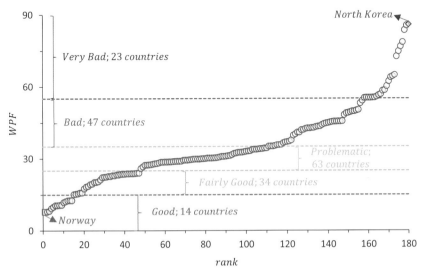

Figure 8.1 World Press Freedom Index, 2020
Source: Created using data from https://rsf.org.
Notes: WPF = World Press Freedom Index; 180 countries included.

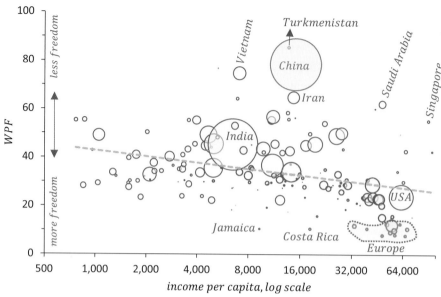

Figure 8.2 World Press Freedom Index and income per capita, 2020
Sources: Created using data from https://rsf.org and World Development Indicators online.
Notes: Income is GNI per capita, PPP (constant 2017 int. $), most recent in 2017–18, log scale; WPF is World Press Freedom Index; bubbles proportional to population; 167 observations; dashed line is trendline; coefficient = –3.66; explained variance is 8.8 percent; Europe = Switzerland, Norway, Ireland, Denmark, the Netherlands, Germany, Sweden, Belgium, Finland, Portugal, and Estonia.

such countries as Turkmenistan, China, Vietnam, Iran, Saudi Arabia, Cuba, and Singapore (see partially Figure 8.2).

The World Press Freedom Index is constructed by pooling qualitative information on responses by experts to a questionnaire organized by Reporters without Borders with quantitative data on abuses and acts of violence against journalists. The questionnaire consists of 87 questions focusing on pluralism, media independence, environment and self-censorship, legislative framework, transparency, and the quality of infrastructure. The data on abuses keeps a detailed track of abuses and violence against journalists and media outlets, which is translated into an index based on intensity of abuses in a certain time period. Summaries of the situation in the included countries and examples of abuses are available on the Reporters without Borders website. In 2020, for example, North Korea "keeps the population in ignorance," China "used the crisis to further tighten its control of the media," and in the Philippines "President Rodrigo Duterte … often threatens journalists … with death" and the "Heal As One Act … gives the government powers to prosecute any reporter or news organization publishing a report that displeases the Duterte government." (The "crisis" referred to in China is the Coronavirus [COVID-19] pandemic. Also note that the situation in the Philippines is still only classified as "problematic" [score of 43.54 and rank 136], rather than "bad" or "very bad.")

To investigate the relationship between freedom of the press and economic prosperity, Figure 8.2 provides a bubble diagram relating income per capita (PPP = purchasing power parity corrected [see Chapter 1], log scale, horizontal axis) and the World Press Freedom Index score (vertical axis), where the bubbles are proportional to population size. Reliable income per capita information is missing for 13 countries (including North Korea, Syria, Cuba, Yemen, Venezuela, and South Sudan), so these countries are missing from the diagram. The relationship between income per capita and the WPF Index is clearly negative, which means that richer countries tend to have more freedom of the press. The estimated coefficient is highly significant, but explains only 8.8 percent of the variance in the World Press Freedom Index. In view of their income per capita level, Jamaica and Costa Rica have high levels of press freedom (low WPF Index). In contrast, freedom of the press is low (high WPF Index) relative to income per capita in Vietnam, Turkmenistan, China, Iran, Saudi Arabia, and Singapore.

8.6 The Economic Freedom Index

Since 1995, the Heritage Foundation, a Washington DC think tank, has been publishing the *Economic Freedom Index* (EFI), which can be viewed as a summary of economically relevant institutions. The 2020 index is calculated for 186 countries and consists of four main categories, subdivided into 12 main aspects (see Table 8.2). The scores range from 0 to 100 for all aspects, where a higher score indicates more economic freedom. The overall score is the simple average of all 12 aspects, which are thus considered to be equally important. The website of the Heritage Foundation explains the used methodology and calculations in detail (see www.heritage.org).

The first main category is the *Rule of Law*, consisting of the aspects property rights, judicial effectiveness, and government integrity. The score for property rights is based on

Table 8.2. Structure of the Economic Freedom Index, 2020

Category A: Rule of Law
        Aspect 1: Property Rights
        Aspect 2: Judicial Effectiveness
        Aspect 3: Government Integrity
Category B: Government Size
        Aspect 4: Tax Burden
        Aspect 5: Government Spending
        Aspect 6: Fiscal Health
Category C: Regulatory Efficiency
        Aspect 7: Business Freedom
        Aspect 8: Labor Freedom
        Aspect 9: Monetary Freedom
Category D: Market Openness
        Aspect 10: Trade Freedom
        Aspect 11: Investment Freedom
        Aspect 12: Financial Freedom

physical property rights, intellectual property rights, strength of investor protection, risk of expropriation, and quality of land administration. The score for judicial effectiveness is based on judicial independence, quality of the judicial process, and favoritism in obtaining judicial decisions. The score for government integrity is based on irregular payments and bribes, transparency of government policymaking, absence of corruption, perception of corruption, and government and civil servant transparency. All these issues combined generate an overall score for the Rule of Law.

The second main category is *Government Size*, consisting of the aspects tax burden, government spending, and fiscal health. The score for the tax burden takes into consideration the top marginal tax rate for individual and corporate income, as well as the total tax rate as a percent of income (GDP). The score for government spending starts at 100 if government expenditure is 0 (as a percent of GDP) and declines in a quadratic fashion to reach 0 if government expenditure is 58 percent or higher. The main idea is that excessive government spending is a serious drag on economic dynamism. On the other hand, the foundation points out that countries with very high scores for government spending (that is, very low levels of government expenditure) can provide few public goods and will thus receive low scores for other aspects of the Economic Freedom Index, like property rights and investment freedom. The fiscal health score is based on the average government deficit in the most recent three years and the level of government debt (both as percent of GDP).

The third main category is *Regulatory Efficiency*, consisting of the aspects business freedom, labor freedom, and monetary freedom. The score on business freedom takes into consideration aspects of starting a business, obtaining a license, closing a business, and getting electricity. Issues that play a role for these aspects include the number of procedures, the time it takes (in days), and the costs involved (as percent of income per capita). The score on labor freedom takes into consideration the ratio of minimum wage relative to average value-added per worker, hindrance to hiring additional workers, rigidity of hours, difficulty of firing redundant employees, notice period, severance pay, and labor force participation rate. The score for monetary freedom is based on the average inflation rate for the most recent three years and the extent of government manipulation of prices through direct control and subsidies.

The fourth (and final) main category is *Market Openness*, consisting of the aspects trade freedom, investment freedom, and financial freedom. The score on trade freedom is based on a trade-weighted average tariff rate and an evaluation of nontariff barriers (quantity restrictions, regulatory restrictions, customs restrictions, and direct government intervention). The score on investment freedom deducts points for restrictions typically imposed on investment, such as national treatment of foreign investment, foreign investment code, restrictions on land ownership, sectoral investment restrictions, expropriation without fair compensation, foreign exchange controls, and foreign investment controls. Finally, the score for financial freedom is based on the extent of government regulation of financial services, the degree of state intervention in banks and other financial firms, government influence on the allocation of credit, the extent of financial development, and the openness to foreign competition.

As briefly discussed above, a wide range of institutional characteristics are incorporated in different aspects of the Economic Freedom Index. Table 8.3 provides some summary

Table 8.3. Economic Freedom Index; summary statistics, 2020

Variable	Min	Max	Mean	Median	St dev	# obs
EFI 2020	4.2	89.4	61.6	61.6	11.3	180
A Rule of Law						
1 Property	10.1	96.8	56.6	56.6	18.5	185
2 Judicial	5	92.9	45.1	43.4	18.6	185
3 Integrity	13.1	96.1	43.8	38.7	21.2	185
B Government Size						
4 Tax	0	99.8	77.3	78.5	13.1	180
5 Spending	0	96.5	66.0	71.0	22.9	183
6 Fiscal	0	99.9	69.1	80.0	30.3	182
C Regulatory Efficiency						
7 Business	5	96.2	63.3	63.6	15.8	185
8 Labor	5	90.9	59.4	60.0	14.4	184
9 Money	0	87.0	74.6	76.9	10.9	184
D Market Openness						
10 Trade	0	95.0	73.8	76.3	13.1	182
11 Investment	0	95.0	57.2	60.0	22.3	184
12 Financial	0	90.0	49.0	50.0	19.3	181

Source: Authors' calculations using www.heritage.org data.
Note: EFI = Economic Freedom Index.

statistics for the overall index and the various aspects in 2020. The overall score ranges from a low of 4.2 in North Korea to a high of 89.4 in Singapore. Only 180 countries are included in the overall score because of missing information for six countries (Iraq, Libya, Liechtenstein, Somalia, Syria, and Yemen). The mean and median overall score is 61.1, which is close to the scores reached by Russia, Honduras, and Barbados.

As Table 8.3 shows, not all aspects contribute equally to the overall score. The mean and median scores are lower than the overall mean and median scores for all Rule of Law aspects (property rights, judicial effectiveness, and government integrity), as well as for labor freedom, investment freedom, and financial freedom. In all these aspects it thus seems harder to reach a high score compared to the other aspects. This holds in particular for tax burden, fiscal health, monetary freedom, and trade freedom, where the mean and median scores are much higher than the overall average. This is reflected by the extremely high or low scores. For example, there are 12 aspect scores above 99, in particular for fiscal health (Afghanistan, Azerbaijan, Bulgaria, Estonia, Hong Kong, Kuwait, Macau, and Micronesia) and for tax burden (Bahrain, Qatar, Saudi Arabia, and United Arab Emirates). Similarly, there are 18 aspect scores equal to zero, in particular for Cuba (government spending), Eritrea (fiscal health, investment freedom), Kiribati (government

Table 8.4. Economic freedom aspects correlation matrix, 2020

	A1	A2	A3	B4	B5	B6	C7	C8	C9	D10	D11
A1 Law-Property	1.00										
A2 Law-Judicial	0.85	1.00									
A3 Law-Integrity	0.89	0.84	1.00								
B4 Gov-Tax	−0.11	−0.12	−0.25	1.00							
B5 Gov-Spend	−0.27	−0.20	−0.38	0.40	1.00						
B6 Gov-Fiscal	0.36	0.27	0.31	0.02	0.03	1.00					
C7 Reg-Business	0.80	0.73	0.73	0.10	−0.14	0.31	1.00				
C8 Reg-Labor	0.47	0.45	0.39	0.25	0.00	0.18	0.53	1.00			
C9 Reg-Money	0.52	0.42	0.42	0.15	−0.04	0.30	0.47	0.41	1.00		
D10 Open-Trade	0.64	0.55	0.62	0.16	−0.10	0.31	0.63	0.35	0.43	1.00	
D11 Open-Inv	0.68	0.58	0.65	−0.12	−0.10	0.31	0.55	0.27	0.52	0.59	1.00
D12 Open-Fin	0.73	0.62	0.70	−0.06	−0.13	0.30	0.60	0.33	0.47	0.62	0.81

Source: Calculations based on The Economic Freedom Index 2020, www.heritage.org.
Notes: See Table 8.2 for full name of economic freedom aspects; negative correlations in red; correlations above 0.5 green and shaded.

spending), North Korea (tax burden, government spending, fiscal health, monetary freedom, trade freedom, investment freedom, financial freedom), Lebanon (fiscal health), Libya (government spending), Micronesia (government spending), Syria (investment freedom), and Venezuela (fiscal health, monetary freedom, investment freedom).

As indicated by the extreme score examples, where North Korea scores zero points on seven aspects, there is substantial correlation between the aspect scores, as summarized in Table 8.4. Out of the 66 off-diagonal correlations, only 13 (20 percent) are negative. The other correlations are positive, with 24 correlations (36 percent) above 0.5. As already pointed out above, most negative correlations are relative to government spending (eight in total), indicating that high scores for government spending come at a price of low scores in other aspects (integrity, property rights, judicial effectiveness, and so on). The other negative correlations are relative to the tax burden (five in total), again indicating that high scores here come at the expense of low scores elsewhere, although not as strongly as for government spending. The next section analyzes these aspects in more detail.

8.7   Income Per Capita and Institutions

What is the relationship between institutions and economic development as measured by income per capita? This section analyzes the question using the Economic Freedom Index and its aspects in two ways, namely by relating these to levels of income per capita (PPP) and long-run economic growth using World Bank data. It begins with the overall Economic

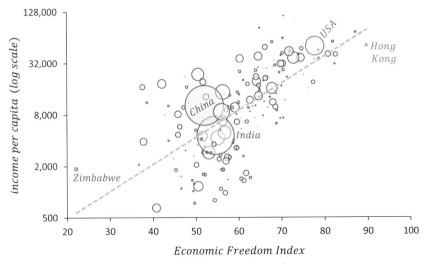

Figure 8.3 Economic Freedom Index and Income per capita
Sources: Created by the authors using Economic Freedom Index data (www.heritage.org) and World Bank Development Indicators online.
Notes: Income is GNI per capita (PPP, in constant 2011 $); bubbles proportional to population; 174 countries; data is for 2011 to maximize the number of observations.

Freedom Index before later analyzing the various aspects in more detail. The World Bank has provided reliable PPP income per capita data since 1990. Data is used in constant 2011 international dollars, which has a maximum number of observations available in 2011, so that year is used for the discussion in levels, resulting in 174 observations. Regarding the relationship with long-run economic growth, the implied compounded annual growth rate is calculated based on the first observation and last observation for a country in the period 1990–2018, resulting in 150 observations. This growth rate is related to the 2011 Economic Freedom Index (see the discussion below and section 8.8).

Figure 8.3 depicts the relationship between the Economic Freedom Index and the level of income per capita (using a log scale), with bubbles proportional to population size. The relationship is clearly positive, indicating that a higher score on the Economic Freedom Index is associated with a higher level of income per capita. The estimated coefficient is 0.0729 and highly significant, suggesting that a one-point-higher economic freedom score is associated with a rise of about 7.3 percent in income per capita. The regression explains about 44 percent in the variance of the log of income per capita. The highest freedom score is for Hong Kong (89.7), while the lowest score is for Zimbabwe (22.1).

Figure 8.5 depicts the relationship between the Economic Freedom Index and the long-run growth rate of income per capita (in percent per annum), again with bubbles proportional to population size. In stark contrast to our discussion above on the *level* of income per capita, there seems to be *no* relationship between the Economic Freedom Index and the long-run *growth rate* of income per capita. The regression line basically has a slope of 0 and explains 0 percent of the variance in the long-run growth rate. Long-run growth rates are high, for example, for Zimbabwe, China, and Latvia, which have very different

BOX 8.2 THE HERITAGE FOUNDATION CLAIMS ECONOMIC FREEDOM BOOSTS GROWTH

In a report discussing the highlights of the 2020 Economic Freedom Index, the Heritage Foundation claims that "Economic Freedom boosts growth" (p. 1). The main argument is illustrated in Figure 8.4, where for different time periods of 5, 15, and 25 years the average growth rate is determined for two groups of countries, namely those "gaining economic freedom" and those "losing economic freedom." For all three time periods, the countries gaining economic freedom have a higher growth rate than the countries losing economic freedom, namely 2.7 versus 1.7 percent for the 25-year period, 2.8 versus 1.9 percent for the 15-year period, and 2.2 versus 1.2 percent for the 5-year period. The box thus concludes that "economic freedom boosts growth" because higher growth rates are associated with rising levels of economic freedom.

The claim that economic freedom boosts growth is in contrast to the finding in Figure 8.5 that there is *no* relationship between economic freedom and long-run growth. Our main objection is regarding the used methodology. Of interest here is to determine if the level of economic freedom at a certain point in time – for example, at the beginning of the period under investigation or halfway through this period – has predictive power for explaining differences in growth rates. This turns out *not* to be the case, as shown for the 2011 level of economic freedom in Figure 8.5 (see also Table 8.5). Instead, the Heritage Foundation looks at *changes* in the Economic Freedom Index in a given period relative to average economic growth rates, which is an *ex post endogenous* classification of countries (based on observed outcomes). The score on institutional aspects of economic freedom as provided by the Heritage Foundation is to a large extent

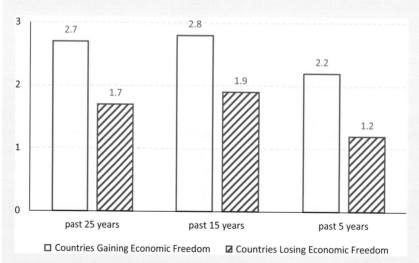

Figure 8.4 Economic growth and countries gaining or losing economic freedom, 2020
Source: Created using "Highlights of the 2020 Index of Economic Freedom" data, p. 1, www.heritage.org.

BOX 8.2 (cont.)

based on qualitative assessments of these institutional aspects (see section 8.6). There is an understandable tendency of people making these evaluations to raise the score if economic growth is high and to lower the score if economic growth is low. This creates the positive association depicted in Figure 8.4 in contrast to the absence of predictive power shown in Figure 8.5. This issue is discussed in more detail in the main text of sections 8.7 and 8.8.

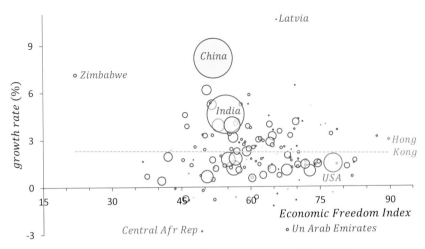

Figure 8.5 Economic Freedom Index and long-run growth, 1990–2018
Sources: Created by authors using Economic Freedom Index data (www.heritage.org) and World Bank Development Indicators online.
Notes: Income is GNI per capita (PPP, in constant 2011 $); bubbles proportional to population in 2011; 150 countries; long-run growth based on first and last observation in the 1990–2018 period.

economic freedom scores. Similarly, long-run growth rates are low for the Central African Republic and for the United Arab Emirates, again with very different economic freedom scores. In general, the current level of economic freedom provides basically no information on expected future growth rates. This is in contrast to the general view of institutionalists like North, Acemoglu, Robinson, and Johnson and the claim by the Heritage Foundation (see Box 8.2) that "economic freedom boosts growth." The final part of this section analyzes the robustness of the finding that economic freedom is positively related to the level of income per capita but not to the long-run growth rates of income per capita for the different aspects of economic freedom. The next section continues the explanation of this finding using the work of Glaeser *et al.* (2004).

Table 8.5 analyzes the robustness of the findings for the overall Economic Freedom Index for the 12 individual aspects using a regression analysis. The finding that economic freedom is highly positively associated with the *level* of income per capita is illustrated in the left-hand part of the table (with the exception of the tax burden and fiscal health). The

Table 8.5. Economic freedom, income per capita, and economic growth

Indicator	Income per capita level (log)		Income per capita long-run growth	
	coefficient	R^2	coefficient	R^2
EFI 2020	0.0729[***]	0.4408	−0.0032	0.0003
A1 Law-Property	0.0349[***]	0.4835	−0.0079	0.0097
A2 Law-Judicial[#]	0.0371[***]	0.4094	−0.0036	0.0015
A3 Law-Integrity	0.0411[***]	0.5189	−0.0087	0.0093
B4 Gov-Tax	−0.007	0.0057	0.0186	0.0146
B5 Gov-Spend	−0.013[***]	0.0715	0.0031	0.0013
B6 Gov-Fiscal[#]	0.0048	0.0148	0.0092[*]	0.0192
C7 Reg-Business	0.0433[***]	0.4056	0.0054	0.0024
C8 Reg-Labor	0.0175[***]	0.0642	0.0031	0.0007
C9 Reg-Money	0.0433[***]	0.1149	−0.0242	0.0149
D10 Open-Trade	0.0545[***]	0.2773	0.0083	0.0023
D11 Open-Inv	0.0258[***]	0.2607	0.0014	0.0003
D12 Open-Fin	0.0365[***]	0.3345	−0.0051	0.0024

Sources: Calculations based on the Economic Freedom Index (www.heritage.org) and World Bank Development Indicators online.

Notes: See Table 8.2 for full name of economic freedom aspects; income is GNI per capita (PPP, in constant 2011 $); level impact in 2011, 174 countries; long-run growth based on first and last income observations in the 1990–2018 period, 150 countries; [#] aspect data are from 2017, year of introduction of this aspect; [***] significant at 1 percent (dark shade); [*] significant at 10 percent (light shade).

highest share of the variance of the log of income per capita explained (51.9 percent) is for Rule of Law – government integrity, but it is also high for the overall index, property rights, judicial efficiency, and the freedom indicators (trade, investment, and finance). The finding that economic freedom is *not* related to the long-run *growth* of income per capita is illustrated in the right-hand part of the table. With the exception of Government Size – Fiscal Health, which is mildly significant, *none* of the estimated regression coefficients is significant. Moreover, the one exception (fiscal health) is only able to explain 1.9 percent of the variance in long-run growth rates (and at the 10 percent significance level this might, in view of the number of regressions, be a statistical artifact). In short, the finding regarding the absence of predictive power for long-run economic growth for aspects of the economic freedom index is robust. The important question following on from this, "do institutions cause growth," is addressed in the next section.

8.8   Do Institutions Cause Growth?

The title in this section is taken from the work of Glaeser *et al.* (2004), referred to within this section as GLPS (author last name initials: Glaeser, Lopez-de-Silanes, Porta, and Shleifer).

There are two main approaches. The first builds on the work of North (1981, 1990), Hall and Jones (1999), Acemoglu *et al.* (2001, 2002), Rodrik *et al.* (2004), and many others to argue that good institutions which put restrictions on government behavior, such as respecting property rights, cause economic growth. The second approach builds on the work of Lipset (1960), Barro (1999), Alvarez *et al.* (2000), Djankov *et al.* (2003), and Przeworski (2004), and others to argue the *reverse* idea that growth in income per capita and human capital causes institutional improvements. The discussion below brings us back to the *Reversal of Fortune* discussion of Chapter 4 (Acemoglu *et al.* 2001 and 2002) and in the end will lead to a similar conclusion regarding the importance of human capital incorporated in migration flows.

Based on North (1981), GLPS (p. 275) emphasize two aspects of institutions, namely that they should (i) provide some type of constraint on governments and (ii) be permanent or at least durable features of the environment. They argue that the empirically used measures of institutions reflect neither of the two aspects above. Sections 8.5 and 8.6 already discussed some measures of institutions. They have common features as the institution measures analyzed by GLPS, who focus in particular on the Polity measure of *constraints on the executive* as the "best" measure of institutions (see Box 8.3). In many cases, measures of institutional quality depend on the *subjective* assessment of property rights, judicial effectiveness, government integrity, and so on. As a consequence, the data tend to reflect what actually happened in a country rather than some permanent rules of the game. To the extent that dictatorial regimes score high for certain aspects of the quality of institutions (as seen in section 8.6), this reflects the choice of dictators and not political constraints (in violation of aspect (i) above). This observation explains the high correlation of the measures of institutional quality with income per capita levels observed in section 8.7. It also explains why measures of institutional quality tend to *change* over time and can in fact be quite *volatile*, as discussed by GLPS and in Box 8.3 (and in violation of aspect (ii) above). The executive constraints measure, for example, moves up and down with high variability between the minimum of 1 and the maximum of 7 in the period 1950–2018 for both Haiti and Nigeria (see Figure 8.6 in Box 8.3), making it hard to see how this variable is indicative of the quality of institutions imposed by durable constraints on the executive.

GLPS take executive constraints as the variable most clearly associated with the "institutions cause growth" approach and education (schooling) as the variable most clearly associated with the reverse causality approach of "economic growth causes institutional improvements" and proceed in two main steps. First, they use ordinary least squares (OLS) regressions to argue which variable (and thus which approach) is more powerful in predicting economic growth (see Table 8.6). Second, they repeat the exercise while using instrumental variables to deal with endogeneity problems (see Table 8.7). They also include control variables when needed and discuss many other variations not reported here. In all cases, they conclude that institutions *do not* cause growth.

Table 8.6 analyzes the power of initial conditions for executive constraints and years of schooling to predict economic growth in the period 1960–2000. Control variables include the share of the population living in the temperate zone and the initial income per capita level. Both control variables are highly significant and indicate that a larger share of the

BOX 8.3 EXECUTIVE CONSTRAINTS AND THE VOLATILITY OF INSTITUTIONS

The Center for Systemic Peace (CSP) was founded in 1997 and analyzes problems of political violence within the global system (see www.systemicpeace.org). It provides detailed information on the Integrated Network for Societal Conflict Research (INSCR) data page, including the Polity data on executive restraints discussed in the Glaeser *et al.* (2004) paper (GLPS, see section 8.8). The latest version (Polity 5) provides information up to 2018. According to the Dataset Manual (Marshall and Gurr 2020, p. 61), the *executive constraints* variable "refers to the extent of institutional constraints on the decision-making powers of the chief executive, whether an individual or collective executive." The variable ranges from 1 (unlimited executive authority; when there are "no regular limitations on the executive's actions") to 7 (executive parity or subordination; when "the accountability groups have effective authority equal to or greater than the executive"). In hectic times, a numerical code outside the 1 to 7 range is given to identify specific issues. (The codes are –66, –77, and –88 to identify "interruption," "interregnum," and "transition" periods, respectively. These are ignored here.)

GLPS argue that institutions provide constraints on the government and should thus be fairly constant over time and adjust only gradually. This claim is briefly analyzed for the executive constraint variable (xconst) in the period 1950–2018 for all relevant countries (that is, excluding countries and territories without any observations in this period). In total, there are 179 countries with 9,265 observations for an average of 52 observations per country (ranging from 2 for South Sudan to the maximum of 69 for 40 countries). The average score for all countries is 4.2 and the standard deviation for all countries is a substantial 2.32. At the country level, there are 44 countries (25 percent of the total) who receive the same score throughout the entire period. In most cases (34 out of 44) this is the maximum score of 7 points (usually for the advanced nations), but there are also countries with a constant score of 1 (Saudi Arabia, Qatar, and Uzbekistan), 2 (Sudan North), 3 (Angola, United Arab Emirates, Vietnam, and Singapore), or 5 (South Sudan and Namibia).

In all other cases (135 countries, or 75 percent of the total), the executive constraints score varies within this time period. If these countries are ranked in terms of variability using the standard deviation, the most volatile country is Spain ($sd = 2.93$), followed by Paraguay ($sd = 2.89$), Portugal ($sd = 2.84$), and Somalia ($sd = 2.80$). However, this does not tell the whole story. Spain, for example, switched one time from a minimum score of 1 during the Franco era (up to 1974) to a maximum score of 7 from 1978 onward (and no score in the period 1975–1977). Something similar holds for Portugal (and to a lesser extent for Paraguay and Somalia). For this reason, Figure 8.6 shows the evolution of the executive constraints score for three examples: Taiwan, Haiti, and Nigeria. In line with the GLPS argument that institutions improve as nations develop successfully, the score for Taiwan gradually rises, namely from 2 up to 1974; to 3 until

BOX 8.3 (cont.)

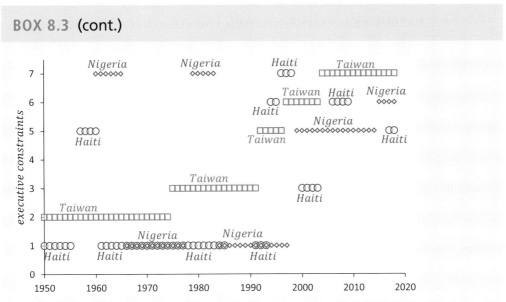

Figure 8.6 Executive constraints in Haiti, Nigeria, and Taiwan, 1950–2018
Source: Created using Center for Systemic Peace data (www.systemicpeace.org).

1991; to 5 until 1996; to 6 until 2003; and to the maximum of 7 from 2004 onward. The other two countries move up and down swiftly. Haiti is discussed in more detail by GLPS and has: a score of 1 for six years; a gap for one year; a score of 5 for four years; a score of 1 for 25 years; a gap for five years; a score of 1 for three years; a score of 6 for two years; a score of 7 for three years; a gap of one year; a score of 3 for four years; a gap for two years; a score of 6 for four years; a gap for seven years; and a score of 5 for two years. The score for Nigeria is only slightly less erratic, moving from a maximum of 7 to a minimum of 1, back to a maximum of 7, to return to a minimum of 1, up to a score of 5 and eventually 6, with two small gaps in between. It is indeed hard to see how this volatility is indicative of the quality of institutions imposed by constraints on the executive.

population in the temperate zone raises economic growth and that there is convergence of income per capita in this period (initially rich countries grow more slowly than initially poor countries). More importantly, the initial level of executive constraints has no power to predict economic growth at all (similar to the observations in section 8.7), while the initial level of schooling is a strong predictor of economic growth, indicating that an initially more educated population leads to faster economic growth.

The OLS results in Table 8.6 do not deal with the long-recognized problem that the quality of institutions and income per capita are both endogenous variables. A methodology using valid instruments (see Chapter 2) is needed to adequately deal with this. GLPS credit Acemoglu *et al.* (2001, 2002) for invigorating the discussion on the link

Table 8.6. Economic growth, executive constraints, and human capital (schooling)

Explanatory variable	Dependent variable: growth of income per capita (GDP), 1960–2000		
share of population living in temperate zone (1995)	0.0253[***]	0.0175[***]	0.0255[***]
	(0.0039)	(0.0049)	(0.0048)
log of initial income per capita	−0.0079[***]	−0.0092[***]	−0.0189[***]
	(0.0025)	(0.0034)	(0.0034)
initial executive constraints	0.0013		0.0008
	(0.0009)		(0.0008)
log of initial years of schooling		0.0073[***]	0.0096[***]
		(0.0024)	(0.0028)
number of observations	72	71	57
R^2	0.34	0.38	0.55

Source: Selection from Glaeser *et al.* 2004, table 5.
Notes: Robust standard errors in parentheses; OLS regressions, including constant (not shown); [***] significant at 1 percent (shaded).

between institutions and growth. Chapter 4 outlines their Reversal of Fortune hypothesis, where log settler mortality or population density is used as an instrument. As GLPS point out, however (Glaeser *et al.* 2004, p. 289, emphasis added):

> ... even if one agrees that mortality risk or indigenous population density shaped the European settlement decisions, it is far from clear that what the Europeans brought with them when they settled is limited government. *It seems at least as plausible that what they brought with them is themselves, and therefore their know-how and human capital.*

Based on the work of Spolaore and Wacziarg (2013) and Putterman and Weil (2010), Chapter 4 analyzes not only selection effects for the Reversal of Fortune hypothesis, but also the importance of ancestry-adjusted years of agriculture and ancestry-adjusted years of state history incorporated in migration flows of the past 500 years.

After a detailed discussion of the validity and suitability of instruments, GLPS eventually continue with an instrumental variable approach incorporating both executive constraints and years of schooling as instruments. Both variables are averaged for the period under investigation (1960–2000). (This is customary in the literature.) Table 8.7 presents a selection of their first-stage and second-stage results using log settler mortality and French legal origin as instruments, while controlling for the share of population living in the temperate zone. In the first stage, log settler mortality and French legal origin are important for determining executive constraints, while log settler mortality and the share of the population in the temperate zone are important for determining the years of schooling. Most importantly, in the second stage, the predicted years of schooling *are* important for determining the level of income per capita, while the predicted executive constraints *are not*. In the instrumental variable framework, therefore, human capital is a more important variable for predicting economic development than political institutions. Throughout the paper GLPS emphasize the

Table 8.7. Economic development, instrumental variable approach

| | Dependent variable | | |
| | Second-stage regression | First-stage regression | |
Explanatory variable	log income per capita (GDP) in 2000	executive constraints	years of schooling
years of schooling (1960–2000)	0.7894*** (0.2753)		
executive constraints (1960–2000)	−0.3432 (0.2577)		
share of population living in temperate zone (1995)	−1.6969 (1.2053)	−0.1195 (0.7202)	3.4975*** (0.8044)
log settler mortality		−0.8212*** (0.2053)	−1.0183*** (0.2293)
French legal origin		−1.4124*** (0.4258)	−0.377 (0.4757)
number of observations	47	47	47
R^2	0.31	0.53	0.70

Source: Selection from Glaeser *et al.* 2004, table 11.
Notes: Robust standard errors in parentheses; regressions include constant (not shown); *** significant at 1 percent (shaded).

role of dictators to get the process of economic development started, such that they conclude: "Our evidence suggests ... that ... countries that emerge from poverty accumulate human and physical capital under dictatorships, and then, once they become richer, are increasingly likely to improve their institutions" (Glaeser *et al.* 2004, p. 298).

8.9 Conclusions

This chapter briefly analyzed and discussed various aspects of institutions and contracts which represent the rules of the game that constrain human interaction. It emphasized that institutions and contracts are prevalent throughout all societies and many different fields of economics, so it necessarily focused on the most important considerations from an economic development perspective. Sections 8.2 and 8.3 began with the work of Coase to explain the nature of firms and the importance of social costs and property rights. According to Coase, firms exist to lower transaction costs by organizing activities within the firm rather than relying on costly market contracts. Similarly, from a social perspective, the Coase Theorem claims that if property rights are well-defined and there are no transaction costs at all, the economic outcome is efficient and independent of the distribution of property rights. Remember that Coase emphasizes that there *are* transaction costs and property right may *not* be well-defined, so the economic outcome is *not* efficient and *not* independent of the distribution of property rights.

Section 8.4 briefly reviewed the links between institutions and economic development. It emphasized the importance of institutions to channel information, enforce property rights and contracts, and promote competition. It also showed that institutions should cater to the specific needs and circumstances of a country (not one-size-fits-all) and that the building of institutions is a cumulative, time-consuming process. As a consequence, institutions must adjust to the needs of countries at different stages of development at a certain point in time, as well as to the needs of a given country as it develops over time.

Sections 8.5 and 8.6 covered aspects of certain types of institutions. Regarding the World Press Freedom index, they focused on the importance of access to reliable and independent information and illustrated the large differences that exist around the world, and showed that press freedom tends to improve as income per capita rises, but that the association is weak and the variation is substantial. These sections also outlined the key components of a wide range of institutions incorporated in the Economic Freedom Index, with Rule of Law, Government Size, Regulatory Efficiency, and Market Openness as main components, each subdivided into three aspects for a total of 12 institutional aspects. The correlation between the aspects is usually (highly) positive, except for two aspects (tax burden and government spending), where high scores tend to come at the cost of low scores for other aspects.

Section 8.7 analyzed the connections between institutions and income per capita. It showed that the quality of institutions is highly correlated with the *level* of income per capita, but *cannot* predict the growth rate of income per capita. Building on these observations, section 8.8 takes the last step using the work of Glaeser *et al.* (2004) in answering the question: "do institutions cause growth?" The answer is negative. Essentially, the argument is that if countries start to develop successfully, potentially because a dictator made the right choices, the quality of institutions tends to improve over time. The role of physical and human capital accumulation is crucial in the process (as measured by schooling; see also Chapter 7). For explaining the Reversal of Fortune hypothesis, the human capital incorporated in migration flows is of crucial importance, as discussed in Chapter 4.

Further Reading

A well-written account of human history, what factors have stimulated growth and inequality, including how and why humanity has only recently escaped the Malthusian poverty trap, is provided by Oded Galor in *The Journey of Humanity: The Origins of Wealth and Inequality* (New York/London: Dutton/ Penguin, 2022). According to Galor, the quality of institutions, among other factors, is very important.

Classic contributions in this area are mentioned in the chapter, including Coase (1937, 1960) and North (1981, 1990). The work of Coase and North (with Robert Fogel) is clarified on the Nobel Prize website. See: www.nobelprize.org/prizes/economic-sciences/1991/summary/ and www.nobelprize .org/prizes/economic-sciences/1993/summary/.

An accessible introduction to the role of institutions in economic development is provided by Voight, while Przeworski and Limongi focus on the connection between political regimes and economic growth. See: Voight, S. 2019. *Institutional Economics* (Cambridge University Press); and Przeworski, A. and F. Limongi. 1993. "Political Regimes and Economic Growth," *Journal of Economic Perspectives*, 7(3), 51–69.

Money and Finance

9.1 Introduction

This chapter is partially based on earlier work (see van Marrewijk 2012, Part III.A and III.B and Brakman and van Marrewijk 2021). When (developing) countries are trading with other countries, they are confronted with financial interactions and forces that affect the way they do business and limit the possibilities and effectiveness of certain types of policies. The power of these financial forces is enormous. According to the Bank for International Settlements (2019), the *daily* turnover on financial markets for all instruments on a net-net basis in April 2019 was US$6.6 trillion, which is equivalent to about 8 percent of total world income in one *year*.[1] This chapter briefly discusses the main interactions, forces, limitations, and possibilities.

Section 9.2 opens with a discussion of the main aspects of exchange rates, the price of one currency in terms of another. Section 9.3 emphasizes the importance of forward-looking markets for understanding the power of financial forces. These aspects are combined in section 9.4, which examines covered and uncovered interest rate parity – crucial for understanding the possibilities and limitations of monetary policy as explained in section 9.5. Using this theoretical basis, section 9.6 reviews the main policy choices made in recent history up until the present. Next, section 9.7 turns to the practical issues of trade financing and trade financing gaps, also in relation to international (vehicle) currencies in section 9.8. Sections 9.9 and 9.10 draw the chapter to a close with a brief discussion on finance, investment, and development, before focusing on the impact of microfinance in a randomized evaluation. Section 9.11 concludes.

9.2 Exchange Rates

When engaging in international trade flows the exporters and importers at some point in time are confronted with *exchange rates* when they have to exchange goods or services valued in one currency in exchange for another currency. It is important to realize that an exchange rate is a price, namely the price of one currency in terms of another currency. This price is determined simply by demand and supply in the foreign exchange market. As

---

[1] Using World Bank Development Indicators online GDP income for 2018 as a reference.

Table 9.1. Some international currency symbols

Country	Currency	Symbol	ISO code
Australia	dollar	A$	AUD
Canada	dollar	C$	CAD
China	yuan	¥	CNY
EMU countries	euro	€	EUR
India	rupee	Rs	INR
Iran	rial	RI	IRR
Japan	yen	¥	JPY
Kuwait	dinar	KD	KWD
Mexico	peso	Ps	MXP
Saudi Arabia	riyal	SR	SAR
Singapore	dollar	S$	SGD
South Africa	rand	R	ZAR
Switzerland	franc	SF	CHF
United Kingdom	pound	£	GBP
United States	dollar	$	USD

there are many countries with convertible currencies, there are many exchange rates, such as the exchange rate of a Singapore dollar in terms of European euros or the exchange rate of a Japanese yen in terms of British pounds.

Since the exchange rate is a price, a rise in the exchange rate indicates that the item being traded has become more expensive, just like any other price rise indicates. Therefore, if the exchange rate of a Singapore dollar in terms of European euros rises, this indicates that the Singapore dollar has become more expensive. Various specialized symbols have been introduced to identify specific currencies, such as $ to denote (US) dollars, € to denote European euros, £ to denote (British) pounds, and ¥ to denote Japanese yen or Chinese yuan. Table 9.1 lists some of these international currency symbols, as well as the three-letter international standard (ISO) code to identify the currencies.

As discussed below, there are various types of exchange rates, one of which is the *spot* exchange rate – the price of buying or selling a particular currency at this moment. Table 9.2 lists some spot exchange rates as recorded on December 3, 2019, at 11:55:00 AM (UTC+01:00 time).[2] The fact that a high level of precision is needed by listing not only the day on which the spot exchange rates were recorded but also the exact time and the time zone signals an important general property of exchange rates: they are *extremely variable*. The website from which the information was taken updates every five seconds. Real-time transactions are updated even more frequently. This makes exchange rates rather special prices, as the variability in the quoted prices is much higher than for goods and services traded on the market place (such as the price of diapers in the supermarket), although generally of the same order of magnitude as many other prices in financial markets.

---

[2] UTC = Universal Time Coordinated, successor to Greenwich Mean Time.

Table 9.2. Spot exchange rates on December 3, 2019 at 11:55:00 am (UTC+01:00)

Price of	Bid spot rate	Ask spot rate	In terms of currency	Country	Spread %
1 USD	1.32993	1.33007	CAD	Canada	0.0105
1 USD	0.98960	0.98976	CHF	Switzerland	0.0162
1 USD	14.66009	14.66686	ZAR	South Africa	0.0462

Source: www.oanda.com.

Table 9.2 lists the exchange rate of the US dollar relative to three countries, namely Canada, Switzerland, and South Africa. There are actually two rates quoted: (i) the *bid* rate, that is, the price at which banks are willing to buy one US dollar (what they are bidding for one dollar); and (ii) the *ask* rate, that is, the price at which the banks are willing to sell one US dollar (what they are asking to sell you one dollar). These quotes are for large amounts only. The difference between the buying and selling rate is called the *spread*. It generates revenue for the currency trading activities of the banks. In practice, the spread is quoted relative to the bid price. So, based on Table 9.2, a Swiss bank might quote USD 0.98960–76, indicating the bank is willing to buy dollars at 0.98960 and willing to sell dollars at 0.98976. Obviously, banks from other countries can also buy and sell US dollars for Swiss francs – that is, trading in these currencies is not only limited to Swiss and American banks. Note that the spread between the bid price and the ask price, the margin for the banks, is very small. For the US dollar–Canadian dollar in our example it is only 0.0105 percent. As shown in Table 9.2, the spread is slightly bigger for trade in the US dollar–Swiss franc (0.0162 percent) and substantially larger for trade in the US dollar–South African rand (0.0462 percent). In general, the spread decreases with the intensity with which the two currencies involved are traded. Since the spread is so small, we henceforth assume that the bid price is equal to the ask price (such that the spread is zero) and refer to *the* exchange rate of the US dollar in terms of Canadian dollars, Swiss francs, or South African rands. For financial trading, however, the spread is crucially important.

Figure 9.1 illustrates the variability of exchange rates for a longer time period (2000–20) for the exchange rate of the US dollar in Canada, South Africa, and Switzerland using daily data. There are clearly big differences in the price of the US dollar over time, as well as big differences in variability between countries. In Canada, for example, the US dollar exchange rate varied from a low of 0.9168 on November 7, 2007 to a 76 percent higher value of 1.6128 on January 18, 2002. In South Africa, on the other hand, the US dollar exchange rate varied from a low of 5.615 on December 24, 2004 to a three times higher value of 16.8845 on January 20, 2016.

Over the period as a whole, the US dollar *depreciated* relative to the Swiss franc, meaning that it has become less expensive for the Swiss to purchase American dollars. Initially, there is also a depreciation of the US dollar relative to the Canadian dollar, but that trend is reversed to an *appreciation* (US dollar becomes more expensive) around 2008 and 2013,

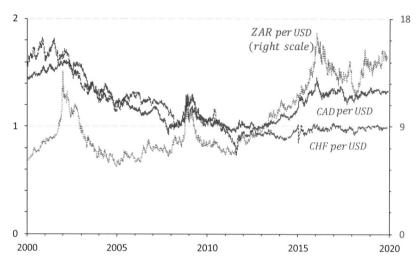

Figure 9.1 Swiss franc, Canadian dollar, and South African rand; daily data, 2000–2020
Data source: www.federalreserve.gov.
Notes: CHF = Swiss franc; CAD = Canadian dollar; ZAR = South African rand (on right-hand side vertical axis); exchange rates relative to US dollar.

such that the net effect over a 20-year period is small. Relative to the South African rand, the US dollar has appreciated over this time period, with large fluctuations over time and peaks in 2002, 2009, and 2016.

As shown above, exchange rates vary considerably over time, even within one day. The same is *not* true for the exchange rate at different locations for a given point in time. Since currencies are homogenous goods (a yen is a yen, no matter where it comes from) and the spreads are very small, if the Japanese yen exchange rate was high in one location, say New York, and low in another location, say London, at the same point in time, traders could make a profit by (electronically) rapidly buying yen in London (where they are cheap) and selling them in New York (where they are dear). As a result of this *arbitrage* activity, the price of yen would rise in London and fall in New York. Profit opportunities exist until the price is equal in the two locations. In view of the small spreads, the ability to swiftly move large funds around the globe electronically and the huge trading volume equality occurs almost instantaneously.

This does not only hold for direct arbitrage for a particular exchange rate, but also for so-called *triangular arbitrage* for different pairs of exchange rates. This is illustrated in Table 9.3. Suppose we know the price of one US dollar in terms of Canadian dollars (1.3300), Swiss francs (0.9897), and South African rands (14.6635). In view of arbitrage opportunities, this suffices to calculate all cross exchange rates as given in Table 9.3. We know, for example, that one Swiss franc must cost 14.8164 South African rand, because 14.6635 rands is worth one US dollar and one US dollar is worth 0.9897 Swiss francs, such that one Swiss franc is worth 14.6635/0.9897 = 14.8164 rands; similarly for the other table entries. Box 9.1 briefly discusses arbitrage in connection to Donald Trump's claims of Chinese currency manipulation in 2016.

Table 9.3. Cross exchange rates; spot, 3 December 2019 at 11:55:00 AM (UTC+01:00)

Price of 1	(Country)	In terms of			
		CAD	CHF	USD	ZAR
CAD	(Canada)	1.0000	0.7441	0.7519	11.0252
CHF	(Switzerland)	1.3439	1.0000	1.0104	14.8164
USD	(United States)	1.3300	0.9897	1.0000	14.6635
ZAR	(South Africa)	0.0907	0.0675	0.0682	1.0000

Data source: See Table 9.2.
Notes: For ISO codes, see Table 9.1; based on average bid and ask price of USD.

BOX 9.1 CHINA: ARBITRAGE, REAL EXCHANGE RATES, AND CURRENCY MANIPULATION?

Arbitrage ensures that goods cost the same in different countries if currencies reflect their real value. Suppose a hamburger costs USD 4 in the USA. If you exchange this to Chinese yuan at an exchange rate of CNY 7 per USD, you receive CNY 28 and should be able to buy a similar hamburger in China. If, instead, the hamburger costs CNY 35 in China, the dollar is undervalued. Suppose S is the nominal spot exchange rate, P is the average price of American goods, and P^* is the average price of Chinese goods, then the *real* exchange rate RER can be defined as $RER = SP^*/P$. If the ratio is larger than one, Chinese yuan are overvalued. If arbitrage works, the ratio should move toward one. Since in practice nations trade with many countries, the real exchange rate concept is applied to all trading partners (using trade shares as weight) to determine the real *effective* exchange rate, which provides a summary of a currency's value relative to all trading partners.

Figure 9.2 depicts the nominal exchange of Chinese yuan relative to the US dollar, as well as the real effective exchange rate (index; 2010 = 100) for the period 1990–2020. It can be used, for example, to evaluate Donald Trump's claim during the presidential elections in 2016 that China is a currency manipulator (see www.staradvertiser.com/2016/12/29/breaking-news/what-it-means-if-trump-names-china-a-currency-manipulator/). If true, this suggests that China artificially influenced the value of the yuan to boost its competitive position, thus creating an undervalued currency. Note that the nominal dollar exchange rate rose sharply from about CNY 4.8 to 8.6 in 1994 (a depreciation of the yuan), then remained stable at about 8.3 for a long time until 2004 (pegged to the US dollar), after which it started to decline to about 6.1 in 2014 (an appreciation of the yuan) and rise to about 7.0 at the end of 2019 (a depreciation of the yuan).

BOX 9.1 (cont.)

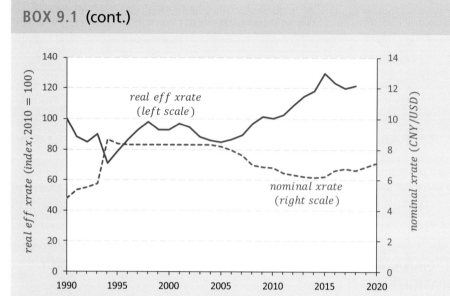

Figure 9.2 Real effective exchange rate and nominal exchange rate; China, 1990–2020
Source: Created using World Bank Development Indicators data.
Notes: xrate = exchange rate; nominal = official rate.

The real effective exchange rate takes currency changes and price changes relative to all of China's trade partners into consideration. It is 100 by construction in 2010 and also in 1990. The latter might be taken as an "equilibrium" year as China's current account balance switched from a deficit in 1989 to a surplus in 1990. (Except for 1993, China's current account balance remained a surplus ever since. It reached a peak in relative terms in 2007 [9.9 percent of GDP] and has virtually disappeared since then [0.4 percent of GDP in 2018].) The real effective exchange rate is below 100 for the period 1991–2008 and has been rising substantially above 100 since then. Although it's important not to be too dramatic about minor deviations, if anything this suggests that the Chinese yuan has been overvalued rather than undervalued since about 2013. Trump's claim of currency manipulation during the presidential election in 2016 was therefore not valid, although it might have been valid around 1994.

9.3   Forward-Looking Markets

The large variability of exchange rates illustrated in Figure 9.1 potentially poses problems for agents active on the foreign exchange market. Suppose, for example, that you represent a Japanese firm and have sold 1,000 watches for delivery and payment in France in three months' time at a total price of €150,000. At the current exchange rate of ¥133.49 per euro, the payment of €150,000 is worth ¥20,023,500. Since the total cost of producing and delivering the watches for your company is about ¥19 million Japanese, you stand to make a profit of about ¥1 million on this transaction, so your boss will be pleased. However, payment (in euro) takes place only three months later. To your surprise and dismay, the euro turns out to have considerably depreciated relative to the Japanese yen in this period, such that three months later the spot exchange rate for the euro is only ¥120.49. The payment of €150,000 is now worth only ¥18,051,000, which means that your company made a loss of about ¥1 million yen, rather than a profit of ¥1 million. Your boss is not pleased.

Could you have avoided the ¥1 million loss? Yes, you could have, but it required you to take action three months earlier on a forward-looking market using a forward-looking instrument. In this case, for example, you could have sold the €150,000 on the forward exchange market three months earlier at a then-agreed-upon forward price of, say, ¥131.24 per euro. This would have *guaranteed* you a revenue of ¥19,686,000 upon payment and ensured a profit of about ¥700,000. That is, you could have *hedged* your foreign exchange risk exposure on the forward exchange market.

Since many other economic agents face exposure to similar or opposite foreign exchange risks (which they would like to hedge too) and other economic agents would like to take a gamble (*speculate*) on the direction and size of changes in the exchange rate, a whole range of forward-looking markets has developed, with associated rather exotic terminology. It is possible to distinguish, for example, between three so-called *plain vanilla* instruments, namely *forwards*, *swaps*, and *options*. According to the Bank for International Settlements (2002, p. 34), the term plain vanilla refers to instruments "which are traded in generally liquid markets according to more or less standard contracts and market conventions." Combinations of the basic instruments can then be used to construct tailor-made financial instruments, such as currency *swaptions* (options to enter into a currency swap contract).

The spot exchange rate is the price at which you can buy or sell a currency today. The forward exchange rate is the price at which you agree upon today to buy or sell an amount of a currency at a specific date in the future. (The *futures* market is slightly different from the forward market in that only a few currencies are traded, with standardized contracts at certain locations [such as the Chicago Mercantile Exchange, the largest futures market] and specific maturity dates.) A swap involves the *simultaneous* buying and selling of an amount of currency at some point in the future and a *reverse* transaction at another point in the future. A currency swap applies this to a stream of profits. Finally, an option gives you the right to buy or sell a currency at a given price during a given period.

Figure 9.3 illustrates the movement of the spot rate and the three-month forward exchange rate of the British pound relative to the euro from January 1 to May 24, 2016 (the figure depicts the price of one euro in terms of British pounds). Obviously, the forward rate and the spot rate move, in general, quite closely together (note that the scale on the vertical axis does not start at zero). Over the period 2009–16, the forward rate of the euro was mostly higher than the spot rate (about 77 percent of the time), that is, the euro was

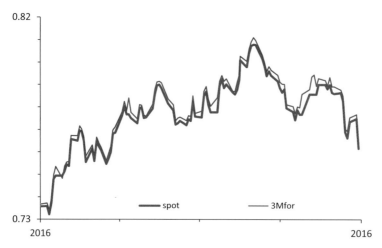

Figure 9.3 British pound to euro spot and three-month forward exchange rates, 2016
Source: Based on Datastream data.
Notes: Daily data from January 1 to May 24, 2016 (average rates); 3Mfor is three-month forward rate; note that vertical scale does not start at zero.

selling at a *premium*. If the opposite holds, that is, if the forward rate is below the spot rate, the currency is said to be selling at a *discount*. The existence of a forward premium is driven by an expected appreciation of the currency, while a forward discount is driven by an expected depreciation of the currency. To get a better (and comparable) view of the degree to which the euro was selling at a premium or a discount in this period, it is possbible to calculate the annualized forward premium for different maturities. Let S denote the spot exchange rate, F the forward rate, and let the duration be measured in months. Then this is given by:

$$forward\ premium\big|_{annual,\%} = \frac{(F - S)/S}{duration/12} \qquad 9.1$$

Figure 9.4 illustrates the forward premium for the three-month forward rate since 2009 (right-hand scale), as well as the spot rate of the euro (left-hand scale). It shows that the changes from one period to the next can be quite large and that the predicted percentage change of appreciation or depreciation (as measured by the forward premium) can be substantial (almost +10 percent, for example, on April 30, 2010, which is clearly outside the scale in the figure).

9.4   Interest Rate Parity

When you have a large sum of money to invest, you are interested in the return on your investment from different opportunities. When these opportunities are located in different countries, the exchange rate plays an important role in determining where to invest. This evaluation leads to the interest rate parity condition, which is crucial for international

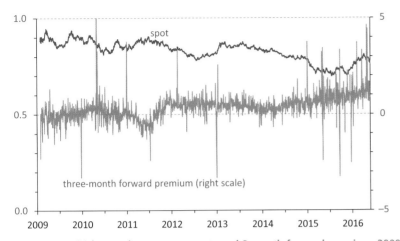

Figure 9.4 British pound to euro spot rate and 3-month forward premium, 2009–2016
Source: Based on Datastream data.
Notes: Daily data from January 1, 2009 to May 24, 2016 (average rates); three-month forward premium annualized, in percent.

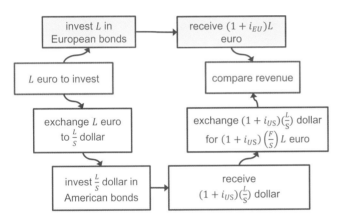

Figure 9.5 Two investment options

money markets. There are two types of interest rate parity conditions, namely covered and uncovered. This section starts with the former and then discusses the latter.

Suppose you live in Europe and want to invest in government bonds. For simplicity, just two options are considered, namely European bonds and American bonds. Assume that the two assets are *perfect substitutes*, implying in particular that there is no difference in perceived riskiness of one asset relative to the other. For concreteness, you have a large sum L of euros to invest for one time period and care only about the return in euros. Figure 9.5 shows two possible investment options.

- Option I: you can purchase a European bond. If the European interest rate is equal to i_{EU}, you will receive $(1 + i_{EU})L$ euros by the end of the period.
- Option II: you can purchase an American bond. Since these are denominated in dollars, you will have to be active on the foreign exchange market. First, by exchanging your L

euros on the spot market for L/S US dollars, where S is the spot exchange rate of the US dollar (its price in euros). Second, by investing these L/S dollars in American bonds. If the American interest rate is equal to i_{US}, you will receive $(1 + i_{US})(L/S)$ dollars by the end of the period. You are, however, not interested in the return in dollars, but only in the return in euros, so you will have to convert these dollars at the end of the period back to euros. This poses a problem because at the moment you are making your investment decision (option I or option II), you do not yet know what the future spot exchange rate of the dollar is going to be. This is where the forward exchange market provides a solution. Since you know exactly how many dollars you will receive one time period from now if you choose option II (namely $(1 + i_{US})(L/S)$ dollars), you will also know exactly how many euros you will receive if you sell these dollars before making your investment decision at the forward exchange rate F on the forward exchange market, namely $(1 + i_{US})(F/S)L$ euros.

In short, you know exactly the return to your investment if you choose option I and the return to your investment if you choose option II. Obviously, many other economic agents make similar calculations as you do (possibly trying to benefit from arbitrage opportunities) and all of you will invest in the asset with the highest return. If the two assets are perfect substitutes and both are held in equilibrium, the return to the two assets must therefore be the same to ensure that the market does not prefer one asset over the other, that is, we have the following equilibrium condition:

$$\frac{F(1 + i_{US})}{S}L = (1 + i_{EU})L \quad \Rightarrow \quad \frac{F}{S} = \frac{1 + i_{EU}}{1 + i_{US}} \qquad 9.2$$

Obviously, the time frame for equation 9.2 must be consistent, so if F is, for example, the three-month forward rate, then i_{EU} and i_{US} must be three-month interest rates. Except for interest rates, we will use the convention that lower-case letters refer to the natural logarithm of upper case letters. The second equality of condition 9.2 can be written more tersely by taking the natural logarithm and using the approximation $\ln(1 + X) \approx X$ (where the symbol $\approx$ should be read as "is approximately equal to"), to get:

$$f - s \approx i_{EU} - i_{US} \qquad 9.3$$

Equation 9.3 states that the logarithmic difference between the forward rate and the spot rate must be equal to the difference between the domestic and the foreign interest rate. It is known as the *covered interest parity condition*, because you have fully covered your return in foreign currency on the forward exchange market. It provides a powerful and crucial empirical relationship between interest rates and (spot and forward) exchange rates in international money and finance analysis.

Under the given circumstances, there are more options available to you. One of these options (called option III below) is *not* to hedge your risk on the forward exchange market. For clarity of exposition, it is better to now explicitly add a subindex t to denote time. Let's compare your revenue from option I, that is, buy the European bond, with the revenue from option III: buy the American bond and do not hedge on the forward exchange market. Nothing has changed for option I, so:

- revenue from buying European bond: $(1 + i_{EU,t})L$.

Before you can purchase the American bond you have to convert your euros to dollars at the exchange rate S_t, which will give you L/S_t dollars. In the next period your revenue will therefore be $(1 + i_{US,t})(L/S_t)$ dollars. You have decided not to hedge your foreign exchange risk, so in the next period you will have to exchange your currency on the spot exchange market. In this period, when you have to make your investment decision, you obviously do not know next period's spot exchange rate. To make your decision you will therefore have to form some expectation today about the future spot exchange rate. This can be a simple (single number) or a complicated (distribution function) expectation. Let's denote the expected value of your forecasting process by S_{t+1}^e, then we conclude:

- *expected* revenue from buying American bond: $\frac{S_{t+1}^e (1 + i_{US,t})}{S_t} L$.

We cannot draw immediate conclusions from comparing these two revenues, because we know the return to investing in the European bond for sure, whereas the return to investing in the American bond is uncertain. Only under the additional assumption of *risk-neutral* economic agents, hypothesizing that agents just focus on the expected value of the return and do not care at all about the underlying distribution of risk, should the sure return to the European bond be equal to the expected return of the American bond. Under that assumption, and after a similar logarithmic transformation and approximation as discussed above, we arrive at the *uncovered interest parity condition*:

$$s_{t+1}^e - s_t \approx i_{EU,t} - i_{US,t} \qquad 9.4$$

Equation 9.4 says that the difference in home and foreign interest rates must be equal to the expected appreciation of the foreign currency. As such, the equation is pretty useless for empirical testing because it contains the expectation of the future exchange rate and expectations cannot be directly measured. (It is possible, of course, to get indirect measures from surveys, consensus forecasts, and so on.) Alternatively, you can view it as a simple method to define these expectations under the assumption of risk neutrality. In combination with the covered interest parity condition 9.3, however, it is trivial to see that the forward exchange rate should be equal to the expected value of the future spot exchange rate:

$$f = s_{t+1}^e \qquad 9.5$$

Equation 9.5 still does not give us a testable hypothesis unless we are willing to go one step further, namely by assuming *rational expectations*. Under rational expectations economic agents make no systematic forecast errors. They will, of course, not be able to exactly predict the future exchange rate, but their prediction should reflect all information available to them at the time they are making the prediction. Any forecast errors must therefore be uncorrelated (that is, not systematically related) with the information set available at the

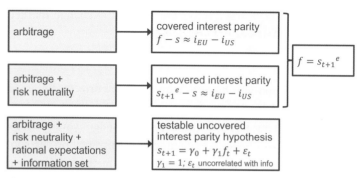

Figure 9.6 Assumptions, interest parity, and market efficiency

time of the prediction. Under the additional assumption of rational expectations, the uncovered interest parity condition can therefore be tested by estimating a regression similar to (see Frenkel 1976):

$$s_{t+1} = \gamma_0 + \gamma_1 f_t + \varepsilon_t \qquad\qquad 9.6$$

Where ε_t is the (forecast) error term. (For econometric reasons, the actual test is usually in deviation from s_t.) Under the hypothesis of risk neutrality and rational expectations, we expect the parameter γ_1 to be equal to unity and the forecast error to be uncorrelated with the information available at time t. Empirical estimates of equations like 9.6 are frequently called tests of *market efficiency*. There are different types of market efficiency, where the joint hypothesis of risk-neutrality and rational expectations is dubbed the *simple efficiency hypothesis* by Sarno and Taylor (2002, p. 10). Figure 9.6 schematically summarizes our discussion. Box 9.2 illustrates some of the economic and financial connections associated with interest rates, inflation, currencies, capital controls, and economic growth for Argentina.

9.5   The Policy Trilemma

In theory, it is possible to distinguish between two types of exchange rate regimes, namely *fixed* exchange rates and *flexible* exchange rates. In practice, there is a sliding scale (with associated colorful typology) from one hypothetical extreme to the other. As the names suggest, the difference between fixed and flexible exchange rates is the extent to which the exchange rate is allowed to change in response to market pressure. Under fixed exchange rates, the central bank of a country has set the exchange rate at a particular level and it will not allow the currency to appreciate or depreciate relative to that level. To maintain the fixed exchange rate, the central bank must be ready to intervene in the foreign exchange market by buying or selling reserves or by increasing or decreasing the interest rate (see van Marrewijk 2012). Under flexible exchange rates, on the other hand, the central bank does not intervene in the foreign exchange market and allows the currency to freely appreciate or depreciate in response to changes in market demand and supply.

BOX 9.2 ARGENTINA: INTEREST RATES, INFLATION, AND CAPITAL CONTROLS

Inflation rates in Argentina have been high in the twentieth century. The *average* inflation rate in the period 1975–90, for example, was about 550 percent *per year*, which implies that prices rise by about 40 percent per month (based on World Bank Development Indicators online GDP deflator). The peak of inflation was in 1989 at more than 3,000 percent. As Figure 9.7 illustrates, after a period of free-market reform and privatization, the inflation rate became low or negative until 2001 and combined with an exacerbating economic crisis starting in 1998, eventually leading to a large contraction of about 11 percent in 2002.

A series of deposit runs forced the Argentine authorities to impose a deposit freeze (capital controls) in December 2001, combined with partial default and abandoning convertibility. The peso lost most of its value and in 2002 inflation rose to 31 percent and the interest rate to 52 percent, while unemployment rose sharply. Economic growth returned under the guidance of Roberto Lavagna (Minister of the Economy), who moderated inflation and stabilized the exchange rate, with the help of a commodity price boom. Under the Kirchner presidencies (first Néstor and then his wife Cristina Fernández), inflation rates crawled back up despite price and capital controls, with a slowdown of the economy and a second default in 2014.

Based on this legacy, Mauricio Macri became president in 2015, and then released exchange restrictions and lifted price and capital controls. The subsequent rise in inflation rate was accompanied with rising interest rates (to 40 and 37 percent in 2018, respectively). Despite negative real interest rates, economic growth was halted and

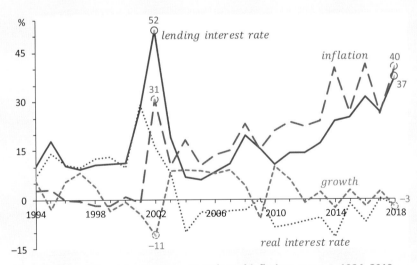

Figure 9.7 Argentina: interest rates, growth, and inflation; percent, 1994–2018
Source: Created using World Development Indicators data.
Notes: inflation is GDP deflator; growth is GDP growth.

BOX 9.2 (cont.)

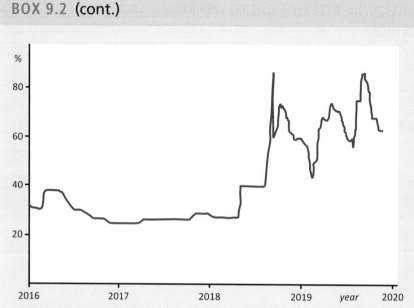

Figure 9.8 Argentina Reference interest rate; seven-day LELIQ rate, 2016–2020
Source: Created using Central Bank of Argentina data (https://tradingeconomics.com).

turned negative (–3 percent) in 2018. As the interest rate developments since then (see Figure 9.8) show, the situation became unstable in August 2018 (see The Economist 2018). The peso depreciated sharply as financial markets started to worry that the government would struggle to refinance its debt and get re-elected in view of the required high interest rates to attract creditors, which might repel voters. These worries became a reality in October 2019 when Alberto Fernandez rather than Maurizio Macri was elected. Interest rates rose sharply as Argentina tightened capital controls (re-introduced in September 2019) substantially: savers could only buy US$200 per month, rather than US$2,000 per month (Do Rosarion and Millan 2019).

The history of the international economic order on exchange rate regimes and capital market integration is closely connected (see Mundell 1968, Eichengreen 1996, and Obstfeld and Taylor 2003). To better understand this connection, it is useful to distinguish between three possible policy objectives that a nation might try to achieve (see Beugelsdijk *et al.* 2013 for a similar analysis):

1. Monetary policy independence.
2. A fixed exchange rate.
3. International capital mobility.

The first objective is desirable as it allows a country to determine its monetary policy independently of other countries, based on its own economic circumstances. The second objective is desirable as it provides price stability for international transactions and a clear point of reference. The third objective is desirable as it allows spreading of investment risks and access to the most profitable projects internationally.

It turns out that only two of these three policy objectives can be achieved at any one point in time, at the expense of the third objective. Focusing on the EU and the USA, this can be illustrated most effectively by recalling the uncovered interest rate parity condition with transaction costs (using a zero risk premium, see equation 9.7):

$$i_{EU,t} = i_{US,t} + \left(s_{t+1}^e - s_t\right) + \textit{transaction costs} \qquad 9.7$$

where the subindex t denotes time, $i_{EU,t}$ is the EU interest rate, $i_{US,t}$ is the US interest rate, s_t is the (log) US dollar exchange rate (price of one dollar in terms of euros), and s_{t+1}^e is the (log) expected value of next period's US dollar exchange rate.

If there is complete international capital mobility (objective 3 holds), the transaction costs are very low, such that equation 9.7 reduces to the uncovered interest parity condition itself: $i_{EU,t} = i_{US,t} + \left(s_{t+1}^e - s_t\right)$. This implies that expected changes in the exchange rate are the only reason for an interest rate differential between the EU and the USA. With full international capital mobility, policymakers must therefore *choose* between monetary policy independence (reaching objective 1, as measured by a deviation between EU and US interest rates) and a fixed exchange rate (reaching objective 2).

Figure 9.9 illustrates how satisfying two policy objectives (squares) necessarily implies sacrificing the third policy objective (circle).

If, for example, the monetary authorities decide to fix the exchange rate (such that $s_{t+1}^e - s_t = 0$), this automatically implies $i_{EU,t} = i_{US,t}$, making monetary policy independence impossible. Similarly, if they decide to strive for monetary policy independence, this automatically makes a fixed exchange rate impossible since $s_{t+1}^e \neq s_t$ when $i_{EU,t} \neq i_{US,t}$. The only way in which objectives 1 and 2 can be achieved simultaneously is by giving up objective 3, in which case equation 9.7 with fixed exchange rates reduces to $i_{EU,t} = i_{US,t} + \textit{transaction costs}$. A country can then steer its own interest rate (retain policy autonomy) and have a fixed exchange rate at the cost of immobile capital, which

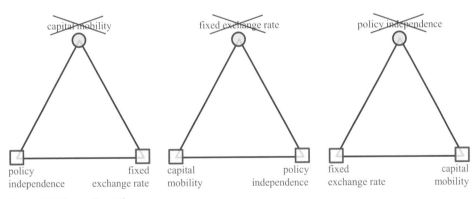

Figure 9.9 The policy trilemma

prevents portfolio investors from directing capital flows to or from the EU so as to benefit from the interest rate differential. Although intermediate solutions are possible for monetary policy independence and capital controls (some capital controls buy you some monetary independence, see also Table 9.4 below), this does not hold for fixed exchange rates.

The incompatibility among objectives 1–3 was pointed out by Nobel laureate Robert Mundell in the early 1960s. It is called the *incompatible trinity, incompatible triangle,* or *policy trilemma,* and provides us with a categorization scheme that helps us to understand changes in the international economic order over time. Figure 9.9 illustrates the trilemma. In each triangle of the figure the two squares indicate the objectives pursued by the government, whereas the circle at the top of the triangle indicates the policy objective that cannot be met. The trilemma indicates that there is a price to pay for policymakers when they want to achieve full capital mobility, fixed exchange rates, or policy autonomy. Box 9.2 illustrates the connections for a real-world case such as Argentina.

9.6   Exchange Rate Policy

This section briefly explains how the policy choices have changed over time by focusing on the most recent main international monetary regimes (see also Eichengreen 1996 and Obstfeld and Taylor 2003).[3] Figure 9.10 gives an overview of these regimes and their duration, and a summary of the main characteristics:

- Gold Standard (±1870–1914)
- World Wars and Recession (1914–45)
- Bretton Woods (1945–71)
- Floating Rates (1971–now)

9.6.1   Gold Standard (±1870–1914)

Toward the end of the nineteenth century, when the UK was the world's leading economy and London the undisputed global financial center, an increasing share of the world economy moved to the gold standard. This was a stable and credible fixed exchange rate regime in which countries valued their currency in terms of gold. It started in Britain in 1844 when the Bank Charter Act established that Bank of England Notes, fully backed by gold, were the legal standard. It became an international standard in 1871 when Germany established the Reich mark on a strict gold standard, soon followed by many other European nations, and eventually by Japan (1897), India (1898), and the USA (1900). With countries issuing bank notes directly backed by gold, and by allowing gold to be freely imported and exported across borders according to the gold standard rules, the exchange rates between the currencies became fixed. Suppose, for example, that the Federal Reserve pegs the price of gold at $35 per ounce and the Bank of England at £7,

---

[3] General historical information in this section is based on Wikipedia, http://en.wikipedia.org.

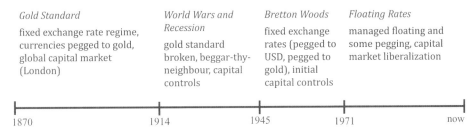

Gold Standard	World Wars and Recession	Bretton Woods	Floating Rates
fixed exchange rate regime, currencies pegged to gold, global capital market (London)	gold standard broken, beggar-thy-neighbour, capital controls	fixed exchange rates (pegged to USD, pegged to gold), initial capital controls	managed floating and some pegging, capital market liberalization

1870   1914   1945   1971   now

Figure 9.10 Overview of international monetary regimes

then the exchange rate of the British Pound in terms of US dollars must be $35/7 = 5$, otherwise profitable arbitrage opportunities arise. In practice, taking the costs of shipping and insuring gold in transit into consideration, the exchange rates could fluctuate within narrow margins called *gold points*. The gold standard functioned as a disciplining device for countries, which led to a convergence of interest rates and a global capital market centered in London, in exchange for a reduction in policy autonomy.

The gold standard worked quite well at the end of the nineteenth and beginning of the twentieth centuries, but there are also several drawbacks to the gold standard. First, although currency backed by gold generally leads to relatively stable prices, the rate of inflation is determined not only by macroeconomic conditions, but also by the random discoveries of new gold supplies. There have been considerable fluctuations linked to these events (see Cooper 1982). Second, the international payments system requires gold as reserves. As economies are growing, central banks strive for an increase in the buffer stock of their gold reserves (otherwise there would be deflation). Simultaneous competition for gold by central banks might bring about unemployment through a reduction in their money supply. Third, the gold standard gives countries with a large gold supply, such as Russia and South Africa, the ability to influence the world's macroeconomic conditions by selling gold. Fourth, and perhaps most importantly, the gold standard puts undue restrictions on the use of monetary policy as a means for fighting unemployment under special circumstances, such as a worldwide recession (this is true for any fixed exchange rate regime).

9.6.2   World Wars and Recession (1914–1945)

The pillars of the international economic system – the gold standard, multilateral trade, and the interchangeability of currencies – crumbled down one by one during the First World War (1914–18), the Second World War (1939–45), and particularly during the Great Depression, which started in October 1929 and lasted throughout the 1930s. To finance its war efforts, Britain ended the convertibility of Bank of England notes in 1914. Nations printed more money than could be redeemed in gold, hoping to win the First World War and redeem the excess out of reparations payments. Losing the war, Germany was indeed required by the Treaty of Versailles to pay large punitive damages, of which in the end it could only effectively transfer a fraction (see Brakman and van Marrewijk 1998, ch. 1). To deal with these difficulties, the Bank for International Settlements was established in 1930 under the Young Plan. Many nations, including the USA and the UK, instituted capital controls to prevent the movement of gold. Britain returned to the gold standard at the prewar gold price in 1925, which entailed a significant deflation for the economy, much to the dismay of British economist John Maynard Keynes, who called the gold standard a "barbarous relic."

The credibility of the gold standard was broken by the First World War, such that countries were no longer willing to give up their policy autonomy for a well-functioning international economic system, focusing instead on domestic political goals. Consequently, when the Great Depression hit in 1929, many countries engaged in non-cooperative, competitive beggar-thy-neighbor devaluations and instituted capital controls. This greatly exacerbated the crisis, caused the international trade system to collapse, and put millions of people out of a job, with unemployment rates of more than 30 percent. Both the punitive damages required from Germany in the Treaty of Versailles and the economic consequences of the nationalistic policies imposed during the Great Depression are seen as major contributing factors in causing the outbreak of the Second World War. While the war was raging, politicians and advisors started to work on a plan to avoid this happening again.

During the Great Depression in the 1930s, the "beggar-thy-neighbor" policies, in which each country tried to transfer its economic problems to other countries by depreciating its own currency and imposing high tariffs (see, for example, the Hawley–Smoot Act of the USA in 1930), led to an almost complete collapse of the international trade system, further exacerbating and prolonging the economic crisis. The impact of the beggar-thy-neighbor policies on international trade is aptly illustrated by the "spider web spiral," measuring the size of world imports in each month by the distance to the origin (see Figure 9.11). In a period of only four years, world trade flows dropped to one-third of their previous level (from January 1929 to January 1933, world imports fell from 2,998 to 992 million US gold $ per month).

9.6.3 Bretton Woods (1945–1971)

The foundations for a new international economic order were laid at the Mount Washington hotel in Bretton Woods, New Hampshire, when the delegates of 44 allied nations signed the Bretton Woods Agreement in July 1944. The delegates set up a system of rules, institutions, and procedures and established the International Monetary Fund (IMF) and the World Bank. Planning for the new order had been under way some three years since the US President Franklin Roosevelt and the British Prime Minister Winston Churchill signed the Atlantic Charter in August 1941. There was no question toward the end of the Second World War that the balance of power had shifted toward the USA, politically and economically, as well as militarily. This meant that, although there was some compromise toward the British plan designed by John Maynard Keynes, the structure of the Bretton Woods system was based on the plans designed by American Harry Dexter White, who would remain a powerful initial influence at the IMF as the first US Executive Director.

The pillar of the US vision for the post-war economic order was free trade and a prevention of beggar-thy-neighbor policies. William Clayton, Assistant Secretary of State

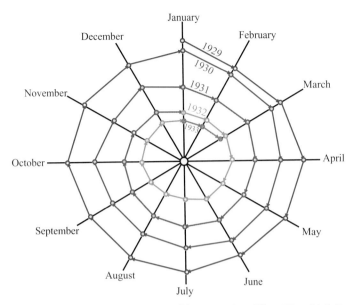

Figure 9.11 Spider web spiral: world imports in million US gold dollar, 1929–1933
Source: League of Nations 1933.
Note: Values in January (1929–33): 2,998; 2,739; 1,839; 1,206; 992.

for economic affairs, apparently summed up this point by saying: "we need markets – big markets – around the world in which to buy and sell." Free trade involved lowering tariffs and other trade barriers, a task for the GATT/WTO, and a stable international monetary system to foster the development of trade and capital flows. To do this, the gold standard was re-established indirectly through the role of the US dollar as international reserve currency. The US government fixed the price of gold at $35 per ounce and made a commitment to convert dollars to gold at that price (for foreign governments and central banks). In conjunction with the strength of the US economy, this made dollars even better than gold as international reserves, since dollars earned interest and gold did not. Other countries pegged their currency to the US dollar at a *par value* and would buy and sell dollars to keep exchange rates within a *band* of plus or minus 1 percent of parity. To avoid the beggar-thy-neighbor devaluation problem, member countries could only change their par value with IMF approval, which required a decision by the IMF that the balance of payments was in "fundamental disequilibrium." A decrease in the value of a currency was called a *devaluation*, an increase a *revaluation*. This terminology still holds for all fixed exchange rate regimes. For floating regimes, *appreciation* and *depreciation* are used respectively.

9.6.4 Floating Rates (1971–Now)

Increasing pressure on the Bretton Woods system during the 1960s and early 1970s caused its collapse. Massive sales of gold by the Federal Reserve and European central banks led to the installment of a two-tier gold market on March 17, 1968. Private traders could buy and sell gold at a price determined by market forces on the London gold market, while central banks would continue to transact with one another at the (lower) official gold price of $35 per ounce. The latter was only used to a limited extent. Speculation against the dollar forced the German Bundesbank to purchase $1 billion during a single day on May 4, 1971, and another $1 billion during the first hour of the next trading day alone (see Krugman and Obstfeld 2003, p. 560). Germany gave up and allowed the mark to float. It became clear that the dollar had to be devalued. This was, however, difficult under the Bretton Woods system because it implied that all other currencies, which were pegged to the dollar, had to be revalued with approval from the IMF and all other countries, many of whom were reluctant to do so. Richard Nixon, the US president, forced the issue on August 15, 1971 by formally ending the convertibility of US dollars to gold and imposing a 10 percent tax on all imports into the USA until an agreement was reached. Although this *Smithsonian agreement* to devalue the dollar by about 8 percent came in December of 1971 (at the Smithsonian Institution in Washington, DC), it was unable to save the Bretton Woods system. After renewed speculative attacks, there was another 10 percent devaluation of the dollar on February 12, 1973, followed by a decision of a floating exchange rate of the US dollar relative to the most important international currencies on March 19, 1973.

Table 9.4 summarizes the policy choices made by most countries concerning the policy trilemma explained in section 9.5 for each of the four most recent international monetary systems. During the Gold Standard there was a broad consensus to give up on policy autonomy in exchange for capital mobility and maintaining fixed exchange rates. This broke down during the World Wars and Recession era, as most countries pursued activist monetary policies to try to solve domestic problems at the cost of either imposing large capital controls or giving up on fixed exchange rates. In the Bretton Woods era there was again broad consensus to maintain fixed exchange rates, this time by sacrificing capital mobility (which was limited directly after the Second World War and then gradually increased). For the Floating Rates era, the table depicts the more recent policy choices as

Table 9.4. The policy trilemma and the international economic order

Era	Resolution of trilemma – countries choose to sacrifice:			Notes
	Policy autonomy	Capital mobility	Fixed exchange rate	
Gold Standard	most	few	few	broad consensus
World Wars and Recession	few	several	most	capital controls especially in Centr. Europe, Lat. America
Bretton Woods	few	most	few	broad consensus
Floating Rates	few	few	many	some consensus; currency boards, dollarization, etc.

Source: Obstfeld and Taylor 2003.

they have evolved over time, in which many countries have been willing to give up on fixed exchange rates in return for policy autonomy and capital mobility.

9.6.5   Current Exchange Rate Regimes

Although the present international monetary system is called the Floating Rates era, this does not mean that all currencies are freely determined by market forces. On the contrary, almost all countries at some time or another engage in some type of foreign exchange market intervention, either through their legal framework, direct intervention, or their interest rate policy. As summarized in Table 9.5, the IMF currently identifies 10 different exchange rate regimes. Figure 9.12 shows the number of countries in each of the

Table 9.5. IMF exchange rate classification system

Hard pegs	
No separate legal tender	The currency of another country circulates as the sole legal tender (formal dollarization).
Currency board arrangements	A monetary regime based on an explicit commitment to exchange domestic currency for a specified foreign currency at a fixed exchange rate. The domestic currency will be issued only against (fully backed) foreign exchange.
Soft pegs	
Conventional pegged arrangement	The country formally (de jure) pegs its currency at a fixed rate to another currency or a basket of currencies. The exchange rate may fluctuate within narrow margins.
Stabilized arrangement	A spot market exchange rate that remains within a margin of 2 percent (except for outliers) for six months or more and is not floating.
Crawling peg	The currency is adjusted in small amounts at a fixed rate or in response to changes in selected indicators.
Crawl-like arrangement	The exchange rate remains in a narrow margin of 2 percent relative to a statistically identified trend for six months or more and is not floating.
Pegged exchange rate within horizontal bands	The exchange rate is maintained within margins of at least +1 percent around a central rate.
Floating arrangements	
Floating	The exchange rate is largely market determined, without an ascertainable or predictable path for the rate.
Free floating	Exchange rate intervention occurs only exceptionally and aims to address disorderly market conditions.
Residual	
Other managed arrangement	A residual category if the exchange rate regime does not meet the criteria for any of the other categories.

Sources: IMF 2020, table 1 and Habermeier *et al.* 2009.
Note: System used since 2009.

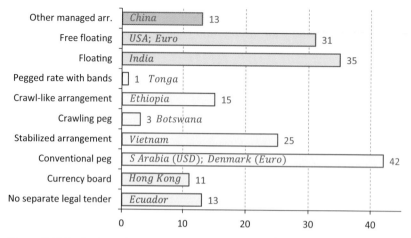

Figure 9.12 De facto exchange rate arrangements; April 30, 2019
Data source: IMF 2020, table 2.
Notes: # of countries; selected countries for each regime, see also Table 9.5.

10 categories as identified on April 30, 2019, with some selected countries in each category for illustration purposes. It indicates that many countries have opted for a floating or free floating arrangement, while at the same time many other countries are engaged in various forms of fixed and managed exchange rate regimes.

9.7   Trade Finance

Compared to domestic trade, cross-border trade activities are more risky, which raises costs as firms learn about foreign markets, regulations, and product customization (see Foley and Manova 2015). In addition, traders experience a longer delay between production and payment, while banks screen traders more carefully, which raises the costs of credit (see Ahn *et al.* 2011). Trade finance is credit (including open account, cash-in-advance, and bank-intermediated instruments) that banks offer to firms to facilitate global trade. The payment contract is influenced by export and import market characteristics, costs, timing, and default risk. As a result of the above properties, trade finance has characteristics that differ from other types of credit (see DiCaprio and Yao 2017). These characteristics include: (i) short tenor (the amount of time left for repayment or until a contract expires); (ii) availability (not all banks have the know-how to offer trade finance); and (iii) stability (the first line of credit to be pulled in case of a liquidity shortage).

Historically, attention for difficulties traders encounter when they want to finance their activities rises in times of a credit crunch (such as the Great Recession, which started in 2008) as a way to explain the exacerbation of a crisis since banks transfer the shock (their shortage of funds) to their borrowers (credit rationing). In contrast, since 2013, the Asian Development Bank (ADB) has been collecting information on trade finance difficulties during regular times as an obstacle in the development process. These efforts now seem to

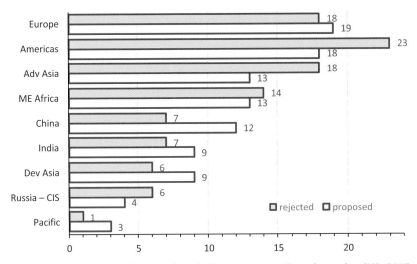

Figure 9.13 Proposed and rejected trade finance transactions; by region (%), 2017
Source: Created using data from ADB 2017.
Notes: Adv Asia = Advanced Asia (Hong Kong, Japan, S. Korea, Singapore); ME = Middle East; Dev Asia = Developing Asia, excl. China and India; CIS = Commonwealth of Independent States (Azerbaijan, Belarus, Kazakhstan, Kyrgyzstan, Armenia, Moldova, Russia, Tajikistan, Uzbekistan).

lead to a bi-annual *Trade Finance Gaps, Growth and Jobs Survey*, used in this section as the main source of information. It is suitable that the ADB became active in this area since the dominant bank-intermediated trade finance instruments are Letters of Credit, for which Asia and the Pacific is by far the dominant region (see DiCaprio and Yao 2017).

The global regional distribution of proposed and rejected trade finance transactions is reasonably stable and depicted for 2017 in Figure 9.13. Ordered by proposed transactions, Europe is the largest region (19 percent), followed by the Americas (North and South, 18 percent). At the continent level Asia is dominant (close to 50 percent), but in the figure it is subdivided into many sub-regions (advanced Asia, developing Asia, China, and India), while the Middle East is combined with Africa. Relative to their share in proposed transactions, the share of rejected transactions is large in the Americas, advanced Asia, Middle East & Africa, and in the Commonwealth of Independent States. It is relatively low in the other regions.

Figure 9.14 focuses on the distribution of proposed and rejected transactions by firm size. Multinationals and large corporations take care of almost half of the proposed transactions and only one-quarter of the rejected transactions. In contrast, micro and small and medium-sized enterprises take care of only 12 percent of the proposed transactions and almost double that (22 percent) of rejected transactions. The midcap firms are in between. The probability of a rejected transaction is thus substantially larger for smaller firms.

In subsequent work, the ADB analyzed some of the causes and consequences of rejected trade finance transactions. Figure 9.15 starts with the causes of rejection and shows that many projects lack additional collateral or are simply unsuitable for support. Other important reasons for rejection are the inability of banks to really know their customers,

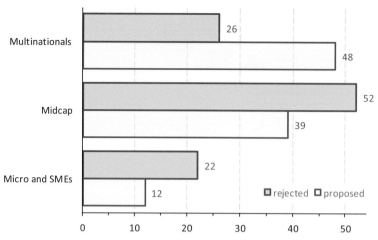

Figure 9.14 Proposed and rejected trade finance transactions; by firm size (%), 2017
Source: Created using data from ADB 2017.
Notes: Multinationals includes large corporations; SMEs = small and medium-sized enterprises.

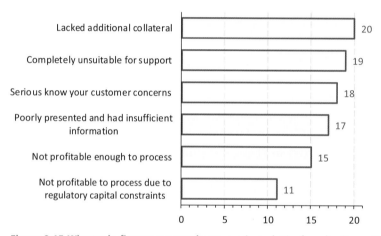

Figure 9.15 Why trade finance proposals were rejected; % of applications, 2019
Source: Created using data from ADB 2019.

poor presentation, and insufficient information. Less frequent reasons are a lack of profitability of the finance transaction and regulatory capital constraints.

In most cases, the consequence of rejected trade finance proposals is that the transaction does not take place. An imperfect indication is provided in Figure 9.16, which lists the outcome of the respondents of a question regarding the outcome of efforts to seek alternative finance. In almost half of the cases (47 percent), respondents were unable to find appropriate alternative finance, while in 18 percent of the cases they found alternative, informal, or digital finance (in 10, 7, and 1 percent of the cases, respectively), but opted not to use it. Hence, about 65 percent of the rejected trade finance transactions failed to materialize. The remaining projects were financed eventually, about 18 percent through

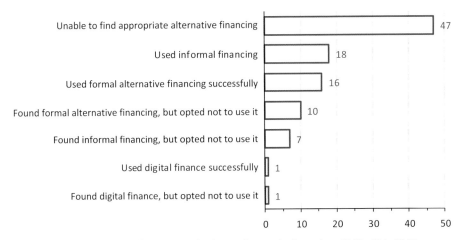

Figure 9.16 Outcome of efforts to seek alternative trade financing; SMEs (%), 2019
Source: Created using data from ADB 2019.
Notes: % of respondents; SMEs = small and medium-sized enterprises.

informal financing, 16 percent through alternative formal financing, and 1 percent through digital financing.

The Asian Development Bank (2019) estimates that the global trade finance gap is large but stable at $1.5 trillion. The global regional distribution is fairly stable, but the gap is particularly large for smaller firms. This shortage in trade finance needs continues to hamper international trade, particularly for the smallest firms in developing countries. The Asian Development Bank (2019) finds no evidence that improved technology is reducing the gap.

9.8 International Currencies

It has already been noted in section 9.6 that the dollar performs the role of an international currency. The current section briefly looks at the consequences of this characteristic of the world economy. International currencies perform the same roles as national currency, but are also used outside the country of origin. Table 9.6 gives a widely accepted typology.

International currencies act as a medium of exchange just as a national currency would do, but at a larger scale. These are the so-called *vehicle* currencies that facilitate currency exchanges. If businesses need to exchange for example the Bhutan ngultrum into the Rwandan franc the US dollar is in the middle and two exchanges take place because there is no market that exchanges both currencies directly. So the ngultrum is exchanged into dollars, and dollars into francs. The US dollar is the main currency in this respect. According to the Bank for International Settlements (2019), 88 percent of all trades in April 2019 involved the US dollar. Closely related to this function is that these currencies are a safe store of value in unstable local markets. It protects private actors against extreme inflation, and the trust in the US government can be higher than in a local government.

Table 9.6. Functions of international currencies

Sector	Functions		
	Medium of exchange	Store of value	Unit of account
Private sector	Vehicle currency Liquid & safe asset markets	Nominal securities issuance Banking and cash hoarding	Denomination of securities Trade invoicing
Official sector	Intervention currency Lender of last resort	Reserves	Exchange rate peg

Source: Based on Gourinchas *et al.* 2019.

It is well known that in financial markets there is a home-market effect, which means that investors have a bias in favor of investments in the home market currency. For international currencies, this is different. US firms – even if they are small – can easily borrow money from foreign investors because foreign investors have little difficulty lending in US dollars. This gives US borrowers an advantage that firms in other countries – for example, developing countries with a less developed financial market – do not have. This is partly an explanation of one of the Obstfeld and Rogoff (2000) puzzles.

The special position of international currencies and in particular of the US dollar is also reflected in the denomination of securities and invoice share of these international currencies. Gopinath (2016) documents that for many countries a large share of imports and exports is denominated in the US dollar. If trade is denominated in a particular currency, traders can reduce the exchange rate risk by also holding funds and securities in the same currency.

For central banks – the official sector – the special role of international currencies implies that if they have to intervene in currency markets it is efficient to do so using a currency that most market players use – that is, an international currency. As a consequence, holding reserves in these currencies is a precaution for when the need arrives to intervene.

A reserve currency gives the country of origin, the hegemon, an advantage. Exchange rate risks are in general not as severe as for other countries, running a current account deficit for extended periods of time is not as problematic as for other countries (a deficit is needed to provide the world with a sufficient amount of the reserve currency), and it has easier access to global capital markets compared to other countries. For unstable countries with governments that are unable to handle the economy, such a currency provides a safe haven. But what are the disadvantages?

It turns out that an appreciation of the dollar is transmitted in import and export prices throughout the world, while at the same time insulating the USA from these price changes. Gopinath *et al.* (2019) find that a 1 percent appreciation of the dollar results in a 0.6–0.8 percent decline in (world) trade. The special position of the reserve currency also affects the discussion of the trilemma in section 9.5 (see Rey 2016). The position of a strong reserve currency such as the dollar affects the policy trilemma. As discussed in section 9.5, a flexible exchange rate should allow a country to perform independent monetary policy, but a strong reserve on which a country relies interferes with this as monetary conditions are sensitive to monetary policies in the hegemon country – in practice, the USA. So, reserve currencies enable unstable countries to find safe havens, but also make them dependent on the policies of another country – in practice, the USA.

9.9 Finance, Investment, and Development

Foreign direct investments (FDI) are an important source of investments for many countries. If a foreign investor acquires a controlling stake in a firm, it is an FDI. If the investment does not result in a controlling stake in the firm, it is called a portfolio or equity investment. The threshold to qualify as FDI is in practice at 10 percent or higher. FDI can be a greenfield investment (the construction of a new production facility) or a Merger&Acquisition (M&A) (a takeover of an existing firm). Most FDI is in the form of M&As (see Antràs and Yeaple 2014).

The distribution of FDI flows is shown in Figure 9.17 for four groups of countries, determined by the World Bank (2020 classification) on the basis of income per capita (Atlas method), as follows:

- High-income countries; 2019 GNI per capita $12,536 or more; consists of 83 countries in total, including most of Europe, the USA, Japan, and South Korea.
- Upper-middle-income countries; 2019 GNI per capita between $4,046 and $12,535; consists of 56 countries in total, including China, Brazil, Indonesia, and Russia.
- Lower-middle-income countries; 2019 GNI per capita between $1,036 and $4,045; consists of 50 countries in total, including India, Bangladesh, Nigeria, and the Philippines.

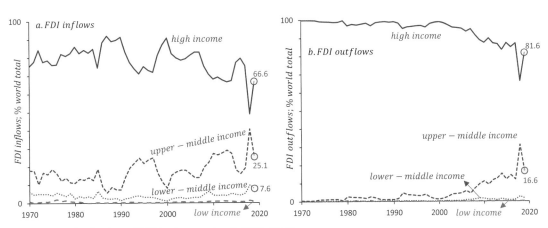

Figure 9.17 Distribution of FDI by income level; 1970–2019
Source: Created using World Development Online data.
Notes: FDI inflows are net inflows (BoP, current USD) as percent of the world total; FDI outflows are net outflows (BoP, current USD) as percent of the world total; see the main text for details on country classification.

- Low-income countries; 2019 GNI per capita $1,035 or less; consists of 29 countries in total, mostly in Sub-Sahara Africa, but also Afghanistan, North Korea, and Haiti.

Figure 9.17 indicates that the high-income countries of Europe, the USA, and Japan are both the main source (panel b, outflows; 81.6 percent in 2019) and the main destination (panel a, inflows; 66.6 percent) of FDI flows. The panels also show variability over time (as is common for investment flows) and that the share of high-income countries is declining over time. Moreover, taken together, the high-income countries are the main *net investors* in the rest of the world (outflows are larger than inflows for all years, on average by about 16 percentage points). As panel a of Figure 9.17 shows, the upper-middle-income countries, including China and Mexico, have been the most important recipients of these FDI flows and their share of the total has been rising over time (from about 10 percent to about 25 percent, with a peak of 40 percent in 2018). Panel a also shows that lower-middle-income countries (like India) play only a modest role in FDI inflows (about 4 percent of the world total), while low-income countries (in Sub-Sahara Africa) play almost no role at all (only about 0.5 percent of the world total). Finally, panel b shows that upper-middle-income countries (like China) have begun to play a more important role as a source of FDI flows since the new millennium.

Why do investors engage in FDI? The literature distinguishes between two main forces: a *horizontal* motive and a *vertical* motive. With horizontal FDI a firm copies the production facility at home in the foreign market in order to serve customers in that market, hence the term "horizontal." With vertical FDI a firm establishes a foreign branch that produces an intermediate step in the production process for the final product, hence the term "vertical." With horizontal FDI a firm is looking for interesting markets – for example, a market with sufficiently many wealthy customers to buy a certain type of product. For this type of investment low costs in the foreign market are less important than a developed market. For vertical FDI cost differences tend to be most important. This includes, for example, low local wages for labor-intensive parts of the production process, but can also be based on other types of cost advantages. In practice, one finds combinations of both motives.

The horizontal versus vertical typology structures the discussion on FDI. Figure 9.17 shows that most FDI takes place between advanced countries, which suggests that the dominant motive for FDI is not that firms are looking for low-cost destinations to set up an establishment, but for interesting markets. This observation does not imply that the vertical FDI motive is absent; many FDI flows are between developing and advanced countries. For these flows the vertical FDI motive is usually important. What is striking in Figure 9.17 is that middle-income developing countries increasingly participate in FDI. The question arises why firms do not simply export and import, but take the trouble to set up a foreign establishment? Dunning (1981) describes the main aspects of multinational ownership in his famous *OLI* framework. The *O* stands for Ownership advantages and indicates that a firm has know-how that other firms do not have, like patents, technology, and management practices. The *L* stands for Location advantages in the foreign market. A foreign market might have advantages such as low wages or large markets that compensate for the additional cost of setting up an additional facility. Finally, the *I* stands for Internalization advantages and indicates that because of transaction frictions it is beneficial to produce in-house, instead of outsourcing. All three advantages together are necessary to explain the existence of multinational firms.

What are the effects of FDI on the destination markets? These investments can contribute to further development by increasing capital in the host markets. There is, however, also a risk of crowding-out; if FDI is financed locally it could make investments for domestic firms more difficult if lenders prefer FDI over local firms. The effects of FDI on economic growth in the host countries is also ambiguous. Multinational firms – on average – pay higher wages, and are more innovative and skill-intensive than local firms, but the effects are only positive when FDI is accompanied by a mature financial sector (see Alfaro *et al.* 2004).

FDI can also have positive effects on local firms through knowledge spillovers that increase productivity in local firms. Furthermore, local firms can benefit from multi-national activity through forward and backward linkages. Forward linkages refer to the supply of high-quality intermediate products by multinationals. Backward linkages refer to the demand for local inputs by multinationals. Of course, there are also negative effects of multinational production. The additional demand for finance might crowd out local firms, they can monopolize local markets and raise wages such that the most qualified workers are no longer available to local firms. The net effects of FDI are not clear-cut (see Alfaro and Chauvin 2020 for a recent survey). See Chapter 18 for a further discussion.

9.10   The Miracle of Microfinance?

As already mentioned in Chapter 8, Mohammed Yunus observed that very small loans could make a disproportionate difference to a poor person. Because the size of the loans and the lack of collateral make such loans uninteresting for regular banks, he started Grameen Bank in 1976 and used his government connections to pioneer the concepts of microcredit and microfinance. These efforts to make a difference earned him the Nobel Peace Prize in 2006.

After an initial period of praise for reducing poverty by making microfinancing available, support dwindled as stories of problems, such as suicides linked to high debts, became available. Reddy Subrahmanyam, an Indian official, even argues that "the industry [has] become no better than the widely despised village loan sharks it was intended to replace" (quoted in Banerjee *et al.* 2015, p. 23). Using a randomized control trial methodology (see Chapter 11), Banerjee *et al.* (2015; referred to as BDGK in this section) evaluate the effectiveness of microfinance in the city of Hyderabad (population about 10 million in 2020), India. This section summarizes their findings.

The BDGK experiment focuses on the expansion of microfinance by Spandana in Hyderabad, starting in 2005. After identifying 104 poor neighborhoods, 52 were randomly selected to open a Spandana branch (treatment neighborhoods), while the other neigborhoods were not (control neighborhoods). After 15 to 18 months, the first comprehensive "endline" household survey was conducted. During this time period other microfinance institutions entered both the treatment and control neighborhoods, and it was possible for people living in control neighborhoods to borrow from Spandana microfinance in a treatment neighborhood (see below for details). Two years later, a second "endline" survey was conducted among the same households. By this time, both Spandana and other microfinance institutions were active in both the treatment and control neighborhoods.

In line with other microfinance institutions, the main Spandana product is a group loan (first introduced by Grameen Bank). A group consists of 6–10 women, while 25–45 groups form a "center." The loans are small (10,000 rupees for the first loan) and the women must meet certain conditions to be eligible.[4] The group is jointly responsible for the loan, which is repaid with interest in 50 weeks. The interest rate is 12 percent and the annual percentage rate (APR) is 24. Perhaps remarkably, these interest rates were low by typical microfinance standards. If all members of a group repay their loans they are eligible for a next loan (up to 2,000 rupees higher than the previous loan, with a maximum of 20,000 rupees). The groups are formed by the women and Spandana does not require a group to (pretend to) start a business. Nonetheless, small businesses in the rapidly growing Hyderabad environment of the time were common: 32 businesses per 100 households, compared to an OECD-country average of 12 percent who say that they are self-employed. Business owners and their families spend on average 76 hours per week working in the business.

Table 9.7 provides summary information for access to credit (in percentage points) for the two endline surveys for treatment and control neighborhoods, as well as their difference (and its significance). At the first endline survey, access to Spandana microfinance is significantly higher for the treatment neighborhoods than for the control neighborhoods (17.8 versus 5.1 percent). Since there is only a small and insignificant difference in access to other microfinance institutions (13.7 versus 14.9 percent), the access to microfinance overall is significantly higher in the treatment neighborhoods (26.7 versus 18.3 percent). Access to other bank credit and to total credit is similar for the treatment and control neighborhoods, while access to informal credit is significantly lower for the treatment neighborhoods (70.9 versus 76.1 percent). At endline 1, therefore, people in treatment neighborhoods had better access to microfinance because of Spandana and partially used this to reduce expensive informal borrowing.

Table 9.7 also shows for the endline 2 survey that there are no differences in access to microfinance, other bank, informal, and total credit between treatment and control neighborhoods. The main difference is that people in treatment neighborhoods had significantly better access to Spandana microfinance credit and less access to other microfinance credit

---

[4] Clients (i) must be female, (ii) must be between 18 and 59 years old, (iii) must have resided in the same area for at least one year, (iv) must have valid identification and residence proof, and (v) at least 80 percent of women in a group must own their home. The last requirement is not related to collateral and does not require a formal property title.

Table 9.7. Access to (micro)finance in Hyderabad experiment (percentage points)

Credit access	Endline 1			Endline 2		
	Treatment	Control	Difference	Treatment	Control	Difference
Microfinance Institutions (MFI)						
Spandana	17.8	5.1	12.7[***]	17.4	11.1	6.3[**]
Other MFI	13.7	14.9	−1.2	22.9	26.8	−3.9
Any MFI	26.7	18.3	8.4[***]	33.3	33.1	0.2
Other bank	8.2	7.9	0.3	7.4	7.3	0.1
Informal	70.9	76.1	−5.2[**]	60.5	60.3	0.2
Total	84.4	86.7	−2.3	90.4	90.4	0.0

Source: Based on Banerjee *et al.* 2015, table 2.

Notes: [***] and [**] significant at 1 and 5 percent, respectively; see Banerjee *et al.* 2015 for control variables; see main text for details.

(although this difference is not statistically significant), and about equal access to microfinance in total (33.3 versus 33.1 percent). The main difference between treatment and control neighborhoods in endline 2 is therefore the length of access to microfinance, leading to higher loans (not shown).

BDGK continue to discuss how differences in access to microfinance (endline 1) and differences in length to microfinance access (endline 2) have almost no effect on all important economic and social variables. Treatment households are not more likely to have a business and do not have significantly more businesses. The majority of small businesses make little profit and microfinance does nothing to help them. There is only some creation of marginal businesses in the first year. There is no difference in self-employment and salaried labor, no difference in hours worked for all adults and teens, and no difference in consumption variables. (Except for higher consumption of durables and lower consumption of temptation goods and festivals for treatment households in endline 1; this disappears in endline 2.) Moreover, there is no difference in social outcomes: no change in the probability of school enrollment, no difference in spending on private school fees, no difference in the number of hours worked by girls or boys aged 5 to 15, and so on. In short, there is basically no evidence that microfinance leads to important changes in decision making or in social outcomes.

9.11   Conclusions

This chapter highlighted the interrelations between countries through trade and finance and illustrated some of the policy consequences. It presented a short history of exchange rate regimes, illustrated international vehicle currencies, and discussed capital and investment flows.

A key link between a country and the rest of the world is through the exchange rate. Prices in different countries have to be translated into one another's currencies. As trade takes time (order now, pay later), expectations about exchange rates become important, which establishes a link between the exchange rate and interest rates: the covered and uncovered interest parity conditions.

The links between exchange rates is crucial for understanding the possibilities and limitations of monetary policy and finance opportunities for firms that are internationally active. Firms in more unstable countries have a more difficult time financing their international operations. International financial relations also limit policy choices for a government. This is the so-called policy trilemma. One can only choose two out of the following three policy wishes: monetary policy independence, a fixed exchange rate, and full international capital mobility. The case of Argentina shows how difficult this choice is (see Box 9.2).

The majority of FDI flows is still between high-income countries, but upper-middle-income countries (like China) are becoming more important over time, not only as a destination of FDI, but also (more recently) as a source of FDI. Such flows are important for economic development, which makes it painful to observe that poor countries and lower-middle-income countries only receive a small share of FDI flows.

The chapter concluded with a discussion of the impact of access to small loans by microfinance institutions. It appears that this access has basically no impact on businesses, education, health, or women's empowerment, either in the short run or in the long run. This puts a question mark on the miracles of microfinance.

Further Reading

For a primer on money creation in the modern economy, see the Bank of England: www.bankofengland.co.uk/quarterly-bulletin/2014/q1/money-creation-in-the-modern-economy.

For a further discussion of exchange rates, the international role of the US dollar, and the policy trilemma, see: Ilzetzki, E., C. Reinhardt, and K. Rogoff. 2022. "Rethinking Exchange Rate Regimes," in G. Gopinath, E. Helpman, and K. Rogoff (eds.), *Handbook of International Economics: International Macroeconomics* (Amsterdam: Elsevier), vol. 6.

The historical importance of the policy trilemma is discussed in: Irwin, D. A. 2012. *Trade Policy Disaster: Lessons from the 1930s* (Cambridge, MA: MIT Press).

For information on the reasons for giving the Nobel Peace Prize for micro financing to Muhammed Yunus and the Grameen Bank, in particular "for their efforts to create economic and social development from below," see: www.nobelprize.org/prizes/peace/2006/summary/.

PART III
Human Development

· ·

Part III consists of five chapters with a focus on important aspects of human development. Chapter 10 opens with a discussion on measuring poverty and the speed of its decline, as well as gender equality, and measuring income inequality with an overview of recent changes, both globally and within and between countries. Chapter 11 introduces *poor economics*, which attempts to better characterize and understand the economic lives of the poor and the decisions they make. This approach uses randomized control trials as its main methodology, briefly discussed in terms of advantages and disadvantages and applied in other chapters. Chapter 12 analyzes population and migration issues by discussing developments in world population, birth rates, death rates, and population pyramids. The impact of demographic transition is then linked to present and future demographic dividends. Problems of migration in terms of refugees and internally displaced persons can be big, but are usually small relative to the demographic forces analyzed previously. Chapter 13 focuses on the importance of education for economic development by discussing the biology of learning and the links with development. The chapter addresses the gender gap in education and the quality of university and basic skills education before discussing a teaching model on tracking students, peer effects, and teacher payoffs (which is then taken to the data). Chapter 14 concludes with a discussion of health issues, including life expectancy, its links with development, differences in health care, and a characterization of the main causes of death. The chapter includes an evaluation of infant, child, and maternal mortality, before discussing two health experiments on deworming and providing school meals.

10 | Poverty, Inequality, and Gender

10.1 Introduction

After correcting for price differences, the country with the *highest* level of income per capita in 2018 is Qatar, an oil-rich nation in West Asia with a population of about 2.8 million people with an *average* income level of \$94,820 per person (GNI PPP in constant 2017 international \$). In 2018, Macao had an even higher income level per capita (\$120,376), but the focus here is on Qatar since Macao is a small special administrative region of the People's Republic of China with a population of 0.6 million. The country with the *lowest* income per capita level in 2018 is Burundi, a nation in Africa of about 11.2 million people with an average income level of \$763 per person. The average income level per person in Qatar is thus 124 times higher than the average in Burundi. In other words, the average person in Burundi earns in one year what the average person in Qatar earns in only three days. Income inequality between countries is thus enormous and from a Qatar perspective the average person in Burundi lives in poverty.

Income inequalities are actually even higher than the above paragraph suggests and poverty is even more extreme since the focus (as emphasized) is on the *average* person in a country. Within Burundi there are actually also rich people, like Pierre Nkurunziza (1964–2020), who was President for 15 years (2005–2020). This means there are actually many people in Burundi *below* the \$763 average income per capita level and income inequality within countries should also be taken into consideration. Similarly, within Qatar there are people with income levels far beyond the average of \$94,820, such as Sheikh Tamim bin Hamad al-Thani, the billionaire Emir of Qatar since 2013 and head of the board of directors of the Qatar Investment Authority (an enormously rich sovereign wealth fund). Compared to this, almost all people in Burundi live in extreme poverty.

There are many different types of poverty and inequality, not only in terms of income and wealth, but also in terms of access to education, health, opportunities, finance, and so on. Moreover, people and families with high income and wealth levels have unequal access to the power to make decisions and influence policies, at home and abroad. This, in turn, leads to a perpetuation of unequal outcomes as their siblings, uncles, aunts, children, grandchildren, and so on have access to earlier accumulated wealth, power, education, firms, and networks beyond what other people have access to. As a result, there are rich families around the world, such as the Walton family in America, the Slim family in Mexico, the Dumas family in France, the Ambani family in India, the Kwok family in Hong

Kong, the Hartono family in Indonesia, and so on. A simple way to illustrate this inequality is to realize that it is possible to identify the happy few very rich individuals and families mentioned above, but not the millions (or billions) of people at the other extreme: they remain "nameless" people. In this respect it is admirable that the World Bank usually tries to identify people by name or location to take away the anonymity, such "Baruani," "Tungise," and "young woman in city" in the report on gender equality (World Bank 2012, pp. 2, 2, and 7, respectively; see section 10.6). Nonetheless, it is too easy to forget the Baruanis and Tungises and remember the Waltons and Slims.

This chapter discusses and analyzes some aspects of poverty and inequality. Section 10.2 starts by analyzing differences in economic growth rates in the period 1950–2016 and the connection with (initial) income levels (convergence or divergence). Section 10.3 continues with a discussion of poverty issues, such as poverty lines, the number of people in poverty, and headcount ratios. Based on this information, section 10.4 shows and explains that poverty has been declining globally since 1970, independently of the chosen poverty line. Section 10.5 briefly analyzes how (income) inequality can be properly measured by imposing some desirable properties and discussing which measures satisfy these properties (and which measures do not). Section 10.5.1 uses this information to analyze the connections between development and income inequality. Section 10.5.2 provides an overview of changes of within-country income inequality before section 10.6 analyzes several issues of gender equality. This chapter concludes with an analysis of the relationship between economic development and income inequality in China in section 10.7 and the chapter's findings are summarized in section 10.8.

10.2   Income and Growth

This section starts with an analysis of the connection between a country's initial income level and the long-run growth rate of income per capita. As discussed in Chapter 5, Angus Maddison provides a good source of data using income per capita levels corrected for PPP. His work is continued in the Maddison Project Database by the University of Groningen, of which the 2018 version is used here. The principal period is the 66 years from 1950 to 2016 for which information is available for 140 countries, together comprising about 95 percent of the world population. For each country in this period, the annual *compounded* growth rate of income per capita is determined. If y_t is income per capita in period t, we thus determine the number x (in percent) such that $(1 + x)^{66} = y_{2016}/y_{1950}$.

Figure 10.1 provides information on the distribution of long-run growth rates at the country level. The average long-run growth rate of income per capita is 2.0 percent per year and the median is 1.9 percent. The range is from a minimum of –1.2 percent for the Central African Republic to a maximum of 5.5 percent for Equatorial Guinea. Most countries (89 percent of the total) are in the 0 to 4 percent growth range, while the standard deviation is 1.2 percent. Eight countries grow *slowly* (below 0 percent) and seven countries grow *fast* (above 4 percent). Six of the eight slow-growing countries are in Africa (Liberia,

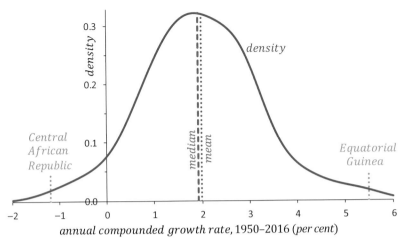

Figure 10.1 Distribution of country long-run growth rates per capita; kernel density, 1950–2016
Source: Calculations based on Maddison Project Database 2018.
Notes: 140 countries included; for Cuba, N. Korea, and Palestine data for 2015 instead of 2016 is used; real income is based on GDP per capita in 2011 USD with benchmark 2011 (rgdpnapc variable); based on normal distribution with bandwidth $(4/3)^{1/5}\hat{\sigma}n^{-1/5}$, where $\hat{\sigma}$ is standard deviation and n is the number of observations (140).

Madagascar, Niger, Central African Republic, DR Congo, and Djibouti), joined by one country in the Americas (Haiti) and one in Asia (Afghanistan). Most fast-growing countries are in Asia (China, S. Korea, Taiwan, and Singapore), joined by two countries in Africa (Equatorial Guinea and Botswana), and one in Europe (Malta).

In this chapter on inequality, also of interest is the connection between the initial income level and the long-run growth rate. This is a question of *convergence*, where the basic idea is that if initially poor countries *on average* have *higher* long-run growth rates than initially rich countries, they will catch-up and income inequality at the country level will not exacerbate over time. The reverse holds if this is not the case. Chapter 4 analyzed this question from a very long-run perspective, but this chapter concentrates on the period 1950–2016. Figure 10.2 illustrates the connection between initial income level (on the horizontal axis, using a log scale) and the long-run growth rate (on the vertical axis, in percent) using a bubble diagram, where the size of the bubbles is proportional to the size of the population in 2000. The conclusions on convergence are summarized in the two regression lines in the figure.

The first regression line is a standard regression line, which is horizontal. Try to look at Figure 10.2 while making all countries equally important by imagining all bubbles to be of equal size. If you draw a regression line through this imaginary figure, the standard regression line results. Its slope (coefficient is 0.0004) is not statistically different from zero and the regression explains 0.00 percent of the variance in growth rates. On the basis of this information, therefore, it makes sense to conclude that there is *no* relationship between the initial income level and the long-run growth rate. Initially poor countries do not *on average* grow faster than initially rich countries and there is no long-run convergence of income.

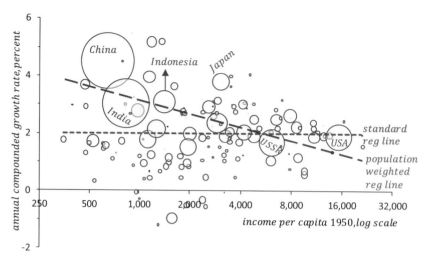

Figure 10.2 Initial income per capita and long-run growth rates, 1950–2016
Source: See Figure 10.1.

Notes: Bubble size proportional to population in 2000; reg line = regression line; 140 countries included; data for Cuba, N. Korea, and Palestine for period 1950–2015.

If you now look again at Figure 10.2, you will notice that some of the biggest bubbles, such as China and India, which are countries with a large population, are in the upper-left corner. These countries are thus initially poor (hence in the left part of the figure), but clearly have above-average growth rates (hence in the upper part of the figure). An alternative to the standard regression line, therefore, is to determine a *population-weighted* regression, where the importance of an observation is weighted by the size of the population. This line is also depicted in Figure 10.2. Its slope is clearly negative (equal to –0.673) and highly significant; this line explains about 29.7 percent of the weighted variance in long-run growth. It is therefore possible to conclude that there is evidence of convergence of income in the period 1950–2016 at the country level when the size of the population is taken into consideration.

10.3   Poverty

The Economist Intelligence Unit regularly gathers information on the cost of living in 133 large cities around the world. It compares more than 400 individual prices for products and services, such as food, drink, clothing, home rents, transport, schools, recreational costs, and so on. In the year 2015, Singapore was the world's most expensive city to live in and Lusaka (Zambia) was the least expensive (The Economist 2016). Other expensive cities are located in Europe, Southeast Asia, and North America, such as (in order, starting with the most expensive): Zurich, Hong Kong, Geneva, Paris, London, and New York. Other less expensive cities are located in South Asia, Africa, and Central Asia, such as (also in order, as above): Bangalore, Mumbai, Karachi, Chennai, Algiers, and Almaty. If you have $200 in your pocket in Singapore, you are therefore "poorer" than if you have the same amount of money in Lusaka. To determine if someone is poor, the focus is generally on the goods and services this person can afford to buy at that location. There is therefore a need to correct for the price differences in different locations and use purchasing power parity (PPP) exchange rates. It is customary in most countries and at international organizations to determine a "poverty line" of real income to define poverty. If your income level is below this line, you are poor (headcount index). If it is above, you are not.

How high should the poverty line be? To a large extent, this is arbitrary and subjective. There must be a lower bound, of course, because you need to have enough real income to purchase a minimum nutrition requirement in order to stay alive. To varying degrees, you also want to include clothing and shelter in the minimum requirements. The poverty line is also subjective. In general, the real poverty income line that countries use to identify poor people is higher in the advanced economies, where some goods that are luxuries in developing countries may be considered necessities. Moreover, even if you have a median income level in an advanced economy, you may still feel rather poor when you are walking around in Monaco and staring at the yachts in the harbor and the Rolls-Royces, Ferraris, and Bentleys in the streets.

The remainder of this section focuses on the international poverty lines of $1.90 per day and $3.20 per day in international 2011 PPP dollars, as defined by the World Bank. (The $1.90 per day line is more or less equivalent to the $1 per day line popularized in the early 1990s.) For persons from advanced economies these are low real income levels indeed, so the focus is on poverty rates in the developing world. Figure 10.3 depicts the evolution of poverty since 1981 in absolute numbers in four main developing regions as identified by the World Bank (see Chapter 1 for a brief description of these world regions). Panel a focuses on the $1.90 per day poverty line and panel b on the $3.20 per day poverty line. For ease of comparison the vertical scale in the two panels is identical. Using either poverty

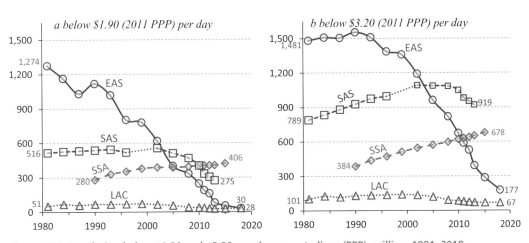

Figure 10.3 Population below $1.90 and $3.20 per day poverty lines (PPP); million, 1981–2018
Source: Based on World Development Indicators online.
Notes: EAP = East Asia & Pacific, SAS = South Asia; SSA = Sub-Sahara Africa, LAC = Latin America & Carribean; relative to 2011 PPP $.

line, most poor people were living in East Asia & Pacific (EAP) in 1981, followed by South Asia (SAS) and Sub-Sahara Africa (SSA).

It is clear from Figure 10.3a that the evolution over time has differed drastically between the developing regions. As a consequence of (mainly) the economic development of China, poverty declined enormously in East Asia, lifting more than 1.2 billion people above the $1.90 per day threshold by 2018. In contrast, poverty in Africa increased from 280 million in 1990 to 406 million in 2015. To a large extent this is due to a rapid increase in Africa's population size, as discussed below and in Chapter 12. The South Asian experience is somewhere in between these two extremes: the number of poor people continued to rise to about 555 million in 2002 and then declined to about 275 million in 2013. Compared to the other regions, poverty in Latin America is more modest, while the developments are similar to those in South Asia, namely a small rise initially (to 77 million in 1999) and a steady decline since then (to 28 million in 2018). Figure 10.3b shows similar movements at the higher $3.20 per day poverty line, with an enormous decline of poverty in East Asia since 1990, a rise of poverty in Africa, and an initial rise followed by a steady decline in South Asia and Latin America. At the world level, the number of people in poverty at the $3.20 line rises to about 3 billion in 1990, where it stays until 2002 and then starts to decline and hovers around 2.4 billion people from 1981 to 2002, and then starts to decline rapidly to below 2 billion in 2015.

The above discussion has focused on *absolute* poverty (that is, the number of people below a poverty line). We can, and to some extent should, also investigate *relative* poverty (that is, the share of the total population below a poverty line). This requires us to take into consideration the rising size of the total population, which in this period rose substantially in the four regions, namely by 2.6 billion people from 3.3 to 5.9 billion (see also Chapter 12). This is done in Figure 10.4, which shows the poverty headcount ratio as a percent of the population in the various regions, both for $1.90 per day (panel a) and for $3.20 per day (panel b). Clearly, the fight against poverty has been more successful in

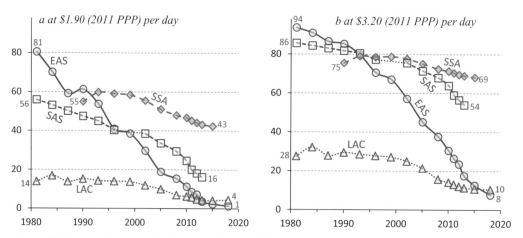

Figure 10.4 Poverty headcount ratio at $1.90 and $3.20 per day; % of population, 1981–2018
Source: See Figure 10.3.

relative terms: the share of people below a poverty line has declined in all regions. This even holds for Africa since the new millennium: the absolute number of poor people in Africa is still rising, but the relative number is already declining. For the four developing regions as a whole, the share of the population below $1.90 per day has declined by 37 percentage points in the period 1990–2013, from 51 to 14 percent. Similarly, the share of the population below $3.20 per day has declined by 40 percentage points, from 77 percent in 1990 to 37 percent in 2013. A formidable improvement indeed.

There is a final important point to note on the developments in Latin America and the Middle East & North Africa, and the developing countries of Europe & Central Asia (data not shown in the figures). Both the absolute number of poor people and the share of the population living in poverty is (most of the time) substantially lower in these regions than in the other regions discussed above. In 2018, for example, the $1.90 headcount ratio is 1 percent in Europe & Central Asia, 4 percent in Latin America, and 7 percent in the Middle East & North Africa. Moreover, the spectacular poverty decline in East Asia already leads to lower headcount ratios than in Latin America and the Middle East & North Africa.

It can be concluded that poverty rates declined in the developing world as a whole since 1981. The decline is impressive for both poverty lines, particularly in relative terms. A number of other poverty lines (such as $6 a day or $10 a day) can, of course, be defined. As the next section shows, however, the fight against poverty has been successful in the past three decades, independent of the exact way in which poverty is measured (see Chen and Ravallion 2010). At the regional level, large differences can be observed: the decline of poverty has been spectacular in East Asia, substantial in South Asia, and less impressive in Africa.

10.4   Declining Global Poverty

Section 10.2 showed that, once the size of the population is controlled for, initially poor countries have on average been growing faster than initially rich countries since 1950. Poverty rates in the developing world have been falling rapidly since 1980, although this drop has been unequally distributed across the world, with Africa, in particular, lagging behind. So far this chapter has focused on countries as the unit of analysis and has added results for individual countries to arrive at regional and global results. But this is the wrong approach to answer questions on changes of global income inequality. In that case, the individual human being is the unit of analysis in order to ensure that the same weight is given to a banker in Manhattan and a peasant in Tanzania. To do that, it is necessary to take *within-country* differences in the distribution of income into account.

An enormous variation in the degree of income inequality exists, both across countries and over time. In order to analyze changes in global income inequality, it is necessary to combine information on changes in within-country income inequality with appropriate levels of population in these countries, in order to aggregate this information to a global distribution of income for different time periods. It is easy to see that this is a formidable task

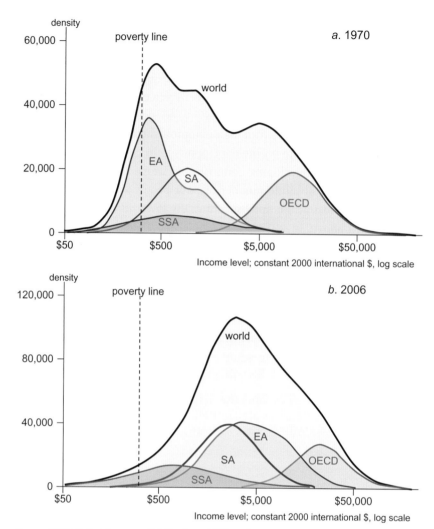

Figure 10.5 Global income distribution, 1970 and 2006
Source: Based on Pinkovskiy and Sala-i-Martin 2009.
Notes: The poverty line corresponds to $312 a year, or $1 a day in 2006 prices; EA = East Asia; SA = South Asia; SSA = Sub-Sahara Africa; not all regions included separately.

as it requires estimating an annual income distribution for individual countries based on country surveys and then integrating these country distributions for all levels of income (see Sala-i-Martin 2006). Figure 10.5 is the end result of the analysis and provides the inequality estimates for 191 countries in 1970 and 2006 (see Pinkovskiy and Sala-i-Martin 2009). Panel a provides the income distribution for the world as a whole and for four major regions (East Asia, South Asia, Sub-Sahara Africa, and the OECD countries) in 1970. Panel b does the same for 2006. Note that the vertical density scale in 2006 is twice that of 1970 to compensate for the rising population level. Also note that the income scale is logarithmic, such that income levels increase ten-fold at each step. To reflect on the previous discussion of poverty lines, the figures also depict a poverty line (in this case of $1 a day, PPP in 2006 prices).

A comparison of panels a and b of Figure 10.5 shows that the global distribution of income has shifted to the right. This indicates that there has been economic progress for most people in the sense that, in general, the income levels have risen. Note, however, that it is quite possible for the income levels of *some* people to fall despite the general rise in income. The figures clearly demonstrate that the poverty rate has fallen over time. When comparing the share of the population below the poverty line in 1970 (the share of the density mass to the left of this line) with that in 2006, an enormous decline in the poverty rate can be observed, in accordance with the previous discussion (in this specific case, from 26.8 to 5.4 percent of the world population). More importantly, note that the exact location of the poverty line is not important for this conclusion: if the poverty line would have been a little bit to the left or a little bit to the right the same conclusion would still be reached.

Looking at the shape of the global income distribution in 1970 (panel a), there are three "humps." From left to right, the first hump may be associated with East Asia and the second hump with South Asia, both with Sub-Sahara Africa as part of these humps. The third hump may be associated with the Soviet Union (not shown in the figure). The shape of the global income distribution in 2006 (panel b), in contrast, is characterized by a single hump (or peak), as one would expect in general from the income distribution of a single country. Looking at the performance of individual regions in the two panels, it can be seen that East Asia was the poorest region in 1970, but clearly moved up in the world's income distribution in the period 1970–2006 (with on average higher income than South Asia and Sub-Sahara Africa in 2006). South Asia more or less held on to its relative position in the world's income distribution and reduced poverty considerably. Sub-Sahara Africa, in contrast, shows little growth in income and a small reduction in poverty rates. The OECD countries, finally, more or less held on to their top position in the world income distribution. (If you compare the relative size of the OECD region in the income distributions of 1970 and 2006, it is obvious that the *relative* population size of the OECD countries is falling. Similarly, that of Africa is rising.) It is not directly clear from just looking at the two panels of Figure 10.5 if world income inequality has fallen or not. To answer that question, it is necessary to first determine *how* to measure income inequality, which is covered in the next section.

10.5 Measuring Income Inequality

Suppose we observe a distribution of income levels for a group of people. Two examples are given in Table 10.1 for two groups of 10 people, labeled situation 1 and situation 2. In both cases all income levels are positive, they are ordered from low to high, and the average income level is equal to 310. How do we determine how equal or unequal the income levels are distributed in these situations? How does income inequality in situation 1 compare to that in situation 2? To answer these questions, we need a measure of income inequality. This section discusses some issues and measures associated with this.

Table 10.1. Hypothetical Income inequality

Order	Situation 1		Situation 2	
	Income	share	Income	share
1	60	0.019	20	0.006
2	80	0.026	40	0.013
3	100	0.032	60	0.019
4	130	0.042	90	0.029
5	200	0.065	160	0.052
6	310	0.100	270	0.087
7	370	0.119	330	0.106
8	500	0.161	460	0.148
9	650	0.210	610	0.197
10	700	0.226	1060	0.342
Average	310		310	
Some income inequality measures				
10/10	11.67		53.00	
20/20	9.64		27.83	
Gini	0.406		0.522	
MLD*	0.323		0.610	
Theil	0.269		0.461	

Note: * MLD = mean logarithmic deviation.

A good income inequality measure should fulfill some minimum requirements.

- First, it should be *anonymous* in the sense that it should not matter if Mrs. Winfrey or Mr. Slim has the highest income level, just the level of income is important.
- Second, it should be *scale independent*: if everyone's income level is doubled, the measure of income inequality should not change.
- Third, it should be *population independent*: the size of the group should not affect the inequality measure.
- Fourth, it should satisfy the *transfer principle*: if some income is transferred from a rich person to a poor person (while still preserving the income order), the measured inequality should decrease (strong form) or not increase (weak form).

Notice that situation 2 in Table 10.1 can be transferred to situation 1 by taking away $9 \times 40 = 360$ units from person 10 and giving 40 units to each of 1 to 9 (this can be broken up in nine separate transfers). A good income inequality measure should therefore give a lower value to situation 1 than situation 2. The simplest income inequality measures are *shares* and *ratios*, where shares are calculated as the share of income earned by the top 10 or 1 percent (ranging from zero to one) and ratios are taken for "higher over lower" (ranging from one to infinity). The 10/10 ratio, for example, is the ratio of the share of total income earned by the 10 percent of people with the *highest* income level over the share of total income earned by the 10 percent of people with the *lowest* income level; similarly for the 20/20 ratio. If everyone earned the same income level the ratios would be one, which is therefore the minimum value. The ratio is easy to interpret (this group earns four times as much as that group), but has no upper limit. In situation 1 in Table 10.1, the 10/10 ratio is 11.67. In situation 2 it is much higher: 53.00. Similarly, but slightly less drastic, for the 20/20 ratio. Note, however, that these ratios do not satisfy the (strong) transfer principle.

The most often used income inequality measure is the *Gini coefficient* (see Gini 1912). It can be graphically illustrated by constructing the *Lorenz curve*, with the (ordered) cumulative population on the horizontal axis and the cumulative income level on the vertical axis. In situation 1, for example, the poorest person (10 percent of the population) earns 1.9 percent of all income, so the point $(0.10, 0.019)$ is part of the Lorenz curve. The next poorest person earns 2.6 percent of all income, so the cumulative income level earned by the poorest 20 percent of the population is $1.9 + 2.6 = 3.5$ percent, and the point $(0.20, 0.035)$ is also part of the Lorenz curve. Continuing in this fashion for situation 1 gives the Lorenz curve as depicted in Figure 10.6. If all people earned the same income level, the Lorenz curve would coincide with the $45°$ line (diagonal). The deviation between the diagonal and the Lorenz curve determines the Gini coefficient: it is calculated as area $A/(A + B + C)$ in situation 1 and by area $(A + B)/(A + B + C)$ in situation 2. The Gini ranges from 0 (complete equality) to 1 (complete inequality). An advantage of the Gini is that it can be shown to be a distribution-free inequality index that represents the views on inequality of a society with very general distributional preferences (see Sen 1974).

A disadvantage of the Gini coefficient is that it is not decomposable into population groups or income sources. If we look, for example, at the extent of income inequality for the world as a whole we are combining within-country income differences and between-country income differences. We would therefore like to know the relative

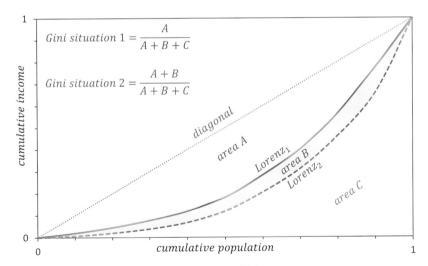

Figure 10.6 The Lorenz curve and the Gini coefficient
Note: The figure depicts situation 1 in *Lorenz₁* and situation 2 in *Lorenz₂* (see Table 10.1).

contribution of each component to total global inequality. Similarly, if we observe changes in the income distribution over time leading to changes in total income inequality, we would like to know if these changes were caused by changes within countries or between countries. The two most often used income inequality measures that are also decomposable are the *mean logarithmic deviation* (MLD) and the *Theil index*, both special cases of the *generalized entropy* (GE) measure.[1] Equations 10.1 to 10.3 provide the definition of these measures for discrete and continuous data, where $\bar{x}$ is the average income level. Table 10.1 also provides the value of the Gini, MLD, and Theil index for situations 1 and 2.

$$MLD = \frac{-1}{N}\sum_{i=1}^{N} ln\left(\frac{x_i}{\bar{x}}\right); \quad MLD = -\int ln\left(\frac{x}{\bar{x}}\right)dF \qquad 10.1$$

$$Theil = \frac{1}{N}\sum_{i=1}^{N}\frac{x_i}{\bar{x}} ln\left(\frac{x_i}{\bar{x}}\right); \quad Theil = \int \frac{x}{\bar{x}} ln\left(\frac{x}{\bar{x}}\right)dF \qquad 10.2$$

$$GE(\alpha) = \frac{1}{\alpha(1-\alpha)}\left(1-\frac{1}{N}\sum_{i=1}^{N}\left(\frac{x_i}{\bar{x}}\right)^{\alpha}\right); \quad GE(\alpha) = \frac{1}{\alpha(1-\alpha)}\left(1-\frac{\int x^{\alpha}dF}{\bar{x}^{\alpha}}\right); \quad \alpha \neq \{0,1\} \qquad 10.3$$

10.5.1   Development and Income Inequality

Chapter 5 on the long-run perspective of globalization suggests that income inequality is rising over time; see in particular section 5.5 on the widening perspective of leader versus laggard income per capita over the past 1,000 years. An important part of the globalization debate is focused on the question of whether globalization fosters income inequality. This question is addressed in two steps. This section focuses on changes in global income inequality, while the next section analyzes changes in within-country income inequality. The discussion is based on Rougoor and van Marrewijk (2015; see this article for references), who also make a projection of expected changes in global income inequality for the next 40 years. The discussion in this section groups countries together in larger regions and focuses on the Gini coefficient as a measure of inequality. It ranges from zero (when all people in the world have the same income level in a certain period) to one (when one person earns all income and everyone else earns nothing).

Around 200,000 years ago, when Homo sapiens first walked on the Earth, global income inequality must have been very small as most people were simply trying to stay alive. The Gini coefficient is then close to zero. Since then global income inequality has been rising, particularly in the past two centuries, driven by the strong and continuous growth of a small number of (OECD) countries after the Industrial Revolution. This resulted in a twin-peaks world income distribution (see section 10.4), characterized by a large number of people (countries) with a low income level and a smaller group of people (countries) with a high income level, and not much in between.

---

[1] The related Atkinson (1970) index can also be decomposed. The Theil index is sometimes referred to as the Theil T index and MLD as the Theil L index, where *Theil T = GE*(1) and *Theil L = GE*(0).

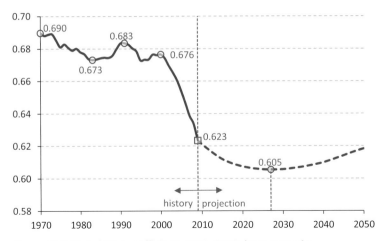

Figure 10.7 Global Gini coefficient; 1970–2050, base scenario
Source: Based on Rougoor and van Marrewijk 2015.

From the 1970s onward, "equalizing" factors proved stronger than "disequalizing" factors and a trend toward lower global inequality started, largely because of a decline in between-country income inequality. Major equalizing factors were the faster-than-world-average income growth in China and South Asia combined with a slower-than-world-average population growth in Europe and the Western Offshoots. Major disequalizing factors were slower-than-world-average income growth in Sub-Sahara Africa (combined with faster-than-world-average population growth in that region) and faster-than-world-average income growth in the Western Offshoots.

Figure 10.7 illustrates the decline in global income inequality since the 1970s using data on income per capita for 176 countries, as well as information on the distribution of income within each country. The decline is slow at first and not monotonic; the Gini coefficient falls by about 2.4 percent from 1970 to 1983 and then rises again by 1.5 percent from 1983 to 1991. In the new millennium, the decline in global income inequality is more rapid: the Gini coefficient falls by about 7.9 percent from 2000 to 2009.

Rougoor and van Marrewijk (2015) develop several global growth scenarios up to 2050 in order to project global income inequality in the next 40 years. Figure 10.7 also provides the projection of global income inequality up to 2050 for a "base scenario." Economic growth, driven by productivity increases, naturally plays a large part in this process, but given the long time horizon, demographic developments do so as well. For example, the population of Africa is projected to double in the coming four decades. At the same time, Asian countries profit from a beneficial age structure, as many advanced countries have over the past decades. These countries are now starting to struggle with aging populations and fertility rates below replacement levels. All these developments directly (through economic growth) or indirectly (through the share of working age population) affect global income inequality.

Up until 2050, Asia's income share is expected to rise by about 15 percentage points and that of Africa and Oceania by less than 1 percentage point. The income shares of Latin

America and North America decline by about 4 percentage points, that of Europe by about 9 percentage points. These changes are, of course, the result of changes in the total population, the working population, and production per worker. Total population more than doubles in Africa, compared to about 30 percent for most of the rest of the world, except for Europe, which has a stagnant population. Africa is the only continent where the share of the working population increases by 6.6 percentage points. In the other continents it declines, ranging from 1.5 percentage points for Latin America to 11.2 percentage points for Europe.

The base scenario projects a reversal of the current trend toward lower global income inequality. (Several alternative scenarios and measures of income inequality lead to similar conclusions.) The turning point is expected to be reached around 2027. Rising income levels in many Asian economies and continuing high population growth rates in Sub-Sahara Africa are the most important drivers behind this trend reversal. By 2050, global income inequality is expected to have returned to levels similar to that of 2010. To analyze the dynamics behind this development, a closer look at the data is required. This is done by constructing a World Distribution of Income, which is the result of a so-called kernel density function in which all income groups are population-weighted and effectively integrated into one global income distribution. Figure 10.8 has the income level (log scale) on the horizontal axis and millions of people on the vertical axis. The area under the lines is equal to the total world population in the respective years.

Each consecutive world distribution of income is larger (larger area under the graph) and shifted to the right relative to the one before. This corresponds to a growing world population and rising income levels. Because of these two large-scale developments most

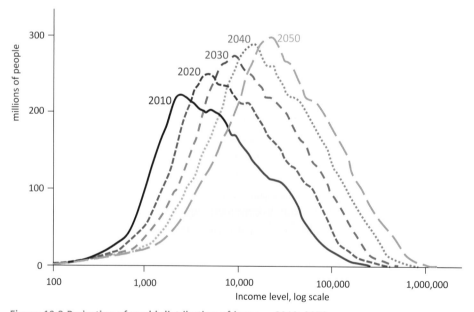

Figure 10.8 Projection of world distribution of income, 2010–2050
Source: Rougoor and van Marrewijk 2015.

other shifts are small in comparison and therefore hardly visible. Figure 10.9 takes this approach one step further and looks at different regions (based on the World Bank classification) in relation to one another. Sub-Sahara Africa (SSA), South Asia (SA), East Asia (EA), and the OECD countries are shown as distributions for 2010 and 2050.

First, note that considerable shifts are visible, both in individual distributions and in distributions in relation to each other. All distributions shift to the right, but South Asia and East Asia move relatively faster. A consequence of this is that East Asia has more overlap with the income distribution of the OECD countries in 2050 than it had in 2010. The same holds for South Asia.

Second, note that the continent distributions shift relative to one another. Some of these shifts result in an overall decrease of inequality and some result in an overall increase of inequality. With respect to South Asia and East Asia, the situation is more complex. While these countries *catch up* to OECD countries, they simultaneously *pull away* from most other African and Asian countries (the latter are not shown in the graph). For example, China has over the past few decades grown faster than the OECD average. At the same time, it outgrew most African countries, resulting in a diverging trend relative to Africa and a converging trend relative to the OECD. The net result for global income inequality depends on the relative size of such trends.

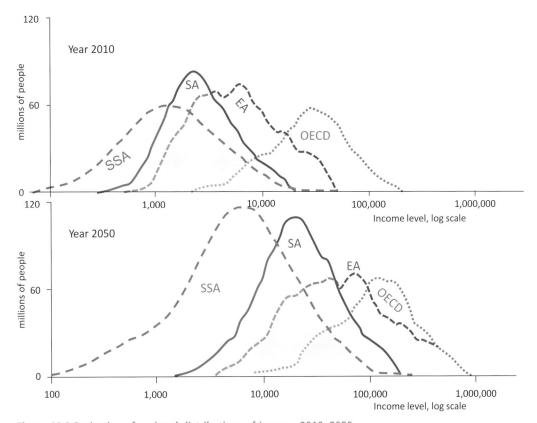

Figure 10.9 Projection of regional distributions of income, 2010–2050
Source: Rougoor and van Marrewijk 2015.
Notes: EA = East Asia; SA = South Asia; SSA = Sub-Sahara Africa.

Finally, note that the OECD countries and East Asia (mainly China) show a modest population growth. South Asia (India) and Sub-Sahara Africa are projected to significantly increase in population.[2] This impacts global inequality in at least two ways. First, a rapid increase in population is often associated with a higher youth dependency ratio and subsequent lower economic growth. Countries with an extremely high population growth are thus at risk of (economically) lagging behind countries with a lower population growth. A similar observation can be made for very low population growth, which results in a larger old-age dependency ratio (most relevant for OECD countries such as Germany and Japan). Second, population size also directly influences inequality measures such as the Gini coefficient. The bulk of low-income countries are situated in Sub-Sahara Africa. As the population in Sub-Sahara Africa grows more rapidly than in the rest of the world the relative weight of the continent increases. Therefore, inequality would increase *even if* GDP per capita is assumed to stay the same in all countries over the entire period.

To conclude, from a long-term perspective, global income inequality has been mostly rising. Since the 1970s, global income inequality has been falling (thanks in large part to the economic rise of China and India). This recent trend is likely to reverse again in the 2020s, mainly as a result of the rising share of world population in Africa, which is still lagging behind.

10.5.2   Within-Country Income Inequality

The discussion in section 10.5.1 has ignored changes in within-country income inequality. The UNU-WIDER database on World Income Inequality (WIID3.b1) is used to analyze these changes, focusing on the quintile distribution of the included studies if this is provided. Since the objective is to determine long-run trends in within-country income inequality, we want to compare the first information for the country as a whole that is available for any country with the last (most recent) information.[3] We also want to incorporate the quality of the observations, as indicated by the database in the four classes "not known," "low," "average," and "high." We therefore compare the first observation of average or high quality with the last observation of average or high quality. Only if observations of average or high quality were *not* available did we select low or not known quality (in that order).[4] On the basis of these observations, we calculated implied Gini coefficients to determine if within-country income inequality is rising or falling for the country under consideration. See Box 10.1 for alternative information on within-country wage inequality.

---

[2] Population growth between 2010 and 2050 according to UN Population Department (2011): OECD from 1.23 to 1.40 billion, East Asia from 1.89 to 2.01 billion, South Asia from 1.63 to 2.31 billion, and Sub-Sahara Africa from 0.85 to 1.95 billion people.

[3] Studies covering only part of a country or only rural or urban areas are therefore excluded. The only exception is for Germany, where the distribution of the West in 1968 and of Germany as a whole in 2011 is used. This choice does not affect the findings below.

[4] If the rules resulted in two or more estimates for the same year, the highest quality estimate was chosen. In case of a tie, the most recently modified or updated one was chosen. In case of a further tie the first entry in the database was chosen.

BOX 10.1 GLOBALIZATION AND AMERICAN WAGES

When reviewing the globalization and wages debate in light of new empirical evidence, with a focus on the US experience, Haskel *et al.* (2012) note five major changes affecting globalization and technology since the mid-1990s: (i) political barriers to trade have been declining; (ii) natural barriers to trade have been declining (ICT); (iii) US productivity growth has increased; (iv) GDP growth in middle- and low-income countries (such as China and India) has increased; and (v) trade and investment flows (with developing countries) have increased dramatically. Paul Krugman therefore reverted his earlier position that those flows were simply too small to have a significant impact (see Krugman 2008). Although the size of the flows is much larger now and could have an impact, Haskel *et al.* nonetheless conclude that "there is only mixed evidence that trade in goods, intermediates, and services has been raising inequality between more- and less-skilled workers" (2012, p. 120). They do point to technological change (greater tradeability of services and larger market sizes abroad) to explain the US phenomenon of the rising relative earnings of "superstars" (the top 1 percent of the income distribution).

Haskel *et al.* (2012) clarify the evolution of the trade and wages debate by showing the cumulative percentage changes since 1991 in mean real (price adjusted) money earnings for working adults in the USA for five different education groups. The real wages for higher-educated workers rose rapidly from 1990 to 2000, initially for those with an advanced degree, soon followed by those with a Bachelor's degree. The remaining education levels (some college, high school, and less than high school) lagged behind in this period, thus prompting the debate on the relation between trade and wages suggesting rising inequality in the advanced economies reviewed above. Since 2000,

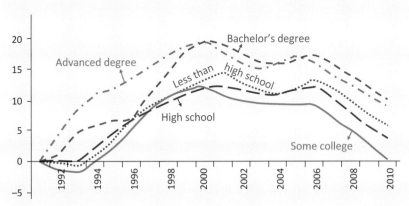

Figure 10.10 Changes in US real income; working adults, by education, 1991–2010
Source: Based on Haskel *et al.* 2012.
Notes: Cumulative percentage changes relative to 1991 in mean real money earnings for working adults (aged 25 and above) by educational cohort in terms of the highest level of education attained (adjusted for price inflation and smoothed to three-year averages); see Beugelsdijk *et al.* 2013, ch. 14.

BOX 10.1 (cont.)

however, the real wages for the higher education levels have been doing less well than for the lower education levels. Particularly the two lowest education levels (less than high school and high school) have been catching up in relative terms. As trade flows continued to rise rapidly in this period and wage inequality fell during the same period, it thus becomes hard to blame trade flows for rising inequality. Note that the medium-education level (some college) has been doing worst of all education levels during the period 1991–2010. This process is called polarization of the labor market in the labor economics literature (lovely and lousy jobs) and linked to technological change in the labor market (routine tasks and nonroutine tasks; see Autor *et al.* 2003, Goos and Manning 2007, and Goos *et al.* 2009). Finally, real wages declined in the period 2000–2010 despite the rise in productivity mentioned above. The consequence is, of course, higher earnings for capital in the USA (corporate profits reached 12.4 percent in 2010, the highest percentage recorded in 60 years; Haskel *et al.* 2012, p. 123).

Table 10.2 summarizes the findings for the 148 countries with more than one observation.[5] Panel a provides summary statistics on the year and Gini index of the first and last observation, as well as the change in the Gini index. The median first observation is in the year 1988 (average is 1985). The median last observation is in the year 2009 (average is 2007). The median difference between the first and last observation is thus 21 years (average is 22). The median Gini index for the first observation is 0.361 (average is 0.373) and for the last observation is 0.339 (average is 0.353). For the average country, therefore, the median Gini index has *fallen* by 0.019 or a modest 5 percent (the average by 0.020, also 5 percent) over a period of 21 years. Indeed, the Gini index fell for most countries (96 out of 148 or 65 percent). The largest decline was in Armenia from 1996 to 2011 (by 0.283 or 50 percent). The largest increase was in Rwanda from 1985 to 2006 (by 0.202 or 76 percent).

The information above does not necessarily imply that the declining within-country income inequality as summarized in Table 10.2a translates into a decline in global income inequality if these trends continue in the future. This depends, among other things, on (i) regional differences and (ii) the trend for the most populous nations. Regarding (i), Table 10.2b provides further information by detailing the changes in the Gini index for the six continents. Big differences cannot be observed between the continents regarding the change in the Gini index: the decline is small and holds for about two-thirds of the countries. The only exception is North America, where the two countries involved (Canada and USA) both experienced an increase in within-country

---

[5] There are 23 countries with just one observation, which are thus not included in the table. For these countries, the median observation is in 2003 (average in 1999) and the median Gini index is 0.408 (average is 0.420). The within-country income inequality is thus substantially higher for these countries than for the countries included in the table.

Table 10.2. First and last quintile information and associated Gini coefficients

a. First and last observation year and Gini coefficient

| Statistic | First observation | | Last observation | | Change |
	Year	Gini	Year	Gini	Gini[*]
Average	1985	0.373	2007	0.353	−0.020
Median	1988	0.361	2009	0.339	−0.019
Minimum	1951	0.175	1978	0.186	−0.283
Maximum	2007	0.651	2012	0.647	0.202
Standard deviation	13.8	0.100	5.9	0.083	0.074
Observations	148	148	148	148	148
Population weighted average Gini index[#]		0.3598		0.3597	−0.000

b. Change in Gini coefficients per continent

Statistic	Asia	Africa	Europe	Latin America	Oceania	North America
Average	−0.016	−0.027	−0.007	−0.039	−0.045	0.060
Median	−0.009	−0.035	−0.018	−0.036	−0.023	0.060
Minimum	−0.283	−0.205	−0.110	−0.265	−0.177	0.056
Maximum	0.094	0.202	0.122	0.098	0.042	0.063
Standard deviation	0.075	0.086	0.062	0.069	0.093	0.005
Observations	41	35	40	26	4	2
Falling inequality	23	25	25	20	3	0
Falling percent	56	71	63	77	75	0

Source: Rougoor and van Marrewijk 2015.
Notes: Calculations based on UNU-WIDER World Income Inequality Database (WIID3.0b, September 2014); [*] The Gini index falls for 96 out of 148 countries (65 percent) and rises for the other 52 countries; [#] The population-weighted average Gini index uses the total population in 2000 as weights (data from World Development Indicators; plus Maddison 2001 for Taiwan). The observations for no-longer-existing countries (Czechoslovakia, USSR, and Yugoslavia) are excluded from calculating the weighted average.

income inequality. Regarding (ii), Table 10.2a also provides a "population-weighted average Gini index," which thus takes the size of the population in a country into consideration. It shows that although there is a majority of countries where income inequality declined, this is almost perfectly compensated by the fact that income inequality increased for some populous nations, such as (in order of population size) in China (by 19 percent), the USA (by 15 percent), Indonesia (by 17 percent), Bangladesh (by 21 percent), and Nigeria (by 9 percent).[6] As a consequence, the population-weighted average Gini index is *constant* at 0.360.

---

[6] Income inequality on average *declined* by less in other populous countries, such as (in order of population size, starting with the largest) in India (by 5 percent), Brazil (by 10 percent), Russia (by 7 percent), Pakistan (by 12 percent), and Mexico (by 22 percent).

To conclude, over the period 1988–2009, there is no clear trend in changes in within-country income inequality; the population-weighted average Gini index is constant.

10.6   Gender Equality

Women live longer than men in all regions of the world (see also Chapter 12), but tend to be disadvantaged relative to men in many other ways, despite impressive progress in recent decades. Gender gaps for girls and young women in education have closed rapidly in many countries for primary and secondary education and have even reversed to gender gaps for young men in universities in a range of countries (see Chapter 13). Labor force participation has also improved for women in many countries, in large part because of reductions in fertility. Other gender gaps are more persistent. Females are more likely to die, for example, than males in many developing countries. The World Bank (2012, p. xxi) estimated these deaths at 3.9 million women and girls under the age of 60 each year, because they are never born, die in early childhood, or die in their reproductive years. Moreover, the number is growing rather than declining in Sub-Sahara Africa. Similarly, primary and secondary school enrollment remains much lower for girls than for boys in Sub-Sahara Africa and parts of South Asia. Women are also more likely to work as unpaid family laborers in the informal sector, tend to farm smaller and less profitable plots, tend to operate smaller and less profitable firms, and in general tend to earn less than men. In addition, women tend to have less say over decisions in their households and less control over household resources, and tend to be under-represented in the upper echelons of society. In short, there is a need for improving gender equality as such in order to stimulate development.

The World Bank has reported a *gender equality* index on a scale from 1 (low) to 6 (high) since 2006 (see Box 10.2 for a discussion on gender equality). The gender equality index "assesses the extent to which the country has installed institutions and programs to enforce laws and policies that promote equal access for men and women in education, health, the economy, and protection under law." Figure 10.11 illustrates the link between income per capita and gender equality by using a bubble diagram (proportional to population). Unfortunately, the gender equality score is only available for a limited number of countries as it is not reported for countries with high income levels and information is missing for a wide range of developing countries (34 countries with below-world-average income per capita levels, together representing 2.3 billion people, including China, Brazil, and the Philippines). As a result, Figure 10.11 shows information for 82 developing countries, together representing 3.4 billion people. (Four countries are excluded because income per capita data is unavailable: South Sudan, Yemen, Somalia, and Eritrea.)

Figure 10.11 indicates that the world average gender equality is 3.24, ranging from a minimum of 1.5 for three countries (Afghanistan, South Sudan, and Yemen) to a maximum of 4.5 for six countries (Armenia, Georgia, Kyrgyz Rep., Moldova, Rwanda, and Vietnam).

BOX 10.2 GENDER EQUALITY BASED ON OPPORTUNITY OR OUTCOME?

According to the World Bank (2012, p. 4):

Gender refers to the social, behavioral, and cultural attributes, expectations, and norms associated with being a woman or a man. Gender equality refers to how these aspects determine how women and men relate to each other and to the resulting differences in power between them.

The key dimensions of gender equality are (i) endowments, (ii) opportunities, and (iii) actions. The accumulation of endowments includes education, health, and physical assets. They can be used to take up economic opportunities and generate income, as well as to take actions to affect individual and household well-being. Gender (in)equality is different from other types of (in)equalities in three main ways. First, it is difficult to measure the welfare of men and women living in the same household separately. Second, based on biological factors and social behavior, preferences, needs, and constraints can differ between men and women. Third, gender issues cut across other problems based on income and class. This raises the issue of whether gender equality should be measured as equality of opportunity or equality of outcome.

Proponents of gender equality based on equality of opportunity argue that we have to be careful in focusing on outcomes since there are differences between men and women regarding risk behavior, attitudes, preferences, and choices. As a result, not all differences in observed outcomes arise from differences in opportunities, which is the issue that really matters. Proponents of gender equality based on outcomes argue that differences in preferences and attitudes are largely based on "learned" behavior caused by culture, environment, and differences in power and status between men and women. It is therefore virtually impossible to define equality of opportunity without considering how actual outcomes are distributed. Both views make a valid point, but in practice it is difficult to measure opportunities separate from outcomes. The starting point is therefore to measure the equality of outcomes and then analyze the extent to which deviations are based on differences in opportunities.

As the trendline indicates, there is a positive association between gender equality and income per capita. The slope of the line is 0.3278, which indicates that a 10 percent higher level of income per capita is associated with a rise of about one-third point on the gender equality index. The trendline explains about 16 percent of the variance in gender equality, so there is substantial variation determined by other factors, as illustrated in the figure for Afghanistan and Rwanda.

As the World Bank (2012) emphasizes, promoting gender equality is not only an important development objective in its own right, it is also smart economics for which the World Bank identifies four policy priorities, namely: (i) reduce gender gaps in human

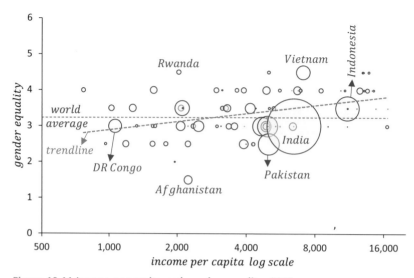

Figure 10.11 Income per capita and gender equality, 2018
Source: Created using World Development Indicators online.
Notes: Gender equality score from 1 (low) to 6 (high), most recent in 2005–2018 period; income per capita is GNI PPP (constant 2017 int. $), most recent 2017–2018, log scale; bubbles proportional to population, 2018; 82 countries included.

capital (especially for female mortality and education); (ii) close gender gaps for access to opportunities, earnings, and productivity; (iii) shrink gender differences in voice and agency within society; and (iv) limit the reproduction of gender inequality across generations. A few examples to achieve these policy priorities are listed here (see World Bank 2012, p. xxiii). Vietnam has been able to reduce excess mortality among young girls by expanding access to clean water and sanitation. Pakistan has used conditional cash transfers to get girls from poor families to school. Colombia subsidized day-care programs for working mothers. Ethiopia granted joint land titles to wives and husbands. Morocco reformed family law to equalize ownership rights of husbands and wives over property acquired during marriage. Uganda facilitates the transition from school to work with job and life skills training programs. And so on.

As an illustration of progress made over time regarding gender equality, Figure 10.12 depicts the female minus male life expectancy at birth for a selection of countries and the world as a whole. Under normal circumstances, female life expectancy at birth is *higher* than male life expectancy. This is shown in the figure using the world average, where female life expectancy is 3.9 years higher than male life expectancy in 1960, rising to 4.5 years in 1990 and hovering around that value since then. There are only five countries in the period 1960–1991 where life expectancy is *reversed*, indicating that males live longer than females. An indication of progress is, therefore, that since 1992 female life expectancy is higher than male life expectancy for all countries in the world, without exception.

Figure 10.12 also shows the five countries where life expectancy was reversed at some point in time, all located in South Asia. A good example of steady progress over time is provided by Bangladesh, where female life expectancy in 1960 was 1.45 years lower than

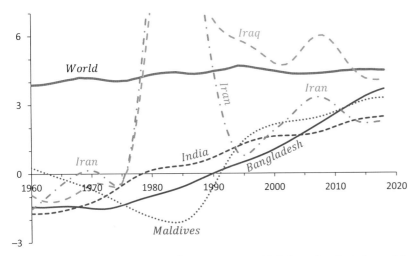

Figure 10.12 Female minus male life expectancy at birth (years); selected countries, 1960–2018
Source: Created using World Development Indicators online.
Note: Peak for Iran and Iraq in 1984 not visible.

male life expectancy. Relative to the world average, where life expectancy for females in 1960 was 3.87 years higher, this creates a gender gap of 5.32 years (3.87+1.45). Bangladesh gradually managed to diminish the gender gap relative to the world by 85 percent (to 0.82 years in 2018), along the way eliminating the reversal in 1991. Similar, but slightly less spectacular, progress was made in India, which eliminated about two-thirds of the gender gap relative to the world (from 5.61 years in 1960 to 2.02 years in 2018; eliminating the reversal already in 1979). A similar overall relative improvement as in India for the period as a whole is visible for the Maldives, although in this case there is a long initial period of deterioration of the gender gap from 1960 to 1984 before rapid improvement takes place.

The female minus male life expectancy lines for Iran and Iraq in Figure 10.12 provide a spectacular illustration of other issues that are important for explaining deviations and changes. Initially, female life expectancy is below male life expectancy in both countries. This reversal is eliminated for both countries in 1976 (and for Iran briefly in 1968–1971). After that, female life expectancy relative to male life expectancy rises enormously for both countries, reaching peaks far above the world average in 1984 (namely 15.0 years for Iran and 12.3 years for Iraq, compared to 4.4 years for the world average in that year). The underlying reason in both countries is that life expectancy for men dropped dramatically because of the Iran–Iraq hostilities culminating in the Iran–Iraq War (1980–1988), which resulted in a reduction of male life expectancy in Iran of almost nine years (from 55.6 in 1976 to 46.8 in 1985) and in Iraq of almost seven years (from 61.2 in 1976 to 54.4 in 1984) (see also the subsequent fluctuations in the figure for both countries). This concludes the discussion on gender equality. The next section analyzes the relationship between economic development and income inequality from a Chinese perspective.

10.7   Income Inequality in China

An important potential problem threatening China's impressive economic development is rising income inequality.[7] The indicator of economic success used here is China's income level per capita relative to the world average. Remember that this indicator provides no information regarding the distribution of the gains within society, which might create conflicts.

The analysis here is based on the UNU-WIDER World Income Inequality Database (WIID), which collects information on inequality estimates for almost all countries in the world from 1867 onward. The latest version (January 2017, WIID 3.4) has 8,817 estimates for 182 countries, of which 175 estimates are for China, starting in 1953. Of these observations, 42 percent are classified as low quality, 41 percent as average quality, 18 percent as high quality, and 12 percent as unknown quality. As expected, the quality of the observations tends to increase over time (see panel a of Figure 10.13), even though the first unknown classification occurs in 2006. The present discussion is based on all different types of quality available, but the level of quality is clearly identified in the graphs below.

Several issues need to be taken into consideration when compiling inequality measures (see UNU-WIDER). First, we need to know if the inequality measure is on an income or consumption/expenditure basis. There are advantages of and advocates for either approach: Deaton and Zaidi (2002) favor the consumption approach, while Atkinson and Bourguignon (2000) do not. Second, we have to be clear on what to include in the definition of income and consumption. Regarding income-based inequality measures, it is preferred if these are based on disposable income rather than total income, if available. Third, there are some conceptual issues. The household should be the basis for the analysis, while the household size should be taken into consideration, since we are interested in the economic well-being of individuals, not of households. (Since various and changing "equivalence scales" are used, UNU-WIDER prefers to focus on income per capita estimates, also because they are the most widely available.) Finally, we should choose an appropriate income inequality measure. Although various options satisfying certain restrictions (anonymity, scale independence, population independence, and satisfying the transfer principle; see section 10.5) are available, the focus here is on the Gini index (see again section 10.5).

The early inequality measures available tend to be based on gross income as a welfare definition (12 percent of the observations), while later measures are based on disposable income (67 percent of the observations). Consumption-based estimates (15 percent of the observations) are more recent (see panel b of Figure 10.13). The remaining 10 percent of the observations are based on other welfare definitions. Regarding the equivalence scale used, household per capita estimates are by far the most common (87 percent of the observations), while 5 percent are without adjustment and 9 percent are in another

---

[7] This section is based on van Marrewijk 2019.

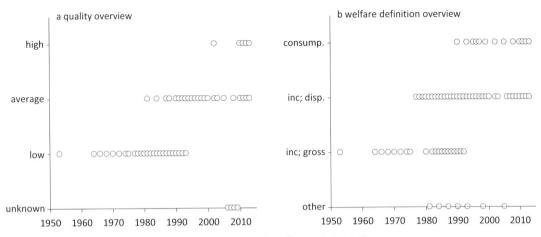

Figure 10.13 China inequality information; quality and welfare, 1953–2015
Source: Based on data from UNU-WIDER.
Notes: inc. = income; disp. = disposable; consump. = consumption.

category. The data also indicate if there are age restrictions for the included people in the study (for China there never is, so all studies are based on "all" population) and the type of area covered, classified as "all" for the country as a whole (27 percent of the observations), "urban" (37 percent of the observations), and "rural" (35 percent of the observations).

On the basis of the above information and in view of our interest in the change of income inequality over time, we will focus on inequality measures based on disposable income using household per capita as equivalence scale. This implies we use the preferred income measure (disposable income), which is most widely available, and the preferred equivalence scale (household per capita), which is also most widely available, but cannot include the earliest income inequality measures in the period 1953–1975 (since these are based on gross income instead of disposable income). We must, of course, distinguish the different types of studies regarding area covered. In total, there are 114 studies with a Gini index available meeting our criteria, namely 21 studies for the country as a whole, 46 rural studies, and 47 urban studies. These are illustrated in panels a, b, and c, respectively, in Figure 10.14, and discussed below.

We start with an analysis of the Gini index (on a scale from 0 to 100) for the country as a whole: see panel a of Figure 10.14. The first observation is in 1978 at the start of the Economic Reform process and the last observation is in 2012. The early observations are of low quality, most of the middle observations are of average quality, and a large share of the recent observations are of high quality, combined with a number of observations of unknown quality. Although there are, of course, variations between the studies, there is a consistent trend visible over time, supported by studies of different quality classifications. The Gini index of income inequality in China rises substantially over time. The regression line provided in panel a explains 74 percent of the variance in the Gini coefficient and has a slope of 0.7122 (see Table 10.3). On the basis of the regression line, which combines

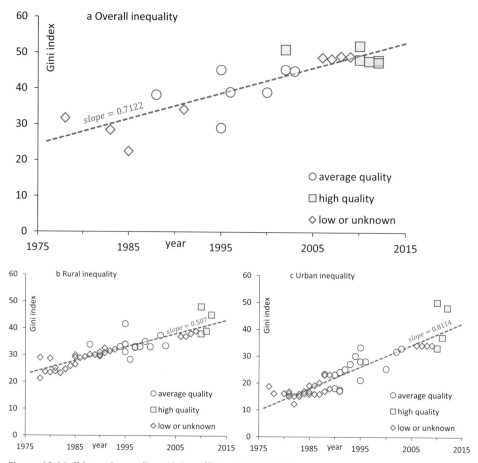

Figure 10.14 Chinese inequality; Gini coefficient, 1975–2015
Source: Based on data from UNU-WIDER.
Notes: Regression explains 74.1, 78.0, and 82.2 percent of variance for panels a–c, respectively; number of observations is 21, 46, and 47 for panels a–c, respectively; dashed lines are regression lines.

information from all available studies, the Gini index for China as a whole rose from 26.5 percentage points in 1978 at the start of the Economic Reform process to 52.9 percentage points in 2015.

Panel b of Figure 10.14 shows the Gini index for studies on rural income inequality in China. The first observation is again in 1978 and the last observation in 2012. As for the country as a whole, the quality of the studies tends to improve over time and the Gini index tends to rise over time. The regression line provided in panel b explains 78 percent of the variation in the Gini coefficient and has a slope of 0.5070 (see Table 10.3). On the basis of this regression line, the Gini index for rural China rose from 24.3 percentage points in 1978 to 43.1 percentage points in 2015. The increase is thus less sharp for rural China than for the country as a whole.

Panel c of Figure 10.14 shows the Gini index for studies on urban income inequality in China. The first observation is in 1977 and the last observation in 2012. As for the country

Table 10.3. China Gini index regressions, 1977–2015

	Country	Rural	Urban
intercept	−1382	−979	−1593
(t value)	(−7.16)	(−12.10)	(−14.19)
slope	0.7122	0.5070	0.8114
(t value)	(7.38)	(12.49)	(14.40)
R^2	0.741	0.780	0.822
# observations	21	46	47

Source: Time regressions based on UNU-WIDER data.
Notes: Disposable income studies only; dependent variable is Gini index (scale from 0 to 100).

as a whole and for rural China, the quality of the studies tends to improve over time and the Gini index tends to rise over time. The regression line provided in panel c explains 82 percent of the variation in the Gini coefficient and has a slope of 0.8114 (see Table 10.3). On the basis of this regression line, the Gini index for urban China rose from 12.2 percentage points in 1978 to 42.3 percentage points in 2015. The increase for urban China is thus sharper than for the country as a whole and much sharper than for rural China.

The findings for the Gini disposable income inequality are briefly summarized as follows:

• China's overall income inequality has risen substantially since 1978.
• China's rural income inequality has also risen substantially since 1978, but not as fast as for China as a whole.
• China's urban income inequality was low in 1978, but has been rising faster since then relative to China as a whole and much faster relative to rural China.
• Since 2017, China's urban disposable income inequality is about equal to China's rural disposable income inequality.[8]

The remark that China's urban inequality was low in 1978 is clear when comparing panels b and c of Figure 10.14. Note that China's overall income inequality is higher than either the rural or the urban inequality because of the differences in income levels in these areas.[9] China's rapid economic development has thus been accompanied by rising disposable income inequality. This is not a new phenomenon (see Box 10.3).

---

[8] If you take the regression results (too) seriously, then urban inequality surpasses rural inequality in July 2017.
[9] In the new millennium, using NBS data, urban average income is about three times higher than rural average income. The UNU-WIDER data provide no solid basis for analyzing the change in urban versus rural average (or median) income over time, since only a few studies provide data (the earliest is 1995) and different sources provide quite different results for the same year.

BOX 10.3 DEVELOPMENT AND INCOME INEQUALITY

The World Bank's 2009 World Development Report was entitled *Reshaping Economic Geography* and focused on the links between economic development on the one hand and the advantages of physical geography (resources, waterways, climate; first-nature geography) and man-made geography (clustering, agglomeration, and spillovers; second-nature geography) on the other. The role of concentration of economic activities in specific locations for development plays an important role in this study. Countries embarking on a successful development path generally concentrate economic activity increasingly in cities and specific clusters of activity, which attract migration flows from the countryside, usually create slums, and may grow into large agglomerations. During this initial stage of development, income inequality measures within the country and between regions in the country generally increase. At later stages of development, the migration flows slow down or stop, the worst slum problems are addressed, and measures of income inequality decline again.

This is illustrated in Figure 10.15 for the USA in 1840–1960 (the arrows for the USA indicate a time-direction as per capita income rises over time; similarly for the other countries), for Spain in 1860–1975, for Sweden in 1920–1961, and for Japan in 1955–1983. In all cases, but to varying degrees and at varying speeds, regional income inequality first rises and then reaches a peak before declining again. This parallels the current developments in China, where income inequality has been rising since 1981

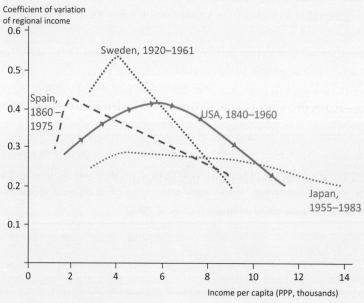

Figure 10.15 Development and income inequality, some historical examples
Sources: Based on World Bank 2009; see also Beugelsdijk *et al.* 2013, ch. 14.

along with the concentration of economic activity in rapidly growing, large cities. As the Chinese government increasingly pays attention to the frictions caused by rising income inequality, economic and policy forces are trying to reverse the process of rising Chinese income inequality and according to some studies they are succeeding (see Cai and Du 2011).

10.8 Conclusions

This chapter analyzed issues related to poverty, inequality, and gender. Section 10.2 showed that there are large differences between countries in terms of long-run growth rates in the period 1950–2016. It also showed that there is conditional convergence (initially poor countries grow faster than initially rich countries) when taking the population size of countries into consideration. Section 10.3 discussed poverty lines, absolute poverty, and headcount ratios to argue in section 10.4 that poverty has been declining globally since 1970, independently of the chosen poverty line.

Section 10.5 first imposed some desirable properties measures of inequality should possess and then discussed some measures that fulfill these properties, such as the Gini index and Generalized Entropy (including Mean Log Deviation and Theil index), and some (less appropriate) measures that do not, like percentiles and ratios. The section discussed the link between development and income inequality from a long-run perspective to show that global income inequality has been (i) mostly rising, (ii) declining somewhat since the 1980s because of the economic development of China and India, and (iii) is likely to start to rise again around the mid-2020s because of lagging Africa. Associated with this discussion, the section then evaluated changes in within-country income inequality since the 1950s to find that inequality has been rising in some countries and falling in others without a clear net effect for the world as a whole.

Section 10.6 discussed issues of gender equality, in particular what it is, how it can be measured, and the many topics to which it is related. Some of these topics will be covered in more detail later, such as demography (Chapter 12), education (Chapter 13), and health (Chapter 14). In general, striving for gender equality is important for its own sake as well as smart economics. Section 10.7 discussed in detail the changes of within-country income inequality in China as an important example of a rapidly developing country. It showed that successful development in China is associated with rising income inequality, particularly in the cities. This is a common feature of rapidly developing countries, which tends to reverse over time as development progresses and issues of within-country inequality tend to become more important.

Further Reading

Various institutions deal with poverty, inequality, and gender, analyzing and discussing different aspects. See, for example, the OECD website: www.oecd.org/social/inequality-and-poverty.htm or the World Bank: https://datatopics.worldbank.org/world-development-indicators/themes/poverty-and-inequality.html. Both sites are also good starting points for literature surveys.

Frank Cowell is a good starting point on how to measure inequality. See: Cowell, F. 2011. *Measuring Inequality* (Oxford University Press). The UN University World Institute for Development Economics Research (UNU-WIDER) presents up-to-date information on income inequality for (almost) all countries in the World Income Inequality Database (WIID). See: www.wider.unu.edu/project/wiid-%E2%80%93-world-income-inequality-database.

Specialist Branko Milanovic provides a technical account of how to correctly measure income inequality. See Milanovic, B. 2005. *Worlds Apart: Measuring International and Global Inequality* (Princeton University Press).

Bordo, Taylor, and Williamson (2003) provide a detailed historical perspective, while Bourguignon and Morrison (2002) analyze global inequality in the nineteenth and twentieth centuries. For the colonial roots of current inequality, see Acemoglu, Johnson, and Robinson (2001), and for the connection to geographical aspects, see Easterly and Levine (2003). Finally, Rodrik (2003) presents an interesting series of country studies. See: Bordo, M., A. Taylor, and J. Williamson. 2003. *Globalization in Historical Perspective* (University of Chicago Press); Bourguignon, F. and C. Morrison. 2002. "Inequality among World Citizens: 1820–1992," *American Economic Review*, 92(4), 727–44; Acemoglu, D., S. Johnson, and J. Robinson. 2001. "The Colonial Origins of Comparative Development," *American Economic Review*, 91(5), 1369–401; Easterly, W. and R. Levine. 2003. "Tropics, Germs, and Crops: How Endowments Influence Economic Development," *Journal of Monetary Economics*, 50(1), 3–40; and Rodrik, D. 2003. *In Search of Prosperity: Analytic Narratives on Economic Growth* (Princeton University Press).

11 Poor Economics

11.1 Introduction

Poor Economics is the title of a book written by Abhijit Banerjee and Esther Duflo (2011). Its subtitle is: *A Radical Rethinking of the Way to Fight Global Poverty.* The first chapter shows that in the fight to reduce poverty, development economics has focused on the big questions, such as the ultimate cause of poverty, whether democracy is good for the poor, and if foreign aid is needed. They point to Jeffrey Sachs (2006; *The End of Poverty*), who argues that poor countries may be stuck in poverty traps, which requires investments they cannot pay for, hence foreign aid is needed. They also point to William Easterly (2007; *The White Man's Burden*), who argues that aid has done more bad than good as it prevents people from finding their own solutions.

Banerjee and Duflo argue that poverty is a complex problem and it is not easy to answer the big questions, hence they make no attempt to do so. Instead, they break down the complexity by systematically analyzing structured smaller problems using *randomized control trials* (or experiments, see below) to see what works for specific problems under certain conditions. These problems arise in many different areas, like health, education, family planning, and dealing with environmental problems. Reducing poverty is then a step-by-step process based on this analysis.

The effort to reduce poverty in small steps based on experiments started in Kenya in the mid-1990s under the guidance of Michael Kremer. It was extremely influential within the field as well as in policy circles, involving international organizations (like the World Bank) and development aid agencies (like nongovernmental organizations). The highest recognition was bestowed on October 14, 2019 by the Royal Swedish Academy of Sciences, when it announced that the 2019 Nobel Prize in Economics was won by Abhijit Banerjee, Esther Duflo, and Michael Kremer "for their experimental approach to alleviating global poverty," because "[i]n just two decades, their new experiment-based approach has transformed development economics, which is now a flourishing field of research" (see www.nobelprize .org/prizes/economic-sciences/2019/press-release/).

This chapter provides an overview of the *Poor Economics* approach in general. Some experiments and results will be discussed in more detail in Chapters 13 and 14 (see also the discussion on microfinance in Chapter 9). Section 11.2 starts with a description of the economic lives of the poor – for example, regarding family size, how they spend their money, and how they earn their money. Section 11.3 continues with a summary of the main understanding of the decisions poor people make based on the insights derived from the Poor Economics experiments. Section 11.4 explains what randomized control trials are and discusses the most important issues that play a role in these experiments. Section 11.5 briefly reviews the start of this literature by Michael Kremer in Kenya before turning to the main problems associated with randomized control trials. Section 11.6 discusses the problem of external validity, while section 11.7 summarizes the main limitations of randomized control trials, which in many cases are shared by other (micro-economic data-based) empirical methods. Section 11.8 concludes.

11.2   The Economic Lives of the Poor

Banerjee and Duflo (2007) briefly describe the economic lives of the poor based on detailed data from 14 surveys in 13 countries (the average survey is around 1997, ranging from 1988 to 2005).[1] To identify poor people, they use the $1 per day purchasing power parity (PPP) poverty line of 1985, which translates to $1.08 a day in 1993 (the data they use) and is more or less equivalent to the $1.90 per day poverty line in 2011 discussed in Chapter 10. Banerjee and Duflo show that poor families tend to be large, with a median family size of around seven or eight persons. This large size is in part because it is common for adults to live together with parents and siblings (to spread the fixed costs of housing across a larger number of people) and in part because there are many children. Determining fertility is not easy (because of the number of adults in a family), but the median ratio of young people (below 18) to older people (above 51) is around six. The poor of the world thus tend to be young people.

Family size is illustrated in Figure 11.1 using data from the Poor Economics website for rural areas for the 14 countries for which information is available for two groups of people, namely those living on $1 per day or less ("poorest" people) and "richer" people living on $6–10 per day. Evidently, the poorest people tend to have larger families as the average number of persons is higher than for the richer families in all 14 countries. The difference is particularly large in South Africa (nine- versus three-person households) and small in Indonesia (seven- versus six-person households). The simple average family size for the 14 countries is about eight persons for the poorest people and about five persons for richer people. The largest families can be found in the Ivory Coast, namely about eight persons for richer people and no fewer than 12 persons for the poorest people.

11.2.1   How the Poor Spend Their Money
Since poor people tend to be underfed and weak, which affects their ability to work, one might expect they spend virtually all of their income on food and calories. To a fair extent,

---

[1] All information in this section and the next is based on Banerjee and Duflo (2007).

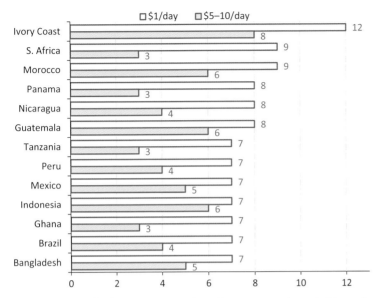

Figure 11.1 Family size; average number of persons per household, rural
Source: Created using (rounded) data from Poor Economics website (www.pooreconomics.com).
Note: Ordered by family size for $1 per day.

this is not the case and poor people feel they have the freedom to make some choices. This is illustrated in Figure 11.2, again using data from the Poor Economics website for rural areas. This time there are nine countries for which information is available for the two groups of people. Three observations are clear when looking at the data. First, the poorest people spent a larger fraction of their income on food (61 percent on average) than richer people (38 percent on average), as you would expect. Second, this observation holds for all countries, but the variation in the difference is large, ranging from 14 percentage points difference in Nicaragua (59–45 percent) to 38 percentage points difference in Guatemala (50–12 percent). Third, the variation in the share of income spent on food by the poorest people is also substantial, ranging from 45 percent in Bangladesh to 71 percent in South Africa.

Spending around 61 percent of income on food items is a large share, but leaves room for other choices. Typically, virtually nothing is spent on movies, theaters, or video shows, between 4 and 6 percent of income is spent on alcohol and tobacco, and, perhaps remarkably, up to around 10 percent is spent on festivals (like weddings and religious festivals), although the latter share tends to decline if the family owns a radio or television. Related to this, if extra income is available not all of it is spent on extra food items, which implies that the income elasticity is less than one (estimates vary considerably). Moreover, poor people make choices regarding their calorie intake. In terms of calories per rupee for grains in India, for example, millet is the best buy, but around 20 percent of grain spending is on rice (which is about twice as expensive) and 10 percent on wheat (more expensive still). In addition, about 7 percent of income is spent on sugar, which is even

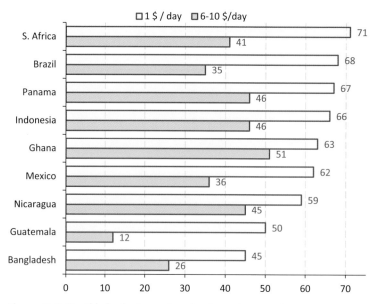

Figure 11.2 Monthly budget spent on food; rural, percent
Source: Created using data from Poor Economics website (www.pooreconomics.com).
Note: Ordered by share of income spent on food for $1 per day.

more expensive than grains and has no other nutritional value. Even for extremely poor people, a 1 percent rise in food expenditure roughly translates into half spent on more calories and half spent on more expensive (better-tasting) calories.

Asset ownership varies substantially across countries. This holds for the ownership of radio and television (which rapidly rises as income rises) and ownership of land (usually small plots for which ownership ranges from 1 to 85 percent in the surveys); similarly for ownership of durable goods, like bicycles, clocks, watches, electric fans, and sewing machines. Even simple items can be scarce. In Udaipur (a city in India), for example, most extremely poor people own a bed or cot, but only about 10 percent have a chair or stool.

In terms of health (see Chapter 14), the extremely poor in India consume about 1,400 calories per day, which is about half the recommended amount for a man with moderate activity. As a result, most extremely poor adults are underweight (as measured by the body mass index), many are anemic (an insufficient number of red blood cells), diarrhea is frequent among children, and many have vision problems (related to poor nutrition and diseases). As a consequence, many poor families (between about 10 and 45 percent) report a member in the last month being bedridden or requiring a doctor. The costs associated with these problems imply that many poor people sometimes had to cut the size of their meal, while about 37 percent of adults went without a meal for an entire day in the last year.

Spending on education among poor people is low, around 2 percent of the budget. The majority of children tend to go to school, although the variance is large (see Chapter 13). Spending is low because most children attend public schools that do not charge a fee. The quality of these schools is low, so some extremely poor families still spend money on sending their children to private schools.

11.2.2   How the Poor Earn their Money

The typical poor family consists of entrepreneurs – that is, people who have some type of business for which they are the residual claimant of the earnings. A large proportion of the entrepreneurs operate a farm, but one can also think of the many families operating an eatery in India or a sari-sari store in the Philippines. (The word sari-sari is tagalog [one of the main languages in the Philippines] for *variety*. These small, family-run stores are ubiquitous, operated from home mini grocery stores.) Many poor people have multiple occupations. Women cook in the morning and sell clothes in the afternoon. Other people are self-employed in agriculture, but only around 19 percent of the families describe this as their main source of income. Most occupations are as daily laborer – that is, someone who works for daily wages, usually as a low-skilled worker. A strikingly large share of available time (around 10 percent) is spent on gathering fuel, either to sell or for own use at home.

To find nonagricultural work, the poorest households frequently report that someone lived outside the family for part of the year. This temporary migration is usually not very far and is short in duration; the median is about one month and only a small fraction is longer than three months. Permanent migration seems to be relatively rare, except for some countries (Indonesia, with subsidies).

Based on the above, from an efficiency point of view, two issues become apparent: (i) a lack of specialization; and (ii) small scale. Members of poor families tend to be not-specialized in their work. They do some agriculture, some selling, some sowing, some temporary work elsewhere in bursts, and so on. In general, they are not active in jobs requiring higher levels of skills that are accumulated over time and earn higher wages. When they operate businesses, the scale is usually small, both in agriculture and other types of businesses. Most businesses have no paid staff and if they do it is on a small scale and frequently a family member. The businesses also have few assets and the assets they have are simple, like tables, scales, and pushcarts. Even nonmotorized vehicles are rare.

11.3   Understanding the Economic Lives of the Poor

Poor families do borrow money, but rarely have access to loans from a formal lending source. Instead, poor people tend to borrow money from shopkeepers, relatives, money lenders, and other villagers. Interest rates from these informal sources are high. Interest is usually charged per month at about 3 or 4 percent, which translates to an interest rate of 43 to 60 percent per year! Under these circumstances the best advice is *not* to borrow money, but most poor families are forced to do so anyway. The high interest rate is not because of high default rates, but because of high contract enforcement costs, also related to the small size of loans (which makes this market of little interest to financial institutions). Related to this, the savings market for the poor also functions poorly as most do not have access to savings accounts, savings at home are unsafe (and too tempting), and informal arrangements are only a partial solution. Moreover, many poor families own land, but land records are incomplete and formal titles are frequently absent. This makes it hard to sell the land or mortgage it for loans (see also De Soto 2003).

Access to formal insurance is limited. Most poor families have no health insurance or life insurance. This is only partially compensated by informal insurance based on loans between neighbors and relatives, where the loan conditions are affected by the economic situation. As a consequence, in times of economic stress – for example, related to health problems and costs – the effective insurance consists of eating less and taking children out of school. Even if governments formally provide some health care for free, there are still practical costs involved in terms of travel, paying for medicines, and (sometimes) fees charged illegally. Some countries provide food-for-work programs, but access is usually limited and payments are low.

The provision of infrastructure, like roads, electricity, schools, and health facilities (water and sanitation), has a local public good character. The availability of infrastructure varies enormously between countries and is generally somewhat better in urban than in rural environments. Even if facilities are made available, however, the quality tends to be bad and absenteeism is a big problem. Chaudhury *et al.* (2005), for example, report an average absence rate among teachers of 19 percent and among health workers of 35 percent. Similarly, an evaluation of the quality of schools found that more than 93 percent of children go to primary school, but 35 percent cannot read a simple second-grade-level paragraph, 40 percent cannot do subtraction, and 65 percent cannot do division. As a consequence, some poor families still send their children to private schools and many go to private health care providers.

Based on the above, Banerjee and Duflo continue by explaining some of the decisions poor people tend to make. There is little specialization in employment, for example, because of risk-spreading and the inability to raise capital. There are many entrepreneurs because these activities are easier to organize than finding a suitable job. As an example, you can buy some fruits or vegetables and sell them on the streets. For that reason, these businesses tend to be extremely small. The spending on alcohol, tobacco, and festivals, instead of spending all income on food, is a deliberate choice representing revealed preference, and perhaps partially represents an effort to keep up appearances with the neighbors. Investment in education is possibly low because illiterate parents might not be able to recognize that their children are not learning much in primary schools. Savings are low because access to bank accounts is limited and hoarding money at home is risky, it might get stolen, or it is hard to resist the temptation to spend it on other items or a craving. Migration is only short term because people want to remain close to their social network, which is the only source of informal insurance. And so on.

11.4   Randomized Control Trials

Suppose you are a government agency in a developing country and want to determine the effectiveness of a proposed policy, say giving school books for free to children attending primary schools. Effectiveness is determined by comparing costs (of providing books for free) with outcomes. To do so, you have to determine the outcome you are striving for. In this case, it might be the test scores of students who get their books for free or it might be the additional years of school participation. Let's say it is the latter, so your objective is to stimulate attending primary school and you measure this in terms of the number of years children go to primary school.

The effectiveness of any policy can only be determined by comparing it to some other policy. There are many alternatives, but in this case the other policy might simply be *not* giving school books for free. This is an attempt to answer a *causal* question: what is the impact of giving books for free? It is also a *counterfactual* question: what would have happened if the books were *not* given for free? It is a counterfactual question because at any given point in time an individual is either given the books for free, or not. For any given individual, it is therefore impossible to provide an answer, but it *is* possible to estimate the impact of the policy by comparing the *average* outcome for individuals who are given books for free with the *average* outcome for individuals who are not. In terms of effectiveness, it is first vital to determine if individuals who get books for free attend primary school more often and then how costly that is.

An important problem associated with comparing the averages of the two groups is that of *selection bias*. Any difference between the averages consists of two components, namely: (i) the impact of the policy (which is what we are trying to estimate); and (ii) any other factors that may influence the outcome. In our example, the likelihood of attending school may depend on the distance to school, which affects the (time) costs of attending school. In rural areas, the average distance to school is larger than in urban areas, hence the likelihood of attending school is lower in rural areas. Suppose there are only two school locations, village A and city B, and the average impact of distance is that individuals in village A attend school 0.2 years less on average than in city B. Moreover, suppose that the *true* effect of giving books for free is to attend school 0.22 years more on average. If the book policy is evaluated by giving books for free in city B only, the average difference in school attendance is $0.20 + 0.22 = 0.42$, which is much *higher* than the true policy effect. If the book policy is evaluated by giving books for free in village A only, the average difference in school attendance is $0.22 - 0.20 = 0.02$, which is much *lower* than the true policy effect.

The solution to this problem is to try to eliminate the selection bias in order to credibly estimate the causal effect of the book policy. One way to do this is to *randomly* assign individuals to a *treatment* group (who are given the books for free) and a *control* group (who do not get the books for free). As a result of such a *randomized control trial*, the only systematic difference between the groups arises from the treatment, which allows us to estimate the impact of the book policy in an unbiased way. Such trials have a long history in science, starting with a clinical trial by James Lind in 1747 to determine the value of oranges and lemons in treating scurvy in sailors (Thomas 1997). They are the gold standard in clinical trials in a *blinded* version, meaning information which may influence the participants is withheld until after the trial is complete. Early work in economics includes the negative income tax experiments of Hausman and Wise (1985) before becoming more popular in other fields, in particular in development economics.

The description above is simple, but the practice of randomized control trials, or *field experiments*, is more challenging. In contrast to clinical trials, blinded trials are usually not possible in economics. In our book policy example, it is clear whether or not you have to pay for the books and the focus is on how your behavior changes as a result of this information. In general, many other factors may affect the measured outcome, such as income or wealth of your family, whether you live in the mountains or in a valley, the political connections of your family, access to navigable water, and so on. As a result, a substantial amount of the work involved in conducting proper field experiments is to identify and adequately control for all of these differences. This effort is usually summarized in tables indicating that the differences between the treatment group and the control group for a range of influential variables is not statistically significant, such that any difference between the average outcome can only be attributed to the treatment itself (the book policy in our example).

Another difficulty is the *unit of analysis*. For example, either a random selection can be made of (i) individual students, (ii) individual families, or (iii) individual schools to be allocated to the treatment group as our unit of analysis. In all cases, the impact is slightly different and it is necessary to adequately control for any selection bias. In the case of individual students as our unit of analysis, a student may get books for free while his or her brother or sister (sibling) does not. In the case of individual families as our unit of analysis, all siblings will be treated the same, but their classmates may either receive free books, or not (as in the case of individual students). For equity reasons, one may think it is unfair that two students in the same school receive different treatment, where one student has to pay for the books and the other does not. At the school level, this problem disappears if individual schools are the unit of analysis and all students of that school either receive books for free, or not. At the aggregate level, the equity problem obviously does not go away (since some students receive books for free and others do not); it only becomes less visible (more obscure). There may also be other reasons (cost efficiency) to select schools as the unit of analysis (as is done frequently).

11.5   Kremer in Kenya

At the macroeconomic level there is clear evidence that accumulating human capital, measured by the number of years of education, is important for economic development (see Chapter 7). At the empirical microeconomic level this raises problems like the selection effects into education, the differences in time and place of the returns to schooling as measured by the number of years, and the most effective policies to improve enrollment and student learning.

In an attempt to answer the microeconomic questions, Nobel laureate Michael Kremer started the randomized control trial revolution in development economics in Kenya in the mid-1990s, financed by Internationaal Christelijk Steunfonds Afrika (ICS, a nongovernmental organization) and in collaboration with a range of co-authors. Kremer (2003) provides preliminary results of some of the experiments. Some experiments estimated the impact of additional school inputs, like textbooks and flip charts. Other experiments estimated the impact of health interventions, like deworming and school meals. Another experiment provided teachers with financial incentives based on the test scores of their students.

As the above experiments illustrate, an advantage of the randomized control trial method is to determine systematically the (cost-) effectiveness of different types of policies, which can then be implemented on a wider scale, or not. The provision of textbooks, for example, increased the test score by about 0.2 standard deviations for the top students, but did not affect the scores for the bottom 60 percent. Kremer (2003, p. 103) argues that this is related to the bottom students having difficulty understanding the textbooks, which are written in English rather than the mother tongue or Swahili and at a level far ahead of the typical rural student. A field experiment to evaluate the effectiveness of flip charts instead of textbooks found no improvement. The health interventions (deworming and school meals) improved school attendance, but not test scores. The financial incentive increased teacher efforts to prepare for the test, leading to higher test scores, but did not improve scores for unrelated exams. Chapter 13 returns to these issues.

11.6 External Validity

Randomized control trials in development economics are usually small scale, say involving village A in valley B of country C at time T. In many cases, the focus is on causal claims: if *this* treatment is provided, then *that* is the consequence. An important aspect discussed and analyzed in the literature is therefore that of *external validity*: does the suggested causal inference also apply under different circumstances? In the example above: does it apply for different villages in this valley, for villages in another valley, for villages in valleys in other countries, for different time periods, and so on? Issues that may play a role in this respect are context dependence, the scale of the experiment, (government) implementation, general-equilibrium effects, spillovers, and randomization and piloting bias. These problems, which are of more general concern for micro-econometric work, are discussed, for example in Duflo (2004), Duflo *et al.* (2007), Banerjee and Duflo (2009), and Banerjee *et al.* (2017).

Context dependence is usually addressed by *replication*. If the result holds for several experiments under different circumstances, for different countries, at different sites, and for different time periods, we are usually inclined to think that it holds more generally. Although with this type of inductive reasoning one can never be really sure, replication *is* important. Wagner (2011, p. 406), for example, recommends never considering "results based on one sample of firms from one country and from one period of time as a stylised fact," while Hamermesh (2000, p. 376) argues that "the credibility of a new finding that is based on carefully analyzing two data sets is far more than twice that of a result based only on one." See also van den Berg, van Marrewijk, and Tamminen (2018).

A more challenging problem is that of *general-equilibrium* effects. Most randomized control trials can be interpreted within a partial-equilibrium framework, taking many prices, distributions, and the like as given. If the trial suggests a specific treatment for dealing with a problem, what happens if we scale up the treatment to the national level? At such a large scale, wages and prices may be affected and may have (unwanted) distributional consequences. One way to deal with this problem within the experiment is to randomize at the market level rather than at the individual level, or to randomize in two stages (at the individual level and at the market level) (see Crépon *et al.* 2013). It is possible to handle spillover issues also at a higher level of aggregation (see Miguel and Kremer 2004).

Randomization bias refers to the problem that people who agree to participate in an experiment may be different from the general population. *Piloting bias* refers to the problem that findings in a small experiment with lots of monitoring and control may not always be replicable at a larger scale. Dealing with these types of problems is usually context-specific. Banerjee *et al.* (2017), for example, report on an iterative procedure of design and experiment followed by redesign and experiment to eventually end up with two policies for India's school system that worked to scale up to millions of children.

11.7   Limitations of Randomized Control Trials

The use of randomized control trials (RCTs) in development economics has become much more popular since the mid-1990s and has a range of advantages, as outlined above and discussed elsewhere (see in particular Chapters 13 and 14). In a critical evaluation of the use of RCTs in general and in development economics in particular, Nobel Prize laureate in economics Angus Deaton (2020) argues that: "The RCT is a useful tool, but I think it is a mistake to put method ahead of substance" (p. 1). He summarizes his two main points as follows:

* RCTs are affected by the same problems of inference and estimation that economists have faced using other methods, as well as by others that are peculiarly their own.
* No RCT can ever legitimately claim to have established causality.

He elaborates on these points in detail to argue that RCTs have no special status as a research method, that they have strengths and weaknesses shared by other methods, and that there simply are "good studies and bad studies, that's all" (p. 2).

Deaton starts by stating that the best method to learn something about any topic always depends on the context, but that (p. 2):

My own personal favorites are cross-tabulations and graphs that stay close to the data; the hard work lies in deciding what to put into them and how to process the data to learn something that we did not know before, or that changes minds. An appropriately constructed picture or cross-tabulation can undermine the credibility of a widely believed causal story, or enhance the credibility of a new one; such evidence is more informative about causes than a paper with the word "causal" in its title. The art is in knowing what to show.

Indeed, this textbook includes carefully constructed graphs and tables based on data to illustrate the main links between different phenomena. This involves hard work in gathering and analyzing the data, experimentation in presenting the data, and discarding many efforts in the process. Depending on the circumstances, other methods can be useful to continue the story. This might be an RCT, or another method.

It is a misconception to think that statistical inference is simpler in RCTs. A problem at the data collection stage is that RCTs require tracking respondents and dealing with outliers, challenging tasks that require time and skills not all authors involved in RCTs possess. At the inference phase there are two main issues: randomization; and the method used for determining significance.

Randomization is difficult, as Deaton discusses with a simple example. Suppose there are four villages, A, B, C, and D, two of which are to be treated for an RCT and two not. If we let the village elders decide based on bidding or bribing, we have a clear self-selection problem for our experiment, say resulting in villages A and B receiving treatment, which would be unacceptable. Suppose, instead, that we randomly select the villages to be treated by rolling the dice. Since there are only six possibilities, there is a one/sixth chance that the randomly selected outcome is that villages A and B receive treatment. It is absurd that this selection is fine in the random selection case, but not in the first case. The probability of such a problematic outcome reduces, of course, if we have more villages to choose from, but we usually have to randomize along several dimensions, which creates new challenges. Remember that it is good to make the treatment and control groups look like one another, but it requires information and deliberate allocation to achieve this.

Regarding inference, the results of RCTs are usually based on calculating t-values for the difference between two means, which has a t-distribution only under certain conditions. In particular, we need assumptions that limit skewness (the third moment, see Chapter 2) or the presence of outliers on one side of the distribution. If an outlier is present it is this extreme observation being either in the treatment or control group that determines the outcome of the RCT. A related problem is the use of inaccurate p-values (see Young 2019). As a consequence, the results of RCTs should be presented as estimates (just like any other method), and not as facts.

Deaton also points out the *external validity* problem, in particular regarding replication and the idea of universal applicability (see also section 11.6). With respect to replication: if something works in 60 experiments there is *no guarantee* that it will work in the 61st experiment. With respect to the idea of universal applicability, Deaton (2020, p. 9) notes: "No one thinks that an estimate of the average income in America will be accurate a decade from now, yet an estimate of an average treatment effect, which is also a sampling-based estimate of a mean, is often treated as if it is likely to hold elsewhere, at least in the absence of evidence to the contrary." Again, this problem applies also to other empirical studies – for example, when we assume that an estimated elasticity of labor supply is also valid in a different country or period. Related to this issue is the observation that policies that are implemented on a large scale based on a few experiments might be less successful than expected.

Regarding *causality*, Deaton points out that even within the context of a specific RCT causal conclusions always depend upon a strong set of auxiliary assumptions (and a model), which are not consequences of the data. Moreover, even given the set of auxiliary assumptions leading to the theoretical claim of causality for a specific RCT, this claim cannot always be transferred to another situation. That is the limited external validity of causality. Finally, Deaton makes several interesting ethical observations, not discussed within the boundaries of this section.

11.8   Conclusions

This chapter briefly reviewed the Poor Economics revolution in development economics, which focuses on effectively solving smaller problems in an experimental setting to reduce poverty. An advantage of the approach is that it tends to stay close to the day-to-day problems of real people. How do they live, how do they spend or earn their money, and how do they make their decisions? As a result, we learn about these processes and problems, which creates effective policy solutions. The chapter also briefly discussed the structure of randomized control trials and how the movement started in Kenya, before analyzing the main challenges facing the approach: external validity and the limitations of randomized control trials. Some of the experiments are discussed in more detail in Chapters 13 and 14.

So how about the attention for "big" versus "small" development questions discussed in the introduction to this chapter (section 11.1)? As is the case in other fields of economics, the focus tends to cycle somewhat over time. The World Bank, for example, started out focusing on the small questions, doing projects for ports, schools, roads, power plants, and so on. A problem in effectively evaluating such projects regarding poverty reduction is created by price distortions, which required calculating and effectively implementing shadow prices as well as discounting costs and benefits. This turned out to be infeasible. As Deaton (2020, p. 16) points out: "The remedy was to switch from the small to the large, to fix the distortions first, and to get the macroeconomy right before doing project evaluation. Structural adjustment was the result." The only true reduction in global poverty arises from economic growth, in recent decades particularly in China and India. Associated with growth are small improvements: more schools, roads, jobs, hospitals, and so on, without understanding exactly how and why. The Poor Economics revolution should be seen as a response to return to the small development questions to better understand the spread of growth to reduce poverty. However, Deaton (2020, p. 16) warns: "No one, as far as I am aware, suggested that RCTs were the key to economic growth; it is hard to tell a story in which RCTs had any relevance for poverty reduction in China."

After this introduction to Poor Economics, the next three chapters focus on important aspects of human development, namely population, education, and health (in that order).

Further Reading

Abhijit Banerjee, Esther Duflo, and Michael Kremer received the Nobel Prize in Economics for their "experimental approach to alleviating poverty." The main ideas underlying this work are explained in this chapter and in: Banerjee, A. V. and E. Duflo. 2011. *Poor Economics: A Radical Rethinking of the Way to Fight Global Poverty* (New York: PublicAffairs). Some applications of their work are available in Chapters 13 and 14. See also Duflo for an overview of field experiments in development economics: Duflo, E. 2006. "Field Experiments in Development Economics," in R. Blundell, W. Newey, and T. Persson (eds.), *Advances in Economics and Econometrics: Theory and Applications, Ninth World Congress* (New York: Cambridge University Press), vol. 2, pp. 322–48.

A detailed and accessible account of the work on Poor Economics by Banerjee, Duflo, and Kremer, as well as on the connections and interactions between the contributors, is available on the Nobel Prize website (including additional references): www.nobelprize.org/prizes/economic-sciences/2019/summary/.

12 Population and Migration

12.1 Introduction

In 2020, there were about 7.8 billion people on our planet. This chapter analyzes the links between economic development (measured by income per capita) and demographic factors, like birth rates and death rates. Associated with these links are (i) a demographic transition model, which (ii) produces a period of rapidly rising population levels, and (iii) associated changes in the age structure of populations, leading to (iv) additional economic benefits known as the demographic dividend. This chapter analyzes the size and structure of these effects for the world as a whole and the main countries and regions. It also analyzes the relative importance of international migration, both voluntary and involuntary (through refugees), for determining the size of the population. This analysis helps us to better understand recent economic developments (1950–2015) in different parts of the world, as well as expected future developments (2015–2050) for Europe, China, India, and Africa.

Section 12.2 reviews the evolution of population levels at the world scale for the most recent 2,000 years. Section 12.3 then analyzes the changes in the distribution and (projected) growth rates over the main countries and regions for the period 1950–2050. It shows that population growth has been rapid at the world scale for the most recent 200 years, with a peak in growth around 1968 and a decline since then. This is indicative of demographic transition at the world scale, as analyzed in sections 12.4 and 12.5. Different countries and regions are in different phases of demographic transition, where Europe is in the final stages and Africa is in the early stages. This helps us to better understand differences in population age structure (as analyzed in population pyramids in section 12.6), as well as differences in the share of working age population (relative to young and old population), which gives rise to a demographic dividend (for China) or reverse dividend (for Africa) (see section 12.7). The chapter concludes with an analysis of migration flows in section 12.8, involuntary migration in section 12.9, and a discussion of Syrian refugees in Europe in section 12.10.

12.2 World Population

According to the UN Population Division, the total world population reached 7.8 billion in 2020. This is a substantial increase of about 1 percent relative to 2019. It means that about

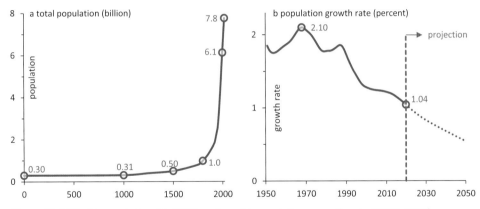

Figure 12.1 World population (0–2020) and world population growth rate (1950–2050)
Source: Based on data from UN Population Division 1999.
Note: Projections are for the medium variant.

220,000 people are added to the world population *each day*, leading to a total increase of about 80 million people *per year*. This, in turn, means that about the entire population of Germany is added to the world population each year.

From an historical perspective, this increase in population is high. According to the UN Population Division (1999), there were only about 300 million people on our planet some 2,000 years ago (in the year 0). This means that it took Homo sapiens about 200,000 years to reach the 300 million mark (see Chapter 3). Including our predecessors in the discussion, it took mankind some 7 million years to reach that level (see again Chapter 3). From then on, the rise in world population from 300 million in the year 0 to 7.8 billion in the year 2020 occurred mostly in the most recent 200 years (see panel a of Figure 12.1). World population was stagnant in the first 1,000 years, rising from 300 million in the year 0 to 310 million in the year 1000. It began to increase slowly in the next 500 years (rising from 310 million in the year 1000 to 500 million in the year 1500). The 1 billion mark was reached in 1804, after which world population began to increase rapidly to 2 billion in 1927, 3 billion in 1960, and so on.

A quick look at panel a of Figure 12.1 might give the impression that the world population is about to "explode" and reach ever-higher levels. This is not true, as indicated in panel b of the figure, which shows the growth rate of world population for the period 1950–2015 and the UN Population Division projected growth rate up to the year 2050. The growth rate of world population peaked at 2.1 percent in 1968 and has declined (with ups and downs) substantially since then to reach 1.05 percent in 2020. The decline is expected to continue to a growth rate of 0.50 percent in 2050. In fact, the UN's projected world population growth rate is a further decline to 0.11 percent in 2100. This last part of the projection is not shown in panel b of Figure 12.1 as it is too far into the future and the deviation between realization and projection is becoming ever larger. This issue is discussed next, but first note that panel b also adequately illustrates that projected demographic trends are always smooth (see the dotted line), while the actual growth rates are full

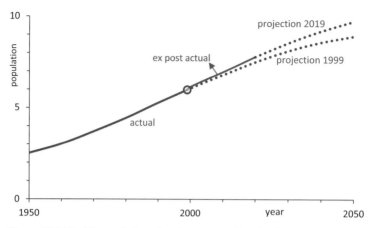

Figure 12.2 World population; development and projections, 1950–2050
Sources: 1999 projections based on data from UN Population Division 1999 and 2015 projections on UN Population Division 2015.
Note: Medium variant.

of ups and downs (even at the world scale) for political reasons, famines, wars, and other unexpected events.

Figure 12.2 illustrates that changes in expected demographic trends can quickly lead to drastically different projected outcomes and substantial deviations from reality. In 1999, the world population reached 6 billion people, which prompted the UN Population Division to publish *The World at Six Billion*, including projected developments of world population up to the year 2150. Figure 12.2 shows the actual development of world population up to 1999 and the UN's projection from 1999 onward to 9.75 billion in 2050. Twenty years later (in 2019), the UN made a new projection of world population based on the updated information becoming available in the period 1999–2019. It is therefore possible to compare the ex post actual realization of world population with the prediction in 1999 for these years, as well as compare the new projection of 2019 with the projection of 1999 up to the year 2050. The deviations tend to be modest initially, but then quickly add up over time to substantial deviations.

After 11 years (in the year 2010), the projected world population was 6.79 billion, while the actual population was 6.96 billion. The world population rose by an additional 167 million people in those 11 years compared to what was expected in 1999. Similarly, the 2019 projection for 2020 is 295 million people higher than the 1999 projection, while the new projection for 2050 is 825 million people higher. It illustrates that demographic trends can be predicted with some accuracy, but that small changes in underlying processes (as explained later in this chapter) lead to substantial deviations within a few decades. For this reason, the figure only shows the projection up to 2050 and not beyond. The UN's 1999 prediction actually extends all the way to 2150, with an expected world population at that time of 9.75 billion. In the updated 2019 prediction, this level will be reached around 2050, or 100 years earlier! The main reason for the increase in projected population estimates is that the impact of the HIV/AIDS epidemic turned out to be less devastating in 2019 than feared in 1999.

Table 12.1. World population in 2050 estimates for different variants in 2019 (million)

	population	deviation		population	deviation
Medium variant	9,735	0	Instant-replacement	9,418	–317
High variant	10,588	853	Zero-migration	9,735	0
Low variant	8,907	–828	Constant-mortality	9,330	–405
Constant-fertility	10,543	808	No change	10,101	366

Source: UN Population Division 2015.
Notes: Population in million; deviation in million relative to medium variant.

The UN Population Division is, of course, well aware of the uncertainties and deviations associated with demographic trend projections. For that reason, it analyzes a number of different trends for all the countries in the world using various scenarios (variants). For illustration purposes, Figure 12.2 uses the medium variant, which represents the UN's best guesstimate of population developments in all countries taking all likely changes regarding birth rate, death rate, and migration flows into consideration. Table 12.1 provides the estimated world population (in millions) in 2050 for eight variants analyzed by the UN in 2019, as well as the deviation from the medium variant. Five variants differ only regarding the assumed fertility (medium, low, high, constant, and instant-replacement). The differences in the estimated world population in 2050 relative to the medium variant ranges from –828 million people for the low variant to +853 million people for the high variant. These extremes are not likely to occur, but it gives a feel for the range of possibilities. In addition, there is a zero-migration variant (which has mainly distribution consequences), a constant-mortality variant (which would reduce world population by 405 million people), and a no change (relative to 2015–2019) variant for fertility and mortality (which would increase world population by an extra 366 million). Keeping these caveats in mind, the remainder of this chapter analyzes and discusses the implications of the medium variant only.

12.3 Main Countries and Regions

After section 12.2 provided a clear view of the development of world population (up to the year 2050), this section analyzes the (likely) developments of population levels in different parts of the world. To do so, the world is divided into seven main countries and regions (see Table 12.2). From a country perspective, the populations of both China and India are about 1.4 billion people in 2020, which is more than four times as much as the USA, the third-ranked country. So for the sheer size of their population, the countries of China and India are included separately. The other entities are mostly the main continents (Africa, Europe, and Latin America), with the exception of what is labeled *Offshoots* in Table 12.2, which groups together four countries (the USA, Canada, Australia, and New Zealand) with a

Table 12.2. Population in main countries and regions; 1950, 2020, and 2050 projection

Region	Total population (million)			Percent of world total		
	1950	2020	2050	1950	2015	2050
China	544	1,439	1,402	21.9	18.5	14.4
India	376	1,380	1,639	14.8	17.7	16.8
Africa	228	1,341	2,489	9.0	17.2	25.6
Latin America	169	654	762	6.7	8.4	7.8
Offshoots	183	399	464	7.2	5.1	4.8
Europe	549	748	710	21.7	9.6	7.3
Other Asia	477	1,834	2,268	18.8	23.5	23.3
World	2,536	7,795	9,735	100.0	100.0	100.0

Source: Based on data from UN Population Division 1999.
Notes: Projection for 2020 based on medium variant; Offshoots are the USA, Canada, Australia, and New Zealand; Latin America includes Caribbean (LAC); Other Asia includes small populations from Oceania (less than 1 percent of the total).

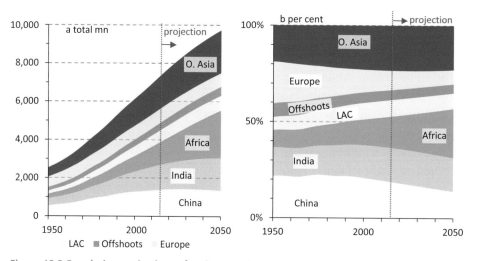

Figure 12.3 Population projections of main countries and regions, 1950–2050
Source: Based on data from UN Population Division 1999, World Population Prospects.
Notes: Projections based on medium variant; Offshoots are the USA, Canada, Australia, and New Zealand; Latin America includes Caribbean (LAC); Other Asia includes small populations from Oceania.

similar demographic and historical experience. This follows Angus Maddison (2001), who refers to these four countries as the *Western Offshoots* (see also Chapter 5). The remaining (rest of the world) region is called *Other Asia*, as it consists mainly of Asian countries (excluding China and India), combined with small populations from Oceania (less than 1 percent of the total population in Other Asia).

Figure 12.3 illustrates the population developments in the seven main regions from 1950 to 2050, both in an absolute sense (millions, see panel a) and a relative sense (percent of world total, panel b). Similarly, Table 12.2 provides the absolute and relative numbers for three time periods: 1950, 2020, and 2050. Below is a summary of the findings from a closer look at the figures and percentages from Figure 12.3 and Table 12.2 for two main periods, namely actual developments and projected developments.

Actual developments for the period 1950–2020:

- The population level was growing in all main countries and regions.
- The growth rate was much lower in Europe than in the world as a whole, leading to a substantial reduction of Europe's share in world population (from 21.7 to 9.6 percent).
- The growth rate was somewhat lower than the world average in the Offshoots and China, leading to a decline in the share of world population of about 2 and 3 percent for the Offshoots and China, respectively.
- The growth rate was higher than the world average for Africa, Latin America, Other Asia, and India, which therefore have a rising population share. This holds in particular for Africa, which had the highest growth rate and increased its share of the world population by 8.2 percentage points (from 9.0 to 17.2 percent).

Projected developments for the period 2020–50:

- The population level is expected to decline in China and in Europe (by 37 million in both cases), while a rise is expected in all other main countries and regions.
- The growth rate is expected to be *below* the world average for *all* countries and regions, except for *Africa*. As a consequence, Africa's share of the world population is expected to rise substantially from 17.2 percent in 2020 to 25.6 percent in 2050.

Combining the above observations, the developments in Europe and China contrast strongly with the developments in Africa. The dynamics of these developments (in terms of birth rate and death rate) are analyzed in section 12.5, but first, section 12.4 discusses demographic terms and transition.

12.4 Demographic Transition

Demographers use a variety of precisely defined terms in their models to adequately express and predict expected changes in population developments. Table 12.3 provides a glossary of a selection of these demographic terms. The focus here is on the size of the population as determined by the population growth rate. This, in turn, depends on three main variables: the crude birth rate, the crude death rate, and the net migration rate (equal to immigration minus emigration). All these variables are expressed as a number per 1,000 population.

$$population\ growth\ rate = crude\ birth\ rate - crude\ death\ rate + net\ migration\ rate \qquad 12.1$$

As equation 12.1 indicates, the population growth rate (per 1,000) is the difference between the crude birth rate and the crude death rate (also known as the rate of natural increase) plus the net migration rate. Sections 12.8 to 12.10 analyze net migration flows. For the

Table 12.3. Glossary of demographic terms, selection

Variable	Definition
Crude birth rate	Number of births over a given period divided by the person-years lived by the population over that period. It is expressed as number of births per 1,000 population.
Crude death rate	Number of deaths over a given period divided by the person-years lived by the population over that period. It is expressed as number of deaths per 1,000 population.
Rate of natural increase	Crude birth rate minus the crude death rate. Represents the portion of population growth (or decline) determined exclusively by births and deaths.
Net migration rate	The number of immigrants minus the number of emigrants over a period, divided by the person-years lived by the population of the receiving country over that period. It is expressed as net number of migrants per 1,000 population.
Median age	Age that divides the population in two parts of equal size, that is, there are as many persons with ages above the median as there are with ages below the median.
Life expectancy	The average number of years of life expected by a hypothetical cohort of individuals who would be subject during all their lives to the mortality rates of a given period. It is expressed as years.
Infant mortality	Probability of dying between birth and exact age 1. It is expressed as deaths per 1,000 births.
Mortality under age 5	Probability of dying between birth and exact age 5. It is expressed as deaths per 1,000 births.
Dependency ratios	The total dependency ratio is the ratio of the sum of the population aged 0–14 and that aged 65+ to the population aged 15–64. The child dependency ratio is the ratio of the population aged 0–14 to the population aged 15–64. The old-age dependency ratio is the ratio of the population aged 65 years or over to the population aged 15–64. All ratios are presented as number of dependents per 100 persons of working age (15–64).

Source: UN Population Division 1999.

moment, therefore, this section focuses on (crude) birth and death rates, which are empirically more important for determining population growth rates than net migration rates for most countries in the world.

Section 12.2 described how the world population at first grew slowly for many years, after which the growth *rate* increased rapidly around 1800, reached a peak around 1968, and then started to decline again. Section 12.3 showed that expected population trends up to 2050 differ widely for the main countries and regions. The *demographic transition* model connects population developments with economic developments. It is based on empirical observations of birth and death rates made at the beginning of the twentieth century by the American Warren Thompson (1887–1973) and Adolphe Landry (1874–1956) of France. The model is illustrated in Figure 12.4 using four stages. (Sometimes five stages are identified, but the fifth stage is then uncertain, so it is excluded here.)

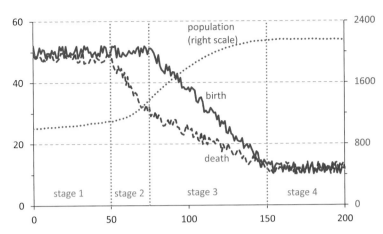

Figure 12.4 Demographic transition

- Stage 1. Birth and death rates are high and volatile, such that population growth is low and fluctuating. It is a stage of low economic development (before the Industrial Revolution), with mostly agricultural workers.
- Stage 2. The death rate starts to fall, especially among children, as a result of improvements in health care and sanitation. It is a stage of emerging economic development in which birth rates remain high. As a consequence, the difference between birth and death rates starts to rise and the population starts to grow more quickly.
- Stage 3. Birth rates start to fall as well, not only because of the availability of contraceptives and an increase of women's status, but also because fewer children are needed on the farm to work as a result of mechanization. It is a more advanced stage of economic development in which the population still rises rapidly, but the speed of population growth starts to decline toward the end of this stage as the gap between birth rate and death rate narrows.
- Stage 4. Birth rates and death rates are both low, stabilizing the population at a higher level than before the demographic transition began. It is a stage of higher economic development with, on average, an older population.

During the demographic transition, the structure of the population changes, with a rising share of young people and a falling share of older people in stage 2, followed by a declining share of young people and a rising share of older people in stages 3 and 4. Sections 12.5 to 12.7 analyze these aspects and their economic consequences. Taking these aging aspects into consideration would slightly alter Figure 12.4, without affecting the main message.

Is there empirical support for the link between the level of economic development and demographic variables? Yes, there is, as illustrated in Figure 12.5 for the crude birth rate (panel a) and crude death rate (panel b) in 2015. In both panels, the horizontal axis depicts income per capita (PPP, log scale) for the 185 countries included in the figures. In panel a, note that birth rates clearly decline if income per capita rises; the estimated income elasticity is –7.42 and a regression explains 75 percent of the variance in birth rates. The

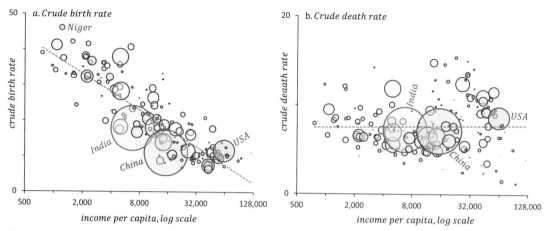

Figure 12.5 Birth rate, death rate, and income per capita, 2019
Source: Created using World Development Indicators online data.
Notes: Income per capita is GNI PPP in constant 2017 $ (2019 or most recent), log scale; crude birth rate and death rate per 1,000 population (2018 or most recent); vertical scales differ in the panels; 185 countries included; bubbles proportional to size of population.

birth rate is highest in Niger (46.1) and lowest in South Korea (6.4). In panel b, note that the relationship between income per capita and death rates is basically absent (note the different vertical scales for panels a and b); the trendline is horizontal and "explains" 0.04 percent of the variance in death rates. The death rate is highest in Bulgaria (15.4) and lowest in Qatar (1.2). This is, of course, related to the aging populations of higher-income countries. The next section looks into these issues in more detail for the world as a whole and the main countries and regions.

12.5   Birth Rate, Death Rate, and Transition

To illustrate the (projected) relevance of demographic transition, this section uses information on birth rate and death rate for the world as a whole and a selection of main countries and regions for the period 1950–2050, as shown in panels a–f of Figure 12.6. Each panel is briefly discussed in turn. Again, birth rates and death rates are per 1,000 population and all panels have the same scale (dividing the numbers by 10 therefore gives percentage growth rates).

Panel a shows the developments for the *world* as a whole. In 1950, the world birth rate was about 37 and the death rate about 19, leading to a rate of natural increase of around 18. The world birth rate declines for the whole period; fairly rapidly in the period 1950–2015 (from 37 to 20) and more slowly since then (to 15 in 2050). Note that there are some fluctuations in the decline of the birth rate in the first half of the 1960s and second half of the 1980s. These are largely related to developments in China (see panel e). The world death rate declines from 1950 to 2015 (from 19 to 8) and is expected to rise (because of an aging world population) to about 9 in 2050. As a result, the rate of natural increase peaked at 21 in 1968 and declines to 6 in 2050. The rate of natural increase is

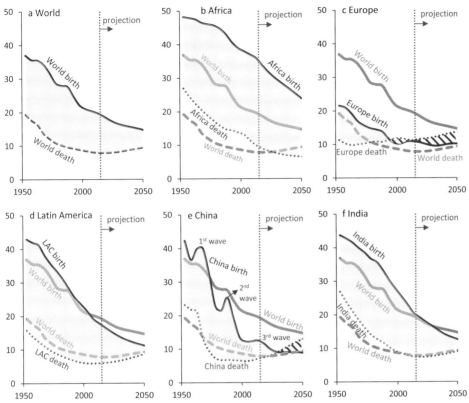

Figure 12.6 Crude birth and death rates; selected countries and regions, 1950–2050
Source: Based on data from UN Population Division 2015.
Notes: Projections from 2015 onward based on medium variant; five-year averages projected in center year; Latin America includes Caribbean (LAC); shaded area is rate of natural increase, striped if it is a decline.

indicated clearly in the figure by the shaded area. For ease of reference, the world birth and world death lines are included in light grey in all other panels of Figure 12.6.

Panel b shows the demographic developments in *Africa*. The birth rate is much higher than the world average throughout the whole period. Although the African birth rate is declining steadily, starting at 48 in 1950 and declining to 36 in 2015 and 24 in 2050, the gap with the world average birth line is steadily rising until the early 2000s and only starts to decline from there on. Africa's death rate is also higher than the world average in 1950 (27 compared to 19) due to poor health care and sanitation. Improvements in these conditions combined with a young population implies that death rates in Africa decline for the whole period (to 10 in 2015 and 6 in 2050) and are expected to drop below the world average in the second half of the 2020s. As a consequence of these developments, the rate of natural increase is much higher than the world average for the whole period, namely 21 in 1950, 26 in 2015, and 18 in 2050. As a result, Africa's share of the world population is rising fast (see section 12.3).

Panel c depicts the demographic developments in *Europe*, which contrast sharply with the African developments. Europe's birth rate is substantially below the world average for the whole period, with an initial decline from 21 in 1950 to 10 around the year 2000, where it is expected to stabilize with some fluctuations up to 2050. Europe's death rate is the reverse of Africa's. Initially it is substantially below the world average (11 instead of 19 in 1950). After reaching a minimum of 10 in the first half of the 1960s, the aging population implies that Europe's death rate starts to rise (to 11 in 2015 and 13 in 2050), such that it is higher than the world average from 1980 onward. As a result of these developments, Europe's natural rate of increase falls from 10 in 1950 to become negative from 1995 onward (reaching −3 in 2050), leading to a sharp decline of Europe's share in the world population (see section 12.3).

Panel d shows the developments in *Latin America and the Caribbean*. They are actually quite similar to the world averages. This holds in particular for the death rate, which is always slightly below the world average; starting from 16 in 1950 to reach a minimum of 6 around 2005 and rising to 8 in 2050. The birth rate in Latin America starts a bit higher than the world average (43 compared to 37 in 1950) and declines a bit faster to drop below the world birth rate around 2005 (and reach 11 in 2050). As a consequence, Latin America's rate of natural increase is initially higher than the world average (particularly in the 1950s and 1960s), but is below the world average from 2015 onward.

Panel e shows the developments in *China*, which are clearly the most dramatic and wildly fluctuating of the analyzed countries and regions. The fluctuations are mostly related to Mao Zedong's Great Leap Forward policies (1958–1962), a campaign to rapidly transform the country from an agrarian economy to a modern society through industrialization and agricultural collectivization in which private farming was prohibited. Food production slowed to a halt, which resulted in the Great Chinese Famine in the years 1959–1961, in which millions of people starved to death. The policies were reversed under the leadership of Liu Shiaoqu and Deng Xiaoping. The consequences are visible for both China's birth rate and its death rate. Regarding the latter, the regular decline in the death rate came to a halt in this period, to then quickly decline afterwards.[1] In the period 1980–2005, the Chinese death rate stagnates at around 6, after which it starts to rise rapidly as a result of the aging population to 13 in 2050; it is expected to be above the world average death rate from 2020 onward. The fluctuations are even more visible in China's birth rate. There is a strong decline in births during the Great Famine as people try not to have children when the circumstances are bleak, followed by a peak to (partially) make up for lost children in the period immediately afterwards (second part of the 1960s). This large number of births then leads to a new peak some 25 years later (second part of the 1980s), which in turn leads to a more modest peak 25 years later again (around 2015). A new, even more modest, ripple effect will occur in the second half of the 2030s, and so on. Interfering with these developments is China's one-child policy, which was introduced in 1979 and is beginning to be formally phased out from 2015 onward. The net result is a wildly fluctuating birth rate that is below the world average from 1975 onward. In

---

[1] Note that the graphs are based on five-year averages, which mitigates the enormous peak in the death rate of 1960.

combination with the developments for China's death rate, the rate of natural increase also fluctuates wildly, is consistently below the world average from 1990 onward, and is negative from 2030 onward.

Panel f, finally, shows the developments in *India*, which are somewhat comparable to those in Latin America and the world as a whole. India's birth rate is initially higher than the world average (44 compared to 37 in 1950), but then declines more rapidly (to 20 in 2015 and 13 in 2050), to drop below the world average from 2025 onward. Similarly, India's death rate is initially higher than the world average (27 compared to 19 in 1950), but then declines more rapidly to drop below the world average in the beginning of the 2000s. India's low point in death rate of around 7 is reached in the first half of the 2020s. As a combination of these two effects, India's natural rate of increase is initially above the world average, to drop below the world average from 2030 onward. In addition, India's population is expected to be larger than China's (and thus the largest in the world) from about 2022 onward.

All six panels of Figure 12.6 show the demographic transition model in action. This framework developed in section 12.4 provides a better understanding of developments of birth rates, death rates, and rates of natural increase relative to the level of economic development of a country or region and relative to the world average, although dramatic events like the Great Leap Forward in China may interfere and to some extent dominate more regular demographic developments. Section 12.6 will now analyze the age structure of a population during the demographic transition, before section 12.7 analyzes the economic *demographic dividend* associated with demographic transition.

12.6 Population Pyramids

A popular and instructive way to illustrate the changing population structure of a country or region during the demographic transition is to construct a so-called population pyramid. An example of three such pyramids for the world as a whole in 1990, 2015, and 2050 is given in Figure 12.7. The size of the population (in millions) is measured on the horizontal axis; for males to the right of the origin and for females to the left of the origin. The population of both sexes is divided into five-year age groups, namely 0–4 years old, 5–9 years old, and so on. All people above 100 years of age are grouped together.[2] The age groups are depicted on the vertical axis, from 0 to 100. The figure also indicates three broader age groups, labeled *young* (0–14 years old), *working age* (15–64 years old), and *old* (65 years and older). This distinction is analyzed in more detail in section 12.7.

The sharpest (most "pointy") population pyramid in Figure 12.7 is the 1990 pyramid, in which each older age cohort is clearly smaller than the previous one. There were, for

---

[2] The UN Population Division does not provide a detailed breakdown for the 80+ population before 1990, which is why 1990 was chosen as the first year.

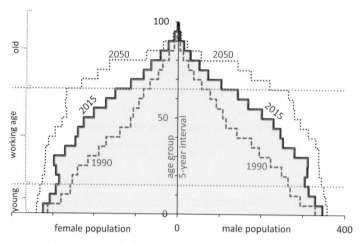

Figure 12.7 World population pyramids; 1990, 2015, and 2050
Source: Based on data from UN Population Division 2015.
Notes: Projections for 2050 based on medium variant; million population per five-year age group.

example, 313 million females in the 0–4 year age group in 1990, followed by 281 million females in the 5–9 year age group, 258 million in the 10–14 year age group, and so on. The respective numbers for males in 1990 are 330, 294, and 270 million. Such a sharp pyramid is indicative of a rapidly rising population, with a large fraction of young people and a small fraction of older people. More specifically, about 33 percent of the population in 1990 was in the young category (0–14 years old) and only 6 percent in the old category (65+), leaving about 61 percent in the working age category (15–64 years old).

The 2015 population pyramid is shaded for clarity. It is bigger and less sharp than the 1990 pyramid. The fact that it is bigger indicates that the world population is increasing, because the sum of all areas represents the entire world population. The fact that it is less sharp indicates that the population growth rate is declining, resulting in a smaller share of young people (26 percent compared to 33 percent in 1990) and a rising share of older people (more than 8 percent compared to 6 percent in 1990). The net result is a rise in the working age population (close to 66 percent, compared to 61 percent in 1990).

The 2050 population pyramid is again bigger than the 2015 pyramid (so the population level is still rising) and even less sharp (so the population growth rate is still declining). By 2050, the share of young people will have declined below 22 percent and the share of older people will have risen above 14 percent. The net result is a decline in the working age population from 66 to 64 percent.

As an example for an individual country, Figure 12.8 provides similar population pyramids for China in 1990, 2015, and 2050.[3] Let's first focus on the shaded China "pyramid" of 2015, which does not look like the regular pyramids for the world as a whole

---

[3] Detailed examples of population pyramids for all countries in the world for all years from 1950 up to 2100 are available at www.populationpyramid.net.

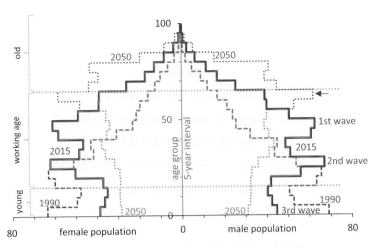

Figure 12.8 China population pyramids; 1990, 2015, and 2050
Source: Based on data from UN Population Division 2015.
Notes: Projections for 2050 based on medium variant; million population per five-year age group.

discussed above because of the peaks and gaps. For the 2015 pyramid, the peaks are labeled 1st, 2nd, and 3rd wave on the male side. The 1st wave corresponds with the peak in China's birth rate in the second half of the 1960s (see panel e of Figure 12.6). It thus relates to the population in the 45–49 years old bracket for 2015. Similarly for the 2nd wave in the second half of the 1980s, which corresponds with the 25–29 years old bracket for 2015, and the smaller 3rd wave after 2010, which corresponds with the 0–4 years old bracket for 2015. The 1st and 2nd waves are also visible for the 1990 pyramid (in the 20–24 years old bracket and the 0–4 years old bracket, respectively), but not identified separately to avoid cluttering the diagram; similarly for 2050.

The corresponding broader age categories (in percent of the total population) for young–working age–old are 29-66-5 in 1990, 17-73-10 in 2015, and 14-62-24 in 2050. This indicates a rapidly declining young population and a rapidly rising older population, with initially a rising share of the working age population and then a declining share of the working age population. Section 12.7 analyzes this aspect in more detail, also regarding China's aging population in general. To conclude this section, however, note the large aging problem China faces around 2050 in particular. This problem is identified in Figure 12.8 by the red arrow pointing to the 60–64-year-old male population for the 2050 pyramid. This age bracket is clearly large in 2050 as it relates to the 2nd wave; in fact, by this time the male and female population in the 60–64-year-old bracket is 9.4 percent of the total Chinese population. In the next five years (from 2050 to 2055), it will be replaced in the working age share of the population by the much smaller 10–14-year-old age bracket of 2050, which implies an enormous decline in the share of the working age population by almost three percentage points in just five years' time. A similar drastic reduction in the share of the working age population is related to the 1st wave and will occur at the end of the 2030. These issues are now analyzed in more detail in the next section.

12.7   Demographic Dividend

Associated with the age structure of a population as shown in the population pyramids of section 12.6 is a broader implication regarding the economic growth prospects of a country. If the population of a country is rapidly growing, the share of the young population which is not yet economically active is large, while the share of the older population which is no longer economically active is small. As shown below, these two effects do not cancel out for the share of the economically active working age population, which actually varies during the demographic transition.

The terms "young," "old," and "working age" are, of course, debatable and may vary over time and with the level of economic development of a country. As noted above, standard practice is used here, namely, classifying the 0–14-year-old population as young and the 65+ bracket as old, which leaves the 15–64-year-old bracket for the working age population. This is covered in more detail below.

Regarding the young population: on the one hand, in many developing countries people of 15 years and older are (forced to be) economically active at work, at the farm, or otherwise because they no longer (can afford to) go to school. Likewise, in many (economically) advanced countries, the mandatory minimum schooling age is up to 18 years old, while most people continue their studies into their 20s. On the other hand, many people in the 15–19-year-old age bracket continue to go to school, also (and increasingly so) in developing countries. Similarly, many people in advanced countries in the 15–24-year-old age bracket go to school *and* are economically active through part-time jobs.

Regarding the older population: the formal retirement age in many advanced countries is around 65 years old for men and (on average) a few years less for women (OECD 2015). The 2019 EU average normal retirement age for a man with a full career from age 22 was 64.3 years (see Figure 12.9). This is higher than for most developing countries listed in the figure, which is below 60 years for Saudi Arabia, Brazil, India, and Indonesia, equal to 60 years for South Africa, China, and Russia, and equal to 65 years in Argentina. Many countries are increasing the retirement age in view of longer life expectancies. For the EU the normal retirement age is expected to rise to 66.2 years in the near future. Most developing countries still have a young population and are not yet planning a similar increase. The exceptions are Russia (a rise from 60 to 64 years) and Indonesia (a rise from 56 to 65 years). Whether people actually stop working at the retirement age is, of course, a different matter. For the OECD countries as a whole, the average employment rate in 2019 was 72.5 percent for people aged 55–59, falling to 49.6 percent for people aged 60–64, and 22.3 percent for people aged 65–69 (see OECD 2019). Many poor developing countries have no effective pension scheme or retirement age, so people stop formal employment if they are no longer physically able to work or are no longer in demand by employers. They may then still be economically active in the informal sector, growing food close to home, taking care of grandchildren, and so on.

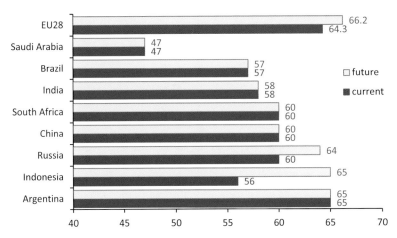

Figure 12.9 Current and future normal retirement age, 2019
Source: Based on data from OECD 2019.
Notes: The normal retirement age is calculated for a man with a full career from age 22; EU28 is European Union 28 countries; scale starts at 40.

The above discussion shows that the age borderlines of 15 and 65 to determine dependency ratios of young versus working age population or old versus working age population or total dependents (young + old) versus working age population are vague and to some extent arbitrary (see Table 12.3 for formal definitions). It is clear, however, that in general younger people are not yet economically active and are dependent on others for food, clothing, care, and shelter. Similarly, older people tend to become no longer economically active and become more dependent on others (although not necessarily financially) for food, clothing, care, and shelter. The remainder of this section focuses on this issue. The borderline ages of 15 and 65 can, of course, be altered, but this does not change the main message analyzed below.

Figure 12.10 illustrates the evolution of the share of the young population (panel a) and the old population (panel b) from 1950 to 2050 for the world as a whole and a selection of regions and countries. To avoid cluttering the diagram, Europe and the Offshoots have been grouped together (with a rather similar age structure from 1975 onward), as well as Latin America and Other Asia (with a rather similar age structure from 1985 onward). (Similarity in age structure in this context refers to the share of working age population – see below.) For the world as a whole, the share of the young population peaked at 38 percent in 1965, declined to 26 percent in 2015, and will continue to decline below 22 percent by 2050. The opposite holds for the share of the old population, which reached a minimum of 5 percent in 1960, increased to 8 percent in 2015, and will continue to rise above 14 percent by 2050.

For the main regions and countries, the developments are (on average) rather similar to the world trends in Latin America, India, and Other Asia. The share of the *young* population is *lower* than the world average and the share of the *old* population is *higher* than the world average throughout the entire period for Europe and the Offshoots. These countries thus

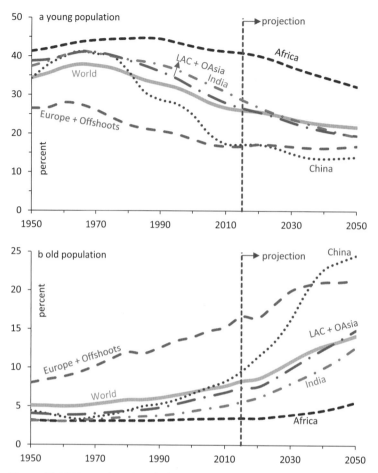

Figure 12.10 Young (0–14) and old (65+) population; percent of total, 1950–2050
Source: Based on data from UN Population Division 2015.
Notes: Projections from 2015 onward based on medium variant; Offshoots are the USA, Canada, Australia, and New Zealand; LAC+OAsia = Latin America and Caribbean plus Other Asia.

have a relatively old population. The reverse holds for Africa, which has a higher young population and a smaller old population. The developments are again most dramatic in China, where the share of the young population is initially higher than the world average, reaches a peak above 41 percent in 1965, declines below the world average in the 1980s, reaches 17 percent in 2015, reaches a minimum below 14 percent around 2040, and then slowly starts to rise again. Almost the opposite holds for the share of the old population in China, which is initially below the world average, reaches a minimum close to 3 percent around 1965, rises above the world average in the early 2000s, is almost 10 percent in 2015, and approaches 25 percent by 2050. The share of the young population in China even declines below that of Europe and the Offshoots in the 2020s, while the share of the old population in China even rises above that of Europe and the Offshoots at the end of the 2030s. In the years ahead (2015–2050), China thus has by far the most rapidly aging population.

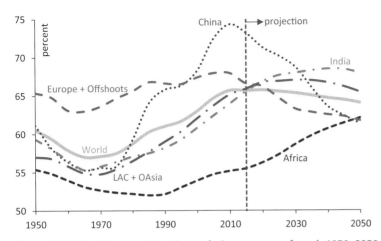

Figure 12.11 Working age (15–65) population; percent of total, 1950–2050
Source: Based on data from UN Population Division 2015.
Notes: Projections from 2015 onward based on medium variant; Offshoots are the USA, Canada, Australia, and New Zealand; LAC+OAsia = Latin America and Caribbean plus Other Asia; vertical scale does not start at zero.

$$income\ per\ capita = \frac{income}{population} = \underbrace{\left(\frac{working\ age\ population}{population}\right)}_{A} \underbrace{\left(\frac{workers}{working\ age}\right)}_{B} \underbrace{\left(\frac{income}{workers}\right)}_{C}$$

12.2

Figure 12.11 shows the combined effect of the young and old population developments for the share of the working age population.[4] For the world as a whole, the share of the working age population reached a minimum of 57 percent around 1965 and has been rising since then to a peak of almost 66 percent around 2010, where it will stay until 2020 and then gradually start to decline. Since income per capita is by definition the product of three ratios (see equation 12.2), this means that for a given income per worker (C) and share of workers in the working age population (B), a rise in the share of the working age population (A) directly translates into rising income per capita levels. From a dynamic perspective, for a given growth rate of income per worker and a given share of workers in the working age population, a rise in the share of the working age population translates into a rise in the growth rate of income per capita, which is the approach taken by Rougoor and van Marrewijk (2015). As such, a rise in the share of the working age population during the demographic transition implies a boost in income per capita levels and growth rates, which is referred to as the *demographic dividend* (see Bloom *et al.* 2003 for an overview). There does not seem to be a generally accepted term for the opposite of a demographic dividend when the share of the working age population is low. (The term demographic deficit cannot

---

[4] Some demographic literature prefers to discuss dependency ratios, a monotone transformation defined as the share of (young, old, or total) dependents divided by the share of working age population. However, this section focuses on the more direct measure of the share of the working age population (see also Rougoor and van Marrewijk 2015).

be used as it seems to have different meanings for different researchers.) For clarity of exposition, the world's share of the working age population is taken as a benchmark and the term *dividend* is used if a country's share is higher than the world average and the term *reverse dividend* if it is lower. The dividend and reverse dividend are measured in percentage point deviations from the world average.

For the main regions and countries identified in Figure 12.11, it can be seen that there is a small reverse dividend for Latin America, India, and Other Asia for the period 1950–2015, while there will be a small dividend for the period 2015–2050, particularly for India. The opposite holds for Europe and the Offshoots, where there was a demographic dividend up to 2015 and there will be a reverse dividend from then on. Africa is again a clear outlier as it has a substantial reverse dividend for the whole period 1950–2050. In fact, Africa's share of the working age population reached a minimum of 52 percent in 1985 (at which stage the reverse dividend was more than 8 percentage points) and has been rising steadily since then to about 56 percent in 2015 and 62 percent by 2050. Africa's reverse dividend is more than 10 percentage points for the period 2005–2015. The most dramatic events occur again in China, which has a share of the working age population fairly close to the world average up to 1980, after which this share rapidly rises above the world average, particularly in the 1980s and in the first decade of the new millennium (related to the two birth waves already discussed in sections 12.5 and 12.6). The peak of China's share of working age population of more than 74 percentage points occurs around 2010, leading to a demographic dividend of 9 percentage points. There are thus enormous deviations in the timing of the demographic dividend for different countries and regions. This holds in particular around 2010 when Africa has a reverse dividend of 10 percentage points, while China has a dividend of 9 percentage points, for a total deviation of 19 percentage points.

It is, of course, not easy to translate differences in demographic dividend into differences in income growth rates. As analyzed throughout this textbook (see in particular Chapters 1 and 7), economic growth depends on the timing of many country-specific factors, related to factor-driven economies, efficiency-driven economies, and innovation-driven economies, as well as the ups and downs of the global economy, such as the rapid restoration after the destructions of the Second World War, the global oil price shocks, or the trade decline after the Great Recession of 2008. One way to illustrate the demographic dividend, while controlling for global effects, is to analyze income developments relative to the world as a whole. To do so, relative income is defined as a country's income per capita (GDP in constant 2010 USD) divided by the world average income per capita in that year, using percentage points and a log scale. (It is, unfortunately, not possible to use the superior PPP income data as it is not available in 1960–1990.)

Figure 12.12 illustrates the connection between the demographic dividend and relative income for China (panel a) and Sub-Sahara Africa (panel b). Sub-Sahara Africa, rather than Africa, is used for the illustration here, as the income per capita information provided by the World Bank focuses on the Sub-Sahara part of Africa, which excludes countries in North Africa (where demographics and economic developments tend to be different from the rest of Africa). Data are available from 1960 onward. This is combined, obviously, with

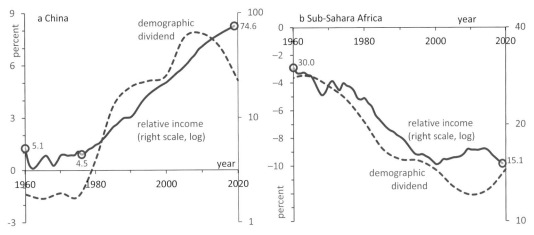

Figure 12.12 Demographic dividend for China and Sub-Sahara Africa, 1960–2019
Sources: Based on data from UN Population Division 1999 and World Development Indicators online.
Notes: Demographic dividend is a country's share of 15–64-year-old population in percent minus the world's share of 15–64-year-old population, five-year observations; relative income is income per capita (GDP in constant 2010 USD) relative to the world average income per capita in percentage points.

Sub-Sahara Africa's demographic dividend, which differs slightly from that of Africa as a whole as given in Figure 12.11.

In China there is a mild reverse dividend in the 1960s and first part of the 1970s. As panel a of Figure 12.12 shows, relative income in China slightly declines (with considerable variations related to the Great Leap Forward and Cultural Revolution policies) from 5.1 percent of the world average in 1960 to 4.5 percent in 1976 (the year Mao Zedong dies). From then on, China develops an enormous demographic dividend relative to the world as a whole, with an associated sharp rise in relative income levels, from 4.5 percent of the world average in 1976 to 74.6 percent in 2019. Panel b of Figure 12.12 shows that Sub-Sahara Africa has a large and growing reverse demographic dividend relative to the world as a whole for the entire period, which leads to a decline of relative income from 30.0 percent of the world average in 1960 to 15.1 percent in 2019.

The implications of this analysis regarding the demographic dividend of the main regions and countries for the period up to 2050 are as follows. First, in view of a switch from dividend to reverse dividend around 2015, it will become increasingly difficult for Europe and the Offshoots to keep up with income per capita developments in the world as a whole. Second, in view of a sharp decline in demographic dividend and return to a reverse dividend at the end of the 2030s, China's high income per capita growth rates can be expected to decline sharply in the 2020s and 2030s, while remaining above the world average. Third, in view of its continued reverse dividend, it will be difficult for Africa to keep up with income per capita growth rates in the rest of the world. In fact, Africa's switch to a demographic dividend region is only expected around 2060. Fourth, in view of its rising demographic dividend, income per capita growth rates in India are likely to be above the world average in the decades to come; India's peak of demographic dividend is around 4 percentage points in the 2040s.

12.8   Migration

So far, the discussion in this chapter has concentrated on birth rates, death rates, mortality, and fertility and ignored international migration flows. Indirectly, migration flows imply international mobility of other inputs, such as many different types of human capital and skills. These inputs are embodied in the migrating population and acquired through years of schooling, studying, practice, training, and on-the-job learning-by-doing. The remainder of this chapter briefly discusses the (relative) size of international migration flows.[5]

People mainly migrate for one of two reasons:

First, fighting and other violence associated with (civil) war, persecution of minorities, drugs trade, and so on may force people to leave their homes and seek safety and shelter elsewhere. See section 12.9 for a brief discussion of this type of migration.

Second, there may be differences in the reward for specific types of labor in different locations. In principle, this creates an incentive for people to migrate from locations with low real wages to those with high real wages. In view of the enormous differences between countries in terms of income per capita (see Chapter 7), the real-wage-difference migration incentive is strong.

Note that the main economic consequences of migration flows based on real wage differences can be analyzed using a similar framework as discussed in Chapter 6. In principle, therefore, migration flows are welfare enhancing.

There are three main obstacles to migration flows based on real wage differences. First, people need to actually have the (educational) skills required to benefit from the real wage difference and be aware of its existence. In many cases, they do not have the required skills or lack information regarding opportunities in other countries. Second, there are many legal obstacles to migration flows, both within and between countries. Many advanced countries, for example, have a quota system, which limits the number of people that can legally enter the country. Third, there are large costs and uncertainties associated with international migration. Many people in Africa, for example, simply lack the resources or financial security to be able to engage in migration efforts.

United Nations (UN) evidence indicates that although the absolute numbers have increased, world migrants (that is, foreign-born) comprise only about 3.5 percent of the world population (UNIOM 2020). This low number seems inconsistent with popular opinion that the level of migrants is much larger, primarily as a result of the low number of migrants in developing countries. Indeed, in some individual countries these numbers are much larger. In 2019, for example, the share of international migrants was 7.2 percent in South Africa, 20.0 percent in Sweden, 21.3 percent in Canada, 37.1 percent in Singapore, and 78.7 percent in Qatar (UNIOM 2020).

Historians have identified two modern "waves" of migration.

---

[5] Sections 12.8–12.10 are based on van Marrewijk 2017, ch. 9; see also Beugelsdijk *et al.* 2013, ch. 1.

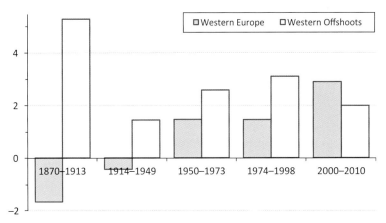

Figure 12.13 Relative migration flows; Western Europe and Western Offshoots, 1870–2010
Data source: Beugelsdijk *et al.* 2013.
Notes: Net migration in the period (Maddison 2001, table 3.4) is divided by the (simple) average population and length of the period, normalized per 1,000 inhabitants; updated for the period 2000–10 with data from UN Population Division, Migration Section; Western Europe consists of Belgium, France, Germany, Italy, Netherlands, Norway, Sweden, Switzerland, and the UK.

The first took place between 1820 and 1913. More than 50 million migrants departed (mostly) from Europe to Australia, Canada, South America, and the USA. Almost 60 percent of the migrants went to the USA. Most were young and relatively low-skilled. After 1850, most migrants came from Ireland.

The second "wave" started after the Second World War, and has not yet ended. Between 1913 and 1950, migration was only a fraction of what it had been during the nineteenth century. The USA remained the main destination country. Immigration grew from a low of 252,000 per year in the 1950s to 916,000 in the 1990s, but the source countries changed dramatically. Before the 1950s, most immigrants came from Europe, in the 1990s most came from Asia and, from 1990 onward, also from the eastern European countries. During this second wave immigration restrictions became more binding than before. Many countries began to use a quota, and allow in migrants for reasons such as a family reunion or specific labor needs. Within Europe, most migration flows are in the form of intra-EU migration. From 1990 to 2010, the stock of migrants in Europe increased from 49 to 70 million, compared to an increase from 28 to 50 million in North America. In general, labor markets are less globally integrated than trade and capital markets.

To get an idea of the expected size of future migration flows, Figure 12.14 provides estimates of a global region's total change in population, both absolute and as a percentage, as a result of migration flows over the period 2013–50. The graph is based on the UN International Migration Report 2013 and compares the estimated population size of a global region in 2050 (medium variant) with the estimated population size of that region if there is no international migration (zero migration variant).

The largest net recipient of people is North America, which is estimated to have a 68 million higher population as a result of international migration flows by 2050. The

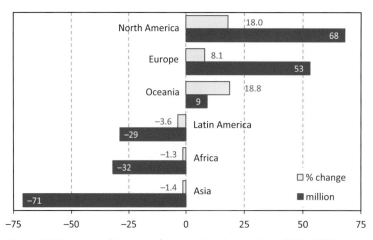

Figure 12.14 Expected impact of international migration, 2013–2050
Source: Based on data from UN Population Division 2013.
Notes: Million indicates expected increase in a region's total population (medium variant) as compared to a zero migration scenario; % change indicates the change in percent of a region's total population relative to the zero migration scenario.

relative impact is also substantial, with an expected increase in population of 18 percent. The second-largest net recipient is Europe, with a 53 million higher expected population or an 8 percent increase. The third net recipient is Oceania. In absolute terms, the rise in population is more modest (9 million), but in relative terms it is the largest (19 percent). All three net recipient regions consist largely of advanced countries.

The migration flows come from mostly developing regions, namely 71 million from Asia, 32 million from Africa, and 29 million from Latin America. In relative terms these flows are more modest, namely 1.3 percent for Africa, 1.4 percent for Asia, and 3.6 percent from Latin America. In general, these expected migration flows support the idea that people tend to move toward locations with higher real wages. In terms of change in total population, the impact is modest for developing regions, but quite substantial for the advanced regions.

12.9   Refugees and Internally Displaced Persons

The UN High Commissioner for Refugees (UNHCR), the UN Refugee Agency, was established in 1950 to help Europeans displaced by the Second World War, initially for a period of three years. The never-ending arrival of new conflicts and humanitarian crises has unfortunately made UNHCR necessary up to the present day. Initial examples are the Hungarian crisis in 1956 and the decolonization of Africa in the 1960s. Later examples are the displacement crises in Asia and Latin America in the 1970s and 1980s, 30 years of refugee crises in Afghanistan, and the turmoil in the Middle East (Syria and Iraq) in the twenty-first century.

The UNHCR website provides regular updates of "populations of concern to UNHCR" for global regions (see Figure 12.15). At the beginning of 2019, the total

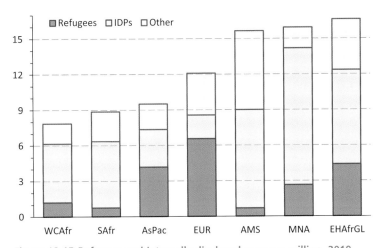

Figure 12.15 Refugees and internally displaced persons; million, 2019
Source: UNHCR 2019.
Notes: Persons in 1,000s; Refugees includes people in refugee-like situations; IDPs = Internally Displaced Persons; Others includes asylum seekers and various other groups; WCAfr = West and Central Africa; SAfr = Southern Africa; AsPac = Asia & Pacific; EUR = Europe; AMS = Americas; MNA = Middle East & North Africa; EHAfrGL = East and Horn of Africa and Great Lakes.

number of people of concern was 86.5 million. Only a minority of these (about 24 percent) are (international) refugees (20.4 million, including people in a refugee-like situation). The largest group concerns Internally Displaced Persons (IDPs) – that is, people who have not crossed an international border in search of safety and shelter (43.5 million or 50 percent). Other groups consist, for example, of asylum seekers, stateless persons, and others of concern to UNHCR. For simplicity, Figure 12.15 distinguishes only between three main groups: Refugees (24 percent), IDPs (50 percent), and Others (26 percent). Note that from a migration perspective only the (international) refugees should be discussed. From a humanitarian perspective, however, IDPs should also be included.

By far the largest number of refugees and IDPs is in the Middle East (10.8 million, or more than 25 percent of the world total). Almost 8 million of these people are IDPs as a result of the conflicts in Iraq, Syria, and Turkey. Other large concentrations of displaced persons, with a majority of IDPs, are in Latin America (5.8 million), East and Horn of Africa (5.8 million), and Central Africa (5.4 million). Southwest Asia has 4.3 million displaced persons, of which the majority (58 percent) are refugees. Despite the attention provided in the media to the European refugee crisis (see section 12.10), the total number of displaced persons in all European regions taken together is 4.2 million persons, fewer than in any of the regions mentioned so far, and less than 10 percent of the world total. The numbers are even lower for North America and East Asia and the Pacific. The conclusion is, therefore, that the displaced person problem is largely a developing economies problem, concentrated in the Middle East, Africa, and Latin America. Taken together, these regions account for more than 30 million (or more than 70 percent) of globally displaced persons.

12.10   Syrian Refugees in Europe

The Syrian refugee crisis started in 2011 when the initially peaceful demonstrations against the Assad regime (inspired by the Arab Spring) were met with torture and violence by the police and military and civil war erupted. There are many different rebel groups involved in the fighting, including the notorious so-called Islamic State. By 2015, the fighting has resulted in more than 200,000 casualties. Various foreign nations are involved in the conflict, including support for the rebels from the USA, France, and the UK and support for the Assad regime from Iran, Iraq, and Russia. This section first outlines developments up to August 2015, and then moves on to a 2020 update.

As usual when violence erupts, a stream of refugees is created by people who try to find safety and shelter elsewhere. A large number of these try to seek asylum in European countries, traveling by various dangerous routes in order to get there. Many drown, particularly when they try to cross the Mediterranean to reach Italy from Libya. The Syrian refugee crisis became the center of media attention in Europe during 2015. As Figure 12.16 shows, a large number of Syrian nationals already applied for asylum in 2014, with a peak of more than 18,000 per month in September and October of 2014. These numbers were dwarfed, however, by the number of asylum seekers in 2015, with about 51,000 applications in July 2015 and more than 73,000 in August 2015. The total number of applications reached more than 440,000 by August 2015.

One of the sources of friction is the distribution of the Syrian refugees over the European countries. As Table 12.4 shows, in absolute terms (left-hand part of the table) almost 109,000 (25 percent) seek asylum in Germany, followed by Serbia (17 percent), Sweden (16 percent), and Hungary (12 percent). All other countries together take care of the

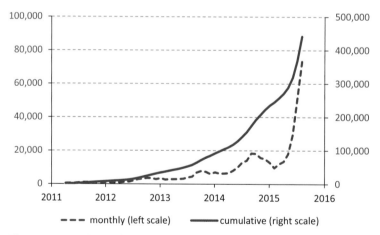

Figure 12.16 Syrian asylum seekers in Europe, 2011–2015
Source: Based on UNHCR data (downloaded October 10, 2015).
Note: Number of asylum applications by Syrian nationals for 37 European countries (excludes East Europe, such as Russia, Belarus, and Ukraine).

Table 12.4. Distribution of Syrian refugees in Europe, August 2015

Top 10 absolute		Top 10 relative	
Country	Asylum applications	Country	Applications / million
Germany	108,897	Serbia (and Kosovo)	10,777
Serbia (and Kosovo)	77,207	Sweden	7,232
Sweden	69,427	Hungary	5,471
Hungary	54,125	Montenegro	4,767
Austria	20,877	Cyprus	2,601
Netherlands	18,096	Austria	2,462
Bulgaria	15,714	Denmark	2,356
Denmark	13,230	Malta	2,249
Switzerland	8,683	Bulgaria	2,163
Belgium	8,230	Germany	1,350
Other 27 countries	47,228	Other 27 countries	185
Total	441,714	Total	822

Source: Based on UNHCR data (downloaded October 10, 2015).
Notes: Number of asylum applications by Syrian nationals for 37 European countries, cumulative April 2011–August 2015; relative: per million population.

remaining 132,000 (30 percent). Note that, with the exception of Germany, all countries in the top 10 in absolute terms are small countries in terms of population. Each of them has more asylum applications than large countries, such as the UK, France, Spain, and Italy. In response to this uneven distribution, the European Union (EU) decided to redistribute 120,000 refugees in September 2015. On the basis of the absolute number of refugees who applied for asylum from Syria alone reported in Table 12.4, this is a modest redistribution only, unlikely to solve this problem in the long run.

The picture of the uneven distribution of Syrian refugees across Europe changes only modestly when looking at the top 10 recipients in relative terms (per million population of the receiving countries). Again, Germany is the only large country involved, with 1,350 applications per million (compared to 822 for the European countries on average). Germany is again accompanied by nine relatively small countries, where Montenegro, Cyprus, and Malta are new on the list (replacing the Netherlands, Switzerland, and Belgium). (Note that the Netherlands, Switzerland, Norway, and Macedonia are also above the European average.) The highest relative number of applications is in Serbia (13 times the European average), followed by Sweden (nine times) and Hungary (seven times).

The influx of such a large number of refugees and the rapid increase during 2015 to more than 73,000 in one month clearly puts pressure on the absorption capacity of European countries and the willingness of populations to accommodate these refugees. In addition, there are migrants from other countries (such as Somalia, Afghanistan, and Nigeria) also

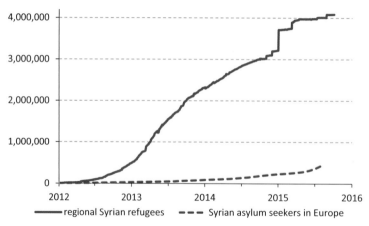

Figure 12.17 Regional versus European Syrian refugees
Source: Based on UNHCR data (downloaded October 10, 2015).
Notes: Regional Syrian refugees is number of registered Syrian refugees in Turkey, Lebanon, Jordan, Iraq, Egypt, and North Africa; asylum seekers in Europe is number of asylum applications by Syrian nationals for 37 European countries.

entering Europe, some as refugees and some for economic reasons.[6] The problems associ-ated with distinguishing between different types of migrants also create tensions. Germany, for example, estimated in September 2015 that about one-third of the asylum seekers in Germany who claim to be Syrian are not actually from Syria (Volkskrant 2015). The flows depicted in Figure 12.16 are thus both overestimating the problem (as it includes nonSyrians) and underestimating the problem (as it excludes many other refugees).

Keeping the above remarks in mind, it is still useful to put the European Syrian refugee problem into proper perspective. To do that, Figure 12.17 repeats the cumulative graph of European asylum seekers from Figure 12.16 and combines it with a graph of the number of *regional* Syrian refugees registered in Turkey, Lebanon, Jordan, Iraq, Egypt, and North Africa. The total number of regional Syrian refugees exceeded 4 million by September 2015, no less than nine times the total number of Syrian asylum seekers in Europe. Turkey alone hosted close to 2 million Syrian refugees (more than four times all of Europe combined), while Lebanon hosted more than 1 million (more than twice the European total). Notwithstanding the fact that a large number of these refugees might still find their way to Europe and apply for asylum there, this indicates that the Syrian refugee problem in Europe is dwarfed by the regional problems created in Turkey, Lebanon, and Jordan. It is also dwarfed by the humanitarian problems the refugees themselves are facing every day.

This section concludes with an overview of developments in the Syrian refugee crisis up to 2020. Since 2015, the number of Syrian refugees has increased further from 4.9 to

---

[6] The European Agency for the Management of Operational Cooperation at the External Borders of the Member States of the European Union (Frontex, http://frontex.europa.eu) reported that about 540,000 migrants entered the EU in January–August 2015, with the largest share coming from Syria. The data shown in Figure 12.16 add up to slightly more than 219,000 Syrian asylum seekers in that period, or about 41 percent of the total. Note that the Frontex numbers may include some double counting.

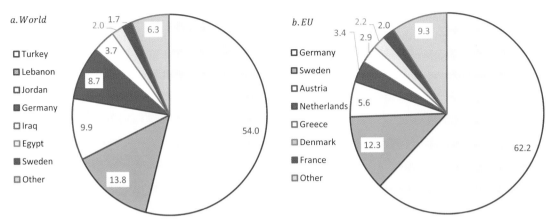

Figure 12.18 Syrian refugees in the world and the European Union; percent, 2020
Source: Created using UNHCR data.
Notes: panel a depicts Syrian refugees in other countries in the world, the percentages are relative to the total of 6.62 million refugees (begin 2020); panel b depicts Syrian refugees in EU countries (including the UK), the percentages are relative to the total of 0.92 million refugees.

6.6 million in 2020 (it has been stagnant at the latter level for two years). Figure 12.18 depicts the worldwide distribution of these referees (panel a) and across the EU (panel b) in percentages at the start of 2020. By far the largest share of Syrian refugees is still in Turkey (3.6 million or 54.0 percent of the total), followed by Lebanon (13.8 percent), Jordan (9.9 percent), Germany (8.7 percent), and Iraq (3.7 percent). With the exception of Germany, all the top five countries are neighbors of Syria. Taken together, the neighboring countries have 5.4 million Syrian refugees or 81.4 percent of the total. The developments since 2015 have therefore not changed the regional focus of the Syrian refugee crisis. Egypt and Sweden are the only other countries listed in panel a, while all other countries combined (including the USA, China, India, and Russia) take care of only 6.3 percent of the Syrian refugees.

Taken together, the EU countries (including the UK) take care of 0.92 million Syrian refugees, which is 13.9 percent of the total. Panel b of Figure 12.18 depicts the distribution of these 0.92 million refugees across the EU. By far the largest share of Syrian refugees in the EU is taken care of by Germany (62.2 percent), followed by Sweden (12.3 percent), Austria (5.6 percent), and the Netherlands (3.4 percent). The other countries listed in panel b are Greece, Denmark, and France (in that order), while the remaining 21 other countries combined (including Spain, the UK, Italy, and Poland) take care of only 9.3 percent of the Syrian refugees.

12.11   Conclusions

This chapter analyzed how the large increase in the world population is a relatively recent phenomenon which occurred mainly in the most recent 200 years. Word population growth peaked at 2.1 percent in 1968 and is expected to decline to almost zero by 2100. This is an example of demographic transition at the world level in four main stages, from initially high birth and death rates, to falling death rates, to also falling birth rates, to ultimately low birth and death rates. The main stages are related to the level of economic development, which explains why different countries and regions are at different stages of the demographic transition process, with associated differences in population age structure in different time periods. In connection with these developments, this chapter analyzed how the share of the working age population first falls, then rises, and then ultimately falls again during the demographic transition. These changes have a direct impact on the process of economic development, known as the demographic dividend (if the share of the working age population is high) or reverse dividend (if this share is low).

The demographic transition framework and the associated demographic dividend helps us to better understand various economic and population developments in different parts of the world. It explains, for example, why Europe's population is falling while that of Africa is rising, why relative income per capita in China rises (demographic dividend) and in Africa declines (reverse dividend), and why relative income per capita is expected to rise in India in the next three decades.

The chapter also discussed the size and direction of migration flows. Voluntary migration is primarily based on differences in real wage rates and flows from developing to advanced countries. Involuntary migration by refugees and internally displaced persons is largely concentrated in the Middle East, Africa, and Latin America.

Further Reading

The UN Population Division of the Department of Economic and Social Affairs provides up-to-date information and estimates on future population developments in the World Population Prospects, including maps, graphs, profiles, and interactive data. See: https://population.un.org/wpp/.

The UN High Commissioner for Refugees (UNHCR) is a global organization dedicated to saving lives, protecting rights, and building a better future for refugees. Its website (www.unhcr.org) provides information on current crises, like the Ukraine emergency and the Yemen emergency. It also provides data in its main publications on Global Trends (numbers of refugees, asylum seekers, and internally displaced persons), the Global Report (key results and achievements of the UNHCR), and Global Appeal (financial requirements, priorities, and budget activities). See www.unhcr.org/data.html.

A wealth of information on the economic aspects of migration can also be found on the OECD website, which provides not only detailed data, but also current research: www.oecd.org/migration/. A solid overview of the impact of educational programs in developing countries using the Poor Economics approach of Chapter 11 is provided in: Kremer, M. 2003. "Randomized Evaluations of Educational Programs in Developing Countries: Some Lessons," *American Economic Review*, 93(2), 102–6.

13 | Education

13.1 Introduction

As the above quotes indicate, mankind has emphasized the importance of education for long-run economic development and prosperity for a long time. The return on investment in education, which includes knowledge spillovers, is high and important for development (see Chapter 7). It is thus painful to realize that even in the year 2020 there are still about 260 million out-of-school children and adolescents worldwide, mostly in developing nations (see section 13.9). As our life span has expanded (see Chapter 14), so has the time we spend learning at school. The rising complexity of today's society requires us to master new and more complicated skills. It is essential to learn the basic skills associated with completing primary education. For most tasks, it becomes ever-more important to acquire more advanced skills associated with completing secondary education. For an expanding range of more complicated tasks the skills associated with completing tertiary education are required. This chapter evaluates these requirements and their relationship with economic development, taking the quality of education into consideration. It also analyzes and evaluates how the teaching process works in more detail, through learning effects, peer effects, target level, and teacher effort. A well-functioning school system using motivated and well-educated teachers is essential for development in all nations.

Section 13.2 starts with a brief discussion of the biology of learning, which emphasizes the importance of early childhood development. Section 13.3 continues, with an overview of the connections between economic development and educational attainment. Building on these results, section 13.4 evaluates the remarkable connections between development

---

[1] The short version (which is more to the point) is apparently frequently incorrectly attributed to Confucius (551–479 BC) (see Hung 2017).

and the gender gap, measured as the difference between female and male educational attainment. After this quantitative analysis, sections 13.5 and 13.6 discuss the quality of education for universities and more basic skills, respectively. The quality of education rises substantially with the level of economic development and is particularly low in the poorest countries. Section 13.7 discusses a teaching model focusing on direct peer effects and indirect peer effects through teacher effort and learning targets, in combination with tracking and nontracking schools. Section 13.8 reviews the results of field experiments in Kenya based on this teaching model, which concludes that tracking schools perform better than nontracking schools for various reasons. Section 13.9 summarizes the World Bank's views on the promise of education for economic development. Section 13.10 concludes.

13.2   The Biology of Learning

The ability to learn is not only guided by genetic endowments, but also by experience and interacting with environmental inputs.[2] The brain is *malleable* (capable of being shaped) throughout life, but most development is completed by the late teens. A *synapse* is a connection in the brain (the point at which a nervous impulse passes from one neuron to another). The fastest synaptic growth occurs before age 3, including the period before you are born. Initially, the brain develops more synapses than it needs, followed by a stage at which synapses used more often become permanent and those used less often are discarded. As a result, a 3-year-old has far more brain synapses than an adult (about 1,000 trillion versus 100–500 trillion). More complex brain structures (series of synapses or neural circuits) develop sequentially and cumulatively. Linguistic development, for example, depends on lower-level neural circuits most malleable earlier in life. Higher cognitive functions, most malleable up to adolescence, in turn use linguistic development as a building block.

Since the brain is more malleable early in life and brain development is sequential and cumulative, establishing sound learning foundations is crucial for skill development. The cumulative aspect is crucial here: skills *beget* skills, which also means that weak foundations create learning gaps. The most efficient way to learn is through exploration, play, and interaction (with peers and caring adults). This creates an especially important task for family members, nursery schools, and primary schools: they must lay the foundation of a nurturing and stable environment in which children are encouraged to play, interact, and experiment so they can develop the necessary skills for the rest of their lives. It also implies that disruptions in this process from all sorts of stress or negative emotions tend to have long-term negative consequences. The next section continues with a discussion of the general links between education and development at the country level.

---

[2] This section is based on World Bank 2018, Spotlight 1, pp. 68–70.

13.3   Education and Development

It seems reasonable to expect that as economic development rises at the country level (measured by income per capita), the education levels of its inhabitants rise as well. This is illustrated in Figure 13.1 for the share (in percent) of the population of 25 years or older that attained or completed three levels of education, namely at least primary education, upper secondary education, and Bachelor (or equivalent) in panels a, b, and c, respectively, relative to economic development using bubble diagrams (proportional to population). Table 13.1 provides summary statistics and information on the trendlines of Figure 13.1. Before this is discussed in more detail, it is important to realize that causality in the diagrams probably runs both ways. As countries become richer, they have more funds available to spend on different types of schooling, so education levels tend to rise. On the other hand, Chapter 7 showed that economic growth tends to rise if the initial education level (measured as human capital) is higher, thus leading to higher income levels. More importantly, Chapter 8 highlighted that schooling and the accumulation of human capital is one of the most important driving forces for economic growth, in contrast to institutional indicators. From a policy perspective, therefore, investing in education is of the utmost importance.

Completing primary education is crucial for acquiring basic skills (like reading, writing, and arithmetic) to be able to function in elementary (goods and labor) markets (see section 13.2). The simple average for the 103 countries depicted in panel a of Figure 13.1 suggests that 78 percent of the population completed primary education, but the population-weighted average is only 69 percent. In other words, about 31 percent of the population above 25 years of age has not even acquired the basic skills to properly function in elementary markets. The variation is wide, ranging from a minimum of 10.9 percent in Burundi to a maximum of 100 percent for several countries. There are four countries where less than 20 percent of the 25+ population has completed primary education. All are in Africa (Burundi, Niger, Mali, and Guinea), with a population-weighted average income level of $1,636. At the other extreme, there are four countries with a 100 percent score for completion of primary education. All are in Europe (Germany, Latvia, Sweden, and the UK), with a population-weighted average income level of $50,879.

As the discussion of the extremes suggest and panel a of Figure 13.1 shows, the level of completed primary education indeed rises as income per capita rises. The slope of the trendline in panel a (which explains 55.3 percent of the variance) is 16.5, which indicates that if income per capita rises by about 10 percent, the share of the population completing primary education rises by about 1.65 percentage points. Obviously, as indicated in the panel, a score above 100 percent is not possible, so for higher income levels the observations tend to cluster together close to this upper boundary. Some countries have observations fairly close to what you might expect on the basis of the trendline, such as India, Indonesia, Brazil, and the USA. Other countries are fairly high above the line (such as DR Congo and Uzbekistan) or below the line (such as Burundi and Ethiopia). In such cases,

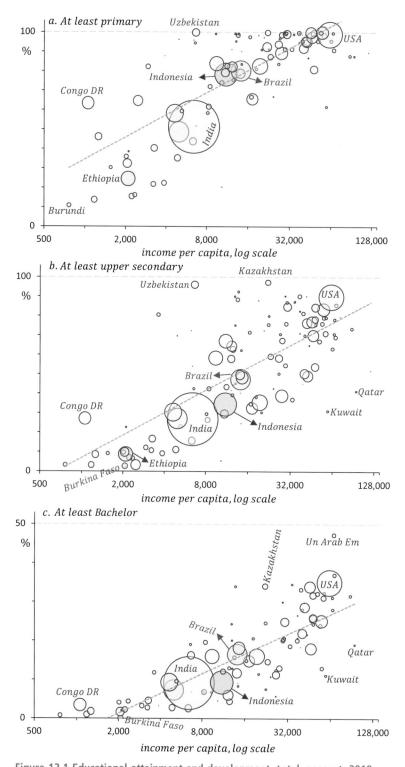

Figure 13.1 Educational attainment and development; total, percent, 2019

Source: Created using World Development Indicators online.

Notes: Educational attainment, total population 25+ (percent), most recent observation in 2011–19 period; income per capita is GNI PPP (constant 2017 int. $), most recent 2017–18, log scale; bubbles proportional to population, 2019; # of observations is 103, 116, and 98 for panels a, b, and c (at least primary, upper secondary, and Bachelor, respectively); dashed lines are trendlines, see Table 13.1 for further details.

Table 13.1. Education and development; summary statistics, 2019

	Primary	Upper secondary	Bachelor
Minimum	10.9	2.8	0.0
	(Burundi)	(Burkina Faso)	(Burkina Faso)
Maximum	100.0	97.4	47.3
	(several)	(Kazakhstan)	(United Arab Emirates)
Mean	78.2	52.7	16.4
Median	89.5	54.4	15.3
Standard deviation	25.4	27.3	10.8
Pop-wgh mean	68.7	42.7	14.3
Observations	103	116	98
Trendlines of Figure 13.1			
Slope	16.514^{***}	16.726^{***}	7.361^{***}
R^2	0.553	0.497	0.610

Source: See Figure 13.1.
Notes: Educational attainment, total population 25+ (percent), most recent observation in 2011–19 period; pop-wgh mean is population-weighted average; *** significant at 1 percent.

it seems worthwhile to investigate why (given the level of education) income levels are not higher (Congo and Uzbekistan), or how it is possible (given the income level) to improve education levels (Burundi and Ethiopia).

Completing upper secondary education is important for acquiring more substantial communication and interaction skills for functioning properly in more complicated markets, as required for basic manufacturing industries. Having a large share of the population with access to these skills is thus particularly important for emerging economies in the early stages of development. The simple average for the 116 included countries of the share of the population completing upper secondary education is 53 percent, while the population-weighted average is 43 percent. This implies that less than half the population has acquired the necessary skills to function in more complicated markets. The variation is high, ranging from a minimum of 2.8 percent for Burkina Faso to a maximum of 97.4 percent for Kazakhstan. The slope of the trendline in panel b of Figure 13.1 (which explains 49.7 percent of the variance) is 16.7, which indicates that if income per capita rises by about 10 percent, the share of the population completing upper secondary education rises by about 1.67 percentage points. The observations for India, Indonesia, Brazil, and the USA are again fairly close to the trendline. Countries like Uzbekistan, Kazakhstan, and DR Congo have relatively high upper secondary education levels. In contrast, countries like Kuwait and Qatar have relatively low upper secondary education levels.

Panel c of Figure 13.1 illustrates the share of the population completing at least a Bachelor (or similar) degree as an indication of the type of skills required to function properly in more advanced and complicated markets, such as aeronautics, pharmaceuticals, ICT, and the like. The scale of this panel is only half that of the other panels because a much smaller share of the population has the opportunity and ability to complete this level of education. In fact, the simple average for the 98 included countries for the share of the population with at least Bachelor-level education is only 16.4 percent and the population-weighted average is 14.3 percent. Even for the high-income countries only about one-third of the population has reached at least Bachelor level. The observations in panel c vary from a minimum of zero for Burkina Faso to a maximum of 47.3 for the United Arab Emirates, which is a clear outlier relative to the trendline in the graph. The slope of the trendline in panel c (which explains 61.0 percent of the variance) is 7.4, which indicates that if income per capita rises by about 10 percent, the share of the population completing Bachelor education level rises by about 0.74 percentage points. Countries with relatively high Bachelor education levels are Kazakhstan and United Arab Emirates. The latter is in contrast to the similar Arab oil countries Kuwait and Qatar, which have relatively low Bachelor education levels.

13.4 The Gender Gap in Education

Chapter 10 briefly reviewed aspects of gender equality. This section analyzes the gender gap for the three different levels of education discussed in section 13.3. It measures the gender gap as the difference in educational attainment of the 25+ population in percentage points for women and men – that is, the female attainment minus the male attainment. A negative score thus indicates that a lower share of women than men have attained that education level. A positive score indicates the opposite. It is important to keep in mind that substantial deviations from zero, either positive or negative, are indicative of a development problem. More specifically, a large negative score indicates that women are not given sufficient opportunity to reach their full potential in economics markets, as summarized in section 13.3, while a large positive score indicates that men are not given sufficient opportunity to reach their potential.

The discussion is organized in a similar way as in section 13.3, by illustrating the gender gap for the three educational attainment levels in relation to economic development in panels a, b, and c of Figure 13.2 using bubble diagrams (proportional to population). Table 13.2 provides summary statistics and information on the trendlines visible in Figure 13.2.

Starting with the primary education level in panel a of Figure 13.2, a large *negative* gender gap can be noted, indicating that women in many countries are not given the opportunity to go to school and acquire basic skills like reading, writing, and arithmetic. The primary education gender gap range is enormous, from –29.1 percentage points in Togo to +6.0 percentage points in Kuwait. The mean gender gap is –5.6, but the population-weighted mean is substantially higher at –11.5 percentage points (thanks in large part to India). The gender gap is largest for countries in Africa and South Asia, like Togo, DR Congo, Ethiopia, Nepal, India, and Pakistan. The large majority of countries has a *negative* primary education gender gap, namely 83 out of 103 or 81.4 percent of the included countries, indicating women are disadvantaged in primary education. Weighed by

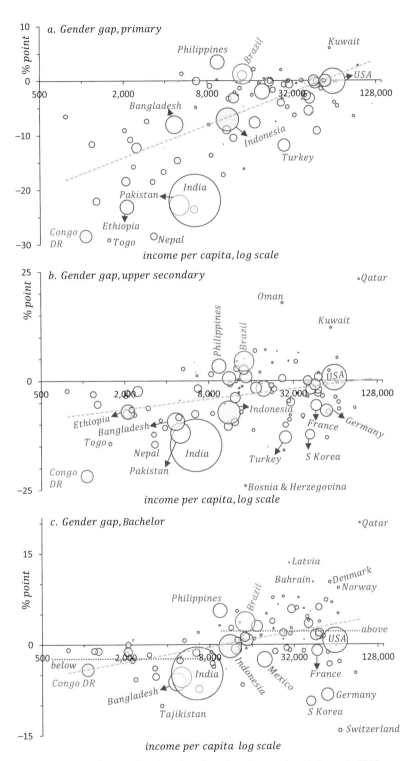

Figure 13.2 Gender gap in education; female minus male attainment, 2019

Source: Created using World Development Indicators online.

Notes: Gap = female − male attainment in percentage points, most recent observation in 2011–19 period; income per capita is GNI PPP (constant 2017 int. $), most recent 2017–18, log scale; bubbles proportional to population, 2019; # of observations is 102, 115, and 97 for panels a, b, and c (at least primary, upper secondary, and Bachelor, respectively); dashed lines are trendlines, see Table 13.2 for further detail; panel c "below" and "above": see main text.

Table 13.2. Gender gaps in education; female minus male attainment, summary statistics, 2019

	Primary	Upper secondary	Bachelor
Minimum	−29.1	−24.0	−14.2
	(Togo)	(Bosnia & Herzegovina)	(Switzerland)
Maximum	6.0	23.2	20.1
	(Kuwait)	(Qatar)	(Qatar)
Mean	−5.6	−3.1	0.8
Median	−2.9	−2.7	0.7
Standard deviation	7.7	6.9	5.1
Pop-wgh mean	−11.5	−7.2	−1.9
Share country negative	81.4	70.4	46.4
Share population negative	87.2	77.9	68.3
Observations	102	115	97
Trendlines of Figure 13.2			
Slope	4.285***	1.684***	1.814***
R^2	0.395	0.077	0.163

Source: See Figure 13.2.

Notes: Gender gap in percentage points of total 25+ population; pop-wgh mean is population-weighted average gender gap; share country negative is the percent of included countries with negative gender gap; share population negative is the percent of the population with a negative gender gap of the included countries; *** significant at 1 percent.

population size, this share rises to 87.2 percent (see Table 13.2). By implication, there are 19 countries with a *positive* gender gap (indicating men are disadvantaged), although the deviation from zero is usually modest, with the exception of Kuwait and the Philippines. The negative gender gap is strongly reduced as economic development rises: the slope of the trendline is about 4.3 and explains about 40 percent of the variance in the primary education gender gap. This means that the gender gap is reduced by about 0.43 percentage points if income rises by 10 percent.

Panel b of Figure 13.2 shows the gender gap for upper secondary education. Again, there is a substantial negative gap for a range of African and South Asian developing countries, like DR Congo, Nepal, India, Pakistan, and Togo. This time, however, there are substantial negative gaps for a range of emerging economies and advanced countries, like Bosnia & Herzegovina, Turkey, South Korea, and (to a lesser extent) Germany and France. The overall gender gap for upper secondary education is again negative, indicating that in particular women are not given the opportunity to acquire more substantial communication and interaction skills: the simple mean is −3.1 percentage points and the population-weighted mean is −7.2 percentage points. The majority of countries has a negative upper secondary education gap (81 countries or 70 percent of the included countries), which rises if population size is corrected for (to 78 percent, see Table 13.2). Note, however, that a range of countries has a substantial positive gender gap for upper secondary education, so the male population might not be able to reach its potential. This holds in particular for the Arab countries Kuwait, Oman, and Qatar, which all score above 12 percentage points. As with primary education, the negative gender gap for upper secondary education falls as economic development rises. This time, however, the impact is much weaker: the slope is only about 1.7 (instead of 4.3) and the share of variance explained is only about 8 percent (instead of 40 percent). This means that the negative gender gap is reduced by only 0.17 percentage points if income per capita rises by about 10 percent.

Panel c of Figure 13.2 shows the gender gap for the Bachelor and higher education level. In some respects, the graph is similar to that of panels a and b; in other respects, it is drastically different. It is similar because the gender gap rises as economic development rises. The effect is similar to that of panel b because the slope of the trendline is about 1.9 (instead of 1.7) and the share of the variance explained is about 16 percent (instead of 8 percent). It is drastically different in several ways.

First, the trendline intersects the horizontal axis at an income level of about $10,000, which means that the gender gap tends to be *negative* below this level (disadvantaging women) and *positive* above this level (disadvantaging men) (the exact point of intersection is $10,017). As the figure shows, this income level is close to that of Indonesia, which has a modest gender gap of –0.31.

Second, as a consequence of the first observation, the overall gender gap for Bachelor-level education is modest: the simple mean is +0.8, while the population-weighted average is –1.9. Similarly, the share of countries with a negative Bachelor-level gender gap is close to half (46 percent), although the population-weighted share is more substantial (68 percent, thanks to India).

Third, there is high variation in the Bachelor-level gender gap among the emerging and advanced economies. Some Arab and European countries have high *positive* Bachelor-level gender gaps, such as Qatar, Latvia, Bahrain, Denmark, and Norway (all above 9 percentage points, with Qatar even at 20 percentage points). In these countries, a strong effort seems to be needed to ensure that more men achieve at least Bachelor-level education. On the other hand, some advanced economies have high negative Bachelor-level gender gaps, like Germany, South Korea, and Switzerland (all below –8 percentage points, with Switzerland even at –14.2 percentage points). In these countries, a strong effort seems to be needed to ensure that more women achieve at least Bachelor-level education.

Fourth, and related to the third observation, if attention is restricted to higher levels of income per capita, say *above* $10,000, there is enormous variation in the Bachelor-level gender gap, but no longer a rise if income per capita rises. In fact, a formal regression for this group of countries is not statistically significant, as indicated by the horizontal "above" dotted line in panel c of Figure 13.2 (equal to the simple average for this group of 68 countries). Moreover, a similar procedure for the group of countries with an income per capita level *below* $10,000 is also not significant, as indicated by the horizontal "below" dotted line in panel c (equal to the simple average for this group of 29 countries). The overall conclusion is therefore that the Bachelor-level gender gap is only weakly related to economic development and is important in both directions (negative *and* positive).

13.5   The Quality of University Education

The analysis in sections 13.3 and 13.4 focuses on the level of education and the share of people who attain this level. It does not take into consideration the *quality* of education. This section discusses the quality of university education and the next section examines the quality of more basic skills. It is well known that there are big differences in the quality of universities between countries. Depending on the country, there are also big differences within countries, as well as differences in access to public and private universities by different groups of people. A simple indicator of limited access is the enormous tuition fee for graduate students charged at Harvard University, the highest ranked (private) university in the discussion below. In the 2020–21 academic year, Harvard charged $51,904 per year in tuition fees alone, clearly beyond the financial reach of most families.[3]

The information in the discussion below uses three main sources of information. First, data from www.statista.com is used to get information on the number of universities in a country in January 2020 (available for 25 countries with most universities). Second, there are several prominent international rankings of universities which provide an indication of the quality of the university. This section uses the Academic Ranking of World Universities (ARWU), also known as the Shanghai ranking as it was initiated by Shanghai Jiao Tong University (although it is now run by an independent organization). Other rankings (QS and Times Higher Education) lead to similar results. ARWU uses six indicators of a university's quality and publishes a ranking of the top 1,000 universities.[4] Third and finally, information from the World Development Indicators online is used on the size of a country's population and its (PPP) income per capita level to put the above information into proper perspective.

Table 13.3 starts in column 1 by listing how many universities a country has in 2020. India has the largest number of universities (4,354), followed by the USA (3,228) and China (2,596). Clearly, the list is dominated by countries with large populations (median population is 82 million). Tunisia, with a population of only 11.6 million, is an exception. The total number of universities for the countries in the table is exactly 23,000. Taken together, these countries represent about 5.2 billion people in 2018, which is about 69 percent of the world population in that year. This therefore gives a rough indication of the total number of universities in the world if we extend proportionally, namely about 33,500.

Column 2 in Table 13.3 lists a country's number of top 1,000 universities in the ARWU ranking. Given our estimate of about 33,500 universities in the world as a whole, the top 1,000 represents roughly the top 3 percent of the world's universities. The USA has most top 1,000 universities (206), followed by China (144) and the UK (65). Taken together, the 25 countries in the table have a total of 772 top 1,000 universities. The third column of

---

[3] See www.gse.harvard.edu/financialaid/tuition; note that there are grants available for talented students.

[4] The indicators are: number of staff and alumni winning Nobel Prize or Field Medal, number of highly cited researchers, number of articles in *Nature* and *Science*, number of articles in Science Citation Index and Social Science Citation Index, and per capita performance.

Table 13.3. Number of (top) universities; 25 countries, 2020

#	Country	# universities (1)	# top 1,000 (2)	(2) / (1) %	# universities per mn (rank)	# top 1,000 per mn (rank)
1	India	4,354	15	0.34	3.2 (20)	0.01 (21)
2	USA	3,228	206	6.38	9.9 (05)	0.63 (05)
3	China	2,596	144	5.55	1.9 (23)	0.10 (15)
4	Indonesia	2,304	0	0.00	8.6 (08)	0.00 (22)
5	Brazil	1,335	22	1.65	6.4 (14)	0.11 (14)
6	Mexico	1,205	2	0.17	9.5 (06)	0.02 (20)
7	Russia	1,091	11	1.01	7.6 (11)	0.08 (17)
8	Japan	992	40	4.03	7.8 (10)	0.32 (09)
9	Iran	653	12	1.84	8.0 (09)	0.15 (12)
10	France	608	30	4.93	9.1 (07)	0.45 (08)
11	Germany	455	49	10.77	5.5 (17)	0.59 (07)
12	Poland	398	8	2.01	10.5 (03)	0.21 (10)
13	Malaysia	384	5	1.30	12.2 (02)	0.16 (11)
14	S Korea	375	32	8.53	7.3 (12)	0.62 (06)
15	Canada	367	28	7.63	9.9 (04)	0.76 (04)
16	Pakistan	343	4	1.17	1.6 (24)	0.02 (19)
17	Ukraine	315	0	0.00	7.1 (13)	0.00 (22)
18	Colombia	290	1	0.34	5.8 (15)	0.02 (18)
19	Philippines	277	0	0.00	2.6 (21)	0.00 (22)
20	UK	276	65	23.55	4.2 (18)	0.98 (01)
21	Spain	260	40	15.38	5.6 (16)	0.85 (02)
22	Nigeria	249	0	0.00	1.3 (25)	0.00 (22)
23	Italy	238	46	19.33	3.9 (19)	0.76 (03)
24	Turkey	211	11	5.21	2.6 (22)	0.13 (13)
25	Tunisia	196	1	0.51	16.9 (01)	0.09 (16)
	Sum total / average	23,000	772	3.36	4.4	0.15

Sources: Data from www.statista.com (# of universities, January 2020), www.shanghairanking.com (# of top 1,000 universities, 2020), and World Development Indicators online (population 2018).
Notes: Table is ordered by the number of universities in a country; shaded cells: above average of sum total.

Table 13.3 indicates the "success rate" of a country in reaching the top 1,000 list by providing the share of top 1,000 universities relative to the total number of universities (in percent). The average for the 25 countries taken together is 3.36 percent. If a country scores higher than this average the cell in Table 13.3 is shaded, otherwise it is not. There are enormous differences in this success rate. The highest score is for the UK (23.55 percent), followed by Italy (19.33 percent) and Spain (15.38 percent). At the same time, there are four countries in the list (Indonesia, Ukraine, Philippines, and Nigeria) without any top 1,000 universities – that is, none of the 3,145 universities in these countries is classified as a top 1,000 university. Note that all four are developing countries. This is a first indication that economic development is important for establishing top universities and that some countries choose to be more selective in granting "university" status to an educational institute than other countries.

The last two columns in Table 13.3 focus on relative measures by listing the number of universities and the number of top 1,000 universities per million population. Both columns list the rank of a country within the table in parentheses. For the 25 countries taken together, there are about 4.4 universities per million population and 0.15 top 1,000 universities. The relative number of universities is highest for Tunisia (16.9 per million), followed by Malaysia (12.2) and Poland (10.5). It is relatively low for Nigeria, Pakistan, and China (in that order, starting with the lowest).[5] The relative number of top 1,000 universities in the table is highest for the UK (0.98), followed by Spain (0.85) and Italy (0.76). Apart from the four countries without any top 1,000 universities, it is relatively low in India, Mexico, and Pakistan (in that order – again, starting with the lowest).[6] Before analyzing the connection with economic development more closely, this section first discusses some of the other countries with top universities.

Table 13.4 provides information on the distribution of top universities according to the ARWU ranking for the top 50, top 100, top 200, and top 1,000 universities (roughly corresponding to the top 0.15, 0.30, 0.60, and 3.0 percent of all world universities). The 11 shaded countries are "new" as they are not listed in Table 13.3. All are small countries in terms of population (Australia is largest, with 25 million people), and most are in Europe (six countries), followed by Asia (four countries). Moreover, all are high-income countries, indicating that universities in advanced countries are much more likely to be among the top universities.

Table 13.4 also indicates a difference between countries in terms of the general quality of universities. China, for example, has 144 top 1,000 universities, of which 15 percent (22 universities) reach the top 200, 4 percent (six universities) reach the top 100, and 1 percent (two universities) reach the top 50. There is therefore, even within the top 1,000 category, a wide variation in quality; similarly for most other countries in the table. Some countries, however, have a much more focused average quality of their universities. The Netherlands is a good example. It has 13 universities in the top 1,000, equivalent to all main Dutch government-funded universities (there are only a few other universities). Of these, about 70 percent (nine universities) are in the top 200, 30 percent (four universities) are in the top 100, and 0 percent are in the top 50 (highest ranked is Utrecht University at 52). Almost all universities are therefore in the 50–200 range, indicating a high quality level for all universities. Countries with a similar profile include Switzerland, Belgium, and Israel.

---

[5] The correlation between the number of universities per million and income per capita (GNI PPP) for the countries in Table 13.3 is moderately positive, namely 0.21.

[6] The correlation between the number of top 1,000 universities per million and income per capita (GNI PPP) for the countries in Table 13.3 is high, namely 0.86 (as discussed below).

Table 13.4. Countries and top universities; ARWU Shanghai ranking, 2020

	Country	# top 50	# top 100	# top 200	# top 1,000
1	USA	30	41	65	206
2	China	2	6	22	144
3	UK	7	8	20	65
4	Germany	0	4	10	49
5	Canada	2	4	9	28
6	Netherlands	0	4	9	13
7	France	3	5	8	30
8	Australia	1	7	8	34
9	Switzerland	1	5	7	9
10	Japan	2	3	7	40
11	Sweden	1	3	5	14
12	Belgium	0	2	4	8
13	Israel	0	1	4	7
14	Denmark	1	2	3	6
15	Italy	0	0	3	46
16	Norway	0	1	2	5
17	Singapore	0	2	2	4
18	Saudi Arabia	0	0	2	4
19	Hong Kong	0	0	2	7

Source: www.shanghairanking.com.
Notes: Table ordered by number of top 200 universities; eight countries with only one top 200 university excluded (Finland, Russia, S. Korea, Brazil, Ireland, Spain, Portugal, and Austria); shaded countries are not listed in Table 13.3.

The choice of university within these countries is less important than, say, in the USA or China, where quality varies enormously.

Figure 13.3 illustrates the relationship between economic development and the relative quality of university education as measured by the number of universities in the ARWU top 1,000 list per million population. The figure only includes countries with at least one university in the top 1,000. A complete picture is provided by imagining bubbles for all other countries in the world spread across the horizontal axis. Ethiopia is the first developing country in the graph (income per capita of only $2,094) with a top 1,000 university, followed by Pakistan ($4,992) and India ($6,427). The power trendline in the figure clearly shows that the relative number of top universities rises beyond the $30,000 level of income per capita. The highest relative score (3.17) is received by the richest country in the figure. Other countries with a relatively high score are Iceland, New Zealand, Luxembourg, Austria, Finland, and Sweden (in that order). The next section now turns to a discussion of the quality of more basic skills.

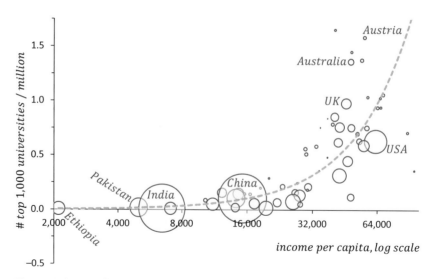

Figure 13.3 Top universities per million population and income per capita, 2020
Sources: Based on www.shanghairanking.com (university ranking 2020) and World Development Indicators online (income per capita in GNI PPP constant int. 2017 $ [most recent 2017–18] and population [2018]).
Notes: Dashed line is a power trendline $(y = \alpha x^\beta)$ with $\beta = 1.6301$, which explains about 74 percent of the variance; 62 countries, but Macao and Iceland not shown (3.17 and 2.84, respectively); bubbles proportional to population.

13.6   The Quality of Basic Skills Education

The World Bank (2018) discusses the quality of education in detail, with an emphasis on more basic skills and learning inequalities. An example is provided in Figure 13.4, which shows that poor children in Africa learn less. The figure depicts the quality of reading achievement in grade 6 in nine African countries based on a test with three classifications: not competent, low competency, and high competency. The figure shows the percentages of each score for four types of students in a country, along gender (boys and girls) and income (rich and poor; where rich are children from the 20 percent richest families and poor are children from the 20 percent poorest families).

A remarkably high share of African children do not meet the minimum reading requirements in grade 6 and are classified as "not competent." The average "not competent" score in the figure is 57 percent, ranging from a minimum of 19 percent for rich boys in Senegal to a maximum of 100 percent for poor girls in Nigeria. In other words: not one (in percentage terms) of the poor girls in Nigeria (and there are many of them) managed to reach the minimum reading requirements. The other side of the coin is students who manage to score "high competency," the average of which is only 18 percent, ranging from a high score of 56 percent for those rich boys in Senegal to a minimum of 0 percent for poor girls in Nigeria, poor boys in Nigeria, and poor boys in Cameroon.

Looking at the differences between rich and poor students, there are enormous variations. For the "not competent" classification, the score is about 38 percentage points *higher* for poor children than for rich children (slightly worse for girls than for boys).

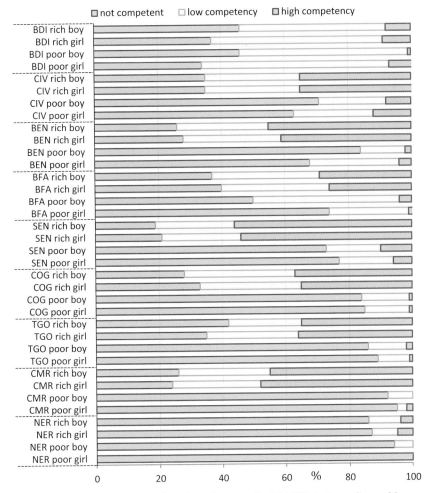

Figure 13.4 Poor children in Africa learn less; grade 6 PASEC test, reading achievement
Source: Created using World Bank 2018, figure O.3, data for 2014.
Notes: Poor = poorest 20 percent; rich = richest 20 percent; BDI = Burundi; CIV = Côte d'Ivoire; BEN = Benin; BFA = Burkina Faso;
SEN = Senegal; COG = Congo Republic; TGO = Togo; CMR = Cameroon; NER = Niger.

Similarly, the percentage of children who score "high competency" is about 29 percentage points *lower* for poor children than for rich children (slightly better for boys). These observations hold for all countries, but the deviations are particularly strong in Cameroon, Togo, Congo Republic, and Senegal. The only exception is in Burundi, where poor girls score "not competent" slightly less than rich girls (34 versus 37 percent). The summary is that children in primary school in Africa learn poorly, particularly poor children.

The discussion is continued in Figure 13.5 with an overview of the extent to which primary school students meet minimum proficiency thresholds for mathematics and reading (median percentage). The left part of the figure focuses on income per capita and the right part on geographic region (excluding high-income countries). As income levels

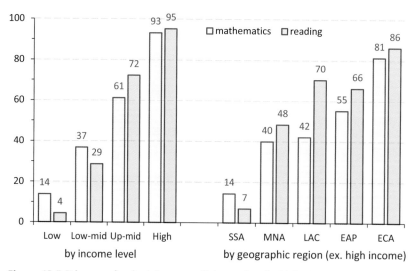

Figure 13.5 Primary school minimum proficiency threshold; by income and region, percent
Source: Created using World Bank 2018, figure O.5.
Notes: Median percentage of students in late primary school who score above a minimum proficiency level on a learning assessment for mathematics and reading; SSA = Sub-Sahara Africa; MNA = Middle East & North Africa; LAC = Latin America & Caribbean; EAP = East Asia & Pacific; ECA = Europe & Central Asia.

rise, the percent of students meeting the proficiency requirement rises as well; for reading from 4 percent for low-income countries to 95 percent for high-income countries and for mathematics from 14 percent for low income countries to 93 percent for high-income countries. In terms of geographic regions, Sub-Sahara Africa scores worst (14 percent for mathematics and 7 percent for reading), followed by the Middle East & North Africa, Latin America & Caribbean, East Asia & Pacific, and Europe & Central Asia. This partially reflects differences in income per capita.

To conclude the discussion on the relationship between the level of economic development and the quality of basic education skills, this section uses the Programme for International Student Assessment (PISA) scores for 15-year-old students to test their abilities for reading, mathematics, and science as put together by the Organisation for Economic Co-operation and Development (OECD). Since the correlation between the reading, mathematics, and science test scores is high (0.95 or more), the focus is on the mathematics test only, as illustrated for 77 countries in Figure 13.6. The mathematics test score rises substantially as economic development improves; a doubling of income per capita raises the test score by about 64 points and the trendline explains about 55 percent of the variance in the score.

Figure 13.6 indicates that, given their level of income per capita, countries such as Ukraine, Russia, Japan, and Singapore score relatively well on the test. In contrast, countries like Dominican Republic, Panama, Saudi Arabia, and Qatar are relatively less impressive. These countries should be able to learn from the teaching structure and incentives used in other countries to improve the effectiveness of their educational system. Before an analysis of ways to do this in more detail based on field experiments in section 13.8, section 13.7 first explains the teaching model underlying these experiments.

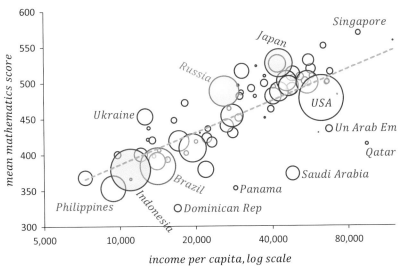

Figure 13.6 Income per capita and quality of education; PISA test mathematics, 2018
Sources: Created using data from OECD 2019 and World Development Indicators online.
Notes: Income per capita is GNI PPP (constant 2017 int. $), most recent 2017–18, log scale; bubbles proportional to population, 2019; mean score for mathematics PISA 2018; vertical scale starts at 300; 77 observations. The observation from a biased selection of tests in China based on Beijing, Shanghai, Jiangsu, and Zhejiang only is excluded from the graph; if included, it would create a clear outlier with the highest score (591).

13.7 A Teaching Model

Chapter 11 discussed how the Poor Economics revolution started in Kenya. Section 13.8 analyzes the empirics of some schooling experiments in Kenya in more detail based on the work of Duflo, Dupas, and Kremer (2011). This section explains the underlying structure of their teaching model in three steps. Subsection 13.7.1 starts, by discussing the effect of tracking on direct peer effects. Subsection 13.7.2 continues, with an analysis of indirect peer effects through the impact of teaching targets and teacher effort on learning effects. Subsection 13.7.3 evaluates how teacher payoffs determine teaching targets and teacher effort, before subsection 13.7.4 concludes with a discussion for the allocation of the median student.

13.7.1 Direct Peer Effects and Tracking

The model here focuses on the impact of tracking on learning outcomes through peer effects, teaching targets, and teacher effort. *Tracking* refers to the impact of assigning students to a curricular track by dividing them into two streams (an upper stream and a lower stream) based on earlier results. These earlier results are referred to as the *initial score*, denoted by the variable x. There are thus two types of schools – namely, tracking schools (which divide students into upper and lower streams) and nontracking schools (which do not). In line with empirical evidence, assume that the distribution of the initial score within schools is single-peaked and symmetric around the median x_m. (More

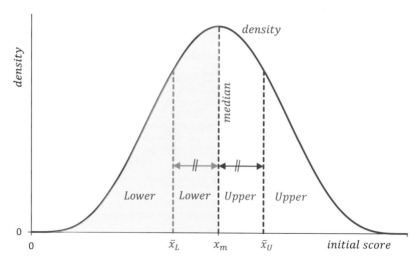

Figure 13.7 Initial score; density, median, and averages

precisely: the density function is continuous, strictly quasi-concave, and symmetric around the median. Examples are the normal distribution and a beta distribution with $\alpha = \beta > 1$.) As illustrated in Figure 13.7, this implies that the mean of the distribution is equal to the median.

Schools, parents, students, employers, and the government are interested in what students learn at school. This is referred to as the *educational outcome* and measured with the (test score) variable y. For student i, the educational outcome y_i is affected by many issues, but this subsection focuses on two main variables: the student's own ability as measured by her initial score x_i; and the effect of learning from other students through peer-to-peer interactions denoted by $peer(.)$. Assume that the peer effect rises monotonically with the average ability of the other students in the class denoted by $\bar{x}_{-i}$, where $^-$ indicates the average and $_{-i}$ indicates all students except student i. This is summarized in equation 13.1, which adds the independently and identically distributed random variable ε_i to the equation, which represents all other class-specific factors affecting the education outcome (symmetric and single peaked).

$$y_i = x_i + peer(\bar{x}_{-i}) + \varepsilon_i \qquad\qquad 13.1$$

The impact of tracking on the direct peer effect is easy to understand. Nontracking schools do not divide the students into streams, so the average initial score for these schools is simply the median x_m. In contrast, tracking schools divide the students into an upper stream and a lower stream depending on the initial score x relative to the median x_m. As a consequence, the *shaded area* in Figure 13.7 depicts the distribution of initial scores for the *lower*-stream students, where $\bar{x}_L$ denotes the *average* score for the lower-stream students. Similarly, $\bar{x}_U$ denotes the average score for the upper-stream students. As the distribution is symmetric around the median, we know that the distance from the median to $\bar{x}_L$ is equal to the distance from the median to $\bar{x}_U$, as indicated by the arrows in the figure. Since the direct peer effects rise monotonically with the average initial score, we have:

$$peer(\bar{x}_L) < peer(x_m) < peer(\bar{x}_U) \qquad\qquad 13.2$$

The direct peer effects for tracking schools thus benefit the upper-stream students who learn more from peer-to-peer interaction than students at nontracking schools, at the expense of lower-stream students who learn less from peer-to-peer interaction than students at nontracking schools. From this perspective, (parents of) students in the lower stream oppose tracking, while (parents of) students in the upper stream favor tracking. It is now time to get teachers involved in the process.

13.7.2 Effort, Target, and Learning Effects

The educational outcome in subsection 13.7.1 focuses only on direct peer effects. This section now broadens the scope by analyzing the activities and impact of teachers in the learning process. It focuses on two main issues: the *effort e* teachers put into the learning process; and the *target* teaching level x^* to which the teacher orients instruction. In the discussion below, teachers optimally *choose* the effort and target levels in the learning process. In general, their choice depends on the distribution of the initial scores for the relevant group of students, which depends on the peers in their class. Equation 13.3, which broadens the learning process by incorporating the impact of teacher effort and target, therefore refers to these as *indirect* effects.

$$y_i = x_i + \underbrace{peer(\bar{x}_{-i})}_{\text{direct effect}} + \underbrace{effort(e) \times learn(|x^* - x_i|)}_{\text{indirect effects}} + \varepsilon_i \qquad\qquad 13.3$$

The indirect effect consists of two parts, $effort(e)$ and $learn(|x^* - x_i|)$, which combined enter the educational outcome multiplicatively. The impact of teacher effort is simple as we assume $effort(e)$ to be a rising concave function of e (see also Box 13.1); hence the higher the teacher effort, the higher the educational outcome. The target teaching level x^* interacts with a student's ability level as measured by the initial score in the learning process in a straightforward way: the larger the (absolute) distance between x_i and x^*, the lower the gain in educational outcome; the $learn(.)$ function is declining in distance $|x^* - x_i|$. Moreover, beyond some distance there may be no learning at all.

Figure 13.8 illustrates the impact of the target teaching level on learning for a bell-shaped learning function. If the teacher sets the target teaching level equal to x_1^*, the learning curve becomes $learn_1$. Note that the rise in educational outcome is highest for x_1^* and falls as x deviates from this target teaching level. In this case, if x falls outside of *range*, which is equivalent to $|x_1^* - x| > range/2$, there will be no learning effect based on teacher effort and teaching target at all. If the teacher sets the target teaching level equal to x_2^*, the learning curve becomes $learn_2$. Obviously, for any given student, for example for a student with initial score x_0, the chosen target teaching level matters a great deal for the educational outcome. The student in question clearly prefers target x_1^* over target x_2^* since $learn(|x_1^* - x_0|) > learn(|x_2^* - x_0|)$, but other students prefer different choices. A clear

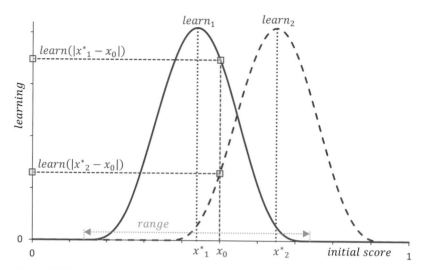

Figure 13.8 Target teaching level and learning effect

advantage of tracking schools over nontracking schools is that tracking allows teachers to better cater to the needs of students, as shown in the next subsection on teacher choices.

13.7.3   Payoff, Target, and Effort

As indicated in subsection 13.7.2, teachers *choose* the optimal effort level e^* and the target teaching level x^*. This choice is guided by maximizing their payoff based on the educational outcomes y minus a cost function based on their effort, taking the distribution of initial scores of their class and the educational outcome determined by equation 13.3 into consideration. The *shape* of the payoff function is crucial for characterizing their optimal choices. As discussed in Box 13.1, the focus here is on *concave* payoffs, *convex* payoffs, and the borderline case of *linear* payoffs (which are both concave and convex). (Assume that the cost function depending on effort is convex.) In the linear case there is no specific preference for the distribution of educational outcomes. In contrast, in the convex case higher educational outcomes are relatively preferred, while in the concave case lower educational outcomes are relatively more important.

Let's start by discussing the target teaching level for *nontracking* schools as illustrated in Figure 13.7. Since there is only one class, the distribution of the initial score is symmetric around the median. In the *linear* payoff case all educational outcomes are weighed equally, so the teacher chooses the target teaching level to maximize the mass of students impacted by this choice. In other words, in the linear case the teacher of the nontracking school chooses $x^* = x_m$. With *convex* payoffs higher educational outcomes are relatively more important, so in the convex case the teacher of the nontracking school chooses a target level above the median: $x^* > x_m$. The reverse holds for *concave* payoffs, in which case the teacher of the nontracking school chooses a target level below the median: $x^* < x_m$.

How about *tracking* schools, which divide students into upper and lower streams? In this case, we would like to characterize the target levels x_L^* for the lower stream and x_U^* for the

BOX 13.1 CONVEX AND CONCAVE FUNCTIONS

In economic analysis, the curvature of functions is frequently important. An example is provided in the teaching model of section 13.7 regarding the shape of the payoff for the teacher as a function of the education outcome y in determining the optimal choice of effort e^* and the target teaching level x^*. The main (related) concepts here are *convex* functions and *concave* functions. The relationship is simple: if a function is convex, then *minus* this function is concave, and vice versa.

To define and illustrate the above, Figure 13.9 starts, with a concave function $f(y)$ for the teacher payoff. Suppose we take two arbitrary points a and b in the domain of the function (see Figure 13.9). By definition, the function f is *concave* if the line connecting the points $(a, f(a))$ and $(b, f(b))$ is *below* (or at most equal to) the function f for all connecting points, as shown in the figure. If $a \neq b$ and the inequality is strict for all points (excluding a and b), the function f is *strictly* concave, as is the case in Figure 13.9. In loose terms, a concave function f is hill-shaped.

Figure 13.9 also shows a convex function $g(y)$ for the teacher payoff. This time, if we take two arbitrary points a and b in the domain, the function g is *convex* by definition if the line connecting the points $(a, g(a))$ and $(b, g(b))$ is *above* (or at most equal to) the function g for all connecting points. If the inequality is strict, g is *strictly* convex. In loose terms, a convex function g is valley-shaped. Moreover, a function g is (strictly) convex if, and only if, $-g$ is (strictly) concave.

As also illustrated in Figure 13.9, a *linear* function is a borderline case for both types of functions as it is both convex *and* concave. In terms of payoff, a linear function gives no special preference for any particular outcome, while the convex function g focuses attention on high outcomes y as the function g rises rapidly for such outcomes, in contrast to the concave function f.

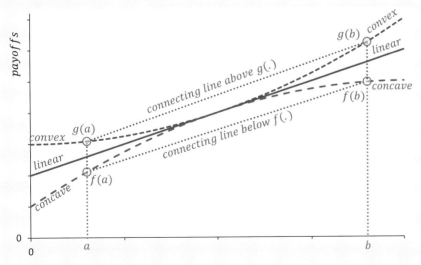

Figure 13.9 Convex, concave, and linear functions

upper stream. We start again with analyzing *linear* payoffs by looking at Figure 13.7. Note that neither the distribution of the upper stream nor that of the lower stream is symmetric around some variable, so it is not easy to pinpoint the exact target levels x_L^* and x_U^* (in general $x_L^* \neq \bar{x}_L$ and $x_U^* \neq \bar{x}_U$). However, we *do* know that the distribution of the upper stream is the mirror image of that of the lower stream around the median x_m. In combination with the fact that with linear payoffs all educational outcomes are weighed equally, this implies that the choice of the target for the teacher in the upper stream must be the mirror image of that of the lower stream. In other words, both targets are at equal distance to the median: $x_m - x_L^* = x_U^* - x_m$. Moreover, this distance is within the range of effective learning – that is, less than *range*$/2$ (see Figure 13.8).

It is now straightforward to characterize the target teaching levels in the case of convex or concave payoffs, as illustrated in Figure 13.10. In the case of *convex* payoffs (see panel a), the teachers in both streams put relatively more weight on higher educational outcomes, implying (relative to linear payoffs) that the target teaching level for the lower stream moves up (and hence closer to the median) and the target teaching level in the upper stream moves up as well (and hence further away from the median) – that is, $x_m - x_L^* < x_U^* - x_m$. The opposite holds with *concave* payoffs, as shown in panel b of Figure 13.10. (Both results have an additional requirement. In the convex case the third derivative of payoffs must be non-negative. In the concave case, the third derivative of payoffs must be nonpositive.)

The impact of the shape of the payoff function on teacher effort is in line with the above discussion. With *linear* payoffs, when educational outcomes are weighed equally, teacher effort is *equal* in the upper stream and in the lower stream. In contrast, with convex payoffs higher educational outcomes are relatively more important, so teacher effort is higher in the upper stream than in the lower stream. The opposite holds for concave payoffs.

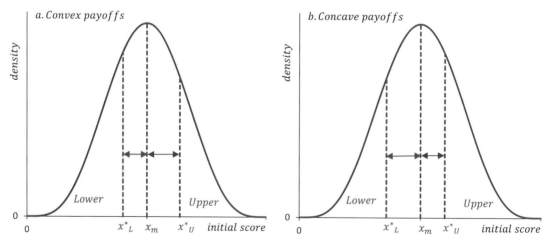

Figure 13.10 Target teaching levels with convex and concave payoffs

13.7.4   The Median Student

Before this section continues with an empirical evaluation of the model, it briefly discusses the impact for a median student x_m to be either assigned to the upper stream or to the lower stream of a tracking school. According to equation 13.3, the difference for the educational outcome consists of two parts – namely, the direct effect and the indirect effect. The direct peer effect is always negative if the student is assigned to the lower stream since $peer(\bar{x}_L) < peer(\bar{x}_U)$ (see subsection 13.7.1).

If teacher payoffs are *linear*, teacher effort is the same in the upper stream and in the lower stream, while the distance from the median initial score to the teaching target is also the same with linear payoffs. In short, with linear payoffs there is no difference between the two streams for the median student regarding the indirect effect. Combined with the negative direct effect this again means that the median student is worse off when assigned to the lower stream.

If teacher payoffs are *concave* or *convex* the difference of the indirect effect is ambiguous. With concave payoffs teacher effort is higher in the lower stream, while the median student is closer to the target teaching level in the upper stream. The reverse holds for convex payoffs. In both cases, the median students must overcome the negative direct effect from being allocated to the lower stream.

13.8   Tracking, Peer Effects, and Teacher Incentives

According to Duflo, Dupas, and Kremer (2011), Kenya has a centralized school system with national exams that is biased to the needs of initially higher-achieving students, rather than the typical student. This is partially based on abolishing school fees, which created an inflow of new, less-prepared students at the bottom of the class. Most teachers are hired through the civil service system and face weak incentives to perform well, leading to high absence rates. There are also short-term contract teachers with stronger incentives to perform well in order to be re-hired in the future, possibly as civil service teachers. The incentives schools and teachers *do* have is for their students to perform well on the primary school exit exam. Students who repeat grades and drop out before that time are not taken into consideration, so this is equivalent to a system of *convex* payoffs (see section 13.7 and Box 13.1).

13.8.1   Experimental Design

The Duflo, Dupas, and Kremer study reports on the effects of reducing class size by providing schools with funds to hire an additional first-grade teacher on a contractual basis. Of the primary schools in western Kenya which received funds to hire an extra first-grade teacher, 121 schools had a single first-grade class which they split into two sections (one of which was taught by the new teacher). In 60 randomly selected schools, students were assigned to sections based on initial achievement, creating an upper stream and a lower stream (*tracking* schools). In the other 61 schools, students were assigned to sections randomly (*nontracking* schools). After the student allocation, the contract teacher and civil service teacher were randomly assigned to a section or stream.

The experiment lasted 18 months, namely the second half of 2005 and all of 2006. As a result of the randomization there are no statistically significant differences between tracking and nontracking schools in school characteristics (enrollment, number of government teachers, pupil/teacher ratio, and performance in the national exam) and class size before and during the program (including female ratio). To evaluate the performance of students, they were tested after 18 months on math skills and a language test (60 in each school; 30 per section, randomly selected). To measure persistence effects of the program, students were tested again one year after the program ended.

13.8.2   Peer Effects for Nontracking Schools

The fact that students were randomly assigned to the two sections in nontracking schools implies that their peer group is also randomly assigned. In combination with the variation in the composition of the groups, this allows us to estimate the peer effect in a regression given by:

$$y_{ij} = \kappa \bar{x}_{-ij} + X_{ij}\beta + \varepsilon_{ij} \tag{13.4}$$

In this specification, y_{ij} is the endline test score for student i in school j (in standard deviations of the distribution of scores in nontracking schools), κ is the peer effect parameter to be estimated, $\bar{x}_{-ij}$ is the average peer initial score of the section to which a student is assigned, X_{ij} is a matrix containing a constant and control variables, β is the control parameter vector to be estimated, and ε_{ij} is a stochastic error term (clustered at the school level).

Table 13.5 reports the effect of peer quality for the endline tests (math, literacy, and total scores). The table controls for school fixed effects and a range of individual control variables (not reported). In all cases the peer effect is positive, significant, and important, with estimates ranging from about 0.30 to 0.35. Students benefit from stronger peers as performance clearly improves if the average quality of classmates rises.

Table 13.5. Effect of peer quality; nontracking schools only

	Total score	Math score	Literacy score
average baseline score of classmates	0.346[**] (0.150)	0.323[**] (0.160)	0.293[**] (0.131)

Source: Based on Duflo *et al.* 2011, table 4.

Notes: Dependent variable is normalized test score (mean 0 and standard deviation 1 in nontracking schools); robust standard errors clustered at school level in parentheses; regressions include school fixed effects and individual controls: age, gender, being assigned to contract teacher, and own initial score; 2,188 observations; [***], [**], and [*] significant at the 1, 5, and 10 percent level, respectively.

13.8.3   Tracking and Student Learning

The division between tracking and nontracking schools and between upper stream and lower stream for the tracking schools allows us to investigate the impact of tracking on learning, not only in general, but also for specific groups of students. The basic estimation strategy is provided in equation 13.5, where y_{ij}, X_{ij}, β, and ε_{ij} are similar as before, T_j is a dummy variable equal to one if school j is a tracking school, and B_{ij} is a dummy variable equal to one if student i in school j was in the bottom half of the initial score for that school (B_{ij} is also included in the control variables X_{ij}).

$$y_{ij} = \alpha T_j + \gamma T_j \times B_{ij} + X_{ij}\beta + \varepsilon_{ij} \qquad 13.5$$

The parameters α and γ measure different effects of tracking. For nontracking schools $T_j = 0$ and equation 13.5 simply estimates the impact of the control variables on the endline test score. For tracking schools $T_j = 1$, so the parameter α measures the general effect of tracking on the endline test score. The parameter γ only enters if both $T_j = 1$ *and* $B_{ij} = 1$ – that is, if the student is in the bottom half for tracking schools. As a result, the parameter γ measures the deviation in the impact of tracking for this group of students (relative to the top half). The discussion below reports similar results if the group of students is divided into four quartiles (bottom quartile, second quartile, third quartile, and top quartile), where the deviations are relative to the third quartile.

Table 13.6 summarizes the impact of tracking on student performance, both the short-run effects (columns 1–3) and the longer-run effects (columns 4–6). The table reports the tracking effects for the total score, but similar results hold for the math and literacy scores. The table controls for a range of individual effects (not reported, except for assignment to contract teacher).

The first row of Table 13.6 reports the parameter α of equation 13.5. This general effect for students in tracking schools is positive, important, and significant in all cases. The learning effect of tracking is also persistent and even somewhat stronger in the longer run than the short run (around 0.21 versus 0.18 on average, respectively). The final row of the table reports the impact on a student's endline test score for being assigned to a contract teacher. This effect is also positive, important, and significant in all cases because contract teachers exert higher effort than civil service teachers. The benefit of being assigned to a contract teacher is also persistent, but declining over time as it is around 0.18 on average in the short run and 0.094 on average in the longer run (perhaps because of the mix of teachers at a later stage).

The second row of Table 13.6 reports the parameter γ of equation 13.5, which analyzes if the benefits of tracking differ for the bottom half of students relative to the top half (columns 2 and 5). The other rows report the outcome of a similar exercise if the group is divided into four quartiles (relative to the performance of the third quartile). In all cases, the estimated coefficients are not significant, which indicates that all these groups of students benefit from tracking in a similar way. The next subsection delves somewhat deeper into this question.

Table 13.6. The impact of tracking on student learning (total score)

	Short-run effects (after 18 months in program)			Longer-run effects (a year after program ended)		
	(1)	(2)	(3)	(4)	(5)	(6)
Tracking school	0.176**	0.192**	0.182*	0.178**	0.216***	0.235***
	(0.077)	(0.093)	(0.093)	(0.073)	(0.079)	(0.088)
Bottom half		−0.036			−0.027	
×tracking school		(0.07)			(0.06)	
Bottom quarter			−0.045			−0.117
× tracking school			(0.08)			(0.09)
Second quarter			−0.013			−0.096
× tracking school			(0.07)			(0.07)
Top quarter			0.027			−0.028
× tracking school			(0.08)			(0.07)
Assigned to contract teacher	0.181***	0.18***	0.18***	0.094***	0.094***	0.094***
	(0.038)	(0.038)	(0.038)	(0.032)	(0.032)	(0.032)

Source: Based on Duflo *et al.* 2011, table 2.

Notes: Dependent variable is normalized test score (mean 0 and standard deviation 1 in nontracking schools); robust standard errors clustered at school level in parentheses; all regressions include individual controls: age, gender, being assigned to contract teacher, dummies for initial half/quarter, and initial score percentile; short-run effects have 5,279 observations, longer-run effects have 5,001 observations; ***, **, and * significant at the 1, 5, and 10 percent level, respectively.

13.8.4   Median Student, Target, Effort, and Payoffs

As suggested in Table 13.6 and just discussed, tracking seems to benefit all students in tracking schools in a similar way when they are divided into halves or quartiles. Duflo, Dupas, and Kremer (2011) analyze this aspect in more detail by investigating the impact of a student's percentile in the initial score on the outcome of the endline test. More specifically, they focus on the median student. As analyzed in subsection 13.7.4 using the theoretical model, with linear payoffs the median student is worse off when assigned to the lower stream instead of the upper stream because the direct peer effect is negative while the indirect peer effects are equal in the upper and lower streams (equal teacher effort and equal distance of the target teaching level to the median. It is therefore possible to apply a regression discontinuity design (see Chapter 2) to determine if the median student is indeed worse off when allocated to the lower stream of tracking schools, as would be the case under linear payoffs. If so, there should be a clear break (a discontinuity) at the median level, with lower endline test scores to the left and higher endline test scores to the right.

After a range of testing procedures, Duflo, Dupas, and Kremer argue (and illustrate) that there is *no* discontinuity at the median initial score level. This rules out the possibility of linear payoffs. They also rule out concave payoffs (related to differences in teacher effort

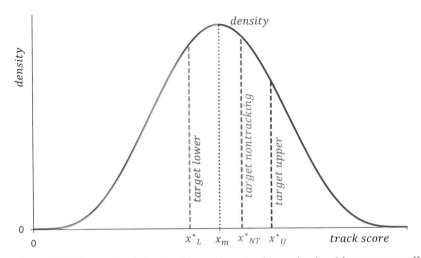

Figure 13.11 Target levels for tracking and nontracking schools with convex payoffs

based on the size of payoffs, not discussed in the model in section 13.7). In combination with the empirical evidence reported at the beginning of this section in favor of convex payoffs, they conclude (2011, p. 1763):

> Taken together, the test score results are consistent with a model in which students influence each other both directly and indirectly through teacher behavior, and teachers face convex payoffs in pupils' test scores, and thus tend to target their teaching to the top of the class. This model can help us interpret our main finding that tracking benefits all students: for higher-achieving students, tracking implies stronger peers and higher teacher effort, while for lower-achieving students, tracking implies a level of instruction that better matches their needs.

This conclusion is illustrated in Figure 13.11. For nontracking schools, convex payoffs imply that teachers set their target teaching level x_{NT}^* above the median: $x_{NT}^* > x_m$. Recall that teachers in the nontracking schools have the same incentives for both sections, so they follow the same strategy in both sections. In contrast, teachers in tracking schools are confronted with upper-stream and lower-stream students and cater to their specific needs in combination with convex payoffs. For the upper-stream students this implies that the target teaching level rises relative to nontracking schools ($x_U^* > x_{NT}^*$; which depending on their initial score may either benefit or hurt them), while teacher effort rises and the direct peer effect is positive (which benefits all of them). For the lower-stream students, the direct peer effect is negative, as is the reduction in teacher effort. They benefit, however, from the lower teaching target $\left(x_L^* < x_m < x_{NT}^* \right)$, which much better caters to their needs. For the median student just allocated to the lower stream this compensates sufficiently for the negative direct peer effect and lower teaching effort because the target teaching level in the upper stream is more distant (since $x_m - x_L^* < x_U^* - x_m$, as illustrated in Figure 13.11).

13.9 Education's Promise

This section briefly summarizes the World Bank's (2018) main position on the role of education in development. Human capital, a term referring to all sorts of different skills incorporated in human beings through nature, nurture, education, and training, has long been identified as crucial in the intricate processes of economic development. If it leads to effectively acquiring these useful skills, education entails the promise of a better, productive, and meaningful life by promoting employment, earnings, and health while reducing poverty. This benefits individuals as well as society. In chase of this promise, schooling rates in developing countries have been rising rapidly over the past decades, in particular for primary education. These schooling rates are, however, still substantially lower than for advanced countries (see section 13.3).

As the World Bank (2018, p. 8) puts it: "The ultimate barrier to learning is no schooling at all." For various reasons (including costs, a lack of schools, unequal opportunities, and conflict), there are millions of children who do *not* attend school, such that education's promise remains elusive. The UN Educational, Scientific, and Cultural Organization (UNESCO) estimates that about 260 million people are out of school worldwide. As Figure 13.12 shows, this number has been declining only slowly since 2014 and consists of about 60 million children of primary school age, about 60 million adolescents of lower secondary school age, and about 140 million youth of upper secondary school age. Enabling access to schooling for these people remains a primary target.

Even for the children who *do* attend school, it is important to acknowledge that schooling is not the same as learning (see sections 13.5 and 13.6). In many developing countries learning outcomes (as measured by tests) are poor, particularly for disadvantaged (rural,

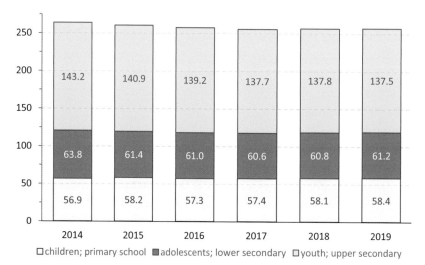

Figure 13.12 Out-of-school children, adolescents, and youth; world total (million), 2014–2019
Source: Created using UNESCO UIS data, http://data.uis.unesco.org.
Note: Numbers in millions.

female, and/or poor) students. As a result, education systems can widen social gaps, rather than narrowing them. Schools are failing students for four main reasons. First, children are often not prepared to learn when they arrive at school because of malnutrition, illness, poverty, and the lack of parental support, which undermines early childhood learning. The effects on brain development are long-lasting, which needs to be taken into consideration (see section 13.2). Second, teachers often lack subject knowledge, pedagogical skills, or motivation to be effective, leading to high teacher absence rates. Regarding the latter, the World Bank (2018, p. 10) notes: "Across seven African countries, one in five teachers was absent from school on the day of an unannounced visit by survey teams, with another fifth absent from the classroom even though they were at school." Third, school inputs may not reach the classroom or may not be used. Examples include textbooks that were distributed but locked away in cupboards and laptops that did not make it to the classroom or were rarely used when they did. As a result, the same measure of school inputs can lead to drastically different outcomes. Fourth, poor school management does not help teachers actively solve problems. The quality of management is lower in developing countries and within these countries it is lower for schools. In combination with a lack of meaningful autonomy, school management functions poorly in many developing countries.

To improve learning outcomes, it is vital to strive to solve the above four main problems by aligning actors to make sure the whole system works by removing technical and political barriers. From a technical perspective, for example, you need reliable metrics to evaluate learning outcomes, so a first step is to make sure these are in place. This is crucial to answer related questions on the effectiveness of alternative programs (for example, in a randomized control trial – see section 13.8). Similarly, if a new curriculum is introduced based on active and creative learning, it must be supported by teacher training to implement the new method effectively. Moreover, the incentives for teachers should be in line with educational outcomes and the incentives for school management should be to improve the efficiency of the system as a whole. All of this should be done, of course, within a country context. A system of high teacher autonomy that works well in Finland (highly qualified teachers) may not work in Sub-Sahara Africa, where teachers are poorly educated, unmotivated, and ill-managed.

13.10   Conclusions

Providing children and adolescents with high-quality education opportunities in schools populated by well-educated and motivated teachers is essential for economic development for all countries in the world. From a biological point of view, it has been shown above that this process already starts at early childhood, which means family members, nursery schools, and primary schools must lay the foundation of a nurturing and stable environment in which children are encouraged to play, interact, and experiment so they can develop the skills they need for the rest of their lives (see section 13.2). It is thus no surprise that educational attainment at all levels is highly correlated with economic development (see section 13.3). It is probably also no surprise that the gender gap (measured as the difference between female and male educational attainment) is *negative* at the primary education level (indicating that women are disadvantaged relative to men) for most countries and this gap declines rapidly as economic development rises. It is remarkable, however, that for higher levels of education (secondary and tertiary) the gender gap is *positive* for many countries and hardly related to economic development. As a result, a range of countries should work harder to reduce *negative* gender gaps in higher education (providing women with better opportunities) and a range of other countries should work harder to reduce *positive* gender gaps (providing men with better opportunities).

Sections 13.5 and 13.6 have shown that there is enormous variation in the quality of education at all levels. They highlighted, for example, the poor quality of primary education in Africa and its relationship with gender and the income level of the family. They also noted that the quality of education is strongly related to economic development, both for basic skills and at the university level. Countries may differ in their general education strategy, where some countries strive to provide the same high-quality level at all universities, while other countries allow for more variation, with peaks and troughs in quality. Variations at the country level for given income levels indicate that there is room for improvement in many countries, regarding both basic skills and higher education.

Sections 13.7 and 13.8 attempt to evaluate and provide a better understanding of the learning process through teacher–student interaction. The focus is on direct learning effects from peers, as well as on indirect effects related to teacher effort and the teacher target level. The discussion is connected to the possibility of tracking student ability, which creates the potential for a suitable selection of peers. The empirical evaluation suggests that tracking schools perform better for all students as they allow teachers to choose a more suitable target level of teaching. Section 13.9 concluded with a summary of the four main issues identified by the World Bank for improving learning outcomes (children must be prepared to learn, teachers must be motivated and have necessary skills, school inputs must be used, and school management must solve practical problems).

Further Reading

The UN Educational, Scientific, and Cultural Organization (UNESCO) advances peace, sustainable development, and human rights through five main areas (education, natural sciences, social/human sciences, culture, and communication/information). It brands itself as a Laboratory of Ideas by providing webinars and open courses, as well as publications on education issues and Global Reports, such as the Science Report and the Global Education Monitoring Report. See: www.unesco.org/en.

A wealth of information on the economic aspects of education around the world can also be found on the OECD website, which provides not only detailed data, but also current research: www.oecd .org/education/.

14 | Health

14.1 Introduction

One measure of (gains in) human health is life expectancy at birth. At the world level, male life expectancy at birth rose from 50.7 years for men and 54.6 years for women in 1960 to 70.4 years for men and 74.9 years for women, a rise of about 20 years in both cases. There are, however, substantial differences across countries and over time. In 2018, for example, male life expectancy for men in the Central African Republic was 50.6 years, while it was 87.7 years (that is, 37.1 years higher!) for women in Hong Kong in the same year. The highest rise in life expectancy from 1960 to 2018 was for women in the Maldives (from 37.4 to 80.5 years, a rise of 43.1 years) and the lowest rise was for men in Ukraine (from 65.6 to 66.7 years, a rise of 1.0 year). It thus matters a great deal where you live and if you are a man or a woman, both for life expectancy at a point in time and gains over time.

You expect, of course, that health indicators improve as economic development rises, if you have more doctors available, and if expenditure rises. In general this is true, but the relationships are far from perfect. Male life expectancy in the USA in 2018, for example, is 76.1 years (about 8 percent higher than the world average). Health expenditure in the USA is high (17.1 percent of GDP), as is the number of physicians per 1,000 people (2.6). However, life expectancy for men is slightly higher in Bahrain (76.3 years), even though health expenditure is only 4.7 percent of GDP and there are only 0.9 physicians per 1,000 people. Similarly, life expectancy for men is higher in Albania than in the USA, even though its level of income per capita is only 21 percent of that of the States. This chapter analyzes these issues in more detail, in combination with health care indicators, the main causes of death, and specific health issues, like infant mortality, deworming, and school meals. Moreover, the chapter analyzes the health and economic impact of the COVID-19 pandemic.

Section 14.2 starts the analysis with an overview of differences in life expectancy for global regions, as well as changes over time and differences between men and women. Section 14.3 analyzes these issues in more detail from a national perspective and relates life expectancy and the gap between female and male life expectancy to the level of economic development as measured by income per capita. As expected, life expectancy is substantially higher if income per capita rises. Section 14.4 analyzes the (far from perfect) connection with health indicators, such as the number of doctors available and health expenditure as share of income. Section 14.5 discusses the main causes of death for different countries and relates this to the level of economic development. Section 14.6 digs deeper into the issues of infant, child, and maternal mortality and immunization, which turn out to be strongly related to income per capita as well as life expectancy. Sections 14.7 and 14.8 discuss health experiments for deworming and school meals and relate them to technical and competitive externalities. Section 14.9 analyzes the consequences of the COVID-19 pandemic, which was ongoing at the time of writing this chapter (October 2020). It discusses the spread of the virus, its death rate, its economic costs, and the (initial) poverty consequences. Finally, section 14.10 concludes.

14.2   Regional Life Expectancy

Life expectancy at birth indicates the number of years a newborn infant would live if prevailing patterns of mortality at the time of its birth were to stay the same throughout its life. As such, this measure is a simple indicator of the quality of life and the health care systems in a country at that point in time. In times of rising economic development and progressing health care systems, this measure tends to underestimate *true* life expectancy of people born at that point in time as it does not take into consideration improvements in health care later in life. This section reports changes in life expectancy since 1960 and differences across regions, countries, and gender (see also Chapter 10).

Figure 14.1 provides information on changes in life expectancy since 1960 for groups of countries, while Table 14.1 provides information on 1960 and 2018. Panel a of Figure 14.1 depicts information on the world as a whole and the (high-income) OECD countries, both for females (solid lines) and males (dashed lines). Over a period of 58 years (data are available from 1960 to 2018), there have been enormous improvements in life expectancy because of better hygiene, economic development, better (more) food, and health care improvements. At the world level, life expectancy rose for men by 19.7 years (from 50.7 years to 70.4 years) and for women by 20.3 years (from 54.6 years to 74.9 years). This amounts to an astonishing rise of 0.34 years *per year* on average for men and 0.35 years *per year* on average for women. To put that into proper perspective: if this rise continued for the rest of this century, it implies at the world level that life expectancy for men born in 2100 will be about 98 years and for women 104 years! Also note that life expectancy for women is about 4.5 years longer than for men. At the world level, this has been rising slowly from 3.9 years in 1960 (see below).

Figure 14.1a also shows life expectancy for men and women in the high-income OECD countries. As expected, this is higher than the world average, namely by about 7.1 years for men (77.5 versus 70.4 years) and 7.9 years for women (82.8 versus 74.9 years) (see Table 14.1). It is clear from the graph that the world average has been catching up to the OECD average for both men and women: in 1960, men in the OECD lived 13.7 years longer than the world average and women 15.6 years longer. The other panels of Figure 14.1 show life expectancy for global developing regions (excluding high-income countries). For ease of reference, each panel also shows the world average developments (thin lines).

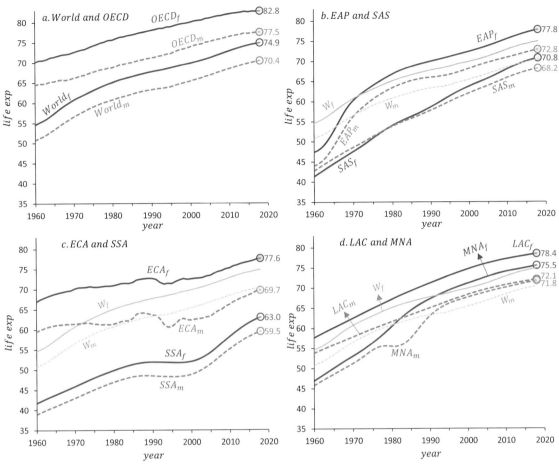

Figure 14.1 Life expectancy at birth (years); female and male, global regions, since 1960
Source: Created using World Development Indicators online.
Notes: Life expectancy at birth in years; W = world; f = female; m = male; EAP = East Asia & Pacific; SAS = South Asia;
ECA = Europe & Central Asia; SSA = Sub-Sahara Africa; MNA = Middle East & North Africa; except panel a, all global
regions exclude high-income countries; horizontal axis starts at 35.

Panel b of Figure 14.1 shows developments in East Asia & Pacific (EAP, including China) and South Asia (SAS), both of which are remarkable. The developments in EAP are remarkable for the speed with which the initial gap in life expectancy relative to the world average is closed in the 1960s and early 1970s at rates which approach and sometimes even exceed one year per year. For example, life expectancy for women in EAP was 4.77 years shorter than the world average in 1965 and 3.76 years shorter than the world average in 1966. This process is strongly influenced by the recovery in China from the devastating consequences of the Great Leap Forward policies, leading to the Great Famine (see Chapter 7). In combination with the rapid economic developments in EAP in this time period, this ensured that life expectancy is higher in EAP than the world average since 1972, leading in 2018 to a higher life expectancy for men by 2.4 years and for women by 2.9 years. This is the biggest improvement relative to the world average for both men and women of all global developing regions.

Table 14.1. Life expectancy at birth (years); global regions, 1960 and 2018

	Women				Men			
	Life expectancy		Gap to world		Life expectancy		Gap to world	
	1960	2018	1960	2018	1960	2018	1960	2018
EAP	47.4	77.8	−7.2	2.9	44.0	72.8	−6.7	2.4
ECA	67.0	77.6	12.4	2.8	59.5	69.7	8.8	−0.7
LAC	57.6	78.4	3.0	3.6	53.8	72.1	3.1	1.7
MNA	47.0	75.5	−7.6	0.6	45.8	71.8	−4.9	1.4
OECD	70.2	82.8	15.6	7.9	64.4	77.5	13.7	7.1
SAS	41.4	70.8	−13.2	−4.1	42.8	68.2	−7.9	−2.2
SSA	41.8	63.0	−12.8	−11.8	38.9	59.5	−11.8	−10.9
World	54.6	74.9	0.0	0.0	50.7	70.4	0.0	0.0

Source: See Figure 14.1, also for global region abbreviations.
Note: Shaded cells indicate negative gaps.

The developments in SAS are remarkable as it is the only global developing region where life expectancy for men is initially higher than for women (by 1.4 years in 1960) (see the discussion in Chapter 10). This negative gender gap in SAS is reversed by 1979 and in 2018 women in SAS are expected to live 2.6 years longer than men. The gap in life expectancy relative to the world average is reduced substantially, from 7.9 to 2.2 years for men and from 13.2 to 4.1 years for women.

Panel c of Figure 14.1 shows developments in Europe & Central Asia (ECA) and Sub-Sahara Africa (SSA). For ECA there is a large gap in life expectancy between men and women, with a peak of 10.9 years in 1994 (71.5 years for women versus 60.6 years for men, see Figure 14.2). This is caused by a stagnation of life expectancy for men during the Soviet Union era, followed by a decline after the collapse of the Soviet Union in 1991. There have been improvements for men since then and the gap to women is closed to 7.9 years in 2018 (but still largest of all global regions, see Figure 14.2). For SSA there are general improvements in life expectancy for both men and women for most of the period, except for a clear stagnation from about 1985 to 2000. The stagnation is associated with the acquired immunodeficiency syndrome (AIDS) caused by the human immunodeficiency virus (HIV), which had devastating consequences for African countries in particular. As a consequence, the gap to world average life expectancy has been barely reduced for both men and women during the period, resulting in the largest gaps by 2018 (see Table 14.1).

Panel d of Figure 14.1 shows developments in Latin America & Caribbean (LAC) and Middle East & North Africa (MNA). For people in LAC, particularly for men, the positive gap relative to the world average has been slightly reduced over time. This results in a widening gender gap. For MNA improvements in life expectancy have been fast, leading

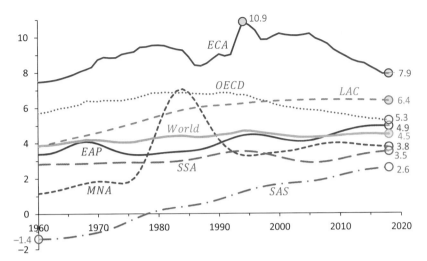

Figure 14.2 Female minus male life expectancy (years); global regions, since 1960
Source: See Figure 14.1, also for region abbreviations.

from a negative gap relative to the world in 1960 to a positive gap in 2018. There is a noteworthy period of stagnation of life expectancy for men at the end of the 1970s and early 1980s related to international conflicts (see Chapter 10).

Figure 14.2 summarizes the evolution of the gender gap (female minus male life expectancy) for the global regions. For the world as a whole, the gender gap has increased slightly from 3.9 to 4.5 years. The only decline of the gender gap was in OECD countries (from 5.7 to 5.3 years), possibly related to the reduction in smoking habits in this period (men used to smoke much more than women). The figure clearly shows the closing gender gap in South Asia, the enormous gap in Europe & Central Asia, the gradually rising gap in Latin America, and the war-related peak in the Middle East. Overall, this section has shown that gaps in life expectancy have been reduced since 1960, but it still matters a great deal where you are born and which gender you are. In 2018, for example, men in Sub-Sahara Africa had a life expectancy of 18.0 years less than men born in OECD countries (59.5 versus 77.5 years), while for women this difference was almost two decades (63.0 versus 82.8 years). The next section briefly analyzes economic development and life expectancy for nations.

14.3 Life Expectancy and Development

At the national level there is, of course, even more variation in life expectancy than at the regional level. This section focuses on differences in 2018 (the most recent year) and relates these to differences in income per capita, corrected for price differences (PPP). There is detailed combined data for 183 countries, together representing more than 7.5 billion people or about 99 percent of the world population.

Table 14.2. Life expectancy at birth and development; top and bottom five, 2018

Country	Income per capita	Female life expectancy	Country	Income per capita	Male life expectancy
Bottom five					
Cen. Afr. Rep	959	55.0	Lesotho	3,151	50.6
Sierra Leone	1,594	55.1	Cen. Afr. Rep.	959	50.6
Nigeria	4,929	55.2	Chad	1,555	52.6
Chad	1,555	55.4	Nigeria	4,929	53.5
Lesotho	3,151	57.0	Sierra Leone	1,594	53.5
Top five					
France	46,537	85.9	Italy	42,776	81.2
Spain	40,419	86.3	Japan	42,564	81.3
Macao	120,376	87.1	Iceland	54,378	81.3
Japan	42,564	87.3	Switzerland	67,888	81.9
Hong Kong	62,985	87.7	Hong Kong	62,985	82.3

Source: See Figure 14.1.

Notes: Cen. Afr. Rep. = Central African Republic. The differences in life expectancy are enormous. Women in Hong Kong, for example, live about 32.7 years longer than women in Central African Republic (87.7 versus 55.0 years, or a difference of 59 percent in relative terms). Similarly, men in Hong Kong live about 31.7 years longer than men in Lesotho (82.3 versus 50.6 years, or a relative difference of 63 percent). If we combine across sexes the differences are even larger: women in Hong Kong live about 37.1 years longer than men in Lesotho (87.7 versus 50.6 years, or a relative difference of 73 percent).

Table 14.2 provides an overview of the top five and bottom five countries in terms of both female and male life expectancy, as well as income per capita. The five countries with the *lowest* life expectancy are all in Africa, with Nigeria as the most populous country. The list of countries is the same for men and women, only the order differs slightly. The average income level for the bottom five countries is $2,438. For women, Central African Republic has the lowest life expectancy (55.0 years), while for men it is Lesotho (50.6 years).

The top five countries (with *highest* life expectancy) are located in Europe and East Asia. The highest score is achieved in Hong Kong, namely 82.3 years for men and 87.7 years for women. Various populous countries are on the top lists, including Japan, Spain, France, and Italy. The average income level for the top five countries is above $54,000 or more than 22 times as high as for the bottom five. This indicates that the level of economic development and life expectancy are clearly related.

The connection between economic development as measured by income per capita and life expectancy at birth is illustrated for women in all 183 countries in Figure 14.3 using a bubble diagram. The dashed line in the figure is a regression line with a slope of 5.763, indicating that a 10 percent rise in income per capita is associated with a rise of about 0.58 years in female life expectancy. It explains 73 percent of the variance in

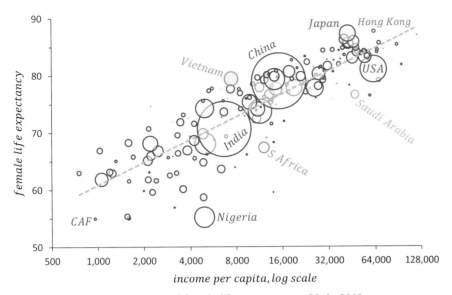

Figure 14.3 Income per capita and female life expectancy at birth, 2018
Source: See Figure 14.1.

Notes: Female life expectancy at birth in years (most recent in period 2016–18); income per capita is GNI PPP in constant 2017 $ (most recent in period 2017–19); bubbles proportional to population; 183 countries included; CAF = Central African Republic; dashed line is a regression; horizontal axis starts at 50.

female life expectancy. There is thus a strong positive relationship between income per capita and female life expectancy. Countries with relatively low female life expectancy (given the level of income per capita) include Central African Republic, Nigeria, South Africa, Saudi Arabia, and the USA (see Figure 14.3). Countries with relatively high female life expectancy are concentrated in East Asia, including Vietnam, China, Japan, and Hong Kong.

A diagram depicting *male* life expectancy relative to income per capita looks similar to Figure 14.3, only shifted down a bit because of the lower life expectancy for men than for women.[1] An alternative way to illustrate this is by depicting the gender gap (female minus male life expectancy) relative to income per capita (see Figure 14.4). Here there is basically *no* relationship between income per capita and the gender gap in life expectancy.[2] All gender gaps are positive (women live longer than men in all countries). The lowest is 0.7 years in Bhutan, followed by 1.2 years in Guinea. The highest gender gaps (above 10 years) are all in former communist countries, namely Belarus, Russia, and Ukraine (from high to low). The discussion in this section at the national level is based on a snapshot at a point in time (2018). To complement, Box 14.1 provides a brief discussion of life expectancy at birth from an historical perspective for a selection of countries.

---

[1] A regression line for male life expectancy relative to income per capita has a slope of 5.328 and explains 70 percent of the variance in male life expectancy.

[2] A regression line has a not-significant slope and only explains 6 percent of the variance in the gender gap.

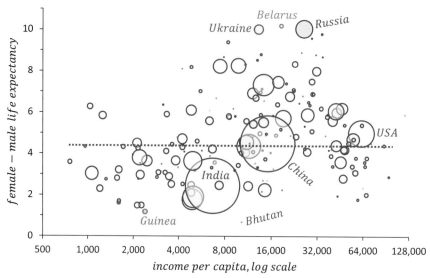

Figure 14.4 Income per capita and female minus male life expectancy at birth, 2018
Source: See Figure 14.3.
Notes: 183 countries included; dotted horizontal line depicts population-weighted average.

BOX 14.1 LIFE EXPECTANCY IN HISTORICAL PERSPECTIVE

The main text discusses changes and differences in life expectancy since 1960. Maddison (2001) provides estimates for a selection of countries going back much further in time (about 2,000 years). An overview is given in Table 14.3 and briefly discussed in this box, as well as more detailed information on the developments in England and Wales since 1841.

The average person born in Roman Egypt around 2,000 years ago could expect to live only about 24 years. The main reason for this low estimate from a modern perspective is the high child mortality, especially in the first year of life (see section 14.6). Once you survived the first five years, life expectancy rose significantly. There was not much improvement in the next 1,000 years. As Maddison (2001, p. 17) puts it: "In the year 1000, the average infant could expect to live about 24 years. A third would die in the first year of life, hunger and epidemic disease would ravage the survivors." As Table 14.3 indicates, for a selection of more advanced countries, progress since then was slow. People in fourteenth- to fifteenth-century England had a life expectancy of about 24 years, rising to 34 years in the sixteenth century and about 41 years in the early nineteenth century. In France, similarly, life expectancy was only about 25 years in the eighteenth century, rising to 39 years in the nineteenth century. In Japan, today's powerhouse in terms of longevity, life expectancy was only about 32 years until deep in the nineteenth century.

There is detailed information on the life expectancy of different groups of people in England and Wales from 1841 onward. Figure 14.5 illustrates progress on life expectancy across time for males in two ways. First, the solid line "1841" indicates expected age

BOX 14.1 (cont.)

Table 14.3. Life expectancy at birth; selected countries and periods, both sexes combined

Location	Period	Life expectancy at birth
Roman Egypt	33–258	24.0
England	1301–1425	24.3
England	1541–1556	33.7
France	1740–1749	24.8
England	1801–1826	40.8
France	1820–1829	38.8
Japan	1776–1875	32.2

Source: Maddison 2001, table 1.4 [selection].

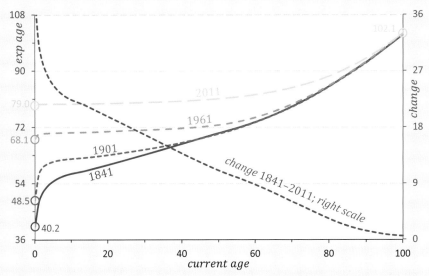

Figure 14.5 Average age expected to reach by current age; En2gland & Wales, males
Source: Created using Decennial Life Tables, Office of National Statistics, www.ons.gov.uk.
Note: The figure shows expected age to be reached given current age in 1841, 1901, 1961, and 2011 (left-hand scale; horizontal axis starts at 35) and change from 1841 to 2011 in expected age given current age (right-hand scale).

(vertical left axis) for an individual male of a given age (horizontal axis) in the year 1841. For example, at birth in 1841 (current age = 0), a boy has a life expectancy of 40.2 years. Life expectancy rises rapidly if you manage to survive the first few years in 1841, namely (not indicated in the figure) to 47.7 years for 1-year-olds, 50.8 years for 2-year-olds, and so on. This rapid rise (of more than one year extra life expectancy per year of extra current life) drops below one from 5-year-old boys onward. In 1841, the minimum of 0.23 extra years of life per extra year of current life is reached for 12- and 13-year-old boys. From then on it rises gradually to approach one from below for very old men (it is 0.9 or higher above 98-year-old men).

BOX 14.1 (cont.)

The 1901, 1961, and 2011 lines in Figure 14.5 are similar to the 1841 line just described for the years indicated by the numbers. The changing shape of the lines in childhood indicate that the problem of high child mortality is strongly diminishing over time and has virtually disappeared by 2011, when male life expectancy at birth is 79.0 years. There is still some increase in life expectancy in 2011 if you manage to survive the first year (a rise of 0.37 years for 1-year-old boys), but virtually no improvement for a long time thereafter. In fact, it is rounded to an increase of 0.0 all the way up to 38-year-old men and only rises above 0.3 above 69-year-olds. Again, it approaches one from below for very old men, ultimately resulting in a life expectancy of 102.1 years for 100-year-olds.

The second way in which Figure 14.5 illustrates progress of life expectancy across time is with the dashed "change 1841–2011" line (vertical right axis), which shows the change (in years) of expected age given current age from 1841 to 2011. At birth, for example, this increase is 79.0 years (in 2011) minus 40.2 years (in 1841) = 38.8 years (just outside the right-hand-side scale of 36). Evidently, this change is positive throughout the range (indicating rising life expectancy for all ages), but declines rapidly as current age rises. For 100-year-olds (the maximum in the figure), the rise in life expectancy is very small, namely about half a year only. More specifically, if you were a 100-year-old man in 1841, your life expectancy would be 101.5 years, which is only mildly below the 102.1 years of 2011. In other words, progress in life expectancy for older people has been modest in almost two centuries.

14.4   Health Care

An important reason for high life expectancy in high-income countries is the availability of a better health care system and access to more expensive medicines and treatments. This section briefly elaborates on this in an absolute and relative sense, starting in Figure 14.6 with the relationship between income per capita and the number of physicians available per 1,000 people.

As indicated by the dashed lines in Figure 14.6, there is a break in the relationship between income and physicians. For low income per capita levels (below $3,000), the number of physicians is low (about 0.1 per 1,000) and does not rise with income. Only when income per capita exceeds a threshold level of about $3,000 does the number of physicians clearly start to rise, namely by about 0.12 physicians per 1,000 people if income per capita rises by about 10 percent. India, for example, has an income level of about $6,700 per capita and about 0.9 physicians per 1,000 people. Similar figures for China are about $15,000 and 2.0 physicians, while the USA has about $62,500 and 2.6 physicians. The variation in this relationship is, however, substantial. Russia, for example, has about 42 percent of the USA's income level per capita, but substantially more physicians per

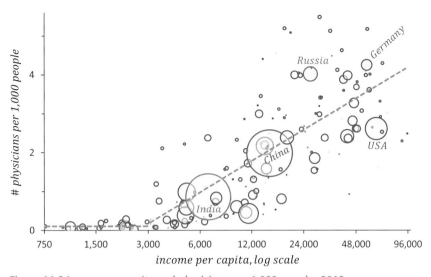

Figure 14.6 Income per capita and physicians per 1,000 people, 2018
Source: Created using World Development Indicators online data.
Notes: Physicians per 1,000 people (most recent in period 2013–18); income per capita is GNI PPP in constant 2017 $ (most recent in period 2017–19); bubbles proportional to population (2019); 171 countries included; Lithuania and Georgia outside vertical range (6.4 and 7.1, respectively); dashed line is population-weighted average below $3,000 and trendline above.

1,000 people (4.0 versus 2.6). Similarly, with about 88 percent of the USA's income level, Germany has 4.2 rather than 2.6 physicians.

If the number of physicians starts to rise as income per capita rises (after exceeding a threshold level), as shown in Figure 14.6, you might expect that the *share* of income spent on health care rises as well. First, because the number of doctors rises and doctors tend to be expensive in all countries. Second, because costly medicines and treatments become available as income levels rise. Third, because you are able to afford spending on health care as income levels rise and you have fulfilled the basic needs already (food, clothing, and shelter). As Figure 14.7 shows, this both *is* and *is not* true. Panel a of the figure shows the relationship between income per capita and current health expenditure as a percentage of GDP. Panel b does the same for domestic government health expenditure (different vertical scale).

It is clear from both panels of Figure 14.7 that high-income countries tend to spend a high share of income on health care. The Japanese government, for example, spends 9.2 percent of GDP on health care (panel b) and the US government 8.6 percent, compared to 2.9 percent for the Chinese government and 1.0 percent for the Indian government. There are, however, also poor countries where the government spends a large share of income on health care, such as Malawi (income per capita about $1,000) which spends 3.0 percent of GDP. The overall relationship is therefore U-shaped, as indicated by the curved trendline in panel b. This U-shaped pattern is even stronger in panel a, which looks at all health expenditures. It is substantially higher in Japan (10.9 percent) than in China (5.2 percent) and India (3.5 percent), but health expenditures rise again for countries with lower levels of income per capita, such as Malawi (9.6 percent) and Afghanistan (11.8 percent). Panel a also illustrates that health expenditures are extremely high in the USA, namely 17.1 percent of GDP or 6.1 percentage points higher than in Japan (which is 10.9).

Table 14.4. Life expectancy and health care indicators correlation, 2017–2018

	A	B	C	D
A *female life expectancy*	1			
B *male life expectancy*	0.963	1		
C *health expenditure (%GDP)*	0.456	0.432	1	
D *gov health exp (% GDP)*	0.707	0.687	0.747	1
E *physicians (per 1000 people)*	0.723	0.658	0.498	0.648

Source: See Figures 14.1, 14.6, and 14.7.
Note: 169 countries included.

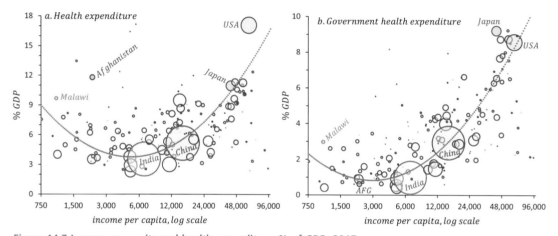

Figure 14.7 Income per capita and health expenditure; % of GDP, 2017
Source: Created using World Development Indicators online data.
Notes: Health expenditure (% of GDP, 2017); domestic government health expenditure (% of GDP, most recent in period 2015–17); income per capita is GNI PPP in constant 2017 $ (most recent in period 2017–19); bubbles proportional to population (2019); 178 countries included; curves based on population-weighted quadratic regression using log of income per capita.

The difference between the two panels in Figure 14.7 is accounted for by private health expenditures and expenditures by other organizations (private, for short). The population-weighted average of these private expenditures is about 3.0 percent. Since the government tends to play a more important role in health care systems of higher-income countries, the private health expenditures as a percent of GDP tend to decline as income levels rise. A clear exception (and outlier) is the USA, where private expenditure is 8.5 percent of GDP. Other countries with high private and organizational expenditures are Afghanistan (11.2 percent) and Sierra Leone (11.6 percent).

This section concludes by pointing out that the health care indicators discussed here are far from perfect. Table 14.4 illustrates this by providing simple correlations between life expectancy and the health indicators for 169 countries (see Box 14.2 for other indicators). As expected, the correlation between female and male life expectancy is extremely high (0.963). The number of physicians per 1,000 people and government

BOX 14.2 HEIGHT, HEALTH, STUNTING, WASTING, AND Z-SCORES

You may read about the prevalence of *stunting* in developing countries as an indicator of poor health. According to the dictionary, stunting means "to prevent from growing or developing properly"; a stunted child is thus relatively short for his or her age, which in general has adverse functional consequences. To operationalize the concept, we take the raw score *x* for height and calculate the *z*-score (also known as standard score or normal score) by subtracting the mean score μ and dividing by the standard deviation σ of the reference population, that is: $z = (x - \mu)/\sigma$. A child is *stunted* if the *z*-score for height is lower than –2, or more than two standard deviations below the WHO Child Growth Standards median (for the respective child age group). Similarly, *wasting* is defined as low-weight-for-height and a child is called *wasted* if the *z*-score for weight falls below two standard deviations of the reference population (identified by the height of the child). It is a strong predictor of mortality for children under 5 years of age (see also section 14.6).

Human height is correlated with income per capita levels, as illustrated in Figure 14.8 for adult male height using a bubble diagram proportional to population. On average, the shortest men live in Timor-Leste (159.8 cm) and the tallest men in the Netherlands (182.5 cm). Even though the upward-sloping trendline in the figure explains a substantial share of the variance in male height (45.7 percent), there is substantial variation to remain explained. This seems to be related to other geographic and regional circumstances. Men are relatively short, for example, in South Asia and Southeast Asia, as shown by India, Indonesia, and Japan in the figure. On the other hand, men are relatively tall in Europe: the top 17 countries with tallest men are all in Europe, while only Australia, Canada, and New Zealand make it to the top 35 (the rest are all European countries).

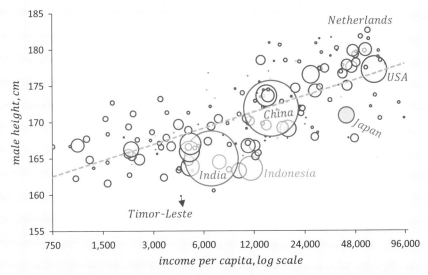

Figure 14.8 Income per capita and male mean height
Sources: Created using data from NCD RisC (www.ncdrisc.org/data-downloads-height.html) for mean height of men aged 18 or older by birth year (1996) and World Development Indicators online.
Notes: Income per capita is GNI PPP in constant 2017 $ (most recent in period 2017–19); bubbles proportional to population (2019); 184 countries included; dashed line is a trendline (slope is 3.1952; explains 45.7 percent of variance)..

health expenditures as a percent of GDP are highly, but far from perfectly, correlated with life expectancy (ranging from 0.658 to 0.723). The correlation of total health expenditures as a percent of GDP and life expectancy is only moderate (0.432 for men and 0.456 for women). The USA, for example, spends 17.1 percent of GDP on health and has a life expectancy for men of 76.1 years, which is less than 38 other countries included in Table 14.4 which on average spend only half as much on health as the USA (8.6 versus 17.1 percent of GDP). From the reverse perspective, Afghanistan spends 11.8 percent of GDP on health (and Kiribati 10.8 percent), but life expectancy for men is only 63.0 years (64.0 years in Kiribati), which is less than 138 of the 168 other countries (131 for Kiribati) included in the table.

To better understand why very poor countries spend a larger fraction of income on health care than middle-income countries, it is vital to better understand the types of problems these countries are dealing with. Section 14.5 does this by analyzing different types of mortality and section 14.6 by focusing on mothers and infants.

14.5   Main Causes of Death

The World Bank identifies three main causes of death, which refers to the share of all deaths for all ages by underlying causes, namely:

- *Noncommunicable diseases*, which includes cancer, diabetes mellitus, cardiovascular diseases, digestive diseases, skin diseases, musculoskeletal diseases, and congenital anomalies.
- *Injuries*, which includes unintentional and intentional injuries.
- *Communicable diseases and maternal, prenatal, and nutrition conditions*, which includes infectious and parasitic diseases, respiratory infections, and nutritional deficiencies such as being underweight and stunting.

Taken together, these three main causes of death add up to 100 percent. The discussion in this section first focuses on the relationship between the level of economic development and noncommunicable diseases (about 71 percent of all deaths) and then on the relationship between economic development versus communicable diseases and maternal, prenatal, and nutrition conditions (about 20 percent of all deaths). The remaining injuries category (about 9 percent of all deaths) is not explicitly analyzed; this cause of death tends to slowly decline as income per capita rises, with Iraq and Qatar as clear outliers (28.4 and 25.9 percent of all deaths, respectively).

Figure 14.9 illustrates that most people die of noncommunicable diseases, including cancer, diabetes, and cardiovascular diseases, and that this cause of death rises significantly as income per capita rises, as illustrated by India and the USA in the figure. More specifically, if income per capita rises by 10 percent, then the share of communicable diseases as cause of death rises by about 1.5 percentage points. An underlying reason for this is the rise in life expectancy as income per capita rises (see sections 14.2 and 14.3) and the fact that diseases like cancer, diabetes, and cardiovascular diseases become more causes of death for aging populations. As Figure 14.9 indicates, Nigeria and Qatar have relatively

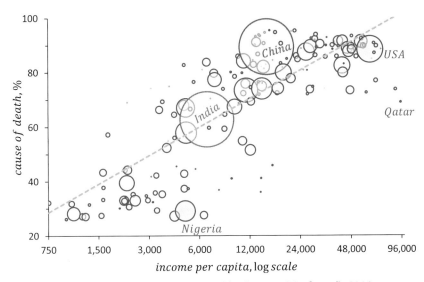

Figure 14.9 Cause of death; noncommunicable diseases (% of total), 2016
Source: Created using data from World Development Indicators online.
Notes: Cause of death (% of total); income per capita is GNI PPP in constant 2017 $ (most recent in period 2017–19); bubbles proportional to population (2019); 175 countries included; dashed line is a trendline (explains 63 percent of variance).

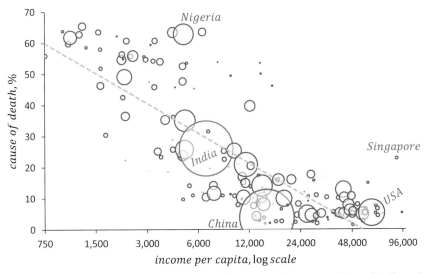

Figure 14.10 Cause of death; communicable diseases and MPN conditions (% of total), 2016
Source: See Figure 14.9.
Notes: MPN conditions = maternal, prenatal, and nutrition conditions; cause of death (% of total); income per capita is GNI PPP in constant 2017 $ (most recent in period 2017–19); bubbles proportional to population (2019); 175 countries included; dashed line is a trendline (explains 63 percent of variance).

few deaths from noncommunicable diseases (about 29 and 69 percent, respectively), while China has relatively many (89.3 percent).

Figure 14.10 shows the relationship between communicable diseases and maternal, prenatal, and nutrition (MPN) conditions relative to income per capita. It is (largely) the mirror image of Figure 14.9 (see India and the USA) since communicable diseases and MPN conditions as a cause of death decline rapidly with economic development, namely by about 1.4 percentage points if income per capita rises by 10 percent. Countries with a relatively high share of communicable diseases and MPN conditions are Nigeria and Singapore (62.7 and 22.7 percent, respectively), while China has a relatively low share (3.8 percent). The next section analyzes these problems in more detail.

14.6   Infant, Child, and Maternal Mortality

The main underlying cause for lower life expectancy in developing countries is high infant and under-5 child mortality, in combination with maternal mortality because of complications at birth. The infant mortality rate refers to the number of infants dying before reaching 1 year of age, per 1,000 live births. The under-5 child mortality rate is the probability per 1,000 live births that a newborn baby will die before reaching age 5, if subject to age-specific mortality rates of the specified year. The maternal mortality rate is the number of women who die from pregnancy-related causes while pregnant or within 42 days of pregnancy termination per 100,000 live births.

As one might expect, infant, child, and maternal mortality are correlated (see below). This holds in particular for infant mortality and under-5 child mortality. In fact, most of under-5 child mortality *is* infant mortality and takes place in the first year. As a result, for 193 countries with data available in 2019 more than 82 percent (population-weighted) of under-5 child mortality is caused by infant mortality. Moreover, the correlation between infant mortality and under-5 child mortality is extremely high (0.991). The focus here is therefore on infant mortality only, as the picture for under-5 child mortality is virtually the same.

The relationship between infant mortality and economic development (as measured by income per capita) is illustrated in Figure 14.11 using a bubble diagram. Infant mortality is clearly a problem of developing nations and rapidly falls as income rises, ranging from a minimum of 1.6 for Iceland to a maximum of 81.0 for the Central African Republic. The population-weighted average infant mortality for the countries in the figure is 20.7 deaths per 1,000 live births, but it is below this average for all countries with an income level above $17,600 per capita. Figure 14.11 graphically shows this relationship with the dashed line based on a power function regression with a coefficient of –0.802, which explains about 75 percent of the variance in infant mortality. The figure also shows that, given their level of economic development, infant mortality is high in countries like Pakistan (55.7 deaths per 1,000 live births) and Nigeria (74.2 deaths).

Figure 14.12 shows the relationship between maternal mortality and economic development. The population-weighted average maternal mortality is 138 per 100,000 live births, ranging from a minimum of two for Belarus, Poland, Italy, and Norway to a maximum of 1,140 for Chad. There is again a clear negative relationship with income as indicated by the dashed line based on a power function regression (which explains about 74 percent of the variance in maternal mortality) and the fact that all countries with an

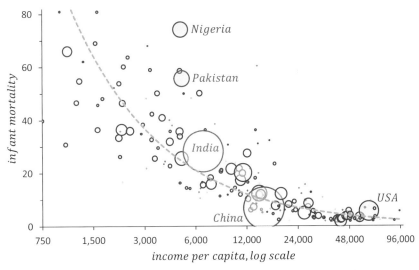

Figure 14.11 Income per capita and infant mortality (per 1,000 live births), 2019
Source: Created using data from World Development Indicators online.
Notes: Infant mortality per 1,000 live births; income per capita is GNI PPP in constant 2017 $ (most recent in period 2017–19); bubbles proportional to population (2019); 176 countries included; dashed line is power function regression (coefficient is −0.802).

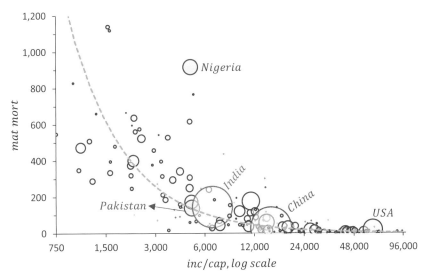

Figure 14.12 Income per capita and maternal mortality (per 100,000 live births), 2019
Source: See Figure 14.11.
Notes: Maternal mortality per 100,000 live births; income per capita is GNI PPP in constant 2017 $ (most recent in period 2017–19); bubbles proportional to population (2019); 176 countries included; dashed line is power function regression (coefficient is −1.259; explains 74.1 percent of variance).

income per capita level above $16,500 have maternal mortality below the population-weighted average of 138. Given its income level (and in line with its infant mortality rate), maternal mortality is again high in Nigeria (917 deaths per 100,000 live births). In contrast, Pakistan performs much better in terms of maternal mortality (140 deaths, close

Table 14.5. Income, life expectancy, immunization, and mortality correlation, 2019

	A	B	C	D	E	F	G
A ln (*income per capita*)	1						
B *female life expectancy*	0.841	1					
C *male life expectancy*	0.824	0.964	1				
D *immunization DPT*	0.449	0.560	0.536	1			
E *immunization HepB3*	0.376	0.494	0.469	0.958	1		
F *immunization measles*	0.451	0.576	0.534	0.884	0.880	1	
G *maternal mortality*	−0.728	−0.856	−0.802	−0.530	−0.484	−0.545	1
H *infant mortality*	−0.806	−0.942	−0.894	−0.593	−0.537	−0.577	0.881

Source: World Development Indicators online.
Notes: 170 countries included; income per capita is GNI PPP in constant 2017 $ (most recent 2017–19); life expectancy in years; immunization DPT (% of children, ages 12–23 months), HepB3 (% of 1-year-old children), measles (% of children ages 12–23 months); maternal mortality per 100,000 live births; infant mortality per 1,000 live births; shaded cells are negative.

to the world average) than in terms of infant mortality (55.7 deaths, about 170 percent higher than the world average).

According to the World Health Organization, we now have vaccines to prevent more than 20 life-threatening diseases.[3] Immunization is one of the best health investments money can buy and about 2–3 million deaths are prevented every year from diseases like diphtheria, tetanus, pertussis, influenza, and measles. Nonetheless, about 20 million infants each year have insufficient access to vaccines. To summarize the connections between immunization, life expectancy, income per capita, and (infant and maternal) mortality, Table 14.5 provides correlations with three common types of immunizations, namely DTP (diphtheria, tetanus, and pertussis [whooping cough]), hepatitis B, and measles.

As indicated by column A in Table 14.5, income per capita is highly positively correlated with life expectancy (more than 0.824) and mildly positively related to immunization (from 0.376 to 0.451), while infant and maternal mortality are highly negatively correlated (less than −0.728). Columns B and C show that life expectancy is positively related to immunization (from 0.469 to 0.560) and strongly negatively related to maternal and infant mortality (less than −0.802). Columns D, E, and F indicate that immunizations are highly correlated with other immunizations (at least 0.880) and mildly negatively related to maternal and infant mortality (from −0.593 to −0.484). Moreover, maternal and infant mortality are highly correlated (0.881), as are female and male life expectancy (0.964). In short, all these issues are related, but in reality different social, cultural, and economic circumstances may play an important role. This has been demonstrated frequently with outliers in figures, such as Russia in Figure 14.4, the USA in Figure 14.7a, and Nigeria and Pakistan in Figure 14.11, as well as the contrast with Figure 14.12. The next two sections analyze some health issues in more detail.

---

[3] See www.who.int/health-topics/vaccines-and-immunization for this paragraph.

BOX 14.3 **SEX RATIO AT BIRTH**

The sex ratio at birth refers to the number of male births per female births. This ratio tends to be slightly higher than one, indicating that more men are born than women. Perhaps that is nature's way to compensate for the lower life expectancy of men. At the country level there is substantial variation in this ratio as a result of nature, nurture, and active interference (through abortion and otherwise). In October 2020, the World Bank had information available for the year 2017 for 194 countries. The simple average was 1.051 male births per female birth. This is shown as the horizontal line in Figure 14.13, which relates the sex ratio to income per capita for 181 countries.

The number of male births per female births ranges from 1.011 for Namibia and 1.0118 for Mozambique, Togo, and Sierra Leone (all in Africa) to a maximum of 1.126 in China and high ratios in several other Asian nations, like Azerbaijan (1.124), Vietnam (1.118), Armenia (1.109), India (1.100), and Pakistan (1.087). As Figure 14.13 shows, there is a mild positive relationship between sex ratio and income per capita, partially because the sex ratio tends to be low for most poor African countries and partially because the sex ratio is high for a number of middle-income countries in Asia. The high ratios in countries like China, India, Vietnam, and Pakistan are particularly noteworthy.

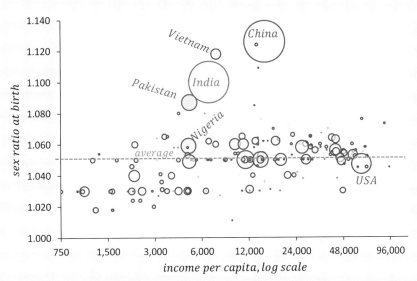

Figure 14.13 Income per capita and sex ratio at birth (male births per female births), 2017
Source: Created using World Development Indicators online.
Notes: Sex ratio is male births per female births; income per capita is GNI PPP in constant 2017 $ (most recent in period 2017–19); bubbles proportional to population (2019); 181 countries included.

14.7 Deworming

Miguel and Kremer (2004) analyze the consequences of a deworming experiment in Kenya. Information presented in this section is taken from their paper. Intestinal worm infections

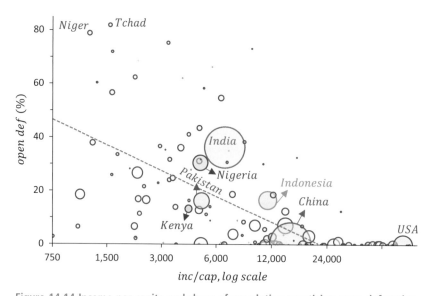

Figure 14.14 Income per capita and share of population practicing open defecation; rural (%), 2017
Source: Created using World Development Indicators online data.
Notes: open def = share of urban population practicing open defecation (% of rural population); income per capita is GNI PPP in constant 2017 $ (most recent in period 2017–19); bubbles proportional to population (2019); 152 countries included; dashed line is trendline based on countries with income per capita below $22,000.

affect hundreds of millions of people around the world. This includes hookworm, round-worm, whipworm, and schistosomiasis (also known as snail fever or bilharzia). Most people have light infections, but a minority has heavy infections, which can lead to serious problems. Low-cost therapies can kill most worms effectively (except for whipworms), but reinfection is rapid, so drugs must be taken every six months or once a year. School-aged children account for the bulk of worm transmission, in particular if they are less likely to use latrines and have poor hygiene practices. Open defecation is largely a rural problem; the simple average open defecation percentage in 2017 for 159 countries was 2.4 percent for the urban population and 13.7 percent for the rural population. The relationship between income per capita and open defecation in rural areas is illustrated in Figure 14.14. Even for rural areas, open defecation is virtually absent if income per capita is above $22,000; exceptions are Mauritius (0.2 percent), Turkey (1.2 percent), and Panama (12.6 percent). As a result, open defecation is prevalent in Sub-Sahara African countries, like Niger (79 percent) and Chad (82 percent). In rural Kenya, it was 13.4 percent in 2017.

The life span of intestinal worms is fairly short; around one year for roundworm and whipworm, two years for hookworm, and three years for schistosomiasis. In the absence of frequent reinfection, worm burdens are thus likely to fall rapidly. Medical treatment in a certain area can thus have positive externalities if it interferes with disease transmission. As Miguel and Kremer point out, previous studies randomized treatment at the individual level and underestimated the treatment effect because the control group with which the treated were compared benefited from positive externalities. They solve this problem in two ways: first, by randomization at the school level; and, second, by identifying cross-school externalities. The study analyzes 75 schools with about 30,000 students. Schools were

Table 14.6. Deworming health externalities, January–March 1999

	Group 1		Group 2	
	Pupils treated in 1998	Pupils untreated in 1998	Pupils treated in 1999	Pupils untreated in 1999
Any moderate-heavy worm infection, 1999 (girls < 13 years and all boys)	0.24	0.34	0.51	0.55
School participation rate, May 1998–March 1999	0.872	0.764	0.808	0.684

Source: Miguel and Kremer 2004, table VI, selection.
Note: Numbers are shares of respective total.

divided randomly in three groups; Group 1 received treatment in 1998 and 1999, Group 2 received treatment in 1999, and Group 3 started to receive treatment in 2001. In 1998, therefore, Group 1 were treatment schools and Groups 2 and 3 were comparison schools, while in 1999 Groups 1 and 2 were treatment schools and Group 3 schools were comparison schools. Depending on infection levels and according to medical standards, treatment schools received medicines for different worm infections and worm prevention education, which emphasized the importance of hand washing.

For girls below 13 years of age and all boys among the Group 1 schools, about 78 percent of the pupils received any medical treatment in 1998 and among the Group 2 schools about 55 percent received any medical treatment in 1999. Girls of reproductive age (13 years and older) usually did not receive treatment because drugs could possibly cause birth defects, hence this group is treated separately. Within Groups 1 and 2, it is thus possible to distinguish between pupils who receive treatment and pupils who do not. This is windicated in Table 14.6, which shows the extent of any worm infections in 1999 and the school participation rate in May 1998 to March 1999. The treated pupils in Group 1 schools had the least worm infections in 1999, namely 24 percent, followed by untreated pupils in Group 1 schools (34 percent), treated pupils in Group 2 schools (51 percent), and untreated pupils in Group 2 schools. This indicates there are significant spillovers within schools as untreated Group 1 pupils are much less affected than treated Group 2 pupils. Moreover, Table 14.6 suggests that there is an important effect upon school participation because participation rates are higher for treated than for untreated pupils within Groups 1 and 2, as well as higher for Group 1 than for Group 2 for both treated and untreated pupils.

Miguel and Kremer (2004) continue with a detailed analysis of the impact of deworming on health and school attendance. They find important externalities associated with deworming treatments regarding both health and attendance for untreated students, both within schools and for neighboring schools. The overall deworming program reduced school absenteeism by at least one-quarter and was much cheaper than alternative ways of boosting school participation. Note that the externalities of treatment can only be adequately estimated by randomization at higher levels, such as schools, rather than at the individual level, which is an important factor to take into consideration when organizing field experiments. The type of externality is also important, as explained in the next section.

14.8   School Meals

Vermeersch and Kremer (2005) analyze the effects of subsidized school meals on school participation and education for preschools in Kenya. This section is mainly based on their paper. The principal idea for providing school meals is that it improves educational achievement by improving child nutrition and by providing incentives for families to send their children to school. An important provider of school meals is the World Food Program (see Box 14.4). Vermeersch and Kremer analyze 50 informal rural preschools in western Kenya, where 25 randomly selected schools received fully subsidized in-school breakfast on every school day for all pupils attending preschool. The meals were prepared by a cook specifically hired so the meals would not take too much time from the teacher.

The Kenyan government provides teacher training, but does not otherwise subsidize preschools. Parents pay fees for the teacher salary and some costs. Parents can enroll their children, but the official school fee is collected in a staggered way, by which teachers can send the children whose parents had not paid "enough" fees back home. As a result, there is a strong correlation between school participation and the amount paid by parents. The experiment took place in a poor region of Kenya where teacher salaries are low. In the area, most preschools are related to a primary school and usually several preschools are available within walking distance (4 km). Since the free meals provided by treatment schools create an incentive to transfer children to treatment schools, the authors use an intention-to-treat estimator. They define treatment as the availability of free breakfast at the school (preprogram) of a child's older sibling as the choice of school is highly correlated between siblings. This ensures that their composition is exogenous to the feeding program.

Preschool classes run for a few hours per day, usually from 08:30 to noon. Absence is high for both teachers and pupils; teachers are absent about 30 percent of the time and enrolled children are absent more than half of the time. As a result, the average class has an enrollment of 85 pupils, but only 35 attend on a typical day. Table 14.7 indicates the impact of free school meals on school participation, which was checked on-site at most six times in 2000 and at most seven times in 2001; the score for school participation varies from 0 (never present) to 1 (always present). As the table indicates, preprogram there was no difference between treatment schools and the comparison schools (column 1). Average school participation increased substantially for treatment schools in both years, although the effect was stronger in 2000 than in 2001. The authors also analyze the impact of treatment on test scores, which were only higher if the teacher was relatively experienced.

Vermeersch and Kremer explain that the smaller effect in 2001 was related to competition among schools, which in this setting is a different type of externality than discussed in section 14.7. During 2001, an increasing number of comparison schools started organizing school meals on their own (funded by parents); more specifically, this number rose from

BOX 14.4 WORLD FOOD PROGRAM RECEIVES 2020 NOBEL PEACE PRIZE

The UN World Food Program (WFP) was awarded the Nobel Peace Prize in 2020 for "its efforts to combat hunger, for its contribution to bettering conditions for peace in conflict-affected areas and for acting as a driving force in efforts to prevent the use of hunger as a weapon of war and conflict" (see www.nobelprize.org/prizes/peace/2020/prize-announcement). Located in Rome (Italy) and working together with its two Rome-based sister organizations (Food and Agriculture Organization and International Fund for Agricultural Development), the WFP is the largest humanitarian organization saving lives and changing lives.

WFP often works under difficult conditions to provide food assistance in emergency situations, including war, conflict, drought, floods, earthquakes, hurricanes, crop failures, and so on. In 2019, the WFP assisted 97 million people in need, which requires a well-functioning emergency organization: "On any given day, WFP has 5,600 trucks, 30 ships and nearly 100 planes on the move, delivering food and other assistance to those in most need." Two-thirds of the WFP's work is "in conflict-affected countries where people are three times more likely to be undernourished than those living in countries without conflict" (Information and quotes from www.wfp.org/overview).

The connections between hunger, food, conflict, and peace are specifically pointed out by the Nobel Prize Committee. In response, WFP Executive Director David Beasly points out: "Where there is conflict, there is hunger. And where there is hunger, there is often conflict. Today is a reminder that food security, peace and stability go together. Without peace, we cannot achieve our global goal of zero hunger; and while there is hunger, we will never have a peaceful world" (see www.wfp.org/news/world-food-programme-awarded-nobel-peace-prize-statement-wfp-executive-director-david-beasley).

The WFP is also intensively involved in providing school meals, with more than six decades of experience. Better health and nutrition allows children to learn and perform better. The WFP's ultimate objective is to transfer ownership to national governments, which has already happened in more than 44 countries. Even so, 17.3 million children in 2019 spread over 59 countries received school meals and snacks from the WFP, whereas another 39 million children in 65 countries were reached through capacity building in cooperation with national feeding programs. (For information on this paragraph, see www.wfp.org/school-meals.)

one preprogram to 14 by September 2001. Another competition effect was on prices. Treatment schools were instructed not to raise their official fees, which they did not. However, the official fees are hardly relevant and treatment schools did become more stringent in fee collection; the total increase in payment (mostly for the teacher) was about one-tenth of the cost of the food delivered to schools. In addition, comparison schools close

Table 14.7. Average school participation

	Preprogram	All 2000	All 2001
Treatment	0.001	0.085[***]	0.055[**]
	(0.029)	(0.022)	(0.024)
Constant	0.377[***]	0.274[***]	0.287[***]
	(0.021)	(0/015)	(0.059)
Observations	49	50	50
R^2	0.00	0.24	0.24

Source: Vermeersch and Kremer 2005, table 6, columns 1, 2, and 7.
Notes: Standard errors in parentheses; for each child in the sample average participation was computed over the relevant visits, then for each school the participation rates of children were averaged; one school did not have a preintervention visit in early 2000; the last column includes geographical dummy variables for administrative divisions (not reported); [**] and [***] significant at 5 and 1 percent, respectively.

to treatment schools responded by lowering their fees. As a result, the estimated effects on the rise in school participation seem to be a lower bound of what would happen if free school meals were provided to all schools.

14.9 COVID-19 Crisis

According to the World Health Organization (www.who.int, October 14, 2020): "Covid-19 is the infectious disease caused by the most recently discovered coronavirus. This new virus and disease were unknown before the outbreak began in Wuhan, China, in December 2019. Covid-19 is now a pandemic affecting many countries globally." Common symptoms of COVID-19 are fever, dry cough, and tiredness, while there is a range of less common symptoms. Some people become infected but have only mild symptoms. Currently, most people (around 98 percent) recover from the disease, although some have been treated in hospital. Fatality rates are low, but differ between groups of people. Older people and people with underlying medical problems (like high blood pressure and diabetes) are more likely to become seriously ill. The time between exposure and the moment when symptoms start is usually around five to six days. The disease spreads primarily from person to person by coughing, sneezing, or speech. It is, however, a new virus in humans and the possible animal source of COVID-19 has not yet been confirmed with certainty, and new variants constantly appear. The World Health Organization is following the developments closely (see https://covid19.who.int/).

14.9.1 Spread of the Virus

From its origin in China, COVID-19 spread across the globe rapidly. As of October 14, 2020, the World Health Organization has reported more than 37.7 million cases worldwide, resulting in slightly more than 1 million deaths. On that day, the overall average death rate was about 28.6 deaths per 1,000 cases (see subsection 14.9.2). The spread of the disease

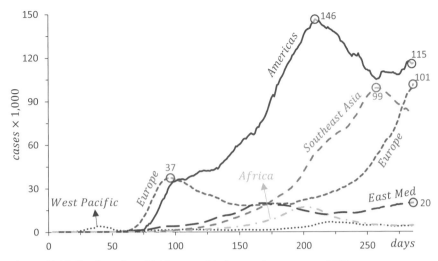

Figure 14.15 Number of covid-19 cases; 14-day moving average, 2020
Source: Created using World Health Organization data (www.who.int, downloaded October 14, 2020).
Notes: cases × 1,000, 14-day centered moving average; days = day number in 2020 (January 1 = 1); East Med = Eastern Mediterranean.

is illustrated in Figure 14.15 for the number of cases and in Figure 14.16 for the number of deaths using 14-day centered moving averages for six World Health Organization regions (this excludes "other," which is less than 0.002 percent of all cases and deaths).

The first notable peak in the number of cases is in February for West Pacific (including China), with a maximum of about 4,000 cases per day, associated with a similar peak in the number of deaths (around 100 per day). As is clear for both cases and deaths, China manages to control the epidemic after this initial peak very well (the small peak after 200 days for West Pacific is for other countries) using a strong lockdown, which has a severe effect on the economy.

COVID-19 spreads from China first to Europe and then to the Americas. The initial peak in Europe in April 2020 is around 37,000 cases per day and about 4,100 deaths per day; both are much higher than in China-West Pacific. Depending on the country, this leads to strong lockdowns to contain the disease and severe economic damage. The measures work well and the numbers of cases and deaths therefore decline. As a result, the containment measures are lifted to avoid unnecessary economic damage, which leads to a new wave of COVID-19 cases (above 100,000 per day October 2020). The number of deaths in Europe also starts to rise again, but much less dramatically. There are two underlying reasons for the deviation. First, many more people are tested in the second half of the year, so the likelihood of being classified as a COVID-19 case, given that you indeed have the disease, rises substantially. Second, the rise in knowledge of how to handle the disease improves substantially as hospitals, doctors, and nurses become more experienced.

Both Figures 14.15 and 14.16 show that after the European peak in April 2020, COVID-19 becomes an important problem in the Americas, first in North America and somewhat later also in South America. The peak in the number of cases in the Americas in July

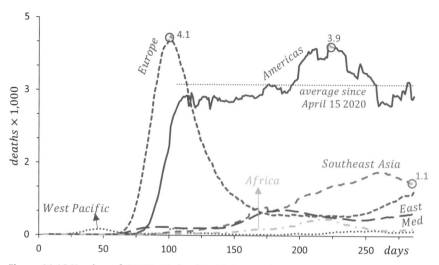

Figure 14.16 Number of COVID-19 deaths; 14-day moving average, 2020
Source: See Figure 14.15.
Notes: deaths × 1,000, 14-day centered moving average; days = day number in 2020 (with January 1 = 1); East Med = Eastern Mediterranean.

2020 is about 146,000 cases per day, followed by a weak decline and a rise to 115,000 per day in October 2020. The peak in the number of deaths in the Americas at the end of July 2020 is about 3,900 per day. More importantly, however, the number of deaths per day remains high for the Americas, with a peak in February 2022 (5,820 on February 4), but has been declining since then.

In general, in 2022, the infection rates have come down all over the world. Differences between regions remain, but overall, measures to prevent further infections, group immunization, and vaccines appear to be working.

14.9.2   Death Rate

How deadly is COVID-19? As indicated above, there were slightly more than 6 million deaths worldwide as of May 2022. Combined with about 520 million cases in total, this implies a death rate of about 12 people per 1,000 cases. How reliable is this estimate, and is it high or low?

Compared to the deadliest relatively recent pandemic, the H1N1 influenza pandemic in 1918–20, the death toll for COVID-19 is still modest. The 1918 pandemic is commonly referred to as the *Spanish Flu*, although it was not restricted to Spain and probably originated in New York (Olson *et al.* 2005). According to the Centers for Disease Control and Prevention (www.cdc.gov), about 500 million people were infected with the Spanish Flu, leading to an estimated death toll of at least 50 million people. This translates roughly to a death rate of 100 people per 1,000 cases. So far, both the number of cases and the number of deaths of COVID-19 is significantly lower than for the Spanish Flu, certainly in relative terms (world population in 2020 is about 7.8 billion people, more than four times the level of about 1.8 billion in 1918).

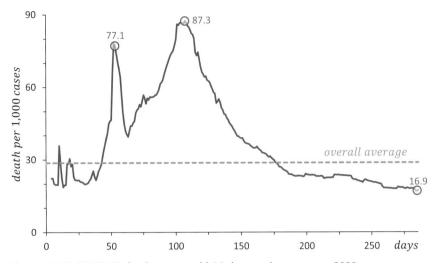

Figure 14.17 COVID-19 death rate; world 14-day moving average, 2020
Source: See Figure 14.15.
Notes: Deaths per 1,000 cases, ratio of sum of 14-day centered moving averages of Figures 14.15 and 14.16; days = day number in 2020 (January 1 = 1); overall average on October 14, 2020 was 28.6.

The estimated COVID-19 death rate is not reliable. This is illustrated for the world as a whole in Figure 14.17, which depicts a 14-day moving average death rate (solid line) compared to the overall average estimate (dashed line). Evidently, there are wild variations in the implied death rate with a peak of 77.1 at the end of February 2020 (based on Chinese evidence) and a second peak of 87.3 halfway through April 2020 (based on European data). Since then, the estimate declines steadily to drop below the overall average at the end of June and reach about 17 in October 2020. The main reason for the initial wild fluctuations is related to the lack of testing facilities available in many countries for a proper diagnosis of the disease, implying that only a fraction of all cases are properly registered. This improves as time goes by, which leads to a decline in the associated death rate. Moreover, treatments of COVID-19 improve as knowledge about the disease accumulates, leading to a decline in mortality.

14.9.3   Economic Costs and Poverty

A common response to contain the outbreak of the COVID-19 pandemic in many countries was to encourage "social distancing" by keeping a minimum distance away from other people (about 1.5 to 2 meters) and limiting the size of groups of people. To reduce interaction between people, restrictions were imposed on transportation and traveling. If such measures were not feasible in the workspace or shops, they were combined with (partial) lockdowns of businesses and firms, leading to strong negative economic effects and reductions in output. The associated economic costs are enormous.

The International Monetary Fund (IMF) regularly updates its estimates of real GDP growth. Figure 14.18 uses data available on October 16, 2020 to determine the expected *change* in real GDP growth (the 2020 estimate minus the 2019 realization) as an indicator

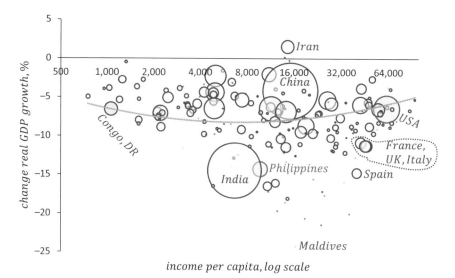

Figure 14.18 Income per capita and expected change in real GDP growth; 2019, %
Sources: Created using IMF data (October 16, 2020) for expected change in real GDP growth (%) and World Development Indicators online for income per capita.
Notes: GNI PPP in constant 2017 $, most recent in period 2017–19 and population (2019); bubbles proportional to population; 183 countries included; the curved line is a population-weighted quadratic regression.

for the severity of the economic impact of the COVID-19 crisis.[4] The figure relates this to the level of economic development as indicated by income per capita (using a log scale). The overall economic damage is enormous: the population- weighted average real GDP growth of the countries in the figure in 2019 was 3.76 percent, which dropped to an expected growth rate of –4.00 percent in 2020 for a decline of 7.75 percentage points. Figure 14.18 shows that the variation is large, from a minimum of –24.3 percent in the Maldives (an island nation largely dependent on tourism) to a maximum of 1.5 percent in Iran. Moreover, the curve indicates that middle-income countries, like India and the Philippines, tend to be more severely affected than very-low-income countries (like DR Congo) and high-income countries (like the USA).[5] A partial explanation for this is provided in Box 14.5, which indicates that the extent to which jobs are "teleworkable" (can be done from home) rises as income per capita rises.

In October 2020, the World Bank published a report on the impact of COVID-19 (in combination with armed conflict and climate change) in the fight against extreme poverty, entitled "Reversals of Fortune" (a reference to the articles discussed in Chapter 4). As shown in Chapter 10, extreme poverty had been falling for decades prior to 2020, although the speed of the decline slowed down as poverty became increasingly concentrated in Sub-Sahara Africa. As a result, according to the preCOVID-19 scenario, the World Bank was expecting global extreme poverty (living below $1.90 per day, see Chapter 10) to fall from

---

[4] Extreme outliers were excluded, namely countries with higher than 20 percentage points real GDP growth in 2020 (Guyana) and countries below –20 percentage points (Macao, Libya, Fiji, and Lebanon).

[5] The (highly significant) estimated coefficients are about –8.4 for income per capita and 0.5 for its square.

Table 14.8. COVID-19 and poverty line at $1.90 per day, 2019–2021

Year	PreCOVID-19		COVID-19 baseline		COVID-19 downside	
	# Poor (mn)	Deviation[*]	# Poor (mn)	Deviation[*]	# Poor (mn)	Deviation[*]
2019	643	0	643	0	643	0
2020	615	0	703	88	729	114
2021	586	0	697	111	736	150

Source: World Bank 2020, figure 1.3.
Notes: Number of poor in millions; [*] deviation = extra number of poor people (in million) relative to preCOVID-19 benchmark.

689 million people in 2017 to 643 million people in 2019 and 586 million people by 2021, for a total decline of more than 100 million people at about 25 million per year.

Table 14.8 depicts the revised expectations in the fight against poverty using a COVID-19 base scenario and a COVID-19 downside scenario, as well as the deviations relative to the preCOVID-19 scenario. The impact is enormous. In the baseline scenario, the World Bank expects 88 million extra people in extreme poverty in 2020 and 111 million extra in 2021. In the downside scenario, these numbers rise to 114 million in 2020 and 150 million in 2021. In short, COVID-19 partially reverses hard-won gains in the fight against global poverty. Associated with this is a rise in inequality. An important underlying reason is that a lockdown in most developing countries means you simply do not have any income at all, in contrast to most advanced nations where there are many social support programs. Of the 88 million extra people in extreme poverty under the baseline scenario, most are in South Asia (49.3 million) and Sub-Sahara Africa (26.2 million); similarly for the 114 million extra people in extreme poverty under the downside scenario, namely 56.5 million in South Asia and 40.0 million in Sub-Sahara Africa. As the World Bank points out (2020, pp. 5, 6): "Overall, some 72 million of the projected new poor in the baseline scenario will be in middle-income countries – more than four-fifths of the total new poor." This is in line with Figure 14.18 and Box 14.5.

14.10 Conclusions

This chapter analyzed various relationships between economic development and the quality of health. In general, there is a positive relationship, such that advanced countries, for example, have higher life expectancy at birth than developing countries. There are substantial differences between countries and gender in life expectancy. There have been enormous gains in life expectancy since 1960 (about 20 years for both sexes), in particular for East Asia & Pacific and North Africa & Middle East. The relationship between income per capita and life expectancy is strongly positive, while there is basically no relationship between income per capita and the gender gap (female minus male life expectancy). On average, women live more than four years longer than men, but the gender gap is

BOX 14.5 WORKING AT HOME

A common response in many countries to contain the spread of COVID-19 was "social distancing" by means of a (partial) lockdown and work from home as much as possible. This raises the question, of course, to what extent different types of jobs are "teleworkable" and can be done from home, or not. Examples of jobs that (mostly) *cannot* be done from home include: cleaning, maintenance, food preparation, production, installation, construction, health care, and transportation. Examples of jobs that (to a large extent) *can* be done from home include: computer and mathematical occupation, education, training, legal occupations, and business and financial operations. As the above suggests, it tends to be easier for higher-paying jobs to be teleworkable than for lower-paying jobs. Dingel and Neiman (2020) classify the extent to which different types of jobs are teleworkable and use their classification to determine the extent to which different economies have teleworkable jobs. At the national level the result is illustrated in Figure 14.19, which clearly shows that the ability to work from home rises as income per capita rises; the regression line explains about 79 percent of the variance in teleworkability. In other words: a (partial) lockdown tends to affect less developing countries more strongly than high-income countries.

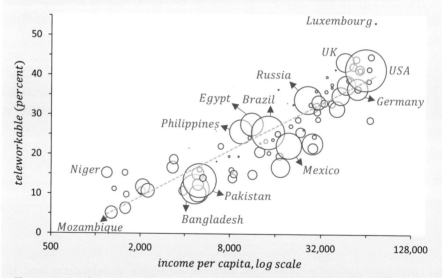

Figure 14.19 Teleworkable jobs (percent of total) and income per capita, 2018
Sources: Created using data from Dingel and Neiman 2020 for teleworkable (percent) and World Development Indicators online for income per capita.
Notes: GNI PPP in constant 2017 $, most recent 2017–18 and population (million, 2018); 86 countries included; dashed line is a regression with slope 8.5454 which explains 79 percent of the variance in teleworkability.

particularly large in Russia, Belarus, and Ukraine. For the world as a whole, the gender gap in life expectancy has been fairly stable for decades.

The number of physicians per 1,000 people rises substantially with income per capita once a threshold level (of about $3,000) has been reached. Health expenditures as a share of income follow a U-shaped pattern, both at the government level and in total. As a consequence, the poorest developing countries tend to spend a larger share of income on health than do middle-income countries, although the share in high-income countries is larger still. The main underlying reason is that the poorest countries have to deal with a range of health issues related to their unique circumstances. This becomes clear when analyzing the main causes of death, where we distinguish between (i) noncommunicable diseases, (ii) injuries, and (iii) communicable diseases and maternal, prenatal, and nutrition (MPN) conditions. It turns out that the share of noncommunicable diseases (including cancer, cardiovascular diseases, and diabetes) rises substantially with income per capita, while communicable diseases and MPN conditions decline rapidly as a cause of death and are thus typical developing-country problems.

From an historical perspective, the main rise in life expectancy has been achieved by lowering infant, child, and maternal mortality problems. One consequence is that gains in life expectancy have been particularly large for younger people and are substantially smaller for older people (see Box 14.1). Another consequence is that the main reason for lower life expectancy in developing countries today (2020) is still because of high levels of infant, child, and maternal mortality, which is negatively related to income per capita and immunization programs. An associated problem is gender selection and survival issues at birth. By nature, there are slightly more male births per female births worldwide (about 5 percent higher), but this ratio is substantially larger in some countries, like China, Vietnam, India, and Pakistan (about 10 percent or more), which is not a natural phenomenon.

The chapter discussed two health experiments in a broader context. The first experiment focuses on the effectiveness of deworming campaigns, which is related to hygiene problems typical for developing countries, on health improvement and school attendance. The broader perspective here is the realization that the experiment has spillover effects from the treated to the comparison group which must be taken into consideration for a proper evaluation (at a higher level of aggregation). The second experiment focuses on the effect of providing free school meals for boosting school attendance. The broader perspective in this case relates to the competition effects, since treated schools tend to raise their prices, while comparison schools nearby tend to lower their prices and start to organize school meals themselves. Such competitive externalities have to be taken into consideration when evaluating policy effectiveness.

The chapter concluded with a discussion of the impact of the COVID-19 pandemic, which started in China and spread across the globe rapidly in 2020. It evaluated the spread of the disease and its death rate before focusing on the economic costs and poverty consequences. The predicted economic costs in terms of the global decline in real GDP are enormous (almost 8 percent). Middle-income countries tend to be affected more strongly than high-income countries, most likely because the share of jobs that is teleworkable (can be done from home) rises as income per capita rises. As a result, many millions of people, particularly in middle-income countries, are pushed back below the extreme poverty line, by about 88 million in 2020 and 111 million in 2021 (in the baseline scenario). The economic and poverty consequences of a health pandemic can therefore be enormous.

Further Reading

The World Health Organization website of the United Nations (www.who.int) provides detailed data and regular updates on current health issues, like the COVID-19 crisis and the Ebola virus disease. The annual World Health Statistics report presents the most recent health statistics for member states.

A wealth of information on the economic aspects of health around the world can be found on the OECD website. This site provides detailed data and acces to current research: www.oecd.org/health/.

PART IV
Connections and Interactions

· ·

Part IV consists of five chapters and focuses on connections and interactions between different parts of the development process. Chapter 15 starts with a discussion of agriculture in connection with (rural) development, by reviewing agricultural production and employment in an historical perspective in relation to the Lewis model of development. After an evaluation, this chapter continues with a discussion of development in the agricultural sector before concluding with agricultural policies. Chapter 16 evaluates the rising importance of location for economic development by analyzing the role of urbanization and agglomeration in the development process, both from an historical perspective and more recently. Chapter 17 continues in this spatial direction by discussing regularities (Zipf's Law and the Gravity Equation) in a geographical economics framework with multiple equilibria and path dependence. A discussion in a broad historical perspective emphasizes the rising importance of human interaction over time while building on geo-human interaction. Chapter 18 discusses firm heterogeneity and focuses on the rising importance of multinational firms for economic development. It provides an overview of empirical regularities before explaining the Melitz model, which helps to understand horizontal and vertical foreign direct investment (fragmentation). The chapter reviews the links with (wage) inequality and concludes with a discussion of multinationals and development. Chapter 19 concludes the book with a discussion of sustainability in connection with development and the environment by analyzing scale, competition, and technology effects, multilateral agreements and the natural resource curse, as well as the main differences between renewable and nonrenewable natural resources.

15 | Agriculture and Development

15.1 Introduction

It is hard to overstate the importance of agriculture in economic development. If one takes a long-term view, the gradual change from hunter-gatherer societies to sedentary food production created a food surplus and enabled people to spend time on other activities than the daily hunt for food. This extra time could be used for innovation in the agricultural sector itself, but also for other activities.

This was not a linear process (see Diamond 1997 and Chapter 3). Sedentary food production was not an invention, but was gradually discovered at different places around the globe and in different periods in history. Hunter-gatherers would go hunting for some time during the year and return to places to check on crops and gradually discovered ways to make food production more reliable. The whole process of domestication from hunter-gatherer societies to sedentary food production took thousands of years and really took off around 8500 BC in the so-called Fertile Crescent.

As Diamond (1997) documents, there are many reasons why the Fertile Crescent was so successful in this process, but important factors were no doubt that the number of crops and animals that could be domesticated was larger in this area compared to other regions in the world and this made the transition from hunter-gatherer lifestyles to sedentary food production relatively easy. Furthermore, the East–West orientation of the European continent ensured that similar climatic circumstances at the same time during the year made the spreading of knowledge also relatively easy. Once food production became settled, it also affected the development of cities. Around food markets population density increased, which stimulated further development and enabled local knowledge spillovers and specialization in production.

Although the history of agricultural development is fascinating by itself, this chapter is not a survey of the history of agriculture (see Chapter 3 for some details). Agriculture, by creating a food surplus, is the basis of economic development. To some extent, this explains why developing countries have relatively large agricultural sectors, because economic development goes hand-in-hand with a reduction of the agricultural sectors in total production. Section 15.2 evaluates agricultural production and employment at the world level and for global regions. Section 15.3 discusses the links between agriculture and development from a contemporaneous perspective and section 15.4 from an historical perspective, including the Rostow stages of development. Section 15.5 explains the theoretical structure of the Lewis model of development, of which section 15.6 provides an evaluation. Section 15.7 discusses the links with urbanization, including the Harris-Todaro model, while section 15.8 evaluates developments within the agricultural sector. Section 15.9 discusses agricultural policies and section 15.10 concludes.

15.2   Agricultural Production and Employment

Table 15.1 shows a breakdown of total population for regions in the world into agricultural employment and value-added. What is clear from the table is that especially in developing countries a large share of the total population is allocated to the agricultural sector. In Africa, for example, more than half of the population is working in the agricultural sector, whereas in Europe or the Americas this share is only 6 and 9 percent, respectively. This indicates that agriculture in Africa, and to a somewhat lesser extent Asia, is a dominant sector. In all regions the share of employment in agriculture is declining in the last two decades. This is to a large extent caused by technological progress; the agricultural sector is slowly becoming more capital intensive. Revealing in this respect is the fact that in all regions the value-added per agricultural worker is rising such that despite the declining share of employment in the agricultural sector, the share of value-added as a percent of GDP is more or less constant in this period.

In Africa, more than 60 percent of the population lives in rural areas, whereas in Europe this fraction is below 30 percent. This suggests a relationship between the importance of agriculture for an economy and the degree of urbanization. This is indeed the case. Economic development and urbanization are linked. This will be discussed in section 15.7 and analyzed in more detail in Chapter 16.

Some of the most important crops in the world are rice, maize (or corn), wheat, and potatoes. Rice is the most widely consumed cereal grain staple food. It was first domesticated in China and production is concentrated in Asian countries, like China, India, Indonesia, Bangladesh, Vietnam, and Thailand. Maize is a cereal grain domesticated in the Americas and widely grown there, as well as in China. Wheat is a cereal grain first domesticated in the Fertile Crescent and used as an ingredient in a wide range of foods, including bread. It is intensively produced in Europe, China, India, and North America. Potatoes are root vegetables domesticated in the Americas, but now most intensively produced in Europe, China, and India.

Figure 15.1 depicts the evolution of world production of the above four crops since 1961 in million tonnes. In 1961, the production of all four crops is around 230 million tonnes (highest for potatoes). Since then, production has grown by about 2.2 percent per year for rice and wheat, 0.6 percent per year for potatoes, and 3.1 percent per year for maize (where production started to rise particularly fast in the new millennium). As a result, the production of maize is now substantially higher than rice and wheat, while the production of potatoes is substantially lower. Note that the production weight ranking is not equivalent to the production value ranking, which would put rice on top.

Table 15.1. Agriculture, population, employment, and value-added, 1997–2017

Region	1997	2007	2017
World			
Population (mn)	5,905	6,705	7,631
Rural population (mn)	3,220	3,343	3,413
Agriculture; employment (%)	40	35	29
Agriculture; value-added/worker	1,810	2,296	3,331
Agriculture; value-added (% GDP)	4	3	4
Africa			
Population (mn)	754	963	1,276
Rural population (mn)	501	606	740
Agriculture; employment (%)	58	56	51
Agriculture; value-added/worker	1,069	1,319	1,663
Agriculture; value-added (% GDP)	16	15	16
Americas			
Population (mn)	800	905	1,007
Rural population (mn)	196	194	191
Agriculture; employment (%)	13	11	9
Agriculture; value-added/worker	5,938	8,311	11,187
Agriculture; value-added (% GDP)	2	2	2
Asia			
Population (mn)	3,594	4,071	4,561
Rural population (mn)	2,300	2,329	2,279
Agriculture; employment (%)	49	42	32
Agriculture; value-added/worker	1,270	1,724	2,798
Agriculture; value-added (% GDP)	7	7	7
Europe			
Population (mn)	727	732	746
Rural population (mn)	213	203	190
Agriculture; employment (%)	11	8	6
Agriculture; value-added/worker	9,412	13,012	19,390
Agriculture; value-added (% GDP)	3	2	2
Oceania			
Population (mn)	30	35	42
Rural population (mn)	9	11	13
Agriculture; employment (%)	18	16	14
Agriculture; value-added/worker	9,633	14,972	20,392
Agriculture; value-added (% GDP)	4	3	3

Source: Food and Agricultural Organization (FAO) data, www.fao.org/faostat/en/#country, accessed July 16, 2020.
Note: Value-added per worker in constant USD.

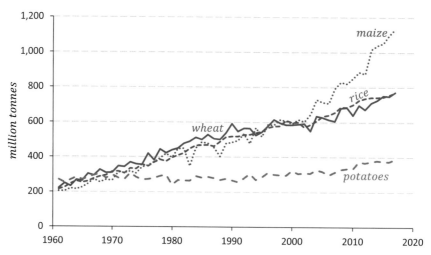

Figure 15.1 World production of maize, rice, wheat, and potatoes since 1961
Source: Created using FAOSTAT data.
Note: Production in million tonnes.

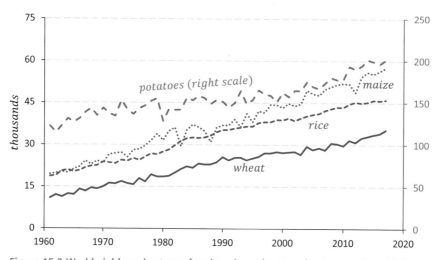

Figure 15.2 World yield per hectare of maize, rice, wheat, and potatoes since 1961
Source: Based on FAOSTAT data.
Notes: Hectograms (100 grams) per hectare; left scale is 30 percent of right scale.

Figure 15.2 shows the evolution since 1961 of the world yield per hectare (in thousand hectograms) for rice, maize, wheat, and potatoes. In 1961, the yield is lowest for wheat (about 11,000), similar for rice and maize (about 19,000), and by far the highest for potatoes (122,000; and therefore depicted on the right-hand scale of the diagram for clarity). Since then, yields have grown for all four crops, which reflects a rise in productivity. Productivity growth has been lowest for potatoes, namely about 0.9 percent per year. Since this is higher than the total rise in production of 0.6 percent (see above and Figure 15.1), the world area for growing potatoes must have been falling by about 0.2 percent per year.[1] The production of rice per hectare increased by about 1.6 percent per year. Since rice production rose by 2.3 percent per year the world rice area must have been rising by about 0.7 percent per year. Maize productivity rose by about 1.9 percent per year, which means the world maize area increased by about 1.1 percent per year (since production rose by 3.1 percent per year). Finally, productivity growth for wheat was highest at about 2.1 percent per year, which is almost equal to the rise in world production of 2.2 percent per year, so the world wheat area increased only slowly by about 0.1 percent per year. In all cases, the majority of the rise in world production is caused by a rise in production per hectare, not by a rise in the area of cultivation.

15.3 Agriculture and Development

As countries develop economically, agricultural output tends to become less important, while other sectors tend to become more important. The contemporaneous relative decline of agriculture is illustrated in Figure 15.3 for 182 countries in 2019 using a bubble diagram proportional to population. The decline over time is discussed in section 15.4. The simple average share of the agricultural sector (percent of GDP) is 10.0 percent and the population-weighted average is 11.3 percent; it ranges from a minimum of 0 percent in Macao to a maximum of 57.4 percent in Sierra Leone. As Figure 15.3 shows, there is a clear decline in the share of agriculture as income per capita rises. The slope of the trendline in the figure (which explains 66.4 percent of the variance) is –7.59; this means that a 10 percent higher income per capita level lowers the share of agriculture in GDP by about 0.76 percentage points. Sierra Leone is a clear outlier, with a high share of agriculture.

   As the share of agriculture declines, the share of other sectors rises. Chapter 7 already discussed this for industry, when it pointed out that the share of industry is typically hill-shaped as development progresses, first rising and then declining again. As Figure 15.4 illustrates for 2019, the share of the services sector in the economy typically rises as development progresses. A method for distinguishing between goods and services is to argue that services, such as getting a haircut, are produced and consumed simultaneously, although not necessarily at the same place. A simpler, but effective, method is to argue that if you can drop it on your foot it must be a good. The simple average share of services in GDP for 182 countries in 2019 was 56.6 percent, while the population-weighted average was 53.7 percent. The variation is large, with a minimum of 12.1 percent for Haiti to a maximum of 94.2 percent for Macao. The slope of the trendline in the figure (which only explains about 33 percent of the variance) is 6.32, which means that a rise of 10 percent in income per capita raises the share of services in the economy by about 0.6 percentage points.

   The observation that the services sector becomes more important as countries develop is consistent with the data in Table 15.1. The share of the workforce in agriculture in more

---

[1] Small deviations in the calculations in the text are the result of rounding.

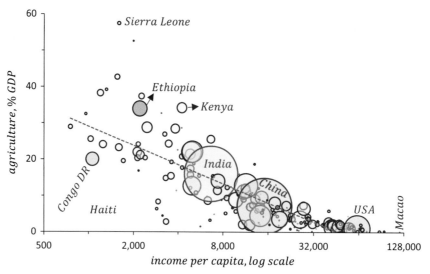

Figure 15.3 Income per capita and agriculture value-added; percent of GDP, 2019
Source: Created using data from World Development Indicators online.
Notes: Income per capita is GNI PPP (constant 2017 $, 2019 or most recent); agriculture includes forestry & fishing (% of GDP, 2019 or most recent); bubbles proportional to population (2019); 182 countries included; dashed trendline explains 66.4 percent of variance.

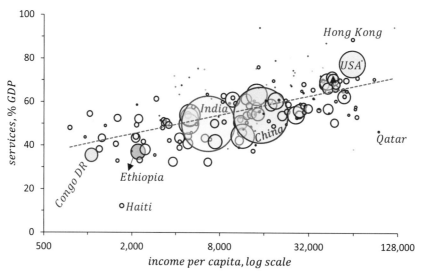

Figure 15.4 Income per capita and services value-added; percent of GDP, 2019
Source: Created using data from World Development Indicators online.
Notes: Income per capita is GNI PPP (constant 2017 $, 2019 or most recent); services, value-added (% of GDP, 2019 or most recent); bubbles proportional to population (2019); 182 countries included; dashed trendline explains 32.7 percent of variance.

developed parts of the world decreases. These nonagricultural workers must find employment elsewhere, either in industry or in the services sector. Note that a correlation between development and urbanization has already been suggested (see section 15.7). Figure 15.4 is consistent with this observation: higher levels of development are associated with higher levels of urbanization (a lower share of the rural population). The services sector in particular is located in cities. Think, for example, of the banking sectors in New York or London. The stylized facts support this relationship between development and urbanization.

15.4   Agriculture in Historical Perspective

If the discussion in section 15.3 is rephrased in a time dimension, there should be a decline of the agricultural sector as a share of income over time as countries start to develop successfully. The World Bank Development Indicators online provide information on this share from 1960 to 2019 for *every* year for only 39 countries (accounting for 4.35 billion people, or about 56 percent of the world population). The discussion in this section begins for these countries as illustrated in Figure 15.5, which focuses on the average in panel a and a selection of countries in panel b. The simple average share of the agricultural sector declines by about 22 percentage points from 35 percent in 1960 to 13 percent in 2019. This is a decline of almost 0.4 percentage points every year. The shaded area in panel a indicates the 95 percent confidence interval for the average, which is about 11.4 percentage points wide in 1960 and falls to 6.8 percentage points in 2019.

Panel b of Figure 15.5 shows the decline of the agricultural sector for three countries that have been developing successfully. All three countries have an agricultural sector above 40 percent of GDP in the 1960s. The decline is strongest and earliest for South Korea (to 1.7 percent in 2019), the first country to start developing (and the richest country of the three currently). The decline is also strong in China (to 7.1 percent in 2019), the second country to start developing. The decline is weakest (but still substantial) in India (to 16.0 percent in 2019), the last country of the three to start developing (and the poorest of the three

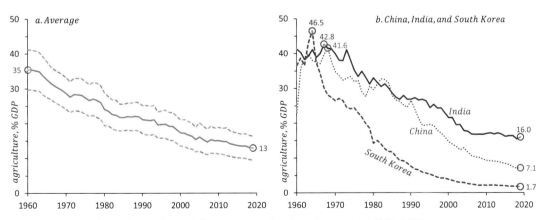

Figure 15.5 Agriculture share of GDP (%); average and selected countries, 1960–2019
Source: Created using World Bank Development Indicators online.
Notes: Agriculture includes forestry and fishing; panel a is average for 39 countries and 95 percent confidence interval; panel b is for selected countries.

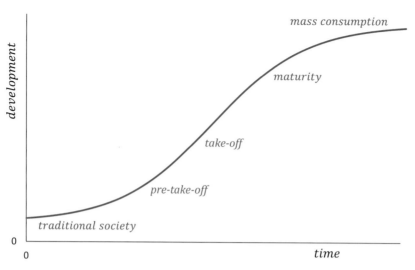

Figure 15.6 Rostow stages of development
Source: Based on Rostow 1962.

currently). All three countries show how the relative importance of the agricultural sector declines over time.

The discussion above suggests that one can distinguish phases of development that often begin with the development of the agricultural sectors. Rostow (1962), for example, describes various stages of economic development, and tries to answer the question surrounding what conditions are needed for traditional, agricultural societies to begin a process of development. Figure 15.6 illustrates the stages of development he identifies:

- Traditional societies that are characterized by subsistence agriculture.
- Preconditions for take-off in which an agricultural surplus enables countries to invest in, for example, irrigation, canals, and ports, and possibly start exporting.
- Take-off: Urbanization increases, enabling knowledge spillovers and innovation.
- Drive to Maturity: An industrial base becomes established and multiple industries develop. This makes large-scale investment in social infrastructure possible (such as schools and universities).
- Age of mass consumption: The industrial sector dominates the economy. Consumption is directed to high-value products, such as cars. Employment is increasingly found in cities and no longer in the rural agricultural sector.
- A final stage in which the marginal utility of consumption goods diminishes and growth declines.

Economic historians always had a keen interest in the role of agriculture in the development process. Countries that later successfully industrialized started with a strong agricultural sector (Adelman and Morris 1988). The central idea in this analysis is that an industrial take-off starts with a Green Revolution (Crafts 1988). This happened in Japan in the nineteenth century and in Taiwan and South Korea in the twentieth century (Wade

1990). Experiences like this suggest that an agricultural revolution is of crucial importance before a next phase of development can start (Rosenstein-Rodan 1943). The Lewis (1954) model is one of the first that indicates how this takes place.

15.5   The Lewis Model of Development

Arthur Lewis (1954) analyzed economic development in a two-sector model. The modern sector – a capitalist sector – develops by using labor from the agricultural sector. In his model, the agricultural sector is underdeveloped. It is a subsistence sector and the capitalist sector can draw labor from this subsistence sector. The high labor supply elasticity implies that initially wages do not increase. For the capitalist sector, this is beneficial. Without wage increases the return on capital is high and capital can be reinvested in order to gain from investments. The increase in the capital stock and the related demand for labor in the subsistence sector leads to growth. The process becomes self-sustainable. At some point, the subsistence sector is no longer able to supply the necessary labor and further increases in demand for capitalist labor start to increase wages. This is sometimes referred to as the Lewis turning point. Recent evidence suggests that China might have reached such a turning point (Zhang *et al.* 2011, but see Das and N'Diaye 2013 for an opposing view). In the seminal article of Johnston and Mellor (1961), the central claim that an agricultural surplus is a necessary condition for economic development is further developed.

15.5.1   The Story
The arguments provided by Johnston and Mellor are as follows (in summary):

1. Providing increased food supply: Developing countries have high population growth rates and an accompanying growth in demand for food that goes with it. Providing food for a growing population is a necessary condition for economic growth. In the early stages of development, the income elasticity for the demand for food can also be high. Insufficient supply of food can increase food prices and reduce real wages. In principle, the gap in food supply could be covered by imports, but developing countries often lack a sufficient amount of foreign exchange.
2. Enlarged agricultural exports: Once food supply is sufficient, growth in agricultural exports increases farm income, creates a source of foreign exchange, and enables countries to benefit from the international division of labor.
3. Transfer of manpower from agriculture to nonagricultural sectors: A larger agricultural surplus allows a transfer of manpower from the agricultural sector to the nonagricultural sector. A more diversified production structure has the benefit of making an economy less vulnerable to fluctuations in the agricultural sector.
4. Agriculture's contribution to capital formation: Economic progress without sufficient capital to finance investments in the manufacturing sector or investments in the

necessary infrastructure is not possible. In practice, the size of these funds is larger than can be obtained from the agricultural sector alone (except perhaps in mineral/oil-exporting countries), but capital formation without a substantial agricultural surplus is impossible.

5. Increased rural net cash income as a stimulus to industrialization: This is related to the former condition of capital formation. An expansion of the nonagricultural sector not only depends on sufficient investment, but also on expected demand for products in the nonagricultural sector. A large domestic market is essential.

In later work, this line of reasoning has been expanded, but the essence of Lewis's story still stands (see Mellor 1995, 1996); in the early phases of economic development, a well-functioning agricultural sector is a necessary condition for development by creating a surplus that can be used in the industrial sector. The data on developing countries, provided in section 15.3, reflect this relationship between economic development and the size of the agricultural sector; it becomes relatively smaller along the development path.

15.5.2   The Model

This section gives a brief description of the Lewis model based on Ray (1998, section 10.2, which is inspired by Ranis and Fei 1961). In the Lewis model, the economy consists of a traditional agricultural sector and a modern industrial sector. The labor market in the agricultural sector is characterized by excess labor supply. As a consequence, a typical farm employing more family members to work the fields no longer increases production. This seems puzzling at first because from micro-economics we know that wages equal the marginal product of labor and if marginal product becomes zero why are wages still positive? The answer is income sharing within the family. Wages in the traditional sector can best be interpreted as family wages that are shared by the family as a whole. If there is unemployment, it is hidden within the family. The industrial sector produces manufactured goods and uses surplus labor from the agricultural sector. The scale of production in the industrial sector is initially too small to use all excess labor from the agricultural sector. The model is illustrated in the two panels of Figure 15.7.

Panel a depicts the industrial labor market, with the industrial labor force measured from left to right. Panel b depicts output in the agricultural sector, with the agricultural labor force measured from right to left, starting at the point L, which indicates total labor supply (given). This enables us to combine the graphs; more labor in the agricultural sector is associated with less labor in the industrial sector. Total labor is distributed over the two sectors, and the length of each horizontal axis gives total labor.

Inspection of panel b shows that the economy is characterized by surplus labor. Moving from right to left initially increases output in the agricultural sector along the output curve, but from point B onward, additional labor does not increase output any further. The average wage – if all labor is employed in the agricultural sector – is $\bar{w} = output/L$. The straight line depicts the total wage bill (except between points C and L, where it is the curved line – see below). The tangent line on the production function indicates where

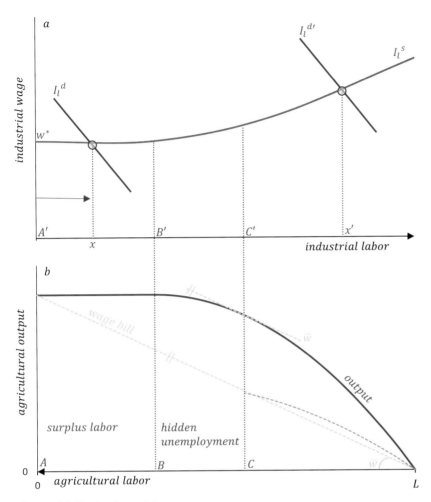

Figure 15.7 The Lewis model

the marginal product of labor equals $\bar{w}$. To the left of point C marginal labor productivity is smaller than $\bar{w}$ and to the right it is larger than $\bar{w}$. With this information, we can divide the agricultural sector into three areas. There is a *surplus labor* section from A to B (where additional workers do not increase output), a *hidden unemployment* section from B to C (where the marginal product of labor is smaller than $\bar{w}$), and a "normal" section to the right of point C (where the marginal product of labor is larger than $\bar{w}$ and there is no hidden unemployment).

The starting point of the analysis is all the way to the left in panel b; all labor is employed in the agricultural sector.

If we move labor out of agricultural employment into industry (as indicated by the arrow in panel a), it can safely be assumed that it does not affect agricultural output because we are in the excess labor supply area. Wages do not change and stay at $\bar{w}$, but employment in the agricultural sector falls. The wage bill – the part of output that is paid to the farmers – reduces along the straight line and the vertical difference between the straight line and the production function is a surplus (the part of output that is not paid to farmers). Note that total output is not reduced until point B is reached. Each worker gets a share of total output. In the excess labor phase each worker takes his/her share of output with him/her if a relocation to the industrial sector takes place. If L_A is the number of workers in the Agricultural sector and L_I the number of workers in the industrial sector, then $\bar{w}.L = \bar{w}.(L_A + L_I) = output$.

Given that the $\bar{w}$ does not change, the output per worker equals $\bar{w}$, in both sectors. The assumption is that the workers employed in industry can still buy their package of food because this worker is no longer employed in agriculture, but in industry. The wage that ensures this is depicted in panel a of Figure 15.7 by the horizontal section at w^*, where the industrial wage is corrected for the relative price between agricultural products and industrial products. As long as we are in the surplus labor section, growth of the industrial sector does not increase wages.

If more workers are relocated to the industrial sector, we move to the hidden unemployment phase. Beyond point B total output in the agricultural sector begins to decline, as does the average agricultural surplus. At wages w^* relocated workers are no longer able to buy a food bundle $\bar{w}$ because the average surplus falls. The consequence is that food prices rise. Industrial wages are no longer competitive and have to go up; this is the first turning point B' in panel a. This does not restore original average food consumption because food production has gone down. A solution is to let the relocated workers also consume industrial products in order to compensate for the loss of food products. Whether this is possible depends on the circumstances of the country. If $\bar{w}$ is at the subsistence level, this is not possible without loss of life.

This process continues until point C, where the hidden unemployment phase ends. From this point onward, agricultural wages become larger than $\bar{w}$. As agricultural wages go up, we are no longer moving along the straight line in panel b, but wages increase, also increasing the wage bill. The curved line starting at C indicates this. The wage offered in the industrial sector has to increase faster in this phase as shown in panel a; this is the second turning point.

Until now, we ignored labor demand in the industrial sector. The downward sloping curves I_I^d and $I_I^{d'}$ in panel a give two possibilities, each representing a phase in the development process. The I_I^d curve shows demand in the surplus labor phase; in this case industrial labor demand does not raise industrial wages. Equilibrium with the I_I^s curve is reached at x. As the industrial sector starts to develop further (by investing profits in an expanding capital stock), demand for labor rises and the demand curve shifts up. Initially (within the surplus labor section), this does not increase wages. Only if the economy moves beyond the surplus labor phase does the industrial wage start to rise, as illustrated by the industrial labor demand curve $I_I^{d'}$, leading to equilibrium x'.

The important message here is that development starts by using the surplus labor from the agricultural sector, which enables workers to relocate to the industrial sector without affecting food supply. Ray (1998) provides further details and discusses some loose ends of the model. A problem, for example, is taxation of the farm. Total farm output remains constant in the surplus labor phase. If some farm workers relocate to the industrial sector, why would the remaining farm workers share the average output with the relocated workers? They could keep it and wages would become larger than $\bar{w}$. So, implicitly, some taxation must take place.

15.6   Evaluation of the Lewis Model

What is the final judgment on the Lewis model after more than 60 years? Gollins (2014) provides an answer. The main criticism of the model is that Lewis was not transparent regarding its micro-foundations. The model is full of assumptions that need further clarification. The capitalist sector is initially a price taker on the labor market, the supply of capital is fixed in the short run, capital can only be used in the capitalist sector, and there is excess supply (or unemployment) in the subsistence sector. In subsequent literature more formal models have been developed (see Fei and Ranis 1964 for an early contribution and Wang and Piesse 2013 for a more recent contribution; see Gollins 2010 for a survey of this literature). The graphical representation in section 15.5 gives some idea of what elements are modeled in these theoretical models.

In general, the idea of two-sector dualism can still describe important aspects of a development process. Many people in economies that are heavily dependent on agriculture have low (real) wages. Although the wages are not necessarily at subsistence levels, the average productivity of labor in many of the lowest-income countries is less than half of that of the nonagricultural sector (Gollins 2014, p. 75). What is more difficult is the dualist nature of the model. The gap between a subsistence sector and a capitalist industrial sector seems too stark. In practice, many sectors exist, and within a sector different types of activities can be distinguished, each with different characteristics. Also in formal modeling the use of unemployment or excess supply of labor is difficult from a theoretical point of view. Including unemployment in the model is not straightforward and, in practice, especially in low-wage economies, individuals are seldom truly unemployed, but develop all sorts of activities to survive (Banerjee and Duflo 2007).

The Lewis turning points are also not undisputed. First, there is growth without wage increases – which is not very beneficial for a society. Next, wage increases hinder the growth process, which is also undesirable. The aim of development is welfare improvements for the people within an economy and real wage increases are important in this respect. Gollins (2014, p. 85) concludes:

His [Lewis] model offers a crude but persuasive depiction of the growth process, in which growth occurs through the reallocation of labor and other resources across sectors. The model puts structural transformation processes at the heart of economic growth – a view that has captured renewed attention over the past few years. There is abundant empirical support for the proposition that structural transformation does, in an accounting sense, explain a large fraction of growth and income levels.

15.7   Development and Urbanization

The Lewis model and its variants provide us with a narrative of how development could start. Note that the relocation of agricultural workers to the industrial sector has another important consequence. This is illustrated in Table 15.2, which compares the (largest) top 20 cities in 2016 with the predicted top 20 cities in 2030. From the table, it is clear that many of the fastest-growing cities can be found in developing countries, such as India, China, Bangladesh, Pakistan, Egypt, Nigeria, and Congo. The Lewis model gives an indication of what the reason could be – namely, migration from rural to urban areas. As shown in Chapter 17, manufacturing tends to agglomerate in cities where wages are higher compared to rural areas.

In line with the Lewis model, Figure 15.8 illustrates the correlation between a lower share of employment in agriculture and a larger share of the urban population in a bubble diagram for 185 countries. The simple average share of the urban population is 59 percent and the population-weighted share is 55 percent, ranging from 12.7 percent in Burundi to 100 percent in Macao, Kuwait, Singapore, and Hong Kong. The simple average share for agricultural employment is 35 percent and the population-weighted share is 46 percent,

Table 15.2. Development of the largest cities; urban population size, 2016–2030

Rank	City in 2016	Size	City in 2030	Size
1	Tokyo, Japan	38.1	Tokyo, Japan	37.2
2	Delhi, India	26.4	Delhi, India	36.1
3	Shanghai, China	24.5	Shanghai, China	30.8
4	Mumbai (Bombay), India	21.4	Mumbai (Bombay), India	27.8
5	São Paulo, Brazil	21.3	Beijing, China	27.7
6	Beijing, China	21.2	Dhaka, Bangladesh	27.4
7	Mexico City, Mexico	21.2	Karachi, Pakistan	24.8
8	Kinki M.M.A. (Osaka), Japan	20.3	Al-Qahirah (Cairo), Egypt	24.5
9	Al-Qahirah (Cairo), Egypt	19.1	Lagos, Nigeria	24.2
10	New York – Newark, USA	18.6	Mexico City, Mexico	23.8
11	Dhaka, Bangladesh	18.2	São Paulo, Brazil	23.4
12	Karachi, Pakistan	17.1	Kinshasa, DR Congo	20.0
13	Buenos Aires, Argentina	15.3	Kinki MMA (Osaka), Japan	20.0
14	Kolkata (Calcutta), India	15.0	New York – Newark, USA	19.9
15	Istanbul, Turkey	14.4	Kolkata (Calcutta), India	19.1
16	Chongqing, China	13.8	Guangzhou, Guangdong, China	17.6
17	Lagos, Nigeria	13.7	Chongqing, China	17.4
18	Manila, Philippines	13.1	Buenos Aires, Argentina	17.0
19	Guangzhou, Guangdong, China	13.1	Manila, Philippines	16.8
20	Rio de Janeiro, Brazil	13.0	Istanbul, Turkey	16.7

Source: Based on UN Human Settlements Program 2016.

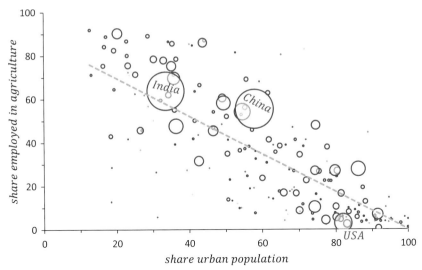

Figure 15.8 Employment in agriculture versus urban population, 2017
Sources: Created using data from https://ourworldindata.org and World Development indicators online.
Notes: Share of population living in urban areas (percent of total); share employed in agriculture (percent of total employment); bubbles proportional to population;185 countries included; dashed line is a trendline (slope is –0.8705; explains 56 percent of the variance in agricultural employment).

ranging from 0.06 percent in Macao to 91.7 percent in Burundi. The slope of the trendline (which explains 56 percent of the variance) is –0.87, indicating that if the degree of urbanization rises by one percentage point the share of agricultural employment declines by about 0.87 percentage points. This suggests that in the reallocation process urbanization and the attractiveness of cities is important. One can think of well-paid jobs in the services sector or industry which are mostly found in cities. These higher urban wages are also consistent with the Lewis development model of section 15.5.

The development process as indicated by the Lewis model also provides us with a problem. As the development process takes off in the model, the industrial sector grows and people who were initially employed at farms migrate to attractive new jobs in urban industrial areas. In many large cities, however, large slums are present. Living circumstances in these slums are often appalling. The UN defines a slum household as a group of individuals living under the same roof in an urban area who *lack* one or more of: durable housing of a permanent nature that protects against extreme climate conditions; sufficient living space, which means not more than three people sharing the same room; easy access to safe water in sufficient amounts at an affordable price; access to adequate sanitation in the form of a private or public toilet shared by a reasonable number of people.

Figure 15.9 shows the evolution of the urban population living in slums from 1990 until 2014 for a few selected regions. The data are available from 1990 to 2014. Asia and Latin America have between 20 and 30 percent of urban populations living in slum households. In Sub-Sahara Africa; on average more than half of urban populations are living in slum households. In some individual countries (not shown in the figure), such as Sudan, South Sudan, and the Central African Republic, more than 90 percent of households live in slums.

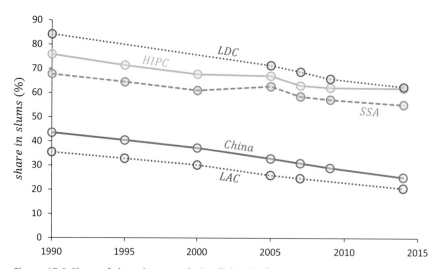

Figure 15.9 Share of the urban population living in slums, since 1990
Sources: Created using data from World Development indicators online and https://ourworldindata.org (2014 data, except for China).
Notes: Share of urban population living in slums (percent of urban population); LDC = Least Developed Countries (UN classification); HPC = Heavily Indebted Poor Countries; SSA = Sub-Sahara Africa (excluding high income); LAC = Latin America and Caribbean (excluding high income).

Slums tend to concentrate in the most heavily indebted poor countries, or the least developed countries.

Over time, the share of the urban population living in slums has been falling. China is an example: the share of the urban population in slum households fell from 44 to 25 percent between 1990 and 2014. Although the shares are declining, they are still high. This raises the question of why people choose to migrate to the city and live in a slum. The classic Harris-Todaro model gives a first indication of what the reason could be for why cities are attractive. It explains why people move from the rural agricultural areas to cities. The central idea is that migrating from the agricultural sector, which offers in the surplus labor stage a wage of $\bar{w}$, is risky. Migrants are hoping for a job in the city (industrial sector), but this is not certain, especially in developing countries. They may or may not get a job in industry. The alternative is unemployment. But the unemployed have to survive too, and might end up in the so-called informal sectors of the city.

The Harris-Todaro model explains why migration still happens. The model introduces expected wages from migration. If p indicates the probability of getting a job in the industrial formal sector with wage w_f and $(1 - p)$ is the probability of finding a job in the informal sector with wage w_i, the expected wage w_e of migrating to the city is equal to $w_e = pw_f + (1 - p)w_i$. As long as $w_e > \bar{w}$, migration still takes place because the expected wages are higher than subsistence wages in the surplus labor stage. As explained above, initially the industrial wages in the first phase of development are identical to $\bar{w}$, which makes massive migration unlikely in the early phases of development. But once the turning points have been crossed, migration from rural to urban areas becomes an important characteristic of the economy in developing countries. If the expectations are over-optimistic, this could lead to over-migration to cities with the risk of creating destitute city areas, which is something that can be observed in many cities in developing countries.

15.8   Developments in the Agricultural Sector

Up until now, we treated the agricultural sector as the basis for development. Work in the higher-paying industrial and services sectors is preferred over a job in the agricultural sector. This is, of course, not a complete description of the sectors in modern economies. Technological development in the agricultural sector can benefit society similarly as developments in any other sector. Self and Grabowski (2007) analyze how developments in the agricultural sector can contribute to economic growth for the period 1960 to 1995. In a cross-section analysis they test whether, for example, fertilizer and tractor intensity (a measure of technological progress) and years of schooling, as a measure of human capital, affect growth rates positively. The results are in general positive; technological progress in the agricultural sector has a positive effect on long-term growth (see also Gollins 2010 for a survey). What is often a source of concern in empirical studies like these is causality; does innovation in the agricultural sector precede economic growth or is it the other way around? Growth could make investment in innovation in the agricultural sector possible.

Tiffin and Irz (2006) use the concept of Granger causality. In a panel of 85 advanced and developing countries to deal with causality, does lagged growth predict progress in the agricultural sector, or is it the other way around? For most countries in their sample, the direction of causality runs from agricultural value-added to income. This leads Tiffin and Irz to conclude that in most cases growth in agricultural productivity must precede wider economic growth. Granger causality is not, however, an undisputed concept to determine causality. As always, some omitted variables could affect both growth and innovation in the agricultural sector and conclusions on causality are difficult. So, in practice, we should be reluctant to draw too strong conclusions. Gollins (2010, p. 3850) concludes: "To sum up, the empirical evidence linking agricultural development to economic growth in the cross-country data is highly suggestive but offers few examples of convincingly identified causal links."

15.9   Agricultural Policies

The challenge for policymakers is to move the agriculture sector beyond its traditional subsistence roots to a modern (capital-intensive) sector that contributes in its own right to economic growth. In many countries, this process is high on the policy agenda. In modern economies, a capital-intensive agricultural sector can contribute to economic growth. The sector in the Netherlands is a case in point. In this country, Wageningen University is an institution especially dedicated to focusing on increasing productivity in the agricultural sector. But there are also countries where this process does not take off or is stalled.

Pingali (2006) refers in particular to Eastern India and provides the following reasons why development of the agricultural sector stalls:

- low and inelastic demand for agricultural output due to low population density and poor market access conditions;
- poor provision of public goods in rural areas;
- lack of R&D in agriculture;
- high share of agro-climatically constrained land resources; and
- institutional barriers to enhancing productivity growth.

In addition, in many countries, the so-called urban bias can be observed. The development story of Lewis and others states that the agricultural sector is the basis for development in urban-based industrial sectors. This lesson has been internalized by many policymakers and has, according to many observers, resulted in an urban bias regarding development policies, where urban areas receive a disproportionally large share of public spending. The reasons for this urban bias in policy are many. In their survey, Bezemer and Headey (2008) mention the following:

- The benefits of the agricultural sector are often external to the agricultural sector itself and benefit the industrial sector. Investments in the agricultural sector are thus not perceived as necessary.
- In terms of the colonial history of many developing countries, the rural population traditionally had little political clout in the former colonies. As a result, high land taxes were introduced that transferred rural income to urban areas.
- Rural populations are often isolated and far apart, so building political pressure groups is difficult. As a result, in rural areas investments in efficient infrastructure are lacking, and access to good education is difficult. Public investments have an urban bias.
- Price distortions (subsidies for specific commodities) that favor the urban population often work against agriculture.

The consequence of the urban bias is a neglected agricultural sector in developing countries, which could, as agricultural development and long-term growth rates are positively linked, affect growth rates in general. It could also lead to over-urbanization and slumps in developing countries where cities attract rural–urban migrants, but are unable to support, house, and employ all inhabitants.

A second aspect is a bias in international trade policy. Advanced economies tend to protect their farming sector by giving subsidies and installing import tariffs on agricultural products. Table 15.3 illustrates this for the European Union (EU), one of the largest markets in the world for agricultural products. Especially products where the EU has domestic

Table 15.3. European Union applied MFN tariffs in agriculture, 2015 and 2019

Product	2015	2019
WTO agricultural products	14.4	14.2
WTO nonagricultural products	4.3	4.2
Animals and meat products	20.2	19.0
Dairy products	36.1	32.3
Fruit, vegetables, and plants	13.1	13.0
Coffee, tea, cocoa, and preparations	12.5	11.5
Cereals and preparations	15.7	17.2
Oilseeds, fats, oil, and products	6.4	6.3
Sugars and confectionary	25.7	27.0
Beverages, spirits, and tobacco	13.6	12.9
Cotton	0.0	0.0
Other agricultural products n.e.s.	5.2	5.9

Source: Based on data from http://capreform.eu/the-protective-effect-of-eu-agricultural-tariffs/.
Notes: MFN = Most Favored Nation; n.e.s. = not elsewhere specified; memo items, trade-weighted averages in 2018: WTO agricultural products 8.1 percent and WTO nonagricultural products 2.7 percent.

producers are heavily protected, such as dairy products and sugar. Agricultural sectors with limited domestic production such as cotton have far lower rates of protection. The suggestion is that countries protect sectors that compete with imports and are more lenient on tariffs for imports where a domestic sector is absent or small.

Many reasons exist why countries protect the farming sector. Protection of and subsidies to the capital-intensive agricultural sector in OECD countries limit market access of the agricultural sector in developing countries to markets in the advanced countries (and thus limit competition). Some countries don't like to be too dependent on food imports for safety reasons: relative poverty among farmers can be high even in the EU and income subsidies and import tariffs help to protect and raise income in the farming sector. It is a way to fight rural poverty in general. Of course, these measures hurt domestic consumers by making agricultural products more expensive, but also affect foreign producers of agricultural products as market access becomes more difficult. In addition, reduced demand from consumers in the EU or OECD countries keeps prices of farm products in developing countries lower than they would have been without market restrictions. This lowers farm income in developing countries and limits the possibility of further investment in innovation. It therefore adds to poverty in developing countries since, as Table 15.1 shows, a large share of the population in developing countries depends on agriculture as their main source of income.

Agricultural recovery can only take place if these distortions are removed. As Anderson (2010) documents, for many African countries, anti-farm policy biases have been addressed, and have reduced the policy biases against agriculture that existed in the late 1960s and 1970s. Still, distortions against the agricultural sector remain. Pingali (2010, p. 3877) estimates that in constant (2000) US dollars, transfers from African farmers to the rest of the economy peaked in the 1970s, at over $10 billion per year, or $134 per farm worker. This was substantially reduced over time. In the period 2000–04, the farm transfer declined to, on average, $6 billion per year, or $41 per farm worker. He notes, however, that the amount is still larger than the amount of public investments or development aid during the same period. Furthermore, it remains necessary to strongly argue within the international trading system that export taxation and the remaining barriers to (regional) trade come to an end, as this would greatly benefit African agriculture in particular (Binswanger and McCalla 2010). Despite these observations Pingali (2010) is relatively optimistic regarding the future of agriculture in developing countries. As countries develop, demand for agricultural products will also grow, raising prices and enabling further investments. Reduced import tariffs between developing countries will not only stimulate trade, but will also make these countries less susceptible to shocks such as the occasional droughts. Furthermore, technological progress in the agricultural sector will increase productivity and contribute to economic growth in general.

15.10   Conclusions

This chapter emphasized the importance of the agricultural sector for economic development. It showed the importance of agriculture in production and employment today, as well as its declining relative importance over time, particularly for countries where the development process takes off. Taking a long-term view, the agricultural surplus is a necessary condition for economic development. This was shown on the basis of the Lewis model, which explicitly links economic development to the agricultural surplus. In particular, the surplus has to be large enough to start investing in the modern sector. The Lewis model is full of assumptions that can be criticized (the capitalist sector is a price taker, the supply of capital is fixed in the short run, capital can only be used in the capitalist sector, and there is excess supply in the subsistence sector), but the idea that structural transformation processes lie at the heart of economic growth remains crucial for development.

It is important to note that the agricultural sector still plays a role in development after the "take off" has taken place; it has a separate contribution to economic growth. For developing countries, the challenge is to prevent policy biases that work against further developments of the agricultural sector, such as the urban bias. From an international perspective, the protectionist measures that still characterize the world economy deserve special attention. The advanced economies are protectionists in terms of the agricultural sector. In this respect, development aid could start at home, and make agricultural markets more accessible for agricultural products from the developing world.

Further Reading

A well-written account of human history, what factors have stimulated growth and inequality, including how and why humanity has only recently escaped the Malthusian poverty trap, is provided by Oded Galor in *The Journey of Humanity: The Origins of Wealth and Inequality* (New York/London: Dutton/Penguin, 2022). According to Galor, the Green Revolution has been crucial for economic development.

The Food and Agriculture Organization of the United Nations provides detailed information and updates on the links between agriculture and economic development in its "The State of the World" (SO) publications, including Fisheries and Acquaculture (SOFIA), the World's Forests (SOFO), Food Security and Nutrition (SOFI), Food and Agriculture (SOFA), and Agricultural Commodity Markets (SOCO). See: www.fao.org/publications/flagships.

16 Urbanization and Agglomeration

16.1 Introduction

Economic activity is unevenly distributed across space (see, for example, Chapters 1, 10, and 17). A visible manifestation of this uneven distribution is the rising share of the number of people living in cities. According to the *World Urbanization Prospects* (UNDESA 2019), this share rose from 30 percent in 1950 to 56 percent in 2020 and will continue to rise to 68 percent in 2050 (see Figure 16.1). In terms of the number of people involved, the rise is enormous: from 750 million people living in cities in 1950 to 4.4 billion in 2020. This number is expected to rise further to 6.7 billion in 2050. As a result of global urbanization, the rural population is rising more slowly: from 1.8 billion in 1950 to 3.4 billion in 2020. The rural population is currently (2020) at its peak; it is expected to decline to 3.1 billion in 2050.

There are two basic explanations for the uneven distribution of economic activity. *First nature* explanations deal with the role of physical geography (see Chapters 3 and 4). *Second nature* explanations build around human and economic interactions as the main driver of the uneven distribution. Some of the second nature approaches center around the role and development of history, psychology, or politics. From an economics perspective, second nature explanations arise from the economic interactions between firms, households, or workers in a market economy. There are two main fields: geographical economics (see Chapter 17) and urban economics (this chapter). A solid and recent introduction to both fields is provided by Brakman, Garretsen, and van Marrewijk (2020).[1]

Modern urban economics centers around the two key concepts of a spatial equilibrium (see section 16.5) and agglomeration economies (see section 16.6). These concepts help us to better understand how cities are internally shaped and organized, why a system of heterogeneous cities can exist, and which forces determine where footloose firms and households prefer to locate. Before analyzing these concepts, this chapter starts in section 16.2 with a discussion of urbanization, followed by section 16.3 with an overview of the current level of urbanization and a summary of 5,000 years of urban development in section 16.4. After discussion of the spatial equilibrium and

---

[1] Parts of this chapter are based on Brakman, Garretsen, and van Marrewijk 2020. Other parts, relating to the urbanization of China, are based on Brakman, Garretsen, and van Marrewijk 2016.

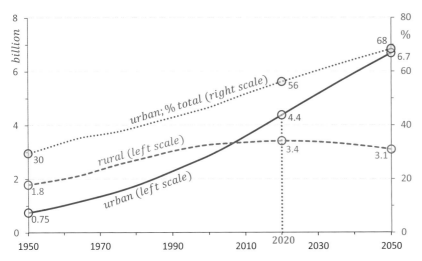

Figure 16.1 World urban and rural population; billion and % of total, 1950–2050
Source: Created using UNDESA 2019 data.
Notes: rural = world rural population (billion); urban = world urban population (billion); urban share is percent of total (right scale).

agglomeration economies, section 16.7 continues with a review of urbanization since 1960 and section 16.8 with a more detailed analysis of the connection between income per capita and urbanization. In section 16.9, this analysis is related to a discussion of urbanization in China and India. Section 16.10 concludes by reviewing the main policy implications of urbanization.

16.2   What Is Urbanization?

The most important source of information for global trends on population and urbanization is the UN Population Division from the Department of Economic and Social Affairs. The most recent *World Urbanization Prospects* (UNDESA 2019) is used for data throughout the chapter, for the evaluation of policy implications in section 16.10, and for this discussion of urbanization.

In simple terms, urbanization refers to the rising share of the population living in cities. However, criteria and definitions to identify and measure cities and urban areas vary across countries. The "city proper" defined by administrative boundaries may exclude suburban areas where a large share of the city's working population lives. Moreover, two or more adjacent cities governed by different local authorities may form a single urbanized area. As much as possible, the UN (UNDESA 2019) therefore uses *urban agglomeration* (see Box 16.1) to refer to a contiguous territory inhabited at urban levels of residential density and *metropolitan area* to refer to agglomeration and surrounding areas at a lower settlement density (with strong economic and social linkages to the central city).

It is important to realize that there are three main sources of urban growth:

- *Natural increase*: The urban population rises if the number of births is higher than the number of deaths. The balance depends on fertility, life expectancy, and the age distribution. Fertility rates in cities are usually lower than in rural areas because women have better access to education and modern family planning methods. Mortality rates are usually also lower in cities because of better health care and a younger age distribution.
- *Migration*: The urban population rises if in-migration is higher than out-migration. In many countries, the size of these flows is large (see, for example, the discussion of implied migration in China in section 16.7). Migrants are usually younger than average, so rural–urban migration tends to increase the average age in rural areas and reduce it in urban areas. Migrants may be forced to settle in slum areas within the city. The Harris-Todaro model helps to understand why migration takes place nonetheless (see Chapter 15).
- *Reclassification*: When cities grow, they need more space and may incorporate neighboring settlements and their population formerly classified as rural. Moreover, within rural areas settlements may grow from rural (villages) to urban (cities) after passing a threshold level.

As the above sources indicate, the phenomenon of urbanization has important and complex consequences. As the United Nations (UNDESA 2019, p. 10) summarizes:

> Urbanization is a complex socio-economic process that transforms the built environment, converting formerly rural into urban settlements, while also shifting the spatial distribution of a population from rural to urban areas. It includes changes in dominant occupations, lifestyle, culture and behaviour, and thus alters the demographic and social structure of both urban and rural areas. A major consequence of urbanization is a rise in the number, land area and population size of urban settlements and in the number and share of urban residents compared to rural dwellers.

The urbanization process is shaped by (public and private) planning projects and investments in buildings and infrastructure. A rising share of economic activity is concentrated in cities, which become hubs for the flow of trade, information, and investments and the location of high-quality services not available in rural areas. Before analyzing these aspects of urbanization in more detail, section 16.3 provides an overview of the current state of urbanization.

16.3 Urbanization and Development Today

Using the most recent information available in December 2020, there is a clear positive relationship between economic development and urbanization (see the bubble diagram in Figure 16.2). The income per capita used in the figure is in constant 2010 USD (and not corrected for PPP), as this information extends further back in time and is also used in

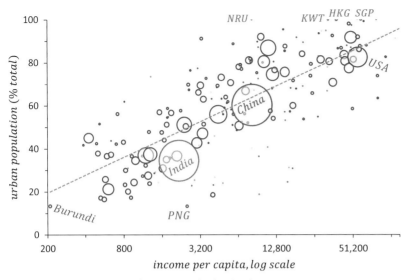

Figure 16.2 Economic development and urbanization, 2019
Source: Created using World Development online data.

Notes: Income per capita is GDP in constant 2010 USD (2019 or 2018); urbanization is urban population 2019 (percent of total); bubbles proportional to population (2019); 193 countries included; slope of dashed trendline (explains 54 percent of variance) is 11.915; PNG = Papua New Guinea; NRU = Nauru; KWT = Kuwait; HKG = Hong Kong; SGP = Singapore.

sections 16.7 to 16.9. The lowest income level in the figure is in Burundi, where only 13.4 percent of the population lives in cities. The only country with a lower population share (13.3 percent) is the developing economy of Papua New Guinea. In contrast, the entire population of Monaco is urban, while its income level per capita is so high (almost 200,000) it is not depicted in the figure for clarity. Other countries with a 100 percent urban population are (from poorest to richest): Nauru, Kuwait, Hong Kong, Macao, Singapore, and the Cayman Islands. With the exception of the tiny isolated island state of Nauru in the Pacific, all of these are high-income countries. (Nauru is 21 km^2; for comparison: Rhode Island, the smallest state in the USA, is more than 190 times as large.)

The relationship between economic development and urbanization is strong, but far from perfect. The trendline in Figure 16.2 explains 54 percent of the variance in the degree of urbanization and has a slope of about 11.9; this implies that a 10 percent higher level of income per capita is associated with a rise in urbanization of about 1.2 percentage points. The current global system of cities as identified by urban agglomerations and some expected future changes is discussed in Box 16.1. Before urbanization and development are discussed in more detail, section 16.4 evaluates the history of urban development.

16.4   5,000 Years of Urban Development

Recent evidence shows that our Neanderthal ancestors were already engaged in human building projects as long as 175,000 years ago, when they created large mysterious cave structures about 300 meters from the cave entrance (Jaubert *et al.* 2016). It is, of course, a

BOX 16.1 WORLD URBAN AGGLOMERATIONS

The United Nations (UNDESA 2019) provides global estimates on the size of urban agglomerations. Figure 16.3 depicts the 2015 distribution of urban agglomerations of at least 300,000 inhabitants.[2] The bubbles are proportional to population size and the figure shows nine of the top 10 largest urban agglomerations by name. (Nonlisted Osaka in Japan [partially hidden by Tokyo] is ranked seventh, with 19.3 million inhabitants.) Tokyo in Japan is the world's largest agglomeration with more than 37 million inhabitants, followed by Delhi in India (25.9 million), Shanghai in China (23.5 million), and Mexico City in Mexico (21.3 million). Three countries have two urban agglomerations in the top 10, namely Tokyo and Osaka in Japan, Delhi and Mumbai in India, and Shanghai and Beijing in China.

Figure 16.3 also shows the *tropical* zone (light-shaded) in between the Tropic of Capricorn in the south (about *minus* 23.44 degrees latitude) and the Tropic of Cancer in the north (about *plus* 23.44 degrees latitude). The remainder is referred to here as *temperate zone*. Most urban agglomerations (about two-thirds) in 2015 are in the

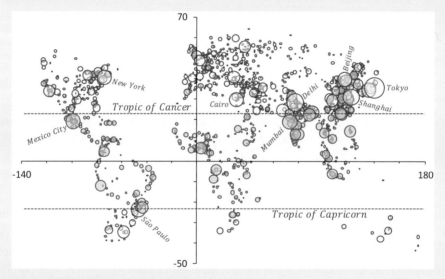

Figure 16.3 World urban agglomerations in 2015
Source: Created using data from UNDESA 2019.
Notes: Only 1,772 cities of 300,000 or more people included; equilateral projection; bubbles proportional to population size.

2 If possible, data classified according to the concept of urban agglomeration are used. However, some countries do not produce data according to the concept of urban agglomeration, but instead use that of metropolitan area or city proper. If possible, such data are adjusted to conform to the concept of urban agglomeration. When sufficient information is not available to permit such an adjustment, data based on the concept of city proper or metropolitan area are used.

BOX 16.1 (cont.)

temperate zone, mainly in the northern hemisphere, including North America, Europe, and large parts of Asia (including most of China and the north of India). The tropical zone includes mostly developing countries in Middle America, South America, Sub-Sahara Africa, parts of India, and Southeast Asia. The number of urban agglomerations in the tropical zone has been rising three times faster than in the temperate zone (from 40 in 1950 to 574 in 2015). Up to 2035, three countries, namely India, China, and Nigeria, are expected to account for about 35 percent of the growth in urban population. Delhi in India is expected to become the largest urban agglomeration (taking over from Tokyo) in the second half of the 2020s. Delhi is also expected to become the first urban agglomeration to pass the 40 million inhabitants mark in the first half of the 2030s.

long way to go from these early structures to something close to what we would now call a city. There is an ongoing debate about what constitutes a city (involving trade, self-sufficiency, and plumbing) and what is thus the world's oldest city, either continuously inhabited, or not (see Compton 2015, also for the discussion below). It is clear, however, that city development is related to the Agricultural Revolution, which started in the Fertile Crescent around 8500 BC (see Chapter 3). The oldest city is thus located somewhere in the Fertile Crescent. Familiar names are Damascus (Syria) and Jericho (Palestine), with early settlements dating as far back as 9000 BC (but not continuous settlements). Less familiar is Byblos (Lebanon), founded in 7000 BC, with continuous habitation since 5000 BC. Or possibly Aleppo (Syria), with settlement dating back only to 6000 BC, but with evidence of wandering nomad domestic camps up to 5,000 years earlier.

Another issue that creates occasional controversy is the question: what is the largest city in the world? Various sources arrive, of course, at slightly different answers, but the review here is based on the influential work of Chandler (1987), who uses a range of methods to estimate the size of a city and includes the surrounding suburban or urbanized area. Figure 16.4 illustrates the evolution of the size of the largest city for the past 5,000 years using a log scale. Memphis (Egypt) was probably the largest city in 3000 BC, with a modest population size (according to modern standards) of 30,000 inhabitants. Ur (Iraq) took over some 1,000 years later, with a population of around 65,000 people, followed by Babylon (Iraq) around 600 BC with 200,000 people.[3] Figure 16.4 shows that the size of the world's largest city started to rise particularly fast after 1200 AD.

In view of the size of its population, not only currently but throughout history, it comes as no surprise that Chinese cities played an important role in the "largest city" competition.

---

[3] A few cities in the first 2,000 years of Figure 16.4 that took over the "largest city" banner have been omitted here, but without clear information on the number of inhabitants.

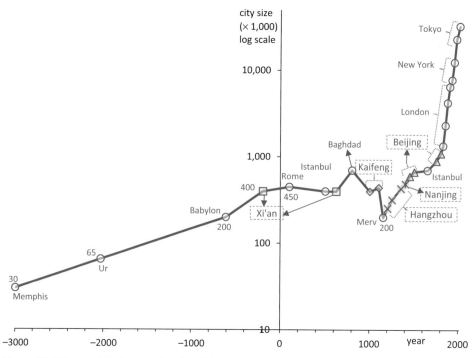

Figure 16.4 The world's largest city since 3000 BC
Source: Based on data from Chandler 1987, updated for Tokyo metropolis in 2015.
Notes: Chinese cities in dotted boxes with larger text size and different markers; nonChinese cities with circular markers.

Chandler identifies five Chinese cities as largest city at some point in time. All five are located in current East–Central China (see Figure 16.5). The first Chinese city that is the largest in the world is Xi'an (or Chang'an, Shaanxi province), one of the Four Great Ancient Capitals of China and well known for its terracotta warriors. It was the largest city with 400,000 people around 200 BC and again (with the same size) around 600 AD. Kaifeng (Henan province), a former capital of the Song dynasty, was the largest city of the world around 1000–1100 AD, with a population size of about 400,000 people. Hangzhou (Zhejiang province), the southern terminus of the Grand Canal, had the honor of being the world's largest city from 1200 to 1350, with a population rising from 255,000 to 432,000 in that period. It was briefly replaced by Nanjing (Jiangsu province), another of the Four Great Ancient Capitals, around 1400, with a population of 487,000. Nanjing was replaced by the province-city Beijing, yet another of the Four Great Ancient Capitals, which was the largest city around 1450–1500 and again around 1750–1800. Its population rose from 600,000 to 1.1 million in this time period.[4] Beijing was replaced by London (the first city to reach 5 million), New York (the first city to reach 10 million), and Tokyo (the first city to reach 20 and 30 million).

---

[4] The missing city of the "Four Great Ancient Capitals" is Luoyang (Henan province).

Figure 16.5 China, its neighbors, and the world's largest Chinese cities in history

16.5   Spatial Equilibrium

As summarized in section 16.1, the two key concepts of urban economics are the spatial equilibrium and agglomeration economies. This section focuses on the spatial equilibrium, first within cities and then between cities. Section 16.6 reviews agglomeration economies.

16.5.1   Spatial Equilibrium within Cities

The core of urban economics analyzes the economic organization of space within cities. Building on the Von Thünen (1826) framework, the foundations were laid by William Alonso, Richard Muth, and Edwin Mills, which explains why the analysis is known as the Alonso-Muth-Mills model. This framework is used, for example, to explain where to live within the city, what rental rate is paid, the impact of (public) transportation methods, how much land to consume, population density, the price for housing, the consequences of heterogeneity (rich or poor, cultural differences), and the impact of amenities (parks, museums, schools, and the like). To get a feel for the underlying forces, below is a simple model to explain the rent curve within a city. All issues above can be analyzed as variations of this example. Applying the equilibrium concept is straightforward: In a spatial equilibrium within cities, economic agents do not have an incentive to move to another location *within* the city.

Suppose a city has N people each using L units of land. The total amount of land needed for the city population is thus NL. The geographic structure of the city is simple: all individuals work in the Central Business District (CBD) in the center and live elsewhere. The area surrounding the CBD is a featureless plane, implying that all points at the same distance from the city center will have the same endogenous economic variables in equilibrium; the equilibrium is characterized by concentric circles around the city center. As a result, there is a maximum distance d_{max} that people will be living away from the city center. This implies a total land area of πd_{max}^2 (from circle geometry) which must be equal to NL. In other words: $d_{max} = \sqrt{NL/\pi}$.

Each individual working in the city center receives a wage rate W and chooses at which distance d from the city center she lives. Two variables are important for making this decision. First, she has to pay transport costs $t(d)$ to travel from home to the city center (actual costs and opportunity costs). Transport costs rise as the distance increases, so $t' > 0$ (a ′ indicates a derivative). Second, people living at distance d from the city center have to pay rent $r(d)$ per unit of land; total rent payments are thus $r(d)L$. This function will be *endogenously* determined by the spatial equilibrium.

$$\max_{C,d} U(C) \qquad\qquad 16.1$$

$$C = W - t(d) - r(d)L \qquad\qquad 16.2$$

$$r'(d) = -\frac{t'(d)}{L} < 0 \qquad\qquad 16.3$$

All individuals want to maximize the same concave utility function U depending on consumption C: see equation 16.1 (marginal utility is positive but diminishing: $U' > 0$ and $U'' < 0$). Consumption C is equal to disposable income, which is the wage rate W minus transportation costs $t(d)$ and minus rent costs $r(d)L$: see equation 16.2. Using two alternative methods, Technical Note 16.1 shows that the crucial first-order-condition for an optimum is given in equation 16.3. This equation indicates that from an optimization perspective *the slope of the rent curve is determined by marginal transport costs*. People are only willing to pay higher transport costs for living further away from the city center if these higher costs are exactly offset by lower rent costs. Since all individuals are similar and can choose to live anywhere within the city, the *spatial equilibrium* imposes this condition.

To close the model and determine the rent level at any location within the city, we need to (i) specify the transportation costs and (ii) determine the value at any location point within the city. This is illustrated in Figure 16.6, where we use (i) linear transport costs, such that $t(d) = \tau d$, and (ii) determine the rent level at the edge of the city from some alternative land use, such as agricultural production, which provides a rent level $\bar{r}$. The construction of the entire rent curve within the city is now simple. The value at the city

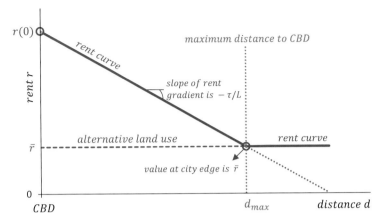

Figure 16.6 Construction of rent curve with linear transport cost
Source: Brakman *et al.* 2020, figure 4.4.

edge (at distance d_{max}) is equal to $\bar{r}$. From there on, the slope of the rent gradient must be equal to $-\tau/L$, as given by condition 16.3. This determines the rent level at any location within the city. In particular, it determines the rent level $r(0)$ in the city center, which is equal to $\bar{r} + \tau d_{max}/L$. Obviously, for large cities d_{max} is higher, so the rent in the city center is higher. General predictions are that (i) rents decline with distance to the city center and (ii) the speed of decline depends on the transport costs. Ample empirical evidence has supported these findings.

16.5.2 Spatial Equilibrium between Cities

Even a casual look at a map reveals that cities vary in size. The analysis in subsection 16.5.1 can be extended by looking at systems of cities, which tend to be fairly stable over time (compare an old map with a new map of the same country). Initially small cities tend to remain small, while initially big cities tend to remain big. This can be explained if the distribution is the result of a spatial equilibrium *between* cities in which economic agents do not have an incentive to move to another city.

The literature of urban systems builds on Henderson (1974), which explains why cities of different sizes may co-exist (depending on sectoral specialization). Extensions of this framework applying the spatial equilibrium concept are needed to explain empirical city-size distributions, which tend to follow a power law (see Box 16.2 and Chapter 17 for more detail). More advanced models allow for heterogeneity of economic agents and cities within a spatial equilibrium framework in which cities are incompletely specialized and house a large variety of people. Davis and Dingel (2020), for example, create a general framework in which heterogeneous individuals with a continuum of skills select a sector to work in and choose a location within a city to live among a range of cities. They do so by maximizing their utility taking all these variables into consideration.

In the Davis and Dingel model, larger cities have agglomeration economies (see section 16.6) and are more expensive to live in. Assuming that higher-skilled

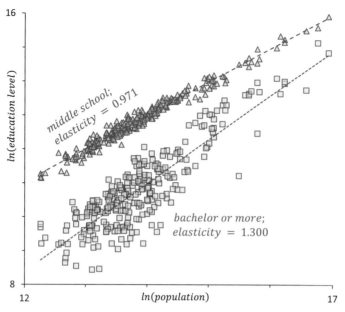

Figure 16.7 Example of urban sorting elasticity test in China, 2010
Source: Based on Brakman *et al.* 2014.

individuals are not only more productive, but also *relatively* more productive in skill-intensive sectors, there is a sorting of skills. Since the most skilled workers can afford to choose the most attractive locations, there will be a range of highly skilled people located in large cities (like Shanghai) who cannot be found in smaller cities (like Suzhou in Jiangsu province), followed by a range of workers with similar skill levels found in both cities. Since skilled people work in skill-intensive sectors, larger cities contain relatively more skilled workers and relatively more skill-intensive sectors. Within this framework, the sorting of skills and sectors can be tested, for example, with an elasticity test and a pairwise comparison test.

The elasticity test simply evaluates if people with higher skill levels are relatively more abundant in larger cities. This is illustrated for Chinese cities in 2010 in Figure 16.7 using log scales and two skill levels: middle school and Bachelor or more (based on Brakman *et al.* 2014).[5] The figure also reports elasticities, which is the percentage increase in people with certain skill levels if the size of the city rises. The number of people with a lower education level (middle school) rises about as fast as the size of the city (the elasticity is 0.971; close to one). The number of people with a higher education level (Bachelor or more) rises faster than the size of the city (the elasticity is 1.300; above one). This illustrates the sorting of higher-skilled workers in larger cities. Table 16.1 reports the population elasticities of six educational groups for cities in China in 2000 and 2010. In general, the

---

[5] See Brakman *et al.* 2014 for details on the data that are used and definitions of spatial units: www.cesifo-group .de/DocDL/cesifo1_wp5028.pdf. The primary data sources here are the population census of 2000 and the population census of 2010.

Table 16.1. Population elasticities in Chinese cities, 2000 and 2010

Educational attainment	City level year	
	2000	2010
Illiterate	0.930 (0.035)	0.846 (0.039)
Primary school	0.946 (0.023)	0.890 (0.022)
Middle school	1.012 (0.010)	0.986 (0.010)
High school	1.012 (0.028)	1.033 (0.016)
College	1.029 (0.038)	1.092 (0.026)
Bachelor or more	1.326 (0.054)	1.300 (0.041)
Observations	1,506	1,626
R-squared	0.889	0.899
Education FE	Yes	Yes

Source: Brakman *et al.* 2014.
Notes: Standard errors in parentheses, clustered by spatial unit.

BOX 16.2 POWER LAWS AND ZIPF'S LAW

Vilfredo Pareto (1896) "discovered" the first power law in economics when studying the distribution of income. He has a distribution function named after him. The reasoning is as follows. He found that for large values of x (thus for large income levels), the number of people with an income level *larger* than x is proportional to $x^{-\gamma}$ for some value of γ. Using the notation $P(.)$ to denote probabilities, and $F(x) = P(X < x) = 1 - ax^{-\gamma}$ for the cumulative distribution, it follows that the *counter-cumulative* distribution equals $P(X > x) = 1 - F(x) = ax^{-\gamma}$ for sufficiently large x. The density function is then $f(x) = a\gamma x^{-(1+\gamma)}$.

The lower the power law exponent γ, the fatter the tails of the distribution. For the distribution of income, this means that low γ implies more inequality between people in the top quantiles of income. If the power law exponent γ is close to one ($\gamma \approx 1$), as is the case for the distribution of city sizes in some countries, we say that *Zipf's Law* holds, named after the Harvard linguist George Kingsley Zipf (who analyzed, for example, the frequency of words in books).

An easy way to illustrate a power law distribution is by plotting the counter-cumulative distribution using a logarithmic scale for the horizontal axis. This is done in Figure 16.8 for the distribution of city sizes in Turkey. If a variable has a power law distribution, the counter-cumulative distribution should be approximately a straight line in the right-hand tail of the distribution (above some minimum level). This clearly is the case in Figure 16.8. Only cities above 300,000 people are included; the slope of the line (which explains 99.5 percent of the variance) is -1.0613, suggesting that the city-size distribution in Turkey follows Zipf's Law. This is analyzed in more detail in Chapter 17.

BOX 16.2 (cont.)

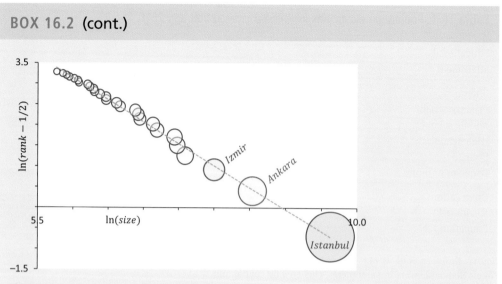

Figure 16.8 Urban power law in Turkey, 2020
Notes: 27 cities included; size measured in 1,000s; bubbles proportional to size; dashed trendline has slope −1.0613 and explains 99.5 percent of variance. The graph uses *ln* (*rank* − 1/2) rather than *ln* (*rank*) for technical reasons (see Gabaix and Ibragimov 2012).
Source: Based on data from UN Department of Economic and Social Affairs 2019.

estimated elasticities confirm that larger locations have relatively more skilled inhabitants: the elasticities are higher for more skilled educational groups in both years. Moreover, this trend is stronger in 2010 than in 2000, which may be indicative of a more market-oriented economy.

16.6   Agglomeration Economies

To put the discussion on agglomeration economies into proper perspective, Figure 16.9 shows the relationship between *city wages* (measured as mean annual earnings for male workers) and *city size* (measured as the number of people within 10 km of the average worker) for 76 Spanish cities. There is a clear positive relationship between wages and city size. The figure thus *suggests* that people might prefer larger cities like Madrid and Barcelona since wages are higher. But if only wages mattered, everybody would end up living in one large city (Madrid), where wages are highest. Apparently, people's location choice not only depends on wages. The fact that larger cities are also more expensive immediately comes to mind. Even so, the wage differentials are substantial, as De la Roca and Puga (2017, p. 1) point out: "workers in Madrid earn 31,000 euros annually on average, which is 21% more than workers in Valencia (the country's third largest city), 46% more than workers in Santiago de Compostela (the median sized city), and 55% more than workers in rural areas."

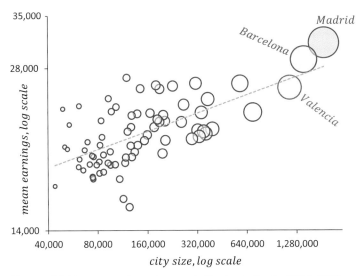

Figure 16.9 Mean annual earnings and city size in Spain, 2004–2009
Source: Brakman *et al.* 2020, figure 6.1, based on data provided by Diego Puga.
Note: The dashed trendline with a slope of 0.1121 explains 39 percent of the variance.

From the firm perspective, Figure 16.9 raises the question of why firms want to locate in large cities if wages, and hence labor costs, are higher there. Somehow, it must be beneficial to choose Madrid or Barcelona as a firm location, despite higher wages. The main reason must be that larger cities offer "agglomeration rents," which explains why firms do not necessarily opt for locations with the lowest wages. Whether it is true that cities somehow make firms and workers more productive is a key question analyzed in urban economics. The answer depends on the strength of agglomeration economies at the city level. Figure 16.9 also hints at the possibility that larger cities display stronger agglomeration economies where wages and productivity are higher. It is far from obvious why causality should run from city size to city wages. Both wages and city size are endogenous variables and the associated endogeneity problem is an important issue in urban economics.

The main concept that links firm productivity and wages to city size is *agglomeration economies*, which refer to the fact that firms operate under increasing returns at the location level (cities). By moving to a larger location, a firm and its workers become more productive, because they benefit from location-specific increasing returns to scale. Terminology is briefly explained below, before discussing the main sources and mechanisms of agglomeration economies. Chapter 17 analyzes the reasons and consequences of agglomeration economies in more detail.

16.6.1 Terminology

Agglomeration economies are an example of increasing returns to scale, indicating that a rise in the level of output produced decreases the average costs per unit of output for the firm: size matters. If costs decline for reasons within the firm only, we speak of *internal* returns to scale. If they decline for reasons at the sector or city level, we speak of *external* increasing returns to scale. Agglomeration economies are a prime example of external returns to scale. As such, agglomeration economies can be either positive or negative with respect to city size. Larger and more densely populated cities make it easier for firms located there to share and find relevant information. These information spillovers are an example of *positive* agglomeration economies. Similarly, congestion costs that increase with city size are an example of *negative* agglomeration economies.

We also distinguish between pure and pecuniary agglomeration economies. *Pure* (or *technological*) agglomeration economies occur if an increase in industry-wide output in a city alters the technological relationship between inputs and output for each individual firm in that city. It therefore has an impact on the firm's production function. The market structure can then be perfect competition since the size of the individual firm does not matter. *Pecuniary* agglomeration economies are transmitted by the market through price effects for the individual firm, which may alter its output decision. Two examples, dating back to Marshall (1891), are the existence of a large local market for specialized inputs and labor market pooling. A large industry can support a market for specialized intermediate inputs and a pool of industry-specific skilled workers, which benefits the individual firm. These spillovers do not affect the technological relationship between inputs and output (the production function). Finally, agglomeration economies can be *static*, as in the cases referred to above, but also *dynamic*. In the dynamic case, the average costs per unit of output fall if the *cumulative* output of the sector rises.

16.6.2   Sources and Mechanisms

The main categorization of the *sources* for agglomeration economies dates back to Alfred Marshall (1891, see Box 16.3). The *Marshallian trilogy* identifies three main sources of agglomeration economies: (i) information or knowledge *sharing*; (ii) labor market *pooling*; and (iii) the sharing of (specialized) *inputs*. Additional sources of agglomeration economies are also identified (see Rosenthal and Strange 2004, table 2, and Combes and Gobillon 2015): namely (iv) *natural advantages* (such as differences in factor endowments at the city level; (v) *home market effects* at the sector level (larger markets provide a source of

---

BOX 16.3 MARSHALL AND KALDOR IN CAMBRIDGE

The British economist Alfred Marshall (1842–1924) was the founder of the Cambridge School of Economics and of modern mainstream economics via his *Principles of Economics*, first published in 1890. In his view (successful) industrial districts are characterized by many small and highly specialized firms. The benefits of agglomeration within a district are found in the sharing of information and inputs and thus are tied to the specialization structure of the city. The shared access to information and (labor) inputs provides a strong incentive for firms to cluster within the district, thereby saving on transaction and transport costs. The increasing returns "mantle" in Cambridge was passed on from Marshall to Nicholas Kaldor (1908–86), who broadened the scope of the increasing returns analysis by turning to models of imperfect competition and economic growth.

pecuniary agglomeration economies); (vi) *consumption externalities* (various city-specific amenities explain why consumers prefer certain cities); and (vii) *rent-seeking* (this behavior may lead to cities that are too large, in contrasts to the other sources which focus on efficiency-enhancing effects; see Ades and Glaeser 1995, Henderson 2003, and Baldwin and Robert-Nicoud 2007).

In an influential paper, Duranton and Puga (2004) focus on *mechanisms*, rather than sources, as a more precise description of what affects agglomeration economies. They note (p. 2066): "consider, for instance, a model in which agglomeration facilitates the matching between firms and inputs. These inputs may be labeled workers, intermediates, or ideas. Depending on the label chosen, a matching model of urban agglomeration economies could be presented as a formalization as either one of Marshall's three basic sources of agglomeration economies even though it captures a single mechanism."

Duranton and Puga identify three basic mechanisms: sharing, matching, and learning. *Sharing* refers to indivisibilities. An opera house, for example, is only economically feasible in large cities. *Matching* refers to the quality of a match between worker and employer in labor market models, where large cities offer a higher probability of a successful match. *Learning* refers to the need for face-to-face contact, where large cities with more contacts lead to a higher quality of learning. In empirical research, the distinction between sources and mechanisms is not always clear cut, but the Marshallian typology has been mostly replaced by the mechanisms identified by Duranton and Puga.

Since agglomeration economies cannot be directly observed, they must be approximated to assess their empirical relevance. This means that one cannot test directly for the presence of a source or mechanism. The main *catch-all* concept that has been used in empirical research related to city size is the density of a location. In a survey, Combes and Gobillon (2015, p. 2) define agglomeration economies as the "effect that increases firms' and workers' income when the size of the local economy grows." They also make the observation that despite the theoretical identification of sources and mechanisms for agglomeration economies, empirical research still relies on composite and indirect measures that make it impossible to directly test for a source or mechanism.

16.7   Global Urbanization since 1960

Since 2007, more than half of the world population lives in cities. At the global level, urbanization is a relatively recent phenomenon. In 1960, only about 34 percent of the world population lived in cities, rising to 56 percent in 2019 (see Figure 16.10). As expected, there is a high positive correlation between the share of the rural population and the share of income or employment generated in agricultural activities (see Chapter 15). Since the latter is negatively correlated with general development levels (as measured by income), there is a positive correlation between income levels and urbanization. This is illustrated in Figure 16.10 for the OECD member countries, where the share of the urban population was 62 percent in 1960, rising to 81 percent in 2019 (still 25 percentage points higher than the world average).

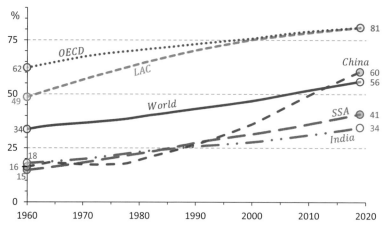

Figure 16.10 Urbanization; selected countries and regions (% of total), 1960–2019
Source: Based on data from World Development Indicators online.
Notes: Urbanization: urban population (% of total); OECD = Organisation for Economic Co-operation and Development countries; SSA = developing Sub-Sahara Africa; LAC = developing Latin America and Caribbean.

Figure 16.10 also depicts urbanization developments in China and India, by far the two largest countries in terms of total population, and in Latin America (LAC) and Sub-Sahara Africa (SSA; referred to as Africa in the discussion below). In 1960, the degree of urbanization was similar and substantially below the world average in China, India, and Africa, namely around 15–18 percent. It was substantially higher in 1960 in Latin America, about 49 percent (higher than the world average). The developments over time are rather diverse. Latin America closed up the gap with the OECD countries as the urban population share rises steadily to 81 percent in 2019. In India, the developments are stable: the urban population share rises steadily every year and reaches 34 percent in 2019. In Africa, the urbanization process is also relatively stable, but urbanization is more rapid than in India: the urban population share almost triples to 41 percent in 2014. The urbanization rate is higher in Africa than in India from 1984 onward. In China, the developments are much more dramatic (see also below). Initially, the urban population share rises from 1960 to 1964 (from 16.2 to 18.3 percent), but then it declines until 1972 (to 17.2 percent) and slowly crawls back until 1977 (to 17.5 percent). From 1979 onward, the urban population share starts to rise quickly (more than 0.7 percentage points per year) and even stronger from 1996 onward (more than 1.0 percentage points per year), reaching 60 percent in 2019 and surpassing the world average in 2013.

Figure 16.11 shows the impact on the absolute number of people living in cities (panel a) and in rural areas (panel b). For the OECD countries, the urban population rose by 119 percent or 597 million people in the period 1960–2019 (from about 500 to 1,100 million), while the rural population declined by 14 percent or 44 million people (from 305 to 261 million). A similar process is observed in Latin America, where the urban population rose rapidly from about 100 to 500 million and the rural population is almost stagnant (a slight increase only of 13 million people). The Indian urban population also rose rapidly, by almost 500 percent or 390 million people (from 81 to 471 million). In contrast to the OECD countries and Latin America, however, the rural population also

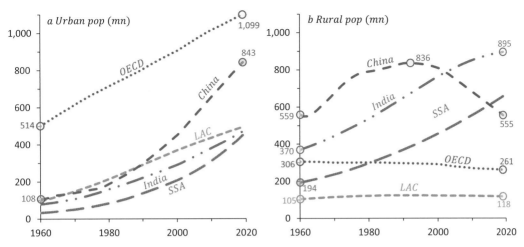

Figure 16.11 Urban and rural population; selected countries and regions (million), 1960–2019
Source: Based on data from World Development Indicators online.
Notes: Urban population (million) and rural population (million); OECD = Organisation for Economic Co-operation and Development countries; SSA = developing Sub-Sahara Africa; LAC = developing Latin America and Caribbean.

increased rapidly, by 142 percent or 526 million people (from 370 to 895 million). In absolute terms, the population increase in India is thus larger in the villages than in the cities. Similar observations hold for Africa, where the urban population rose by 417 million (more than a 12-fold rise) and the rural population even more, namely by 462 million people (from 194 to 656 million). Together, India and Africa are responsible for 71 percent of the worldwide increase in the rural population (of 1.39 billion people), while taking care of only 25 percent of the rise of the worldwide urban population (of 3.26 billion people).

China is responsible for the most spectacular urbanization process, as it takes care of the largest urban population increase in this period, namely by 680 percent or 735 million people (from 108 to 843 million). The *increase* in the number of people living in Chinese cities is thus almost twice the total population of the European Union in 2020. In the Chinese rural areas, the population *de*creased slightly by 1 percent or 4 million people. Those numbers are distorted, however, by the fact that there was a peak of 836 million people in the Chinese rural population in 1991 (meaning an increase of 50 percent in the period 1960–91) and an even larger decline since then (by 282 million people in the period 1991–2019). Under the simple assumption that the Chinese population growth is the same in the cities and the rural areas, the implied migration flow from the villages toward the cities in China is 542 million people in the period 1960–2019 (this includes "migration" of people for villages that pass the threshold of becoming a city). If the population growth rate is higher in the rural areas, the implied migration flows are even larger.

China's (urban) development is dramatically different before and after the *Economic Reform* (ER) process started by Deng Xiaoping in December 1978, as illustrated in Figure 16.12 (panel a in levels and panel b in changes). Before 1979, the urban population share is stagnant (at about 17.5 percent), as is income per capita relative to the world average (at about 4.2 percent). In the early 1960s, income declines as a result of the *Great Leap Forward*, causing the death of millions of people, while urbanization rises slowly.

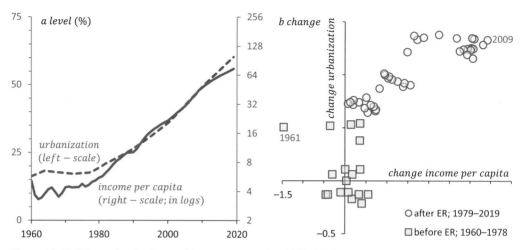

Figure 16.12 China: urbanization and income per capita, 1960–2019
Source: World Development Indicators online.
Notes: Urbanization: urban population (% of total); income per capita: GDP in constant 2010 USD (% of world average GDP in that year); changes in percentage points.

From 1966 to 1976, the effects of the *Cultural Revolution* become visible, in part with forcible relocation of people to the countryside and a decline in urbanization.

Mao's death in September 1976 led to a reinstatement of Deng Xiaoping, who soon afterwards adopted Economic Reform policies to expand rural incentives, encourage enterprise autonomy, reduce central planning, open up to international trade flows with the outside world, establish foreign direct investment in China, and pass new legal codes. This leads to a sharp increase in both the degree of urbanization and relative income per capita since then, with a peak in 2009 when China's income per capita level rises 4.8 percentage points faster than the world average and urbanization rises by 1.34 percentage points.

16.8   Urbanization and Income Per Capita

As indicated in Figure 16.2, Figure 16.12, and briefly discussed in section 16.3, the degree of urbanization tends to go hand in hand with rising income per capita levels, not only for China, but for all countries. In China's case, several researchers have argued recently that China is under-urbanized (see Lu and Tao 2009, Fujita *et al.* 2004, and Au and Henderson 2006a, b). Institutional restrictions on internal migration, notably but not exclusively the Hukou system, are largely held responsible for this outcome (Bosker *et al.* 2012).[6]

---

[6] The Hukou system, which is unique for China, is a visa system that regulates rural–urban migration and the sector of employment, agricultural or nonagricultural. Some agricultural workers can be employed in cities, not only in agricultural employment, but also in jobs such as "equipment operator," "business service personnel," or "production and transport related workers," according to Chan and Buckingham 2008 (p. 583), in general, in jobs "that are considered dirty, dangerous, or low-paying." For a description of what it (still) implies in practice, see Chan and Buckingham 2008 or The Economist 2010. The Chinese government is currently taking measures to relax the Hukou system.

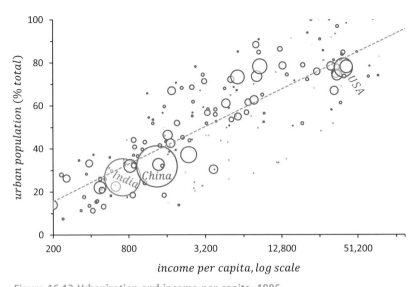

Figure 16.13 Urbanization and income per capita, 1996
Source: Created using World Development Online data.
Notes: Income per capita is GDP in constant 2010 USD; urbanization is urban population (percent of total); bubbles proportional to population; 185 countries included; slope of dashed trendline (explains 64 percent of variance) is 12.52.

The case for China's under-urbanization is illustrated for the year 1996 in the bubble diagram of Figure 16.13, which depicts the log of income per capita (in constant 2010 USD) on the horizontal axis and the degree of urbanization (urban population as percent of the total population) on the vertical axis for 185 countries. The size of the bubbles is proportional to population in 1996. There is, obviously, considerable variation in the degree of urbanization and in the log of income per capita, but on average these two variables are strongly related: the slope of the regression line depicted in the figure is 12.5 and this line explains 64 percent of the variance in urbanization. Since the observation for China is clearly below the regression line, it could be argued that China is "under-urbanized" relative to other countries. A similar case can be made for India, as also illustrated in Figure 16.13.

It's best to avoid a complicated discussion of cause and effect regarding the relationship between urbanization and income per capita (see also Brakman *et al.* 2014), and instead use the cross-section methodology illustrated in Figure 16.13 for 1996 as a method for determining a country's degree of under- or over-urbanization in terms of the deviation (in percentage points) of the cross-section regression line in any given year.

Panel a of Figure 16.14 illustrates the estimated slope coefficient and (minus) the estimated constant for every year since 1960. The estimated slope tends to decline over time (from around 16 to 12), as does (in absolute value) the estimated constant. As panel b of Figure 16.14 shows, these effects are related to the number of countries for which information is available in any given year, which rises from 89 in 1960 to a peak of 201 countries in 2008–11, and then declines somewhat for more recent years (as it usually takes time to gather and process information). This panel also shows that the explained urbanization variance is inversely related to the number of included countries, while a

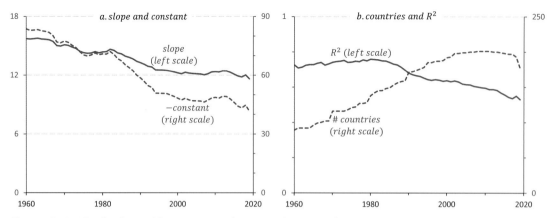

Figure 16.14 Urbanization and income per capita regressions over time, 1960–2019
Source: See Figure 16.13.
Note: Four small countries excluded for which information is only available in 2010, namely Djibouti, Faroe Islands, Liechtenstein, and Turks & Caicos Islands.

comparison with panel a shows that the number of included countries also has an impact on estimated slope and intercept. These issues are taken as given and the next section now turns to a discussion of the degree of over- or under-urbanization in China and India based on this terminology. (It should be noted, however, the same conclusions below are reached if attention is restricted only to the countries for which information from 1960 onward is available.)

16.9   Are China and India Under-Urbanized?

Using the methodology explained in the previous section, Figure 16.15 illustrates the degree of over- or under-urbanization in China and India since 1960. This suggests that China's recently highlighted *under*-urbanization (with a smaller share of the population in cities than what can be expected on the basis of its income per capita level) is a recent phenomenon, starting only in 1987. Before that year, China was actually *over*-urbanized, with a higher share of the population in cities than what could be expected on the basis of its income per capita level. The degree of over-urbanization reached a peak of 23.4 percentage points in 1962 and rapidly declined since then (although it remained substantial throughout the 1960s and 1970s).

China's maximum level of *under*-urbanization occurred in 1996, with 7.5 percentage points fewer people living in cities than what could be expected on the basis of its income level, hence the reason to choose this year for the illustration in Figure 16.13. Since 1996, China's degree of under-urbanization has declined substantially, to only 3.0 percentage points in 2019. The 1962 peak level of over-urbanization is illustrated in Figure 16.16. The most recent level of modest under-urbanization in 2019 is illustrated in Figure 16.2. All in all, it can be seen that China's degree of under-urbanization as emphasized in the recent

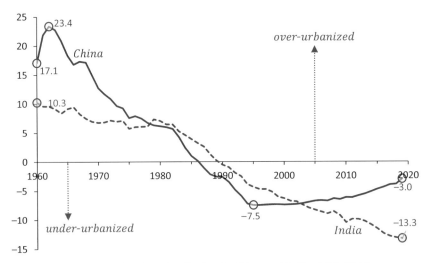

Figure 16.15 Over- and under-urbanization in China and India, 1960–2019
Source: See Figure 16.13.
Note: Deviations in percentage points of urbanization.

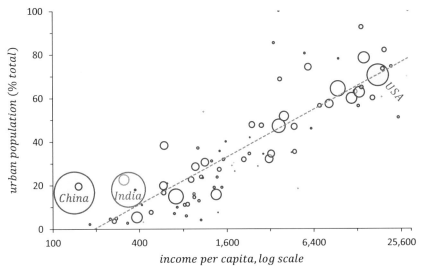

Figure 16.16 Urbanization and income per capita, 1962
Source: See Figure 16.13.
Notes: Slope of dashed trendline (explains 71 percent of variance) is 15.7; 92 countries included.

literature may have been substantial in 1996, but since then has virtually disappeared (in line with the conclusions of Brakman *et al.* 2014). Remarkably, perhaps, China's more substantial degree of over-urbanization in the 1960s seems to have received no attention in the literature.

Figure 16.15 also shows the degree of over- or under-urbanization for India over the period 1960–2019. India's developments are similar to those of China in the sense that it moves from being over-urbanized initially (up to 1989) to being under-urbanized recently (since 1990). India's developments are different in the sense that its degree of over-urbanization was more modest (10.3 percentage points in 1960), while its degree of under-urbanization is more substantial (13.3 percentage points in 2019) and seems to continue to increase. From this perspective, it seems a good suggestion for the literature to start analyzing India's degree of under-urbanization, rather than China's.

16.10   Policy Implications

This chapter has discussed the history of urbanization in ancient times, more recently, and expectations for the future. In all ages, urbanization is linked to economic development, driven by the spatial equilibrium and agglomeration economies. The United Nations (UNDESA 2019) summarize the main policy implications of urbanization in five observations.

The future of the world is urban. The majority of the world population already lives in cities and this share will continue to rise to 68 percent in 2050. For the next three decades, the urban population will rise by about 80 million per year, from 4.4 billion in 2020 to 6.7 billion in 2050. In contrast, the rural population will decline by about 300 million people in the period 2020–50. The rising urban population is based on a combination of natural increase and migration, both rural–urban and international. Cities are the major gateways for these migration flows.

Urbanization is related to sustainable development. Adequately planning and managing urbanization is needed for sustainable economic, social, and environmental development. Public institutions and infrastructure must keep up with the speed of urbanization to prevent rising inequalities, urban sprawl, pollution, and environmental degradation. Moreover, the links with surrounding rural areas must be strengthened to expand opportunities in all regions.

Urbanization is a positive force for growth, poverty reduction, and development. Cities provide educational, housing, health, cultural, and infrastructure services (water, electricity, and internet) that are crucial to achieve the sustainable development goals. Technological innovation is concentrated in cities, which are also the centers of entrepreneurship, trade, and investments. The concentration of economic activity in cities raises productivity through agglomeration economies, which is the main driving force for rural–urban migration.

Government policies can help share the benefits of urbanization more equally. The general benefits of urbanization notwithstanding, governments have a responsibility toward their citizens for inclusive growth. Policies restricting rural–urban migration may be ineffective, or worse. Sustainability requires that cities generate adequate income and decent employment opportunities. Not only must all sorts of infrastructure projects keep up with the speed of urbanization, governments are also obligated to provide education for all, promote healthy aging, ensure property rights, and enable political participation.

Urbanization data is needed for policymaking and planning. The government responsibilities mentioned above and the required actions must be evidence-based. This requires improvements in data collection methods, including civil registration, health information, and the use of *big data*, like remote sensing, satellite images, and geo-referencing. Adequately assessing current and future trends is essential for promoting inclusive and equitable urban and rural development.

16.11   Conclusions

The role of cities in the process of economic development is becoming ever-more important. Most people already live in cities, the largest of which house many millions of urbanites. The importance and size of cities will continue to rise in the near future, particularly in developing countries. This chapter reviewed the essence of cities and how their development started in the Fertile Crescent in combination with the Agricultural Revolution. Urban development is closely related to economic prosperity, both at a point in time and across time.

From a theoretical perspective, the chapter first explained the concept of a spatial equilibrium within cities, where people have no incentive to move to another location within the city, based on the von Thünen framework. Next, it explained the concept of a spatial equilibrium between cities, where people have no incentive to move to another city, based on the Henderson framework. Modern spatial models combine both aspects to better understand the size distribution of cities (Power Laws) and the sorting of skills, sectors, and occupations across cities, where higher skills tend to concentrate in larger cities. This effect is based on various agglomeration economies, based on knowledge sharing, labor market pooling, specialized inputs, natural advantages, home market effects, rent-seeking, and externalities.

The chapter concluded with a more detailed discussion of the links between urbanization and economic development, where it showed that China is no longer under-urbanized (in contrast to some decades ago) while India is, and an overview of the main policy implications of urbanization.

Further Reading

A solid introduction into urban economics is provided in: Brakman, S., H. Garretsen, and C. van Marrewijk. 2020. *An Introduction to Geographical and Urban Economics: A Spiky World* (Cambridge University Press). See especially part II on the spatial equilibrium (chapters 4 and 5) and the empirics of agglomeration (chapter 6).

The UN Population Division of the Department of Economic and Social Affairs provides up-to-date information and estimates on future urbanization developments in the *World Urbanization*

Prospects, which are used throughout the UN and by many international organizations and academic researchers. See: https://population.un.org/wup/.

TECHNICAL NOTE 16.1   LOCATION CHOICE

We can maximize equation 16.1 subject to the budget restriction in equation 16.2 in two ways. First, we can construct a Lagrangean function L using a Lagrange multiplier λ, as in equation A16.1, and determine the first-order conditions with respect to C and d, as in equations A16.2 and A16.3.

$$L = U(C) + \lambda((W - t(d) - r(d)L) - C) \qquad\qquad \text{A16.1}$$

$$U'(C) = \lambda \qquad\qquad \text{A16.2}$$

$$-\lambda(t'(d) + r'(d)L) = 0 \qquad\qquad \text{A16.3}$$

Second, we can directly substitute the budget restriction into the utility function, as in equation A16.4, and maximize only by choice of distance d. That first-order condition is given in equation A16.5.

$$U((W - t(d) - r(d)L)) \qquad\qquad \text{A16.4}$$

$$U'(C)(t'(d) + r'(d)L) = 0 \qquad\qquad \text{A16.5}$$

The first approach indicates that the value of the Lagrange multiplier is equal to the marginal utility of consumption (see equation A16.2). Since the marginal utility of consumption is positive, we therefore conclude from the second condition given in equation A16.3 that there is a relationship between the transportation costs and the rent curve in equilibrium, as given in equation A16.6. The alternative approach (of direct substitution) arrives, of course, at the same conclusion.

$$r'(d) = -t'(d)/L \qquad\qquad \text{A16.6}$$

17 Geographical Economics and Development

17.1 Introduction

Chapters 15 and 16 briefly touched upon geographical issues. They discussed urban–rural interactions (such as rural–urban migration), but without explicitly incorporating geographical considerations. Although they distinguished between two types of locations (rural and urban), they did not discuss where these are located on a map. Distance and the interaction between locations did not enter the discussion. This is an abstraction that allowed the focus to be on the different type of locations, the role of agriculture versus manufacturing, and the urbanization process as such. It did not enable an analysis of an important aspect of the global economic system, namely *agglomeration* or the unequal distribution of population and economic activity across space (see also Chapters 1 and 16).

Millions of people live close together in New York, Moscow, and Beijing. At the same time, there are large, virtually empty spaces available in the USA, Russia, and China. This suggests that for many people distance is important since they *choose* to live close together. The distribution of people and economic activity across space is not only remarkably unequal, it is also remarkably regular, both in terms of a spatial pattern and in terms of the interaction between economic centers. Questions arise regarding why economic activity is unequally distributed, why these regularities occur, and what the impact is on economic development.

It has long been evident that agglomeration and interaction aspects cannot be adequately explained using a neoclassical framework. In particular, economies of scale and imperfect competition, interacting with some type of local advantages, are essential. This implies that it is rather complicated to (endogenously) determine the size of economic activity in different locations in a general equilibrium framework. Such a framework, which needs to combine scale economies and imperfect markets, is difficult to construct from a modeling perspective and was developed only recently. The path-breaking contribution of the American economist Paul Krugman appeared in 1991. Since then, many prominent researchers have published work on refinements, generalizations, and applications in this field now known as *geographical economics* (or *new economic geography*).

In 2008, Paul Krugman received the Nobel Prize in Economics "for his analysis of trade patterns and location of economic activity," which is at the foundation of geographical economics and combines elements from international economics, industrial organization, economic geography, spatial economics, urban economics, and endogenous growth.[1] Since the underlying model and economic structures are not easy to grasp, this chapter introduces Krugman's model by means of an example. The example is then connected to economic development. Is agglomeration beneficial for development, or is a more spread-out distribution better? To some extent the answer is determined by physical geography (so-called *first nature geography*) and to some extent by man-made interactions (so-called *second nature geography*). In practice, these two forms mutually influence each other and it is not easy to determine what is more important. The main aim of this chapter is to show that geography matters.

Section 17.2 starts, with a brief review of the empirics of spatial distributions, followed in section 17.3 with a review of the empirics of spatial interactions, and in section 17.4 with a review of the empirics of agglomeration and development. Section 17.5 explains the structure of geographical economics models by means of an example, while section 17.6 evaluates some issues related to the example and geographical economics in general. Section 17.7 discusses first nature geography in terms of distances in development and section 17.8 second nature geography in terms of man-made barriers. Section 17.9 provides a brief summary of the implications of geographical economics models and connects it to a brief overview of world history. Section 17.10 concludes.

17.2   Spatial Distributions: Power Law / Zipf's Law

Box 16.2 already briefly discussed some details of Power Laws and Zipf's Law, which refers to characteristics of the tail of distribution functions. This section focuses on its application to the spatial distribution of city sizes. This regularity in the distribution pattern is most easily illustrated using an example. In 2020, Delhi was the largest urban agglomeration in India with about 30.2 million inhabitants. Give this city rank number 1. Then take the second largest city (Mumbai, formerly Bombay, with about 20.4 million inhabitants) and give this rank number 2. The third largest city (Kolkata, formerly Calcutta, with 14.9 million inhabitants) is given rank number 3, and so on. Arranging the data for the 181 urban agglomerations with more than 300,000 people this way, you now take the natural logarithm of the population size and of the rank of the city (minus 0.5).[2] This is plotted in a scatter diagram in Figure 17.1. Obviously, there is a negative relationship between population size and rank by construction. The puzzling feature is why this is an almost perfect log-linear straight line. A simple linear regression of the data plotted in Figure 17.1 gives

---

[1] An extensive introduction into this filed of analysis is given in Brakman, Garretsen, and van Marrewijk 2020.
[2] We take the natural log of (rank −0.5) rather than simply the rank for technical reasons as it leads to an unbiased estimate of the slope coefficient (see Gabaix and Ibragimov 2012). The reported high significance is based on an estimated standard error using their methodology. An in-depth discussion can be found in Brakman *et al.* 2020.

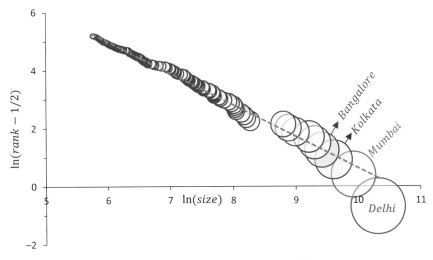

Figure 17.1 Power Law for urban agglomerations in India, 2020
Source: Created using UN Population Division 2019 data.
Note: Bubbles proportional to population size.

$$ln\left(rank - \frac{1}{2}\right) = 11.515 - 1.088\, ln(population) \qquad 17.1$$

The estimated slope coefficient is highly significant and the regression explains 98.7 percent of the variance in city size. This regularity in the distribution of city sizes is called a Power Law. (An alternative name is rank-size rule, based on the visualization in Figure 17.1.) If the estimated coefficient is equal to −1, it is called Zipf's Law (which is approximately the case in India). The city-size distribution does not only follow a Power Law in India in 2020, but also in the USA, Brazil, France, China, Russia, and many other countries in different time periods. Apparently, hitherto poorly understood economic forces play an important role in determining the size distribution of cities, regardless of the economic structure, organization, wealth, and history of a nation. Models that explain the uneven distribution of economic activity have a reality check; does it produce something that resembles a Power Law? Ever since George Kingsley Zipf presented evidence in 1949 on this regularity, scientists have been searching for an adequate explanation.[3]

17.3 Spatial Interaction: Gravity Equation

This section briefly discusses a second spatial regularity, which is related to interactions between economic centers. This spatial interaction is known as the *Gravity Equation*. It can

---

[1] This phenomenon also holds for many other distributions, such as comparative advantage as measured by the Balassa index (see Hinloopen and van Marrewijk 2012).

relate to different types of economic activities, like trade flows, investment flows, and commuting flows, and different types of economic centers, like cities, regions, and countries. Head and Mayer (2014) distinguish between *general* gravity models, *structural* gravity models, and *naïve* gravity models (see van Marrewijk 2017, ch. 16, for an overview). For illustration purposes, this section discusses a naïve gravity model for merchandise export flows from China in 2019. China is the world's largest exporter (see Chapter 6) and exports are measured in billion US dollars. In 2019, the USA was the largest export market for China, with a value of $419 billion. The second largest export market was Hong Kong ($280 billion), followed by Japan ($143 billion), South Korea, Vietnam, Germany, India, Netherlands, and the UK.

The top export markets are a combination of local countries, like Hong Kong, Korea, Japan, and Vietnam, and advanced economies at greater distance, like the USA, Germany, Netherlands, and the UK. Some of China's most important local export markets are relatively small in economic size, like Hong Kong (GDP PPP is $449 billion, in constant 2017 int. $) and Vietnam (GDP PPP is $776 billion). Nonetheless, these markets may be more important for Chinese exports than large economies at greater distance. The GDP of Japan, for example, is 12 times larger than that of Hong Kong, yet Chinese exports to Hong Kong are twice as large as to Japan. In part, this reflects the role of Hong Kong as a trade hub for Chinese exports. In part, this is related to Hong Kong being closer and more closely connected to China than Japan (both in geographical and cultural terms). Similarly, the GDP of Germany is six times larger than that of Vietnam (not a Chinese trade hub), but Chinese exports to Vietnam are 20 percent larger than to Germany because the distance to Vietnam is much lower.

The trade of goods and services from one country to another involves time and effort, and hence costs. Goods have to be physically loaded and unloaded, transported by truck, train, ship, or plane, and packed, insured, traced, etc. before they reach their destination. There they have to be unpacked, checked, assembled, and displayed before they can be sold to the consumer or as intermediate goods to another firm. A distribution and maintenance network has to be established, and the exporter will have to familiarize herself with the (legal) rules and procedures in another country, usually in another language and embedded in a different culture. All of this involves costs, which tend to increase with *distance*. As indicated above, this can be both physical distance, which may be hampered or alleviated by geographical phenomena such as mountain ranges or easy access to good waterways, and political, cultural, or social distance, which also require time and effort before anyone can successfully engage in international business.

The term *transport costs* is used here as a shorthand notation for both types of distance described above. As these costs increase, it will become more difficult to trade goods and services between nations. As a proxy for transport costs, the *weighted distance to China* is used for all Chinese export markets, using the average distance between the main population centers in both countries (provided by CEPII, see Figure 17.2). Also taking into consideration the economic size of the trade partner as

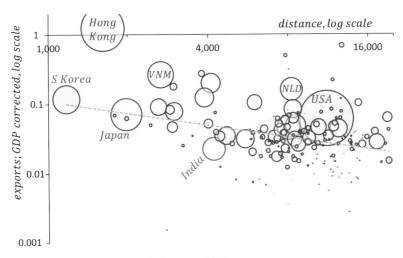

Figure 17.2 China exports and distance, 2019

Sources: Created using data from International Trade Centre (www.intracen.org) for exports (USD billion); World Development Indicators online for GDP PPP (constant 2017 int. $); and CEPII (www.cepii.fr) for distance (km, weighted).

Notes: Bubbles proportional to export flows; 180 countries included; slope of trendline is −0.572; corrected exports calculated as: $ln\,(export_i) - 0.8890 \times ln\,(GDP_i)$.

measured by a country's income level (GDP PPP), a simple regression yields the following result:[4]

$$ln(export) = 1.7336 + 0.8890 \times ln(GDP) - 0.5720 \times ln(distance) \qquad 17.2$$

This simple relationship, which explains 83.4 percent of the variance in Chinese exports, is illustrated with respect to the distance to China in Figure 17.2 – that is, after correcting the size of the exports for the size of the destination market using the estimated coefficient of equation 17.2. The top-left corner reflects countries in the vicinity of China. The slope of the regression line in the figure is −0.5720 as given in equation 17.2. This empirical gravity equation was first applied to international trade between nations by Jan Tinbergen (1962) and holds quite generally for all countries. The relationship is influenced by wealth and development levels, as well as cultural, political, and social organization, and history, such as whether trading partners share a common language or a common border, have a colonial history together, have a trade agreement, and so on.

The gravity model underlines the importance of *distance* in the interaction of economies. This is one of the main objectives of geographical economics; to provide a better understanding of the unequal distribution of economic activity across space and its regularities in terms of distribution pattern and interaction. Zipf's Law illustrates that the spatial distribution of economic activity is characterized by a systematic relationship of large and small locations. But before trying to explain these patterns, it is worthwhile to see whether such patterns matter at all. The next section illustrates the empirical relation between agglomeration and development.

---

[4] The regression is based on 180 Chinese export markets in 2019 for which relevant data is available.

17.4   Agglomeration and Development

Based on differences in wage rates paid in Spanish cities, Chapter 16 briefly reviewed different types of agglomeration economies, namely internal or external, positive or negative, pure or pecuniary, and static or dynamic. Moreover, different sources of agglomeration economies were reviewed (knowledge sharing, market pooling, specialized inputs, natural advantages, home market effects, consumption externalities, and rent-seeking), as well as different mechanisms underlying agglomeration economies (sharing, matching, and learning). This section focuses on the empirical relevance of agglomeration economies for development. Does agglomeration or clustering of economic activities provide some kind of benefit? The answer is: yes.

The elasticities between agglomeration and productivity measures are usually estimated in the range between 0.02 and 0.05, which implies that an average increase of agglomeration with 1 percent raises productivity by 0.02 to 0.05 percent (see Combes and Gobillon 2015 and Ahlfeldt and Pietrostefani 2019 for surveys).[5] The typical specification on which the estimates are based is given in equation 17.3, where w is a measure of wages (or productivity), some measure of agglomeration is used as an explanatory variable, Z are control variables (such as market access [how well a city is connected to other cities] or amenities), ε is an error term, and r is an index of spatial units. These elasticity estimates suggest a strong link between agglomeration/density and productivity/wages.

$$ln(w_r) = \alpha \times ln(agglomeration_r) + \beta \times ln(Z_r) + \varepsilon_t \qquad 17.3$$

Although some consensus exists about the range of outcomes, a meta-study based on 729 estimates from 34 studies reveals that there is large variation under different circumstances, as illustrated in Figure 17.3. According to Melo *et al.* (2009, p. 341), there is "no a priori reason to expect similar estimates of comparable magnitude between sectors, urban areas, or countries." (The causes of variation in the results are partially caused by differences in methods, but Melo *et al.* [2009] also find some evidence of publication bias to publish results confirming positive agglomeration economies.) The relation between agglomeration and productivity has stimulated many governments to start ecouraging agglomeration. Kline and Moretti (2014) analyze a well-known case in the USA in the 1930s. Criscuolo *et al.* (2012) document similar policies for the EU and analyze in detail the composition of regional policies in the UK. Most estimates are for advanced countries in North America and Europe. Evidence for developing countries is more mixed. For the period 2008–12 in Colombia, Duranton (2016) finds, for example, that the elasticity between city size (a measure of agglomeration) and wages is around 5 percent, which is large compared to the findings in advanced countries. Findings for other developing countries, like India and China, are even larger. In developing countries, some factors that

---

[5] The implication is that a doubling of density (employment) increases labor productivity between 1.4 and 3.5 percent (since $100 \times (2^{0.02}-1) = 1.4\%$ and $100 \times (2^{0.05}-1) = 3.5\%$), which is substantial.

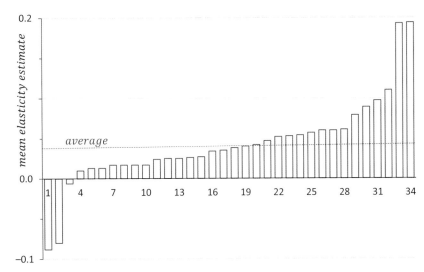

Figure 17.3 Mean estimates of urban agglomeration economies, 34 studies
Source: Based on data from Melo *et al.* 2009, table 1.

are usually less important in advanced countries, like the quality of the road network or the presence of an informal sector in the labor market, might affect the results.

How can we explain the relationship between wages and agglomeration? A good candidate is the geographical economics model developed by Paul Krugman (1991). It includes all the elements that have empirically shown to be important for explaining spatial wages: agglomeration, market access, and transport costs.[6] The next section starts with an instructive example (after reading the example the reader can skip the more technical discussion in section 17.6).

17.5   Geographical Economics: An Example

It is possible to construct a simple example to explain the main structure and implications of the geographical economics approach. Suppose there are two locations (cities, regions, or countries), North and South, and two sectors of production, manufacturing and agriculture. The manufacturing sector produces varieties, that is differentiated products, under internal economies of scale. The cost per unit of output therefore falls as a firm expands its production level. As a result, each firm produces only one variety. A firm can reside either in North or South – that is, a firm has to decide where to produce.

Total demand for each variety of manufactures in this example is exogenous. Assume that each firm sells 4 units to workers in the manufacturing sector and 6 units to the

---

[6] Other explanations are also important in the literature, such as urban economics (see Chapter 16). The Krugman (1991) model is preferred by the authors because it explicitly includes geographical connections, through market access and transportation costs (see Brakman *et al.* 2020 for a survey).

farmers. Total demand for each variety is therefore $10(= 6 + 4)$. The production of agriculture, and hence the demand it generates, is location-specific. Its spatial distribution is exogenously given; assume that 4 units are sold in the North and 2 units in the South. The location of the workers in the manufacturing sector, and hence the 4 units they demand at that location, is not exogenous. The role of the immobile workers is important as they ensure that there is always positive demand in *both* regions, and it implies that mobile workers and firms always have the option to find some demand in all locations. Finally, transport costs between North and South are 1 euro per unit. The firms choose location to minimize transport costs.

We are now able to determine the location decision of each firm. First, we can calculate the regional sales of each firm, given the location of the other firms. In Table 17.1, three (nonexhaustive) possibilities are given; all firms in the North, all firms in the South, or 25 percent of all firms in the North and 75 percent of all firms in the South. Sales in each region are equal to the sales to the workers in manufacturing plus the sales to the farmers. Take, for example, the last row in Table 17.1. The firm sells 5 units in North, namely 4 to the farmers located in North plus $1(= 4 \times 25\%)$ unit to the manufacturing workers located in North. Similarly, the firm sells 5 units in South, namely 2 units to the farmers located in South plus $3(4 \times 75\%)$ units to the manufacturing workers located in South.

Second, using Table 17.1, a decision table can be constructed by calculating transport costs as a function of the firm's location decision given the location of the other firms. Suppose, for example, that all firms are located in North. Table 17.2 indicates that transport costs for a firm locating in South will then be 8 euros, namely 4 for sales to the farmers in North and 4 for sales to all workers in manufacturing located in North (abstracting from sales to its own workers). Similarly, if the firm would locate in North, transport costs would be only 2 for the sales to the farmers in the South. Since transport costs are minimized by locating in the North if all other firms are located in North, the firm decides to also locate production in North. As Table 17.2 shows (second row), a firm will locate in South if all other firms are also located there, whereas (last row) the firm is indifferent between locating in North or South (since transport costs are the same if the firm locates in either region) if 25 percent of the firms are located in North and 75 percent in South.

On the basis of this example, a few distinctive characteristics of the geographical economics approach can be illustrated. The remainder of this chapter returns to each of these observations.

Table 17.1. Geography of sales

	Sales in North	Sales in South	Total Sales
All firms in North	$4 + 4 = 8$	$0 + 2 = 2$	10
All firms in South	$0 + 4 = 4$	$4 + 2 = 6$	10
25% firms in North 75% firms in South	$1 + 4 = 5$	$3 + 2 = 5$	10

Table 17.2. Transport costs

	If location in North	If location in South
All firms in North	0 + 2 = **2** (to farmers in South)	4 + 4 = 8 (to workers & farmers in North)
All firms in South	4 + 2 = 6 (to workers & farmers in South)	0 + 4 = **4** (to farmers in North)
25% firms in North 75% firms in South	3 + 2 = 5 (to workers & farmers in South)	1 + 4 = 5 (to workers & farmers in North)

First, the concept of *cumulative causation*. If a location has attracted more firms than the other location, a new firm has an incentive to locate where the other firms are. Take the first row in Table 17.2. If all firms are located in North, a firm, minimizing transport costs, should also locate there to minimize transport costs. Similarly, for the second row in Table 17.2, the firm will locate in South.

Second, Table 17.2 illustrates the existence of *multiple equilibria*. Agglomeration of all firms in either North or South is an equilibrium. However, we cannot determine beforehand where agglomeration will occur. This depends on initial conditions, that is, the previous location decisions of other firms.

Third, an equilibrium might be *stable or unstable*. The bold entries in Table 17.2 are both stable equilibria; if a single firm decides to relocate, this decision would not influence the location decisions of the other firms. The last row in Table 17.2 describes an unstable equilibrium. If a single firm decides to relocate, the new location will immediately become more attractive for all other firms. This will trigger a snowball effect: all firms will follow the pioneer. In this example, agglomeration is a stable equilibrium, while spreading across locations is not.

Fourth, note that a stable equilibrium can be *nonoptimal*. If all firms are located in North, transport costs are only 2. If all firms are located in South, transport costs are 4 (see the bold entries in Table 17.2). Thus, transport costs for the economy as a whole are minimized if all firms agglomerate in North, whereas agglomeration in South is a stable equilibrium.

Fifth, the tables illustrate the *interaction of agglomeration and trade flows*. With complete agglomeration – that is, all manufactures are produced in a single region – trade between regions will be of the inter-industry type (food for manufactures). In fact, this equilibrium also reflects the so-called *home-market* effect; the combination of economies of scale and transport costs is responsible for the clustering of all footloose activity in a single location. Due to this combination, transport costs can be minimized. The large region ends up with a large market for manufacturing goods, which can be sold without incurring transport costs. The consequence is that this region becomes the exporter of manufactured goods; large regions tend to become exporters of those goods for which they have a large local market, hence the term *home-market effect*. If the manufacturing industry is located in both regions, as described by the last rows in the tables, trade will also be of the intra-industry type.

Besides trading manufactured goods for agricultural products, different varieties of the differentiated manufactured products will be traded between both regions.

17.6   Geographical Development Economics

The example in section 17.5 already explains a part of the two regularities already discussed: Zipf's Law and the gravity model. Zipf's Law is a regularity between large and small agglomerations; the example shows how large and small locations follow by making a few simple assumptions regarding the location of two types of workers and transport costs. In an abstract way, the key characteristic of the gravity model is also present; minimization of transport costs implies that firms like to be near the large(st) markets. That clustering can have welfare consequences is also present in the example; the bold entries may describe the welfare-maximizing distribution of economic activity.

The example in section 17.5 is useful as it illustrates some important aspects of geographical economics. But it is just an example and it is prudent to highlight five missing aspects.

First, the interaction of transport costs, price-setting behavior, and location choice is missing. We simply assume that the demand each firm faces is given and independent of price-setting behavior and transport costs. In fact, prices are completely lacking in the example. There is no analysis of the market structure. In reality, prices, wages, and transport costs will determine the purchasing power of consumers. This interaction drives the location decisions of consumers and producers.

Second, using a two-region model ignores the importance of market access. With more locations, each region is surrounded by other regions that can be served by exports. By weighing the size of all of these regions by distance, we get an impression of the market access of a location. A small location can be attractive if it is surrounded by large and nearby markets; this location has good market access and can be attractive despite its small size.

Third, it is a partial equilibrium model, in the sense that firms do not worry about the necessary labor; wherever they decide to locate labor availability is not the problem. It turns out that assumptions with respect to functioning of the labor market are important. Scale economies and transport costs are important forces. The most important difference is that in this example firms can locate in either region. Consequently, the example gives rise to agglomeration and multiple equilibria.

Fourth, the size of a location matters also in another respect. Figure 17.3 shows that density stimulates income per capita and growth. This phenomenon is called agglomeration economies. It is not only the size of the local market that is important, but also so-called spillovers. Proximity to other people, workers, and firms can make individual workers and firms more productive. The mechanisms that affect productivity are: *sharing, matching, and learning.* Sharing refers to indivisibilities – a hospital, for example, is only economically feasible in large cities. Matching refers to the quality of a match between worker and employer in labor market models, where large cities offer a higher probability of a successful match. Learning refers to the need for face-to-face contact, where large cities with more contacts lead to a higher quality of learning (see Chapter 16 and the survey on modeling, measuring, and estimating agglomeration economies by Combes and Gobillon 2015).

Fifth, the model has a very abstract form of geography. This is deliberate. Krugman (1991) developed a model that results in agglomeration without introducing a possible outcome beforehand. Assuming that a country has one international port of access benefits that location by assumption. The abstract model is interesting because it does not assume that one location is preferred because of some natural geographical characteristic, and still the final equilibrium is characterized by a core-periphery outcome. In reality, these geographical features *are* important.

There are two important elements of geography. The first is geography that is determined by natural characteristics of space. One can think of navigable waterways, mountains, natural harbors, climate, being landlocked, and other features like these that will most likely affect the spatial distribution of economic activity over space. This is what is called *first nature* geography. The second is geography that is initiated by economic behavior itself. This is called *second nature* geography.

The example in section 17.5 shows that the desire to minimize transportation costs can lead to core-periphery outcomes. Transport costs themselves can also be influenced by investing in infrastructure. In practice, both types of geography will shape the spatial structure of economies. Figure 17.2, for example, shows the relationship between Chinese exports and distance to trade partners. Cost minimization is an important factor, which is illustrated by the fact that countries close to China are more important for Chinese exports than countries that are further away. The special position of Hong Kong is most likely a combination of first and second nature geography. The seaside location offers good access to the Chinese market. So, for large parts of China, exporting through Hong Kong is an obvious route. Investments in infrastructure in the international port of Hong Kong, combined with excellent road, rail, and air connections to China, have made Hong Kong more than proportionally important as an export partner for China, as the relatively large size of the Hong Kong bubble in Figure 17.2 illustrates.

Section 17.9 summarizes the main implications of the various geographical economics models and relates these to the historical processes of inequality and agglomeration (see Chapters 10 and 16) through falling transport and interactions costs. The next two sections take a closer look at first and second nature geography. Note that these two faces of geography are often difficult to distinguish from each other in practice.

17.7 First Nature Geography: Distance in Development

Cost minimization is important in the spatial distribution of economic activity. In order to minimize costs, clustering is important, as the example in section 17.5 illustrates. The large market size that results from clustering is beneficial to firms, but it depends on the behavior of all other firms. In this sense, it is an external effect. This is not the end of the story.

Since agglomeration economies cannot be directly observed, they must be approximated to assess their empirical relevance. An often-used *catch-all* concept that has been applied in empirical research related to city size is the density of a location. This is depicted in Figure 17.3, where most of the studies in the survey use population density as a key measure. The idea is, the higher the population density, the more productive a location becomes because of agglomeration economies. In general, as Combes and Gobillon (2015, p. 2) conclude, agglomeration economies are the "effect that increases firms' and workers' income when the size of the local economy grows."

The conclusion is that clustering of economic activity is beneficial, but also that this depends on the size of transportation costs. If a country is characterized by large rural communities and high transportation costs firms are tempted to locate near local markets and the country foregoes on agglomeration economies. This can be illustrated by extending the example from section 17.5 by adding an additional line with two large agricultural regions; no matter where firms locate, if transportation costs are high and the manufacturing sector is small compared to the immobile agricultural sector, high transportation costs cannot be avoided.

17.7.1   Transport Costs

The question now is what determines the size of transportation costs and whether these are high in developing countries compared to advanced countries, as is often assumed to be the case. So what about first nature geography in developing countries? Box 17.1 addresses the relevance of transport costs in general. Atkin and Donaldson (2015) address this question in more detail when they analyze the size of within-country trade costs that separate consumers in remote locations from (global) markets. In their study, Ethiopia and Nigeria are compared to the USA. Using detailed price information from traders for individual products at the origin and destination, they estimate transportation costs within countries. Their methodology avoids common problems in these types of studies. First, the data should refer to individual products. Using aggregate product definitions introduces possible unobserved quality differences between origin and destination because the aggregate product has changed over distance. Also, using aggregate product definitions obscures well-defined origins and destinations of products (the aggregate might refer to different locations). Most importantly, price-setting behavior might bias estimates of transportation costs. For example, sellers might increase mark-ups in remote locations because competition is largely absent and they are able to charge a high price. In these cases, the price difference of a product between the origin and destination reflects price-setting behavior rather than transportation costs. Intra-national transportation costs depend on distance, but also on intra-national borders delineated by, for example, road blocks. Additional costs could also reflect costs that are caused by within-country differences in language or ethnicity.

Starting with price information for a selection of individual products at the origin, literally at the factory door, and prices that are charged for those products at the destination, the methodology of Atkin and Donaldson (2015) separates price-setting behavior

BOX 17.1 **THE RELEVANCE OF TRANSPORT COSTS**

Transport costs are essential in geographical economics. Without transport costs there is no geography, and the whole exercise of transforming economics models into geographical economics models becomes pointless or academic. Adam Smith already noted the importance of locations near the coast: "... so, it is upon the sea-coast, and along the banks of navigable rivers, that industry of every kind naturally begins to sub-divide and improve itself, and it is frequently not till a long time after that those improvements extend themselves to the inland part of the country" (Adam Smith cited in Radelet and Sachs 1998). Redding and Turner (2015), in general, observe that over a long period of time transportation costs have declined, but that these costs remain substantial, especially the costs of moving people around, such that transport costs still affect the location of economic activity.

Anderson and van Wincoop (2004, pp. 691–2) note that transport costs involve more than just transportation; policy barriers (tariffs and nontariff barriers), information costs, contract enforcement costs, costs associated with the use of different currencies, legal and regulatory costs, and local distribution costs (wholesale and retail). Their rough "representative" estimate for industrialized countries is that total trade costs are about 170 percent of their ad valorem tax equivalent. This number breaks down as follows: 21 percent transportation, 44 percent border-related trade barriers, and 55 percent retail and wholesale distribution costs $(1 + 1.7 = 1.21 \times 1.44 \times 1.55)$.

Now that we have seen that transport costs between and within countries are substantial, we might ask whether or not they matter. The answer is, they do. McCallum (1995), finds that Canadian provinces trade more than 20 times the volume of trade with one another than they trade with similar counterparts in the USA. This number is not undisputed; consistent estimates reduce the value of 20 to about 10, which is still high. In general, borders have a large impact on trade costs (see for a discussion on border effects Feenstra 2016 and Head and Mayer 2014). A meta-study that looks at all other studies estimating the effects of trade costs concludes that the "estimated negative impact of distance on trade rose around the middle of the [20th] century and has remained persistently high since then. This result holds even after controlling for many important differences in samples and methods" (Disdier and Head 2008, p. 37).

from transportation costs. Once the data are cleaned from price-setting effects it turns out that intra-national trade costs in Ethiopia and Nigeria are four to five times *higher* than in the USA. The least remote locations in the sample are 50 miles away from the source of production and the most distant locations some 500 miles away from the origin of production. The rough terrain in these countries contributes to the high transport costs. A further possible explanation for the differences between the countries is that the road density and road quality is higher in the USA compared to Ethiopia and Nigeria. Correcting for this only marginally lowers the difference in transportation costs; transportation costs are still three to five times higher in Ethiopia and Nigeria compared to the USA. So, the influence of the rough geography seems an important explanation for the high transport costs.

Other factors that might explain the differences are: old fuel-inefficient truck fleets requiring frequent repairs; poor logistics; long waiting times for loading and unloading trucks; and frequent checkpoints, which sometimes require bribes. Given all these factors, it is safe to conclude that transportation costs for Ethiopia and Nigeria, compared to the USA, are indeed much higher. Note, however, that these factors are mostly man-made. The next section will discuss this in more detail.

What are the consequences? Consumers who live in remote places pay high transport costs. One of the consequences is that participating in globalization becomes difficult. Imported goods are expensive and some goods will not be imported at all in the remote places because they are too expensive. This can negatively affect growth rates in remote locations. Also, the relatively high import costs reduce profits and might hamper market entries of new firms, which reduces competition and raises relative prices. As the example in section 17.5 shows, this could lead to cumulative causation; people migrating toward more central locations, but as Chapter 15 discussed, this can also result in unemployment in the large and growing urban centers.

It is important to realize the income consequences of barriers to trade, which are substantial. Bosker and Garretsen (2012) estimate the relevance of reductions in distance for income per worker and hence for economic development. Table 17.3 shows the results of six *policy experiments* on the change in income per worker (in percent) via changes in access to neighboring countries. Halving distances to all trade partners (a rough proxy for improving the countries' connectivity through cross-border infrastructure projects or more effective border procedures) results in the largest improvements in income per worker, raising it by about 6 percent. Next comes alleviating a landlocked country's

Table 17.3. Policy experiments and income per worker for five African countries

Change in income per worker (percent) as a result of policy experiment

Experiment	1	2	3	4	5	6
Country	no longer landlocked	no longer island	infrastructure +1 s.d.	all distances halved	RFTA with S. Africa	SSA free trade zone
Cape Verde	–	2.76	4.14	6.05	0.16	1.14
Botswana	4.88	–	4.14	6.05	–	0.08
Cen. Afr. Rep.	4.88	–	4.14	6.05	0.04	0.21
Ethiopia	4.88	–	4.14	6.05	–	0.10
Sudan	–	–	4.14	6.05	–	0.16

The effect on income per worker is calculated by multiplying the change in the market access per SSA country by the coefficient on SSA market access as reported in column (8) of table 3 in Bosker and Garretsen 2012.

burden of having no direct access to the coast (raising incomes by almost 5 percent), followed by a 4 percent increase in income per worker as a result of a one standard deviation improvement in a country's infrastructure (which corresponds, for example, to upgrading Ethiopia's infrastructure to resemble that in Botswana). With a resulting increase of 2.8 percent on income, alleviating the remoteness of an island country has the smallest effect.

Columns 5 and 6 of the table show the effects of a newly established regional free trade agreement (RFTA). These are also positive, but much smaller compared to the other policy experiments. Not surprisingly, this effect is larger the larger the number of new partner countries in the RFTA (compare column 5 to 6, or the impact of the SSA-wide free trade zone for Cape Verde to that for Botswana; an SSA free trade zone would more than triple the number of RFTA partners for Cape Verde, whereas "only" doubling it for Botswana).

17.7.2 Slaves, Terrain, and Natural Disasters

Up to this point, this chapter has stressed the link between first nature geography and transportation barriers. First nature geography can also have other complicated (development) consequences. Alsan (2015), for example, explains the low population density in Africa by the prevalence of the tsetse fly in certain areas. This fly transmits a parasite that causes sleeping sickness in humans and nagana in domesticated animals. In areas where the fly was abundant, technological advances in agriculture were lagging behind, resulting in lower population density and fewer urban centers. This was also because in regions where the tsetse fly was prevalent plough agriculture did not develop and as a consequence in these places slaves were more likely to be used in the work force.

Slave trade itself also has consequences. Dalton and Leung (2014), for instance, find that mostly males were engaged as slaves in the transatlantic slave trade, and were shipped to the Americas. This resulted in a shortage of males in West Africa, which to some extent could explain why polygamy is more widespread in West Africa. This bias is not present in East Africa; the Indian Ocean slave trade did not have a male bias. Climate also plays a role. Fenske and Kala (2015) observe that the cooler temperatures near slave-trading ports stimulated slave exports from those ports. The impact of slave trade itself is also substantial. In a seminal study, Nunn (2008) analyzes the long-term consequences of the slave trade on development in Africa. Based on information on a wide range of sources – plantation inventories, marriage records, death records, slave runaway notices – he makes an estimate of the total number of slaves and finds that the regions from which the largest number of slaves were taken are currently the poorest regions. The study also looks at causality; did poor regions opt into slave trade, or did regions become poor because of the slave trade? Using both descriptive evidence and instrumental variables, his conclusion is that the slave trade did have a significant negative influence on the economic development within Africa; the causality runs from slave trade to economic development. Nunn and Puga (2012) show that other complexities can arise. Terrain ruggedness in general increases barriers to trade. It is more difficult to build roads, bridges, and railroads. Within Africa, however, Nunn and Puga observe that greater ruggedness is correlated with higher income instead of lower income. Africa's history with slave trade explains this to some extent.

First nature geography can also affect development through floods. Chaney (2013) documents how abnormal Nile flooding shocks can have consequences for governance and development. Flooding causes sudden drops in agricultural output and sharp price increases of foodstuffs. Food price increases could lead to riots. In these flood-caused periods of social unrest, the political power of religious leaders could increase relative to the power of military leaders and the sovereign. The reason is that political leaders turned to religious leaders to preserve peace. Consistent with this line of reasoning, Chaney (2013) shows that abnormal floods resulted in higher food prices, more social unrest, fewer changes in religious leadership, and more construction of religious buildings. Allocating resources to religious structures can have an impact on economic development because resources are taken away from potentially more productive uses.

Droughts can also have long-term consequences. Hornbeck (2012) studies the economic effects of the drought in the 1930s in the USA – the Dust Bowl. The strong winds in combination with the long period of droughts eroded the topsoil of the American Plains. Land prices fell and stimulated out-migration and diverted immigration. The migrants relocated at coastal areas which became more dense. The demographic consequences are still felt today.

Studies such as those indicated above suggest that first nature geography can have substantial consequences on development, but also that its impact is felt through, sometimes, unexpected channels.

17.8   Second Nature Geography: Man-Made Barriers

Rough geography, such as deserts and mountains in combination with large distances, are important explanations for high barriers to trade. First nature geography is important. What about second nature geography? As concluded in section 17.6, the stylized example of section 17.5 ignores market access, which relates a location to its surroundings through exports. By correcting the size of the surrounding markets for distance, we can calculate total relevant market access of a location; the closer a location is to large markets, the higher its market access. A small location can be attractive if it is surrounded by large and nearby markets; this location has good market access and can be attractive despite its small size.

Brakman, Garretsen, and van Marrewijk (2020) provide a survey of the empirical literature on the effects of (changes in) market access. In general, high wages or income per capita is correlated with market access. A part of transport costs is first nature, but to an important extent changes in market access are the result of policy decisions that enhance access to interesting markets. Below are some examples to illustrate the effects of these *man-made* barriers to trade.

17.8.1   The Westerscheldetunnel

The Dutch government decided to improve access to a more peripheral area in the Netherlands by building the Westerscheldetunnel (Western Scheldt Tunnel) in 2003. Before the tunnel was opened, ferry services connected *Zeeuws-Vlaanderen* and *Midden-Zeeland* (see Figure 17.4). The ferry services stopped operating on the day the tunnel was opened, dramatically reducing travel time and increasing market access. The study of Hoogendoorn *et al.* (2017) estimates how the tunnel affected housing prices at both of its ends. Housing prices can be viewed as a proxy of the attractiveness of locations and as such a signal of whether the tunnel has made concentration of economic activity profitable near the tunnel and whether these locations have become more attractive because of the new connection. The findings suggest that on average a 1 percent increase in accessibility results in a 0.8 percent increase in housing prices. The Hoogendoorn *et al.* analysis shows that:

- A new connection indeed increases accessibility of the locations at both ends of the new tunnel, which confirms the importance of market access.
- For policymakers, it is important not to analyze these policy initiatives in isolation. The increase of attractiveness of locations at the ends of a new connection is at the expense of locations that have, as a result, become relatively more peripheral. This is a serious warning for policymakers who promote a project for their own region. An important question is always: do other regions possibly suffer from such a project and what are the net benefits on a larger scale?

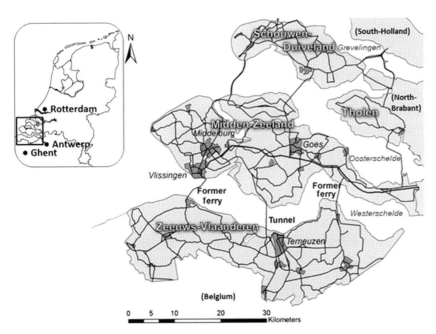

Figure 17.4 The Westerschelde Tunnel in the Netherlands
Source: Hoogendoorn *et al.* 2017.

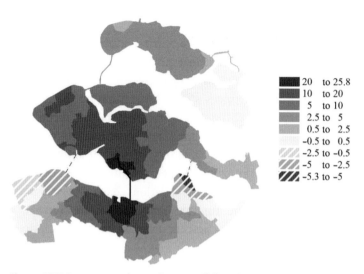

Figure 17.5 Percentage change in accessibility due to the Westerschelde Tunnel
Source: Hoogendoorn *et al.* 2017.
Note: Accessibility is defined as the number of jobs that are accessible, weighted by a distance decay function.

Importantly, in the regions that experienced a decline in accessibility (former ferry locations; see Figure 17.5), this finding implies a *decline* of housing prices.

17.8.2 Somali Pirates

The second, admittedly somewhat extreme, example illustrates the barriers to trade that are the consequence of human behavior: piracy. The return of old-fashioned piracy in some locations of the world is striking. The International Maritime Bureau (IMB), for example, points out that piracy has occurred increasingly frequently since the new millennium, which forces liner-shipping companies to take into consideration the probability of becoming a target for this profitable underground "business" run by specialized criminal organizations. Figure 17.6 illustrates the range of operations in 2011 for the most prominent Somali pirates, who have become a major threat for the Europe–Asia trade route. These pirates started with small-scale operations just off the coast of Haradeere (with a maximum range of about 165 nautical miles in 2005), but expanded quickly to cover the northeast coast of Africa up to the Mozambique Channel, the Sea of Aden, into the Red Sea, and into the Gulf of Oman (with a maximum range of about 1,300 nautical miles in 2011).

To estimate the impact of Somali piracy on international trade flows and welfare, Berden (2011) uses the Global Simulation Model (GSIM, a global partial equilibrium model developed by Francois and Hall 1997). Somali pirates have an economic effect in the model because of higher insurance premiums for vessels sailing through the affected area (in 2008, for example, they were 1,000 percent higher than five years earlier), expenses made for paying ransom for sailors held hostage, costs for keeping naval forces in the area to patrol, costs for legal prosecution, costs for equipping vessels with security on board

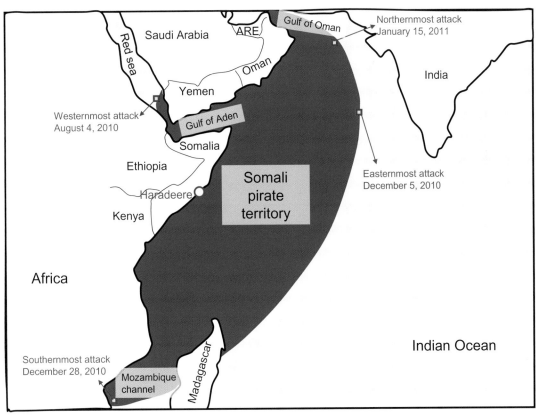

Figure 17.6 Somali pirate territory, 2011
Source: Based on BBC News 2011.

(weapons or armed guards), and additional costs from diverging routes away from the affected area. Two scenarios are analyzed here and it can be concluded that the pirate activities lead to substantial trade and welfare costs, particularly for Europe, China, and Japan. In the first scenario, trade costs increase by 10 percent as a result of the piracy factors mentioned above (a low estimate). In the second scenario, trade costs increase by 20 percent (a more likely case).

Figure 17.7 illustrates the total welfare loss for these two scenarios for different countries or regions (in billion US dollars). Piracy clearly has large negative welfare effects, particularly for the European Union (EU) and China, with a loss of $193 and $133 billion, respectively, in the 20 percent scenario. Brazil is also negatively affected as part of its iron ore exports to Asia pass through the affected area. Table 17.4 depicts the effect of Somali piracy on changes in maritime trade flows. Evidently, trade is in part diverted to other routes (which flourish), while the countries with heavy trade routes through the Somali area are hurt most. EU trade, for example, shifts away from Asia toward Brazil and the Rest of the World (the USA). For China, trade within Asia and to Australia gets a boost, while trade to Europe, the Middle East, and Brazil is diminishing. Saudi Arabia and the United Arab Emirates (ARE) are hurt

Table 17.4. Shipping trade effects of Somali piracy for selected countries (% change)

From	EU	CHN	JPN	BRA	AUS	SAU	ARE	L-AF	L-AS	ROW
					Destination					
EU	0	−36	−43	48	−46	−22	−26	15	−40	9
CHN	−36	0	39	−42	35	−30	−33	−28	48	2
JPN	−42	41	0	−50	27	−32	−35	−35	39	−5
BRA	44	−3	−57	0	25	−36	−39	−37	−55	−7
AUS	−45	37	27	32	0	−37	−40	−39	35	−8
SAU	0	−7	−12	−9	−17	0	−1	7	−11	−7
ARE	0	−7	−12	−8	−16	3	0	8	−10	−7
L-AF	14	−38	−47	−43	−51	−26	−28	71	−41	7
L-AS	−44	44	33	−54	29	−38	−40	−35	42	−5
ROW	7	1	−9	−3	−12	14	10	16	−3	−3

Source: Berden 2011.

Notes: Shaded cells indicate declining trade flows; EU = European Union (27), CHN = China, JPN = Japan, BRA = Brazil, AUS = Australia, SAU = Saudi Arabia, ARE = United Arab Emirates, L-AF = LDCs Africa, L-AS = LDCs Asia, ROW = Rest of World.

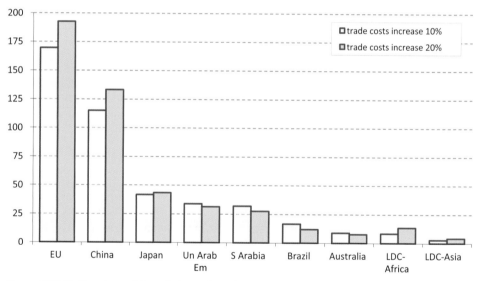

Figure 17.7 Welfare loss of Somali piracy for selected countries (USD billion)
Source: van Marrewijk 2017, figure 16.14, based on data from Berden 2011.

badly since all their seaborne trade passes through the affected area. Clearly, the personal gains to some pirates on the African east coast (the few who get away with it) are at the expense of significant global welfare losses and diverging, suboptimal transport routes.

17.8.3 Other Examples

Piracy is the consequence of human behavior that determines second nature geography; it increases barriers to trade. This is an extreme example that falls into the class of war and conflict. Another telling example is the French Revolution, which took place in 1789 and introduced new Enlightenment values of equality and citizen rights in France. In 1792, the new republic declared war on Austria and its allies, including Prussia. Acemoglu *et al.* (2011) show, for the period between 1700 and 1900, that occupied regions that were subject to institutional reforms inspired by the new French values and experienced longer periods of French occupation between 1793 and 1815 grew faster. Furthermore, urbanization rates were higher in these regions, thus stimulating further spillover effects.

Other examples of man-made factors that determine the spatial distribution of economic activity are related to institutions. In a seminal paper, Rodrik, Subramanian, and Trebbi (2004), for instance, confidently conclude that *institutions rule* (see also Chapters 4 and 8). This line of reasoning can also be found in Easterly and Levine (2003) and Acemoglu, Johnson, and Robinson (2001). A popular version of the importance of institutions can be found in the book *Why Nations Fail*, by Daron Acemoglu and James Robinson (2012), who argue that institutions are key to economic development and that geography only matters if it leaves an imprint on present-day institutions and thereby on economic development.

Figure 17.8 illustrates the correlation between the quality of institutions for a sample of 149 countries. Institutions are measured by the *rule of law*, while contiguity is used to define a country's neighbors. Countries below the diagonal line (such as South Korea) have better own institutions than their neighbors (North Korea). Countries above the diagonal line (such as Yemen) have worse institutions than their neighbors (Oman and Saudi

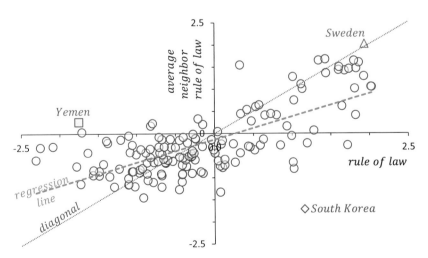

Figure 17.8 Rule of Law; own versus neighbor countries, 2017
Source: World Bank governance data.
Notes: Rule of law ranges from −2.50 (worst) to +2.50 (best); neighbor rule of law based on average for contiguous neighbors using cepii data (cepii.fr); 149 countries included.

Arabia). Countries close to the diagonal line (like Sweden) have similar institutions to their neighbors (Finland and Norway). Bosker and Garretsen (2009) find that (neighboring) institutions and easy access to foreign markets are both important to explain income per capita, but when included together in a single estimation, (neighboring) institutions dominate access to foreign markets as the most important explanation for income per capita.

The studies mentioned above suggest, as with the examples with respect to first nature geography in the previous section, that changes in second nature geography can have substantial consequences on development, but also that its impact is felt through, sometimes, unexpected channels. It seems fair to conclude that market access, institutions, and (physical) geography are important to explain development processes.

17.9   Geography, Transport Costs, and History

There are different types of geographical economics models. Krugman's original model is based on labor mobility between locations. This seems to be a reasonable assumption for analyzing regions or cities within a country, where labor mobility is high and migration restrictions are low (or within a group of countries, such as the European Union, where migration restrictions are low). It seems less suitable, however, to analyze international interactions where migration restrictions are high. There are three main types of other geographical economics models which may be more suitable in an international context (see Brakman *et al.* 2020, ch. 8). There is a *solvable* model based on different factors of production, one of which is mobile between locations (human capital) and one of which is not (less-skilled labor). There is an *intermediate goods* model based on upstream and downstream linkages (see also Chapter 18) without any labor mobility between locations. Finally, there is a *generalized* model incorporating both the Krugman approach and the intermediate goods model as special cases. Fortunately, the main implications of all these models in terms of the relationship between transport costs and agglomeration is similar. Subsection 17.9.1 summarizes these main implications and subsection 17.9.2 connects this to transport costs and history.

17.9.1   Main Implications: Tomahawk Diagram

The main implications of geographical economics models focus on the connection between transport costs and agglomeration of economic activity. For two locations i (labeled 1 and 2) without any inherent geographical advantage for either location, this connection can be summarized in a so-called *Tomahawk diagram*. An example of this is given in Figure 17.9, based on the intermediate goods model. Transport costs are depicted on the horizontal axis using Samuelson's (1952) *iceberg* concept, which assumes that if T goods are shipped only 1 unit arrives at the destination. The fraction $T - 1$ that "melts away" in transit represents transport costs; the higher T, the higher the transport costs, while $T = 1$ means there are no

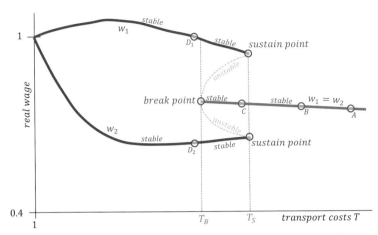

Figure 17.9 Tomahawk diagram example; real wages in an intermediate goods model
Source: Based on Krugman and Venables 1995.
Note: w_i is real wage in location i.

transport costs at all. This method is attractive because we do not have to model a separate transport sector. The vertical axis depicts an *implication* of agglomeration for the model, namely the real wage in location i. The implications can be summarized in three points.

1. Note that transport costs rise in Figure 17.9 if we go from left to right. If transport costs are *high* (above the *sustain* point T_S), we observe only one (solid) line in the figure where $w_1 = w_2$, hence the real wage is the same in the two locations. This occurs because with extremely high transport costs manufacturing goods have to be essentially locally produced, leading to *spreading* of economic activity as the only stable equilibrium, as indicated in the figure. As a result, with high transport costs the two locations are each other's mirror image and the real wage is the same.

2. If transport costs are *low* (below the *break* point T_B), we observe two (solid) lines in the figure with $w_1 > w_2$, hence the real wage is higher in one location than the other. This occurs because with extremely low transport costs it is possible to produce all manufactures in one location (the *core*, with high real wage) and efficiently serve the other market (the *periphery*, with low real wage) at low transport costs. As a result, with low transport costs a core-periphery economic outcome occurs, with high real wages in the core and low real wages in the periphery.

3. With *intermediate* transport costs (in between the break point T_B and the sustain point T_S), we observe three (solid) lines, where one is associated with the core (w_1), one is associated with the periphery (w_2), and one is associated with the spreading equilibrium $(w_1 = w_2)$. This occurs because there are two types of stable equilibria; the spreading equilibrium is stable, as is the core-periphery equilibrium. Which outcome occurs depends on initial conditions, or on the historical path followed by the economy (*hysteresis*, see below).

In short, high transport costs lead to the spreading of economic activity (point 1), low transport costs lead to agglomeration of economic activity in one location (point 2), and intermediate transport costs lead to multiple types of stable equilibria (in which either spreading or agglomeration can occur (point 3). These main implications can be observed in all types of geographical economics models. There is one stable equilibrium (spreading) if transport costs are high, there are two stable equilibria if transport costs are low (the core in location 1, as in Figure 17.9, *or* the core in location 2), and there are three stable equilibria for intermediate transport costs (spreading, core in 1, or core in 2). The term *break point* is used for the lowest transport costs for which spreading is stable and the term *sustain point* is used for the highest transport costs for which a core-periphery structure is stable. There are also unstable equilibria. In the figure, these are indicated for intermediate transport costs by dashed lines. For other transport levels they are not indicated to avoid cluttering the diagram.

17.9.2   Transport Costs and History

The main implications as summarized in the Tomahawk diagram can be connected to historical developments. Assume that transport (and interaction) costs have usually declined throughout history. Long ago, therefore, transport costs were very high and we are at the extreme right of Figure 17.9. Because of the very high transport costs manufacturing must essentially be locally produced and spreading of economic activity is the only stable equilibrium, so the equilibrium occurs at point *A*. The real wage rate is the same in locations 1 and 2.

Over the course of time (hundreds of years), transport costs decline. The question arises: what happens in terms of the spatial equilibrium? The answer is: (almost) nothing. Transport costs are lower, but remain high, and spreading of economic activity is still the only stable equilibrium. This is represented by point *B* in Figure 17.9, where the real wage is still the same in locations 1 and 2. The spatial distribution does not change, but the lowering of transport costs does result in higher real wages for both locations as real wages are higher in point *B* than in point *A*.

The process of falling transport costs continues for hundreds of years. All this time, spreading of economic activity remains a stable spatial equilibrium and the only real consequence we observe is slowly rising real wages. At some point in time, we will pass the sustain point threshold, as indicated by point *C* in Figure 17.9. We are now in the realm of intermediate transport costs with multiple stable equilibria and the question arises: what will happen to the spatial equilibrium? The answer is: nothing! The equilibrium is determined by *hysteresis* – that is, the path the economy follows over time (*path-dependency*). The spreading equilibrium was stable and remains stable so the economy just follows along its trajectory from point *A* to point *B* and point *C*. The real wages are the same in the two locations and continue to rise slowly over time.

As we continue along this trajectory and start to approach the break point, we move into the region where spreading of economic activity is no longer a stable equilibrium, only a core-periphery structure is spatially stable. Something drastic, a so-called *catastrophe*, must happen. Either location 1 becomes the core and location 2 becomes the periphery, or the other way around. Based on the structure of the model, there is no reason to suggest that one location is more likely to become the core than the other. Any small deviation in one direction, say toward location 1, will be self-reinforcing to ensure that location 1 becomes the core and location 2 becomes the periphery. The consequences, however, are substantial as the real wage in location 1 rises enormously (see point D_1 in the figure) and in location 2 falls drastically (see point D_2 in the figure). As a result, income inequality rises fast.

Based on Figure 17.9, Krugman and Venables (1995) argue that the process depicted by the gradual lowering of transport costs T can be used to understand the globalization process from the late nineteenth century until the end of the twentieth century (they call it "history of the world, part I"). In the two-location model, location 1 is the *North* (let's say the OECD countries) and location 2 is the *South* (the developing countries). High transport costs (low levels of economic integration) are combined with real wage equalization. When economic integration really takes off, one region (North) becomes the core region and real wages start to differ between North and South. This so-called *Great Divergence* is what happened during the nineteenth and a large part of the twentieth centuries. Note that as transport costs continue to fall in Figure 17.9, real wages become more equal again. With ongoing integration (think of post-1990 globalization), real wages start to converge (see also Crafts and Venables 2003 and Baldwin 2006). Baldwin (2016) has dubbed the period post-1990 (with the fall of the Berlin Wall in 1989, the entry of China and India into the world economy, and the ICT revolution that enabled the international fragmentation of manufacturing production) as the period of *The Great Convergence.*

Redding and Venables (2004) give some *empirical* evidence on the relevance of the geographical economics approach to "explain" (changes in) economic development across countries. They estimate an equilibrium wage equation where the real market potential is approximated with a gravity trade model and where income per capita is the dependent variable. The distance of countries to markets where they sell and the distance from countries which supply intermediates are crucial determinants for explaining cross-country income differentials. The further away final markets and suppliers of the intermediate products, the lower the income levels in the countries concerned.

Redding and Venables (2004) give a simple example to illustrate the potential impact of transport costs in such a model. They try to answer the *what-if* question: what happens to economic development when transport costs change? If the prices of all goods are set on the world market and transport costs are borne by the producing country, and if intermediates account for 50 percent of the total value, the effects of small changes in transport costs turn out to be large. Transport costs of 10 percent on both final products and intermediate products reduce the value-added by 30 percent. Transport costs of 20 percent reduce value-added by 60 percent. This example makes intuitively clear why Redding and Venables (2004) are able to explain more than 70 percent of cross-variation in income per capita.

17.10   Conclusions

Chapter 15 touched upon geographical considerations in a rudimentary fashion. It discussed urban–rural relations without explicitly dealing with geography. The unequal distribution of economic activity (see Chapter 16) and the associated rising inequality in income distribution (see Chapter 10) is an important empirical regularity that draws much attention. The unequal spatial distribution of people and economic activity is also remarkably regular, both in terms of a systematic pattern across space with respect to city sizes (Zipf's Law) and in terms of the interaction between economic centers (the gravity equation). Questions arise surrounding why economic activity is so unequally distributed, why these regularities occur, and whether the unequal distribution has an impact on development.

The path-breaking contribution of the American economist Paul Krugman (1991) was the first convincing explanation for the unequal spatial distribution of economic activity. Since then, many prominent researchers have worked on refinements, generalizations, and applications in the field now known as *geographical economics* (or *new economic geography*). The approach combines elements from international economics, industrial organization, economic geography, spatial economics, urban economics, and endogenous growth. This chapter explained Krugman's approach by means of an example and summarized the main implications of geographical economics with the Tomahawk diagram. It also linked the stylized conclusions of these models to economic development and inequality. To some extent, the answer is determined by physical geography (first nature geography) and to some extent by man-made geography (second nature geography). The interaction between falling transport costs and second nature geography can explain rising agglomeration and inequality.

Further Reading

A solid introduction into geographical economics is provided in: Brakman, S., H. Garretsen, and C. van Marrewijk. 2020. *An Introduction to Geographical and Urban Economics: A Spiky World* (Cambridge University Press). See especially chapter 10 on the link between various aspects of geography and development, discussed in terms of well-known models of growth and geographical economics.

A good starting point on the links between geography and development is: Krugman, P. 1997. *Development, Geography, and Economic Theory* (Cambridge, MA: MIT Press). The *Journal of Economic Geography* provides up-to-date analyses on recent contributions to these links.

18 Heterogeneous and Multinational Firms

18.1 Introduction

The key actor in economics is the firm. Casual observation shows that firms differ in many aspects. What they produce, how they are organized, how much they sell, for which markets they produce, and how productive they are varies substantially from one firm to another. Over the past two decades, the activities and characteristics of the firm and how firms differ in many relevant aspects has become central in economic analysis. This shift of emphasis was made possible by a much wider availability of detailed micro-level data (first in the USA, and then in many other countries), which allowed empirical economists (led by Bernard and Jensen 1995 and 1999) to analyze firm characteristics for different types of firms.

Section 18.2 reviews empirical evidence on the heterogeneity of firms: how they differ in size, productivity, and organization. Even in a country's strong sectors only a small share of all firms engage in export activities. These exporting firms tend to be larger, employ more workers, use more capital, pay higher wages, use more skilled workers, and have higher productivity than firms that are only active in the domestic market. Similar observations hold for firms that engage in multinational activities or importing activities.

Melitz (2003) provides the first thorough (and enormously influential) theoretical analysis of the consequences of international trade between countries when firms differ in terms of productivity. Section 18.3 analyzes the main structure and outcomes of his approach. An extension of this approach (based on the work of Helpman *et al.* 2004; see section 18.4) can explain the existence of multinational firms.

The main insights into the forces underlying horizontal FDI decisions are analyzed in section 18.4. The combination of transportation costs and plant-level scale economies leads to a proximity–concentration trade-off that explains why firms service some markets through exporting and other markets through multinational activities. This allows us to derive a clear ranking of firms in terms of productivity levels, in which low-productivity firms produce for the domestic market, intermediate-productivity firms also engage in exporting activities, and only the most productive firms become multinationals.

Because of ever-lower transportation and interaction costs and ever-improving communication possibilities, it is now possible for firms to reorganize their production process in different locations, taking the specific advantages of these locations for certain upstream or downstream parts of the process into consideration. Section 18.5 analyzes this fragmentation process, which involves supply chains and leads to vertical FDI. Section 18.6 shows that vertical FDI essentially requires differences in factor prices, such that fragmentation is related to wage inequality in source and destination countries. The heterogeneous firm setting can also be used in this framework (section 18.7). Section 18.8 evaluates the pros and cons of multinationals and FDI. Not all aspects of FDI can be captured by the models, and it is important to realize that the effects of FDI can be many and varied; beforehand it is not always clear that the net effect of FDI is welfare-increasing; it often depends on local circumstances.

18.2   Firm Heterogeneity in Trade

This section begins the chapter proper by providing some empirical information on firm heterogeneity and trade, based on data from Bernard *et al.* (2018). The focus here is on export data, but similar remarks hold for import data. Figure 18.1 shows on the horizontal axis that, on average, only 35 percent of the US manufacturing firms export their products. This differs widely for the 21 manufacturing sectors identified in the figure (bubbles proportional to the number of firms in the sector), ranging from 15 percent for Printing and Related Support to 75 percent for Computer and Electronic Product. We can make four observations. First, on average, it is relatively rare to be an exporting firm as only one in three firms engage in exporting activities. Second, the share of exporting firms differs per sector. Third, assuming that the USA has a "traditional" (technology or factor-abundance based) comparative advantage in computers, the share of exporting firms is positively related to traditional sources of comparative advantage. Fourth, firm heterogeneity is

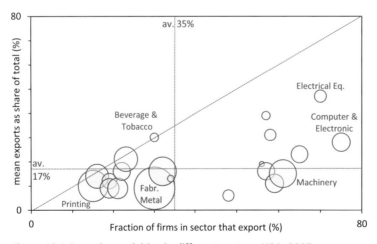

Figure 18.1 Exporting activities in different sectors; USA, 2007
Source: Based on data in Bernard *et al.* 2018.
Notes: 21 sectors; averages refer to Aggregate Manufacturing; bubble size proportional to the percent of firms in total manufacturing for that sector.

substantial; even for the strongest sectors not *all* firms are exporting, while for the weak sectors there are still some firms that *do* export.

Figure 18.1 also indicates (on the vertical axis) the mean exports as a share of total shipments. The average export share is only 17 percent, considerably less than the 35 percent of firms that engage in exporting activities. The lowest share of export revenue is for Paper Manufacturing (6 percent) and the highest share for Electrical Equipment (47 percent). Beverage and Tobacco Products is the only sector where the mean exports as a share of total shipments (30 percent) is not less than the fraction of firms in the sector that exports (also 30 percent). For the majority of firms, the domestic market seems to be more important, but there is substantial variation among the different sectors.

Since not all firms engage in exporting activities, it is worthwhile to investigate to what extent exporting firms differ from nonexporting firms. One way to do this is to analyze information for thousands of firms using regression analysis to estimate the size of the differences. This is done in Figure 18.2, which reports exporter premia over nonexporters in percent. Let's first focus on the simple regressions (the "none" bars). Panel b of the figure shows that exporting firms are larger than nonexporters; they employ about 128 percent more people and shipments are about 172 percent larger. Panel a shows that they have other characteristics as well; the skill per worker is about 6 percent higher, the

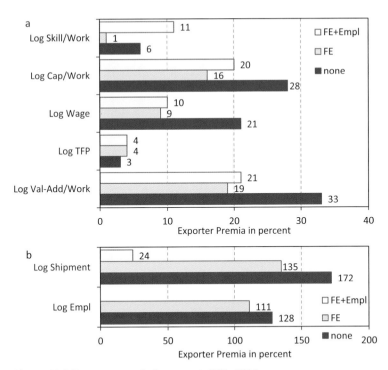

Figure 18.2 Exporter premia in percent; USA, 2007

Source: Based on data in Bernard *et al*. 2018.

Notes: Legend identifies additional covariates in bivariate OLS regressions; FE = Industry Fixed Effects; FE+Empl = Industry Fixed Effects & Log Employment; Skill/Work = Skill per Worker; Cap/Work = Capital per Worker; TFP = Total Factor Productivity; Val-Add/Work = Value-Added per Worker; Empl = Employment; all significant at 1 percent except log skill/work FE.

capital per worker about 28 percent higher, the wages they pay about 21 percent higher, the value-added per worker about 33 percent higher, and the firm's total factor product-ivity (TFP) is about 3 percent higher. The simple regressions lump all firms in all sectors together. To control for differences between sectors, we should look at the "FE" bars, which allow for sector-specific fixed effects. In general, the estimated premia are a little lower (except for TFP), but all are still strong and highly significant (except for skill per worker). Finally, we can also control for the size of the firm by looking at the "FE+Empl" bars, which control for sector fixed effects and employment size. As expected, this reduces the estimated shipment premium (from 135 to 24 percent, see panel b). All other estimated firm characteristic premia in panel a, however, become larger and are highly significant (including skill per worker).

It has already been shown that exporting firms tend to be larger and more productive. This discussion now continues in two steps. First, this section will analyze the extent to which trading firms differ regarding the number of products they trade and the number of countries they trade with – the so-called extensive margin of trade flows. Second, it will analyze the extent to which trade involves within-firm transactions – so-called related party trade, where a firm in one country trades with a parent or affiliate in another country. The discussion is based on evidence for American firms, but similar observations hold for the structure of trade flows for other countries.

Recall that only about one-third of all American manufacturing firms are active in exporting activities (see section 18.2). The differences between these exporting firms regarding the number of products they export, the number of countries they export to, and the value of these exports are enormous, as illustrated in Figure 18.3.

Panel a of Figure 18.3 shows the distribution of the share of exporting firms over the number of products and the number of countries. By far the largest number of exporting firms (35 percent of the total) export only one product to one other country, visualized in

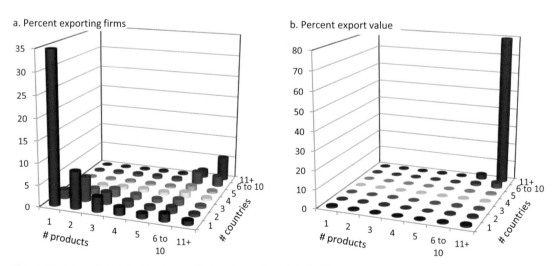

Figure 18.3 Export distribution by product and country; USA, 2007
Source: Based on data in Bernard *et al.* 2018.

panel a by the high bar in the left corner. Less than 9 percent of the firms export one product to two countries, less than 4 percent of the firms export one product to three countries, and only about 1 percent of the firms export one product to 11 or more countries. In total, about 53 percent of the exporting firms export only one product. In the other dimension: about 2 percent of the firms export two products to one country and less than 1 percent of the firms export three products to one country, four products to one country, and so on. In total, about 38 percent of the exporting firms export only to one country. The upper-right corner of panel a shows the share of firms that export many products to many countries. About 16 percent of the firms export six or more products to six or more countries. There is therefore a clear distinction in this panel: the majority of firms (more than 51 percent) export one or two products to one or two countries (lower-left corner), while only a small fraction of firms (less than 6 percent) export 11 or more products to 11 or more countries.

Panel b of Figure 18.3 shows the distribution of the export value over the number of products and the number of countries. This panel is clear: there are only four entries above 1 percent of export value and they are all in the top-right corner for firms that export six or more products to six or more countries; taken together, these 16 percent of firms account for more than 86 percent of all export value (about seven times higher than the average value for exporting firms). By far the highest bar in panel b is for the superstar firms that export more than 11 products to more than 11 countries; taken together, these 5.5 percent of firms account for about 80 percent of all export value (about 15 times higher than the average value for exporting firms). A small fraction of very large firms is thus responsible for the large majority of export revenue. Most of these firms are multinationals.

Multinationals differ from other firms in many aspects. As a framework for their analysis of multinational firms in the most recent *Handbook of International Economics*, Antràs and Yeaple (2014) identify the following stylized facts of multinationals:[1]

1. Multinational activity is primarily concentrated in advanced countries, where it is mostly two-way. Developing countries are more likely to be the destination of multinational activity than the source. Most FDI flows take place between advanced economies, which suggests that the dominant motive for FDI is the Horizontal motive; most FDI is market-seeking rather than low-production-cost-seeking (see also Chapter 9).

2. The relative importance of multinationals in economic activity is higher in capital-intensive and Research & Development (R&D) intensive goods, and a significant share of two-way Foreign Direct Investment (FDI) flows is intra-industry in nature.

3. The production of the foreign affiliates of multinationals falls off in distance, but at a slower rate than either aggregate exports or parent exports of inputs to their affiliates.

4. Both the parents and the affiliates of multinational firms tend to be larger, more productive, more R&D intensive, and more export-oriented than nonmultinational firms.

---

[1] In line with the terminology used in this textbook, their use of "developed economies" has been replaced with "advanced economies" as it more easily distinguishes between the two types of countries.

5. Within multinational firms, parents are relatively specialized in R&D, while affiliates are primarily engaged in selling goods in foreign markets, particularly in their host market.
6. Cross-border Mergers and Acquisitions (M&As) make up a large fraction of FDI and are a particularly important mode of entry into advanced countries.

18.3   The Melitz Model

Building on Hopenhayn's (1992a, 1992b) work on endogenous selection of heterogeneous firms in a sector and Krugman's (1979, 1980) model of trade under monopolistic competition with increasing returns to scale, Melitz (2003) develops an ingenious dynamic model in which (i) less productive firms exit the market, (ii) intermediately productive firms only produce for the local market, and (iii) the most productive firms both export and produce for the local market. The Melitz approach is based on the monopolistic competition model of intra-industry trade with one important difference: instead of all firms having identical technology, a firm may now be identified by its productivity level φ (which differs among firms). There are increasing returns to scale at the firm level due to a (per period) fixed cost f, which we assume to be the same for all firms. Firm productivity heterogeneity arises from differences in marginal production costs. More specifically, for a firm with productivity level φ, the labor costs involved in producing q units of a good are $f + q/\varphi$. As shown below, firms with different productivity levels charge different prices, produce different quantities, and so on. These variables are denoted with a sub-index φ. Below is a simplified version of the model. The essence of the model is that firms have to be productive enough to survive in a market. First, firms must be able to survive in the domestic market. Only firms that are more productive than a minimum productivity level can survive; this level is the productivity cut-off value. All firms that are more productive than this minimum level survive. A natural assumption is that entering a foreign and unfamiliar market is more difficult (it has higher entry costs) than entering the domestic market. The implication is that exporting firms have to be more productive than firms that only serve the domestic market. The highest entry costs are for multinational firms, because they have to build a new plant or take over an existing foreign firm.[2] So, only the most productive firms can become a multinational. The model thus predicts a clear ranking of firms; the less productive firms only sell to the domestic markets, if a firm is productive enough it can also start exporting, and the most productive firms become multinationals. It turns out that the Melitz (2003) model and its extensions can explain many of the stylized facts about exporting firms and multinationals.

18.3.1   Main Structure

The main structure of the model is illustrated in Figure 18.4. There is a large number M of active firms in the economy, each producing a differentiated good under monopolistic

---

[2] Multinational firms are also abbreviated MNE (MultiNational Enterprise); *multinational* is used for clarity.

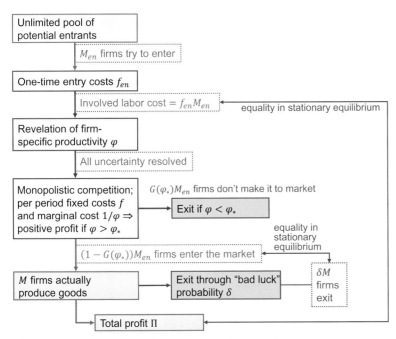

Figure 18.4 Structure of the heterogeneous firms model

competition. Since the firms differ in their productivity levels φ, they have different levels of operating profits.[3] Firm exit at this stage occurs with an exogenous probability of "bad luck" δ, identical for all firms. In each period δM, active firms therefore exit the market. The prospective of earning positive operating profits entices M_{en} firms to try to enter the market out of an unlimited pool of potential entrants. Each of these firms incurs a fixed entry cost f_{en} for their attempt (note that these entry costs differ from the per period fixed costs f).

In equilibrium, the total entry costs $f_{en}M_{en}$ are equal to the total operating profits. The only uncertainty in the model involves the *ex ante* firm productivity level, which is resolved upon investing the one-time entry costs. Once the firm productivity level is known, the entrepreneur can determine if it is possible to earn positive operating profits. If not (that is, if the productivity level is below a certain threshold φ_*), the potential entrant will immediately exit the market (with probability $G(\varphi_*)$). The remaining $1 - G(\varphi_*)$ firms do in fact enter the market successfully. In the stationary equilibrium, the number of entrants is equal to the number of active firms that exit the market δM and the total number of active firms does not change.

The demand for a particular variety of a good is iso-elastic with elasticity parameter $\varepsilon > 1$, such that $q_\varphi = A p_\varphi^{-\varepsilon}$.[4] This leads to a constant mark–up $\varepsilon/(\varepsilon - 1)$ of price over

---

[3] This chapter analyzes a very large (continuum) number of firms, hence it does not use a sub-index i to identify different firms, but instead uses the continuous parameter φ for this purpose.

[4] The constant A is defined as $A \equiv IP^{\varepsilon-1}$, where I is the income level and P is the price index.

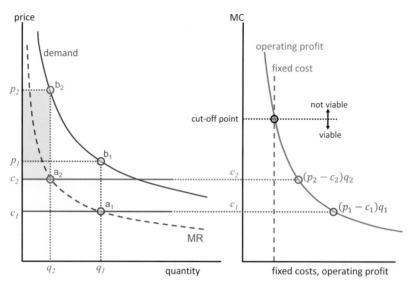

Figure 18.5 Firm heterogeneity, prices, and profits

marginal costs. Setting the wage rate as numéraire ($w = 1$), this implies that a firm with productivity level φ which has marginal costs $1/\varphi$ charges an optimal price $p_\varphi = \left(\frac{\varepsilon}{\varepsilon-1}\right)\left(\frac{1}{\varphi}\right)$. This is illustrated in Figure 18.5 for two firms with different productivity levels: firm 1 is more productive than firm 2 and thus has lower marginal costs ($c_1 < c_2$). The left-hand graph of Figure 18.5 illustrates iso-elastic demand and the associated marginal revenue curve (MR). Firm 1 equates marginal revenue and marginal costs at point a_1, charges optimal price p_1, and earns operating profits equal to area $p_1 b_1 a_1 c_1$. Firm 2 equates marginal revenue and marginal costs at point a_2, charges a higher optimal price p_2, and consequently earns lower operating profits equal to area $p_2 b_2 a_2 c_2$. The right-hand graph of Figure 18.5 depicts these two operating profit levels for the two different marginal cost levels. If we repeat this exercise for all possible different marginal cost levels, we can derive the optimal profit curve for all possible combinations also shown in the right-hand graph. If we substitute the optimal price information in the demand function, we can derive the firm's total revenue r_φ and profits π_φ (see Technical Note 18.1, also for a definition of the constant B):

$$r_\varphi = p_\varphi q_\varphi = \varepsilon B\varphi^{\varepsilon-1}; \quad \pi_\varphi = B\varphi^{\varepsilon-1} - f \qquad\qquad 18.1$$

So far, we have identified firm productivity by the variable φ. Equation 18.1 shows that if we identify firm productivity instead by the monotonic transformation $\varphi^{\varepsilon-1}$, then firm revenue and firm profits are *linear* in firm productivity. Figure 18.6 illustrates the relationship between this measure of firm productivity and firm profits. If firm productivity is close to zero, then the firm makes a per period loss equal to the fixed costs f if it decides to produce. As a consequence, the best this firm can do is exit the market and have zero profits. As productivity rises, firm profits rise as well. Once firm productivity passes a certain threshold level, equal to $\varphi_*^{\varepsilon-1}$ in Figure 18.6, profits become positive and nonzero

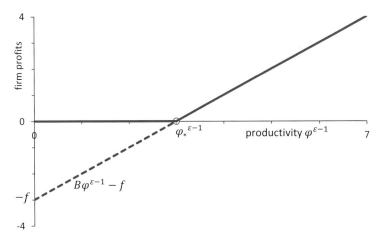

Figure 18.6 Firm productivity and firm profits

production is possible (the firm becomes viable in the market). This point is also illustrated in Figure 18.5. The firm takes this cut-off point as given, but it is determined endogenously in the general equilibrium of this model through entry, exit, and the mass of firms.

18.3.2 Entry, Exit, and Equilibrium

To construct a minimalist dynamic model, we impose an exogenous probability of firm exit (through some shock or bad luck) equal to δ and common for all firms. In each period, δM firms therefore exit the market. This is confronted with an endogenous determination of firm entry. The active firms in the market are earning positive operating profits as given in equation 18.1. This makes it attractive for potential entrants to enter the market. There are two caveats. First, they do not yet know their productivity level. Second, they have to incur a one-time fixed cost (in terms of labor) to enter the market equal to f_{en}. These issues are connected, as we assume that all uncertainty is resolved once the entry costs are paid.

The firm's entry problem is illustrated in Figure 18.7, which shows the *ex ante* probability density function (pdf, see Chapter 2) of a firm's productivity draw φ, which becomes known once the entry costs f_{en} are paid. The probability that the firm is not viable (and does not produce) after paying the entry costs depends on the location of the cut-off level φ_*; more specifically, the probability that $\varphi < \varphi_*$ is equal to the area under the pdf. In all those cases, the firm will have zero operating profits and make an *ex post* loss equal to f_{en}. If productivity is above the cut-off level ($\varphi > \varphi_*$), the firm makes a positive operating profit each period it survives in the market. Per period, the operating profit is $(B\varphi^{\varepsilon-1} - f)$ (see equation 18.1). Since the probability of exit in any period is equal to δ, the probability that the firm is still operative after t periods is $(1 - \delta)^t$. Ignoring discounting for simplicity, the net present value of the operating profits is therefore equal to $(B\varphi^{\varepsilon-1} - f)/\delta$ (since $\sum_{t=0}^{\infty}(1 - \delta)^t = 1/\delta$). If this value is less than the entry costs f_{en}, the entrant will still make an *ex post* loss; only if this value is larger than the entry costs will the entrant make an *ex post* expected profit. The probability of any particular outcome occurring is, of

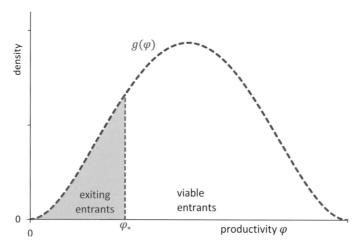

Figure 18.7 Firm entry problem

course, given by the pdf $g(\varphi)$. The *free entry condition* for potential entrants ensures that the ex ante expected value of discounted profits is equal to the entry costs f_{en}:

$$\int_{\varphi_*}^{\infty} \left[(B\varphi^{\varepsilon-1} - f)/\delta \right] g(\varphi) d\varphi = f_{en} \qquad 18.2$$

We can now combine the free entry condition with the zero profit condition regarding viability to endogenously (and uniquely) determine the cut-off productivity level φ_* in autarky:

$$h(\varphi_*) = \frac{\delta f_{en}}{f} \qquad 18.3$$

The monotonically declining function $h(\varphi_*)$ is defined in Technical Note 18.2. Note that the free entry condition determines the average profits (and revenue) of active firms, say $\bar{\pi} = \delta f_{en}/(1 - G(\varphi_*))$. If we denote by $\bar{\varphi}$ the productivity level associated with this average profit level, it can be shown that the economy behaves *similarly* to the representative firm monopolistic competition model with that average level of firm productivity (see, for example, Melitz and Redding 2014). In particular, the number of firms active in the economy is proportional to the market size of the country and the love-of-variety effect is reflected in higher welfare levels for larger markets. The important difference is, of course, that this productivity level is determined *endogenously* within the model and is the appropriate representative of an underlying distribution of heterogeneous firms with many different levels of firm productivity.

18.3.3   Firm Heterogeneity, Trade, and Productivity

What will happen in the economy described above when it is confronted with another, identical economy with which it is able to trade? (This identical economy precludes wage differences between countries, so the focus can be exclusively on the links between heterogeneity, trade, and productivity.) Based on overwhelming empirical evidence, two crucial assumptions can be made.[5] First, the firm must pay a per unit trade cost and ship $\tau > 1$ units in order to ensure that one unit arrives in the destination country. This elegant way to model trade costs was introduced by Samuelson (1952) to avoid the need for explicitly modeling a transport sector. Since it is as if part of the product melts away in transit, it is called *iceberg* transportation costs. Second, the firm faces significant entry costs to get acquainted with the export market, to learn about the foreign legal system, to set up a foreign distribution channel, to adapt the product to foreign standards, and so on (see Roberts and Tybout 1977). We model these export costs as a per period fixed investment cost $f_x > 0$, independent of the firm's export volume.[6] Each firm therefore faces the decision whether or not it is worthwhile to pay the fixed export costs and sell goods in the foreign market. Assume that the firm makes this export decision when it knows its productivity level and that the per period fixed production costs f are the same irrespective of export status.

The symmetry assumption ensures that the two countries have the same wage rates (normalized to unity) and the same aggregate variables. Subsection 18.3.2 showed that in autarky the viability cut-off productivity level φ_* is determined endogenously by the condition $B\varphi_*^{\varepsilon-1} = f$. Section 18.3.1 showed that the constant B, which determines a firm's demand and profitability, is determined endogenously and depends, in particular, on the economy-wide price index P. As a consequence, when the two identical countries engage in international trade under the conditions specified above, this means that this constant differs in the trade equilibrium relative to the autarky equilibrium. We denote this by B_{tr}, where the sub-index tr refers to trade. The discussion below analyzes a trade equilibrium in which a fraction of firms export goods to the other country. As a consequence, more firms are active on a country's market under trade than in autarky, which increases competition and lowers the price index P. This, in turn, implies that the firm's demand and profitability constant is lower under trade than in autarky: $B_{tr} < B$.[7]

The optimal pricing rule is the same constant mark-up over marginal costs, so a firm with productivity level φ charges price $p_\varphi = \left(\frac{\varepsilon}{\varepsilon-1}\right)\left(\frac{1}{\varphi}\right)$ in the domestic market and price τp_φ in the foreign market to cover the higher marginal costs, provided exports are positive. Since the price charged in the foreign market is τ times as high and demand is iso-elastic with elasticity ε, the revenue in the foreign market is $\tau^{1-\varepsilon}$ times the revenue in the domestic markets (equal to $\tau^{1-\varepsilon}\varepsilon B_{tr}\varphi^{\varepsilon-1}$; see equation 18.1). Since operating profits are $1/\varepsilon$ times revenue and a firm will engage in exporting activity if the associated operating profits are larger than the fixed exporting costs f_x, this means a firm will export if: $\tau^{1-\varepsilon}B_{tr}\varphi^{\varepsilon-1} - f_x > 0$. We will denote this export productivity cut-off level by φ_{*x}. In line with the empirical observations discussed in section 18.2, assume that the export cut-off

---

[5] In the absence of these assumptions, trade only has a size-of-market (positive variety) welfare effect, as in Krugman (1980).

[6] In the set-up here, this is equivalent to a one-time export investment cost equal to f_x/δ. See Romer 1994 and van Marrewijk and Berden 2007 for heterogeneity in the fixed entry costs.

[7] This condition is intuitively obvious and formally derived in Melitz 2003.

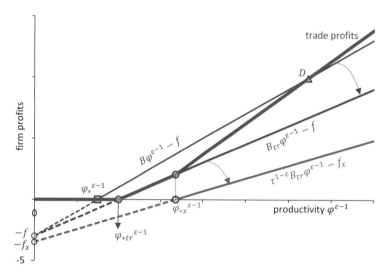

Figure 18.8 International trade viability and profits

level is higher than the viability cut-off level. This means that all firms are active in the domestic market and only a fraction of firms engage in export activity; this implies that the fixed export costs must be sufficiently large, namely $f_x > \tau^{1-\varepsilon}f$.

The trade situation relative to autarky is illustrated in Figure 18.8. In autarky, the profit line intercepts the vertical axis at $-f$ and has a slope equal to B. Firms become viable at the cut-off productivity level φ_* (the square in the figure). Under trade, firms that are active in the domestic market also have a profit line that intercepts the vertical axis at $-f$. This time, however, the slope is equal to B_{tr}, which is smaller than B, hence the profit line rotates clockwise around the point $(0, -f)$ and firms become viable at a *higher* productivity level than under autarky: $\varphi_{*tr} > \varphi_*$. An important consequence of engaging in international trade is therefore that the least efficient firms are forced to exit the market; this holds for all firms in between productivity levels φ_* and φ_{*tr}.

Figure 18.8 also shows the profit line for firms that want to engage in exporting activity. This profit line intercepts the vertical axis at $-f_x$ and has a slope equal to $\tau^{1-\varepsilon}B_{tr}$, which is strictly lower than the slope of the domestic profit line B_{tr}, since $\varepsilon > 1$. As a consequence, the export profit line is rotated clockwise relative to the domestic profit line and shifted along the vertical axis.[8] This implies that only the most productive firms engage in exporting activities. Finally, the thick, solid line in the figure shows the firm's profits under trade, which has two kinks. The first kink occurs at the viability point $\varphi_{*tr}^{\varepsilon-1}$: profits are zero for all firms below this cut-off point. The second kink occurs at the export viability point $\varphi_{*x}^{\varepsilon-1}$: export profits are positive for all firms beyond this cut-off point and these profits are added to the domestic profits. All firms in between these two cut-off points only produce for the domestic market. Note that profits under trade only increase for the most efficient firms with the highest productivity levels (above point D).

---

[8] It is not necessary that $f_x > f$ as drawn in Figure 18.8, as long as $f_x > \tau^{1-\varepsilon}f$.

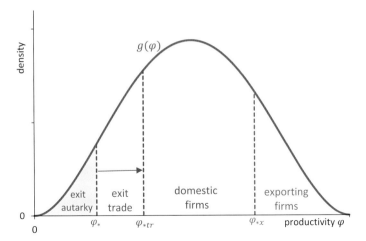

Figure 18.9 Impact of trade and distribution of firms

The main effects of trade for the firms are illustrated in Figure 18.9. The *ex ante* probability of a firm's productivity draw after paying the entry costs f_{en} is given by the pdf $g(\varphi)$. Under autarky, the viability cut-off productivity is equal to φ_* and all firms below this productivity level are forced to exit the market (exit autarky). Under trade, the viability cut-off productivity level increases to φ_{*tr} (as indicated by the arrow in the figure) and all least productive firms (those with productivity levels in between φ_* and φ_{*tr}) are forced to exit the market (exit trade). The export cut-off productivity level is given by φ_{*x}; only the most productive firms (with productivity levels beyond this cut-off value) will engage in export activities (exporting firms) and expand their production level. All firms in between these two productivity levels will only produce for the domestic market (domestic firms); these firms will contract their production level. As noted by Melitz (2003, p. 1712): "The result that the modelling of fixed export costs explains the partitioning of firms by export status and productivity level is not exactly Earth-shattering. This can be explained quite easily within a simple partial equilibrium model with a fixed distribution of productivity levels."

What such a partial equilibrium approach cannot explain, and what is thus, instead, the main contribution of the Melitz model, is the endogenous impact of trade flows on the distribution of productivity levels. It allows us to explain which firms gain or lose from trade competition, which firms exit the market, which firms produce only for the domestic market, and which firms export. In addition, the shift of production toward the more efficient firms creates an additional welfare gain hitherto unexplored.

18.4   Horizontal FDI

The analysis so far has been helpful in determining whether or not a firm will enter the foreign market under firm heterogeneity. It is time to go one step further and determine not only under which conditions a firm will enter the foreign market, but also how it will be active on that market, namely through trade or through (horizontal) foreign direct

Table 18.1. Productivity advantage of multinationals and exporters

	coefficient	t-statistic
Multinationals[*]	0.537	14.432
Nonmultinational exporters[*]	0.388	9.535
Advantage of multinationals over nonmultinational exporters	0.150	3.694
Number of firms	3,202	

Source: Helpman et al. 2004, table 1.
Notes: * Relative to domestic firms. Labor productivity (log of output per worker) differences, controlling for capital intensity and four-digit industry fixed effects, 1996. All results significant at the 1 percent level.

investment (FDI). The exposition here is based on the Helpman, Melitz, and Yeaple (2004) approach and distinguishes between three types of firms, namely (i) domestic firms (producing only for the domestic market), (ii) exporting firms (serving also the foreign market through trade flows), and (iii) multinationals (serving also the foreign market through a subsidiary). It is vital, of course, to have an idea about the main empirical differences between these three types of firms. This is provided in Table 18.1, which shows that (other things being equal) exporting firms are about 39 percent more productive than domestic firms (see also section 18.2), while multinationals are about 54 percent more productive than domestic firms. Consequently (third row of Table 18.1), multinational firms are about 15 percent more productive than exporting firms. There is, therefore, a clear productivity hierarchy: domestic firms are the least productive, multinationals the most productive, and in between are exporting firms.

Figure 18.10 illustrates the findings of Table 18.1 for a somewhat more detailed distinction of four types of firms for Latin America, namely: national firms producing for the domestic market; national firms that also export; foreign firms producing for the domestic market; and foreign firms that also export. Although there is considerable overlap between the different types of firms, the figure clearly shows that the national firms producing for the domestic market are the least productive, while the foreign firms (FDI) engaged in exporting are the most productive.

Inspired by the Melitz model explained above, Helpman, Melitz, and Yeaple (2004) analyze a world with many countries and many sectors and a homogeneous good. The homogeneous good sector is a catch-all numéraire sector, eliminating all income effects. The disadvantage of this approach, which is a common modeling trick, is that all rises in income are absorbed by this sector and have no impact at all on any of the other sectors. In contrast, the analysis itself usually focuses completely on these other sectors.

A sector produces differentiated goods using labor as the only input. As above, a firm incurs a fixed cost to be able to start production and then learns its productivity parameter drawn from an *ex ante* distribution function. It may then either exit (if productivity is not high enough) or start production, in which case it is faced with a fixed overhead cost. A producing firm can either not serve the foreign markets (in which case it is a *domestic*

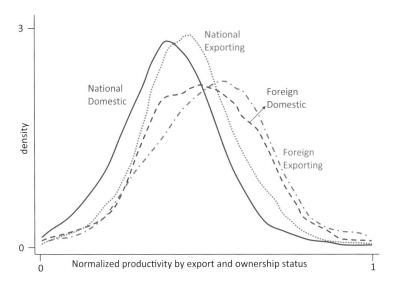

Figure 18.10 Productivity distributions in Latin America, 2006
Source: Chang and van Marrewijk 2013.

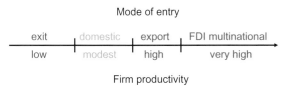

Figure 18.11 Firm productivity and mode of entry

firm) or serve the foreign markets in one of two ways, namely: through *exports* (in which case it incurs an additional fixed cost in each market as well as [iceberg] per unit transport costs); or through foreign direct investment, *FDI* (in which case it incurs higher additional fixed cost in each market than exporting firms, but does not have to pay for transport costs). The fixed costs for firms engaged in FDI are higher per market than for firms engaged in exports because the exporters only have to pay for establishing a distribution and servicing network, while the FDI firms also have to pay for establishing a foreign subsidiary. There is therefore a proximity–concentration trade-off.

Firms with higher productivity can charge lower prices and thus sell more goods and have higher revenue and higher operating profits. Firms with very low productivity cannot earn high enough operating profits to cover the fixed costs and thus exit the market. Similarly, firms with modest productivity cannot recover the additional fixed cost to export to other countries and produce only for the domestic market. For firms with high productivity, it is worthwhile to export to other countries as it recovers the fixed export cost, but only firms with very high productivity are able to recover the very high fixed costs involved in establishing a foreign subsidiary. Figure 18.11 summarizes the theoretical implications of this model, which is in line with the empirical regularities observed in section 18.2 and Figure 18.10.

BOX 18.1 EMPIRICAL EVIDENCE FOR HORIZONTAL FDI

The proximity–concentration trade-off is intuitively plausible and has various implications for the cross-country and cross-sector structure of trade and FDI flows. Brainard (1997) provides an evaluation of the empirical relevance of this trade-off. This box briefly discusses Antràs and Yeaple's (2014) updated version of this work using more complete and more recently available data. Essentially, it attempts to explain as clearly as possible the extent to which firms service foreign markets through exporting. The analysis is based on data for American multinationals servicing 42 different destination countries for a range of manufacturing sectors. Let X_i^j be the exports from the USA to country i in sector j, let S_i^j be the sales of American affiliates in sector j located in country i, and let $s_{x,i}^j$ be the share of exports in serving country i for sector j, defined as: $s_{x,i}^j = X_i^j / (X_i^j + S_i^j)$. The variable $s_{x,i}^j$ is taken as an indication of the extent to which a foreign market is serviced through exports rather than affiliate sales.

The top part of Table 18.2 provides a direct estimate of the impact of the theoretical variables on the attractiveness of exports for servicing foreign markets. The variables "freight costs" and "tariffs" are the logs of the value estimates of shipping costs and tariffs in sector j from the USA to country i. In accordance with the model, a rise in both types of shipping costs makes exporting significantly less attractive. The variables "firm-level costs" and "plant-level costs" are logs of the number of nonproduction workers per representative firm and of production workers per representative plant. They represent the variables f_{en} and f_{pl}, respectively. Again, in accordance with the model, the attractiveness of exporting as a means to service foreign markets significantly falls if firm-level costs rise or plant-level costs decline.

Table 18.2. Proximity–concentration empirics for American multinationals, 2009

Dependent variable $\log(s_{x,i}^j)$ (see the main text for details)

Variable	Coefficient	Standard error
Freight costs	-0.13^{**}	0.04
Tariffs	-0.29^{**}	0.06
Firm-level costs	-0.32^{**}	0.04
Plant-level costs	0.14^{*}	0.05
GDP difference	0.39^{*}	0.17
Schooling difference	0.07	0.09
Capital–labor ratio difference	0.08	0.06
Observations	2315	

Source: Antràs and Yeaple 2014, table 2.3, column 4.
Notes: ** and * indicate significant at 1 and 5 percent levels; 42 countries included in the analysis; no sector or country fixed effects; additional controls not reported.

BOX 18.1 (cont.)

The bottom part of Table 18.2 provides estimates of the degree to which country differences can explain the proximity–concentration trade-off. The variable "GDP difference" is the log of the absolute value of the difference in GDP for the USA and country i. Large differences in country size make exporting significantly more attractive. The variables "schooling difference" and "capital–labor ratio difference" are the logs of differences in the years of schooling and capital–labor ratios for the USA and country i. These variables try to measure differences in factor endowments for the relative attractiveness of exports. Unfortunately, both variables are not statistically significant, which suggests that differences in factor endowments are not important. Note, however, that the specification assumes that the role of endowments for the proximity–concentration trade-off is the same for all sectors. Box 18.3 returns to this issue, with an analysis of the role of comparative advantage in more detail, and allowing factor abundance to interact with a sector's factor intensity.

18.5 Fragmentation and Vertical FDI

After the analysis of heterogeneous firms and horizontal FDI, this section now completes the analysis of multinational firms by discussing vertical FDI. As a result of ever-lower transportation and interaction costs and ever-improving communication possibilities, it is now possible for firms to reorganize their production process in different locations, taking the specific advantages of these locations for certain upstream or downstream parts of the process into consideration. A low-skilled labor-intensive part of the production process may be moved to a country with relatively low wage rates. Similarly, an advanced and technology-intensive part of the production process may be moved to a country abundant in human capital, and so on.

Various colorful names have been given to these developments, such as fragmentation, slicing-up-the-value-chain, global value chains, and supply chains. Since the various parts of the production process need to be fitted together at some point in time, it is often better to locate the various plants in one another's vicinity and not on the other side of the globe. As a consequence, some supply chains combine the advantages of countries at different stages of economic development that are near to each other, such as Germany and the Czech Republic or America and Mexico. Other supply chains use the differences in technical expertise of countries at similar levels of economic development, such as Japan, the USA, and the UK.

Although a firm may fragment the production process domestically, attention is focused on the international dimension of the fragmentation process. The proper term for locating part of the production process in another country is *offshoring*. Firms can decide to organize offshoring activities either within the firm boundaries (integration) or by *outsourcing* to another firm. In the media, the terms offshoring and outsourcing are sometimes confused.

The discussion here of vertical FDI (fragmentation) starts with a simple $2 \times 2 \times 2$ framework of two countries (America A and China C), two types of goods (food and differentiated manufactures), and two factors of production (capital K and labor L).[9] Assume that the two countries have identical technologies and that all firms are equally productive. Both assumptions are relaxed in section 18.7. To avoid the incentive for horizontal FDI activity analyzed in section 18.4, assume there are no transport costs. In line with the case study on hard-disk drives (see Box 18.2), the key new modeling aspect is that we allow for fragmentation of the production process into different stages that are geographically separated. The production process of manufactures consists of two stages:

- *Headquarter services.* Think of the fixed entry costs for firms, such as R&D, marketing, development of specialized machines, financing, and so on. These services are firm-specific, produced under increasing returns to scale, nonrival within the firm, and produced relatively (human-) capital intensively.
- *Manufacturing.* Uses capital, labor, and headquarter services to produce final output under increasing returns to scale. Production costs fall if the supply of headquarter services rises.

The manufacturing firm's decision process is now simple, as illustrated in Figure 18.12. Since both stages of the production process have increasing returns to scale, there will be only one location for headquarter services and one manufacturing location. Headquarter services tend to be located in the country with the ownership advantage, so for an American firm headquarter services will be located in America. This firm then has to decide whether the manufacturing location is in China or also in America. Based on this location decision, it then determines the production levels for both stages of the production process to maximize profits.

The key insight of Helpman (1984) is that there is *no* incentive for vertical FDI if the factor prices are the *same* in the two countries. After all, the incentive to relocate the manufacturing stage of the production process to China must be based on the ability to achieve lower costs by doing so. Since manufacturing is relatively labor-intensive, this will be possible if, for example, the wage rate is lower in China than in America. In the case of factor price equalization, both the wage rate and the rental rate are the same in the two countries and there is no cost advantage associated with vertical FDI at all. Any arbitrarily small costs associated with organizing a production process in two separate countries would thus preclude vertical FDI from being feasible if factor price equalization holds.

International trade leads to factor price equalization in the center of the Edgeworth box (if the distribution of factor endowments is not too different). The same holds in this setting, so if factor endowments are similar, factor price equalization occurs and there will be no vertical

[9] The analysis in this section is based on Helpman 1984 and Helpman and Krugman 1985.

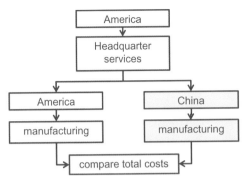

Figure 18.12 Vertical FDI decision process

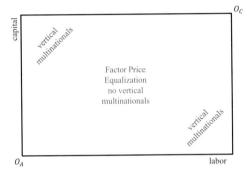

Figure 18.13 Characterization of main vertical FDI regimes

multinationals (in the center of the Edgeworth box in Figure 18.13).[10] On the other hand, if factor endowments differ substantially between countries, firms can lower total costs by fragmenting the production process into two separate stages and locating part of the production process in the other country such that vertical multinationals arise (in the corners of the Edgeworth box in Figure 18.13). In the example here, if labor is sufficiently abundant in China compared to America such that the Chinese wage rate is sufficiently low compared to the American wage rate, it is advantageous for American firms to become vertical multinationals and locate manufacturing production in China. Moreover, in this setting, fragmentation tends to work in the direction of restoring factor price equalization.

18.6 Vertical FDI and Wage Inequality

As discussed in Chapter 10, there is an ongoing debate about the links between globalization and income inequality, both within and between countries. Regarding the economic

---

[10] Some technical details are being skipped over here, but Helpman (1984) shows that for a given relative size of countries the share of intra-firm trade in total trade is rising in differences in factor endowments. He also shows that for some factor endowment regions fragmentation may restore factor price equalization.

BOX 18.2 HARD-DISK DRIVE SUPPLY CHAIN EXAMPLE

The manufacture of hard-disk drives, an essential component for the computer business, is a dynamic industry, with high revenues, product life cycles of less than 18 months, and rapidly falling prices.[11] In 1980, about 80 percent of all drives production was done by US firms and assembled in the USA. Within two decades, less than 5 percent was still assembled in the USA. Ignoring R&D, there are four major steps in the value chain: (i) electronics – this includes semiconductors, printed circuit boards (PCBs), and their assembly; (ii) heads – devices that read and write the data, which are manufactured in stages with labor-intensive subassembly activities, such as head-gimbal assembly (HGA) and head-stack assembly (HSA); (iii) media – the material on which the information is stored;[12] and (iv) motors – which spin the media with extreme precision.

Producers locate the production of the many discrete steps in the value chain around the world for various reasons. The final assembly of the disk, which gives it the "Made in Singapore" or "Made in Thailand" label, is only one (and not necessarily the most important) aspect in this process. As Gourevitch, Bohn, and McKendrick (2000), discussing the structure of Seagate, the world's largest manufacturer of hard-disk drives, put it:

> Although Seagate has kept control over almost all production, it has globally dispersed its operations to an extraordinary degree. A single component may be worked on in five countries and cross two oceans while Seagate is building it up through its value chain. Seagate develops new products (and processes) at seven locations in the United States and Singapore. It assembles disk drives in Singapore, Malaysia, Thailand, and China. In heads, the company fabricates its wafers in the United States and Northern Ireland, and cuts them into bars and assembles them into HGAs in Thailand, Malaysia, and the Philippines. It makes media in Singapore and motors in Thailand. It manufactures printed circuit cables in Thailand and assembles the electronics onto printed circuit boards in Indonesia, Malaysia, and Singapore. It is the largest nongovernment employer in Thailand and Singapore.

Table 18.3 gives four different indicators of nationality of production for the hard-disk drive industry. The large majority (88.4 percent per unit of output) of hard-disk drives is made by US firms. In sharp contrast, only 4.6 percent of the final assembly is done in the USA. Most final assembly of disks now takes place in Southeast Asia (64.2 percent), which means that the bulk of employment is in Southeast Asia (44 percent), rather than in the USA (19.3 percent), although the value of wages paid is much higher in the USA

---

[11] This section is based on Brakman *et al.* 2001.

[12] According to Gourevitch *et al.* (2000, p. 304): "Typically, aluminum blank substrates are nickel-plated and polished before the platters are sputtered and finished. As with heads, media are a very high-technology aspect of HDD production."

BOX 18.2 (cont.)

Table 18.3. Hard-disk drives: indicators of nationality of production

Measure[*]	USA	Japan	SE Asia	Other Asia	Europe	Other
Nationality of firm	88.4	9.4	0.0	2.2	0.0	0.0
Final assembly	4.6	15.5	64.2	5.7	10.0	0.0
Employment	19.3	8.3	44.0	17.1	4.7	6.5
Wages paid	39.5	29.7	12.9	3.3	8.5	6.1

Source: Gourevitch *et al.* 2000, table 2.
Notes: Numbers as percent of world total; [*] nationality of firm (percent of unit output), location of final assembly, employment in value chain, and wages paid in value chain.

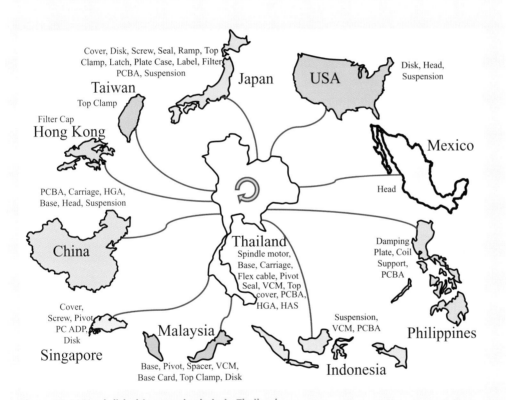

Figure 18.14 Hard-disk drive supply chain in Thailand.
Source: van Marrewijk 2009, adapted from Baldwin 2008 and Hiratsuka 2005.

(39.5 percent) than in Southeast Asia (12.9 percent). Essentially, the hard-disk drive industry currently has two concentration clusters. The first is Silicon Valley in the USA, with a substantial share of research, design, development, marketing, and management (with a smaller counterpart in Japan). The second is in Southeast Asia, which dominates

BOX 18.2 (cont.)

final assembly, most labor-intensive subassemblies, and low-tech components, such as baseplates.

Figure 18.14 illustrates how involved the supply chain network is within Southeast Asia. To do so, the figure shows the sources of parts of a disk drive that is assembled in Thailand by a Japanese affiliate. A range of components, such as the spindle motor and the flex cable, are sourced locally (from Thailand). Many other components are sourced from a range of other countries, most of which are in Southeast Asia. The filter cap comes from Hong Kong, the damping plate from the Philippines, the top clamp from Taiwan, Japan, or Malaysia, the disks themselves from the USA, Japan, or Malaysia, and so on. Each of the listed parts may, of course, consist of other parts and components. Each of these other parts and components may again be sourced from different countries. Trying to complete the interlinkages picture by tracing out the ultimate source of each and every component is basically impossible.

Finally, it is important to remember that once the hard-disk drive is finished, it does not stay in Thailand, but serves as a component in another production process. It could, for example, be part of a computer assembled in China that is subsequently sold as a final good to a consumer in Switzerland or as an intermediate input to a consulting firm in Canada. At each next export step, only part of the value of the product represents value-added of the exporting country. The next section thus investigates value-added trade flows in more depth.

consequences of vertical FDI, the focus of attention is on within-country income inequality. This section briefly discusses some possible consequences of fragmentation for within-country wage inequality. To do so, it distinguishes between two types of workers: high-skilled workers (subindex H) and low-skilled workers (subindex L). Relative to the discussion in section 18.5, we can think of high-skilled workers as being represented by (human) capital K and low-skilled workers by labor L. Regarding factor prices, it is most appropriate to refer to these as wages in this setting, so we let w_{HA} denote the wage rate of high-skilled workers in America, w_{LC} the wage rate of low-skilled workers in China, and so on.

Assume that America is relatively abundant in high-skilled labor and take for granted that the wage rate for high-skilled workers is higher than for low-skilled workers within a country, thus providing an incentive for workers to become high-skilled workers (although we do not model this process; note that we can always assure that $w_H > w_L$ within a country by redefining the units in which high-skilled and low-skilled workers are measured). We focus attention on analyzing whether or not w_{HA}/w_{LA}, the wage rate of high-skilled workers relative to low-skilled workers in America, rises as a consequence of fragmentation. If w_{HA}/w_{LA} rises, we conclude that fragmentation leads to higher wage inequality in America. If not, the reverse holds. This question is also examined from China's perspective. At the end of this section, it is concluded that "anything goes," which means that there are no simple and robust predictions regarding the links between fragmentation and wage inequality.

18.6.1   Rising Wage Inequality in America and Lower Wage Inequality in China

The discussion here begins with the model analyzed in section 18.5, where the variable K is reinterpreted as high-skilled workers, as explained above. The predictions of the effect of fragmentation in this model are straightforward along the neoclassical lines of the Stolper-Samuelson theorem (see Chapter 6). Fragmentation only occurs outside the factor price equalization area of the Edgeworth box. If fragmentation does occur, it works in the direction of restoring factor price equalization since fragmentation increases the relative demand for and reward of the relatively abundant factor of production in each country. Since America is abundant in high-skilled workers, this means that w_{HA}/w_{LA} *rises* and offshoring leads to higher wage inequality in America. Since China is abundant in low-skilled workers, this means that w_{HC}/w_{LC} *falls* and offshoring leads to lower wage inequality in China. The impact is thus rising wage inequality in the source country and lower wage inequality in the destination country.

18.6.2   Offshoring Tasks and Rising Wage Inequality in Both Countries

This subsection now analyzes a model based on Feenstra and Hanson (1996) as discussed in Antràs and Yeaple (2014). Suppose that instead of only two production stages for manufactures there is a continuum of stages indexed by s, ranging from 0 to 1. The marginal cost for stage s is determined by the use of high-skilled and low-skilled labor at this stage: $a_H(s)w_H + a_L(s)w_L$. We order the stages in terms of rising skill intensity $a_H(s)/a_L(s)$ (see Figure 18.15). The stages are combined into final goods using a Cobb-Douglas production function. There is also a fixed cost at each stage in terms of final output (such that the relative cost ordering is not affected). Fragmentation is frictionless. Finally, assume for simplicity that the production of food uses only low-skilled labor.

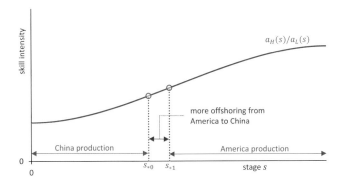

Figure 18.15 Stage offshoring and wage inequality

This model leads to the following conclusions: (i) if endowment differences are small, there is factor price equalization and no incentive for fragmentation of the production process; and (ii) for larger but "not too big" factor endowment differences, fragmentation occurs and restores factor price equalization. More interesting are the additional conclusions. If factor endowments are sufficiently different between countries, there is a critical stage s_*, such that all stages with low-skill intensity (stage 0 to s_*) are produced in China and all stages with high-skill intensity (stage s_* to 1) are produced in America (see Figure 18.15). Since technology is assumed identical in the two countries, this equilibrium implies that the low-skilled wage is higher in America than in China ($w_{LA} > w_{LC}$), while the high-skilled wage is higher in China than in America ($w_{HC} > w_{HA}$).

Suppose that we are in a situation with large endowment differences, such that there is no factor price equalization, as illustrated by the critical stage s_{*0} in Figure 18.15. Next, assume that the supply of both high-skilled and low-skilled workers increases proportionally in China. This increases the range of tasks outsourced to China, say from s_{*0} to s_{*1} in Figure 18.15. The key observation to make is that this raises the demand for high-skilled workers in both countries. The newly outsourced tasks (in the range from s_{*0} to s_{*1}) are *more* skill-intensive than the range of tasks (from 0 to s_{*0}) that were already performed in China, so the relative demand for high-skilled workers increases in China. Similarly, the newly outsourced tasks (in the range from s_{*0} to s_{*1}) are *less* skill-intensive than the range of tasks (from s_{*1} to 1) that continue to be produced in America, so the relative demand for high-skilled workers also increases in America. As a consequence, wage inequality rises in both countries.

18.6.3   Offshorability of Tasks and Lower Wage Inequality in America

This section now continues with a discussion of a model by Grossman and Rossi-Hansberg (2008) in which the degree of offshorability of tasks plays a role (see Antràs and Yeaple 2014). It returns to the benchmark model of section 18.6.1 with headquarter services and manufacturing. This time, however, China is $\gamma < 1$ times less productive than America. The section focuses on a situation with *conditional* factor price equalization (such that $w_{LC} = \gamma w_{LA}$ and $w_{HC} = \gamma w_{HA}$) in which China is so large it produces food, headquarter services, and manufacturing, while America only produces headquarter services and manufacturing. Moreover, suppose headquarter services and manufacturing are both produced from a continuum of tasks involving high-skilled workers and a continuum of tasks involving low-skilled workers (similar to section 18.6.2), with headquarter services relatively more skill-intensive. Finally, suppose that all high-skilled labor tasks cannot be outsourced, while all low-skilled tasks can be outsourced to China using the superior American technology at an offshorability cost requiring $\beta t(s) \geq 1$ units of labor for task s.

If the low-skilled labor tasks are now ordered in terms of rising offshorability costs, a picture similar to that in Figure 18.15 arises, with a critical task s_* such that all tasks below s_* are offshored to China and the remaining tasks are performed in America. The critical task is implicitly defined by the equality of costs for the low-skilled worker for that task:

$w_{LA} = \beta t(s_*)w_{LC}$. A fall in the parameter β can now be interpreted as an increase in the offshorability of low-skilled tasks. This raises the range of outsourced low-skilled tasks, similar to Figure 18.15. This time, however, the wage costs are essentially pinned down by China. This implies that the high-skilled wage rate in America does not change, while the increase in offshorability for low-skilled workers in America is similar to low-skilled labor-biased technological change and raises the low-skilled wage rate. As a consequence, an increase in offshorability lowers wage inequality in the source country.

18.6.4 Conclusion

Section 18.6 has briefly analyzed three different models of vertical FDI leading to different implications regarding the link between offshoring and wage inequality. In one model, offshoring leads to higher wage inequality in the source country and lower wage inequality in the destination country. In another model, offshoring leads to higher wage inequality in both countries. In yet another model, offshoring leads to lower wage inequality in the source country. This implies to some extent that "anything goes," indicating that there are no simple and robust predictions regarding the links between fragmentation and wage inequality. A more detailed look at the construction of the models shows that there are simply too many different model construction possibilities to lead to robust conclusions. This suggests that from an empirical point of view the impact of fragmentation depends on the specific circumstances for the country, time period, and sector under investigation. A broader discussion on globalization and income inequality is provided in Chapter 10.

18.7 Heterogeneous Firms and Vertical FDI

Section 18.2 analyzed the enormous differences between firms in terms of size, productivity, and the number of markets they service. The analysis in section 18.5 is based on representative firms with the same productivity level for each sector and country. This shortcoming can easily be alleviated using the tools developed in section 18.3. To do this, the two-sector model of section 18.5 is needed, but this time using only one type of labor as the factor of production. Assume that both countries produce food (under constant returns to scale) and that America is more productive in food production. This implies that the American wage rate is higher than the Chinese wage rate ($w_A > w_C$) and that the producers of manufactures face a perfectly elastic supply of labor at these wage rates. Manufacturing firms produce headquarter services h one-to-one with labor in America because it is assumed to have a sufficiently large technological advantage for producing these services. Both countries can produce manufacturing m one-to-one with labor, which means China has a comparative advantage in manufacturing since its wage rate is lower.

To produce final output, manufacturing firms combine h and m using a Cobb-Douglas technology. Since firms differ in their productivity level φ (drawn from some underlying distribution after paying a fixed cost), total output for a firm is proportional to $\varphi h^\eta m^{1-\eta}$, where η is the intensity of headquarter services. Continue to assume that the transport of final goods is frictionless. Firms have two location choices.

- *Domestic firm*: produce both headquarter services and manufacturing in America. In this case, there is a fixed cost f associated with headquarter services provision and the marginal production costs are proportional to the American wage rate w_A.
- *Multinational firm*: produce headquarter services in America and manufacturing in China. In this case, there is a higher fixed cost $f_m > f$ reflecting both the headquarter services provision and the costs associated with organizing the fragmentation of the production process. In addition, there is an iceberg transport cost $\tau > 1$ associated with shipping the manufacturing input m from China back to America. The marginal costs of production thus depend on both the American and the Chinese wage rate and are proportional to $w_A^{\eta}(\tau w_C)^{1-\eta}$.

Producers of a variety of manufactures face iso-elastic demand, where ε is the price elasticity of demand. They thus charge a constant mark-up of price over marginal cost. Operating profits depend on the price charged for final goods and the size of the American and Chinese markets. For a domestic firm with productivity level φ and marginal costs w_A, operating profits are equal to $Bw_A^{1-\varepsilon}\varphi^{1-\varepsilon} - w_A f$, where B is some constant (see Technical Note 18.1). A domestic firm will only produce if it is able to recover its fixed costs f. All firms with a productivity level below some viability cut-off level φ_* will thus exit the market, where φ_* is determined by $Bw_A^{1-\varepsilon}\varphi_*^{\varepsilon-1} = f$ (see Figure 18.16).

For a multinational firm with productivity level φ and marginal costs $w_A^{\eta}(\tau w_C)^{1-\eta}$, operating profits are equal to $B\left(w_A^{\eta}(\tau w_C)^{1-\eta}\right)^{1-\varepsilon}\varphi^{1-\varepsilon} - w_A f_m$ (see Figure 18.16). As drawn, the intercept for multinational profits on the vertical axis is lower than for domestic firms (which requires $f_m > f$), while the slope of the multinational profit line is steeper than for domestic firms, which requires $w_A > \tau w_C$ (see Technical Note 18.3). If the American wage

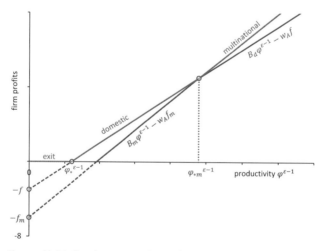

Figure 18.16 Firm heterogeneity and vertical FDI
Note: $B_d \equiv Bw_A^{1-\varepsilon}$ and $B_m \equiv B\left(w_A^{\eta}(\tau w_C)^{1-\eta}\right)^{1-\varepsilon}$.

BOX 18.3 EMPIRICAL EVIDENCE FOR VERTICAL FDI

When discussing empirical evidence for horizontal FDI for US multinationals in Box 18.1, it was noted that differences in capital–labor ratios and schooling did not seem to have significant explanatory power. Taking a closer look at the most actively involved countries, it is evident that the top five countries for US affiliate exports back to the USA are (in this order, starting with the highest): Canada, Mexico, Ireland, the UK, and Singapore. These countries differ substantially in their characteristics and development levels, indicating that strict adherence to a $2 \times 2 \times 2$ framework does not do justice to the rich empirical connections between countries. Evidently, some American firms find it worthwhile to outsource part of the production process to an advanced country like Canada, while other firms do so with respect to a middle-income country like Mexico. At the same time, some firms outsource to neighboring countries (Canada and Mexico), while other firms outsource to countries further away (the UK, Ireland, and Singapore). The comparative advantage of fragmentation for a particular production process depends, of course, on the production process itself and the factor intensity of the fragmented part. In short, it is necessary to interact a country's factor abundance with the factor intensity of the production activity.

To allow for flexibility in our empirical evaluation, we interact endowments with skill intensity. Let X_i^j be the exports from the USA to country i in sector j, let S_i^j be the sales of American affiliates in sector j located in country i, and let $s_{x,i}^j$ be the share of exports in serving country i for sector j, defined as: $s_{x,i}^j = X_i^j / (X_i^j + S_i^j)$. This indicates the extent to which a foreign market is serviced through exports rather than affiliate sales.

The analysis of Box 18.1 is now extended by taking skill interactions into consideration. All variables analyzed before are now used as control variables in this specification,

Table 18.4. Skill interactions for American multinationals, 2009

Dependent variable $\log(s_{x,i}^j)$ (see the main text for details)

Variable	(1)	(2)	(3)	(4)
Skill endowment	−0.03	1.57[*]	1.57[*]	
	(0.29)	(0.63)	(0.64)	
Skill endowment × skill intensity		−10.5[**]	−9.83[**]	08.77[**]
		(3.57)	(3.38)	(2.68)
Skill intensity		13.7[**]		
		(2.74)		
Observations	2,315	2,315	2,315	2,482

Source: Antràs and Yeaple 2014, table 2.4.
Notes: [**] and [*] indicate significant at 1 and 5 percent levels; standard errors in parentheses; 42 countries included in the analysis; country fixed effects only in column 4; sector fixed effects only in columns 3 and 4; additional controls not reported.

BOX 18.3 (cont.)

which allows us to focus on skill endowments, skill intensity, and skill interactions (see Table 18.4). From the vertical FDI analysis in this chapter, the crucial prediction is that the impact of the interaction term should be negative: skill-intensive parts of the production process should tend to be located in skill-abundant countries. Column (1) confirms that skill endowments are not significant if the interaction term is absent. Column (2) includes the interaction term and confirms that American firms tend to export more to skill-scarce countries in skill-intensive sectors. Columns (3) and (4) show that this result is robust to including sector and country fixed effects.

rate is sufficiently high compared to the Chinese wage rate, the profits of becoming a vertical multinational are higher than for a domestic firm if the firm is sufficiently productive. See Box 15.2 for empirical evidence from Spain. In Figure 18.16, the switching point is given by φ_{*m}. All firms above φ_{*m} become vertical multinationals. All firms below φ_* exit the market. All firms in between these two levels are domestic firms (that export to the Chinese market). Note that, in accordance with empirical observations, there is a range of domestic firms active in the market in Figure 18.16, if the multinational profit line is sufficiently steep this range may not exist (see Technical Note 18.3 for the exact condition).

18.8   Multinationals and Development: An Evaluation

So far, this chapter has attempted to explain some stylized facts about firms and multinationals with the help of trade models. These models help us to understand firm behavior and some of the trade-offs firms have to make in order to become internationally active. Looking only at the relevant trade models also poses a risk. One easily overlooks the controversies that often surround multinationals and FDI. These discussions can be organized around the so-called home and host country effects and the possible external effects that surround FDI.

Home country effects concern questions such as employment and wage effects of off-shoring, transfer pricing and tax issues, effects on the trade structure and comparative advantages. Host country effects relate to the general effects on wages and employment. These effects can have consequences for other firms that might see their most productive employees move to multinationals, the effects of remittances and profits that leave the host country, and the effects on knowledge and innovation because the multinational brings new technology into the country. The literature on these topics is large and varied (see Lipsey 2004, or Barba-Navaretti and Venables 2004, for extensive discussions).

For economic development the host country effects are the most noteworthy: do developing countries gain or lose from FDI? The entrance of foreign firms might affect wages in the host countries where they start operating. It has already been observed that multinationals are more productive than local firms or firms that also export, and are therefore able to pay higher wages. Lipsey (2004) observes that most multinationals indeed pay higher wages than domestically owned firms. This does not necessarily imply that wages in the host countries increase. Multinationals might, for example, select the more productive workers who already earned high wages, or multinationals might acquire higher-productive, high-wage firms. If multinationals engage in M&As, the local industry might not benefit if the takeover involves the more productive local firms; there is only a shift in ownership. The multinationals capture the market and could ship profits to the home countries.

If wages indeed increase, the high wages might spill over to domestic firms, affecting the profitability of those firms. These effects are the so-called wage spillover effects.

The evidence on this effect is mixed, but leans toward a positive effect (see also Antràs and Yeaple 2014). For domestic firms, this implies that they have to compete for the best employees with multinationals, which are on average more productive, pay well, and have the means to win the competitive battle of attracting the best and most productive employees. This forces local firms to pay more. Whether the *net* effect of this process is positive or negative from a welfare perspective depends to a large extent on productivity. It has already been established that multinationals belong to the group of most productive firms. Does the higher productivity of multinationals spill over to locally owned firms and does this compensate for the higher wages?

The answer to this question is related to the possibility of international knowledge spillovers. If international knowledge transfers are possible, countries are no longer restricted by their own knowledge, but can benefit from knowledge that is developed in foreign countries and becomes available through trade, but also by the local presence of multinationals. If knowledge spillovers are possible, the productivity of a sector not only depends on the local knowledge or experience of the firms themselves, but also on foreign knowledge that becomes available by the presence of multinationals. A key assumption is that international knowledge is freely available. Grossman and Helpman (1991) show how this process of knowledge spillovers can affect specialization patterns of individual countries. Depending on initial conditions, various patterns are possible, with different growth perspectives. If knowledge spillovers increase growth rates of a sector with a high growth potential, this process of knowledge accumulation will positively affect technological progress or TFP of the industry and will increase the welfare of the country involved. If knowledge accumulates in sectors with low growth potential, the growth effects are smaller.

Coe and Helpman (1995) find that technological progress depends on domestic as well as on foreign R&D capital. They estimate the relationship between openness and the stock of foreign R&D. They find that the elasticity of productivity with respect to domestic R&D is higher in larger countries, but that these larger countries produce an additional return of 30 percent in the smaller (neighboring) countries. This indicates that international R&D spillovers are present in the data; large countries – that are the home base of multinationals – export knowledge. Coe, Helpman, and Hoffmaier (1997) repeat this exercise for 77 developing countries. Despite the fact that these countries initially have low levels of R&D themselves, they benefit from the R&D investments in the advanced countries. This knowledge accumulates in multinationals. The implication is that these knowledge spillovers are facilitated by the presence of multinationals. Coe and Helpman (1995) also interact openness with R&D. So, it is not only R&D that is important in their model, but also the possibility that the impact of knowledge is larger in economies that trade a lot. They find that trade openness has a significant effect on productivity, and that the larger a country's foreign R&D stock is (the stock of foreign knowledge to which it has access), the larger its TFP gains.

Knowledge spillovers can potentially benefit the host country of FDI. There is also a risk: the risk that R&D investments in knowledge by local firms only duplicates knowledge that is already available abroad and within the multinational. Firms that are only active locally might increase their productivity by learning or copying from the multinationals. They might be forced to do so for competitive reasons: they can only survive if their productivity increases. In these cases, overall industry productivity can increase, but it also involves waste because local firms invest in copying and not in developing new products. The risk and waste of duplication is discussed in Grossman and Helpman (1991). A possible way out is to increase the incentive to innovate in order to remain competitive. Countries could use R&D investment to develop new and unique varieties of a product. Governments could provide incentives to avoid waste and develop new products. The Irish case illustrates this process (Barba-Navaretti and Venables 2004). Ireland shifted from being reluctant to allow inward FDI until the 1950s to stimulating and welcoming inward FDI. Tax exemptions and special economic zones attracted foreign capital. The spectacular increase in the number of foreign firms, together with Ireland joining the EU, transformed the economy from a relatively closed economy into one that heavily depends on exports of products that were new to the Irish economy. The share of exports increased to over 70 percent of GDP. The foreign firms rely almost exclusively on export markets. This export orientation spilled over to domestically owned firms.

This section emphasizes that the effects of FDI on an economy are many and varied. It is not *a priori* clear what the net effects are. For some economies, the effects of FDI are welfare enhancing, for others they are not. The survey by Lipsey (2004) provides many case studies that make clear that the overall effects are dependent on local circumstances. Bhagwati (1978) already drew this conclusion; the growth effects of inward FDI could be favorable or unfavorable, depending on local circumstances and the incentives that are introduced by host-country (trade) policies. It should be noted that some *economic* aspects that are relevant for the host countries were highlighted above. The controversies that surround FDI also include issues related to corruption, pollution, labor conditions, and other issues where FDI could be important. These disputes are outside the scope of this textbook, but can be crucial for some countries, as FDI could have destabilizing influences. UNCTAD provides information on these topics (see https://unctad.org/topic/investment/world-investment-report).

18.9   Conclusions

The key actor within economics is the firm. What firms produce, how they are organized, how much they sell, for which markets they produce, and how productive they are vary substantially from one firm to another. Over the past two decades, the activities and characteristics of the firm and how firms differ in many relevant aspects have become central in economic analysis. Thanks to the work of Melitz (2003) and followers, there is now a better understanding of the consequences of heterogeneous firms that differ in their productivity levels for economic development.

This chapter analyzed the main structure and outcomes of his approach, and applied it to understand horizontal and vertical FDI. The combination of transportation costs and plant-level scale economies leads to a proximity–concentration trade-off that explains why firms service some markets through exporting and other markets through multinational activities. Because of ever-lower transportation and interaction costs and ever-improving communication possibilities, it is now possible for firms to reorganize their production process in different locations, taking the specific advantages of these locations for certain upstream or downstream parts of the process into consideration. The chapter analyzed this fragmentation process, which involves supply chains and leads to vertical FDI. The heterogeneous firm setting can also be used in this framework. The chapter also evaluated the pros and cons of FDI. Not all aspects of FDI can be captured by the models, and it is important to realize that the effects of FDI can be many and varied. It is not always clear that the net effect of FDI is welfare increasing. It often depends on local circumstances.

Further Reading

The starting point for the importance of firm heterogeneity is the empirical work of Andrew Bernard and Bradford Jensen (for example, 1995 and 1999). The breakthrough theoretical work is that of Marc Melitz (2003). See Melitz and Redding (2014) for an overview.

Attention for the importance of multinational firms is much older than that of firm heterogeneity, starting with Hymer (1960) and Dunning's (1977) ownership – localization – internalization framework in the international business literature. See Barba-Navaretti and Venables (2004) for an overview.

The UN Conference on Trade and Development (UNCTAD) provides up-to-date information on the relationships between multinational firms and development, in particular in the annual World Investment Report. See: https://unctad.org/publications.

TECHNICAL NOTE 18.1   FIRM REVENUE AND PROFITS

For a firm with productivity φ, we substitute the optimal price $p_\varphi = \left(\frac{\varepsilon}{\varepsilon-1}\right)\left(\frac{1}{\varphi}\right)$ in the demand function $q_\varphi = A p_\varphi^{-\varepsilon}$ and multiply by p_φ to get revenue r_φ:

$$r_\varphi = p_\varphi q_\varphi = \left[\left(\frac{\varepsilon}{\varepsilon-1}\right)\left(\frac{1}{\varphi}\right)\right]A\left[\left(\frac{\varepsilon}{\varepsilon-1}\right)\left(\frac{1}{\varphi}\right)\right]^{-\varepsilon} = \varepsilon(\varepsilon-1)^{\varepsilon-1}\varepsilon^{-\varepsilon}A\varphi^{\varepsilon-1} = \varepsilon B\varphi^{\varepsilon-1} \qquad \text{A18.1}$$

Where the constant B is defined as $B \equiv (\varepsilon-1)^{\varepsilon-1}\varepsilon^{-\varepsilon}A$. Using this to determine profits π_φ gives

$$\pi_\varphi = p_\varphi q_\varphi - \left(f + \frac{q_\varphi}{\varphi}\right) = \frac{p_\varphi q_\varphi}{\varepsilon} - f = \frac{r_\varphi}{\varepsilon} - f = B\varphi^{\varepsilon-1} - f \qquad \text{A18.2}$$

Where the second equality uses the optimal pricing rule and the third and fourth equality uses equation (A18.1).

TECHNICAL NOTE 18.2   AUTARKY EQUILIBRIUM

The cut-off viability condition is given in equation A18.3. Substituting this in the free entry condition (equation A18.4) to eliminate the constant B gives equation A18.5. It can be shown that the function $h(\varphi_*)$ is monotonically declining from ∞ to zero and thus uniquely determines the autarky equilibrium cut-off productivity given by equation 18.3.

$$B\varphi_*^{\varepsilon-1} - f = 0 \qquad \text{A18.3}$$

$$\int_{\varphi_*}^{\infty} \left[(B\varphi^{\varepsilon-1} - f)/\delta\right]g(\varphi)d\varphi = f_{en} \qquad \text{A18.4}$$

$$\int_{\varphi_*}^{\infty} (\varphi^{\varepsilon-1}\varphi_*^{1-\varepsilon} - 1)g(\varphi)d\varphi \equiv h(\varphi_*) = \delta f_{en}/f \qquad \text{A18.5}$$

TECHNICAL NOTE 18.3   VERTICAL FDI

As explained in the main text in section 18.7, operating profits are equal to $Bw_A^{1-\varepsilon}\varphi^{1-\varepsilon} - w_A f$ for a domestic firm and $B\left(w_A^\eta(\tau w_C)^{1-\eta}\right)^{1-\varepsilon}\varphi^{1-\varepsilon} - w_A f_m$ for a firm engaging in vertical FDI. To make vertical FDI and a distribution of firms into domestic firms and multinationals possible, three simple conditions need to be fulfilled. First, we must make sure that the vertical intercept of the profit function is lower for multinationals than for domestic firms. This requires that $f < f_m$, such that the fixed costs are larger for multinationals than for domestic firms. Second, we must ensure that the slope of the profit function is steeper for multinationals than for domestic firms. This requires:

$$w_A^{1-\varepsilon} < \left(w_A^\eta(\tau w_C)^{1-\eta}\right)^{1-\varepsilon} \Leftrightarrow w_A > w_A^\eta(\tau w_C)^{1-\eta} \Leftrightarrow w_A > \tau w_C \qquad \text{A18.6}$$

Where the inequality reversal in the first step arises from the fact that $\varepsilon > 1$. This implies that it is only attractive to become a multinational firm if the wage rate paid in America is sufficiently high compared to the wage rate paid in China, taking the transportation costs τ into consideration. Third, we must ensure that the viability threshold for domestic firms occurs before that of multinational firms is reached, or equivalently that the point where the two profit levels are the same is reached after the viability threshold is reached. If this third condition is not met, we will only observe multinational firms in equilibrium and no domestic firms. We can determine this threshold by equating the profit functions above to zero, which gives:

$$\varphi_*^{\varepsilon-1} = \frac{w_A f}{B w_A^{1-\varepsilon}}; \quad \varphi_m^{\varepsilon-1} = \frac{w_A f_m}{B\left(w_A^\eta(\tau w_C)^{1-\eta}\right)^{1-\varepsilon}} \qquad \text{A18.7}$$

Where $\varphi_*^{\varepsilon-1}$ is the threshold for domestic firms and $\varphi_m^{\varepsilon-1}$ is the threshold for multinationals. The third condition is therefore met if $\varphi_*^{\varepsilon-1} < \varphi_m^{\varepsilon-1}$, which means:

$$\frac{w_A f}{B w_A^{1-\varepsilon}} < \frac{w_A f_m}{B\left(w_A^\eta(\tau w_C)^{1-\eta}\right)^{1-\varepsilon}} \Leftrightarrow \frac{f}{w_A^{1-\varepsilon}} < \frac{f_m}{\left(w_A^\eta(\tau w_C)^{1-\eta}\right)^{1-\varepsilon}} \Leftrightarrow \left(w_A^\eta(\tau w_C)^{1-\eta}\right)^{1-\varepsilon} f < w_A^{1-\varepsilon} f_m.$$

19 Sustainability and Development

This chapter is co-authored by Julia Swart.

19.1 Introduction

Chapter 4 showed that biogeographic conditions, such as climate systems and access to waterways, have a strong influence on economic development. The relationship between these conditions and economic development can, however, vary across space and time. Some countries are strongly affected by abrupt weather circumstances because of higher dependence on the agricultural sector and/or less availability of insurance. Chapter 15, on the other hand, emphasized the link between food production, rural development, and migration decisions.

Although it is clear that biogeographic conditions (henceforth geography) have an effect on the economy (through agricultural productivity, transportation costs, medical costs, and so on), the relationship between geography and economic development only started to receive real attention in the development literature at the end of the 1990s. With the disappearance of the Malthusian model, land as a factor of production also mostly disappeared from the development literature, in particular because of the strong evidence of fast physical capital accumulation in the more advanced countries in the world. Therefore, physical capital and labor were the two dominant factors of production in the economic growth models during the twentieth century.

The diverse experience of developing countries in the past century shows that the standard growth model cannot fully explain the disappointing (sometimes even negative) rates of economic growth for some countries. While trying to explain the weak growth rate of some of these countries, economists returned to geography as an explanatory factor. Bloom and Sachs (1998) pioneered the study of the effect of geography (proxied as the percent of land area in the tropics) on income growth. Since then, geography in general and climate in particular became one of the fundamental determinants of economic growth (alongside institutions and culture).

Although the debate about the fundamental determinants of economic growth continues, the economic growth literature has been benefiting from research on climate change, including the effects on agriculture productivity, incidence of storms, drought, heat waves, and so on. All these factors can affect the economy and are unevenly distributed across the world population and within countries. When climate change affects the agricultural sector, for example, the small farmer without access to insurance mechanisms is one of the most affected persons. All in all, geography has a central place in development policies in a period of climate change. Environmental policies are now acknowledged as essential for long-term development. At the same time, development policies should incorporate the possible environmental impact to avoid costs now and in the future.

A crucial distinction in the literature between developing countries and advanced countries is the degree to which they prioritize environmental issues. Environmental goods, such as clean air and biodiversity, are often seen as luxury goods which inhabitants of countries only desire when they are rich enough. At the same time, developing countries are, in general, relatively more dependent on natural goods (such as agriculture and mines). The combination of dependence on natural goods and lower desire for environmental conservation leads to relatively more environmental degradation in the developing countries. While it might seem contradictory that one does not care about a good which one depends on, such an outcome might make sense in the presence of market failures.

This chapter investigates the links between economic development and the environment. Section 19.2 begins, with a discussion on the relationship between economic development and the environment. Section 19.3 analyzes issues of scale, composition, and technology before section 19.4 turns to the sustainable development goals and section 19.5 examines multilateral agreements. The so-called natural resource curse is analyzed in section 19.6, while section 19.7 discusses renewable versus nonrenewable resources, before section 19.8 concludes.

19.2   Economic Development and the Environment

The quality of our environment today is undoubtedly at a lower level than, say, 1,000 years ago. Economic progress, population growth, and affluence led us to cut down forests, to discard trash and obsolete products, to extract minerals and metals from the ground, to emit pollution into the atmosphere, and various other adverse effects for our planet. It is therefore not surprising that for most of human history economic development was associated with environmental degradation. There was a *trade-off* between development and the environment. That is, in order to preserve the environment, we would have to refrain from economic development. Alternatively, economic development leads to environmental degradation.

In 1968, a group of scientists, industrialists, and economists created the *Club of Rome* to discuss global challenges, such as environmental degradation. A few years later, they published the report *The Limits to Growth* (1972), which was a pioneer study to question the implications of sustained economic growth to the environment. The authors were concerned about irreversible damages that pollution could cause to natural systems. Nonetheless, according to the Club of Rome, at that time, "only the developed nations of the world are seriously concerned about pollution." The authors add: "It is an unfortunate characteristic of many types of pollution, however, that eventually they become widely distributed around the world" (p. 84).

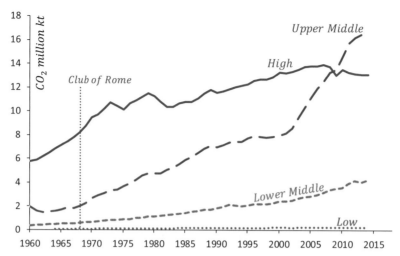

Figure 19.1 Total CO$_2$ emissions by income groups; million kt since 1960
Source: Created using World Development Indicators online.
Notes: CO$_2$ emissions in million *kt*; see main text for income groups.

Pollution, in general terms, has indeed increased throughout the world in the period after the Club of Rome was formed. The authors were also right that pollution is becoming more distributed around the world, with rising environmental damage for some countries. Figure 19.1 shows total CO$_2$ emissions for four income groups since 1960. The classification in income groups is based on the World Bank with the ranking: Low income – Lower Middle income – Upper Middle income – High income.[1] In 1968 (the year the Club of Rome was created), high-income countries were responsible for approximately 63 percent of the world's CO$_2$ emissions. In total, the High-income group emitted around 8 million kt (kt = kiloton, 1,000 tons) of CO$_2$ in that year. More recently (in 2014), these figures have changed to approximately 36 percent of the world's emissions from high-income countries, but an absolute increase to around 13 million kt of CO$_2$. Figure 19.1 clearly illustrates the sharp increase in emissions coming from Upper-Middle-income countries and to a lesser extent from Lower-Middle-income countries.

Total emissions show us the overall burden we are placing on our planet, but they don't tell us much about the way we are living our lives today as compared to the past. A simple figure which gives us an indication about the environmental impact per citizen is emissions per capita. Do high-income countries emit more CO$_2$ because they are wealthier or because they have more people? Figure 19.2 shows data on CO$_2$ emissions per capita by income group since 1960. The figure shows that in 1968 high-income countries emitted approximately 9.55 metric tons of CO$_2$ per capita. This was no less than 27 times higher than for

---

[1] For Low income (34 countries) GNI per capita in 2016 was below $1,006; for Lower Middle income (47 countries) $1,006–3,956, for Upper Middle income (56 countries) $3,956–12,235, for High income (80 countries) $12,235+.

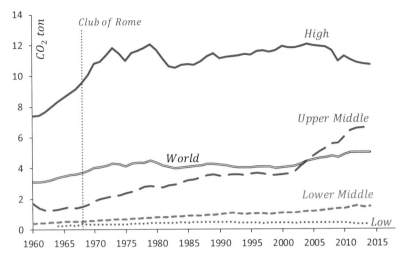

Figure 19.2 CO_2 emissions per capita by income group; metric tons since 1960
Source: Created using World Development Indicators online.
Notes: CO_2 in metric ton per capita; see main text for income groups.

low-income countries (0.35 metric tons per capita). In 2014, these figures have only become worse: high-income countries emitted around 10.71 metric tons per capita of CO_2, which is 33 times higher than for low-income countries, which emitted only 0.32 metric tons per capita. It is clear why many policymakers are concerned about the environmental consequences of economic development in less developed countries. Imagine that all the inhabitants of middle-income countries suddenly had the same CO_2 emissions per capita as the high-income countries in 2014: this would imply that total CO_2 emissions would rise from 34 to 71 million kt.[2] As a result, the CO_2 concentration would increase by 4 ppm (parts per million)[3] in 2014, which is extremely high given the estimates from the IPPC that the Earth's temperature will rise by 2–4.5° C if we double the amount of CO_2 compared to preindustrial levels (280 ppm).

The positive link between economic development and environmental degradation was analyzed in the 1970s by the so-called *IPAT* identity (Ehrlich and Holdren 1971):

$$I = P \times A \times T \qquad\qquad 19.1$$

where *I* represents impact (society's impact on the environment), *P* represents population, *A* represents affluence, and *T* represents technology. Using this identity, emissions can be

---

[2] Calculated using the population size of lower-middle- and high-middle-income countries in the year 2014, which together was approximately 5.4 billion.

[3] Assuming that 46 percent of the CO_2 emissions stay in the air, 54 percent would therefore be stored in plants, rivers, lakes, the oceans, soil, and rocks (30–40 percent alone dissolves into rivers, lakes, and oceans, leading to ocean acidification); also assuming that the concentration of CO_2 in the atmosphere rises by 1 ppm for every 7.8 billion tons of CO_2 in the air.

decomposed in three separate terms. For example, equation 19.2 decomposes CO_2 emissions in population size, income per capita (in GDP), and emissions intensity (CO_2 per GDP).

$$CO_2 = population \times \frac{GDP}{population} \times \frac{CO_2}{GDP} \qquad 19.2$$

The *IPAT* identity suggests that technological progress will not reduce environmental degradation if population growth continues at a high rate. To think in terms of growth rates, totally differentiate equation 19.1 and use ~ to denote the relative change of a variable (so $\tilde{x} = dx/x$) to get:[4]

$$\tilde{I} = \tilde{P} + \tilde{A} + \tilde{T} \qquad 19.3$$

Suppose, for example, that income per capita remains constant (an optimistic scenario from an environmental perspective, given the *IPAT* framework), population continues to grow at around 1.15 percent per year, and pollution intensity decreases at the rate of 0.55 percent per year.[5] What would be the impact on the environment? Substituting these numbers in equation 19.3, the environmental impact would rise at a rate of 0.6 percent per year. Concerns related to population growth, consumption, and environmental impact have intensified in the mid-twentieth century. This is represented by the Neo-Malthusian view. Nonetheless, solutions derived from this view (natality control and reduction in consumption) are quite controversial.

In contrast to this pessimistic view on the environment, the Environmental Kuznets Curve (EKC) approach (see Grossman and Krueger 1995) suggests that pollution rises with income per capita for low levels, but starts to fall for sufficiently high levels. There is thus a critical level $\bar{A}$ such that $\partial I/\partial A > 0$ for $A < \bar{A}$ and $\partial I/\partial A < 0$ for $A > \bar{A}$, where $\bar{A}$ is a threshold level of income per capita, which can be empirically estimated. The intuition behind this turning point in income, leading to an improvement in the environment beyond this point, is that rich countries have a higher willingness and ability to pay for pollution abatement and therefore impose stricter rules for environmental regulation. Poor countries, on the other hand, give priority to economic growth and leave environmental protection as a second step on their development agenda.

Figure 19.3 plots 2015's fossil fuel energy consumption (percent of total) against income per capita for a sample of 133 countries. To find evidence for an Environmental Kuznets Curve, we should find a hill-shaped relationship between these two variables, such that pollution first rises and then falls.[6] This is illustrated in Figure 19.3 by the estimated EKC line on the basis of a simple regression provided in Table 19.1, which explains fossil fuel

---

[4] Log-differentiation simplifies the procedure. First take logs of equation 19.1: $lnI = lnP + ln\ A + ln\ T$. Next, differentiate this equation to get: $\frac{dI}{I} = \frac{dP}{P} + \frac{dA}{A} + \frac{dT}{T}$. This is simplified in equation 19.3 using the ~ notation.

[5] World population growth rate was 1.16 percent in 2017 (World Bank, WDI). Weil (2014) estimates the productivity growth rate in the USA at 0.54 percent per year in the period 1975–2009.

[6] The literature usually refers to an "inverted-U relationship," but then you first have to picture a "U" in your mind and turn it upside-down. Instead, the term "hill shape" is straightforward.

Table 19.1. Environmental Kuznets Curve for fossil fuel energy consumption

Variable	Estimated coefficient	Standard error
constant	−409.61***	55.07
ln (income per capita)	101.56***	13.05
(ln (income per capita))²	−5.25***	0.76

Notes: Dependent variable is fossil fuel energy consumption (percent of total); *** indicates statistically significant at 1 percent level

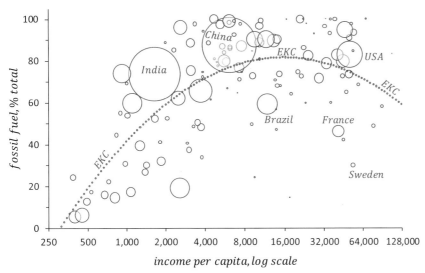

Figure 19.3 Fossil fuel energy consumption and Income per capita, 2015
Source: Created using World Development Indicators online.
Notes: Fossil fuel energy consumption (percent of total); income per capita in GDP (constant 2010 USD); size of bubbles proportional to total population in 2015; data covers 127 countries; EKC is estimated Environmental Kuznets Curve (see Table 19.1).

energy consumption using the log of income per capita and its squared term. The hill shape arises if the estimated coefficient for the squared term is negative.[7]

Based on the estimated Environmental Kuznets Curve in Figure 19.3, countries like India, China, and the USA are relatively polluting (above the line), while countries like Brazil, France, and Sweden are relatively green (below the line). The peak arises close to $16,000, an income per capita level for countries like Chile, Lithuania, and Estonia. In general, for

---

[7] To see this, consider a simple regression, such as provided in Figure 19.3 (where y is pollution and x is income): $y = \alpha + \beta_1 x + \beta_2 x^2 + \varepsilon$. The first derivative is then $\partial y / \partial x = \beta_1 + 2\beta_2 x$ and the second derivative is $\partial^2 y / \partial x^2 = 2\beta_2$. Remember from calculus that if the second derivate is negative, then the graph of the function has a local maximum at $x^{\cdot}$, where $x^{\cdot}$ is determined by setting the first derivate equal to zero. In this case, the second derivative is negative if $\beta_2 < 0$ and the turning point is reached at $x^* = -\beta_1 / 2\beta_2$. Substituting the coefficients from Figure 19.3 implies $x^* = 9.67$, or $exp(x^*) = 15,873$.

this variable, pollution is therefore expected to worsen up to an income per capita level of about \$16,000 and to improve for higher levels. Note, however, that the variation in Figure 19.3 is high, so it might be a good idea to add additional explanatory variables.

19.2.1   Andreoni and Levinson Model

Andreoni and Levinson (2001) provide a theoretical framework for the Environmental Kuznets Curve which is based on a technological link between consumption and abatement. A key condition for the hill-shaped EKC in this model is increasing returns to abatement. A simple version of the model is provided here. Suppose there is an economy with one representative individual, whose utility function U is represented by equation 19.4 and pollution P is a byproduct of consumption as in equation 19.5, where C is consumption and E is environmental effort. Note that pollution in equation 19.5 is divided into two parts. The first part, C, is simply consumption, indicating that the more the individual consumes, the more pollution will be generated. This part can be interpreted as gross pollution before abatement. The second part, $C^\alpha E^\beta$, represents abatement, indicating that the individual can reduce pollution as long as part of the income is dedicated to abatement. How much the individual will spend on environmental effort and consumption is subject to the budget constraint provided in equation 19.6, where M represents income.

$$U = C - P \qquad\qquad 19.4$$

$$P = C - C^\alpha E^\beta \qquad\qquad 19.5$$

$$C + E = M \qquad\qquad 19.6$$

The individual maximizes utility (equation 19.4) subject to the technological restriction (equation 19.5) and the budget restriction (equation 19.6). The solution to this optimization problem is provided in equations 19.7 and 19.8 (see Technical Note 19.1). Given the optimum level of environmental effort E^* and the optimum level of consumption C^*, we can now find the optimum level of pollution by substituting equations 19.7 and 19.8 into equation 19.5 as shown in equation 19.9. Note that the optimum level of pollution is not zero (why not?).

$$E^* = \left(\frac{\beta}{\alpha + \beta}\right)M \qquad\qquad 19.7$$

$$C^* = \left(\frac{\alpha}{\alpha + \beta}\right)M \qquad\qquad 19.8$$

$$P^* = \left(\frac{\alpha}{\alpha + \beta}\right)M - \left(\frac{\alpha}{\alpha + \beta}\right)^\alpha \left(\frac{\beta}{\alpha + \beta}\right)^\beta M^{\alpha + \beta} \qquad\qquad 19.9$$

Equation 19.9 presents the optimum pollution level P^* as a function of income M. These are the two key variables of the model. Technical Note 19.2 shows that the hill-shaped Environmental Kuznets Curve arises if, and only if, there are increasing returns to abatement, that is: $\alpha + \beta > 1$. Intuitively, as countries get richer, abatement becomes more attractive because of the rising returns to abatement. Technology is thus the critical factor leading to environmental conservation. The other factor which could result in environmental conservation (namely, less pollution being a luxury good and a rising preference for less pollution as income increases) does not play a role here.

19.3   Scale, Composition, and Technology

The Andreoni and Levinson (2001) model is consistent with another theoretical explanation for the Environmental Kuznets Curve. This explanation focuses on the roles of scale, composition, and technology and argues that economic progress has an impact on the *scale* and *composition* of output and on the *technology* (technical efficiency) used in the economy. Returning to the *IPAT* identity, the terms *P* (population) and *A* (affluence) represent scale effects. A larger population and higher income, everything else constant, increase the environmental impact. The third term of the *IPAT* identity is the technology effect, that is, the adoption of *cleaner* or *dirtier* technologies. The technology effect can thus be positive or negative for the environment, depending on the type of technology adopted. A critique on the *IPAT* equation is that it does not take into account the interaction between the terms on the right-hand side. That is, *P*, *A*, and *T* are treated independently.

As economies grow, the scale effect, everything else constant, negatively affects the environment. However, a country can change the composition of its output (for example, from manufacturing to services) and the technologies employed. The combination of these three factors imply that economic growth can have a positive or negative impact on the environment:

$$I = f\left(\underbrace{scale}_{+}, \underbrace{composition}_{+/-}, \underbrace{technology}_{+/-} \right)$$ 19.10

where *I* represents environmental impact. The three factors on the right-hand side are not exogenously determined. A country can, for example, decide to substitute away from harmful pesticides because of the deliberate concern for environmental protection.[8] Institutions (in this case, environmental regulation) can thus influence technology. Similarly, a country's changing comparative advantage over time will influence the composition effect.

19.3.1   Green Solow Model

The Andreoni and Levinson model provides theoretical support for the Environmental Kuznets Curve provided there are increasing returns to scale in the abatement technology. The authors provide evidence for rising returns to scale for the USA. Brock and Taylor (2010), however, argue that the empirical evidence also supports constant abatement costs

---

[8]   In August 2018, for example, France banned five pesticides which researchers accredited with killing off bees: www.telegraph.co.uk/news/2018/08/31/france-first-ban-five-pesticides-killing-bees/.

as a fraction of income. They suggest a simple amended version of the Solow model (see Chapter 7) which solves three puzzles of the Environmental Kuznets Curve literature.

1. The first puzzle is that pollution abatement costs are rather stable over time, whereas emissions reductions have fallen significantly. An explanation of the Environmental Kuznets Curve based on richer countries imposing tighter regulations, and thus rising abatement costs, is incompatible with the empirical evidence of constant abatement costs as a fraction of income.
2. The second puzzle is the underlying theoretical explanation of the Environmental Kuznets Curve. Despite supporting empirical evidence (depending on the pollutant), the theoretical literature struggles to explain the data.
3. The third puzzle is the contradicting cross-country empirical findings on the link between income per capita and pollution.

The Brock and Taylor (2010) model builds on the Solow model in which output Y is a strictly concave function $F(K, BL)$ of capital K, labor L, and the labor-augmenting technology B subject to constant returns to scale. The savings rate is denoted by s and depreciation by δ. Assume that the population grows at a constant rate n (such that $\dot{L}/L = n$) and labor-augmenting technological progress occurs at a rate g_B (such that $\dot{B}/B = g_B$).

We add pollution to the Solow model by assuming that pollution emissions E are equal to pollution created ωF minus pollution abated $\omega A(F, \theta F)$, where F are units of economic activity (output), ω are units of pollution, A is abatement, and θF is the abatement effort (where θ can be interpreted as abatement costs relative to income). Assume that the abatement function $A(F, \theta F)$ exhibits constant returns to scale and is strictly increasing and strictly concave in F and θF.

$$E = \omega[F - A(F, \theta F)] \qquad 19.11$$

Equation 19.11 gives the equation for pollution emissions. Assume a constant rise in abatement technology: $\dot{\omega} = -\omega g_A$ for $g_A > 0$, while $\omega(0) = \omega_0$ is the initial pollution emission.[9] Given the above definitions and assumptions, we include pollution and abatement in the Solow model as provided in equations 19.12–19.14. The output available for consumption C or investment I is given in equation 19.12. Writing the variables in intensive units (see Chapter 7) gives the law of motion of capital in intensive units (equation 19.13) and pollution emissions in intensive units (equation 19.14) – see Technical Note 19.3.

$$C + I = [1 - \theta]F \qquad 19.12$$

$$\dot{k} = sf(k)[1 - \theta] - [\delta + n + g_B]k \qquad 19.13$$

$$e = f(k)\omega a(\theta); \quad a(\theta) \equiv (1 - A(1, \theta)) \qquad 19.14$$

---

[9] Technological progress in abatement (for example, better filter systems) implies that pollution ω decreases at rate g_A.

In the steady state, the capital stock in intensive units is constant (say k^*) and solves $\dot{k} = 0$ in equation 19.13. Output in intensive units is then also constant and equal to $y^* = f(k^*)$. Aggregate output $Y = y^* BL$ then grows at the rate $\tilde{Y} = g_B + n$. Assuming that θ (the fraction of economic activity dedicated to abatement) is constant, it follows from equation 19.14 that emissions in intensive units fall at the rate g_A, since $f(k^*)$ and $a(\theta)$ are constant, while ω falls at the rate g_A through improvements in abatement technology. The growth rate of aggregate emissions $E = eBL$ is then (see Technical Note 19.4):

$$\tilde{E} = g_B + n - g_A \equiv g_E \qquad\qquad 19.15$$

Equation 19.15 has two components: a scale effect $g_B + n$ and a technique effect g_a. Aggregate emissions growth rate in the steady state (labeled g_E for future reference) is negative if $g_A > g_B + n$. Thus, whenever technological progress in abatement is larger than the growth rate of aggregate output, the economy is on a sustainable growth path, providing theoretical support for the Environmental Kuznets Curve in an extended Solow growth model.

To illustrate this, consider a Cobb-Douglas production function in intensive form: $f(k) = k^\alpha$. If we divide the left-hand side and right-hand side of equation 19.13 by k, we get the growth rate of capital in intensive units: $\tilde{k} = sk^{\alpha-1}(1-\theta) - (\delta + n + g_B)$, which consists of two parts. Figure 19.4 depicts α times these two parts (and thus visualizes $\alpha\tilde{k}$). The solid downward-sloping curve with arrows is $\alpha sk^{\alpha-1}(1-\theta)$. It depicts savings available for capital accumulation and falls because of the declining marginal product of capital. The dashed horizontal line depicts $\alpha(\delta + n + g_B)$ and indicates what is needed to keep k constant. Capital in intensive units k thus rises if the savings curve is above the line and falls if it is below the line, as indicated by the arrows in the figure. The intersection at the point B determines the steady-state level of capital in intensive form k^*.

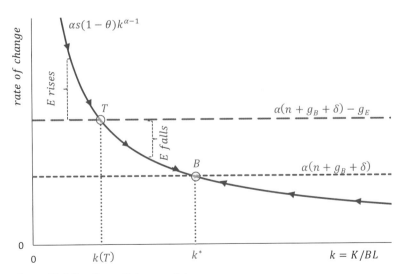

Figure 19.4 The Green Solow model
Note: Based on $f(k) = k^\alpha$; $\alpha = 0.3$; $\theta = 0.2$; $n + \delta + g_B = 0.4$; $s = 0.4$; $g_E = -0.1$.

Note that equation 19.15 depicts the growth rate of aggregate emissions at the steady state k^* only. Outside of the steady state, we have to take the impact of changing k on intensive emissions e as provided in equation 19.14 into consideration. More specifically, assuming that θ is constant (and so a is constant), we have: $\tilde{e} = \tilde{f} + \tilde{\omega}$. Recall that $\tilde{\omega} = -g_A$. Since $f(k) = y$, we have $\tilde{f} = \tilde{y}$. With the production function $y = k^\alpha$, we then get $\tilde{y} = \alpha \tilde{k}$, such that $\tilde{e} = \alpha \tilde{k} - g_A$. Using this to determine the growth rate of aggregate emissions E, we get: $\tilde{E} = \tilde{e} + \tilde{B} + \tilde{L} = \left(\alpha \tilde{k} - g_A\right) + g_B + n = \alpha \tilde{k} + g_E$ (see equation 19.15). The growth rate of aggregate emissions is thus equal to the growth rate g_E in the steady state plus $\alpha \tilde{k}$, which explains why we visualized $\alpha \tilde{k}$ instead of $\tilde{k}$ in Figure 19.4, as it allows us to determine easily what happens with aggregate emissions (without affecting the steady-state analysis since $\tilde{k} = 0$ if, and only if, $\alpha \tilde{k} = 0$). This is the reason for the second, long-dashed horizontal line in Figure 19.4, which is (in this case) an upward shift of the first horizontal line $\alpha(\delta + n + g_B)$ by the amount g_E, where we take growth to be sustainable, such that $g_E < 0$. Note that this second line intersects the downward sloping curve at the (turning) point T in Figure 19.4. For k values to the left of turning point T, the growth rate of aggregate emissions is positive, whereas for points to the right it is negative. The model thus provides a theoretical framework for the Environmental Kuznets Curve in which countries with low output, namely below $y = f(k(T))$, have rising aggregate emissions and countries with a high output have falling emissions (provided, of course, $g_E < 0$).

Theoretically, there is another explanation for the Environmental Kuznets Curve. Politically, there are mixed results. The empirical literature presents evidence that an Environmental Kuznets Curve in combination with the Green Solow model suggests a strong policy implication: economic growth may be seen as a way toward a cleaner environment. Countries first need to reach the turning point level of capital $k(T)$ to solve their environmental problems. From then onward, emissions levels will decrease. Developing countries can use this argument to focus on economic growth first and leave environmental concerns for the future. There are at least two problems with this argument. First, there is the irreversibility problem associated with some environmental goods, such as irreversible biodiversity loss and climate change consequences which cannot be undone. Second, it does not take into consideration the detrimental impact of environmental degradation on current economic prospects. Developing countries, for example, tend to be more dependent on the agricultural sector, which is more affected by natural disasters, climate change, water pollution, and so on. Related to this is the problem that developing countries have lower financial capacity to adapt to environmental damages, which imposes higher production costs. The next section therefore addresses the need for green financing in developing countries.

19.4   Sustainable Development Goals and Financing

The conservation of ecosystems and a clean environment is fundamental for sustained economic growth. Sectors such as fisheries, agriculture, and tourism depend heavily on the environment. These sectors consist of firms of different sizes, ranging from small family businesses to large multinationals. Families depend directly on the environment for their survival by their harvests or fish catch, by the wages they receive when working in these sectors, and by the food supply in the market. They also depend indirectly on the environment via the impact of environmental-dependent sectors on other sectors of the economy and on tax revenues. As a consequence, more countries become actively engaged in protecting the environment as a reflection of the vital role that the environment has on the lives of all citizens. One way to illustrate this rising environmental engagement is via the participation and ratification of environmental agreements, which is discussed in section 19.5.

In September 2015, no fewer than 193 world leaders met in New York under the guidance of the United Nations. They committed to 17 Sustainable Development Goals (SDGs) set up during the UN Conference on Sustainable Development in Rio de Janeiro in 2012. These goals have three general objectives:

1. end extreme poverty;
2. fight inequality and injustice; and
3. fix climate change.

The SDGs expand on the Millennium Development Goals (MDGs), which were part of a global effort starting in the year 2000 to combat poverty, by incorporating new areas such as climate change and sustainable consumption. In 2015, these world leaders set goals and targets to be implemented by 2030. Seven of the 17 targets are directly related to the environment:

- Goal 6: Clean water and sanitation;
- Goal 7: Affordable and clean energy;
- Goal 11: Sustainable cities and communities;
- Goal 12: Responsible consumption and production;
- Goal 13: Climate action;
- Goal 14: Life below water;
- Goal 15: Life on land.

The other 10 goals are (indirectly) also related to the environment (see https://sustainabledevelopment.un.org/sdgs). Environmental conservation depends on individual attitudes and preference, education, technology, regulation, and strong institutions. The government cannot completely control everything individuals do (think about how the way you dress, eat, communicate, dispose of your waste, and so on affects the environment). It is thus fundamental in a sustainable development path to have an economy in which individuals are fully aware of the impact that environmental degradation has on our standard of living. Social factors, such as poverty (goal 1: no poverty) and hunger (goal 2: zero hunger) on the one hand, take the attention away from the environment toward alleviating poverty. (Poor people in Tanzania, for example, use charcoal as the main source of household energy because of its relatively low price.) On the other hand, prioritizing social inclusion with disregard for the environment will only worsen the problems in the near future. In fact, environmental conservation can facilitate social inclusion. In Tanzania, using charcoal to generate energy in inefficient stoves creates significant health and safety problems because combustion of such fuels releases carbon monoxide, sulfur, and other particulate matter. Policies to raise sustainably produced charcoal and the promotion of fuel-efficient stoves can serve the dual purpose of improving social inclusion (by improving the health of poor households) and the environment (see World Bank 2009 for information).

Particulate Matter (PM) is the term used to describe solid and liquid particles suspended in the atmosphere. Potential health problems may arise if these particles are small, in particular smaller than 2.5 micrometers in diameter, since they stay in the air for a long time and may penetrate deep into human lungs. Measuring the intensity of these particles, referred to as $PM_{2.5}$, is thus frequently used as an indicator of air pollution (an inverse indicator of air quality). Figure 19.5 shows data for a sample of 194 countries in the year 2015 with respect to this measure of air pollution and three education variables. Panel a uses primary school enrollment as the educational variable, panel b uses secondary school enrollment, and panel c uses tertiary school enrollment. All three panels suggest a negative relationship between air pollution and education. The relationship is stronger as the level of education rises. Remember that correlation does not imply causality. It is possible that education and air pollution are not directly related, but there is a third variable which affects education positively and air pollution negatively. Such variables are omitted here to keep the exposition simple, but other studies have included control variables and found that higher education, everything else constant, results in less air pollution.

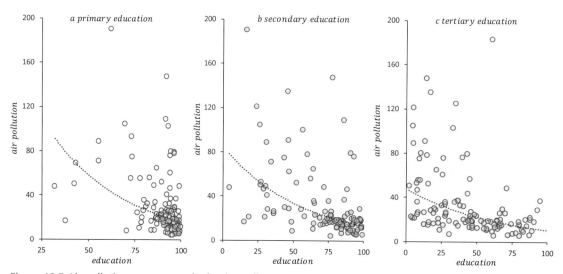

Figure 19.5 Air pollution exposure and school enrollment, 2015
Source: Created using World Bank Development Indicators online.
Notes: Air pollution is mean annual exposure to $PM_{2.5}$ in $\mu g/m^3$; first and secondary enrollment percent net, tertiary percent gross; 194 countries included.

The adoption of sustainable development strategies by developing countries faces a significant financial constraint. The UN Commission on the Sustainable Development Goals therefore gives a central role to financing sustainable development.[10]

The first challenge with respect to financing is to estimate how much financing is needed. Although it is possible to estimate the costs of particular investments, many uncertainties arise when estimating a long-term plan which encompasses different interconnected goals. Setting such a plan needs to take into account the synergies and trade-offs from the interconnected sectors involved.

The second challenge refers to the definition of how much investment is needed and the quality of the investment needed. There are many technological choices to be considered, and most integrated models do not take the quality of the investments into account. Many studies have attempted to estimate the magnitude of investment in different ecological systems (such as oceans and forests) and sectors (such as renewable energy and agriculture). The UN papers (see footnote above) analyze these studies and find that if we are to respect the climate target agreements, we need to invest trillions of US dollars per year in energy transition alone. Management of the global commons (biodiversity, forests, and oceans) requires additional hundreds of billion US dollars per year. Adding it all up leads to an immense effort which is simply not feasible for most developing countries. Therefore, financing for sustainable development requires a coordinated plan, action, and collaboration among advanced and developing countries.

One way to increase financing possibilities for developing countries is to increase private participation. In particular, given the high value of assets of international institutional investors, these investors could contribute to finance sustainable development by fostering infrastructure, innovation, and climate financing. In contrast, institutional investors are at the moment only financing a small portion of sustainable development projects. An important explanation for the lack of financing is bad institutions in developing countries (such as uncertainty with respect to regulations and weak governance). In addition, alternative private financing is limited in developing countries. Equity markets consist of only a small number of firms in developing countries and banks usually are the main source of financing. Banks, however, tend to finance short-term investments and not long-term investments related to sustainable development. Given the low capture of private funding, developing countries still need to rely on public investment. It is estimated, for example, that the public sector finances approximately one-third of infrastructure in developing countries.

Given these realities, the goals require the support of rich countries in terms of financing and access to technology. As usual, when the benefits accrue to all parties involved and the costs to voluntary parties, a free-rider problem is created. The problem is slightly different

---

[10] The discussion below is based on the background papers for the Intergovernmental Expert Committee on Sustainable Development Financing and its deliberations surrounding the post-2015 UN development agenda. These papers were issued by the UN Task Team (UNTT Working Group on Sustainable Development Financing); see https://sustainabledevelopment.un.org/topics/finance/documents.

when environmental issues are taken into account, as rich countries are also directly affected by unsustainable practices in developing countries. Both sides have an intrinsic motivation to act now. The biggest challenge is therefore to coordinate and have collaboration among countries and to create good governance practices for capturing the required financing. Overall, there is a consensus that countries should cooperate to provide the public goods essential for sustainable development. Nonetheless, developing countries should for their own self-interest also mobilize resources and create the internal conditions for more sustainable practices. The next section discusses how developing countries are at least from an external perspective showing a proactive attitude toward the environment.

19.5   Multilateral Agreements: Trade and the Environment

The oldest multilateral environmental agreement dates back to 1857. This agreement was signed by Austria, Baden, Bavaria, Switzerland, and Wurtemberg to respect the regulation of the flow of water from Lake Constance, which is on the River Rhine, near the Alps, situated in Austria, Germany, and Switzerland (Mitchell 2016). However, multilateral environmental agreements were more an exception than a rule in the nineteenth century, with a slowly rising popularity in the twentieth century. Figure 19.6 illustrates the rising use of these types of agreements over time, with a peak in the 1990s of no fewer than 143 new agreements.

Like most international agreements, multilateral environmental agreements are susceptible to enforcement problems. Getting countries to ratify and sign multilateral agreements often requires long negotiations because of free-riding possibilities. Consider, for example, the practice of exporting hazardous waste to developing countries which was prevalent

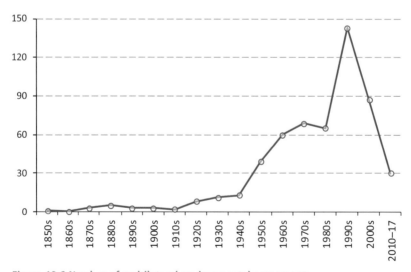

Figure 19.6 Number of multilateral environmental agreements
Source: Authors' calculations based on data from Ronald B. Mitchell. 2002–16, International Environmental Agreements Database Project.

until the beginning of the 1990s. Assume that an advanced country A considers this practice unethical and faces national pressure to stop doing so. If advanced country B does not face similar pressure it will oppose an agreement on transboundary hazardous waste because that would impose an additional cost on the inhabitants of country B. At the same time, it benefits from a cleaner environment when other advanced countries (such as country A) decide to collect and dispose of their own waste. It might also be of benefit if such a measure implies that country A will now develop technologies to dispose of hazardous waste in a more environmentally friendly way. Developing countries, on the other hand, might oppose such an agreement because of the expected loss of income. If so, this country is labeled *short-sighted* because it does not take into account the future loss of income arising from the environmental problems created by nonenvironmentally friendly disposal of hazardous waste (such as health costs).

Free-riding problems can vary in their intensity. Dumping hazardous waste in a developing country possibly hardly affects the sending country. This might result in a Not-In-My-BackYard (NIMBY) attitude, which is to accept the generation of toxic waste as long as the costs associated with it are not incurred by the people generating these costs. Other free-riding problems are more severe. Climate change, for example, affects all countries (in different intensities and different ways) regardless of who has emitted the greenhouse gas emission. The incentive to free-ride in such a case is substantial.

A multilateral environmental agreement often follows a *Polluter-Pays-Principle*. The Basel Convention on the control of transboundary movements of hazardous wastes and their disposal, for example, attempts to assign the costs of handling and disposing of hazardous waste to the producers of such waste. In this way, the agreement creates an incentive for the countries generating such waste to produce less of it. The Polluter-Pays-Principle does not always lead countries to sign an agreement. In climate change, for example, some countries are big polluters, but do not face high enough cost from climate change to justify paying for the largest share of emission reduction. These countries can delay negotiations and object to an agreement based on the Polluter-Pays-Principle. Other countries, on the other hand, are small polluters, but will bear a high cost with climate change (think of small islands in the South Pacific region). These small polluters with high cost are very open to an agreement.

Another principle underlying multilateral environmental agreements is the *Precautionary Principle*. For example, the risk of extinctions of species is uncertain and to some extent unknown. Countries can assume that the risk is significant enough to take actions to prevent the extinctions of species. Thus, precaution can be the basis for an environmental agreement on the ground that lack of scientific evidence today about the future impact on the quality of life and the environment should not serve as an argument for inaction.

Two more principles underlying the negotiation of environmental agreements are the *Principle of common but differentiated responsibility* and the *Principle of intergenerational equity*. The first principle takes into account the differences among advanced and developing countries with respect to their financial capacity and their technological adequacy to deal with particular environmental problems. This principle attempts, therefore, to consider equity aspects within environmental negotiations. The second principle also relates to ethical considerations – not across different current generations, but across current and future generations. It assumes that we have received the environment as it is now from past generations and we therefore have the obligation to provide future generations with a likewise or better environment.

From the above discussion it is clear that multilateral environmental agreements require an interdisciplinary approach. This contains elements of economics, politics, law, philosophy, and environmental sciences, among others. From an economic point of view, these agreements alter the economic relation between countries in two fundamental respects: trade and investment. By doing so, the country-specific impact on the environment can be intensified or restricted (see also the discussion in section 19.3 on the scale, composition, and technique effect).

The European Emissions Trading System (EU ETS) has been criticized, for example, for not being effective enough to curb global greenhouse gas emissions. One reason for this ineffectiveness is that if the system becomes too stringent (which is desirable to limit emissions), we will experience *carbon leakage*, which means that polluting-intensive firms will move out of Europe toward countries with laxer environmental regulation. The net effect of the ETS on aggregate emissions will thus be small (and could even get worse due to a *technique effect*). This concern aligns with the *Pollution Haven Hypothesis*, which states that free trade will lead pollution-intensive industries to move toward countries with laxer environmental regulation. Implicit in the Pollution Haven Hypothesis is that environmental costs, and therefore also environmental policies, are an important source of comparative advantage. In reality, the empirical literature shows that international trade has little impact on the environment (see Cherniwchan *et al.* 2017).

19.6   Natural Resource Curse

Chapter 6 shows that it is beneficial for countries to specialize in the production and export of goods and services for which they have a comparative advantage. Many developing countries are relatively abundant in natural resources. This is illustrated in Figure 19.7 by depicting the composition of wealth for groups of countries (classified using per capita income) for four assets, namely (i) produced capital, (ii) human capital, (iii) natural capital, and (iv) net foreign assets.[11] Each panel of the figure depicts the evolution of the four assets since 1995 for a group of countries, namely for panels a–f: low income, lower-middle income, upper-middle income, high income non-OECD, high income OECD, and world,

---

[11] The World Bank (2018) estimates the wealth of countries by measuring produced capital (comprising machinery, structures, equipment, and urban land); human capital (estimated using household surveys, and including the knowledge, skills, and experience embodied in the workforce); natural capital (comprising energy, minerals, crop and pasture land, protected areas, and forest); and net foreign assets (encompassing financial capital held in other countries). Total wealth is then computed as the sum of the four wealth components.

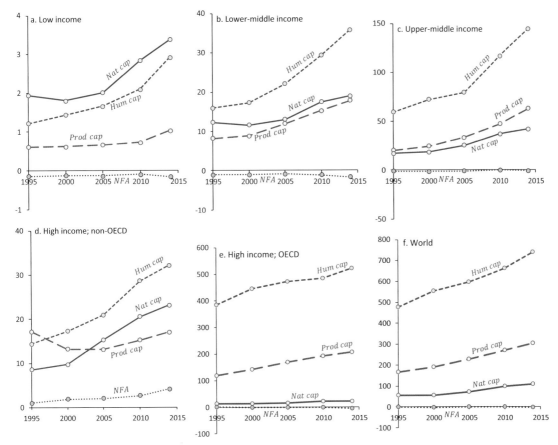

Figure 19.7 Composition of the wealth of nations since 1995
Source: Created using World Bank data (see Lange *et al.* 2018).
Notes: Values in constant 2014 USD, trillion; Nat cap = Natural capital; Hum cap = Human capital; Prod cap = Produced capital; NFA = Net Foreign Assets; different vertical scales.

respectively. Since 1995, natural capital comprises close to 50 percent of total wealth in low-income countries. In lower-middle-income countries, the share of natural capital is substantially lower at around 30 percent. For the high-income OECD countries, the share of natural capital in total wealth is only around 3 percent. In general, therefore, natural capital becomes relatively less important as per capita income rises, with the exception of high-income non-OECD countries, which include oil-wealthy countries such as Kuwait, Saudi Arabia, Qatar, United Arab Emirates, Oman, and Russia. In contrast, Figure 19.7 illustrates that human capital becomes relatively more important as per capita income rises, again with the high-income non-OECD countries as an exception. The share of produced capital, which includes machinery, structures, and equipment, does not vary substantially with per capita income, in line with Kaldor's stylized fact 4 (see Chapter 7).

From the theory of comparative advantage, we expect many developing countries to specialize in the production of resource-intensive goods, in view of their relative abundance in natural resources. This is illustrated in Figure 19.8, which shows the share

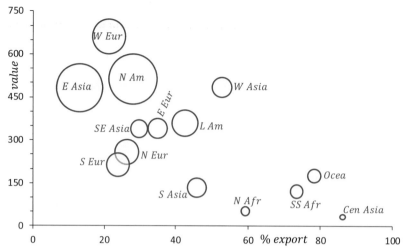

Figure 19.8 Natural resources exports; billion USD and percent of total exports, 2016
Sources: Created using UN Comtrade (commodity exports) and World Development Indicators (GDP).
Notes: Natural resources as percent of total exports and in value (billion USD); bubbles proportional to GDP (in constant 2010 USD);148 countries included; natural resources includes HS commodity codes: 01, 02, 03, 04, 05, 06, 07, 08, 09, 10, 11, 12, 13, 14, 15, 16, 17, 18, 19, 20, 21, 25, 26, 27, 28, 40, 41, 44, 45, 47, 51, 52, 53, 68, 71, 72, and 81; W = West; E = East; N = North; S = South; SE = Southeast; L = Latin; SS = Sub-Sahara; Cen = Central; Am = America; Eur = Europe; Afr = Africa; Ocea = Oceania.

of natural resources in total exports, as well as the value of natural resources exports (with bubbles proportional to total income) for groups of countries. Note that for developing regions like Central Asia, Sub-Sahara Africa, North Africa, West Asia, South Asia, and Latin America, natural resources exports exceed 40 percent of total exports; more specifically, in Sub-Sahara Africa it is about 75 percent, in North Africa close to 60 percent, and in Central Asia about 86 percent.[12] Note that although the *share* of natural resources exports tends to be high in developing countries, the *value* of natural resources commodities exports is high in some advanced regions. West Europe as a whole exported $663 billion in natural resources commodities in 2016 and North America $513 billion.

The information provided above and in Figure 19.8 addresses natural resource exports at the aggregated regional level (for groups of countries). At the national level, some countries are highly dependent on natural resources commodities exports. This holds, for example, for São Tomé and Príncipe, where natural resources commodities represent about 90 percent of all exports in 2016. The main export product is cocoa beans, which constituted 71 percent of all exports in 2016, followed by iron products with 6.7 percent.[13] Countries

---

[12] In our dataset, Central Asia consists of two countries: Kazakhstan and Kyrgyzstan. Kazakhstan's main export is crude petroleum (40 percent of the total in 2016); Kyrgyzstan is relatively more diversified than Kazakhstan. Kyrgyzstan's main export in 2016 was gold (15 percent), other ores (8.4 percent), and precious metal ore (6.7 percent).

[13] In the Atlas of the Observatory of Economic Complexity, you can use a tool to build a visualization of all exports of São Tomé and Principle in 2016 and for other countries and years; see: https://atlas.media.mit.edu/en/visualize/tree_map/hs92/export/stp/all/show/2016/.

like São Tomé and Príncipe are not diversified in their production structure, which makes them vulnerable to commodities price shocks. What do you think would happen if the price of cocoa beans significantly fell in the international market? Given the importance of this product for the trade balance of São Tomé and Príncipe, this would directly impact the income of cocoa beans producers and of the labor force involved in the production of cocoa beans, as well as indirectly affect other sectors of the economy, likely resulting in a depreciation of the currency.

On the basis of the export pattern of countries like São Tomé and Príncipe, it is in fact customary to refer to the *natural resource curse*: the possibility of countries which are highly dependent on natural resources exports to be economically "cursed" by this natural advantage. This contrasts with the idea that natural resources abundance is a blessing and is based on the practical observation that many countries with abundant natural resources seem to be worse off, rather than better off, as a consequence of this abundance. Venezuela and Nigeria are classic examples of the resource curse. This is illustrated in Figure 19.9 as a negative relationship between resource dependency (exports of natural resources commodities as a percentage of total exports) and the log of income per capita for 147 countries in 2016. (Nigeria is listed as an example in Figure 19.9, but Venezuela is not as data are not available.) Note that there is a lot of variation in Figure 19.9 (such that a regression explains only about 18 percent of the variance in log income per capita), but the negative relationship is strong nonetheless (an estimated regression coefficient is highly significant). Does this negative relationship contradict the Ricardian or factor abundance theories of comparative advantage which state that all trading countries are better off with free trade? Not necessarily. The problem is not associated with observed trade flows themselves, but with the response to an inflow of resources related to the natural resources sectors. There

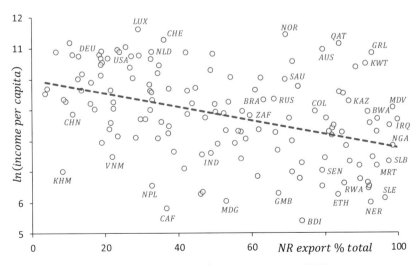

Figure 19.9 Income per capita and natural resources exports, 2016
Sources: Created using UN Comtrade (commodity exports) and World Development Indicators (GDP).
Notes: Natural resources as percent of total exports; income per capita in GDP (constant 2010 USD); 147 countries included; natural resources includes HS commodity codes (see Figure 19.8); see https://unstats.un.org/home/ for a list of country codes.

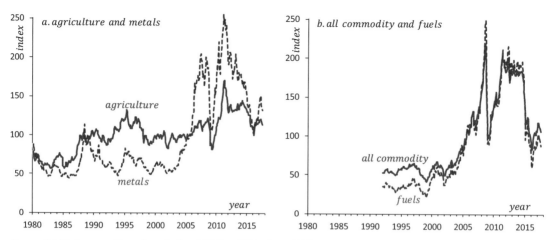

Figure 19.10 Commodity prices; index (2005 = 100), since 1980
Source: Created using IMF monthly data (www.imf.org/external/np/res/commod/index.aspx).
Notes: Agriculture = agriculture raw materials index (incl. timber, cotton, wool, rubber, and hides price indices); metals = metals price index (incl. copper, aluminum, iron ore, tin, nickel, zinc, lead, and uranium price indices); all commodity = all commodity price index (incl. both fuel and nonfuel price indices); fuel = fuel (energy) index (incl. crude oil [petroleum], natural gas, and coal price indices).

are broadly three explanations for the resource curse: (i) commodity prices, (ii) institutions, and (iii) the Dutch disease. These three explanations are now briefly discussed below.[14]

Commodity prices. The first explanation of the resource curse focuses on the volatility of commodity prices. Figure 19.10 shows the evolution over time (an index with value of 100 in 2015) for four groups of monthly commodity prices, namely agricultural raw material index & metals price index in panel a and fuel index & all commodity index in panel b. Regardless of the commodity type, the prices are highly volatile (although fuel prices are even more volatile and have a big impact on the all commodity price index). For example, the all commodity price index *decreased* by 1.5 percent in November 2016 (relative to October 2016) and *increased* one month later by 7.3 percent. Such volatility is detrimental to the suppliers of these commodities, because their income fluctuates accordingly. This causes frictional unemployment, under-utilization of capital, and less investment. Depending on the size of the resource sector, such fluctuations can have a significant impact on economic growth. This reasoning thus argues that the volatility of commodity prices results in a resource curse. That is, countries which are more dependent on natural resources are more exposed to highly volatile prices, which affects their economic prospects.

Institutions. The second explanation for a resource curse focuses on institutions. Look again at Figure 19.9. Norway (NOR) is in the upper-right corner with high income per capita and high share of natural resources exports, well above the regression line. Norway is a resource-rich country (oil in particular), which has not been "cursed" by this factor abundance. To the contrary, being rich in natural resources has been a blessing, with the oil

---

[14] Frankel (2012) identifies six channels: 1 long-term trends in world prices; 2 price volatility; 3 permanent crowding out of manufacturing; 4 autocratic/oligarchic institutions; 5 anarchic institutions; 6 Dutch disease.

resources promoting economic growth. How has Norway escaped the resource curse? Because of good institutions. Norwegian institutions guarantee that oil resources benefit the whole society and not just a small interest group, both in the present and in the future. Given that oil is a nonrenewable resource, Norwegian institutions have taken into account that the oil resources will eventually end by setting policies which favor long-term economic growth and the creation of a Petroleum Fund to benefit future generations. Resource wealth funds are currently adopted by several commodity exporter countries (for example, United Arab Emirates, Norway, Kuwait, Qatar, and Russia). For most of these countries, the size of these funds is not yet enough to create a safeguard buffer against shocks. According to this explanation, countries which face a resource curse are countries without good institutions in place.

Bad institutions are associated with corruption and over-consumption stimulated during periods of resource windfalls. The problem is that when the period of large windfalls slows down in the resource-rich countries, they get stuck with bottlenecks in infrastructure (because of insufficient investment) and in the industrial sector. They therefore cannot keep up with the high consumption levels achieved during the *bonanza* period. Another point of view is that in many resource-rich countries bad institutions make countries more vulnerable to conflicts. Given the concentration of the natural-resource sector (particularly for *point-source resources* such as mining and oil), a few interest groups fight over power to try to appropriate the revenues from the resource sector. (Point-source resources are geographically clustered, which makes it easier to control this type of resource. In contrast, nonpoint-source resources are geographically diffused, such as pasture and agricultural land.)

Dutch disease. The final explanation for a resource curse is the Dutch disease, which refers to negative side-effects after a period of boom in the natural resource sector (such as the discovery of a new mine or oil field or a rise in the commodity price). The name "Dutch disease" originates from the negative effects from the discovery of natural gas in Groningen (the Netherlands) in 1959. After this discovery, the manufacturing sector in the Netherlands declined. The Dutch disease occurs when, as a result of the boom, the resource sector has a significant increase in total exports, which increases the inflow of foreign currency into the country. As a negative side-effect, the country experiences a real appreciation of the currency which is detrimental for other (manufacturing) export sectors. The shift of factors of production toward the commodity sector often starts a deindustrialization process and a reduction of the traded sector. Other side-effects may include a rise in government spending and a current account deficit. The Dutch disease is seen as an explanation for a resource curse because when resources leave the industrial sector, the economy experiences a loss of *learning-by-doing* knowledge generation. When the boom period ends, the country is faced with lower productivity, making it more difficult to catch up again in terms of industrial competitiveness.

Whether the resource curse exists or not is an empirical question. Overall, the three explanations for the resource curse show that being wealthy in natural resources can be a blessing, as it has been for many countries. It depends, however, on good policies to protect the country against commodity price fluctuations, to guarantee investments envisioning long-term sustainable development and against expropriation from interest groups. When bad institutions are in place, experience shows that it is difficult to avoid the resource curse, leading to lower competitiveness and high income inequality.

19.7   Nonrenewable and Renewable Natural Resources

From a country perspective, being wealthy in natural resources can have major short-term and long-term implications. From a global perspective, we have to share the natural resources among ourselves. Two examples are gold and fish. These are different natural resources with distinct usages which face the problem of depletion. The more gold or fish one country has, the less will be available for other countries. An important difference is that gold is a *nonrenewable* resource, whereas fish is a *renewable* resource (although depletable).

Nonrenewable resources have a finite quantity available on Earth within a meaningful timeframe. Examples are oil, gas, uranium, and diamonds. Such resources are not renewable and therefore once used are depleted. We measure the availability of nonrenewable resources by the level of the current *reserves*, which is the quantity that is financially accessible. This is the quantity that can be profitably extracted at current prices and technology. With this definition, although nonrenewable resources cannot increase in the relevant timeframe, current reserves can increase if the price rises or if the extraction technology improves. Current reserves also change if new discoveries are made and resources are used.

Renewable resources can (at least to some extent) be naturally replenished. Examples are fish, trees, and water (although not all water is renewable). Note, however, that most renewable resources are also depletable. If the consumption rate is too high, the resources might not have the time and the natural conditions to replenish themselves. The availability of renewable resources depends therefore also on consumption levels. The change of the stock of a resource S_t is measured as the difference between the quantity of the resource G_t which has grown in the given period and the quantity of the resource E_t which has been extracted:

$$\Delta S_t \equiv S_{t+1} - S_t = G_t - E_t \qquad\qquad 19.16$$

Consider a forest which has been largely cut down for timber use. With only a few trees left, it takes a long time for the forest to regenerate itself, so growth G_t is small. On the other hand, if the forest is kept intact, growth G_t is also small because the trees will be competing with one another for space and sunshine. Somewhere in between these two extremes of a small forest and a large forest (its *carrying capacity*, which is defined as the largest quantity of the resource which prevails if no extraction takes place), we will have the largest growth. Figure 19.11 illustrates this and shows that there is an optimal level of stock S^* such that the quantity of resource growth is maximized. It is possible to keep this

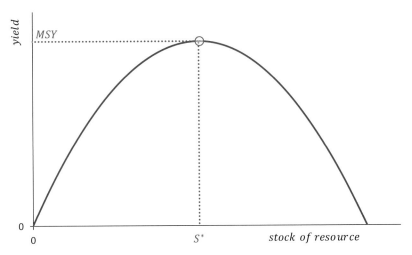

Figure 19.11 Maximum sustainable yield

optimal level of stock in all periods as long as the quantity extracted is equal to the *maximum sustainable yield* (MSY), as indicated in the figure.

The above perspective of resource preservation looks purely into the direct use of the resource. In reality, we need to conserve the environment for many other reasons, such as linkages within the ecosystem (for example, cutting down trees may result in fewer trees tomorrow, but also less wildlife). From a societal perspective, the costs of unsustainable forestry management are huge. Some of the main impacts of deforestation relate to: the livelihoods of individuals who are dependent on products and services derived from the forest; the preservation of species diversity; and the impact of climate change by the rise of carbon release into the atmosphere. In addition, the presence of forests has related positive aspects, such as regulation of local temperatures and precipitation levels.

This section concludes by showing that natural resources are not uniformly distributed across the world. Figure 19.12 plots forest size for all countries in the world in 2015, in ascending and cumulative order. Four countries alone, Russia, Brazil, Canada, and the USA, have 50 percent of all the forests in the world. Forests are also diversified. In Russia, most of the forests are classified as boreal forests (also known as taiga), while Brazil has the largest tropical rainforest. Boreal forests are a biome characterized by coniferous trees, that is, forests in which the total number of tree species is relatively small. Tropical forests, on the other hand, are characterized by high levels of biodiversity in a climate which is hot and wet.

Apart from these differences, all forests contribute to maintaining ecosystems services and regulation of climate change, which is a global public good. In this sense, deforestation around the world has not only localized but also global negative consequences. Forests, resource conservation, and pollution reduction are far-reaching sustainability goals. Individual countries benefit from sustainable practices, but other countries also benefit. This makes the challenge of sustainability much more complex than purely internal economic problems because it requires international cooperation. As section 19.5 shows, many international agreements were signed with the intention to commit countries to a

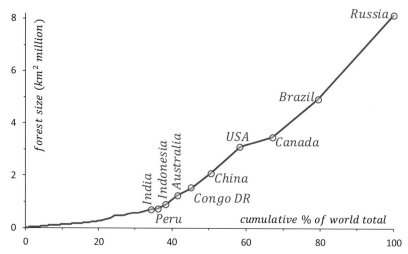

Figure 19.12 Ordering of forest area size, 2015
Source: Created using World Development Indicators online.
Note: 211 countries included.

more sustainable future. Nonetheless, the challenge to take international considerations within national investment decisions is still out there to be addressed.

19.8   Final Remarks

This chapter has focused on sustainability and the environment. It analyzed two main topics within sustainability: the environment and natural resources. Economic development is intrinsically linked to sustainability. Pollution can hamper development by affecting the quality of life and human health (such as water and air pollution), but economic development can also facilitate the adoption of cleaner modes of production (through cleaner technologies and stricter regulation). Similarly, natural resources can affect the development of countries owning this resource, either negatively (resource curse) or positively (resource blessing), while other countries may also depend on these resources (resource scarcity).

The strong connection between development and sustainability has become more apparent in recent years, resulting in more attention in the media, academia, and in the policy field. Figure 19.13 shows an impressive rise in the number of publications in the field of economic development related to *pollution* and *sustainable development*. There are many examples of resource depletion, severe pollution, and ecosystem mismanagement. At the same time, there is growing awareness that countries should not first grow economically and only take care of the environment at a later stage (a recurrent speech used in the past by policymakers from developing countries). The challenges remain enormous for two main reasons: first, the international aspect of sustainability; and, second, the trade-off between long-term benefits of sustainability practices and short-term costs.

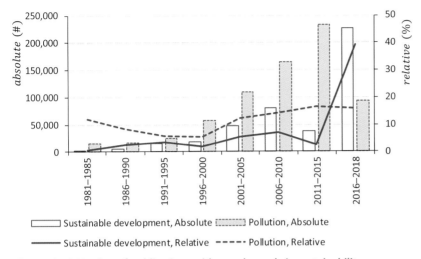

Figure 19.13 Number of publications with search words in sustainability
Source: Created using scholar google search terms "sustainable development," "pollution," and "development economy."
Note: The search was done repeatedly by restricting the years of publications.

The second challenge is clear: policymakers might be aware of the need to implement sustainable practices, but are reluctant to face the associated costs. The international aspect is much more complex and this chapter has only been able to touch upon it. Therefore, this section concludes with a short list of issues for you to reflect upon. First, the bargaining power of countries which own resources that the whole world wants to preserve. Do you expect Brazil to pay for the whole cost of preserving the Amazon forest? How should countries cooperate to preserve natural resources? Second, the free-riding problem in reducing pollution. Who should pay for cleaning up the plastic soup in the ocean flowing to a few coastal areas? Third, the "invisible" actors responsible for pollution related to the "known" actors responsible for pollution. Often, we know who is directly responsible for pollution, such as firm X in India. In addition, there is also an "invisible" group of people motivating firm X to pollute, such as consumers of the final products and governments outside India who have established stricter environmental regulations such that firms do not produce in their own country. This invisible group is harder to trace and assign responsibility to. Consumers, producers, and governments, within and outside the national geographic borders, are intricately connected via investments, trade flows, production, consumption, and ideas. Taken together, all these connections affect both economic development and the sustainability of our planet.

Further Reading

A thorough grounding in the problems and issues of sustainable development, including measurement, is provided by: Rogers, P. P., K. F. Jalal, and J. A. Boyd. 2012. *An Introduction to Sustainable Development* (London: Routledge).

The World Bank provides regular updates on progress (or lack thereof) regarding the 17 Sustainable Development Goals. See: https://openknowledge.worldbank.org/pages/sustainable-development-goals.

Important stylized facts and the theoretical linkages between globalization and the environment are discussed in: Copeland, B. R., J. S. Shapiro, and M. S. Taylor. 2022. "Globalization and the Environment," in G. Gopinath, E. Helpman, and K. Rogoff (eds.), *Handbook of International Economics: International Trade* (Amsterdam: Elsevier), vol. 5. Most importantly: a firm conclusion on whether globalization is good or bad for the environment is not possible and depends on specific circumstances.

TECHNICAL NOTE 19.1   ANDREONI AND LEVINSON MODEL

To maximize equation 19.4 subject to equations 19.5 and 19.6, first substitute equation 19.5 into equation 19.4 to get $U = C^\alpha E^\beta$. Now create the Lagrange function with only restriction 19.6:

$$L = C^\alpha E^\beta + \lambda(M - C - E) \qquad\qquad 19.A1$$

The first order conditions are:

$$\alpha C^{\alpha-1} E^\beta = \lambda \qquad\qquad 19.A2$$

$$\beta C^\alpha E^{\beta-1} = \lambda \qquad\qquad 19.A3$$

Take the ratio of the first order conditions to get $\alpha E = \beta C$. Substitute this in the budget restriction 19.6 to get: $M = C + E = C + (\beta/\alpha)C = ((\alpha + \beta)/\alpha)C$ or $C^* = (\alpha/(\alpha+\beta))M$, which is equation 19.7. Similarly for equation 19.7. Substitution in equation 19.5 to get equation 19.9 is straightforward.

TECHNICAL NOTE 19.2   ENVIRONMENTAL KUZNETS CURVE

To verify if pollution first rises with income and then falls in the Andreoni and Levinson model, we take the first and second derivative of equation 19.9, see equations 19.A4 and 19.A5, respectively.

$$\frac{\partial P^*}{\partial M} = \left(\frac{\alpha}{\alpha+\beta}\right) - (\alpha+\beta)\left(\frac{\alpha}{\alpha+\beta}\right)^\alpha \left(\frac{\beta}{\alpha+\beta}\right)^\beta M^{\alpha+\beta-1} \qquad 19.A4$$

$$\frac{\partial^2 P^*}{\partial M^2} = -(\alpha+\beta-1)(\alpha+\beta)\left(\frac{\alpha}{\alpha+\beta}\right)^\alpha \left(\frac{\beta}{\alpha+\beta}\right)^\beta M^{\alpha+\beta-2} \qquad 19.A5$$

The sign of the first and second derivatives depends on the parameter coefficients α and β. Ignoring the borderline case $\alpha + \beta = 1$, there are two possibilities:

- If $\alpha + \beta < 1$ then $\frac{\partial^2 P^*}{\partial M^2} > 0$; pollution rises monotonically with income.
- If $\alpha + \beta > 1$ then $\frac{\partial^2 P^*}{\partial M^2} < 0$; there is a hill-shaped relationship between pollution and income since $\partial P^*/\partial M > 0$ for M sufficiently close to zero.

TECHNICAL NOTE 19.3   GREEN SOLOW MODEL

To obtain the law of motion of capital in intensive units, start with the identity $k = K/BL$ and differentiate both sides with respect to time (use the quotient rule and the product rule); see equation 19.A5. Next, substitute $n = \dot{L}/L$ and $g_B = \dot{B}/B$ before substituting $\dot{K} = sF(K, BL)(1 - \theta) - \delta K$ and writing the equation in intensive units only (next two equal signs of the equation).

$$\dot{k} = \frac{\dot{K}BL - (\dot{B}L + B\dot{L})K}{B^2 L^2} = \frac{\dot{K}}{BL} - [n + g_B]k = sf(k)[1 - \theta] - [\delta + n + g_B]k \qquad \text{19.A5}$$

To obtain pollution in intensive units, recall equation 19.11 and use the assumption of constant returns to scale for A to get:

$$E = \omega[F - A(F, \theta F)] = \omega F(1 - A(1, \theta)) \qquad \text{19.A6}$$

Now define $a(\theta) \stackrel{\text{def}}{=} (1 - A(1, \theta))$ and write in intensive units to get: $e = f(k)\omega a(\theta)$.

TECHNICAL NOTE 19.4   DERIVATION OF GROWTH RATE

We can write emissions at any time t as given in equation 19.A7, where we made the dependence on time t explicit and $B(0)$, $L(0)$, and $\omega(0)$ are initial conditions for technology level, population size, and pollution intensity, while g_E is the growth rate of emissions (derived below).

$$E(t) = B(0)L(0)\Omega(0)a(\theta)e^{g_L t}k(t)^\alpha \qquad \text{19.A7}$$

Taking logs gives: $lnE(t) = lnB(0) + lnL(0) + \ln\omega(0) + lna(\theta) + g_E t + \alpha \ln(k(t))$. Differentiating this with respect to time gives: $\tilde{E} = g_E + \alpha\tilde{k}$. Substituting the growth rate for intensive capital, namely $\tilde{k} = sk^{\alpha-1}(1 - \theta) - (\delta + n + g_B)$, gives equation 19.15 in the text.

References

Preface

Schultz, T. 1981. *Investing in People: The Economics of Population Quality* (Berkeley, CA: University of California Press).

Chapter 1

Schultz, T. 1981. *Investing in People: The Economics of Population Quality* (Berkeley, CA: University of California Press).

World Bank, World Development Indicators online, www.worldbank.org.

World Economic Forum. 2019. *The Global Competitiveness Report 2019* (Geneva: World Economic Forum).

Chapter 2

Brakman, S., J. H. Garretsen, and C. van Marrewijk. 2019. *An Introduction to Geographical and Urban Economics: A Spiky World* (Cambridge University Press).

Combes, P.-P., G. Duranton, L. Gobillon, and S. Roux. 2010. "Estimating Agglomeration Economies with History, Geology, and Worker Effects," in E. L. Glaeser (ed.), *Agglomeration Economics* (University of Chicago Press), pp. 15–65.

Dachis, B. G. Duranton, and M. A. Turner. 2012. "The Effects of Land Transfer Taxes on Real Estate Markets: Evidence from a Natural Experiment in Toronto," *Journal of Economic Geography*, 12(2), 327–54.

Dinardo, J. and J. L. Tobias. 2001. "Nonparametric Density and Regression Estimation," *Journal of Economic Perspectives*, 15(4), 11–28.

Lee, D. S. and T. Lemieux. 2014. "Regression Discontinuity Designs in Social Sciences," in H. Best and C. Wolf (eds.), *The SAGE Handbook of Regression Analysis and Causal Inference* (London: SAGE), pp. 301–26.

2010. "Regression Discontinuity Designs in Economics," *Journal of Economic Literature*, 48(2), 281–355.

Lewin, K. 1952. *Field Theory in Social Science: Selected Theoretical Papers by Kurt Lewin* (London: Tavistock).

Lord Kelvin (William Thompson). 1883. "Lecture on Electrical Units of Measurement," May 3, https://archive.org/stream/popularlecturesa01kelvuoft#page/73/mode/2up.

Pasteur, L. 1854. Lecture at the University of Lille, December 7.

The Guardian. 2016. "The Top 10 Sources of Data for International Development Research," March 16, www.theguardian.com/global-development-professionals-network/2016/mar/16/the-top-10-sources-of-data-for-international-development-research.

World Bank. 2017. "The Tech Revolution That's Changing How We Measure Poverty," July 27, www.worldbank.org/en/news/immersive-story/2017/07/26/the-tech-revolution-thats-changing-how-we-measure-poverty.

World Food Programme (WFP). 2009. *Emergency Food Security Assessment Handbook*, 2nd edn. (Rome: WFP), www.wfp.org/content/emergency-food-security-assessment-handbook.

Chapter 3

Ashraf, Q. and S. Michaelopoulos. 2015. "Climatic Fluctuations and the Diffusion of Agriculture," *Review of Economics and Statistics*, 97(3), 589–609.

Brakman, S., H. Garretsen, and C. van Marrewijk. 2009. *The New Introduction to Geographical Economics* (Cambridge University Press).

Diamond, J. 1997. *Guns, Germs, and Steel* (London: Vintage).

Olsson, O. and D. A. J. Hibbs. 2005. "Biogeography and Long-Run Economic Development," *European Economic Review*, 49(4), 909–38.

Putterman, L. and D. Weil. 2010. "Post-1500 Population Flows and the Long-Run Determinants of Economic Growth and Inequality," *Quarterly Journal of Economics*, 125(4), 1627–82.

Smith, B. 1998. *The Emergence of Agriculture* (New York: Scientific American Library).

Spolaore, E. and R. Wacziarg. 2013. "How Deep Are the Roots of Economic Development?," *Journal of Economic Literature*, 51(2), 325–69.

Tully, R. B., H. Courtois, Y. Hoffman, and D. Pomarede. 2014. "The Laniaka Supercluster of Galaxies," *Nature*, 513(7516), 71–3.

Wolchover, N. 2012. "Why It Took So Long to Invent the Wheel," *Scientific American*, March 6.

Chapter 4

Acemoglu, D., S. Johnson, and J. Robinson. 2002. "Reversal of Fortune: Geography and Institutions in the Making of the Modern World Income Distribution," *Quarterly Journal of Economics*, 117(4), 1231–94.

2001. "The Colonial Origins of Comparative Development: An Empirical Investigation," *American Economic Review*, 91(5), 1369–401.

Ashraf, Q. and O. Galor. 2011. "Dynamics and Stagnation in the Malthusian Epoch," *American Economic Review*, 101(5), 2003–41.

Beugelsdijk, S., S. Brakman, H. Garretsen, and C. van Marrewijk. 2013. *International Economics and Business* (Cambridge University Press).

Chen, D. and H. Chen. 2013. "Using the Köppen Classification to Quantify Climate Variation and Change: An Example for 1901–2010," *Environmental Development*, 6(1), 69–79.

Glaeser, E., R. La Porta, F. Lopez-de-Silanes, and A. Shleifer. 2004. "Do Institutions Cause Growth?," *Journal of Economic Growth*, 9(3), 271–303.

La Porta, R., F. Lopez-de-Silanes, A. Shleifer, and R. Vishny. 1998. "Law and Finance," *Journal of Political Economy*, 106(6), 1113–55.

Olsson, O. and D. A. J. Hibbs. 2005. "Biogeography and Long-Run Economic Development," *European Economic Review*, 49(4), 909–38.

Putterman, L. and D. Weil. 2010. "Post-1500 Population Flows and the Long-Run Determinants of Economic Growth and Inequality," *Quarterly Journal of Economics*, 125(4), 1627–82.

Sachs, J., and P. Malaney. 2002. "The Economic and Social Burden of Malaria," *Nature*, 415 (February 7), 680–5.

Sachs, J., A. Mellinger, and J. Gallup. 2001. "The Geography of Poverty and Wealth," *Scientific American* (March), 70–5.

Smith, A. 1776. *An Inquiry into the Nature and Causes of the Wealth of Nations*, 1937 edn. (New York: Random House).

Spolaore, E. and R. Wacziarg. 2013. "How Deep Are the Roots of Economic Development?," *Journal of Economic Literature*, 51(2), 325–69.

The Economist. 2014a. "An Astonishing Record," March 22.

2014b. "Comander of His Stage," March 22.

World Health Organization. 2014. *World Malaria Report 2014* (Geneva: WHO Press).

Chapter 5

Albert, M. 1993. *Capitalism against Capitalism* (London: Vintage).

Baldwin, R. E. and P. Martin. 1999. "Two Waves of Globalization: Superficial Similarities, Fundamental Differences," NBER Working Paper No. 6904. National Bureau of Economic Research, Cambridge, MA.

Beugelsdijk, S., S. Brakman, H. Garretsen, and C. van Marrewijk. 2013. *International Economics and Business* (Cambridge University Press).

Findlay, R. and J. G. O'Rourke. 2001. "Commodity Market Integration, 1500–2000," NBER Working Paper No. 8579, National Bureau of Economic Research, Cambridge, MA.

Keynes, J. M. 1919. *The Economic Consequences of the Peace* (London: Macmillan).

Linden, G., K. L. Kraemer, and J. Dedrick. 2011. "Innovation and Job Creation in a Global Economy: The Case of Apple's iPod," *Journal of International Commerce and Economics*, 3(1), 223–39.

2009. "Who Captures Value in a Global Innovation Network? The Case of Apple's iPod," *Communications of the ACM*, 52(3), 140–4.

Maddison, A. 2001. *The World Economy: A Millennial Perspective* (Paris and Washington, DC: OECD).

McDonald, F. and F. Burton. 2002. *International Business* (London: Thomson).

Neary, J. P. 2003. "Globalisation and Market Structure," Presidential Address to the European Economic Association, *Journal of the European Economic Association*, 1(2/3), 245–71.

Obstfeld, M. and A. M. Taylor. 2003. "Sovereign Risk, Credibility, and the Gold Standard: 1870–1913 versus 1925–31," *Economic Journal*, 113(487), 241–75.

O'Rourke, K. H. and J. G. Williamson. 2002. "When Did Globalization Begin?," *European Review of Economic History*, 6(1), 23–50.

1999. *Globalization and History: The Evolution of a Nineteenth-Century Atlantic Economy* (Cambridge, MA: MIT Press).

Sachs, J. and A. Warner. 1995. "Economic Reform and the Process of Global Integration," *Brookings Papers on Economic Activity*, 1(95), 1–118.

Sorge, A. M. and A. van Witteloostuijn. 2004. "The (Non)Sense of Organizational Change: An Essay about Universal Management Hypes, Sick Consultancy Metaphors and Healthy Organization Theories," *Organization Studies*, 25(7), 1205–31.

Stiglitz, J. 2002. *Globalization and Its Discontents* (New York: W. W. Norton).

van Marrewijk, C. and K. Berden. 2007. "On the Static and Dynamic Costs of Trade Restrictions for Small Developing Countries," *Journal of Development Economics*, 84(1), 46–60.

Wacziarg, R. and K. Welch. 2008. "Trade Liberalization and Growth: New Evidence," *World Bank Economic Review*, 22(2), 187–231.

Chapter 6

Balassa, B. 1966. "Tariff Reductions and Trade in Manufactures," *American Economic Review*, 56(3), 466–73.

Bergeijk, P. and C. van Marrewijk. 2013. "Heterogeneity and Development: An Agenda," *Journal of International Trade and Economic Development*, 22(1), 1–9.

Bernard, A., J. Eaton, J. Jensen, and S. Kortum. 2003. "Plants and Productivity in International Trade," *American Economic Review*, 93(4), 1268–90.

Beugelsdijk, S., S. Brakman, H. Garretsen, and C. van Marrewijk. 2013. *International Economics and Business* (Cambridge University Press).

Brülhart, M. 2008. "An Account of Global Intra-Industry Trade," Research Paper Series: Globalisation, Productivity and Technology, Research Paper 2008/08, University of Nottingham.

Chamberlain, E. 1933. *The Theory of Monopolistic Competition: A Re-orientation of the Theory of Value* (Cambridge, MA: Harvard University Press).

Chang, H.-H. and C. van Marrewijk. 2013. "Firm Heterogeneity and Development: Evidence from Latin American Countries," *Journal of International Trade and Economic Development*, 22(1), 10–51.

Grubel, H. and P. Lloyd. 1975. *Intra-Industry Trade: The Theory and Measurement of International Trade in Differentiated Products* (New York: John Wiley).

Irwin, D. 2002. *Free Trade under Fire* (Princeton University Press).

Krugman, P. 1995. "Growing World Trade: Causes and Consequences," *Brookings Papers on Economic Activity*, 1, 327–62.

  1992. *The Age of Diminished Expectations: US Policy in the 1990s* (Cambridge, MA: MIT Press).

Melitz, M. 2003. "The Impact of Trade on Intra-Industry Reallocations and Aggregate Industry Productivity," *Econometrica*, 71(6), 1695–725.

Thurow, L. 1993. *Head to Head: The Coming Economic Battle among Japan, Europe, and America* (London: Allen & Unwin).

van Marrewijk, C. 2017. *International Trade* (Oxford University Press).

Verdoorn, P. 1960. "The Intra-Block Trade of Benelux," in E. Robinson (ed.), *Economic Consequences of the Size of Nations* (London: Macmillan), pp. 291–330.

Chapter 7

Aghion, P. and P. Howitt. 1992. "A Model of Growth through Creative Destruction," *Econometrica*, 60(2), 323–51.

Barro, R. J. 1991. "Economic Growth in a Cross Section of Countries," *Quarterly Journal of Economics*, 106(2), 407–43.

Feenstra, R., R. Inklaar, and M. Timmer. 2015. "The Next Generation of the Penn World Table," *American Economic Review*, 105(10), 3150–82.

Grossman, G. and E. Helpman. 1991. *Innovation and Growth in the Global Economy* (Cambridge, MA: MIT Press).

International Monetary Fund (IMF). 2015. *World Economic Outlook: October Red* (Washington, DC: IMF).

Kaldor, N. 1961. "Capital Accumulation and Economic Growth," in F. Lutz and D. Hague (eds.), *The Theory of Capital* (London: Macmillan), pp. 177–222.

Muth, J. F. 1961. "Rational Expectations and the Theory of Price Movements," *Econometrica*, 29(3), 315–35.

Ramsey, F. P. 1928. "A Mathematical Theory of Saving," *Economic Journal*, 38(152), 543–59.

Romer, P. 1994. "The Origins of Endogenous Growth," *Journal of Economic Perspectives*, 8(1), 3–22.

  1990. "Endogenous Technological Change," *Journal of Political Economy*, 98(5), s71–s102.

Solow, R. 1956. "A Contribution to the Theory of Economic Growth," *Quarterly Journal of Economics*, 70(1), 65–94.

Uzawa, H. 1963. "On a Two-Sector Model of Economic Growth II," *Review of Economic Studies*, 30(2), 105–18.

van Marrewijk, C. 1999. "Capital Accumulation, Learning, and Endogenous Growth," *Oxford Economic Papers*, 51(3), 453–75.

van Marrewijk, C. and K. Berden. 2007. "On the Static and Dynamic Costs of Trade Restrictions for Small Developing Countries," *Journal of Development Economics*, 84(1), 46–60.

Chapter 8

Acemoglu, D., S. Johnson, and J. A. Robinson. 2002. "Reversal of Fortune: Geography and Institutions in the Making of the Modern World Income Distribution," *Quarterly Journal of Economics*, 117(4), 1231–94.

2001. "The Colonial Origins of Comparative Development: An Empirical Investigation," *American Economic Review*, 91(5), 1369–401.

Alvarez, M., J. A. Cheibun, F. Limongi, and A. Przeworski. 2000. *Democracy and Development: Political Institutions and Material Well-Being in the World, 1950–1990* (Cambridge University Press).

Barro, R. J. 1999. "Determinants of Democracy," *Journal of Political Economy*, 107(6), s158–s183.

Coase, R. 1960. "The Problem of Social Cost," *Journal of Law and Economics*, 3(4), 1–44.

1937. "The Nature of the Firm," *Economica*, 4(16), 386–405.

Djankov, S., R. La Porta, F. Lopez-de-Silanes, and A. Shleifer. 2003. "The New Comparative Economics," *Journal of Comparative Economics*, 31(4), 595–619.

Glaeser, E. L., R. La Porta, F. Lopez-De-Silanes, and A. Shleifer. 2004. "Do Institutions Cause Growth?," *Journal of Economic Growth*, 9(3), 271–303.

Hall, R. E. and C. I. Jones. 1999. "Why Do Some Countries Produce So Much More Output Per Worker than Others?," *Quarterly Journal of Economics*, 114(1), 83–116.

Lipset, S. M. 1960. *Political Man: The Social Basis of Modern Politics* (New York: Doubleday).

Marshall, M. G. and T. R. Gurr. 2020. *Polity 5: Political Regime Characteristics and Transitions, 1800–2018, Dataset Users' Manual*, Center for Systemic Peace, April 23.

North, D. C. 1990. *Institutions, Institutional Change, and Economic Performance* (Cambridge University Press).

1981. *Structure and Change in Economic History* (New York and London: W. W. Norton).

North, D. C. and B. R. Weingast. 1989. "Constitutions and Commitment: The Evolution of Institutions Governing Public Choice in Seventeenth-Century England," *Journal of Economic History*, 49(4), 803–32.

Przeworski, A. 2004. "Geography vs Institutions Revisited: Were Fortunes Reversed?", mimeo, New York University, https://as .nyu.edu/content/dam/nyu-as/faculty/ documents/reversal.pdf.

Putterman, L. and D. Weil. 2010. "Post-1500 Population Flows and the Long-Run Determinants of Economic Growth and Inequality," *Quarterly Journal of Economics*, 125(4), 1627–82.

Rodrik, D., A. Subramanian, and F. Trebbi. 2004. "Institutions Rule: The Primacy of Institutions over Geography and Integration in Economic Development," *Journal of Economic Growth*, 9(2), 131–65.

Spolaore, E. and R. Wacziarg. 2013. "How Deep Are the Roots of Economic Development?", *Journal of Economic Literature*, 51(2), 325–69.

World Bank. 2002. *World Development Report 2002: Building Institutions for Markets* (New York: Oxford University Press).

Chapter 9

Ahn, J., M. Amiti, and D. Weinstein. 2011. "Trade Finance and the Great Trade Collapse," *American Economic Review*, 101(3), 298–302.

Alfaro, L., A. Chanda, S. Kalemli-Ozcan, and S. Sayek. 2004. "FDI and Economic Growth: The Role of Local Financial Markets," *Journal of International Economics*, 64(1), 89–112.

Alfaro, L. and J. Chauvin. 2020. "Foreign Direct Investment, Finance, and Economic Development," in M. Spatareanu (ed.), *Encyclopedia of International Economics and Global Trade,* vol. 3: *Foreign Direct Investment and the Multinational Enterprise* (Singapore: World Scientific), pp. 231–58.

Antràs, P. and S. R. Yeaple. 2014. "Multinational Firms and the Structure of International Trade," in G. Gopinath, E. Helpman, and K. Rogoff (eds.), *Handbook of International Economics* (Amsterdam: Elsevier), vol. 4, pp. 55–130.

Asian Development Bank (ADB). 2019. *Trade Finance Gaps, Growth, and Jobs Survey*, September, ADB, Manila.

2017. *Trade Finance Gaps, Growth, and Jobs Survey*, September, ADB, Manila.

Banerjee, A., E. Duflo, R. Glennerster, and C. Kinnan. 2015. "The Miracle of Microfinance? Evidence from a Randomized Evaluation," *American Economic Journal: Applied Economics*, 7(1), 22–53.

Bank for International Settlements (BIS). 2019. *Triennial Central Bank Survey, Foreign Exchange Turnover in April 2019*, September, BIS, Basel.

2002. *Triennial Central Bank Survey: Foreign Exchange and Derivatives Market Activity in 2001*, March, BIS, Basel.

Beugelsdijk, S., S. Brakman, H. Garretsen, and C. van Marrewijk. 2013. *International Economics and Business: Nations and Firms in the Global Economy*, 2nd edn. (Cambridge University Press).

Brakman, S. and C. van Marrewijk. 2021. "Trade, Finance, and Development," in J. Y. Abor, C. K. D. Adjasi, and R. Lensink (eds.), *Contemporary Issues in Development Finance* (London: Routledge), pp. 351–84.

1998. *The Economics of International Transfers* (Cambridge University Press).

Cooper, R. N. 1982. "The Gold Standard: Historical Facts and Future Prospects," *Brookings Papers on Economic Activity*, 1, 1–45.

DiCaprio, A. and Y. Yao. 2017. "Drivers of Trade Finance Gaps," Asian Development Bank Institute Working Paper Series 678.

Do Rosarion, J. and C. Millan. 2019. "Argentina Tightens Currency Controls after Fernandez Victory," Bloomberg, www.bloomberg .com/news/articles/2019-10-28/argentina-tightens-currency-controls-after-fernandez-victory.

Dunning, J. 1981. *International Production and the Multinational Enterprise* (London: Boston, Allen & Unwin).

Eichengreen, B. J. 1996. *Globalizing Capital: A History of the International Monetary System* (Princeton University Press).

Foley, F. and K. Manova. 2015. "International Trade, Multinational Activity, and Corporate Finance," *Annual Review of Economics*, 7(1), 119–46.

Frenkel, J. A. 1976. "A Monetary Approach to the Exchange Rate: Doctrinal Aspects and Empirical Evidence," *Scandinavian Journal of Economics*, 78(2), 200–24.

Gopinath, G. 2016. "The International Price System," Jackson Hole Symposium Proceedings.

Gopinath, G., E. Boz, C. Casas, F. Diez, P.-O. Gourinchas, and M. Plagborg-Moller. 2019. "Dominant Currency Paradigm," NBER Working Paper No. 22943, Cambridge, MA, 2016, updated 2019.

Gourinchas, P.-O., H. Rey, and M. Sauzet. 2019. "The International Monetary System," *Annual Review of Economics*, Advanced Access.

Habermeier, K., A. Kokenyne, R. Veyrune, and H. Anderson. 2009. "Revised System for the Classification of Exchange Rate Arrangements," IMF Working Paper 09/211.

International Monetary Fund (IMF). 2020. *Annual Report on Exchange Arrangements and Exchange Restrictions 2019* (Washington, DC: IMF).

Krugman, P. R. and M. Obstfeld. 2003. *International Economics: Theory and Policy*, 6th edn. (New York, etc.: Addison-Wesley).

Mundell, R. A. 1968. *International Economics* (New York: Macmillan).

Obstfeld, M. and K. Rogoff. 2000. "The Six Major Puzzles in International Macroeconomics: Is There a Common Cause?" *NBER Macroeconomics Annual*, 15(1), 339–90.

Obstfeld, M. and A. M. Taylor. 2003. "Sovereign Risk, Credibility, and the Gold Standard: 1870–1913 versus 1925–31," *Economic Journal*, 113(487), 241–75.

Rey, H. 2016. "International Channels of Transmission of Monetary Policy and the Mundellian Trilemma," *IMF Economic Review*, 64(1), 6–35.

Sarno, L. and M. P. Taylor. 2002. *The Economics of Exchange Rates* (Cambridge University Press).

The Economist. 2018. "Go Fund Me: Markets Bash Argentina's and Turkey's Currencies Again," September 1, www.economist.com/ finance-and-economics/2018/09/01/ markets-bash-argentinas-and-turkeys-currencies-again.

van Marrewijk, C. 2012. *International Economics: Theory, Application, and Policy*, 2nd edn. (Oxford University Press).

Chapter 10

Atkinson, A. 1970. "On the Measurement of Inequality," *Journal of Economic Theory*, 2(3), 244–63.

Atkinson, A. B. and F. Bourguignon. 2000. "Introduction: Income Distribution and Economics," in A. B. Atkinson and F. Bourguignon (eds.), *Handbook of Income Distribution* (Amsterdam: Elsevier), pp. 1–58.

Autor, D., F. Levy, and R. Murnane. 2003. "The Skill Content of Recent Technological Change: An Empirical Explanation," *Quarterly Journal of Economics*, 118(4), 1279–333.

Beugelsdijk, S., S. Brakman, H. Garretsen, and C. van Marrewijk. 2013. *International Economics and Business* (Cambridge University Press).

Cai, F. and Y. Du. 2011. "Wage Increases, Wage Convergence, and the Lewis Turning Point in China," *China Economic Review*, 22(4), 601–10.

Chen, S. and M. Ravallion. 2010. "The Developing World Is Poorer than We Thought, But No Less Successful in the Fight against Poverty," *Quarterly Journal of Economics*, 125(4), 1577–625.

Deaton, A. and S. Zaidi. 2002. *Guidelines for Constructing Consumption Aggregates for Welfare Analysis* (Washington, DC: World Bank).

Gini, C. 1912. "Variabilita e mutabilita," in E. Pizetti and T. Salvemini (eds.), *Memorie di Metodologica Statistica* (Rome: Libreria Eredi Virgilio Veschi).

Goos, M. and A. Manning. 2007. "Lousy and Lovely Jobs: The Rising Polarization of Work in Britain," *Review of Economics and Statistics*, 89(1), 118–33.

Goos, M., A. Manning, and A. Salomons. 2009. "The Polarization of the European Labor Market," *American Economic Review, Papers and Proceedings*, 99(2), 58–63.

Haskel, J., R. Lawrence, E. Leamer, and M. Slaughter. 2012. "Globalization and US Wages: Modifying Classic Theory to Explain Recent Facts," *Journal of Economic Perspectives*, 26(2), 119–40.

Krugman, P. 2008. "Trade and Wages, Reconsidered," *Brookings Papers on Economic Activity*, 39(1), 103–54.

Maddison, A. 2001. *The World Economy: A Millennial Perspective* (Paris: OECD Publishing). See also for the latest updates: www.rug.nl/ggdc/historicaldevelopment/maddison/?lang=en.

Pinkovskiy, M. and X. Sala-i-Martin. 2009. "Parametric Estimations of the World Distribution of Income," NBER Working Paper No. 15433, Cambridge, MA.

Sala-i-Martin, X. 2006. "The World Distribution of Income: Falling Poverty and . . . Convergence," *Period. Quarterly Journal of Economics*, 21(2), 351–97.

Sen, A. 1974. "Informational Bases of Alternative Welfare Approaches: Aggregation and Income Distribution," *Journal of Public Economics*, 3(4), 387–403.

The Economist. 2016. "Daily Chart: Worldwide Cost of Living Survey," March 10.

2013. "The Cost of Living around the World," February 7.

UNU-WIDER. 2021. World Income Inequality Database (WIID), Version 31, May, https://doi.org/10.35188/UNU-WIDER/WIID-310521.

van Marrewijk, C. 2019. "Demography and Inequality in China," in S. Brakman, C. van Marrewijk, N. Salike, and P. Morgan (eds.), *China in the Local and Global Economy* (London and New York: Routledge), pp. 243–83.

World Bank. 2012. *World Development Report 2012: Gender Equality and Development* (Washington, DC : World Bank).

2009. *World Development Report 2009: Reshaping Economic Geography* (Washington, DC: World Bank).

Chapter 11

Banerjee, A. and E. Duflo. 2011. *Poor Economics: A Radical Rethinking of the Way to Fight Global Poverty* (New York: Public Affairs).

2009. "The Experimental Approach to Development Economics," *Annual Review of Economics*, 1(1), 151–78.

2007. "The Economic Lives of the Poor," *Journal of Economic Perspectives*, 21(1), 141–67.

Banerjee, A., R. Banerji, J. Berry, E. Duflo, H. Kannan, S. Mukherji, M. Shotland, and M. Walton. 2017. "From Proof of Concept to Scalable Policies: Challenges and Solutions, with an Application," *Journal of Economic Perspectives*, 31(4), 73–102.

Chaudhury, N., J. Hammer, M. Kremer, K. Muralidharan, and F. H. Rogers. 2005. "Teacher Absence in India: A Snapshot," *Journal of the European Economic Association*, 3(2–3), 658–67.

Crépon, B., E. Duflo, M. Gurgand, R. Rathelot, and P. Zamora. 2013. "Do Labor Market Policies Have Displacement Effects? Evidence from a Clustered Randomized

Experiment," *Quarterly Journal of Economics*, 128(2), 531–80.

Deaton, A. 2020. "Randomization in the Tropics Revisited: A Theme and Eleven Variations," in F. Bédécarrats, I. Guérin, and F. Roubaud (eds.), *Randomized Control Trials in the Field of Development: A Critical Perspective* (Oxford University Press), pp. 29–46.

De Soto, H. 2003. *The Mystery of Capital: Why Capitalism Triumphs in the West and Fails Everywhere Else* (New York: Basic Books).

2004. "Scaling Up and Evaluation," in F. Bourguignon and B. Pleskovic (eds.), *Accelerating Development* (New York: Oxford University Press).

Duflo, E., R. Glennerster, and M. Kremer. 2007. "Using Randomization in Development Economics Research: A Toolkit," in T. Schultz and J. Strauss (eds.), *Handbook of Development Economics* (Amsterdam: Elsevier), vol. 4, pp. 3895–962.

Easterly, W. 2007. *The White Man's Burden: Why the West's Efforts to Aid the Rest Have Done So Much Ill and So Little Good* (London: Penguin Books).

Hamermesh, D. 2000. "The Craft of Labormetrics," *Industrial and Labor Relations Review*, 53(3), 363–80.

Hausman, J. A. and D. A. Wise. 1985. *Social Experimentation* (University of Chicago Press).

Kremer, M. 2003. "Randomized Evaluations of Educational Programs in Developing Countries: Some Lessons," *American Economic Review*, 93(2), 102–6.

Miguel, E. and M. Kremer. 2004. "Worms: Identifying Impacts on Education and Health in the Presence of Treatment Externalities," *Econometrica*, 72(1), 159–217.

Sachs, J. D. 2006. *The End of Poverty: Economic Possibilities for Our Time* (London: Penguin Books).

Thomas, D. P. 1997. "Sailors, Scurvy and Science," *Journal of the Royal Society of Medicine*, 90(1), 50–4.

van den Berg, M., C. van Marrewijk, and S. Tamminen. 2018. "Trade, Productivity and Profitability: On Profit Levels and Profit Margins," *The World Economy*, 41(8), 2149–74.

Wagner, J. 2011. "From Estimation Results to Stylized Facts: Twelve Recommendations for Empirical Research in International Activities of Heterogeneous Firms," *De Economist*, 159(4), 389–412.

Young, A. 2019. "Channeling Fisher: Randomization Tests and the Statistical Insignificance of Seemingly Significant Experimental Results," *Quarterly Journal of Economics*, 134(2), 557–98.

Chapter 12

Beugelsdijk, S., S. Brakman, H. Garretsen, and C. van Marrewijk. 2013. *International Economics and Business: Nations and Firms in the Global Economy* (Cambridge University Press).

Bloom, D. E., D. Canning, and J. Sevilla. 2003. *The Demographic Dividend: A New Perspective on the Economic Consequences of Population Change* (Santa Monica, CA: Rand).

Maddison, A. 2001. *The World Economy: A Millennial Perspective* (Paris: OECD Publishing).

Organisation for Economic Co-operation and Development (OECD). 2019. *Pensions at a Glance 2019: OECD and G20 Indicators* (Paris: OECD Publishing).

2015. *Pensions at a Glance 2015: OECD and G20 Indicators* (Paris: OECD Publishing).

Rougoor, W. and C. van Marrewijk. 2015. "Demography, Growth, and Global Income Inequality," *World Development*, 74(1), 220–32.

UN High Commissioner for Refugees (UNHCR). 2019. *Global Trends: Forced Displacement in 2019* (Geneva: UN High Commissioner for Refugees).

UN International Organization for Migration (UNIOM). 2020. *International Migration Report 2020* (Geneva: UN International Organization for Migration).

UN Population Division. 2019. *World Population Prospects: The 2019 Revision* (New York: United Nations).

2015. *World Population Prospects: The 2015 Revision* (New York: United Nations).

2013. *International Migration Report 2013* (New York: United Nations).

1999. *The World at Six Billion* (New York: United Nations), www.un.org/esa/population/publications/sixbillion/sixbillion.htm.

van Marrewijk, C. 2017. *International Trade* (Oxford University Press).

Volkskrant. 2015. "Een op drie 'Syrische' asielzoekers Duitsland komt niet uit Syrië" ["One in Three Syrian Asylum Seekers Is Not from Syria"], September 25.

Chapter 13

Duflo, E., P. Dupas, and M. Kremer. 2011. "Peer Effects, Teacher Incentives, and the Impact of Tracking: Evidence from a Randomized Evaluation in Kenya," *American Economic Review*, 101(5), 1739–74.

Hung, B. 2017. "False Confucius Quotes," While On Board, https://whileonboard.wordpress.com/2017/04/03/false-confucius-quotes/.

Organisation for Economic Co-operation and Development (OECD). 2019. *PISA 2018 Results: What Students Know and Can Do* (Paris: OECD Publishing), vol. I.

World Bank. 2018. *World Development Report 2018: Learning to Realize Education's Promise* (Washington, DC: World Bank).

Chapter 14

Dingel, J. I. and B. Neiman. 2020. "How Many Jobs Can Be Done at Home?," *Journal of Public Economics*, 189.

Maddison, A. 2001. *The World Economy: A Millennial Perspective* (Paris: Development Centre Studies, OECD).

Miguel, E. and M. Kremer. 2004. "Worms: Identifying Impacts on Education and Health in the Presence of Treatment Externalities," *Econometrica*, 72(1), 159–217.

Olson, D. R., L. Simonsen, P. J. Edelson, and S. S. Morse. 2005. "Epidemiological Evidence of an Early Wave of the 1918 Influenza Pandemic in New York City," *PNAS*, 102(31), 11059–63.

Vermeersch, C. and M. Kremer. 2005. "School Meals, Educational Achievement and School Competition: Evidence from a Randomized Evaluation," Policy Research Working Paper No. 3523, World Bank, Washington, DC.

World Bank. 2020. *Reversals of Fortune: Poverty and Shared Prosperity 2020* (Washington, DC: World Bank).

Chapter 15

Adelman, I. and C. Morris. 1988. *Comparative Patterns of Economic Development, 1850–1914* (Baltimore, MD: Johns Hopkins University Press).

Anderson, K. 2010. "International Trade Policies Affecting Agricultural Incentives in Developing Countries," in P. Pingali and R. Evenson (eds.), *Handbook of Agricultural Economics* (Amsterdam: Elsevier), vol. 4, pp. 3215–52.

Banerjee, A. V. and E. Duflo. 2007. "The Economic Lives of the Poor," *Journal of Economic Perspectives*, 21(1), 141–68.

Bezemer, D. and D. Heady. 2008. "Agriculture, Development, and Urban Bias," *World Development*, 36(8), 1342–64.

Binswanger, H. and A. F. McCalla. 2010. "The Changing Context and Prospects for Agricultural and Rural Development in Africa," in P. Pingali and R. Evenson (eds.), *Handbook of Agricultural Economics* (Amsterdam: Elsevier), vol. 4, pp. 3571–712.

Crafts, N. 1988. "The Assessment: British Economic Growth over the Long Run," *Oxford Review of Economic Policy*, 4(1), i–xxi.

Das, M. and P. M. N'Diaye. 2013. "Chronicle of a Decline Foretold: Has China Reached the Lewis Turning Point?," IMF Working Paper No. 13/26.

Diamond, J. 1997. *Guns, Germs, and Steel* (London: Vintage).

Fei, J. C. H. and G. Ranis. 1964. "Development of the Labor Surplus Economy: Theory and Policy," Economic Growth Center, Yale University. Homewood, IL: Richard D. Irwin, Inc.

Gollins, D. 2014. "The Lewis Model: A 60-Year Retrospective," *Journal of Economic Perspectives*, 28(3), 71–88.

2010. "Agricultural Productivity and Economic Growth," in P. Pingali and R. Evenson (eds.), *Handbook of Agricultural Economics* (Amsterdam: Elsevier), vol. 4, pp. 3825–66.

Johnston, B. F. and J. W. Mellor. 1961. "The Role of Agriculture in Economic Development," *American Economic Review*, 51(4), 566–93.

Lewis, W. A. 1954. "Economic Development with Unlimited Supplies of Labour," *Manchester School*, 22(2), 139–91.

Mellor, J. W. 1996. "Agriculture on the Road to Industrialization," in J. P. Lewis and V. Kallab (eds.), *Development Strategies Reconsidered* (New Brunswick, NJ: Transaction Books for the Overseas Development Council), pp. 1–22.

1995. "Introduction," in J. W. Mellor (ed.), *Agriculture on the Road to Industrialization* (Baltimore, MD: Johns Hopkins University Press for the International Food Policy Research Institute [IFPRI]), pp. 1–22.

Pingali, P. 2010. "Agriculture Renaissance: Making 'Agriculture for Development' Work," in P. Pingali and R. Evenson (eds.), *Handbook of Agricultural Economics* (Amsterdam: Elsevier), vol. 4, pp. 3867–94.

2006. "Agricultural Growth and Economic Development: A View through the Globalization Lens," Presidential Address to the 26th International Agricultural Economists, Australia, August 12–18.

Ranis, G. and J. C. H. Fei. 1961. "A Theory of Economic Development," *American Economic Review*, 51(4), 533–65.

Ray, D. 1998. *Development Economics* (Princeton University Press).

Rosenstein-Rodan, P. N. 1943. "Problems of Industrialization of Eastern and South-Eastern Europe," *Economic Journal* (June–September), 204–7. Reprinted in G. M. Meier, *Leading Issues in Economic Development*, 6th edn. (New York: Oxford University Press, 1995).

Rostow, W. W. 1962. *The Stages of Economic Growth* (Cambridge University Press).

Self, S. and R. Grabowski. 2007. "Economic Development and the Role of Agricultural Technology," *Agricultural Economics*, 36(3), 395–404.

Tiffin, R. and X. Irz. 2006. "Is Agriculture the Engine of Growth?," *Agricultural Economics*, 35(1), 79–89.

UN Human Settlements Program. 2016. *World Cities Report 2016: Urbanization and Development – Emerging Futures* (New York: United Nations).

Wade, R. 1990. "Industrial Policy in East Asia: Does it Lead or Follow the Market?," in G. Gereffi and D. L. Wyman (eds.), *Manufacturing Miracles: Paths of Industrialization in Latin America and East Asia* (Princeton University Press), pp. 231–66.

Wang, X. and J. Piesse. 2013. "The Micro-Foundations of Dual Economy Models," *Manchester School*, 81(1), 80–101.

Zhang, X., J. Yang, and S. Wang. 2011. "China Has Reached the Lewis Turning Point," *China Economic Review*, 22(4), 542–55.

Chapter 16

Ades, A. and E. Glaeser. 1995. "Trade and Circuses: Explaining Urban Giants," *Quarterly Journal of Economics*, 110(1), 195–228.

Au, C.-C. and J. V. Henderson. 2006a. "Are Chinese Cities Too Small?" *Review of Economic Studies*, 73(3), 549–76.

2006b. "How Migration Restrictions Limit Agglomeration and Productivity in China," *Journal of Development Economics*, 80(2), 350–88.

Baldwin, R. E. and F. Robert-Nicoud. 2007. "Entry and Asymmetric Lobbying: Why Governments Pick Losers," *Journal of the European Economic Association*, 5(5), 1064–93.

Bosker, M., S. Brakman, H. Garretsen, and M. Schramm. 2012. "Relaxing Hukou: Increased Labor Mobility and China's Economic Geography," *Journal of Urban Economics*, 72(2), 252–66.

Brakman, S., J. H. Garretsen, and C. van Marrewijk. 2020. *An Introduction to Geographical and Urban Economics: A Spiky World* (Cambridge University Press).

2016. "Urban Development in China," *Cambridge Journal of Regions, Economy, and Society*, 9(3), 467–77.

Brakman, S., S. Hu, and C. van Marrewijk. 2014. "Smart Cities Are Big Cities: Comparative Advantage in Chinese Cities," CESifo Working Paper No. 5028.

Chan, K.-W. and W. Buckingham. 2008. "Is China Abolishing the Hukou System?," *China Quarterly*, 195, 582–606.

Chandler, T. 1987. *Four Thousand Years of Urban Growth: An Historical Census* (Lewiston, NY: St. David's University Press).

Combes, P.-P. and L. Gobillon. 2015. "The Empirics of Agglomeration Economies," in G. Duranton, J. V. Henderson, and W. Strange (eds.), *Handbook of Regional and Urban Economics* (Amsterdam: Elsevier), vol. 5, pp. 247–348.

Compton, N. 2015. "What Is the Oldest City in the World?," *The Guardian*, February 16.

Davis, D. R. and J. I. Dingel. 2020. "The Comparative Advantage of Cities," *Journal of International Economics*, 123.

De La Roca, J. and D. Puga. 2017. "Learning by Working in Big Cities," *Review of Economic Studies*, 84(1), 106–42.

Duranton, G. and D. Puga. 2004. "Micro-Foundations of Urban Agglomeration Economies," in J. V. Henderson and J.-F. Thisse (eds.), *Handbook of Regional and Urban Economics: Cities and Geography* (Amsterdam: Elsevier), vol. 4, pp. 2063–118.

Fujita, M., T. Mori, J. V. Henderson, and Y. Kanemoto. 2004. "The Spatial Distribution of Economic Activities in Japan and China," in J. V. Henderson and J.-F. Thisse (eds.), *Handbook of Regional and Urban Economics* (Amsterdam: Elsevier), vol. 4, pp. 2911–77.

Gabaix, X. and R. Ibragimov. 2012. "Rank-1/2: A Simple Way to Improve the OLS Estimation of Tail Exponents," *Journal of Business & Economic Statistics*, 29(1), 24–39.

Henderson, J. V. 2003. "The Urbanization Process and Economic Growth: The So-What Question," *Journal of Economic Growth*, 8(1), 47–71.

1974. "The Sizes and Types of Cities," *American Economic Review*, 64(4), 640–56.

Jaubert, J., S. Verheyden, D. Genty, M. Soulier, H. Cheng, D. Blamart, C. Burlet, H. Camus, S. Delaby, D. Deldicque, R.L. Edwards, C. Ferrier, F. Lacrampe-Cuyaubère, F. Lévêque, F. Maksud, P. Mora, X. Muth, É. Régnier, J.-N. Rouzaud, and F. Santos. 2016. "Early Neanderthal Constructions Deep in Bruniquel Cave in Southwestern France," *Nature*, Research Letter, June 2, 435(7605), 111–14.

Lu, J. and Z. Tao. 2009. "Trends and Determinants of China's Industrial Agglomeration," *Journal of Urban Economics*, 65(2), 167–80.

Marshall, A. 1891. *Principles of Economics*, 8th edn. (1920) (London: Macmillan).

Rosenthal, S. S. and W. C. Strange. 2004. "Evidence on the Nature and Sources of Agglomeration Economics," in J. V. Henderson and J.-F. Thisse (eds.), *Handbook of Regional and Urban Economics* (Amsterdam: Elsevier), pp. 2119–43.

The Economist. 2010. "Migration in China: Invisible and Heavy Shackles," May 6.

UN Department of Economic and Social Affairs. 2019. *World Urbanization Prospects: The 2018 Revision* (New York: United Nations).

Von Thünen, J. H. 1826. *Der Isolierte Staat in Beziehung auf Landwirtschaft und Nationalökonomie* (Hamburg: Perthes).

Chapter 17

Acemoglu, D., D. Cantoni, S. Johnson, and J. A. Robinson. 2011. "The Consequences of Radical Reform: The French Revolution," *American Economic Review*, 101(7), 3286–307.

Acemoglu, D., S. Johnson, and J. A. Robinson. 2001. "The Colonial Origins of Comparative Development: An Empirical Investigation," *American Economic Review*, 91(5), 1369–401.

Acemoglu, D. and J. A. Robinson. 2012. *Why Nations Fail: Origins of Power, Poverty and Prosperity* (London and New York: Crown Publishers).

Ahlfeldt, G. and E. Pietrostefani. 2019. "The Economic Effects of Density: A Synthesis," *Journal of Urban Economics*, 111(1), 93–107.

Alsan, M. 2015. "The Effect of the Tse Tse Fly on African Development," *American Economic Review*, 105(1), 382–410.

Anderson, J. and E. van Wincoop. 2003. "Gravity with Gravitas: A Solution to the Border Puzzle," *American Economic Review*, 93(1), 170–92.

Atkin, D. and D. Donaldson. 2015. "Who's Getting Globalized? The Size and Implications of Intranational Trade Costs," R&R Econometrica.

Baldwin, R. 2016. *The Great Convergence; Information Technology and the New Globalization* (Cambridge, MA: Belknap Press of Harvard University Press).

2006. "Globalisation: The Great Unbundlings," Prime Minister's Office-Economic Council of Finland.

BBC News. 2011. "The Losing Battle against Somali Piracy," February 10.

Berden, K. 2011. "The Effect of Somali Piracy on Trade Flows and Welfare – a Partial Equilibrium Analysis," mimeo, Ecorys Netherlands BV.

Bosker, M. and H. Garretsen. 2012. "Economic Geography and Economic Development in Sub-Saharan Africa," *World Bank Economic Review*, 26(3), 443–85.

2009. "Economic Development and the Geography of Institutions," *Journal of Economic Geography*, 9(3), 295–328.

Brakman, S., H. Garretsen, and C. van Marrewijk. 2020. *An Introduction to Geographical and Urban Economics: A Spiky World* (Cambridge University Press).

Chaney, E. 2013. "Revolt on the Nile: Economic Shocks, Religion, and Political Power," *Econometrica*, 81(5), 2033–53.

Combes, P.-P. and L. Gobillon. 2015. "The Empirics of Agglomeration Economies," in G. Duranton, J. V. Henderson, and W. Strange (eds.), *Handbook of Regional and Urban Economics* (Amsterdam: Elsevier), vol. 5, pp. 247–348.

Crafts, N. F. R. and A. J. Venables. 2003. "Globalization in History: A Geographical Perspective," in M. D. Bordo, A. M. Taylor, and J. G. Williamson (eds.), *Globalization in Historical Perspective* (University of Chicago Press), pp. 323–64.

Criscuolo C., R. Martin, H. Overman, and J. Van Reenen. 2012. "The Causal Effects of an Industrial Policy," NBER Working Paper No. 17842, Cambridge, MA.

Dalton, J. and T. Leung. 2014. "Why Is Polygamy More Prevalent in Western Africa?," *An African Slave Trade Perspective, Economic Development and Cultural Change*, 62(4), 599–632.

Disdier, A.-C. and K. Head. 2008. "The Puzzling Persistence of the Distance Effect on Bilateral Trade," *Review of Economics and Statistics*, 90(1), 37–41.

Duranton, G. 2016. "Determinants of City Growth in Colombia," *Papers in Regional Science*, 95(1), 101–31.

Easterly, W. and R. Levine. 2003. "Tropics, Germs, and Crops: How Endowments Influence Economic Development," *Journal of Monetary Economics*, 50(1), 3–39.

Feenstra, R. C. 2016. *Advanced International Trade: Theory and Evidence* (Princeton University Press).

Fenske, J. and N. Kala. 2015. "Climate and the Slave Trade," *Journal of Development Economics*, 112(1), 19–32.

Francois, J. and H. Hall. 1997. "Partial Equilibrium Modeling," in J. Francois and K. Reinert (eds.), *Applied Methods for Trade Policy Analysis: A Handbook* (Cambridge University Press), pp. 122–55.

Gabaix, X. and R. Ibragimov. 2012. "Rank-1/2: A Simple Way to Improve the OLS Estimation of Tail Exponents," *Journal of Business & Economic Statistics*, 29(1), 24–39.

Head, K. and T. Mayer. 2014. "Gravity Equations: Workhorse, Toolkit, and Cookbook," in G. Gopinath, E. Helpman, and K. Rogoff (eds.), *Handbook of International Economics* (Amsterdam: Elsevier), vol. 4, pp. 131–95.

Hinloopen, J. and C. van Marrewijk. 2012. "Power Laws and Comparative Advantage," *Applied Economics*, 44(12), 1483–507.

Hoogendoorn, S., J. van Gemeren, P. Verstraten, and K. Folmer. 2017. "House Prices and Accessibility: Evidence from a Quasi-Experiment in Transport Infrastructure," *Journal of Economic Geography*, 19(1), 57–87.

Hornbeck, R. 2012. "The Enduring Impact of the American Dust Bowl: Short- and Long-Run Adjustments to the Environmental Catastrophe," *American Economic Review*, 102(4), 1477–507.

Kline, P. and E. Moretti. 2014. "Local Economic Development, Agglomeration Economies and the Big Push: 100 Years of Evidence from the Tennessee Valley Authority," *Quarterly Journal of Economics*, 129(1), 275–331.

Krugman, P. R. 1991. "Increasing Returns and Economic Geography," *Journal of Political Economy*, 99(3), 483–99.

Krugman, P. R. and A. J. Venables. 1995. "Globalization and the Inequality of Nations," *Quarterly Journal of Economics*, 110(4), 857–80.

McCallum, J. 1995. "National Borders Matter: Canada–U.S. Regional Trade Patterns," *American Economic Review*, 85(3), 615–23.

Melo, P., D. Graham, and R. Noland. 2009. "A Meta-Analysis of Estimates of Urban Agglomeration Economies," *Regional Science and Urban Economics*, 39(3), 332–42.

Nunn, N. 2008. "The Long-Term Effects of Africa's Slave Trades," *Quarterly Journal of Economics*, 123(1), 139–76.

Nunn, N. and D. Puga. 2012. "Ruggedness: The Blessing of Bad Geography in Africa," *Review of Economics and Statistics*, 94(1), 20–36.

Radelet, S. and J. Sachs. 1998. "Shipping Costs, Manufactured Exports, and Economic Growth," mimeo, Harvard University, Cambridge, MA.

Redding, S. and M. Turner 2015. "Transportation Costs and the Spatial Organization of Economic Activity,"in G. Duranton, V. Henderson, and W. Strange (eds.), *Handbook of Regional and Urban Economics* (Amsterdam: Elsevier), vol. 5, pp. 1339–98.

Redding, S. and A. J. Venables. 2004. "Economic Geography and International Inequality," *Journal of International Economics*, 62(1), 53–82.

Rodrik, D., A. Subramanian, and F. Trebbi. 2004. "Institutions Rule: The Primacy of Institutions and Integration in Economic Development," *Journal of Economic Growth*, 9, 131–65.

Samuelson, P. A. 1952. "The Transfer Problem and Transport Costs: The Terms of Trade When Impediments Are Absent," *Economic Journal*, 62(246), 278–304.

Tinbergen, J. 1962. *Shaping the World Economy* (New York: The Twentieth Century Fund).

UN Population Division. 2019. *World Population Prospects: The 2019 Revision* (New York: United Nations).

van Marrewijk, C. 2017. *International Trade* (Oxford University Press).

Zipf, G. K. 1949. *Human Behaviour and the Principle of Least Effort* (New York: Addison Wesley).

Chapter 18

Antràs, P. and S. R. Yeaple. 2014. "Multinational Firms and the Structure of International Trade," in G. Gopinath, E. Helpman, and K. Rogoff (eds.), *Handbook of International Economics* (Amsterdam: Elsevier), vol. 4, pp. 55–130.

Baldwin, R. E. 2008. "Managing the Noodle Bowl: The Fragility of East Asian Regionalism," *Singapore Economic Review*, 53(3), 449–78.

Barba-Navaretti, G. and A. J. Venables. 2004. *Multinational Firms in the World Economy* (Princeton University Press).

Bernard, A. B. and B. J. Jensen. 1999. "Exceptional Exporter Performance: Cause, Effect or Both," *Journal of International Economics*, 47(1), 1–25.

1995. "Exporters, Jobs, and Wages in US Manufacturing: 1976–1987," *Brookings Papers on Economic Activity*, Microeconomics, pp. 67–119.

Bernard, A. B., J. B. Jensen, S. J. Redding, and P. K. Schott. 2018. "Global Firms," *Journal of Economic Literature*, 56(2), 565–619.

Bhagwati, J. N. 1978. "Anatomy and Consequences of Exchange Control

Regimes," Special Conference Series on Foreign Trade Regimes and Economic Development, vol. 11, NBER, Cambridge, MA, www.nber.org/books-and-chapters/foreign-trade-regimes-and-economic-development-anatomy-and-consequences-exchange-control-regimes.

Brainard, S. L. 1997. "An Empirical Assessment of the Proximity–Concentration Trade-Off between Multinational Sales and Trade," *American Economic Review*, 87(4), 520–44.

Brakman, S., H. Garretsen, and C. van Marrewijk. 2001. *An Introduction to Geographical Economics* (Cambridge University Press).

Chang, H.-H. and C. van Marrewijk. 2013. "Firm Heterogeneity and Development: Evidence from Latin American Countries," *Journal of International Trade and Economic Development*, 22(1), 11–52.

Coe, D. T. and E. Helpman. 1995. "International R&D Spillovers," *European Economic Review*, 39(5), 859–87.

Coe, D. T., E. Helpman, and A. W. Hoffmaier. 1997. "North–South R&D Spillovers," *Economic Journal*, 107(440), 134–49.

Feenstra, R. C. and G. H. Hanson. 1996. "Foreign Investment, Outsourcing, and Relative Wages," in R. C. Feenstra, G. M. Grossman, and D. A. Irwin (eds.), *The Political Economy of Trade Policy: Papers in Honor of Jagdisch Bhagwati* (Cambridge, MA: MIT Press), pp. 89–128.

Gourevitch, P., R. Bohn, and D. McKendrick. 2000. "Globalization of Production: Insights from the Hard Disk Drive Industry," *World Development*, 28(2), 301–17.

Grossman, G. M. and E. Helpman. 1991. *Innovation and Growth in the Global Economy* (Cambridge, MA: MIT Press).

Grossman, G. M. and E. Rossi-Hansberg. 2008. "Trading Tasks: A Simple Theory of Offshoring," *American Economic Review*, 98(5), 1978–97.

Helpman, E. 1984. "A Simple Theory of International Trade with Multinational Corporations," *Journal of Political Economy*, 92(3), 451–71.

Helpman, E. and P. Krugman. 1985. *Market Structure and Foreign Trade* (Boston, MA: MIT Press).

Helpman, E., M. J. Melitz, and S. R. Yeaple. 2004. "Export versus FDI with Heterogeneous Firms," *American Economic Review*, 94(1), 300–16.

Hiratsuka, D. 2005. "Vertical Intra-Regional Production Networks in East Asia: A Case Study of Hard Disc Drive Industry," IDE Working Paper.

Hopenhayn, H. 1992a. "Entry, Exit, and Firm Dynamics in Long Run Equilibrium," *Econometrica*, 60(5), 1127–50.

1992b. "Exit, Selection, and the Value of Firms," *Journal of Economic Dynamics and Control*, 16(3–4), 621–53.

Krugman, P. R. 1980. "Scale Economics, Product Differentiation, and the Pattern of Trade," *American Economic Review*, 70(5), 950–9.

1979. "Increasing Returns, Monopolistic Competition and International Trade," *Journal of International Economics*, 9(4), 469–79.

Lipsey, R. 2004. "Home and Host Country Effects of Foreign Direct Investments," in R. E. Baldwin and L. A. Winters (eds.), *Challenges to Globalization: Analyzing the Economics* (University of Chicago Press), pp. 333-82.

Melitz, M. J. 2003. "The Impact of Trade on Intra-Industry Reallocations and Aggregate Industry Productivity," *Econometrica*, 71(6), 1695–725.

Melitz, M. J. and S. J. Redding. 2014. "Heterogeneous Firms and Trade," in G. Gopinath, E. Helpman, and

K. Rogoff (eds.), *Handbook of International Economics* (Amsterdam: Elsevier), vol. 4, pp. 1–54.

Roberts, M. J. and J. R. Tybout. 1977. "The Decision to Export in Colombia: An Empirical Model of Entry with Sunk Costs," *American Economic Review*, 87(4), 545–64.

Romer, P. 1994. "New Goods, Old Theory and the Welfare Costs of Trade Restrictions," *Journal of Development Economics*, 43(1), 5–38.

Samuelson, P. A. 1952. "The Transfer Problem and Transport Costs: The Terms When Impediments Are Absent," *Economic Journal*, 62(246), 278–304.

van Marrewijk, C. 2009. "Collapsing Trade Flows," Inaugural Lecture, Utrecht University.

van Marrewijk, C. and K. G. Berden. 2007. "On the Static and Dynamic Costs of Trade Restrictions for Small Developing Countries," *Journal of Development Economics*, 84(1), 46–60.

Chapter 19

Andreoni, J. and Levinson, A. 2001. "The Simple Analytics of the Environmental Kuznets Curve," *Journal of Public Economics*, 80(2), 269–86.

Bloom, D. E. and J. D. Sachs. 1998. "Geography, Demography, and Economic Growth in Africa," *Brooking Papers on Economic Activity*, 2, 207–95.

Brock, W. A. and M. S. Taylor. 2010. "The Green Solow Model," *Journal of Economic Growth*, 15(2), 127–53.

Cherniwchan, J., B. R. Copeland, and M. S. Taylor. 2017. "Trade and the Environment: New Methods, Measurements, and Results," *Annual Review of Economics*, 9, 59–85.

Club of Rome. 1972. *The Limits to Growth: A Report for the Club of Rome's Project on the Predicament of Mankind* (New York: Universe Books).

Ehrlich, P. R. and J. P. Holdren. 1971. "Impact of Population Growth," *Science, New Series*, 171(3977), 1212–17.

Frankel, J. A. 2012. "The Natural Resource Curse: A Survey of Diagnoses and Some Prescriptions," HKS Faculty Research Working Paper Series, RWP12–014, John F. Kennedy School of Government, Harvard University.

Grossman, G. M. and A. B. Krueger. 1995. "Economic Growth and the Environment," *Quarterly Journal of Economics*, 110(2), 353–77.

Lange, G.-M., Q. Wodon, and K. Carey. 2018. *The Changing Wealth of Nations 2018: Building a Sustainable Future* (Washington, DC: World Bank).

Mitchell, R. B. 2016. "International Environmental Agreements Database Project," http://iea.uoregon.edu/.

Weil, D. N. 2014. "Health and Economic Growth," in P. Aghion and S. Durlauf (eds.), *Handbook of Economic Growth* (Amsterdam: Elsevier), vol. 2, pp. 623–82.

World Bank. 2018. "Building the World Bank's Wealth Accounts: Methods and Data," Environment and Natural Resources Global Practice, World Bank, Washington, DC.

2009. "Environmental Crisis or Sustainable Development Opportunity? Transforming the Charcoal Sector in Tanzania: A Policy Note," World Bank, Washington, DC.

Index